MEDIA TODAY

MASS COMMUNICATION IN A CONVERGING WORLD

— 7TH EDITION —

MEDIA TODAY

MASS COMMUNICATION IN A CONVERGING WORLD

— 7TH EDITION —

JOSEPH TUROW

Routledge
Taylor & Francis Group

NEW YORK AND LONDON

Seventh edition published 2020
by Routledge
52 Vanderbilt Avenue, New York, NY 10017

and by Routledge
2 Park Square, Milton Park, Abingdon, Oxon, OX14 4RN

Routledge is an imprint of the Taylor & Francis Group, an informa business

First edition published by Houghton Mifflin Company 1999
Sixth edition published by Routledge 2016

Library of Congress Cataloging-in-Publication Data
Names: Turow, Joseph, author.
Title: Media today : mass communication in a converging world /
    Joseph Turow, University of Pennsylvania.
Description: 7th edition. | New York, NY : Routledge, 2020. |
    Includes bibliographical references and index.
Identifiers: LCCN 2019014929 (print) | LCCN 2019017299 (ebook) |
    ISBN 9780429489235 (eBook) | ISBN 9781138579835 (hardback) |
    ISBN 9781138593848 (paperback)
Subjects: LCSH: Mass media.
Classification: LCC P90 (ebook) | LCC P90 .T874 2020 (print) | DDC 302.23—dc23
LC record available at https://lccn.loc.gov/2019014929

ISBN: 978-1-138-57983-5 (hbk)
ISBN: 978-1-138-59384-8 (pbk)
ISBN: 978-0-429-48923-5 (ebk)

Typeset in Berkeley
by Apex CoVantage, LLC

Visit the Companion Website: www.routledge.com/cw/turow

For Oriana Avra, Felix David, and Mia Ariel

About the Author

Joseph **Turow** is Robert Lewis Shayon Professor of Communication at the Annenberg School for Communication. Before joining Penn's faculty, he taught at Purdue University. Turow is an elected Fellow of the International Communication Association and was presented with a Distinguished Scholar Award by the National Communication Association. A 2005 *New York Times Magazine* article referred to Turow as "probably the reigning academic expert on media fragmentation." In 2010 *The New York Times* called him "the ranking wise man on some thorny new-media and marketing topics." In 2012 the TRUSTe internet privacy-management organization designated him a "privacy pioneer" for his research and writing on marketing and digital privacy.

Turow received his PhD in Communication from the University of Pennsylvania. He has authored eleven books, edited five, and written more than 150 articles on mass media industries. Apart from *Media Today*, his most recent books are *The Aisles Have Eyes: How Retailers Track Your Shopping, Strip Your Privacy, and Define Your Power* (Yale, 2017) and *The Daily You: How the New Advertising Industry Is Defining Your Identity and Your Worth* (Yale, 2011; Turkish edition, 2015). In 2010 the University of Michigan Press published *Playing Doctor: Television, Storytelling, and Medical Power*, a history of prime-time TV and the sociopolitics of medicine, and in 2013 it won the McGovern Health Communication Award from the University of Texas College of Communication. Other books reflecting current interests are *Niche Envy: Marketing Discrimination in the Digital Age* (MIT Press, 2006), *Breaking Up America: Advertisers and the New Media World* (University of Chicago Press, 1997; paperback, 1999; Chinese edition 2004); and *The Hyperlinked Society: Questioning Connections in the Digital Age* (edited with Lokman Tsui, University of Michigan Press, 2008).

Turow's continuing national surveys of the American public on issues relating to marketing, new media, and society have received a great deal of attention in the popular press, as well as in the research community. He has been interviewed widely about his research, including by NPR's *Fresh Air with Terry Gross*, *The Atlantic*, the

BBC, CBS News, and elsewhere. He has also written about media and advertising for the popular press, including *The New York Times*, *The Atlantic*, *American Demographics* magazine, *The Washington Post*, *The Boston Globe*, and *The Los Angeles Times*. His research has received financial support from the Digital Trust Foundation, the John D. and Catherine T. MacArthur Foundation, the Kaiser Family Foundation, the Robert Wood Johnson Foundation, the Federal Communications Commission, and the National Endowment for the Humanities, among others.

Turow was awarded a Lady Astor Lectureship by Oxford University. He has received several conference paper and book awards and has lectured widely. He was invited to give the McGovern Lecture at the University of Texas College of Communication, the Pockrass Distinguished Lecture at Penn State University, the Chancellor's Distinguished Lecture at Louisiana State University, and the Melvin DeFleur Lecture at Boston University. He currently serves on the editorial boards of the *Journal of Broadcasting and Electronic Media*, *The International Journal of Communication*, and *Media Industries*.

Brief Contents

Detailed Contents

Preface

Our Approach to Studying Media Today

Welcome to *Media Today: Mass Communication in a Converging World!*
As the subtitle suggests, this seventh edition of *Media Today* uses convergence as a lens that puts the reader at the center of the profound changes in the 21st-century media world. Through the convergence lens, readers learn to think critically about the role of media today and about what these changes mean for their lives presently and in the future. The book's media systems approach helps readers look carefully at how media are created, distributed, and exhibited in the new world that the digital revolution has created. In this way, *Media Today* goes beyond the traditional mass communication textbook's focus on consuming media to give students an insider's perspective on how media businesses operate. How exactly does Google profit from web searches? What will the magazine look like in five years?

Joseph Turow—who has been teaching Intro to media for well over a decade—demonstrates the many ways that media convergence and the pervasiveness of the internet have blurred distinctions between and among various media. After looking at the essential history of each media industry, Turow examines the current forces shaping that industry and explores the impact of emerging trends. From newspapers, to video games, to social networking, to mobile platforms, Turow's *Media Today* prepares students to live in the digital world of media, helping them to become critical, media-literate consumers of mass media and, if they go on to work in mass media industries, more alert, sensitive practitioners.

Media Today, Seventh Edition, is characterized by its focus on the following:

- Convergence
- Consumer education
- Comprehensive media industry coverage
- Contemporary student-friendly examples

Convergence

Today it is impossible to write about the workings of the newspaper, television, magazine, recording, movie, video game, advertising, and public relations industries without considering fundamental changes being wrought by websites, blogs, email, video and audio files, social media, and multimedia streams. Consequently, readers will find that every chapter incorporates digital media developments into the main flow of the material.

Consumer Education

The overarching goal of the seventh edition of *Media Today* is to help students become media-literate members of society. Being media-literate involves applying critical thinking skills to the mass media. It also involves reasoning clearly about controversies that may involve the websites students use, the mobile devices they carry, the television shows they watch, the music they hear, the magazines they read, and much more. It means becoming a more aware and responsible citizen—voter, worker, adult—in our media-driven society.

After reading *Media Today*, students should be

- savvy about the influences that guide media organizations,
- up-to-date on political issues relating to the media,
- sensitive to the ethical dimensions of media activities, and
- knowledgeable about scholarship regarding media effects.

Comprehensive Media Industry Coverage

What distinguishes mass communication from other forms of communication is the industrialized—or mass production—process that is involved in creating and circulating the material. It is this industrial process that generates the potential for reaching millions (and even billions) of diverse anonymous people at roughly the same time. *Media Today* uses this production-based approach to scrutinize the media in order to show students how the industrial nature of the process is central to the definition of mass communication.

Media Today also introduces the media as an interconnected system of industries—not as industries totally separate from one another. Of course, an introductory text cannot begin with a sophisticated exploration of boundary blurring. Students have to first understand the nature of the mass communication process. They must become aware that taking a mass communication perspective on the world means learning to see the interconnected system of media products that surrounds them every day in new ways.

Contemporary Student-Friendly Examples

As much as possible, the textbook incorporates stories and events that are happening *now*. In the text, readers will find a wide variety of pop culture examples taken from across different industries—from music, to TV, to video games.

How to Use This Book

Unlike other texts for the introductory course, *Media Today* takes a media systems approach out of the conviction that the best way to engage students is to reveal the forces that guide the creation, distribution, and exhibition of news, information, entertainment, education, and advertising within media systems. Once students begin to understand the ways these systems operate, they will be able to interact with the media around them in new ways.

Many features have been built into the text not only to help students learn about the inner workings of key industries in mass communication but also to help them engage with this media, deepening their understanding of their own roles as both consumers and producers of media.

Chapter Opening Pedagogy

Chapter Objectives

Students are provided with the key learning objectives for the chapter at the very beginning so that they know what is ahead of them.

> **CHAPTER OBJECTIVES**
>
> 1 Discuss what mass media convergence means and why it is important.
> 2 Explain the differences between interpersonal communication and mass communication.
> 3 Explain why an unorthodox definition of mass communication makes the term especially relevant in today's media environment.
> 4 Explain the meaning and importance of culture's relationship with the mass media.
> 5 Analyze the ways in which the mass media affect our everyday lives.
> 6 Explain what the term "media literacy" means.
> 7 List the key principles involved in becoming media-literate.

Vignettes

Relevant and current stories about events or trends in the world of mass communication connect students with what they will read in the chapter and how the information applies to the world in which they live.

> Are you like the "typical" American when it comes to being connected to the internet? According to the Pew Research Center, half of American households have five devices capable of connecting to the internet—for example, a smartphone; desktop computer; laptop; tablet; or streaming device such as a Roku, Xbox, or Apple TV.[1] Pew adds that nearly one in five US households are "hyper-connected"— that is, they contain ten or more of these internet-capable devices. As a result, to quote an Experian report, "throughout the day we are consuming content wherever and whenever we like."[2] In fact, US smartphone users are watching a growing amount of video on their smartphones. That's particularly the case with people between 18 and 24 years old. In 2017 Nielsen found they viewed an average of

> "Whoever controls the media controls the culture."
>
> ALLEN GINSBERG, POET

> "Information is the oxygen of the modern age."
>
> RONALD REAGAN, U.S. PRESIDENT

Quotes for Consideration

Compelling quotes from media figures draw attention to key ideas and spark discussion.

Timelines

Timelines in all the industry chapters help students visually organize the relevant historical information that has shaped that particular industry. Students can go to the book's Companion Website to explore the historical events and figures in more depth using our interactive timeline feature, which links to further resources such as newspaper clippings, photos, video clips, and more.

| 1930s | 1940s | 1950s | 1960s | 1970s |

1931: Emanuel Goldberg and Robert Luther in Germany receive a US patent for a "Statistical Machine," an early document search engine that uses photoelectric cells and pattern recognition to search for specific words on microfilm documents.

1945: Scientist Vannevar Bush publishes the article "As We May Think" in *The Atlantic* magazine predicting the invention of technology that would allow ideas in different parts of text to link to one another.
1946: University of Pennsylvania engineers create ENIAC, the Electronic Numerical Integrator and Computer.

1958: President Eisenhower requests funds to create the US Defense Advanced Research Projects Agency (ARPA).

1962: Len Kleinrock writes an MIT dissertation on "packet switching."
1965: Larry Roberts at MIT sets up an experiment in which two computers communicate to each other using packet-switching technology.
1966: ARPANET project begins in Cambridge, Massachusetts; Larry Roberts is in charge.
1969: ARPANET connects computers at four US universities. The first ARPANET message is sent between UCLA and Stanford University.

1971: Ray Tomlinson creates the first email program, along with the @ sign to signify "at."
1973: ARPANET establishes connections to two universities in the UK and Norway.
1976: Steve Jobs and Steve Wozniak found Apple computers.

Global Media Today & Culture Boxes

Global Media Today & Culture boxes provide stories about current trends in media around the world and help students appreciate the media's global impact. Discussion questions encourage students to think about how different cultural perceptions or experiences may inform the way media are experienced around the world.

GLOBAL MEDIA TODAY & CULTURE

A CASE STUDY OF CONVERGENCE: SONY CORPORATION

What do you think of when you hear the word *Sony*? A video game console? A record company? A Hollywood studio? A series of consumer electronics devices, such as television sets, cameras, headphones, smart mobile devices, Blu-ray, and DVD players? The fact is, it is all of the above and more. The Japanese conglomerate Sony purchased the US record company CBS Record Group in 1988 and the Hollywood studio Columbia Pictures in 1989, and since then it has been consolidating its presence in the global media content business in addition to its core activities centered on consumer electronics. The apparent goal of these acquisitions was to leverage media content and digital devices, reuniting under the same ownership the hardware (electronics) and the software (entertainment) in different media sectors.

In hindsight we can observe that with this strategy they anticipated and embraced the unfolding digital revolution. This strategic move led to synergies among the different businesses they operate in, made possible precisely by the convergence of these different sectors, generated by their digital development and evolution. It can be considered one large example of convergence within one conglomerate operating in the global media landscape, combining previously separate industries now reunited in the same digital environment. What do you think? Can legacy media companies thrive or even survive without embracing convergence and the digital change? How can they embrace convergence and digital change? What are the consequences of convergence for the consumers?

New Media Literacy Questions

Throughout the chapters, students will find media literacy questions that ask them to reflect on what it means to be a consumer of mass media and how that affects their lives.

from other forms of communication is not the size of the audience—it can be large or small. Rather, what makes mass communication special is the way the content of the communication message is created.

THINKING ABOUT MEDIA LITERACY

Mass communication is integral to how our society functions. In what ways does mass communication and the ways it is produced and distributed contribute to society?

mass production process
the industrial process that creates the potential for reaching millions, even billions, of diverse, anonymous people at around the same time

Mass communication is carried out by organizations working together in industries to produce and circulate a wide range of content—from entertainment to news to educational materials. It is this industrial **mass production process** that creates the potential for reaching millions, even billions, of diverse, anonymous people at around the same time. And it is the **industrial nature** of the process—for exam-

Key Terms

Key terms and their definitions have been placed where students need them most—next to their usage in the text. Students can practice their mastery of these terms by using the flash card feature on the Companion Website.

mass production process
the industrial process that creates the potential for reaching millions, even billions, of diverse, anonymous people at around the same time

industrial nature
the aspect of industrialized—or mass production—processes involved in creating the material that distinguishes mass communication from other forms of communication. This industrial process creates the potential for reaching billions of diverse, anonymous people simultaneously

Mass communication is carried out by organizations working together in industries to produce and circulate a wide range of content—from entertainment to news to educational materials. It is this industrial **mass production process** that creates the potential for reaching millions, even billions, of diverse, anonymous people at around the same time. And it is the **industrial nature** of the process—for example, the various companies that work together within the television or internet industries—that makes mass communication different from other forms of communication even when the audience is relatively small and even one-to-one. To help you understand how mass communication relates to other forms of communication, let's take a closer look.

The Elements of Communication

Communication is a basic feature of human life. In general, the word "**communication**" refers to people interacting in ways that at least one of the parties involved

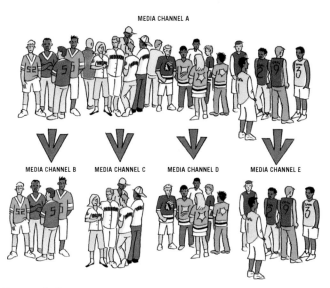

Infographics

Vibrant and instructive art provides students with a visual study tool for understanding key concepts in the text.

Figure 1.1

The arrival of the diverse array of media channels has had a fragmenting effect on audiences—as audience members move to watch, read, or listen to a new channel, fewer people use any single channel.

End-of-Chapter Materials

Activities

Students are given issues to explore and report on based on a debate or topic that was covered earlier in the chapter

 Activity

The section "How to Make Sense of Discussions and Arguments About Media Effects" lists questions to ask yourself. Read this excerpt from an NBC News report about a study of preschoolers' exposure to fast-paced television programming (NBC News, September 12, 2011, www.nbcnews.com/id/44460161/ns/health-childrens_health/t/pants-wearing-sponge-blamed-kids-poor-attention-spans/#.VRXAzvnF98E).

Answer these questions about the research:

1 What question is the researcher asking? Is it interesting and important?
2 In what research tradition does the study fall?
3 How good is the research design?
4 Are the research subjects appropriate, and are there a sufficient number?
5 How convincing is their analysis?

University of Virginia researchers recruited sixty mostly white and middle- or upper-middle-class 4-year-olds and randomly divided them into three groups. One group watched a nine-minute clip of *SpongeBob SquarePants*; a second watched a nine-minute clip of *Caillou*, a realistic PBS cartoon about a preschool boy; and the third drew pictures for nine minutes instead of watching television.

Immediately afterward, the researchers tested what psychologists call "executive function" in the children. "What executive function basically measures is your ability to stay on task, to not be distracted and to persist on task," Christakis explains.

Turns out the PBS and picture-drawing groups performed equally well on the tests; the *SpongeBob* group scored significantly worse. Watching a full half-hour fast-paced cartoon show could be even more detrimental, the study authors write.

Review Questions

End-of-chapter review questions give students the opportunity to recall topics discussed in the chapter and to test their conceptual understanding of these topics.

 Key Terms

You can find the definitions to these key terms in the marginal glossary throughout this chapter. Test your knowledge of these terms with interactive flash cards on the *Media Today* Companion Website.

active audience	digital divide	polysemous
agenda setting	knowledge gap	priming
capitalism	magic bullet or hypodermic	propaganda
colonialism	needle approach	propaganda analysis
co-optation	mainstream approaches	social relations
critical theory	mass media research	two-step flow model
cultivation studies	naturalistic experiment	uses and gratifications
cultural colonialism	panel survey	research
cultural studies	political economy	

 Questions for Discussion and Critical Thinking

1. If the early researchers who concluded media had a "magic bullet" effect on audience were doing research today, how might they use social media to support their theory? What evidence would they see in how people engage with social media that would counter the "magic bullet" theory?
2. In Chapter 1 there was a discussion of the use of media to satisfy "basic human needs" such as enjoyment, companionship, and surveillance. Discuss how the satisfaction of these needs would factor into research applying the "uses and gratifications" framework.
3. The "mean world" syndrome posits that media create the sense that the world is a more dangerous place than it really is. Think of examples of media that have created this sense of a "mean world" in yourself and how you could counter that message.
4. How might you think the impact of video games could be considered using "cultivation theory"?

Expanded in This Edition

- Increases its coverage on how convergence is expanding as digital media take on greater roles in old and new media industries.
- Reinforces its focus on the social implications of many of the new digital-media developments, including for industries, organizations, workers and various segments of the population.
- Enlarges its emphasis on the unstable nature of traditional terms such as magazine, television, radio, book, and movie in an era of digital convergence, thereby encouraging students to think about how the meanings and uses of these terms are changing.

Companion Website

A freshly updated website provides students and instructors with all the tools they will need in their mass communication course: **www.routledge.com/cw/turow.**

For Students

The student website features content-rich assets to help students expand their knowledge, study for exams, and more. Features include the following:

- *Practice quizzes for each chapter*: help students test their knowledge and prepare for exams.
- *Interactive key-term flash cards*: provide students with a fun way to review important terms and definitions.
- *Interactive industry timeline*: brings the timelines from the chapters to life and allows students to learn more about the important people and events that have shaped the media business.
- *Chapter recaps*: summarize the key points and themes of each chapter.
- *Media Today internship and career guide*: offers students information and links to job listings to help them get started in a career in media.
- *Links to further resources*: direct students to key media websites for further study and the latest news on media industries.
- *Media Literacy Questions*: ask students to further reflect on the nature of mass media and its impact in their lives.

For Instructors

The password-protected instructor website provides completely updated instructor support materials in the form of the following:

- *Complete, online, and downloadable instructor's manual revised for this update*: this manual summarizes the key learning objectives of each chapter and provides instructors with discussion starters to help build a dialogue in the classroom.
- *Extensive expanded test bank*: provides multiple-choice, true–false, and fill-in-the-blank questions, as well as new short-answer questions for exams for each chapter.
- *Fully revised PowerPoint presentations*: offer lecture outlines for each chapter, along with a set of slides for every figure in the text.
- *Sample syllabi*: help instructors plan their courses using the new edition.
- *Textboxes* from previous editions of *Media Today* for instructors who would like to continue to incorporate them into their classes.
- *Links to all videos from the Interactive Timelines*, plus additional video recommendations.

Acknowledgments

A book such as this is impossible to create alone, and so there are several people to thank. My wife, Judy, has with every edition been supportive with her encouragement and smart advice. Sharon Black, librarian at the University of Pennsylvania's Annenberg School for Communication, has always been ready to help with the best references available.

At Routledge, I am indebted to my editor, Erica Wetter, whose enthusiasm, suggestions for this revision, and concern throughout the process were an important factor in the high quality of the book. Emma Sherriff was also a key factor in moving this complex project along efficiently. At Apex CoVantage, Project Manager Autumn Spalding was a cheery and vigilant guardian of the book's quality as it moved toward completion.

Nora Paul, Chelsea Reynolds, and Ruth DeFoster at the University of Minnesota each provided helpful and detailed updates to many of the book's features, including the Thinking About Media Literacy questions, the Global Media Today & Culture boxes, the industry chapter timelines, and the end-of-chapter discussion questions and exercises. Additional thanks go to copyeditor Sharon Tripp, proofreader Andrea Harris, and indexer Sheila Bodell.

I would also like to thank all the reviewers (including those who chose to remain anonymous and are not listed here) whose suggestions during the reviewing process helped me greatly as I prepared the seventh edition:

Frank A. Barnas, *Valdosta State University*
Amy Bonebright, *Liberty University*
Nader H. Chaaban, *George Mason University*
Rini Cobbey, *Gordon College*
Raphael Cohen-Almagor, *The University of Hull*
Stephen Dixon, *Newman University*
Sophia Drakopoulou, *Middlesex University*
J. Ann Dumas, *The Pennsylvania State University*
Dave Edwards, *South Central College*
Kevin Ells, *Texas A&M University—Texarkana*
Larissa Faulkner, *Truckee Meadows Community College*
John R. Ferguson, *University of Guelph*
Bradley C. Freeman, *American University in Dubai*
Julian Gurr, *St. Edward's School*
Norsiah Abdul Hamid, *Universiti Utara Malaysia*
Kathleen Hansen, *University of Minnesota*
Rachel Kovacs, *College of Staten Island*
Heather McIntosh, *Minnesota State University, Mankato*
Caryn Murphy, *University of Wisconsin—Oshkosh*

Gail Ramsey, *Montgomery County Community College*
Amy Reynolds, *Kent State University*
John Shields, *Norwalk Community College*
Paolo Sigismondi, *University of Southern California*

To the Student

I hope that you will find *Media Today* fun to read, helpful for understanding the media-saturated world around you, and (if you're so inclined) useful for thinking about a future career in mass media. More likely than not, you've grown up with all or at least most of the media we cover in this book. Your family has probably had newspapers, books, magazines, CDs, radios, and a television set in your home from the time you were born. It's likely, too, that you have had a computer and the internet in your home from the time you were small. In one sense, then, you're already an "expert" at mass media: you've seen a lot of it, you know what you like, and you know what you don't like. At the same time, there's probably a lot about the content mass media present, the industries behind them, and their roles in society that you haven't considered yet.

The purpose of *Media Today* is to introduce you to these ideas, with the expectation that they will help you think about the media you think you already know in entirely new ways. To get the most out of this text, use all the bells and whistles that come with it. The chapter objectives, the marginal glossary, the timelines, the art and photo selections, and the boxed features all have been created with an eye toward making the text itself as clear and relevant as possible. The Companion Website (**www.routledge.com/cw/turow**) will also be of enormous value for learning more about book topics, studying for exams, learning about careers in mass media, quizzing yourself, and more. Get to know all these learning aids, and let us know what you think of them.

Best wishes,

Joe Turow

MEDIA TODAY

1 Understanding Mass Media, Convergence, and the Importance of Media Literacy

CHAPTER OBJECTIVES

1   Discuss what mass media convergence means and why it is important.

2   Explain the differences between interpersonal communication and mass communication.

3   Explain why an unorthodox definition of mass communication makes the term especially relevant in today's media environment.

4   Explain the meaning and importance of culture's relationship with the mass media.

5   Analyze the ways in which the mass media affect our everyday lives.

6   Explain what the term "media literacy" means.

7   List the key principles involved in becoming media-literate.

Are you like the "typical" American when it comes to being connected to the internet? According to the Pew Research Center, half of American households have five devices capable of connecting to the internet—for example, a smartphone; desktop computer; laptop; tablet; or streaming device such as a Roku, Xbox, or Apple TV.[1] Pew adds that nearly one in five US households are "hyper-connected"— that is, they contain ten or more of these internet-capable devices. As a result, to quote an Experian report, "throughout the day we are consuming content wherever and whenever we like."[2] In fact, US smartphone users are watching a growing amount of video on their smartphones. That's particularly the case with people between 18 and 24 years old. In 2017 Nielsen found they viewed an average of 83 minutes daily on those small screens.[3]

Not only are more and more people consuming content on different devices, they are reading, listening, and viewing the same content on different devices. It's quite possible today to start reading an article in a physical magazine—say *Vogue* or *Car and Driver*—and finish reading that article on the magazine's website or app. You might well have started reading a book on your Amazon Kindle during lunch, switched over to reading some of it on your phone's Kindle app on a bus home, and then then picked up where you left off by listening to an Audible continuation on your Echo speaker (Audible and Echo are Amazon-owned) before going to bed. Or how about TV: If you subscribe to cable or satellite television, you probably know that the companies give you the possibility to view a variety of channels live or even on demand just about anywhere through various devices—your TV set, your desktop computer, your laptop, your tablet, your smartphone, your Xbox video game console, your Apple TV, and more. Some companies call this approach "television everywhere." If you don't subscribe to cable or satellite services, you probably know how to cobble together your own version of television everywhere. You can go to several vendors who will let you view many of the same programs via many of the same technologies.

To people involved in media businesses, these changes are exciting and scary at the same time. Many executives realize they are moving into a world that is like no other in history. They increasingly see a world of not just television everywhere but also newspapers everywhere,

> "Whoever controls the media controls the culture."

ALLEN GINSBERG, POET

> "Information is the oxygen of the modern age."

RONALD REAGAN, U.S. PRESIDENT

books everywhere, magazines everywhere, movies everywhere, and more. Many firms are jockeying to shape the new world and define themselves in it. At the same time, they understand that the developments represent only the beginning of what will certainly be a decades-long transformation of the media system in the United States—and the rest of the world. The changes will surely affect you as a citizen, as a consumer, and as a worker, especially if you choose to work in one of the media industries. It's important, then, to ask and answer some basic questions:

- Precisely what is happening that is so transformative?
- Why are those things happening?
- How will it affect me as a citizen, a consumer, and a worker?
- What can I do to help myself, my family, and my society as the changes unfold?

Media Today is about helping you answer these questions. Over the next several chapters we will take an excursion through industries and businesses that relate directly to our everyday lives. We will look at how the media industries got there, what they are doing, and where they seem to be going. We'll explore what is changing about them and what is not. And we'll develop a way of thinking about them that will help you analyze them long after you've read this book. This chapter begins the journey with an exploration of an idea that is at the core of the "everywhere" activities we have just described: media convergence.

Introducing Media Convergence

Let's take the words one at a time. *Media* are platforms or vehicles that industries have developed for the purpose of creating and circulating messages. Think of phones, television sets, movies, music recordings, magazines, and newspapers. *Convergence* occurs when two or more things come together. *Media convergence* takes place when products typically linked to one medium show up on many media. When you can get a Red Sox baseball game broadcast in Boston to show up on your laptop computer and/ or your Android phone in Seattle, that is convergence. When you can transfer an Adele music album from your laptop to your iPod, iPhone, iPad, or Xbox, that is convergence.

Until recently, media convergence was not a common activity. To the contrary, people associated every medium with a particular kind of product. The telephone meant conversations via a special device between two people not located in the same place. Television meant audiovisual programs on a special set with a glass front. Movies meant audiovisual programs made for projection onto a big screen. Newspapers meant printed stories on large sheets of paper circulated daily or weekly. Music recordings were plastic discs or tape cartridges made to be played on phonographs or tape decks.

It's not as if the media were sealed off from one another. Musical recordings showed up on radio all the time. Movie plots sometimes came from books, and theatrical films did show up on television. But these activities involved negotiation by companies that saw themselves in different industries. (The industries that guided particular media and their products were worlds unto themselves.) Moreover, actually moving the products from one medium to another could take a lot of work. One important reason was that the technology—that is, the machinery and materials—of the media industries were very different from one another. Certainly, most members of the audience didn't have the equipment to carry out such transfers. And it was hard to imagine a print magazine such as *Cosmopolitan* sharing a screen with the ABC television program *The Good Doctor*.

"Wait!" you might be yelling at this page (or more likely saying to yourself), "That's still the case. When I hold *Cosmo* or *The Economist* in my hand, I can't put it into my TV set." You're right. But as the phrase "television everywhere" indicates, executives in industries that have historically thought of their content as specific to a particular medium are now trying to get their products—the content you read, watch, and hear—in front of their intended audiences wherever they are. If you're a loyal reader of *Cosmo* or *The Economist* or most any major magazine, you probably know it has a website. It probably has a Facebook page, Twitter feed, and an application ("app") for people to access it on a smartphone, an iPad, or another tablet.

But we're not talking here only of the merger of magazines and the web. Media convergence is taking place with so many media that it is quickly becoming the way media executives do their work, no matter what their industry is. If you're into college sports, you probably have heard about March Madness, the basketball tournament that pits college teams against one another toward finding a National College Athletic Association (NCAA) champion. Until just a few years ago, the only place you could see the matchups outside the stadiums was on your television set, with the CBS television network and Turner's TNT cable network showing various games. But convergence has changed everything. Take what went on during March 2018 as an example. All games except the two "Final Four" national semifinals and the national championship game showed up in their entirety on Turner pay networks TBS, TruTV, and TNT, as well as CBS. (TBS televised the Final Four and CBS aired the championship game.) Viewers with cable or satellite subscriptions could stream the Turner networks on various devices. CBS offered streaming through its subscription service "CBS All Access" (for which nonsubscribers could get a free trial to view the games) on the web, on mobile phones, and on tablets. In addition, the NCAA itself offered a streaming service for a fee through which fans could view all the games on various devices. Truly television everywhere.

Why is media convergence happening now? Why do companies carry it out? When do they do it? How do they do it? When are companies—and workers and industries—winners because of convergence, and when are they losers? How are individuals and society at large affected by the new developments in media today? How might they be affected in the future? Are there government policies or other organized initiatives that try to ensure the best possible outcomes for all involved with the media system?

You probably realize that these questions cannot be answered in two or three paragraphs. Answering them is a project for this book as a whole. The goal is to help you answer these questions not just right now but also in the future as you move through your personal and professional life. To start, it's useful to step back and ask what the media we will be exploring have in common. The answer is that they are all involved in the process of mass communication. Media convergence is, in fact, a central aspect of mass communication today. This chapter will unpack what that means. We will explore and define communication, media, and culture, and we will consider how the relationships among them affect us and the world in which we live. We will also consider why the term "mass communication" remains relevant in the 21st century, contrary to what some writers say.

Introducing Mass Communication

To understand why some writers suggest that the idea of mass communication doesn't connect to what's going on in today's world, we have to look at how the term has traditionally been used. Over the past hundred years, people who wrote about mass communication tended to relate it to the size of the audience. That made a lot of sense at one point. From the mid-19th century onward, new technologies such as high-speed newspaper presses, radio, movies, and television provided access to the huge "masses" of people. Not only were those audiences very large; they also were dispersed geographically, were quite diverse (i.e., made up of different types of people), and typically were anonymous to the companies that created the material. The essential reason that newspapers, radio, television, and other such media were considered different from other means of communication had to do with the size and composition of the audience.

This perspective on mass communication worked well until recently, when the key aspects of the traditional definition of mass communication as reaching huge, diverse groups no longer fit. The reason is that the arrival of many channels—including the growing number of radio and TV stations, the rise of video recorders, the multiplication of cable networks, and the rise of the web—led to **audience fragmentation** (see Figure 1.1). That is, as people watched or read these new channels, there were fewer people using any one of them. Because these new media channels do not necessarily individually reach large numbers of people—the "masses"—some writers have suggested that we can abandon the term mass communication.

However, the view in this book is that mass communication is still a critically important part of society. As we will see, what really separates mass communication

audience fragmentation
the process of dividing audience members into segments based on background and lifestyle in order to send them messages targeted to their specific characteristics

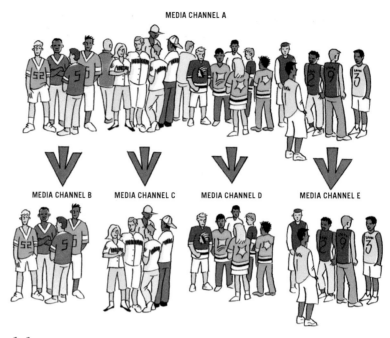

Figure 1.1
The arrival of the diverse array of media channels has had a fragmenting effect on audiences—as audience members move to watch, read, or listen to a new channel, fewer people use any single channel.

from other forms of communication is not the size of the audience—it can be large or small. Rather, what makes mass communication special is the way the content of the communication message is created.

THINKING ABOUT MEDIA LITERACY

Mass communication is integral to how our society functions. In what ways does mass communication and the ways it is produced and distributed contribute to society?

---

mass production process
the industrial process that creates the potential for reaching millions, even billions, of diverse, anonymous people at around the same time

industrial nature
the aspect of industrialized—or mass production—processes involved in creating the material that distinguishes mass communication from other forms of communication. This industrial process creates the potential for reaching billions of diverse, anonymous people simultaneously

Mass communication is carried out by organizations working together in industries to produce and circulate a wide range of content—from entertainment to news to educational materials. It is this industrial **mass production process** that creates the potential for reaching millions, even billions, of diverse, anonymous people at around the same time. And it is the **industrial nature** of the process—for example, the various companies that work together within the television or internet industries—that makes mass communication different from other forms of communication even when the audience is relatively small and even one-to-one. To help you understand how mass communication relates to other forms of communication, let's take a closer look.

The Elements of Communication
Communication is a basic feature of human life. In general, the word "**communication**" refers to people interacting in ways that at least one of the parties involved

understands as **messages**—collections of symbols (words, signs) that appear purposefully organized (meaningful) to those sending or receiving them.

When you signal your needs or thoughts to others, the signals you send are both verbal and nonverbal. When Jane shouts excitedly to her friend Jack and leaps with joy into his arms after she wins a tennis match, that's a form of communication. It's likely that Jack, whose arms she almost breaks, realizes that she wants to tell him something. People who study communication would typically call the interaction just described **interpersonal communication**, a form that involves two or three individuals signaling to each other using their voices, facial and hand gestures, and other signs (even clothes) to convey meaning. When you talk to your parents about your coursework, discuss a recent movie over dinner with friends, or converse with your professor during her office hours, you are participating in the interpersonal form of communication.

Mediated interpersonal communication can be described as interpersonal communication that is assisted by a **medium**—part of a technical system that helps in the transmission, distribution, or reception of messages. The medium helps communication take place when senders and receivers are not face-to-face. The internet is an example of a medium, as are radio, CD, television, and DVD. (Note that the term "medium" is singular; it refers to one technological vehicle for communication. The plural is media.) When you write a thank-you note to your grandmother, send an email to your graduate teaching assistant, or call a friend on the phone, you are participating in the mediated form of interpersonal communication.

Although interpersonal, mediated interpersonal, and mass communication have their differences, they have a central similarity: they involve messages. Eight major elements are involved in every interaction that involves messages: the source, encoding, transmitter, channel, receiver, decoding, feedback, and noise.

Take a look at Figure 1.2. It illustrates how these eight elements appear in the process of interpersonal communication in an imaginary conversation between TV personality Trevor Noah and a student named Sally. Now take a look at Table 1.1. It lays out the ways these elements are similar or different across interpersonal

communication
refers to people interacting in ways that at least one of the parties involved understands as messages

messages
collections of symbols (words, signs) that appear purposely organized (meaningful) to those sending or receiving them

interpersonal communication
a form of communication that involves two or three individuals signaling to each other using their voices, facial and hand gestures, and other signs (even clothes) to convey meaning

mediated interpersonal communication
a specialized type of interpersonal communication that is assisted by a device, such as a pen or pencil, computer, or phone

medium
part of a technical system that helps in the transmission, distribution, or reception of messages

A common sight today is interpersonal communication through both direct and mediated means. Mediated interpersonal communication methods such as FaceTime allow people to keep in touch in a more visual way and across greater distances than was ever possible in the past.

communication, mediated interpersonal communication, and mass communication. The table also presents examples that highlight these similarities and differences.

The main difference between mass communication and the two forms of interpersonal communication relates to the nature of the source and the receiver. In the interpersonal modes, the source and the receiver are individual people—Trevor Noah schmoozing face-to-face with Sally in the library, for example, or Trevor gossiping over the phone with another student named Geraldo. In the case of mass communication, the source is an organization—for example, the Comedy Central television channel (where you can view Trevor Noah's show) or the *Guardian* newspaper. When you read a particular newspaper article or watch a particular program, you may think that sources are individual people, not organizations. After all, the name of the author

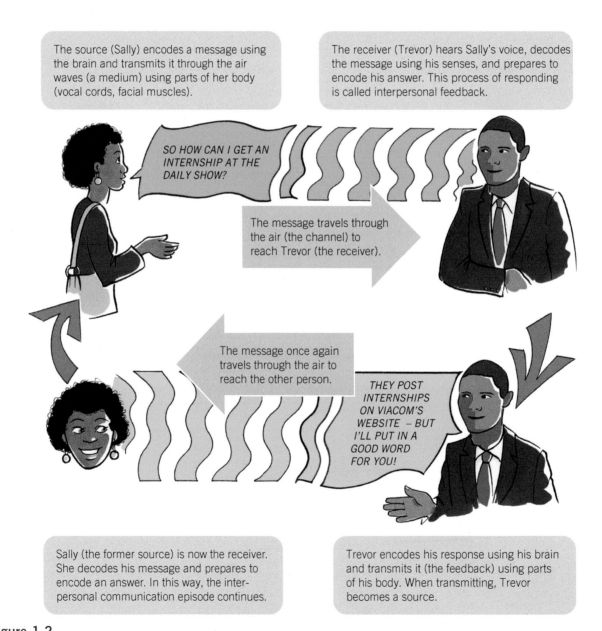

The source (Sally) encodes a message using the brain and transmits it through the air waves (a medium) using parts of her body (vocal cords, facial muscles).

The receiver (Trevor) hears Sally's voice, decodes the message using his senses, and prepares to encode his answer. This process of responding is called interpersonal feedback.

SO HOW CAN I GET AN INTERNSHIP AT THE DAILY SHOW?

The message travels through the air (the channel) to reach Trevor (the receiver).

The message once again travels through the air to reach the other person.

THEY POST INTERNSHIPS ON VIACOM'S WEBSITE – BUT I'LL PUT IN A GOOD WORD FOR YOU!

Sally (the former source) is now the receiver. She decodes his message and prepares to encode an answer. In this way, the interpersonal communication episode continues.

Trevor encodes his response using his brain and transmits it (the feedback) using parts of his body. When transmitting, Trevor becomes a source.

Figure 1.2

In this model of interpersonal communication, information moves from a starting point at the source (Sally), who transmits the message over the channel to the receiver (Trevor) for decoding.

Table 1.1 Comparing Elements Across Different Forms of Communication

Element of communication	General meaning of the element	How do we understand that element in interpersonal communication?	How do we understand that element in mediated interpersonal communication?	How do we understand that element in mass communication?
Source	The originator of the message	It is an individual.	It is an individual.	It is one or more organizations.
Encoding	When the source organizes and prepares to send the message	It takes place in an individual's brain.	It takes place in an individual's brain.	It takes place in an organization using technology.
Transmitter	Performs the physical activity of sending the message	It is the person's vocal cords.	It is the person's vocal cords and technology (e.g., a phone).	It is a person's vocal cords and technology (e.g., a phone).
Channel	Pathway through which the transmitter sends the message	It is the air.	It is the air and technology (e.g., wires).	It is the air and technology (e.g., wires).
Receiver	The person or organization that gets the message	It can be one person or a few individuals in the same location.	It can be one or many individuals in one or more locations.	It is typically many people in different locations.
Decoding	The process by which the receiver makes sense of the message	It takes place in an individual's brain.	It takes place first via technology and then in an individual's brain.	It takes place first via technology and then in an individual's brain.
Feedback	A response to the message	It is immediate and directly to the source.	It is immediate and directly to the source.	It may be immediate or delayed and is generally indirect: other parts of the organization receive it and tell the source.
Noise	A sound in the communication situation that interferes with the delivery of the message	It can be environmental (e.g., noise in a park), mechanical (the person coughs so much the message gets lost), or semantic (the speaker doesn't know the language well).	It can be environmental, mechanical (e.g., park noise or static on the line), or semantic.	It can be environmental, mechanical, or semantic, sometimes caused by organizations.

is on the article, and you can see the actors who work on the show. Why, for example, shouldn't we consider Trevor Noah the "source" on Comedy Central's *The Daily Show*?

The answer is that he is only the most visible of an entire firm of people who prepared the mass media material. If Trevor were in the same room as you telling you about what he just read in the newspaper, he—as an individual—would be a source. But when you watch him do his monologue on *The Daily Show*, Trevor is no longer the source. That's because behind him is an organization that is creating the news satire for him to present. Sure, Trevor is reading the messages, and so it may seem that he should be called "the source." But the writing team of *The Daily Show* helped him write the script, produced and edited the videos he introduces, and prepared his set for the broadcast. Moreover, the photos and clips he satirizes sometimes come from news firms, such as ABC News. So Trevor is really just the most visible representative of an organizational source. And the Comedy Central organization is interacting with other organizations (ABC News, companies that provide it with supplies for the programs, advertisers that support the program, and many more) in order to get *The Daily Show* on the air.

Mass Communication Defined

And so we come at last to the definition of mass communication that we have been building: mass communication is the industrialized production and multiple distribution of messages through technological devices. The industrial nature of the process is central to this definition of mass communication. Figure 1.3 illustrates this point by using *The Daily Show* as an example.

A complex organization within an industry (the source) produces material (messages) and distributes it through a medium using a range of technologies.

An organization presents (exhibits) the material in a particular area, and it reaches a member of the audience who retrieves it using technology.

In this case the material travels to cable firms via satellites (and satellite dishes) and then via cable to homes.

The individual's feedback goes from the computer to WiFi and then via the internet to the production firm.

Members of the production receive the individual and organized feedback and make decisions about future material based on them and many other industry factors.

The audience member chooses to send comments (feedback) to the production firm using a number of technologies. The production firm also hires companies to get organized feedback ("ratings") from many in the audience.

Figure 1.3

In this model of mass communication, the elements (source, message, transmission) are all marked by industrial production and multiple distribution by mass media organizations.

As the definition suggests, mass communication is carried out by mass media industries. Think, for example, of the movie industry, in which many different companies—from production studios to film providers to catering firms—work to make and circulate movies. **Mass media** are the technological instruments—for example, newsprint, the internet, television, and radio (both traditional and satellite)—through which mass communication takes place. **Mass media outlets** are companies that send out messages via mass media—for example, *Time* magazine, foxnews.com, and the NBC television network.

Mass communication's power allows media consumers to share the materials they are reading and listening to with millions of people. This sharing is made possible, of course, because of the industrial nature of the activity and its technology of production and distribution. When complex organizations comprising many workers join to use the latest technology to produce media, those organizations have the potential to circulate the same message to huge numbers of people.

Consider the typical television broadcast of the Grammy Awards, the ceremony in which the recording industry honors its most successful talent. It is typically transmitted via satellite from Los Angeles to broadcast television production facilities in New York and then distributed "live" to every corner of the United States, as well as to many other parts of the world. (In 2018, when it took place in New York's Madison Square Garden, the feed still went through the network's New York broadcast facilities before soaring outward.)

Or consider a typical presidential news conference. It is covered by dozens of newspaper reporters and television and radio news crews. Snippets of the event then will commonly confront Americans around the country in many different forms during that day and the next on national TV news, on internet news and blog sites, on the local news, and in morning papers and throughout the day on hourly radio news reports.

As a third and slightly different example, consider a mega-hit film such as the first of the *Hunger Games* movies. Millions of people around the world saw it in theaters within a few months of its release. In addition, word of the movie's popularity spread around the globe as Lionsgate, its distributor, revved up a publicity and advertising machine. It peppered as many media outlets as possible with word of the high-octane action and digital effects.

The Hunger Games, the presidential news conference, and the Grammy Awards represent only three examples of activities that happen all the time in industrialized countries such as the United States. Linking large numbers of people to share the same materials virtually instantly has become standard practice for the broadcast television, internet, radio, cable TV, and satellite television industries. Just as significant is the sharing that takes place relatively more slowly when newspapers, magazines, books, movies, billboards, and other mass media release their messages. Because of mass media industries and their abilities to mass-produce media content, millions of people within the United States and around the world can receive the same messages within a fairly short time. Think about it—here are huge numbers of people who are physically separated from one another, have no obvious relationship with one another, and most often are unknown to one another. Yet on a daily basis they are watching the same news stories, listening to the same music, and reading the same magazine articles.

mass media
the technological vehicles through which mass communication takes place (note that the term "mass media" is plural and refers to more than one vehicle; the singular version is mass medium)

mass media outlets
companies that send out messages via mass media

Mass Media and Convergence

If you spin out the logic of our descriptions of mass communication and mass media, you can see how closely they are related to the process of convergence that we began to explore at the beginning of this chapter. Recall that we said media convergence takes place when products typically linked to one medium show up on another. We noted that when a Red Sox baseball game broadcast in Boston shows up on your laptop computer in Seattle, that is convergence. Let's take apart that example a bit to show its connection to our definition of mass communication.

It's actually not a hard connection to make. The Boston broadcast is a straightforward case of mass communication: a collection of companies—the Red Sox organization, the local broadcast station, the advertisers, and more—working together to produce the game and distribute it via broadcast television technology. As for the game showing up on your computer in Seattle, remember that the Dish Network makes this possible through Slingbox. That means the satellite firm joins with the technology firm that makes the Slingbox to allow Dish subscribers to tap into Slingbox's potential to send video signals across the internet. Also involved are firms that cooperate with one another in internet distribution of Slingbox signals—the one that provides the connection from the Slingbox in your home to the internet, the firms that carry the video of the game across the internet (we'll discuss how that works in Chapter 6), and the firms that provide you with an internet connection in your Seattle hotel.

Devices such as Google Chromecast and Apple TV allow people to watch the same content, such as a television show or online video, across mobile devices, tablets, computers, and television as a result of digital conversion. As a result, digital conversion has transformed the modern viewing experience.

We have here what might be called the three Cs of mass media convergence: content, corporations, and computers. The first two Cs reflect the definition of mass communication presented earlier. *Content* refers to the "messages"—in this case, the ball game, the announcers' descriptions and interviews, and the commercials shown around all of that. *Corporations* refers to the companies that interact to create and distribute the content. It is the third C—the use of computers by corporations to create and distribute content—that brings convergence into the mass communication picture. To understand how, you need to think about the difference between computer-centered mass media such as the internet and media technologies that don't rely on computers for production and circulation of content.

A crucial difference between computer-centered mass media and other media technologies is that the former are digital rather than analog. A simple way to understand the distinction between digital and analog is to think about what distinguishes an old-fashioned vinyl record from a CD. If you look at a record, you will see grooves. When the phonograph needle moves through the grooves, it picks up vibrations that were made by the sound coming from the singer's vocal cords. When the record was made, a machine cut grooves that reproduced these vibrations into the vinyl. The record grooves, then, hold a literal physical reproduction—an **analog**—of the singer's sound that can be reproduced with the right equipment.

The CD, by contrast, does not contain a physical reproduction of the sound. During the CD's recording process, computers transform the singer's voice patterns into a string of binary digits, or bits (0s and 1s). Each sequence, or string, of 0s and 1s represents a different sound. The strings serve as a code—a symbolic representation of the sound. This **digital** code is placed on the CD in an order that conforms to the sequence of sounds made by the singer. When you turn on your CD player, a laser beam reads the code and sends it to a computer chip in the player. The computer chip is programmed to recognize the code and to understand which strings of numbers represent which sounds. At the speed of light, the chip transforms the code into electrical impulses that, when sent through an amplifier and sound system, reproduce the singer's voice.

The basic idea applies also to digital music files that reside in your laptop computer or your mobile phone. In that case, you don't even have a piece of plastic that carries the tune into the device. Rather, you download a digital file in one of a number of formats (MP3, WAV, AAC, or others), and if your device has the ability to recognize and decode the file, it transforms it into sounds that reproduce the original. If the file you are using is not copy-protected (and MP3 and WAV files are not), you can copy the music from your phone to one of your other players. Being able to move digital files (music or otherwise) from one device to another is an example of the **convergence** of media technologies; it involves the ability of different media to interact with one another easily in parallel digital formats. As a result of convergence, different media can end up carrying out similar functions because they all accept digital information. A laptop computer, a phone, and a tablet (such as the iPad) can take on the functions of a DVD player, a CD player, and a cable television set. That means, for example, that you can start watching the *Hunger Games* movie trilogy on your bedroom cable TV, continue viewing it on your phone during a train ride to work, and finish it during an airplane trip via your iPad. And you can toggle listening to the newest music album by Taylor Swift or Bruno Mars on your phone, your laptop, your tablet, and your CD player (if you still use it).

The digital nature of content also means that you and others can rather easily get the technical capability to alter mass media materials for your own purposes. You can, for example, humorously overlay a *Twilight* scene with a song from the French rapper Guizmo and share it with your friends over the web or in some other way. The ability of members of the audience to easily manipulate the products of mass communication is a recent development, made possible by the rise of digital technology. Realizing this, some media companies invite their audiences to send them materials they can use for their ads, websites, or television shows. Dove soap, for example, has run a contest that involves creating a commercial.

Scholars have pointed to the audience's ability to become part of mass media activities as a new development in the relationship between the audience and the companies that produce and distribute media materials. Some note that audience members are increasingly becoming part of the production process. We will see a lot of this phenomenon as we move through this book.

analog
electronic transmission accomplished by adding signals of varying frequency of amplitude to carrier waves of a given frequency of alternating electromagnetic current. Broadcast and phone transmissions conventionally have used analog technology.

digital
electronic technology that generates, stores, processes, and transmits data in the form of strings of 0s and 1s; each of these digits is referred to as a bit (and a string of bits that a computer can address individually as a group is a byte)

convergence
the ability of different media to easily interact with each other because they all deal with information in the same digital form

Mass Media, Culture, and Society

How Do We Use the Mass Media in Our Daily Lives?

The interest people have in sharing and sometimes manipulating media materials they like speaks to the role these materials play in the most personal parts of our lives. Media industries help us connect ourselves and our friends to parts of the world beyond our private circumstances—worlds of music, politics, war, and much more. Because they do that, mass media industries are a major force in society. To understand what this means, we have to dig deeper into how people use the media and what they get out of them.

Scholars have found that individuals adapt their use of mass media to their own particular needs. Broadly speaking, people use the media in four ways: for enjoyment, for companionship, for surveillance, and for interpretation. Let's examine these uses one at a time.

Enjoyment The desire for enjoyment is a basic human urge. Watching a television program, studying the Bible, finishing a newspaper crossword puzzle, networking on Facebook, or even reading an advertisement can bring this kind of gratification to many people.

News stories, daytime soap operas, sports, and prime-time sitcoms can ignite everyday talk with friends, relatives, work colleagues, and even strangers. During the mid-1990s, for example, many local television stations around the United States were advertising their morning talk programs by saying, "We give you something to talk about." This process of using media content for everyday interpersonal discussions is called using media materials as **social currency**, or coins of exchange. "Did you hear John Oliver's comments about climate change last night on HBO?" someone might ask around the water cooler at work. "Yes, and I disagree with much of what he said," one person might reply, triggering a chain of comments about *Last Week Tonight With John Oliver* that bring a number of people into the conversation.

Of course, another way people can bring mass media material into friendly conversation is by experiencing the content together. If you have attended Super Bowl parties, you have an idea of how a televised event can energize friends in ways that have little to do with what is taking place on the screen. You may even use Twitter to interact with friends—or make friends—around the particular TV shows you are viewing. In this way, the media provide us with the enjoyment we seek as a basic human need.

Companionship Mass media bring a sense of camaraderie to people who are lonely and those who are alone. A chronically ill hospital patient or a homebound senior citizen may find companionship by viewing a favorite sports team on TV or listening to the music of days gone by on the radio. Back when *Grey's Anatomy* was hugely popular, fans might have felt part of a community by reading the blogs written by the show's writers.

Sometimes media can even draw out people who feel troubled and in need of friends. The term "**parasocial interaction**" describes the psychological connections that some people establish with celebrities they learn about through the mass media— typically feeling a sense of bonding with those celebrities. Actors' Facebook pages and Twitter posts might lead fans to feel a special knowledge of and relationship with

Watching televised sporting events, either at someone's home or out at a bar, unites large groups of audience members, who may then go on to talk about the game in various ways that connect them to that larger audience—whether it's talking about the game with coworkers or engaging with other fans (and rivals) on social media. Online activities, such as fantasy football leagues, connect hundreds of thousands of sports fans from around the country, creating a new kind of social currency.

social currency
media content used as coins of exchange in everyday interpersonal discussions

parasocial interaction
the psychological connections that some media users establish with celebrities whom they learn about through the mass media

the person. You might know someone who gets so involved with media images of rock or rap stars that they sometimes act as if they know them well. In a few publicized cases, this feeling has gotten out of control, leading individuals to stalk and even harm the media figures who were the objects of their adulation. In 2009, for example, a man was arrested for trying to get into a vehicle with *American Idol* host Ryan Seacrest while possessing a knife. A month later he was arrested for attempting to approach the star in his workplace. A judge therefore forbade him from coming within 100 yards of Seacrest, his home, his car, or his places of employment.

Surveillance Surveillance users of the media employ them to learn about what is happening in the world. We all do this every day, often without realizing it. Do you turn on the radio, TV, or ask Amazon's Alexa each morning to find out the weather? Do you check the stock listings to find out how your investments are faring? Have you read classified ads in print or online to look for a job, concert tickets, or used furniture? Have you ever called or logged on to Fandango or Moviefone to find out where and when a film is playing? All these activities are illustrations of using the mass media for surveillance. Of course, our surveillance can be more global. Many people are interested in knowing what is going on in the world beyond their immediate neighborhood. Did the flooding upstate destroy any houses? Will Congress raise taxes? What's going on with the negotiations for peace in the Middle East?

surveillance
using the media to learn about what is happening in the world around us

Interpretation Many of us turn to the media to learn not only what is going on but also why and what, if any, actions we should take. When people try to find reasons that things are happening, they are looking for **interpretation**. We may read newspaper editorials to understand the actions of national leaders and to come to conclusions about our stand on an issue. We know that financial magazines such as *Money* and *Barron's* are written to appeal to people who want to understand how investment vehicles work and which ones to choose. And we are aware that libraries, bookstores, and some websites (for example, howstuffworks.com) specialize in "how to" topics ranging from raising children and installing a retaining wall to dying with dignity. Some people who are genuinely confused about some topics find mass media to be the most useful sources of answers. Preteens, for example, may want to understand why women and men behave romantically toward each other but may feel too embarrassed to ask their parents. They may be quite open to different opinions—in the *Twilight* films, in *The View*, in Adele's music, or in *Seventeen*—about where sexual attraction comes from and what the appropriate behavior is.

interpretation
using the media to find out why things are happening—who or what is the cause—and what to do about them

But how do people actually use the explanations they get from the mass media? Researchers have found that the credibility people place on the positions that mass media take depends on the extent to which the individuals agree with the values they find in that content. For example, a person who is rooted in a religiously conservative approach to the Bible would not be likely to agree with a nature book that is based on the theory of evolution; a political liberal probably would not be persuaded by the interpretations that politically conservative magazines offer about ways to end poverty. Keep in mind, however, that in these examples, these people would probably not search out such media content to begin with. Unless people have a good reason to confront materials that go against their values (unless they will be engaging in a debate on the ideas, for example), most people stay away from media content that do not reflect (and reinforce) their own beliefs, values, or interests. And if they do come across materials that go against their values, they may well dismiss them as biased.

THINKING ABOUT MEDIA LITERACY

Think about the kind of mashups of different mass media products that are being produced (for example, the movie trailer from *Ant-Man* and scenes from *The Fly* to create a riff on the *Ant-Man and the Wasp* trailer on Funny or Die.) What was the original intentions of the material being mashed up (the trailer)? What is the intention of the mashup? How does the mix change the way you think about the original?

Multiple Use of Mass Media Content The example of a preteen seeking interpretations of romance from four very different outlets—a movie series, a television talk show, a musical record, and a magazine—raises an important point about the four uses that people make of the mass media: the uses are not linked to any particular medium or genre. If we take television as an example, we might be tempted to suggest that enjoyment comes from certain sitcoms or adventure series, that companionship comes from soap operas, that surveillance is achieved through network and local news programs, and that interpretation can be found in Sunday morning political talk shows such as *Meet the Press*, as well as from daily talk fests such as *The View*. In fact, we may divide many kinds of content in these ways. Communication researchers point out, however, that individuals can get just about any gratification they are seeking from just about any program—or any kind of mass media materials.

You might find, for example, that you use the *NBC Nightly News* for enjoyment, surveillance, and interpretation. Enjoyment might come from the satisfaction of watching reporters' familiar faces day after day (is a little parasocial interaction working here?), surveillance might be satisfied by reports from different parts of the globe, and interpretation might flow from stray comments by the reporters and those they interview about what ought to be done to solve problems.

In thinking about the multiple uses of mass media content, consider too that the application of computer codes to mass media materials allows audience members to carry out enjoyment, companionship, surveillance, and interpretation in ways that did not exist before computer-centered mass communication. With the right tools, users can often manipulate the print, audio, or audiovisual materials to suit their needs and interests. (Think of a person whose keen interest in college sports has led him to create a website with links to the college sports sections of newspaper and TV websites.) Audience members who are connected to the producers of an audio or audiovisual program via a cable or telephone line can respond to those producers via the computer. The producers, in turn, can send out a new message that takes the response—the feedback—into consideration. This sort of manipulation and response—which is much easier in digital than in analog technology—is known as **interactivity**.

How Do the Mass Media Influence Culture?

When we use the term "**culture**," we are broadly talking about ways of life that are passed on to members of a society through time and that keep the society together. We typically use the word "**society**" to refer to large numbers of individuals, groups, and organizations that live in the same general area and consider themselves connected to one another through the sharing of a culture.

interactivity
the ability to track and respond to any actions triggered by the end user in order to cultivate a rapport

culture
ways of life that are passed on to members of a society through time and that keep the society together

What is shared includes learned behaviors, beliefs, and values. A culture lays out guidelines about who belongs to the society and what rules apply to them. It provides guideposts about where and what to learn, where and how to work, and how to eat and sleep. It tells us how we should act toward family members, friends, and strangers and much, much more. In other words, a culture helps us make sense of ourselves and our place in the world.

A culture provides people with ideas about the kinds of arguments concerning particular subjects that are acceptable. In American culture, people likely feel that on certain topics (e.g., vegetarianism) all sorts of positions are acceptable, whereas on other topics (e.g., cannibalism, incest) the range of acceptable views is much narrower. Moreover, American culture allows for the existence of groups with habits that many people consider odd and unusual but not threatening to the more general way of life. Such group lifestyles are called **subcultures**. The Amish of Pennsylvania who live without modern appliances at home represent such a subculture, as do Catholic monks who lead a secluded existence devoted to God.

For better or worse, it is not always easy to find direct evidence of who belongs and what the rules are by simply looking around. The mass media allow us to view clearly the ideas people have about their broad cultural connections with others and where they stand in the larger society. When mass media encourage huge numbers of people who are dispersed and unrelated to share the same materials, they are focusing people's attention on what is culturally important to think about and to talk and

society
large numbers of individuals, groups, and organizations that live in the same general area and consider themselves connected to one another through the sharing of a culture

subcultures
groups with habits that many people consider odd and unusual but not threatening to the more general way of life

---

GLOBAL MEDIA TODAY & CULTURE

A CASE STUDY OF CONVERGENCE: SONY CORPORATION

What do you think of when you hear the word *Sony*? A video game console? A record company? A Hollywood studio? A series of consumer electronics devices, such as television sets, cameras, headphones, smart mobile devices, Blu-ray, and DVD players? The fact is, it is all of the above and more. The Japanese conglomerate Sony purchased the US record company CBS Record Group in 1988 and the Hollywood studio Columbia Pictures in 1989, and since then it has been consolidating its presence in the global media content business in addition to its core activities centered on consumer electronics. The apparent goal of these acquisitions was to leverage media content and digital devices, reuniting under the same ownership the hardware (electronics) and the software (entertainment) in different media sectors.

In hindsight we can observe that with this strategy they anticipated and embraced the unfolding digital revolution. This strategic move led to synergies among the different businesses they operate in, made possible precisely by the convergence of these different sectors, generated by their digital development and evolution. It can be considered one large example of convergence within one conglomerate operating in the global media landscape, combining previously separate industries now reunited in the same digital environment. What do you think? Can legacy media companies thrive or even survive without embracing convergence and the digital change? How can they embrace convergence and digital change? What are the consequences of convergence for the consumers?

argue with others about. In other words, mass media create people's common lived experiences, a sense of the common culture, and the varieties of subcultures acceptable to that common culture.

The mass media present ideas of the culture in three broad and related ways: they help us (1) identify and discuss the codes of acceptable behavior within our society, (2) learn what and who counts in our world and why, and (3) determine what others think of us and what people "like us" think of others. Let's look at each of the ways separately.

Identifying and Discussing Codes of Acceptable Behavior A culture provides its people with notions about how to approach life's decisions, from waking to sleeping. It also gives people ideas about the arguments that are acceptable concerning all these subjects. If you think about the mass media from this standpoint, you'll realize that this is exactly what they do. Newspapers continually give us a look at how government works, as do internet sites such as *Politico* and the *Huffington Post*. TV's *Blue Bloods* and *True Detective* series act out behavior the police consider unacceptable and open up issues in which the rules of police and "criminal" behavior are contested or unclear. Magazine articles provide ideas and a range of arguments about what looks attractive and how to act toward the opposite sex. We may personally disagree with many of these ideas. At the same time, we may well realize that these ideas are shared and possibly accepted broadly in society.

Learning What and Who Counts in Our World—and Why Mass media tell us who is "famous"—from movie stars to scientists—and give us reasons why. They define the leaders to watch, from the US president to religious ministers. News reports tell us who these people are in "real life." Fictional presentations in books, movies, and TV dramas may tell us what they (or people like them) do and are like. Many of the presentations are angrily critical or bitingly satirical; American culture allows for this sort of argumentation. Through critical presentations or heroic ones, though, mass media presentations offer members of society a sense of the qualities that we ought to expect in good leaders.

Fiction often shows us what leaders ought to be like—what values count in society. Actor Liam Neeson excels at playing a strong, smart, and persevering father/husband/ex-husband in the popular *Taken* films and *The Grey*. Sometimes, mass media discussions of fiction and nonfiction merge in curious ways. Dan Coats, in 2015 a US senator from Indiana, linked fact and fiction when in a CNN television interview he responded to a question about Americans' acceptance of certain intelligence activities. "Americans understand the need for these activities," he told the program's anchor. "They watch [the Showtime series] *Homeland* and similar shows." (Coats in 2017 became the director of national intelligence for the Trump administration.)

Determining What Others Think of Us—and What People "Like Us" Think of Others Am I leadership material? Am I good-looking? Am I more or less religious than most people? Is what I like to eat what most people like to eat? Is my apartment as neat as most people's homes? How do I fit into the culture? Mass media allow us, and sometimes even encourage us, to ask questions such as these. When we read newspapers, listen to the radio, or watch TV, we can't help but compare ourselves to the portrayals these media present. Sometimes we may shrug off the comparisons with the clear conviction that we simply don't care if we are different from people who are famous or considered "in." Other times we might feel that we ought to be more in tune with what's going on; this may lead us to buy new clothes or adopt a new hairstyle. Often, we might simply take in ideas of what the world is like outside our direct reach and try to figure out how we fit in.

At the same time that the mass media get us wondering how we fit in, they may also encourage feelings of connection with people whom we have never met. Newscasters, textbooks, and even advertisements tell us that we are part of a nation that extends far beyond what we can see. We may perceive that sense of connection differently depending on our personal interests. We may feel a bond of sympathy with people in a US city that the news shows ravaged by floods. We may feel linked to people thousands of miles away who a website tells us share our political opinions. We may feel camaraderie with Super Bowl viewers around the country, especially those rooting for the team we are supporting.

Similarly, we may feel disconnected from people and nations that mass media tell us have belief systems that we do not share. US news and entertainment are filled with portrayals of nations, individuals, and types of individuals who, we are told, do not subscribe to key values of American culture. Labels such as "rogue nation," "Nazi," "communist," and "Islamic extremist" suggest threats to an American sense of decency. When mass media attach these labels to countries or individuals, we may well see them as enemies of our way of life, unless we have personal reasons not to believe the media portrayals.

Criticisms of Mass Media's Influence on Culture Some social observers have been critical of the way mass media have used their power as reflectors and creators of culture. One criticism is that mass media present unfortunate prejudices about the world by systematically using **stereotypes**, predictable depictions that reflect (and sometimes create) cultural prejudices, and **political ideologies**, beliefs about who should hold the greatest power within a culture and why. Another is that mass media detract from the quality of American culture. A third criticism, related to the first two, is that the mass media's cultural presentations encourage political and economic manipulation of their audiences.

Criticisms such as these have made people think deeply about the role that mass media play in American culture. These criticisms do have their weak points. Some might note that it is too simplistic to say that mass media detract from the quality of American culture. Different parts of the US population use the mass media differently and, as a result, may confront different kinds of images. Related to this point is the idea that people bring their own personalities to the materials they read and watch. They are not simply passive recipients of messages. They actively interpret, reshape, and even reject some of the messages.

Nevertheless, the observations about stereotypes, cultural quality, and political ideology should make us think about the power of mass media over our lives. Many people—most people at one time or another—do seem to see the mass media as mirroring parts of their society and the world beyond it, especially parts they do not know firsthand. Most people do accept what the mass media tell them in news—and even in entertainment—about what and who counts in their world and why. Many seem to believe that the mass media's codes of acceptable behavior accurately describe large numbers of people, even if the codes don't describe their own norms. And they accept the mass media's images as starting points for understanding where they fit in society in relation to others and their connection with, or disconnection from, others. They may disagree with these images or think that they shouldn't exist. Nevertheless, the media images serve as starting points for their concerns about and arguments over reality. There will be further discussion about critical views on the effects of media in Chapter 2.

stereotypes
predictable depictions that reflect (and sometimes create) cultural prejudices

political ideologies
beliefs about who should hold the greatest power within a culture and why

---

THINKING ABOUT MEDIA LITERACY

Throughout your day you consume different types of media. Which are analog? Which are digital? Think about media content that you might use in both analog and digital form (i.e., a print and a downloaded book, an album and a Pandora channel). What are the differences in the consumption experience with the two? Which do you prefer?

Media Literacy

The aim of this book is to help you learn how to seriously examine the mass media's role in your life and in American life. The goal is not to make you cynical and distrustful of all mass media. Rather, it is to help you think in an educated manner about the forces that shape the media and your relationships with them so that you will better evaluate what you see and hear. The aim is to give you the tools you need to become media-literate.

A media-literate person is

- knowledgeable about the influences that guide media organizations,
- up-to-date on political issues relating to the media,
- sensitive to ways of seeing media content as a means of learning about culture,
- sensitive to the ethical dimensions of media activities,
- knowledgeable about scholarship regarding media effects, and
- able to enjoy media materials in a sophisticated manner.

Being media-literate can be satisfying and fun. For example, knowing movie history can make watching films fascinating because you will be able to notice historical and technical features of the films that you wouldn't have otherwise noticed. Having a comparative understanding of different forms of news can help you think more clearly about what you can expect from journalism today and how it is changing. Understanding the forces that shape the entertainment we see and hear, as well as the social controversies around stereotyping and violence in entertainment, can make your daily use of the media a jumping-off point for thinking critically about yourself in relation to images of others in society. All these and other media activities can also start important conversations between you and your friends about the directions of our culture and your place in it. That, in turn, can help you become a more aware and responsible citizen—parent, voter, worker—in our media-driven society (see Figure 1.4).

Principles of Media Literacy

When we speak about **literacy**, we mean the ability to effectively comprehend and use messages that are expressed in written or printed symbols, such as letters. When we speak about **media literacy**, however, we mean something broader. To quote the National Leadership Conference on Media Literacy, it is "the ability to access, analyze, evaluate and communicate messages in a variety of forms."

Much of what we know about the world comes from what we see and hear in the media. Beyond simply mirroring what our world looks like, the media interpret, alter, and modify our reality. To develop media literacy skills and become responsible,

literacy
the ability to effectively comprehend and use messages that are expressed in written or printed symbols, such as letters

media literacy
the ability to apply critical thinking skills to the mass media, thereby becoming a more aware and responsible citizen—parent, voter, worker—in our media-driven society

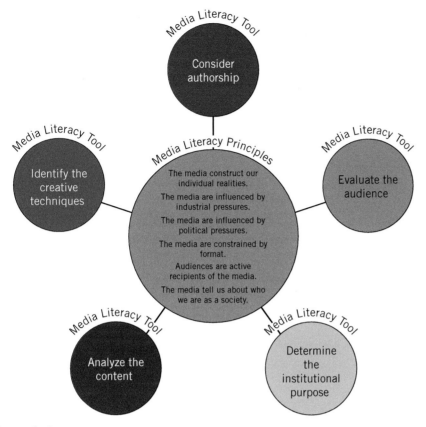

Figure 1.4
Steps to becoming a media-literate citizen.

media-literate consumers who can critically examine the way the media work in our lives, we first need to understand some basic principles about mass media materials—principles that help us engage in and understand the media's role in our daily lives.

Principle 1: The Media Construct Our Individual Realities Along with our personal observations and experiences, media materials help us create our own individual notions of reality. Much of what we see as reality comes from the media we've experienced, and it is sometimes difficult to distinguish between our personal experiences and the world of the media. When we read newspapers, watch TV, and surf the web, we need to be aware that what we are seeing and hearing is not reality—even so-called reality TV. Rather, media materials are created with specific purposes in mind. They are constructions—that is, human creations that present a kind of script about the culture. Even when media materials appear to be particularly "natural" or reflective of reality, many different business decisions and constraints have contributed to the way they are constructed.

Principle 2: The Media Are Influenced by Industrial Pressures We have already noted in this chapter that mass media materials are produced by organizations that exist in a commercial setting. The need to bring in revenues, often to sell advertising, is foremost in the minds of those who manage these organizations. As such, when you decode the media, you need to ask yourself: Who paid for this? What economic decisions went into creating this product? What financial pressures affected the distribution and exhibition of this product?

As we'll see in forthcoming chapters, mass media's industrial implications also involve ownership. If the same company owns a record company, a movie studio, a cable service, a television network, and book and magazine publications, it has a powerful ability to control what is produced, circulated, and therefore seen. Large companies also have the ability to take advantage of media convergence more than do small ones—another factor influencing what is produced, circulated, and seen.

Principle 3: The Media Are Influenced by Political Pressures Politics refers to the way a society is governed. When it comes to mass media, the term refers to a variety of activities. These range from the specific regulations that governments place on mass media, to decisions by courts about what restrictions the government can place on the media, to the struggle by various interest groups to change what media do (often using government leverage). For many media observers, being aware that media operate within a political environment leads to the idea that this environment deeply influences the media content itself. To them, this means we should be aware that the ideas in the media have political implications—that they are ideological.

Principle 4: The Media Are Influenced by Format Media scholar Patricia Aufterheide and others note that every medium—the television, the movie, the magazine—has its own characteristics, codes, and conventions, its own ways of presenting cultural reality.

Although you probably haven't thought about it, it's a good bet that you recognize the differences between the ways these media do things. A report on a presidential press conference looks different depending on whether it was written for a newspaper or a magazine, presented on TV as news, described on a website's blog, or put together for the big screen. You probably also recognize, though, that mass media are similar in some of their approaches to presenting the world—they organize the world into a number of basic storytelling forms that we recognize as entertainment, news, information, education, and advertising. As a media-literate person, you should ask yourself: What about the format of this medium influences the content? What about the format limits the kind of content that is likely to be shown?

Principle 5: Audiences Are Active Recipients of the Media The process of making meaning out of media is an ongoing interaction between the reader and the materials. As individual audience members, we filter meaning through our unique experiences: our socioeconomic status, cultural background, gender, and so on. However, emphasizing the input of the individual does not take away from the broad social importance of the media. Because so many people share mass media materials, large segments of society see mass media as having cultural importance for society as a whole.

Principle 6: The Media Tell Us About Who We Are as a Society People may like what they see about their society, or they may complain about it. They may want people to view media images about themselves and others, or they may fear that others will be influenced negatively by certain products (e.g., stereotypes and violence). Even with an active audience, then, mass media hold crucial importance for society's visions of itself. A media-literate person searches out bias and explores the assumptions and the values in everything that is made through the production, distribution, and exhibition processes.

Media Literacy Tools

To be a critical consumer in a mediated society, you need to equip yourself with tools that enable you to distinguish between different media forms and know how to ask basic questions. From the media literacy principles we discussed previously flow a series of five basic categories of questions that you can use to begin to take apart and explore any media message. Typically, you would apply this questioning process to a specific media "text"—that is, an identifiable production or publication, or a part of one: an episode of *The Vampire Diaries*, an ad for Orangina, an issue of *Wired* magazine, a billboard for Guinness beer, photos and articles about a bank robbery on the home page of a news site, or the Super Bowl telecast. Sometimes a media "text" can involve multiple formats. A new animated Disney film, for example, involves not only a blockbuster movie released in thousands of theaters but also a whole campaign of advertising and merchandising—character dolls and toys, clothes, lunchboxes, and so on—as well as a website, storybooks, games, and perhaps eventually, a ride at one of the Disney theme parks. Consider, too, that with the convergence of digital media, the movie that appears in theaters also will likely appear in other media—as will the games, storybooks, and other products based on it.

Let's take a look at these skill-building categories one at a time. They all involve asking questions about the media. Don't worry if you don't feel comfortable answering them now. You'll feel much more able as you move through this book.

Consider Authorship Ask yourself: Who created this message, and why are they sending it? To explore the idea of "authorship" in media literacy is to look deeper than just knowing whose name is on the cover of a book or all the jobs in the credits of a movie. Companies make media texts just as buildings and highways are put together. Lead companies make the plans and then call on a variety of firms to make the products and do the work, the building blocks are brought together, and ordinary people get paid to do various jobs. Whether we are watching the nightly news, passing a billboard on the street, or reading a political campaign flyer, the media messages we experience are created and circulated by various organizations in which individuals (and often teams of individuals) have written the words, captured the images, and worked the technical marvels.

Disney has maintained a significant merchandise campaign for Star Wars, based both on the old movies and on the new ones. Digital advertising, such as movie trailers, and merchandise encompass only a small part of the promotion process of advertising media such as a blockbuster movie.

Be aware, too, that in this creative process choices are made. If some words are spoken, others are not or are edited out. If one picture is selected, dozens may have been rejected. If an ending to a story is written one way, other endings may not have been explored. However, as the audience, we don't typically get to see or hear the words, pictures, or endings that were rejected. We see, hear, or read only what was accepted. Rarely does anybody ever explain why certain choices were made. Rarely, too, do creators bring up alternative ways to interpret the world we see through our media channels. It is up to us to consider the constructed nature of our media realities and, when possible and important to us, look for a variety of perspectives on the same realities.

Evaluate the Audience This proposition involves two broad questions. The first is, who are the intended targets of these media materials? The second is, how might different people understand these materials similarly and differently?

Thinking about the intended targets gets us back to the point that industries typically construct media materials to make money. As we will see, that often means deciding what types of people would want certain kinds of content and creating products designed to fit these interests. As straightforward as this idea sounds, we will see that it is really quite complex. Entire companies revolve around helping firms describe lucrative target audiences, evaluate their interests, and figure out how to reach them. Other firms make money evaluating whether the audiences that were targeted actually attended to the messages. "Audience research" is, in fact, a big business that is increasingly important to all media industries, from books and newspapers to the internet and video games. The more you learn about it, the more you will understand the multitude of factors that lead to the sometimes different media worlds that different people encounter. Moreover, in a world where convergence is common, media firms are likely to try to follow their target audiences with the same content across a variety of platforms. ESPN, for example, will want you to tune into its cable channel, its internet site, its tablet app, and its phone feed.

As we will see, the companies that produce, circulate, and sponsor media materials often have certain ideas in mind about what specific audiences will share as funny, sad, repulsive, scary, and exhilarating. Even though they contend that these notions are based on research, they also may be rooted in social stereotypes. To understand the forces leading to social stereotypes, it is useful to explore the social histories of the groups particular media firms are constructing and targeting as their audiences. Thinking about audience this way when you confront media materials will force you to dive into some of the most interesting questions about their creation and the roles they play in society.

Determine the Institutional Purpose Ask yourself: Why is this content being sent? This question flows from the previous questions about the audience. We noted that much of the world's media were developed as moneymaking enterprises and continue to operate today as commercial businesses. As we will see, with the rise of digital convergence, companies associated with products from particular industries are trying to make money from those products across various media platforms. We will see in Chapters 8 and 9, for example, how newspaper and magazine publishers are redefining their output for the laptop, the tablet, and the mobile phone—while still trying to sell printed versions of their products. Chapters 8 and 9 also discuss how newspapers and magazines decide how much space they can devote to different kinds of material based on the amount and kinds of advertisements they sell. Chapter 3 sets up the more general idea that what is really being sold through commercial media is not just the advertised products to the audience but also the audience to the advertisers!

Analyze the Content Ask yourself: What values, lifestyles, and points of view are represented in (or omitted from) this message? Because all media messages are constructed, choices have to be made. These choices inevitably reflect the values, attitudes, and points of view of the ones doing the constructing. The decisions about a character's age, gender, or race mixed in with the lifestyles, attitudes, and behaviors that are portrayed; the selection of a setting (urban or rural, affluent or poor); and the actions and reactions in the plot are just some of the ways that values become part of a TV show, a movie, or an ad. As we will discuss in Chapter 3, even the news reflects values in the decisions made about which stories go first, how long they are, what kinds of pictures are chosen, and so on.

Our discussion of scholarly media research in Chapter 2 will provide you with a variety of tools for analyzing content. There, as well as throughout this book, we address two major complaints that many people have about the widespread mass media: (1) less popular or new ideas can have a hard time getting aired, especially if they challenge long-standing assumptions or commonly accepted beliefs; and (2) unless challenged, old assumptions can create and perpetuate stereotypes, thus further limiting our understanding and appreciation of the world and the many possibilities of human life.

Identify the Creative Techniques Ask yourself: What creative techniques are being used to attract my attention? This question relates partly to the need to identify the ways that media materials provide clues to their institutional purpose and choices made. You should think about how a message is constructed to connect with its intended audience, including the creative components that are used in putting it together—words, still images, moving images, camera angle, music, color, movement, and many more components. Apart from the issue of targeting, understanding the creative techniques of mass media will aid your appreciation of the artistry involved. All forms of communication—whether print magazine covers, television advertisements, or horror movies—depend on a kind of "creative language." For example, use of different colors creates different feelings, camera close-ups often convey intimacy, and scary music heightens fear. As we will see, learning the history of a medium involves learning the ways that companies have organized words and images to draw and captivate audiences. Go beyond what you learn here to immerse yourself in the creative languages of media that you love—whether they are comic books, romance novels, hip-hop recordings, cowboy films, daily newspapers, video games on mobile devices, or other elements of media culture. Try to understand how the techniques involved in creating those products change when companies adapt them for other media. What you learn will undoubtedly be fascinating, and it will make your everyday interactions with those media extremely interesting.

THINKING ABOUT MEDIA LITERACY

When you sneak a look at your phone during a class lecture to see updates to your favorite social media feed, which of the basic human needs is it satisfying? Does looking at the same content satisfy different needs at different times? What are some examples?

The Benefits of a Media-Literate Perspective

Armed with the principles of media literacy and the tools to evaluate any media message, you are on your way to developing a media-literate perspective. For those who adopt this perspective, the power held by the mass media raises a host of social issues, including the following:

- Do media conglomerates have the ability to control what we receive over a variety of media channels? If so, do they use that ability? How do their activities affect the way digital convergence is taking place?
- Are portrayals of sex and violence increasing in the new media environment, as some critics allege? Do media organizations have the power to lower the amount of sex and violence? Would they do it if they could?

- Does the segmentation of audiences by media companies lead to better advertising discounts and greater diversity of content for groups that those firms consider more attractive than for groups that those firms consider less important? If so, what consequences will that have for social tensions and the ability of parts of society to share ideas with one another?
- What (if anything) should be done about the increasing ability of mass media firms to invade people's privacy by storing information they gain when they interact with them? Should the federal government pass laws that force companies to respect people's privacy, or should we leave it up to corporate self-regulation? What do we know about the history of corporate self-regulation that would lead us to believe that it would or wouldn't work in this situation?
- Should global media companies adapt to the cultural values of the nations in which they work, even if those values infringe on free press and free speech?

Our exploration of these and related questions will take us into topics that you may not associate with the mass media business—for example, mobile phones, toys, games, and supermarkets. It will also sometimes take us far beyond the United States because American mass media companies increasingly operate globally. They influence non-US firms around the world and are influenced by them. As we will see, their activities have sparked controversies in the United States and abroad that will likely intensify as the 21st century unfolds.

CHAPTER REVIEW

 Visit the Companion Website at www.routledge.com/cwturow for additional study resources.

 ## Key Terms

You can find the definitions to these key terms in the marginal glossary throughout this chapter. Test your knowledge of these terms with interactive flash cards on the *Media Today* Companion Website.

analog	interpersonal communication	parasocial interaction
audience fragmentation	interpretation	political ideologies
channel	literacy	receiver
communication	mass media	social currency
convergence	mass media outlets	society
culture	mass production process	source
decoding	media literacy	stereotypes
digital	mediated interpersonal	subcultures
encoding	communication	surveillance
feedback	medium	transmitter
industrial nature	messages	
interactivity	noise	

Questions for Discussion and Critical Thinking

1. The ease of content production and distribution by anyone, not just media organizations, is one of the major changes in today's media. Think about some of the kinds of materials you create or share and apply the principles of media literacy to them. Which of the principles are particularly relevant to the creation and distribution of personal media and which are not?

2. Think about a television program you normally watch and apply the media literacy tools of "evaluating the audience," "analyzing the content," and "identifying the creative techniques." In what ways do the content and creative techniques clearly reflect the audience (you?) they are likely to be targeting? Now, watch a program you normally would never watch. What clues can you see to what kind of audience it would be trying to target?

3. The array of options for receiving media content is ever expanding. Media names that people used to associate with one technology platform (for example, printed paper or film) we now associate with a number of platforms (for example, websites or mobile phone apps). Pick one of the following: books, movies, television, music, or newspapers. What was the "original" ("legacy") platform? Describe two platforms you associate the medium with now. What are the advantages/disadvantages of newer platforms for consuming that content over the legacy platform?

4. Media literacy is defined by the National Leadership Conference on Media Literacy as "the ability to access, analyze, evaluate, and create media." Why do you think they consider "creating media" to be a part of media literacy?

Activity

The Idea: Do a snapshot of your personal media use. Think about your media consumption for a typical week and compile an inventory of the following:

- The media "delivery systems" you used (These would be anything you use to read, listen to, or watch media—from devices (phone, radio, television) to apps)
- How many people/organizations did you check/follow on
  - Facebook,
  - Twitter,
  - Instagram, or
  - Other?
- How many books or parts of books did you read in paper form?
- How many books did you read online (that is, on a browser) or in an app?
- How many magazines or newspapers did you read in paper (analog) form?
- How many did you read online or in an app?
- How many music CDs did you purchase in physical form?
- How many music downloads did you purchase?
- How many movies did you watch in a movie theater?
- How many movies did you watch on a television?
- How many movies did you stream?
- How much did you pay for:
  - Wireless access for home computer,
  - Smartphone,
  - Movie theater tickets,
  - Access to streaming video,
  - Magazine or newspaper print subscriptions,
  - Online access to newspaper or magazine sites,
  - Cable or satellite television,
  - Recorded music—in any form,
  - Printed books (for pleasure—not school),
  - Digital books,
  - Video/online games, or
  - Media apps (ones that give access to games/publications/entertainment media)?

Comment: What do you feel about this list of media use? What surprises you about the detailing of your media use? Note that these are probably only a few of the media you come into contact with each week. Outdoor ads, cereal boxes, and supermarket floor signs are just a few of the media many of us pass every day.

Making Sense of Research on Media Effects and Media Culture

2

CHAPTER OBJECTIVES

1   Identify and explain what mass media research is.

2   Recognize and discuss the mainstream approaches to mass media research.

3   Recognize the shift from mainstream approaches to critical approaches.

4   Recognize and discuss the critical approaches to mass media research.

5   Recognize and discuss the cultural studies approaches to mass media research.

6   Harness your media literacy skills regarding media research and effects to understand and evaluate the media's presence and influence in your life.

Imagine a communication major, Vert, who is a junior at a college near a large city. She also has a strong interest in protecting the environment; she works part-time for a local organization that checks the safety of the area's landfills, water supply, and air. Vert has recently become alarmed at the barrage of ads for dresses, pants, shoes, and accessories of all kinds that she receives on social media, sees on video and TV channels, and hears on music services. As interested in fashion as her friends, Vert is nevertheless torn between the urge to buy the newest wardrobes she sees and a concern that the constant turnover of clothing in American society may be contributing to the degradation of the environment. The problems come in the energy to make, pack, and ship the new products, as well as in the cost of landfills when they are thrown away.

Vert realizes that her friends are avid viewers of fashion-themed reality programs such as various versions of *Project Runway* on Lifetime, *What the Fashion* on E!, and Vogue Fashion Week videos. They also follow various stores and brands on Instagram, Tumblr, and other social media. Having just learned about media convergence in one of her communication classes, Vert is aware that the fashion programs, photos, and ads that she encounters in one medium also cross over to many other media and so reach their fan base in many ways. Lifetime even released a *Project Runway* DVD for every one of its seasons; they are also on Hulu. She learns, too, that fashion-themed reality TV series can be found in many of the wealthier countries around the world. All this both fascinates and worries Vert. "If people in the richer areas of the globe slowed their interest in fast-changing fashion just a bit," she muses, "that might have a small but growing good effect on the environments where they live."

Vert thinks she may have a way to attack the problem. She herself has become an avid finder of great clothes in local consignment stores. These are places where people offer lightly used garments and accessories they don't want any more for a price they share with the store's owner. If more people her age sold their clothes through those stores instead of throwing them away, and if more people her age bought their clothes through those places, it would place a much lighter load on the environment, she figures. How, though, can the consignment world make itself as fashionable as the new-clothing industry? The answer, she thinks, is to get E!, Lifetime, and some other media channels aimed at people around her age to highlight consignment outlets as wonderful places to find fashion.

"I know lots of college students who watch E! and Lifetime," Vert says to her boyfriend, Jasper, over lunch. "If

> "There are in fact no masses; there are only ways of seeing people as masses."

RAYMOND WILLIAMS, CULTURAL PHILOSOPHER

they saw those channels emphasizing consignment fashion on TV and through the other media they use, I bet it would spark so much interest in social media that new consignment stores would open up all over the place."

"You're being very optimistic," Jasper answers, "but you may be right. The trick, of course, is to get those companies to do it. Why would they?"

Vert finds that a number of friends at the place she works share her concerns about the constant pull of new fashion. Kaj, an economics and environmental studies major, helps her put together a "fact sheet" that demonstrates that increased use of consignment fashion can bring large savings to shoppers, as well as important health benefits to the environment. Fact sheet in hand, Vert drives to her local cable system with a request that they persuade E! and Lifetime to plug "consignment fashion" and use its own media-convergence activities to demonstrate the value of buying clothes that way. The community-relations manager listens politely to her complaints and her suggestion, but he never gets back to her. Kaj and Jasper both hypothesize that a local cable system doesn't have the motivation to plug consignment stores when it is interested in getting ads from local department and specialty clothing stores. The same may be true for the large cable networks, they realize.

Vert is determined not to let the idea drop. But what should she do now? Jasper advises her to start with the basics. "You need to research the effects of TV and of convergence, as well as how cable TV operates. If you go out there and start complaining publicly and offering advice with no real knowledge about the impact of programming or how it's created and distributed, you may come off looking foolish. And the people who run the cable system and the networks will have had their way." Jasper suggests that her first step might be to talk to her advisor. "Get his input into how all this works, what effects fashion images and stories might have, and the best ways to influence the companies that put them on the air and over the internet," he says.

Vert decides to give it a try, so she shares her concerns with her advisor, communication professor Felix Ora.

"It's an interesting topic," Professor Ora says. "In fact, it's an issue I would love to pose to the graduate students in my Media Theory class. Why don't you come to the class next week, and I'll get the students to help you brainstorm?" Vert tells him that's a great idea, but she secretly worries that the grad students might be more inclined to think about "ivory tower" concepts and not about her concerns regarding the cable programs. Nevertheless, she shows up in the graduate class to find that she has hit on a hot-button topic with a substantial proportion of the students, who are eager to express their viewpoints and link them to scholarly research. In this chapter are the kinds of things you might hear if you were in on the discussions.

The Nature of Mass Media Research

Research is the application of a systematic method to solve a problem or understand it better than in the past. **Mass media research** involves the use of systematic methods to understand or solve problems regarding the mass media.

The research we are concerned with in this chapter tries to answer questions that relate to society's bottom line, not to a company's bottom line. Understanding how the research developed also means understanding how the mass media developed and how people responded to them. The research we review here asks about the role mass media play in improving or degrading the relationships, values, and ideals of society and the people who make up that society.

mass media research
the use of systematic methods to understand or solve problems regarding the mass media

The Early Years of Mass Media Research in the United States

Nearly a hundred years ago, two major media issues preoccupied the thinkers of the day. The first was the media's role in helping to keep a sense of American community alive. The second was the media's role in encouraging bad behavior among children—an issue that faded rather quickly, only to reappear many years later.

Searching for Community: Early Critical Studies Research

The early 20th century was a time of enormous social change in American society. The industrial revolution was in full swing, and factories were turning out machine-made consumer products at low cost in numbers that had never been seen before. Many of these factories were located in cities, and they drew millions of workers who streamed out of farming communities in order to take advantage of the higher salaries and better opportunities of urban life.

Even more numerous than the workers who came to the cities from US farms were the immigrants from central and eastern Europe who were teeming into American ports looking for a piece of the American dream. For many, the dream turned out to be a bit of a nightmare, at least at first. A large number of the newcomers, poor and unable to speak the English language, led a difficult, even hand-to-mouth existence that contrasted dramatically with the lives of the wealthy urban industrialists of the day and the relatively modest, yet still quite comfortable, situation of most nonimmigrants.

Mott Street in downtown New York City circa 1900—an area known as "Little Italy" because it was home to many of the Italian immigrants. During this time, newcomers to America banded together to create self-sustaining neighborhoods where inhabitants shared cultural values and the same language, making it difficult to pressure the immigrants into assimilating.

Social observers in this period considered this a very serious situation. It wasn't just the poverty that concerned them. They also worried that this new urban, often non–English-speaking population of immigrants who knew little of American values would endanger the small-town democratic community that they believed had characterized American society before the late 19th century. Could the traditional sense of community—that shared sense of responsibility that people felt toward their neighbors and their nation—be sustained in cities where so few people knew or cared about one another? Could the torrents of immigrants be brought into the mainstream of American society so that they considered its values their own?

You may not agree that the questions these social observers asked were the correct ones. You may feel that these people were romanticizing small-town communities. Or you might argue that those who already lived in the United States did not have the right to impose their "American" values on the new immigrants. These are quite legitimate objections, but at the turn of the 20th century, many people considered US society's biggest problems to be preserving a sense of small-town community and making sure immigrants "assimilated."

The pessimists among them concluded that there really was no hope—that urban society, especially immigrant urban society, would destroy the connectedness that they associated with small-town America. Drawing on late 19th-century European writings on the dangers of the "crowd" (or the "masses" as they were sometimes called), the prejudiced among US citizens saw these urban crowds as having dangerously irrational tendencies. There was, they felt, a good reason to keep immigrants away from US shores.

A group of prominent sociologists at the University of Chicago argued publicly and in their scholarly writings that it was precisely because of the mass media that the situation in "mass society" was not nearly as bleak as some thought. Professors Robert Park, John Dewey, and Charles Cooley suggested that the widespread popularity of newspapers and magazines in the early 20th century allowed for the creation of a new type of community (see Figure 2.1).

Figure 2.1
According to the Chicago School of Sociology, media have power to bring disparate individuals together by broadcasting the same notions of society to large numbers of people who might otherwise never interact, thereby creating a new type of community.

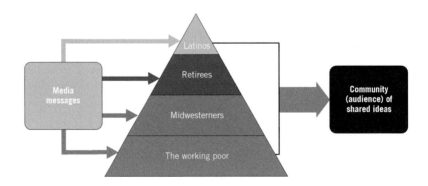

These researchers argued that the media brought together large numbers of geographically separated, diverse individuals who would otherwise be disconnected from one another and from a common notion of society and allowed them to share ideas about the society without assembling in the same geographic area. They said that if media firms acted responsibly, Americans—both newcomers and those here from birth—could learn ideas that were essential to their democracy from the media's messages. Robert Park conducted a study of the immigrant press in the United States and concluded that, far from keeping the foreigners in their own little ethnic worlds, the immigrant newspapers were helping people over time acclimate to American society. Immigrants, he said, were using their foreign-language media to learn how to be good citizens.

Cooley and Dewey were social philosophers. Their work tended to be conceptual rather than empirical. Park, a former newspaper reporter, was more empirically oriented. All three were the most prominent members of what became known as the Chicago School of Sociology. Many of their ideas are fresh and interesting even today. Not everyone agreed with them then (and not everyone agrees with them now). Nevertheless, they were among the first US academics to show how systematically presented ideas and research about the mass media could feed into important social issues.

Fearing Propaganda: Early Concerns About Persuasion

At about the same time that Cooley, Dewey, and Park were writing about ways the mass media could help society maintain an informed democratic public, other researchers were expressing strong concerns about unethical rulers using the power of the mass media to reach huge numbers of people for undemocratic ends.

University of Chicago political science professor Harold Lasswell saw mass media organizations as powerful weapons of persuasion because they reached enormous numbers of geographically dispersed people in very short periods of time. Never before in history had this been possible, Lasswell and other researchers pointed out. They feared that powerful interest groups in a society would use mass media as **propaganda**— messages designed to change the attitudes and behavior of huge numbers of otherwise disconnected individuals on controversial social issues. Under the right conditions, they feared, such propaganda would enable rulers to spread lies through the media and manipulate large numbers of people to support their views. Those in the society who opposed these rulers would be at a substantial disadvantage.

propaganda
messages designed to change the attitudes and behavior of huge numbers of otherwise disconnected individuals on controversial social issues

One reason that such fears abounded in the United States had to do with the successful manipulation of newspaper reports and photographs by both the Allies and the German government during World War I. The head of the US propaganda effort, George Creel, wrote a popular book, *How We Advertised America* (1920), in which he boasted that expertly crafted messages—on billboards, on records, and in movies— had moved huge numbers of people to work for the war effort. In addition, *The Brass Check* (1919), a book by the social critic Upton Sinclair, alleged that major advertisers demanded favorable coverage of their products in newspapers in exchange for ad space purchases. Many liberal thinkers of the day saw these activities as fundamentally threatening to democracy, given that citizens often had no idea of the intentions behind the messages they were seeing and hearing.

Some writers, such as journalist Walter Lippmann, argued that the most important culprits hindering US newspapers' objective portrayal of the world were not propaganda forces. Rather, said Lippmann, the culprits were US journalists themselves. Because they were mere mortals with selective ways of seeing things, and because they worked in organizations with deadlines, restrictions on story length, and the need to grab readers' attentions, news journalists often portrayed predictably patterned (stereotyped), limited views of the world. In his book *Public Opinion* (1922), Lippmann argued that the news media are a primary source of the "pictures in our heads" about the external world of public affairs that is "out of reach, out of sight, out of mind." Lippmann's notion that the media create "the ideas in our heads" about what is going on in the world is referred to as **agenda setting.**

agenda setting
the notion that the media create "the ideas in our heads" about what is going on in the world

Chief of Staff George C. Marshall enlisted well-known director Frank Capra (who later directed *It's a Wonderful Life*, among other films) to create a series of seven propaganda films that the government showed American soldiers during World War II to explain why it was important for them to be fighting in this war. Propaganda analysts would examine films such as these for their efficacy in convincing soldiers that the United States was right to be involved in the war in Europe.

propaganda analysis
the systematic examination of mass media messages that seem designed to sway the attitudes of large populations on controversial issues

Other academic thinkers of the era were more likely to emphasize the propagandistic aspect of the press. Academics of the 1920s and 1930s, such as Leonard Doob, Alfred McLung Lee, Ralph Casey, and George Seldes, saw the importance of systematically exploring the forces guiding media companies and the value of analyzing media content. They felt that by letting people know how media firms operate, they could help citizens protect themselves from the undue power of those firms. They called the activity **propaganda analysis**, a type of content analysis that systematically examines mass media messages designed to sway the attitudes of large populations on controversial issues. In their propaganda analysis studies, specially trained coders examined messages (articles, movies, radio shows) for elements that the researchers believed to be significant.

For example, analysts in the late 1930s were concerned that US newspapers were negatively portraying the communist Soviet Union and potentially harming the chances for a US–Soviet collaboration against Hitler's Germany. To find out what influential newspapers were doing, the researchers might have systematically examined two years of articles about the Soviet Union in major US newspapers. The researchers would be trained (and tested on their ability) to note a variety of topics included in the coverage of that country, from music, to crime, to politics. After analyzing the findings, the researchers would be able to come to quantitative conclusions about the messages about the Soviet Union that major press outlets were presenting to large numbers of Americans.

Some writers on the history of mass communication research have suggested that propaganda analysts took a **magic bullet or hypodermic needle approach** to mass communication (see Figure 2.2). By this, they mean that the propaganda analysts believed

Figure 2.2
The hypodermic needle or magic bullet approach has been used by researchers as a punching bag to illustrate what they believe is a simplistic view of media effects.

that messages delivered through the mass media persuaded all people powerfully and directly (as if they had been hit by a bullet or injected by a needle) without the people having any control over the way they reacted. For example, critics say that propaganda analysts believed that a well-made ad, an emotionally grabbing movie, or a vivid newspaper description would be able to sway millions of people toward the media producers' goals.

But the terms "magic bullet" and "hypodermic needle" are too simplistic to describe the effects that propaganda analysts felt the media had on individuals. For one thing, the propaganda analysts certainly did not believe that all types of messages would be equally persuasive. (They stated, for example, that audiences would more likely to accept messages that reinforced common values than messages that contradicted common values.) For another, they emphasized that propaganda is more likely to work under circumstances of media monopoly than when many competitive media voices argue over the ideas presented. They believed, too, that people could be taught to critically evaluate (and thus not be so easily influenced by) propaganda.

Nevertheless, propaganda analysts of the 1920s and 1930s tended to focus more on media producers and their output than they did on members of society. They assumed that most members of society shared similar understandings of media messages, and they didn't focus on the possibility that individual audience members might interpret messages in different ways. However, another way of seeing media influence—one that suited very different social questions—was developing.

magic bullet or hypodermic needle approach
the idea that messages delivered through the mass media persuade all people powerfully and directly (as if they were hit by a bullet or injected by a needle) without the people having any control over the way they react

Kids and Movies: Continuing Effects Research

By the mid-1920s, large numbers of parents, social workers, and public welfare organizations were worried about whether specific films might be negatively affecting youngsters. Invented just a few decades earlier, the movies had become very much a part of Americans' leisure activities by the 1920s. As children and teenagers became accustomed to moviegoing, adults fretted that the violence, sexual suggestiveness, and misrepresentations of reality in many of the films they watched might bring about a slew of problems in their lives. Among the ills suggested were bad sleep patterns, improper notions of romance, and violent conduct.

These ideas may sound very modern to have been around as early as the 1920s. You may know (and we'll note later in the book) that in recent years television programs, comic books, video games, sports programs, the internet, and songs, as well as movies, have all been accused of encouraging these same problems among US youth.

These early controversies over movies marked the first time that social

Studying children's emotional reactions to different genres of movies is one method that researchers have used to determine media's effects.

researchers carried out systematic research to determine whether these accusations had any basis in reality. The most important of these projects, formally known as Motion Pictures and Youth, is more commonly referred to as the Payne Fund Studies because a foundation called the Payne Fund paid for the project. The research effort was led by Professor W. W. Charters of The Ohio State University and was conducted by the most prominent psychologists, sociologists, and educators of the day. The studies, published in 1933, look at the effects of particular films on sleep patterns, knowledge about foreign cultures, attitudes about violence, and delinquent behavior.

The researchers used a range of empirical techniques, including experiments, surveys, and content analysis. One especially interesting survey was qualitative: a sociologist interviewed female college students about the extent to which and ways in which movies had affected their notions of romance. A noteworthy experiment was aimed at determining whether children who had seen violent films slept more restlessly than those who had seen only nonviolent films. The children in the experiment were shown a movie featuring a lot of fighting, whereas those in the control condition saw a film with no combat at all. To determine the effects of the films on sleep, the researchers had the children sleep where they could observe them. Among other aspects of the children's sleep, the researchers measured their "restlessness" by attaching equipment to their beds that would note how often they moved and turned. They found that the children who had viewed the violent film tossed and turned more than the ones who had not.

Some popular commentators in the 1930s suggested that the results showed that individual movies could have major negative effects on all children—a kind of hypodermic needle effect. Most of the Payne Fund researchers themselves, though, went out of their way to point out that youngsters' reactions to movies were not at all uniform. Instead, these reactions very much depended on specific social and psychological differences among children. A sociologist in the group, for example, concluded that a particular film might move a youngster to want or not want to be a criminal. The specific reaction, the sociologist found, depended to a large extent on the social environment, attitudes, and interests of the child.

The psychologists in the group, for their part, pointed out that the way children reacted to films often depended on individual differences in mental or cognitive ability. So, for example, two researchers looked at children's emotional reactions to a film by hooking them up to instruments that measured their heartbeat and the amount of sweat on their skin. They found that children varied widely in emotional stimulation, and they suggested that differences in response to specific scenes were caused by varied abilities to comprehend what they saw on the screen.

Social Relations and the Media

At Columbia University's sociology department in the early 1940s, a new contribution to this emphasis on people's different reactions to media materials emerged. It was the idea that **social relations**—interactions among people—influence the way individuals interpret media messages. For example, when people watch movies, read newspapers, listen to the radio, or use any other medium, they often talk with other people about what they have seen or heard, and this can affect their opinions about what they have seen or heard. To understand how media content affects one person differently from another, then, we might want to know more about whom people speak to about what they've seen, read, or heard in the media.

It wasn't until the early 1940s that researchers began to think of placing social relations alongside individual social and psychological differences as a major factor in helping determine the different understandings that people draw from the media. Paul Lazarsfeld and his colleagues at Columbia were the first academics to state this

social relations
interactions among people that influence the way individuals interpret media messages

discovery systematically, and their research started in a large-scale survey of the voting attitudes and activities of people in Erie County, Ohio, about the 1940 presidential election.

Lazarsfeld and his colleagues interviewed four similar samples of approximately 600 people about their use of radio and newspapers in relation to the election. The researchers split the people up in this way because they were using a technique called a **panel survey**. In a panel survey, the same individuals are asked questions over time. The purpose is to see whether and how the attitudes of these people change over time. In the early 1940s, panel surveys were an innovative design. Lazarsfeld wanted to find out whether asking people questions once a month during the election campaign (May to November) would lead to their answering questions differently from the way they would answer if the investigators asked them questions a few times during the period, only once during the period, or only at the end of the period. After comparing the answers given by the four samples, Lazarsfeld concluded that surveying people every month did not affect their answers. The good thing about surveying them every month, however (despite its expense), was that the researchers could track the changes in the people's opinions regarding the candidates.

When the Columbia researchers concentrated on the roles that radio and newspapers played in individuals' decisions regarding the campaign, they found that news about the race seemed to change few people's voting intentions. However, when Lazarsfeld and his colleagues turned away from the issue of direct media influence to knowledge about the election, they got a surprise. The researchers were struck by the importance of voters' influence on one another. In short, voters who participated in the survey reported that instead of being exposed to the election through news coverage, they learned what was going on through discussions with friends and acquaintances.

Building from their data in a somewhat shaky manner, Lazarsfeld and his colleagues offered the **two-step flow model** (see Figure 2.3). This model states that media influence often works in two stages: (1) media content (opinion and fact) is picked up by people who use the media frequently, and (2) these people, in turn, act as opinion leaders when they discuss the media content with others. The others are therefore influenced by the media in a way that is one step removed from the actual content.

panel survey
asking the same individuals questions over time in order to find out whether and how the attitudes of these people change over time

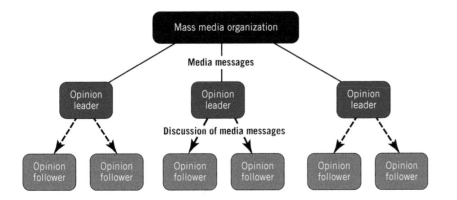

Figure 2.3
The two-step flow model of media influence.

As an everyday example, think of a friend whose taste in movies is similar to yours and who is much more likely than you to keep up with the latest news about films. When the movie companies put out new releases, he not only reads newspaper and magazine reviews but also checks the web and reads the trade press. At least once a week, over lunch, you and that friend talk about the new releases and discuss the possibility of seeing "the best one" that weekend. Clearly, media discussions of the new movies are influencing you through your friend. The two-step flow moves first from the various media to your friend and then to you.

THINKING ABOUT MEDIA LITERACY

Why do you think early researchers had such strong concerns about the impacts of media on children? Can you think of some examples of how these concerns about media's impact on children still exist?

active audience
the idea that people are not simply passive recipients of media messages; they respond to content based on their personal backgrounds, interests, and interpersonal relationships

uses and gratifications research
research that studies how people use media products to meet their needs and interests; it asks (and answers) questions about why individuals use the mass media

Paul Lazarsfeld, his colleague Robert Merton, a graduate student named Elihu Katz, and other members of Columbia's sociology department went on to conduct several other studies on the relationship between opinion leaders, the two-step flow, and the mass media. In addition to these important works, the Columbia program conducted research that examined the relationship between the media and their audiences—research that emphasized the idea of the active audience. By **active audience**, they meant that people are not simply passive recipients of media messages. Rather, they respond to content based on their personal backgrounds, interests, and interpersonal relationships.

The best-known aspect of this research, which came to be known as **uses and gratifications research**, studies how people use media products to meet their needs and interests. The aim of this research was to ask (and answer) questions about why individuals use the mass media. Underlying these studies is the belief that it is just as important to know what people do with media as it is to know what media do to people. You may remember that in Chapter 1 we discussed why people use the media and raised such topics as enjoyment, companionship, surveillance, and interpretation. All these are ideas that sprang from scholarly writings about the uses and gratifications people make of and get from the mass media.

Uses and gratifications research typically employs two research methods. One method involves interviewing people about why they use specific media and what kinds of satisfactions (gratifications) they get from these media. Often such research involves a small population so that the research can be conducted in depth. The second research method involves surveys that try to predict what kinds of people use what media or what certain kinds of people do with particular media.

Consider a researcher who is interested in whether computers in nursing homes can enrich the lives of seniors. He might want to use both of these methods. One way to start such a project would be to go to nursing homes that provide internet access and interview residents about the extent to which they use the internet and what they get out of it. You might object that such a small-scale study is not clearly generalizable to other situations. You're right about that, but the researcher might sacrifice getting a representative sample of the population in return for the ability to really learn the habits and ideas of these people. He then might test what he learns in other circumstances or through large-scale surveys. In fact, the researcher might want to use the survey technique to canvass nursing homes with web access around the country. One goal might be to find out whether certain characteristics of seniors—their age, their health, or their attitudes about the future, for example—predict the kinds and extent of their web use.

The Limits of Propaganda: Limited Effects Research

Amid all this interest in how difficult it is for media to change people's attitudes and behaviors, even propaganda research was turned on its head. Remember how powerful the propaganda analysts of the 1920s and 1930s considered the mass media to be? Well, in the 1940s, social psychologists were pointing out that even media materials specifically designed to persuade people would succeed only under limited circumstances and with only certain types of people.

The issue was by no means just a theoretical one. Propaganda became an important tool during World War II in the 1940s and during the height of the Cold War with the Soviet Union in the 1950s and 1960s. During World War II, military officials became especially interested in the ability of movies, filmstrips, and other media to teach soldiers about the reasons for the war and to increase their motivation to serve. Research on the power of these media was carried out as part of a wide investigation called "The American Soldier."

Because a soldier's duty is to do what he or she is told, a team of social psychologists under the leadership of Carl Hovland conducted careful naturalistic experiments with large numbers of people, a task that is typically difficult to accomplish. A **naturalistic experiment** is a study in which randomly selected people are manipulated in a relatively controlled environment (as in an experiment) without knowing that they are involved in an experiment. Some (who make up the experimental group) see the media message that is being evaluated, whereas others (the control group) do not. Researchers ask both groups the same questions at different points in time. The researchers take care to separate the questionnaire from the viewing so that the subjects don't suspect the relationship between the two. The before/after answers of the two groups are then compared. This approach is usually more reflective of real life than a typical experiment, in which groups of randomly chosen subjects know that they are involved in an experiment and often participate in a laboratory setting.

naturalistic experiment
a study in which randomly selected people are manipulated in a relatively controlled environment (as in an experiment) without knowing that they are involved in an experiment

Hovland and his colleagues used a variety of techniques with different subjects, but all were shown movies explaining America's reason for entering World War II. The 4,200 soldiers involved in the study were not told they were involved in an experiment. Instead, they were told they were being given a general opinion survey; the questionnaires they were given before seeing the film were different from those they received a week after seeing the film (but with some of the same questions) to disguise the real purpose of the questionnaire. Some of the experimental groups were also given questionnaires nine weeks after seeing the movie to study the long-term effects of the film. Control groups did not see the movies, but they were given questionnaires to fill out to see if changes happened without their having viewed the movies.

Hovland's naturalistic experiments showed how difficult it is to change an individual's opinions. As an example, consider the researchers' findings when they evaluated the effects of *The Battle of Britain* (a short film that explored in vivid detail how Britain fought bravely against the Nazis, why the United States went to war to help Britain, and why it was necessary to fight to win) on men enrolled in the military. The team found that the movie had strong effects on what men learned about the battle; how much they learned depended on their educational background. When it came to convincing the men in the study that the British and French were doing all they could to win, however, the film had much less effect; few soldiers who were suspicious of the French and British before they saw the film changed their opinion.

The film was also ineffective in strengthening the overall motivation and morale of the soldiers. Specifically, one item on the questionnaire given after the experimental group saw the film asked whether the soldiers preferred military service at home or joining the fighting overseas. Only 38 percent of the control group said they wanted to fight. For the film group—supposedly fired up by the film—the comparable figure was 41 percent, not a significant difference. Even Hovland (who later went on to run the influential Program of Research on Communication and Attitude Change at Yale University) agreed that the findings did not contradict what by the 1950s was the mainstream verdict about media influence: under normal circumstances, in which all aspects of the communication environment could be held equal, the mass media's ability to change people's attitudes and behavior on controversial issues was minimal.

Consolidating the Mainstream Approach

The seeds planted by the Columbia School, the Yale School, and to a lesser degree the Payne Fund Studies bore great fruit in the 1950s and beyond, as researchers in many universities and colleges built on their findings. We can divide these later approaches into three very broad areas of study: opinion and behavior change; what people learn from media; and why, when, and how people use the media. Let's look at these one at a time.

Studying Opinion and Behavior Change

Many researchers have been interested in understanding why some people's opinions or behaviors are influenced by certain types of content and those of others are not. Some of these researchers became involved in the most contentious issues involving media in the second half of the 20th century—those centering on the effects of TV violence on children and the effects of sexually explicit materials (pornography) on adults.

In general, researchers seem to agree that the ways in which most adults and children react to such materials depend greatly on family background, social setting, and personality. At the same time, they also agree that consistent viewing of violent television shows or movies may cause some children to become aggressive toward others, regardless of family background. Researchers have come to similar conclusions about violent sexual materials, the kind in which men hurt women or vice versa. There is mounting evidence that in the case of some viewers, irrespective of their background or initial attitudes, heavy exposure to such materials may desensitize them to the seriousness of rape and other forms of sexual violence. For example, in one study viewers of sexual violence had less concern about the supposed victim of a violent rape than the control group viewers who hadn't seen such materials. Because most of these findings are based on lab experiments, though, there is a significant amount of debate about whether they apply to the real world.

Studying What People Learn From Media

A large number of researchers have been interested in who learns what from mass media material and under what conditions. There are many facets to this study area, but two particularly important ones stand out. The first is whether media can encourage children's learning of educational skills. The second looks at who in society learns about current national and world affairs from the media.

Can Media Encourage Learning Skills in Children? *Sesame Street*, which made its TV debut in 1969, has been the subject of a great deal of research into what children learn from it. Researchers have found that the program can teach boys and girls from different income levels their letters and numbers and can be credited with improving the vocabulary of young children.

Educational programming, such as *Sesame Street*, has been heavily researched with respect to media effects and how such programming can affect the young children who watch it.

Professor Ellen Wartella, an expert on this topic, summarizes other findings on children's learning of education skills this way:

> Since the success of Sesame Street, other planned educational programs, such as *Where in the World Is Carmen Sandiego*, *Bill Nye the Science Guy*, *Square One Television*, *Reading Rainbow*, *Gullah Gullah Island*, *Blue's Clues* and *Magic School Bus*, have been found both to increase children's interest in the educational content of programs and to teach some of the planned curriculum. In addition, other children's shows, which focus less on teaching cognitive skills but more on such positive behaviors as helping others and sharing toys, can be successful. The most important evidence here comes from a study of preschool children's effective learning of such helping or pro-social behaviors from watching *Mister Rogers' Neighborhood*.

Which Individuals Learn About National and World Affairs From the Mass Media? Researchers who examine what people learn about national and world affairs from the mass media would probably argue that they too are looking at pro-social learning, but of a different kind. The basic belief that guides their work is that a democratic society needs informed citizens if public policies are to be guided by the greatest number of people. Some of their questions center on Walter Lippmann's agenda-setting concept that we discussed earlier in this chapter.

Agenda-setting scholars agree with the mainstream position that differences among individuals make it unlikely that the mass media can tell you or me precisely what opinions we should have about particular topics. They point out, however, that by making some events and not others into major headlines, the mass media are quite successful at getting large numbers of people to agree on what topics to think about. That in itself is important, these researchers argue, because it shows that the press has the power to spark public dialogue on major topics facing the nation.

Professors Maxwell McCombs and Donald Shaw at the University of North Carolina, Chapel Hill, demonstrated this agenda-setting effect in research for the first time in a 1970 article. They surveyed Chapel Hill voters about the most important issues in the presidential campaign. They also conducted a content analysis of the attention that major media outlets in Chapel Hill paid to issues in the presidential campaign. McCombs and Shaw showed that the rankings of the importance that voters placed on certain issues in the presidential election campaign were related not to the voters' party affiliation or personal biases, but to the priorities that the media outlets in Chapel Hill presented at the time.

This one study on the influence of the media agenda on the public agenda led to more than 200 others. The agenda-setting power of the press has generally been shown to operate in both election and nonelection studies across a variety of geographic settings, time spans, news media, and public issues. Researchers have also described an effect called priming as a "close cousin of agenda-setting."

priming
the process by which the media affect the standard that individuals use to evaluate what they see and hear in the media

Priming is the process by which the media affect the standard that individuals use to evaluate what they see and hear in the media. The idea is that the more prominent a political issue is in the national media, the more that idea will prime people (that is, cue them in) that the handling of that issue should be used to evaluate how well political candidates or organizations are doing their jobs.

But the power of agenda setting and priming is by no means the entire story. Researchers have found that mass media agenda setting has the ability to affect people's sense of public affairs priorities and that mass media coverage primes people with respect to the criteria they use to evaluate particular issues. Nevertheless, researchers emphasize that individual backgrounds and interests weaken these effects. That is, these factors bring about a lot of variation in what issues people pick up as important, how they prioritize these issues, and whether they use these issues as evaluation criteria. The weakening of the effects of agenda setting and priming occurs primarily because people's differences lead them to pay attention to different things in the media. As with the Yale studies described earlier, the strongest agenda-setting effects have been found in experimental studies, which suggests that a major condition for obtaining these effects is attention, given that in experiments subjects are essentially forced to pay attention, whereas under naturalistic conditions some people do and others don't, based on their interest in what is going on.

THINKING ABOUT MEDIA LITERACY

Agenda setting is one of the key ideas media researchers have examined over the years. In this era of concerns about media credibility and information accuracy, how does the notion of agenda setting apply? Are agenda setting and propaganda similar or different? Why?

If it is sometimes difficult to get people to pay attention to current events via the headlines, imagine how difficult it is to get them to pay attention to less obvious aspects of our political culture. In fact, in the decades since World War II, researchers have found a wide variation in what individuals learn from the mass media. Education has consistently been a major factor that is positively associated with differences between those who pick up knowledge of public affairs and those who do not. It seems that people are more likely to remember the events and facts that media present if they have frameworks of knowledge from schooling that can help them make sense of the news events they see or hear.

In the late 1960s, Professors Phillip Tichenor, George Donahue, and Clarice Olien of the University of Minnesota came upon a sobering survey finding that relates to the difference in the amount of current events information that different people learn from the media. They found that in the development of any social or political issue, the more highly educated segments of a population know more about the issue early on and, in fact, acquire information about that issue at a faster rate than the less educated segments. That is, people who are information-rich to begin with get richer faster than people who are information-poor, and so the difference in the amount of knowledge between the two types of people will grow wider.

Professors Tichenor, Donahue, and Olien concluded that this growing **knowledge gap** was dangerous for society in an age in which the ability to pick up information about the latest trends is increasingly crucial to success. Because the study found that the information-rich in society were often the well-schooled and well-off financially, a growing knowledge gap might mean that the poorer segments of society could not participate meaningfully in discussions of social issues. It also might mean that they would not know about developments that would help them prepare for—and get—better jobs.

knowledge gap
a theory that holds that in the development of any social or political issues, the more highly educated segments of a population know more about the issues early on and, in fact, acquire information about that issue at a faster rate than the less educated segments, and so the difference between the two types of people grows wider

Studying Why, When, and How People Use the Media

Some of the most basic questions that researchers ask about mass media in society center on who uses them, how, and why. As we noted earlier, it was a group of scholars at Columbia University who created the first notable research program that went

GLOBAL MEDIA TODAY & CULTURE

THE POLYSEMY OF *FINDING NEMO*

Finding Nemo features distinctive character design.
Have you ever watched the film *Finding Nemo*? It is a very successful computer-animated movie distributed by Pixar Animation Studios in 2003, which won the Academy Award for Best Animated Feature and has earned almost $1 billion at the box office worldwide since its release. The movie chronicles the story of a clownfish, Nemo, separated from his father and its adventures before eventually reuniting with him. It delves into the issues of parenthood, growing up, and friendship through the lenses of marine life in the Australian Great Barrier Reef in the Pacific Ocean.

The massive commercial success of the movie stems from its very positive reception from heterogeneous audiences: It was simultaneously acclaimed by kids, their parents, and young moviegoers interested in a date movie, in the United States and internationally. One could say it is polysemic, as it effectively engages concurrently different demographics by providing entertainment to all of them in different ways: Younger audiences enjoy the adventures of the small clownfish Nemo, whereas the parents relate with the challenges of raising their offspring trying to navigate the fine line between guiding them closely and letting them experience their surroundings autonomously. There are different humorous situations and lines intended for all of the different audiences. Although it is intuitive to say the polysemy could be one of the keys to commercial success for entertainment artifacts—a successful movie should make sense and engage a large number of potential viewers—the ability to do so is not easy at all. Do you recall any other movies with a similar approach?

beyond basic factual descriptions of the numbers of newspaper readers and radio listeners to ask what motivated people to use certain kinds of content.

They asked, for example, "Why do people like such programming as radio soap operas and quiz shows?" This question may have gotten sneers from some of their elitist colleagues. Nevertheless, over the decades, this area of study, called **uses and gratifications research**, has received a lot of attention. Recall that its focus is on when, how, and why people use various mass media or particular genres of mass media content.

True to the spirit of the mainstream approach, uses and gratifications research has at its core a belief in the active audience, which again means that individuals are not just passive receivers of messages. Rather, they make conscious decisions about what they like, and they have different reasons for using particular media, depending on different social relationships, as well as on individual social and psychological differences. Moreover, people are physically active when they use media. When it comes to TV, for example, studies have shown that people do not sit quietly, transfixed by the tube, as some cartoon stereotypes would have it. Rather, they move around, do other things, and talk to friends and family.

A huge amount of literature explores how people use a variety of media and why. Researchers such as danah boyd, Mimi Ito, Zizi Papacharissi, and Sonia Livingstone explore people's use of social media in different ways and from different perspectives. A major contemporary theme is that people interact not just with the reading, video, and audio material big companies provide to them but also with the material they create for themselves. That happens particularly, though not exclusively, on social media platforms such as Facebook or Instagram. Henry Jenkins, for example, has studied the way fans of particular TV programs or movies take advantage of the phenomenon of media convergence to spread their interests across different devices.

Much of this work is interesting and important in its own right. Knowing how people use the media and why can help us understand important trends in society. It is also useful to know how people from different backgrounds differ in their uses, because some may need help connecting to the media environment in ways that can benefit them and the larger society. It is useful to know, for example, what percentage of low-income people have been connecting to the internet compared with the percentage of middle-class and wealthy families. The findings that there are sharp differences in income between families that are online at home and those that are not has sparked discussion of a **digital divide** in the United States—a separation between those who are connected to "the future" and those who are being left behind (see Figure 2.4). That, in turn, has led to efforts by governments and corporations to place web-linked computers with instructors in libraries and community centers that are within easy reach of people who cannot afford the internet at home.

digital divide
the separation between those who have access to and knowledge about technology and those who (perhaps because of their level of education or income) do not

THINKING ABOUT MEDIA LITERACY

How do social media such as Facebook and Twitter fit within the two-step flow model? Who do you think are most likely to be opinion leaders and why? Are there any limitations to applying this model to social media? Why or why not?

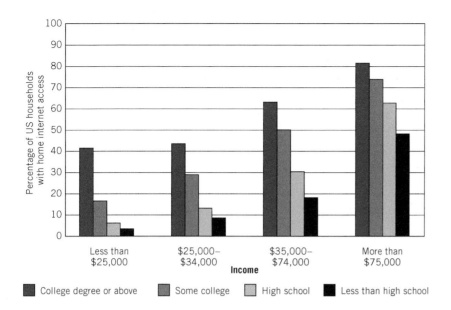

Figure 2.4
Now, more than ever, the gap between those people and communities who can make effective use of information technology and those who cannot is widening. Although a consensus does not exist regarding the extent of this digital divide, most researchers acknowledge that an education-income divide exists at this point in time, as this figure shows.

Activists argue that there is a lot more to do in this area. Of particular concern are economically disadvantaged children in the United States and elsewhere in the world who are falling behind in their ability to be part of the modern world. More than a few of their advocates point out that although providing them with new technology is a beginning, it is not enough. Teaching them how to use the technology in ways that will benefit them and their societies is a critical part of bridging the digital divide.

The Rise of Critical Approaches

As you can see, the **mainstream approaches**—the research models that developed out of the work of the Columbia School, the Yale School, and the Payne Fund Studies—have led to valuable work that has helped many researchers contribute to society's most important debates. At the same time, however, other researchers insist that the questions asked by mainstream approaches are not really the most important ones when it comes to understanding the role of mass media in society.

mainstream approaches
the research models that developed out of the work of the Columbia School, the Yale School, and the Payne Fund Studies

Moving From Mainstream Approaches to Critical Approaches

According to critics of the mainstream approach, there are two major problems with even the best mainstream research. One problem is its stress on change rather than continuity. The other is its emphasis on the active role of the individual—the active audience member—in the media environment and not on the power of larger social forces that control that media environment.

Let's look at the first problem. In referring to a focus on change over continuity, critics of mainstream research mean that much of this research focuses on whether a change will occur as a result of specific movies, articles, or shows. Critics say that this approach ignores the possibility that the most important effects of the media have to do not with changing people, but with encouraging them (or reinforcing them) to continue certain actions or perspectives on life.

Mainstream researchers might focus, for example, on whether a girl will hit her little brother after watching the violent antics of a Three Stooges film or whether a

Karl Marx's *Das Capital* was his manifesto in which he heavily criticized capitalism as an economic model because he felt it was heavily dependent on the exploitation of the working class by business owners and the upper class, creating many cultural and societal problems for countries adopting this economic model. The interaction between capitalism and culture was of great interest to those in the Frankfurt School during the 1930s and 1940s.

woman will learn about politics from a website or TV news program. Now, there's nothing wrong with such questions, the critics allow. But, they add, fascination with these questions of change often hides the importance of the media in encouraging the reinforcement of actions and beliefs among many in society.

Mainstream researchers emphasize that most people's opinions and behaviors don't change after they view television or listen to the radio. What the researchers don't emphasize, the critics point out, is that the flip side of change—reinforcement—may well be a powerful consequence. In fact, the critics argue, reinforcement is often the major consequence of mass media messages. Media may repeat for us values that we have come to love, ideas about the world that we have come to trust, social class relationships that we have come to accept, and beliefs that we have come to accept about the way people who are not like us look and act. These are the ideas that hold a society together, the critics say, so it is a shame that the mainstream researchers have played them down.

But the critics often go further. They argue that mainstream research has placed so much emphasis on the individual's relationships to media—the second major problem we identified—that it has ignored social power. It has neglected to emphasize that there are powerful forces that exert control over what media industries do as part of their control over society.

What really ought to be studied, say the critics, is the way these powerful groups come to influence the most widespread media images in ways that help them stay in power. From this perspective, agenda setting and the digital divide are not just phenomena that point to what people learn and how differently they learn. They are phenomena that help the powerful classes in a society retain their power.

Clearly, we have here a major difference of opinion about how to look at mass media, about where their powers lie, and about which of their aspects should be studied. Many critics of the mainstream approach prefer an avenue of research that recalls the most sophisticated of the propaganda analysts. Like the propaganda analysts, contemporary critical scholars emphasize the importance of systematically exploring the forces guiding media companies. They also place great value on analyzing media content to reveal the patterns of messages that are shared broadly by the population. Like the propaganda analysts, their aim is often to expose to public light the relationships between media firms and powerful forces in society. They want to publicize their findings in order to encourage public understanding and, sometimes, to urge government regulations that would promote greater diversity among creators of media content and in the content itself.

The "critical" label describes a wide variety of projects relating to the mass media. Three prominent perspectives that guide critical researchers are the critical theory of the Frankfurt School, political economy research, and cultivation studies.

The Deep Political Influence of the Media: The Frankfurt School's Critical Theory The Frankfurt School is a shorthand name for a group of scholars who were associated with a place called the School for Social Research during the 1930s and 1940s. This shorthand name comes from the original location of the institute in Frankfurt, Germany. Among the thinkers who made significant contributions to this school of thought are Theodor Adorno (philosopher, sociologist, and musicologist),

Walter Benjamin (essayist and literary critic), Herbert Marcuse (philosopher), and Max Horkheimer (philosopher and sociologist). Each of these philosophers shared the basic view of capitalism set forth by the 19th-century philosopher Karl Marx. According to Marx, **capitalism** is the ownership of the means of production by a ruling class in society. Marx insisted that in societies that accept this economic approach, capitalism greatly influences all beliefs. He further insisted that capitalism and the beliefs it generates create economic and cultural problems. They exploit the working class and celebrate that exploitation in literature and many other aspects of culture. Marx believed that the direction of history was toward labor's overthrow of the capitalist class and the reign of workers in a society in which everyone would receive what he or she needs.

The Frankfurt School focused on the cultural aspect of this issue, and its members were pessimistic about it. Marxist and Jewish, they were exiled from Germany to the United States because of the rise of Nazism during the 1920s and 1930s. In New York (where several worked at the New School for Social Research), the members of the Frankfurt School explored the relationship between culture and capitalism in an era in which economic depression, war, and mass exterminations made it difficult to be optimistic about the liberating potential of culture. Their writings about the corrosive influence of capitalism on culture came to be known as **critical theory**. Writings by Adorno stress the power of "the culture industry" to move audience members toward ways of looking at the world. Writings by Marcuse suggest to researchers how messages about social power can be found in all aspects of media content, even if typical audience members don't recognize them. For example, **co-optation** is a well-known term that Marcuse coined to express the way capitalism takes potentially revolutionary ideas and tames them to express capitalist ideals. For an example of co-optation, consider how advertisers take expressions of youthful rebellion such as tattoos and colored hair and turn them into the next moneymaking fads. Marcuse would say that this sort of activity shows how difficult it is for oppositional movements to create symbols that keep their critical meanings.

Many media scholars today feel that the members of the Frankfurt School tended to overemphasize the ability of mass media to control individuals' beliefs. Nevertheless, over the decades, the philosophies collectively known as critical theory have influenced many writings on mass media.

Political Economy Research **Political economy** theorists focus specifically on the relationship between economics and the culture. They look at when and how the economic structures of society and the media system reflect the political interests of society's rich and powerful. In this vein, professor and media activist Robert McChesney examined ownership patterns of media companies in the early 2000s. He concluded in his 2004 book *The Problem of the Media* that we have reached "the age of hyper-commercialism," where media worry far more about satisfying advertisers and shareholders than about providing entertainment or news that encourages people to understand their society and become engaged in it. McChesney blames government legislators and regulators for allowing the rise of huge media conglomerates that control large portions of the revenues of particular media industries for the purposes of selling advertising time and space. One alarming consequence, he contends, is a journalistic system that focuses more on attracting the attention of audiences than on trying to build an informed society like that imagined by Jefferson and Madison. As alarming to McChesney is the notion that, because US media firms

capitalism
as defined by Karl Marx, the ownership of the means of production by a ruling class in society

critical theory
the Frankfurt School's members' theories focusing on the corrosive influence of capitalism on culture

co-optation
a term coined by Marcuse to express the way in which capitalism takes potentially revolutionary ideas and tames them to express capitalist ideals

political economy
an area of study that focuses specifically on the relationship between the economic and the cultural and that looks at when and how the economic structures of society and the media system reflect the political interests of society's rich and powerful

are so powerful internationally, this commercially driven perspective on journalism is spreading through the world. He and political economist Edward Herman put that idea succinctly in a 1997 book called *The Global Media*:

> Such a [global] concentration of media power in organizations dependent on advertiser support and responsible primarily to shareholders is a clear and present danger to citizens' participation in public affairs, understanding of public issues, and thus to the effective workings of democracy.[1]

Another writer from a political economy perspective, Ben Bagdikian, points out in his book *The Media Monopoly* that huge media firms are often involved in many businesses outside of journalism. Comcast, the parent of NBC News, owns many cable systems, for example. Disney owns theme parks around the world, as well as ABC News. News workers who are employed by these firms may be afraid to cover controversies that involve those operations; in fact, corporate bigwigs may keep them from doing so.

The problem is not just theoretical: When Brian Ross was an investigative reporter for ABC News, he put together a report on child abuse issues in theme parks. He was ordered by executives of the Walt Disney Company, which owns ABC News, not to report on possible problems with child care in Disneyland (Figure 2.5). ABC officials denied that the corporate linkage influenced their decision to pull an investigative report on allegations involving Disney: "Disney: The Mouse Betrayed," a *20/20* segment produced by Brian Ross. It alleged, among other things, that Disney World in Florida fails to perform security checks that would prevent the hiring of sex offenders and has problems with peeping Toms. According to an ABC spokeswoman, news president David Westin's killing of the story had nothing to do with any network reluctance to criticize its parent company. "The fact that this particular story involved Disney was not the reason it did not make air," claimed an ABC spokesperson (www.washingtonpost.com/wp-srv/style/tv/features/abckillsstory.htm).

The work by McChesney, Herman, and Bagdikian looks into the economic relationships within the media system and tries to figure out their consequences for issues of social power and equity. It is concerned with looking at how institutional and organizational relationships create requirements for media firms that lead the employees of those firms to create and circulate certain kinds of material and not others. These scholars might explore, for example, whether (and how) major advertisers' relationships with television networks affect programming. They would look at the extent to which advertisers' need to reach certain audiences for their products causes networks to signal to program producers that shows that aim at those types of people will get preference.

The topics that political economists choose vary greatly. Some, such as Daniel Schiller, explore global issues. An example is the study of factors that encourage the spread of Western (often US) news and entertainment throughout the world. These political scientists consider such activities to be cultural colonialism. **Colonialism** means control over a dependent area or people by a powerful entity (usually a nation) by force of arms. England and France practiced colonialism in places such as India and Vietnam for many years. **Cultural colonialism** involves the exercise of control over an area or people by a dominant power, not so much through force of arms as by surrounding the weaker countries with cultural materials that reflect values and beliefs supporting the interests of that dominant power. The political economists

colonialism
control over a dependent area or people by a powerful entity by force or arms

cultural colonialism
the exercise of control over an area or people by a dominant power, not so much through force of arms as by surrounding the weaker countries with cultural materials that reflect values and beliefs supporting the interests of that dominant power

Figure 2.5

A conflict of interest can arise when conglomerates with a direct stake in businesses outside of journalism own many of the media outlets through which the public is informed, as was the case for Brian Ross's "Disney: The Mouse Betrayed" news segment.

who explore cultural colonialism argue that by celebrating values such as commercialism and immediate gratification, the cultural colonizers encourage markets for goods that reflect those values and so help their own country's business interests.

Other political economists focus on the concerns of media in individual countries. They look, for example, at the extent to which ethnic or racial minorities can exert some control over mainstream media. Their fear is that social minorities often do not get to guide their own portrayals in their nation's main media. The result is underrepresentation and stereotyping of these groups by producers who are insensitive to their concerns. These political scientists urge changes so that minority producers and actors can have input regarding their groups' depictions.

Cultivation Studies Cultivation researchers are also interested in depictions, but in a different way. Such studies are different from political economy studies, in that they focus not on industry relationships, but on the information about the world that

cultivation studies

studies that emphasize that when media systematically portray certain populations in unfavorable ways, the ideas that mainstream audiences pick up about those people help certain groups in society retain their power over the groups they denigrate

people pick up from media portrayals. You might object that this sounds very much like what many mainstream effects researchers do. On the surface it does. Where cultivation researchers differ is in the perspective they bring to the work and how they interpret their findings. **Cultivation studies** emphasize that when media systematically portray certain populations in unfavorable ways, the ideas that mainstream audiences pick up about those people help certain groups in society retain their power over the groups they denigrate. Stereotypes, they believe, reinforce and extend ("cultivate") power relationships.

Cultivation work is most associated with Professor George Gerbner and his colleagues at the University of Pennsylvania's Annenberg School for Communication from the 1960s through the 1980s. Gerbner began his work with the perspective that all mass media material—entertainment and news—gives people views of the world. Those views, he said, are the mass-produced output of huge corporations. These corporations have a vested interest in perpetuating their power along with the power of established economic and cultural approaches in US society. Their power is seen especially in the way violence is used in television entertainment, the most widely viewed entertainment medium in the United States.

The HBO fantasy show *Game of Thrones* came under criticism after airing several episodes with sexual assault against women, sparking a debate over consent and excessive sexual violence on the show.

Across all channels on the tube, argues Gerbner, TV violence is a kind of ritual ballet that acts out social power. Although TV violence may sometimes encourage aggression, most of the time it cultivates lessons about strength and weakness in society. For example, Gerbner contends that the "hidden curriculum" of TV violence tells us that women and blacks, who tend to be the objects of violence, are socially weak. White males, who tend to be perpetrators of violence (including legal violence by the police or military), are socially strong.

Moreover, Gerbner argues, the overall message of TV violence is that we live in a scary, mean world. He and his colleagues found support for this view through a two-pronged research design. First, they conducted a content analysis of many hours of television entertainment programming, using a careful definition of violence and noting who is violent to whom and under what conditions. Next, they conducted a telephone survey of a random sample of the US adult population and asked the people questions about how violent the world is and how fearful they are. They found that heavy viewers of television are more fearful of the world than light viewers. Over time, these viewers also engage in more self-protective behavior and show more mistrust of others than do light viewers.

THINKING ABOUT MEDIA LITERACY

The notion of a "knowledge gap" in society is a concern to researchers. Do you think the current media environment holds promise to help close the knowledge gap? Why or why not?

Gerbner maintains that although this phenomenon affects the individual, it also has larger social implications. The message of fear helps those who are in power because it makes heavy viewers (a substantial portion of the population) more likely to agree to support police and military forces that protect them from that scary world. Not incidentally, those police and military forces also protect those in power and help them maintain control over unruly or rebellious groups in society.

Gerbner's cultivation research and the critical approaches of political economists and the Frankfurt School helped to add another dimension to the way US scholars looked at the mass media. In the past decades, a third broad avenue of inquiry has added to the mix of ideas about media power and consequences. This avenue is widely known as cultural studies.

Cultural Studies

Let's say that you accept the importance of emphasizing the connection between mass media and social power, but you're a bit uncomfortable with what you feel is the too-simplistic perspective of the political economy and cultivation theorists. "Media power isn't as controlling as they would have it," you say. "I don't believe that everybody in society necessarily buys into the images of power that these systems project. People have minds of their own, and they often live in communities that help them resist the aims of the powerful."

If that's your perspective, you would probably find one of the many approaches within cultural studies to be up your alley. The approach taken by cultural studies was developed in Europe and had been used there for many years before it attracted a large following in the United States during the 1980s. Writings in this area often tie media studies to concepts in literature, linguistics, anthropology, and history. **Cultural studies** scholars often start with the idea that all sorts of mass media, from newspapers to movies, present their audiences with technologies and texts and that audiences find meaning in them. Major questions for these scholars center on how to think about what "making meaning" of technologies and texts means and what consequences it has for those audiences in society. As you might imagine, there are many ways to answer these questions.

Historical Approaches to Cultural Studies

One way to answer cultural studies questions is from a historical perspective. Professor Lynn Spigel, for example, explores the expectations that men and women have had for audiovisual technologies in the home and how those expectations have tied into larger social issues. She points out, for example, a historical relationship between home TV use and social fear:

> Communications technologies have promised to bring the outside world into the home since the late 19th century. At the time of industrialization, when urban centers were linked to the first suburban towns, there were endless speculations about the joys and potential pitfalls of a new design for middle-class living which would allow people to be joined together in an electrical public space without ever going outside. Middle-class families could, in this way, enjoy social encounters while avoiding the elements of urban space—such as labor unrest or ethnic immigration—which made them feel most threatened.

cultural studies
studies that start with the idea that all sorts of mass media, from newspapers to movies, present their audiences with technologies and texts and that audiences find meaning in them; scholars then ask questions that center on how to think about what "making meaning" of technologies and texts means and what consequences it has for those audiences in society

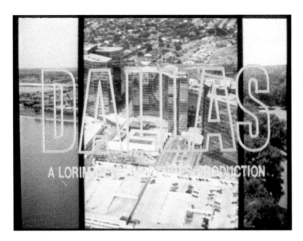

Even though *Dallas* is an iconic television show, its interpretation is still heavily dependent upon the cultural and personal backgrounds of its viewers.

Anthropological Approaches to Cultural Studies

Another way to look at what technologies mean in the context of social class and social power is to take an anthropologist's approach and closely examine the way people use media. Cultural studies researchers tie people's uses of the media to their class, racial, or gender positions within society. Here, for example, is Professor Ellen Seiter writing in 2003 on differences between men and women in the use of television and computers in the home. Consider whether you think the particulars she emphasizes apply today.

Television sets and computers introduce highly similar issues in terms of placement in domestic space, conflicts among family members over usage and control, value in the household budget, and we can expect these to be articulated with gender roles in the family. Some research on gendered conflicts over computers (Giacquinta; Murdock; Haddon) reproduces themes of family-based studies about control of the television set. Already researchers have noted a strong tendency for men and boys to have more access to computers in the home. Television studies such as Ann Gray's, David Morley's and my own work suggest that women in nuclear families have difficulty watching a favorite television show (because of competition for control of the set from other family members, and because of shouldering the majority of childcare, housework and cooking). If male family members gravitate towards the computer as hobbyists, the load of chores relegated to female family members will only increase, and make it more difficult for female members to get time on the home computer. Computers require hours of trial and error experimentation, a kind of extended play demanding excess leisure time. Fully exploring the internet needs time for lengthy downloading, and patience with connections that are busy, so much so that some have dubbed the World Wide Web the World Wide Wait.[2]

Linguistic and Literary Approaches to Cultural Studies

You probably found the paragraphs by Ellen Seiter and Lynn Spigel quite straightforward and easy to understand. The same can't typically be said for the areas of cultural studies that apply linguistic and literary models to the meaning of media texts. They tend to use the complex phraseology of linguistics and the jargon of literary analysts to make their points. That is unfortunate because some of the scholars involved in this area often proclaim that their goal is to encourage viewers and readers to "resist" the dominant models of society that are suggested in the text.

Moreover, these discussions are actually quite interesting and important, once you cut through the language. A major topic of discussion recalls the UK scholar Stuart Hall's interest in "dominant" and "resistant" readings but considers whether they may be even more ambiguous and unstable than Hall had believed.

At one extreme are scholars who believe that a text is open to multiple meanings (they say that it is **polysemous**) because people have the ability to subject media content to endless interpretations based on their critical understanding of the world. So, for example, Professors Elihu Katz and Tamar Liebes interviewed people in Israel and Japan to find out how they understood the popular 1980s US

polysemous
open to multiple meanings

TV series *Dallas*. They found that Japanese viewers, Israeli viewers originally from Morocco, and Israeli viewers originally from Russia had quite different interpretations of the program and its relevance to their lives. According to such findings about multiple interpretations, people in this camp have a clear idea of where they should apply their public interest energies. They would say, for example, that trying to limit the power of media conglomerates is not nearly as important as teaching people how to interpret media critically, in ways that resist any support of the dominant system.

THINKING ABOUT MEDIA LITERACY

Think about the notions of "cultural colonialism" and "cultivation studies." How do they differ? What might be a way that cultivation studies might be applied in the context of cultural colonialism?

Against this notion of a program or book being open to multiple meanings is the opposite idea that the meaning is in the text itself. Scholars with this view argue that the shared culture of a society leads individuals to share the basic meaning of the text. To them, firms that create agendas in news and entertainment have enormous power that cannot be overcome simply by teaching criticism. Active work to limit the power of these conglomerates is also necessary.

Philosophically, many scholars take a position between these two extremes. They accept the notion of polysemy, but they argue that most people's interpretations of media texts are very much shaped by the actual texts themselves and by the industrial and social environments in which these texts are created. They stress that texts are likely to "constrain" meaning in directions that benefit the powerful. That is, because of the way the text is created, viewers or readers notice the "preferred" meaning, the meaning that members of the establishment would likely find most compatible with their own thinking. Certainly, audience members can disagree with this take on the world. Even if they do, however, they may get the strong idea that most other people would not disagree with the text's approaches to racial, gender, ethnic, and religious stereotypes; tales of who is strong and who is weak; or portrayals of what the universe is like, how we (as Americans and humans) fit in, and how we should act toward it. Such scholars might be likely to enthusiastically support media criticism, as well as public actions to limit the power of huge media conglomerates.

Using Media Research to Develop Media Literacy Skills

We now return to the story of Vert. She has heard the grad students discuss everything that you've read in this chapter's pages, as they present ways of looking at the issues about local news that she has brought to them. Each student gives her a thumbnail summary of the history and nature of different aspects of mass communication research. Vert's head is spinning from the variety of ways to look at the same media material and the hundreds of questions it is possible to ask.

You may feel the same way she does. But if you think about it a bit more, you'll see that understanding the history of mass media research provides tools with which to figure out several key questions that you as a media-literate person must grapple with. They range from where you stand with respect to the effects of media on society to how to make sense of the discussions and arguments about media effects to how to get involved in research that can be used to explore concerns you might have about mass media.

Where Do You Stand With Respect to Media Effects?

While reading this chapter, it's likely that you found yourself agreeing with some of the media approaches and disagreeing with others. Maybe you dismissed political economy as a lot of baloney but you felt that uses and gratifications research and some aspects of cultural studies really make sense. That's fine; part of becoming media-literate involves taking an informed stand on why the media are important. Learning about the ways in which people have grappled with concerns about the mass media over the decades can help you sort out your concerns. You personally may be more convinced that the individual interpretations and uses of the media are what make a difference for people. You may not be convinced by those who emphasize social issues, such as political economists, cultivation researchers, and even people involved in studying agenda setting.

It's really important, though, that you do not close your mind to the possibilities. New ideas keep coming up; your ideas about life keep changing as well. You can keep up with what media researchers are saying by reading press articles about them or maybe even by going to journals such as the *Journal of Communication*, *Critical Studies in Media Communication*, *Journalism and Mass Communication Quarterly*, or the *Journal of Broadcasting & Electronic Media*. What you have learned here and what you learn in the future may well affect how you relate to the media yourself, how you introduce your children to different media, and what you tell parents who ask your opinion on how to think about the media's consequences for their children.

How Can You Make Sense of Discussions and Arguments About Media Effects?

When you do read about research in the popular press or in academic journals, think back to this chapter to help you place the work in perspective and critique it. Here are some questions you should ask yourself:

Are the questions the researcher is asking interesting and important? Think of the issues you have learned about in this chapter. How important are the ones dealt with in the study you are considering? Do you wish the researchers had devoted their energies to other topics that you consider more relevant to your life or the life of the country?

Into what research tradition does the study fall? Is it a study of priming, an example of cultivation research, a study of message persuasion, or a representation of another one of the streams of work that we have discussed (see Table 2.1)?

How good is the research design? Whereas journal articles lay out the method used in research quite carefully, press reports of research often don't give you a lot of information about how the work was carried out. Even in the popular press, however, you can often find some of the specific questions the investigators used and some details about the method. When you think about the research design, be skeptical. Think about the type and size of the sample. If the study was an experiment, how realistic was it?

How convincing is the analysis? If the researcher is claiming that the media caused something to happen, are there any other explanations for the findings? Does it appear that the researcher thought about reliability? How valid does the study seem in terms of the real world? These and other questions should roll around in your head as you decide whether to accept the conclusions of the researchers or others who are quoted.

What do you wish the researchers would do next in their research? Asking this question, involving whether or not you like the research, will encourage you to think more deeply than you otherwise might about the role of media in society. Talking with your friends about especially interesting or problematic research is

Table 2.1 Comparing Media Research Theories

Theory/research study	Approach	Participating researchers	Aim	Example
Chicago School	Early philosophy and sociology of media	Dewey, Cooley, Park	Searching for community	The immigrant press
Propaganda analysts	Early concerns about media persuasion	Lasswell, McLung, Casey	The activities of media producers and the resulting content	Content analyses of newspapers
Payne Fund researchers	Early research on children and movies	Charters	Explorations of media effects via multiple methods	How violent movies affect children's sleep patterns
Columbia School	The media and social relations	Lazarsfeld, Katz, Merton	Research on how interpersonal relations intervene in media effects	The "two-step flow" influence of radio and newspapers during a presidential election campaign
American soldier propaganda research	The limits of propaganda	Hovland	Movies, learning, and persuasion	An evaluation of the effects of *The Battle of Britain*
Yale Program of Research on Communication and Attitude Change	The limits of propaganda	Hovland	Research on the conditions that encourage audience persuasion	Experiments to determine whether and when fear appeals were more persuasive than appeals not using fear
Various	Mainstream effects research		Studying behavior and opinion change	
Various	Mainstream effects research		Research on whether television can encourage learning skills in children	Research on what youngsters learn from *Sesame Street*
Various	Mainstream effects research	McCombs and Shaw; Tichenor, Donahue, and Olien	Research on which individuals learn about national and world affairs from mass media	Research on agenda setting; research on the knowledge gap

(continued)

Table 2.1 Comparing Media Research Theories (*Continued*)

Theory/research study	Approach	Participating researchers	Aim	Example
Uses and Gratifications	Mainstream research	Ito, Boyd, Jenkins	Why, when, and how people use the media	Investigations of the active audience, social media audience, digital divide
Frankfurt School	Critical approaches to mass media	Adorno, Marcuse, Horkheimer	The relationship between capitalism and culture	Critical theory about the culture industry
Various	Critical approaches to mass media	Bagdikian, Schiller	Political economy research	Research on media monopolies
Annenberg School	Critical approaches to mass media	Gerbner	Cultivation studies	Research on TV violence and perceptions of a mean world
Various	Cultural studies	Spigel	Historical approaches	Historical relationship between home TV use and social fear
Various	Cultural studies	Seiter, Murdock, Haddon	Anthropological approaches	Differences between men and women in use of TV and computers
Birmingham School	Cultural studies	Stuart Hall	Encoding/decoding	Research on dominant meanings and resistant meaning
Various	Cultural studies	Katz and Leibes	Literary and linguistic approaches	Research on polysemous meanings

another way to play out some of the meanings that the research holds for you and for others in society.

How Should You Explore Your Concerns About Mass Media?

What are the implications of the research for your personal life as well as for public policy? For example, a well-done study of attitudes toward the web and uses of the web by people over the age of 75 might have great meaning to you if you work in a senior center and want to get seniors engaged with the internet. The study might inform members of Congress who are thinking of providing funding to connect senior centers to the web. The study might also be relevant if you have a parent or grandparent over that age, and you have wondered whether and how to introduce email and other web-related technologies to her or him.

A desire to learn the implications of research for her personal life and public policy, you'll remember, is what brought communication major and environmental activist Vert to Professor Ora's graduate seminar. She now understands that all the research perspectives that the students have presented, from mainstream effects and uses and gratifications research, to cultivation research, to political economy and cultural studies, can be relevant to the continual promotion of new fashions on TV and online.

"There are so many possible important approaches to this issue that I almost feel paralyzed just worrying about which to choose," she says to the assembled group. "Where should I begin? How should I begin?"

As they continue discussing her concerns, though, Vert realizes that she must choose the approach to mass media that best fits the concerns she personally has about the media and the specific questions that she is asking. She goes home convinced that what she has had all along is a critical-studies take on the issue.

Vert enlists Kaj, the economics and environmental studies major, to get a group together. With the help of one of the professors, the group will conduct a systematic content analysis of Lifetime and E! programs and commercials, as well as those networks' Facebook pages and social media feeds. One goal is to find whether and how that content is pushing the importance of continually purchasing new fashions. Another goal is to discover when, if ever, the material mentions consignment or thrift stores—and, when it does, how. Part of the challenge for the researchers, of course, will be to figure out exactly what they mean by "pushing the importance of continually purchasing new fashions." After the content research is completed, the group will interview graduate students to prepare a review of agenda-setting and cultivation literature, to make the point that the systematic TV and internet presentations can have a real impact on the way viewers think about their wardrobes and their world. When all that is done—Vert estimates it will take five months—she and her group will examine their findings. If their expectations about the depictions of fashion and the lack of consignment depictions are confirmed, they will present their material to the local cable systems, as well as to reporters and academics. Their hope is that the work will encourage people to use consignment stores. They hope, too, that people will place pressure on the program creators to rethink their depictions of clothes buying and sometimes highlight the value of consignment fashion to individuals and the environment. "Maybe I'm quixotic," Vert tells her group, "but I really do think it can be done."

You may or may not agree with what Vert wants to do. Her story is not an unusual one, though. Every day, all sorts of mass communication research, from all sorts of perspectives, are brought to bear on a multitude of public issues. Local, state, and federal governments draw on the results of mass communication research, and they often commission it. Of course, scholars don't always carry out research with specific public policy questions in mind. Nor, it should be emphasized, do they "cook" their results to conform to their particular political points of view. Nevertheless, as we have seen in this chapter, over the past century academics have asked questions not from the irrelevance of an ivory tower, but as human beings concerned with the best ways to think about some of the most important topics of their day. As you read the rest of this book, consider that you can explore the topics and issues systematically from one or more of the perspectives sketched in this chapter. You might find carrying out such an inquiry fascinating and rewarding.

CHAPTER REVIEW

 Visit the Companion Website at www.routledge.com/cw/turow for additional study tools and resources.

 ## Key Terms

You can find the definitions to these key terms in the marginal glossary throughout this chapter. Test your knowledge of these terms with interactive flash cards on the *Media Today* Companion Website.

active audience	digital divide	polysemous
agenda setting	knowledge gap	priming
capitalism	magic bullet or hypodermic	propaganda
colonialism	needle approach	propaganda analysis
co-optation	mainstream approaches	social relations
critical theory	mass media research	two-step flow model
cultivation studies	naturalistic experiment	uses and gratifications
cultural colonialism	panel survey	research
cultural studies	political economy	

 ## Questions for Discussion and Critical Thinking

1. If the early researchers who concluded media had a "magic bullet" effect on audience were doing research today, how might they use social media to support their theory? What evidence would they see in how people engage with social media that would counter the "magic bullet" theory?

2. In Chapter 1 there was a discussion of the use of media to satisfy "basic human needs" such as enjoyment, companionship, and surveillance. Discuss how the satisfac-tion of these needs would factor into research applying the "uses and gratifications" framework.

3. The "mean world" syndrome posits that media create the sense that the world is a more dangerous place than it really is. Think of examples of media that have created this sense of a "mean world" in yourself and how you could counter that message.

4. How might you think the impact of video games could be considered using "cultivation theory"?

Activity

The section "How to Make Sense of Discussions and Arguments About Media Effects" lists questions to ask yourself. Using journals like *Journal of Communication* or *Journal of Broadcasting and Electronic Media*, find a study that researches media effects.

Answer these questions about the research:

1. What question is the researcher asking? Is it interesting and important?
2. In what research tradition does the study fall?
3. How good is the research design?
4. Are the research subjects appropriate, and are there a sufficient number?
5. How convincing is their analysis?

The Business of Media

3

CHAPTER OBJECTIVES

1   Recognize how mass media personnel consider the audience an integral part of business concerns.

2   Describe the primary genres of the materials created by various mass media industries.

3   Identify and discuss the process of producing, distributing, and exhibiting materials in mass media industries.

4   Explain the way media firms finance the production, distribution, and exhibition of media materials.

5   Harness your media literacy skills to evaluate what media forms mean to you as a media consumer.

Understanding the changing media system and the issues surrounding it can help us to be responsible citizens—parents, voters, workers—in our media-driven society. If you know how news is created, you might be able to read a paper or watch a TV news magazine with a much keener sense of what's going on. If you know how TV entertainment shows get on the air and how and why the firms that produce them are changing, you may be able to come up with strategies for influencing those changes that will benefit social groups that you care about. If you are aware of the strategies of media conglomerates and their relation to convergence, you may have a better understanding of why certain companies want to move into certain businesses. You also may be able to decide whether the government officials you voted for are doing the right thing by allowing or not allowing them to do that.

The difficulty of getting up to speed on these topics is that trying to understand a mass media industry can be a bewildering experience. Let's say that community leaders in the neighborhood where you live have begun to complain about billboard advertising. Some complain about the overwhelming number of signs featuring sexual images or advertising beer. Others object to the new digital boards that border some of the poor neighborhoods near a highway. They protest that those media are so bright and flickering that they interfere with people's ability to sleep. In order to help a community group petition billboard company executives to change their companies' policies, you decide you must learn about the billboard business. You quickly find that billboards on the road are part of the large and growing out-of-home (OOH) advertising industry. Its sectors include signs in sports stadiums, buses, bus stops, railway cars, railway stations, airports, and malls. Moreover, you learn that the billboard companies in your area are some of the biggest in the industry. Their signs can be found around the country and even around the world.

> "If anyone said we were in the radio business, it wouldn't be someone from our company. We're not in the business of providing news and information. We're not in the business of providing well-researched music. We're simply in the business of selling our customers' products."
>
> LOWRY MAYS, FORMER CLEAR CHANNEL CEO

You are faced with a number of crucial questions here. First, how do you get enough of a grasp on the billboard industry to learn about the factors that affect sign content, placement, and lighting policies—and how those policies can be changed? Second, in terms of your interest in changing outdoor advertising policies, is it relevant that many of the objectionable signs are in working-class and poor neighborhoods? Is it also relevant that the outdoor firms in question own signs in many cities? If so, how?

You want to learn as much as possible about the outdoor advertising industry to understand how its policies on beer and sex and lighting in neighborhoods can be changed. But should you also learn about the industry's stadium, transit, and mall businesses? If so, what should you learn? And where do you start? Moreover, must you conduct research on each segment of the industry separately, as if learning about the activities in one segment cannot help you understand the activities in another? If that's the case, you may find yourself thinking it's not worth the time and effort.

This chapter aims to ensure that becoming knowledgeable about the business of media is not as intimidating as it may sound. By learning a small number of general points about the mass media business, you will understand large, many-faceted firms and mass media industries much better than if you started from scratch every time.

Identifying an Audience for Mass Media Content

The consulting firm PWC estimates that in 2017 spending on media in the United States by companies and individuals was $703.6 billion.[1] That number will give you one sense of the large overall size of the media business. As we move through this book, we will see that the revenues of individual media industries come to tens of billions of dollars and sometimes far more. Table 3.1 gives you another sense of the media economy by presenting the top ten biggest media firms in terms of global revenue. You've probably heard of most, if not all, of them. Note that most are based in the United States, though all those plus Germany's Bertelsmann have major activities

Table 3.1 Top Global Media Owners, 2017

Rank	Media company	Headquarters Country
1	Alphabet	USA
2	Facebook	USA
3	Comcast.	USA
4	Baidu	China
5	The Walt Disney Company	USA
6	21st Century Fox	USA
7	CBS Corporation	USA
8	iHeartMedia	USA
9	Microsoft	USA
10	Bertelsmann	Germany

Source: The Zenith Unit of Publicis, "Top 30 Global Media Owners 2017," www.zenithusa.com/top-30-global-media-owners-2017/, accessed February 19, 2018.

Note: The Walt Disney Company bought 21st Century Fox in 2019.

throughout the world. (Bertelsmann, for example, owns the US-based Random House book publishing company.) The one firm on the list that may not be familiar to you is Baidu. It currently brings in most of its revenues from China (it takes up more than 60 percent of the internet search advertising revenues in that country), though it also operates in parts of East Asia and has ambitions to expand more broadly.[2]

No matter where it is based, no media business can exist (or continue to take in revenues) without content that attracts consumers, or **audiences**—the people to whom mass media firms are directing their products. **Media practitioners**—the people who select or create the material that a mass media firm produces, distributes, or exhibits—are keenly aware that their content must be attractive to audiences if money is to flow their way instead of to their competitors. In fact, audiences pose enormous risks as well as great opportunities for success for media practitioners. To best manage these risks and increase their chances of success, practitioners must carefully consider the following questions:

audiences
the people to whom a media product is directed

media practitioners
the people who select or create the material that a mass media firm produces, distributes, or exhibits

1. How should we think about our audience? How should we define our audience?
2. Will the material we are thinking of creating, distributing, or exhibiting to attract that audience generate adequate revenues?
3. Were the people we thought would be attracted to our products in fact attracted to our products? Why or why not?

Defining and Constructing a Target Audience

Executives who are charting the direction of media firms do not think about the members of their audience in the same way that the audience members think about themselves. Take, for example, Kaya. She thinks of herself in a number of ways—as a hard worker who juggles her communication studies major with her 20-hour-a-week job at a local restaurant; as a daughter who visits her parents twice a week; as a moderate churchgoer (about two Sundays a month); as a girlfriend who makes time for her boyfriend, Omar; and as a loyal friend who tries to keep up with high school classmates by phone and email.

Now consider how executives at a fashion magazine and app that Kaya uses—call it *Style & Beauty* (*S&B*)—think of her. Of course, they are not really thinking specifically about Kaya at all. Instead, *S&B* executives focus on the characteristics that they can use to show potential advertisers the types of people they can reach through their magazine, website, and app. *S&B* got some of its data from a questionnaire that Kaya filled out in order to get free makeup after she downloaded the app. Other data came from lists that the app bought from companies that bring together information about millions of people and sell it to media firms.

To *S&B*, Kaya is (among other things) in the 18–34 age group, a female, a student, a small-car owner, Android (Galaxy) phone owner, unmarried, childless, apartment renter, earner of $30,000 a year, the possessor of two credit cards, avid moviegoer, not a big TV watcher, and someone who has taken at least three airplane trips in the past two years. The major reason that *S&B* collects this information it does have about Kaya is that these are some of the characteristics that major advertisers consider when they think about buying ads in the printed magazine and app. A car manufacturer who is thinking of advertising in the magazine doesn't care how many times a month Kaya goes to church or whether she visits her parents (though other advertisers may well consider that information useful as a predictor of buying patterns). The car manufacturer does care about her age, her gender, her income, and the kind of car she presently owns because it believes this information predicts the likelihood that she will buy its brand. Kaya's age and student status make her attractive to advertisers such as car manufacturers, even though she doesn't make a lot of money; they believe these factors indicate that she will make a lot more someday.

Because *S&B* gets a large majority of its revenue from advertising, its executives especially want to keep an app and magazine population that is attractive to advertisers. They therefore use the information they have about Kaya and people like her—and about other groups of users that they have identified as being attractive to advertisers—to help them decide what kinds of materials in the app will keep these people coming back. These identified and selected population segments, then, become the desired audience for *S&B*. Once the company's executives have identified the target segments, they try to learn things about those segments that will lead to an increase in sales of space to advertisers. That, in turn, leads to more research to understand the groups. Figure 3.1 illustrates this process by focusing on Kaya. The example assumes that *S&B* marketers are attracted by what they know about Kaya and want her to be part of their audience. If they didn't find Kaya and people with similar characteristics attractive as consumers, they would produce content that speaks to different interests and that might drive Kaya away.

Thinking about the audience, then, means learning to think of people primarily as consumers of media materials and other products. For media professionals, thinking about people in this way requires a combination of intuition and solid knowledge of the marketplace. As the example of Kaya and *S&B* suggests, when advertisers contribute all or part of a firm's revenue stream, the firm's executives have three challenges: First, they have to create content that will attract audiences. Second, recognizing the importance of convergence, they have to place the content, or content like it, on a variety of media—a printed monthly magazine, an app for smartphones and tablets, a website, Facebook pages, Twitter feeds, Instagram photos, and even brochures for fashion shows that *S&B* puts on in malls. Third, the *S&B* executives also must make sure that the content and the audience it brings in will be attractive

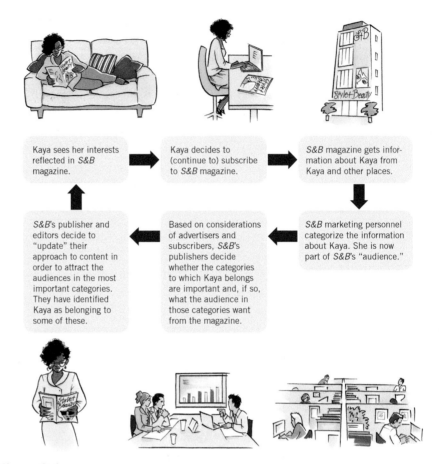

Figure 3.1
Kaya and the constructed audience.

to advertisers on one or several of these media so that money flows to *S&B* instead of to its competitors. To do this, they need to decide whether enough advertisers want to reach that audience in order to provide **adequate revenue**—enough cash to allow the enterprise to pay for itself and give the owners or bankers who put up the money the desired return on their investment.

Sometimes, in fact, media executives reverse the order of the questions. They first ask which audiences advertisers want to reach and then look for ways to attract those audiences. In recent decades, companies have been quite targeted in their audience aims: they try to appeal to particular segments of society rather than to the population as a whole. Often executives have to ask what segments should be the targets— women or men; the rich, the middle class, or the poor; Asians, Latinos, whites, or blacks; people who live in the eastern United States or those who live in the Midwest; or some combination of these and other categories?

Executives try to verify their intuitions and control their risks with research. In conducting this research, they think about the types of people who make up their audience—that is, they construct their audience—in four broad ways: through demographics, psychographics, lifestyle categories, and behavioral information. Increasingly, firms are bringing these data approaches together for personalized targeting in bids to attract audience members and advertisers.

Demographics **Demographics**—one of the simplest and most common ways to construct an audience—refers to characteristics by which people are divided into particular

adequate revenue
enough cash to allow the enterprise to pay for itself and give the owners or bankers who put up the money the desired return on their investment

demographics
characteristics by which people are divided into particular social categories

social categories. Media executives focus on those characteristics, or factors, that they believe are most relevant to understanding how and why people use their medium. **Demographic indicators** include such factors as age, gender, income, occupation, ethnicity, and race. Our fictional *S&B* focuses on the first three when it tells potential advertisers that its app and magazine readership is 90 percent female and 47 percent between 18 and 34 years old and that 37 percent make $100,000 or more per year. The management's hope is that these attractive "demos" will attract lots of upscale advertisers.

demographic indicators
factors such as age, gender, occupation, ethnicity, race, and income

Psychographics Media organizations also differentiate groups by **psychographics**, or by categorizing people on the basis of their attitudes, personality types, or motivations. Let's imagine that the management of *S&B* wants advertisers to understand its audience beyond the demographics of female, high income, and at a point in their lives (i.e., age) when they are likely to acquire new things. The executives hire a research firm to interview a large number of the *S&B* magazine's subscribers and create psychological profiles of them. The researchers find that the readers can be divided into three psychographic types: comparers (25 percent of the audience), who like to read the magazine to see how their clothes stack up against the apparel on the pages; idea hunters (60 percent of subscribers), who read it to help them with their own sense of clothes and cosmetics; and luxury lovers (15 percent), who subscribe because they like to look at the expensive clothes and accessories that appear in the magazine's articles and ads each month. The researchers also find that the three psychographic categories differ in terms of the length of time people remain subscribers. Those readers who are classified as idea hunters stay the longest time (an average of five years), and those classified as luxury lovers stay the shortest time (two years), with the comparers in the middle (three years). The magazine executives can use this construction of the audience to shape their articles to appeal to the idea hunters and comparers and to find advertisers that are interested in any of the groups (see Figure 3.2).

psychographics
a way to differentiate among people or groups by categorizing them according to their attitudes, personality types, or motivations

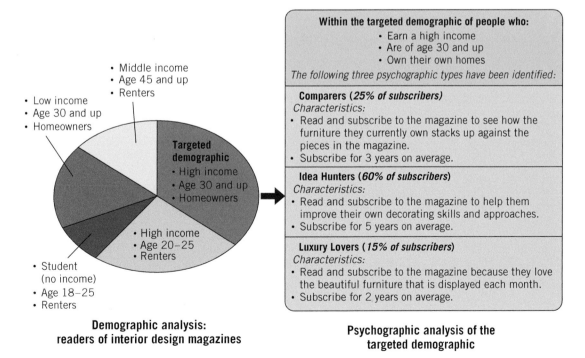

Demographic analysis: readers of interior design magazines

Psychographic analysis of the targeted demographic

Figure 3.2
Psychographic indicators can help media executives further shape their product to attract the audience members their advertisers seek.

lifestyle categories
activities in which potential audiences are involved that mark them as different from others in the population at large

Lifestyle Categories We can also describe media audiences using **lifestyle categories**—that is, by finding activities in which potential audiences are involved that mark them as different from others in the audience or in the population at large. Suppose, for example, that *S&B* magazine conducts another research study that finds that its readers go to restaurants, own expensive cars, and travel outside the United States far more than the average for the US population. In this way, the magazine's employees are categorizing readers from a lifestyle point of view.

THINKING ABOUT MEDIA LITERACY

Which lifestyle category or categories do you think you fit? How might a magazine target its content toward one of the categories? Think of the topic of the exercise—how might a magazine targeting young adults deal with the topic differently than one for senior citizens? Imagine the advertisers that would be interested in one target audience or the other.

Behavioral Information People's wide use of digital media allows many media firms to follow their activities within the firms' websites and apps and even into physical locations. (We will discuss how they do that in Chapter 6; check it out now if you can't wait to learn.) Media firms bring together that behavioral information in ways that they hope will attract advertisers to their cross-platform products. S&B's behavioral tracking may reveal, for example, that the users of its app and website spend more than half an hour a week on S&B material and that they quite often interact with the ads there. The magazine's executives may use these findings to attract advertisers who want to reach audience members who are clearly engaged with both a media firm's products and the ads that surround them.

Personalized Targeting Increasingly, companies are bringing together demographic, psychographic, lifestyle, and behavioral data regarding individual audience members. That allows executives to offer their advertisers the ability to reach people who fit particular profiles that may interest them. A diaper advertiser, for example, may want to reach S&B readers who are young mothers and read S&B's advice columns and articles related to babies and baby products. Typically, a media firm such as S&B will serve the personalized ads without revealing the identity of the audience members to the advertiser. Sometimes, the advertiser will be able to learn the audience members' identities. As you can imagine, these and related issues regarding the rights of audience members to have a say in such activities have created much controversy. It's an important subject we will be taken up in different ways throughout this book, but especially in Chapters 4, 5, and 6.

Keep in mind that what media professionals learn about their audiences through research is relevant only if it relates to making money by attracting advertisers or by keeping them as audience members. The lifestyle characteristics that our fictional magazine found are terrific—just the sort that will attract major automobile, airline, hotel, and restaurant advertisers. The demographics and psychographics are also useful for getting sponsors, as well as for thinking about the kind of content that will keep particular groups as part of the audience. S&B's ability to target individuals with a number of these characteristics might also attract advertisers.

Creating Content to Attract the Target Audience

A key challenge for mass media firms is knowing what kind of content to present to their target audiences and how to present it. Although this may seem straightforward, it actually involves quite a bit of selection, thought, and risk.

Suppose you are in charge of programming for the CBS broadcast television network—that is, in charge of setting the television schedule for the coming year. Your job is to create the menu of shows that the owners of CBS hope will attract tens of millions of viewers to their airwaves every day. Quite a daunting task, isn't it? For one thing, you must try to get a thorough understanding of the audiences your company wants to attract—who they are and what they like. For another, you need to have a strong grasp of the kinds of materials that may be available to meet audience interests at different times of the day. What will grab people's attention? Who can create it? How much will it cost? And (here comes convergence again!) can you make money on the shows beyond the traditional CBS over-the-air network—for example, by charging individuals to access the programs on their tablets or streaming devices such as Roku and Apple TV? How do you even begin to determine whether the ideas that potential creators pitch to you will succeed on these and other platforms?

Sometimes the answers to these questions are based on the intuitions and experiences of the executives in charge. To lower their risk, they may choose creators with a good **track record**—that is, a history of success. They also may choose to produce material that is similar to other material that has recently been successful. For example, if a comedy/horror movie aimed at young adults has recently been successful at the box office, film studio executives might search for another film of the same type, hoping that lightning will strike twice.

When a lot of money is at stake (and it usually is with broadcast TV networks), executives often turn to **research and development (R&D)** activities to systematically investigate potential sources of revenue. These activities involve learning about the leisure habits of different audiences through a number of tools, including surveys, focus groups, or the analysis of existing data.

In **surveys**, a certain number of carefully chosen people are asked the same questions individually over the phone, via the internet, or in person. A **focus group** is an assemblage of eight to ten carefully chosen people who are asked to discuss their habits and opinions about one or more topics. Another method, the **analysis of existing data**, involves systematic investigation of the potential audience for certain kinds of content (who they are, where they are, how much they like the idea, how much they will pay for it) and of the competitors (who they are, how similar their products are, how powerful they are). Based on these results, executives must decide what kinds of materials to create and how—and whether their proposed budget is adequate to create the product and market it successfully against the competition.

Measuring the Content's Success With the Target Audience You might think that whether or not mass media content will find success with its audience would become clear when the material is created and released. This all depends, though, on the mass medium and the exact questions being asked. At its simplest, measuring success may involve counting the sales—how many magazines or movie tickets were sold. In cases in which sales are not involved, such as with radio, broadcast television, and the web, ratings companies conduct regular surveys to count audiences to help executives determine how many people watched particular programs. As we will see later in the text, however, neither counting sales nor conducting ratings surveys is really a simple activity.

track record
the previous successes or failures of a product, person, or organization

research and development (R&D)
departments within companies that explore new ideas and generate new products and services, systematically investigating potential sources of revenue through surveys, focus groups, or the analysis of existing data

surveys
a research tool that seeks to ask a certain number of carefully chosen people the same questions individually over the phone, online, or in person.

focus group
an assemblage of eight to ten carefully chosen people who are asked to discuss their habits and opinions about one or more topics

analysis of existing data
a systematic investigation into the potential audience for the material (who they are, where they are, how much they like the idea, how much they will pay for it) and into the competitors (who they are, how similar their products are, how powerful they are)

Nevertheless, counting sales and audiences is a lot easier than determining why a media product succeeded or failed. Executives often try to find out what went wrong—or what went right—so that they can avoid future mistakes and repeat past successes. That sometimes involves conducting focus groups or surveys to gauge the intended audience's opinions. Often, though, executives discuss their failures and successes with one another. They try to figure out which elements led to success and which led to failure. This is not at all scientific, but it's often the best that people whose business it is to select or create mass media content can do.

Determining a Genre for Mass Media Content

When media practitioners try to determine how to choose or produce content that is appropriate for the audiences they want to reach, they must do so with an understanding of the major categories of content from which they can build their material. Major categories of media content are called **genres**—categories of artistic composition, as in music or literature, marked by a distinctive style, form, or content. The primary genres that media practitioners discuss are entertainment, news, information, education, and advertising. Let's first take a look at each.

Entertainment

The word "**entertainment**" derives from the Latin *tenere*, which means "to hold or keep steady, busy, or amused." The notion of making money by keeping an audience steady, busy, or amused remains central to those in the business of entertainment. Media practitioners, then, define entertainment as material that grabs the audience's attention and leaves agreeable feelings, as opposed to challenging their views of themselves and the world. However, this doesn't mean that people who work in the entertainment business always stay away from informing or persuading. Many movies that are categorized under "entertainment" by their production firms have been written and produced with the intention of making a political point (think of *The Post*, *In the Loop*, or *Selma*) or an educational point (e.g., *The Darkest Hour*, *The King's Speech*, and *Schindler's List*). When media practitioners label a product as "entertainment," though, they are signaling to their audiences that the creators' primary concern is with audience enjoyment, not with any other messages that may be included.

Subgenres of Entertainment One way to understand entertainment is to see it as consisting of four subgenres: festivals, gaming, drama, and comedy. We can see each subgenre, in turn, as having still more subcategories nested within it. Consider, for example, the subgenre gaming, which may include sports (*Monday Night Football*), quiz shows (*Jeopardy!*), and newspaper crossword puzzles, among other forms. Similarly, the subgenre comedy may include situation comedies (*The Big Bang Theory*), stand-up comedy routines (Amy Schumer) and their ancillary products (Schumer's DVD *Mostly Sex Stuff*), certain radio talk shows (*The Howard Stern Show*), and joke lists (Michael Kilgarriff's *1,000 Knock-Knock Jokes for Kids*), among other forms. We can even go further and think of a more specific level—subgenres of these subgenres. We can break situation comedies into school sitcoms (*Glee*), workplace sitcoms (*The Office*), family sitcoms (*Black-ish*), and buddy sitcoms (*Two Broke Girls*). In turn, people who are specialists in sitcoms might be able to create still further subgenres of these categories. Workplace sitcoms might be divided into medical sitcoms (*The Mindy Project*) and office sitcoms (*Parks and Recreation*). Take a look at Figure 3.3 for an illustration of these relationships.

genres
major categories of media content

entertainment
material that grabs the audience's attention and leaves agreeable feelings, as opposed to challenging their views of themselves and the world

Genre	ENTERTAINMENT			
Subgenre	**Festival**	**Drama**	**Gaming**	**Comedy**
Second-level subgenre	Music festival	Workplace drama	Sports	Situation comedy
Third-level subgenre	Popular music festival	Dramas about professionals	Professional sports	Work-based sitcoms
Fourth-level subgenre	Annual popular music festival (e.g., SXSW, Lollapalooza)	Forensic-themed crime dramas (e.g., *CSI*, *Bones*)	NFL football (e.g., *Monday Night Football*, *Sunday Night Football*)	Hospital-based sitcom (e.g., *House*, *The Mindy Project*)

Figure 3.3
Entertainment is divided into subgenres of festival, drama, gaming, and comedy. Under each subgenre are second-, third-, and fourth-level subgenres. You may be able to break down the fourth-level subgenres further. For example, people who write hospital-based sitcoms might be able to describe various subgenres of these sitcoms.

Entertainment Formulas You may have noticed that there are key elements that make up various subgenres: the family situation comedy, the hospital drama, the baseball broadcast, or any other subgenre. This specific combination of elements is called a **formula**—a patterned approach to creating content that is characterized by three major features:

formula
a patterned approach to creating content that is characterized by the use of setting, typical characters, and patterns of action

- Setting
- Typical characters
- Patterns of action

GLOBAL MEDIA TODAY & CULTURE

MERGERS AND ACQUISITIONS: OLIGOPOLIES IN THE MEDIA INDUSTRIES

The telecom giant AT&T merged with the conglomerate Time Warner in 2019. The merged conglomerate's assets comprise HBO, CNN, Warner Bros., and DirectTV, among other major media companies, united under the same ownership. This is not an isolated case. Rather, in the last two decades the media landscape has been increasingly undergoing processes of mergers and acquisition, resulting in fewer competitors operating with multiple companies they own in the different media sectors. As you read this book and learn about the different media industries, you might notice that a few companies have large shares of these markets, from music to movies and advertising, for example.

These are examples of oligopolies: It is an economic term indicating a market where a few players dominate the competitive landscape (whereas monopolies occur when there is only one player, duopolies when there are two), which is vastly different from a perfect competition landscape where there are many players, each with small market shares. What do you think? What could be the reasons for these mergers and acquisitions? Is this the best allocation of resources from an economic point of view? Also, given the central relevance of the media industries in societies, does this concern you that such a concentration of ownership might lead to a lack of diversity? In general, who do you think wins and who loses from the way these markets are structured and work?

setting
the environment in which content takes place

typical characters
those who appear regularly in the subgenre

patterns of action
the predictable activities associated with the characters in the settings

The **setting** is the environment in which content takes place. A football program such as *Monday Night Football* takes place in a stadium and in an announcer's booth. A doctor show such as *The Good Doctor* takes place primarily in a hospital.

The **typical characters** are those who appear regularly in the subgenre. In the football program, the announcers, the athletes, the referees, and the coaches are typical characters. Doctor shows such as *The Good Doctor* are populated by (you guessed it) doctors, patients, and nurses.

The **patterns of action** are the predictable activities associated with the characters in the settings. The football program's patterns of action center on the rules of the game, which are bounded by the clock (sixty minutes plus time-outs and half-time) and the field (the playing zones). The patterns of action in doctor shows aren't as clearly based on rules. Nevertheless, each episode does have its plot patterns, revolving around issues of life and death.

When it comes to reality shows, you can probably suggest different forms of the subgenre depending on whether you are discussing *The Amazing Race*, *Dancing with the Stars*, *The Voice*, or *Survivor*. *Survivor* might be called an "isolation" reality show subgenre, along with such series as *The Apprentice*, *The Biggest Loser*, and *Project Runway*. They contain similar formula elements:

- Setting: a location that isolates a group with minimal interference from the "outside" world
- Typical characters: good-looking individuals of diverse ethnic backgrounds who have certain expected character profiles—selfish or generous, gregarious or loner, crafty or naïve
- Patterns of action: challenges set up by the producers that often set members of the group against one another and lead to individuals being chosen to leave

Keep in mind, too, that formulas can and do change. Media practitioners who use these formulas to create stories for movies, television, video games, or other media are often steeped in the formulas' history. Writers and producers in all mass media often "borrow" plot elements, characters, and settings from previously successful stories. Their hope is that the basic elements of the formula will stay popular and that they can reshape these elements to fit what they believe are the interests of contemporary audiences.

Examples are all around us, but you have to know something about the history of a mass medium to notice them. Perhaps you've seen the remakes of classic horror movies that have appeared in movie theaters over the past few years—for example, *Friday the 13th* (2009), *The Echo* (a 2009 remake of the Philippine film *Sigaw*), *The Wolfman* (2009), and *Halloween* (2007). If you go back to the originals, you will see how the contemporary writers borrowed settings, characters, and plot elements from the originals and then changed them to fit their idea of what audiences of the 2000s would like. Watching TV, going to the movies, reading novels, and even playing video games will take on a whole new dimension once you are aware of this borrowing. If you've seen the movie *Deadpool 2*, you must have noticed how the writers reveled in making snide references to many examples of the superhero formula and its storytelling elements.

In crime dramas such as *NCIS*, there is a fairly set pattern of action involving the finding of human remains and an investigation into the cause of death and identity of the victim, and the show is typically resolved with the identification and capture of the person responsible for causing the victim's death.

THINKING ABOUT MEDIA LITERACY

Imagine there was a police shooting in your town. How would a "hard news" story, an investigative report, and an editorial differ? What would each contain? What would be the informational goals of each?

Apart from updating genres, writers and producers are also eager to find new ways to mix entertainment subgenres to entertain their target audiences. The term "**hybrid genres**" can be used to describe mixed genres; the process of mixing genres within a culture and across cultures is called **hybridity**. Hybrid genres are all around us. Consider, for example, the music of Taylor Swift, which consciously blurs the boundary between country and teen pop music. Hybridity can also take place across cultures. Think of attempts by US producers and writers to mix plots, settings, and characters of Indian Bollywood films with traditional Hollywood plots, characters, and settings. For example, *Bride and Prejudice* is a 2004 movie that inserts an Indian family into the basic plot of the Jane Austen novel *Pride and Prejudice* and follows them through Indian, UK, and US locales. The advertising tagline for the movie, which was filmed in India, the United Kingdom, and the United States, trumpeted this hybridity: "Bollywood meets Hollywood . . . and it's the perfect match."

Beyond combining specific entertainment subgenres, some producers and writers try to get people's attention by blending the rules associated with drama (serious) and comedy (funny) into what some media practitioners call a **dramedy**. Dramedies have shown up fairly frequently on US television in recent years. Think of *The End of the F**ing World*, *Orange Is the New Black*, *Girls*, and *Monk*. These programs don't have laugh tracks, and they can veer from a hilariously funny scene to one that tugs strongly at viewers' heartstrings. *New York Daily News* TV critic David Hinckley zeroed in on that quality in *Monk* when commenting on the series' final episode. The closing drama brings Adrian Monk (Tony Shalhoub) back to the show's original launching point: the unsolved murder of his wife, Trudy. As Hinckley noted,

> Trudy's death gave the show a bed of tragedy and Monk a terrible sadness that passing seasons did not diminish. It also left him with a nightmare of phobias, quirks and general obsessive compulsion. He was afraid of germs, of closed areas, of pretty much anything involving people. But the show's genius, and Shalhoub's, was that all this somehow honed his skills. He solved case after case even as he couldn't crack the one he most cared about.

The finale carried these features to a conclusion that combined formula-driven TV with a wonderful understanding of the program's characters. Hinckley wrote that "it's so well-written and so true to the wonderfully tragicomic tone of the whole show that you won't even mind the fact that the actual plot wrapup is pretty formulaic."

News

News, like entertainment, involves the telling of stories. We often don't think of news in this way, but it is useful to pause and consider this point. When you watch

hybrid genres
a term used by some academic writers to describe mixed genres

hybridity
the process of mixing genres within a culture and across cultures

dramedy
a subgenre that blends the rules associated with drama (serious) and comedy (funny)

NBC Nightly News, in one sense news anchor Lester Holt is telling you a tale with a beginning, a middle, and an end. Of course, Holt reads most of the story and shows short video clips of the accompanying action, whereas other storytelling media genres (such as the sitcom) continuously illustrate the story through acting. The tales that Lester Holt tells during his newscast, however, may not be that different from the sitcom you will be viewing just two hours later on the same network. In fact, many of the ideas for non-news television programming are generated from news. NBC's *Law & Order*, in fact, used to boast that its plots were "ripped from the headlines." The program's ads stopped saying that because of the producers' fear they might be sued for libel by the people whose news stories they adapted. Nevertheless, even casual viewers of *Law & Order* or other drama programs would notice that the program drew on news stories.

Historically, newspapers have been central to the circulation of news in America. But as we'll see in later chapters, big changes taking place are eroding the presence and power of newspapers in people's lives. Today's journalists are learning that they must present news in many media, including audio and video reports on the web. Convergence has become a fact even in the news divisions of the major TV networks. You can find Lester Holt reading the news on your tablet, laptop, and smartphone in addition to on your TV set.

Reporters, directors, editors, producers, and other people who work in the news business are called **journalists**. A journalist is someone who is trained to report non-fiction events to an audience. Journalists' reporting can be in print (newspapers, magazines) or electronic media (radio, TV, the web). Many journalists today take courses in college to learn how to carry out newswork. (You may, in fact, be such a person.) Historically, news reporters didn't necessarily have that kind of training, and today, with the spread of outlets for news on the internet, many people who describe "news" in textual, audio, and/or video form to sometimes large audiences don't have any kind of journalistic training or certification. With the ease of spreading stories on the internet, we also see controversies around the accuracy of news stories from some outlets. In particular, recent elections have witnessed the spread of so-called "fake news": made-up stories by people with an interest in supporting one or another candidate. American intelligence agencies concluded that a large number of these concocted "news" stories were created and initially spread by Russian agents with an interest in affecting American public opinion. At the same time, President Trump made many comments lambasting American mainstream news outlets such as CNN, MSNBC, and *The New York Times* as purveyors of "fake news." The developments led to lots of public discussions about what news means, the importance of accuracy, and a debate about whether it is possible in the United States—where the Constitution protects a press free from government control—to decide who is and who isn't a legally protected "journalist" in today's world.

Subgenres of News How would journalists explain the difference between what they produce and other storytelling genres, such as entertainment? Many would undoubtedly argue that there is one clear distinction: news stories are constrained by facts, whereas entertainment stories are not. The writer of the screenplay for a TV show that is "based on a true story" or "ripped from the headlines" can decide whether a character who is accused of rape is guilty or innocent. The reporter of the real-life news event, however, should never make such a judgment. Building on this basic distinction, news workers divide news broadly into four subgenres:

journalists

individuals who are trained to report nonfiction events to an audience

- Hard news
- Investigative reports
- Editorials
- Soft news

HARD NEWS

Hard news is what most people probably think of as news. It is the firsthand report-age of a battle, the coverage of a congressional bill's passage, or the details of a forest fire. News workers use four guidelines when deciding what is and isn't hard news. An event that fits only one of these guidelines will probably not be considered hard news. Additionally, the more of these guidelines that apply to an event, the more likely news workers are to cover it.

hard news
a news story marked by timeliness, unusualness, conflict, and closeness

- *Timeliness*. A hard news event must have happened recently—typically within the past day or so. A murder that happened yesterday might deserve coverage. A murder that happened last year would not, unless new information about it has been released or discovered.
- *Unusualness*. Hard news events are those that most people would consider unusual. To use the classic example, "Dog Bites Man" is not news, whereas "Man Bites Dog" is.
- *Conflict*. Struggles between opposing forces—conflicts—often lie at the center of hard news stories. Often these struggles are physical; they can be wars or bar-room brawls. Sometimes the conflicts involve wars of words, as between members of Congress. Other times they pit humans against nature (a fire or other natural disaster).
- *The closeness of the incident*. An event is more likely to be seen as hard news if it happens close by than if it takes place far away. Note, however, that closeness carries two meanings: it can mean geographically close (physically near to the audience), or it can mean psychologically close. An incident is psychologically close when members of the audience feel a connection to it even though it takes place far away. Because of Boston's large Irish population, for example, news-paper editors in Boston may consider certain happenings in Ireland to be hard news, whereas editors in areas of the United States with small Irish populations would not cover those events.

Once they have decided that something is hard news, news workers must decide how to present it. Journalists use the word "**objectivity**" to summarize the way in which news ought to be researched, organized, and presented. Most journalists would agree that it is impossible to present a totally objective view of an event if that means a view that is the absolute truth with no personal viewpoints inserted. The fact is that no two people will see the same thing in exactly the same way. Most journalists would say that what they mean by an objective report is a report that presents a fair, balanced, and impartial representation of the events that took place.

Over the decades, journalists have agreed on certain characteristics that an objec-tive story will have. These characteristics give a reporter the tools to describe an inci-dent efficiently in ways that his or her editor (or any other editor) will consider fair and impartial. Here are four major characteristics of an objective story, particularly with regard to print news:

objectivity
presenting a fair, balanced, and impartial representation of the events that took place by recounting a news event based on the facts and without interpretation, so that anyone else who witnessed the event would agree with the journalist's recounting of it; the way in which the news ought to be researched, organized, and presented

Figure 3.4

The inverted pyramid approach to reporting the news begins with the most general statement of the story and grows increasingly more specific.

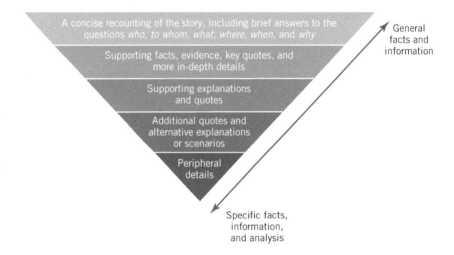

A concise recounting of the story, including brief answers to the questions *who, to whom, what, where, when,* and *why*

Supporting facts, evidence, key quotes, and more in-depth details

Supporting explanations and quotes

Additional quotes and alternative explanations or scenarios

Peripheral details

General facts and information

Specific facts, information, and analysis

- It should be written in a form that journalists call an inverted pyramid (see Figure 3.4). This means that the reporter should place in the first paragraph (the lead paragraph) a concise recounting of the entire story. In the paragraphs that follow, the reporter should give increasingly specific information about the material in the lead paragraph.
- An objective story should be told in the third person: that means writing as if the journalist is a novelist telling the tale but is not involved in it (i.e., the person doesn't use personal pronouns such as "I" or "me").
- An objective story should report at least two sides of a conflict. If a politician is accused of corruption, the objective report must also note the politician's denial of the charges.
- An objective story uses quotes from those involved or from experts on the topic to back up statements.

These characteristics can be used in creating objective news stories for any medium. If you watch television news programs carefully, however, you may note that reporters also convey the idea of objectivity in a visual way. Here are three camera rules for an objective story:

- There should be a title on the screen telling the viewer whom the reporter is interviewing.
- The camera should film the reporter or a person being interviewed from the height of an average person, not from the ground staring up at the person or from above the person staring down.
- The camera should give as much time to a person representing one side of the conflict as it does to a person representing the other side. Anything less would be considered biased.

accuracy
reporting factually correct information

In addition to being objective, hard news reports are held to strict standards of accuracy. **Accuracy** means reporting factually correct information. Many news organizations expect their reporters to check facts with at least two sources before they use them in stories, and many news-oriented magazines employ fact-checkers, who review stories for accuracy before they are released to the public.

BIG BAD WOLF
Master of Disguise, Grimm University

 Note inclusion of name of person being interviewed and their affiliation

Camera angle is even with both Little Red Riding Hood and the Big Bad Wolf. Camera gives equal time to both Little Red Riding Hood and the Big Bad Wolf during the interview

Figures 3.5a and b
TV news producers often use camera rules that allow them to argue their program is "objective."

INVESTIGATIVE REPORTS

Investigative reports are in-depth explorations of some aspects of reality. This news subgenre shares the same standards of objectivity, accuracy, and fairness or balance with hard news. However, a major difference between hard news and investigative reports is the amount of time journalists can devote to the project. When it comes to hard news, journalists typically work on tight schedules; their time limit (deadline) for the completion of an assignment is often only a few hours after they begin it. In contrast, journalists who work on investigative reports have quite a bit more time to do their research, interview their sources, and write their script. Their deadlines can be days or weeks from the time they begin, or even longer.

Investigative reporters often seek to uncover corruption or other problems in government or business, and the tone of the report resembles that of a detective story. A few broadcast television news series, such as *60 Minutes*, *Dateline NBC*, and *20/20*, present this type of material. They spread their output across a variety of digital media, too. Propublica is a nonprofit organization that often creates investigative reports with the cooperation of other journalistic organizations based in print, broadcast, cable, or digital media.

investigative reports
in-depth explorations of some aspects of reality

EDITORIALS

Opinions regarding hard news are usually reserved for editorials. Unlike hard news and investigative reports, an **editorial** is a subgenre of news that expresses an individual's or an organization's point of view. Some editorials are written in the name of (and express the point of view of) the person who wrote the piece, whereas others are written in the name of the entire news organization—for example, the newspaper that printed the piece or the television station that aired it.

News organizations may also allow their reporters and knowledgeable people who do not work for their firm to present editorial comments. **Columnists** are individuals who are paid to write editorials on a regular basis—usually weekly, monthly, or daily. Editorials by the most famous columnists, such as Leonard Pitts, Jonah Goldberg, and Anna Quindlen, are carried by many news outlets across the United States and even around the world. On the web, columnists may show up on journalistic websites (such as CNN.com or Slate) or on **blogs**, online sites written in the style of

editorial
subgenre of news that concentrates on an individual's or an organization's point of view

columnists
individuals who are paid to write editorials on a regular basis—usually weekly, monthly, or daily

blogs
journalistic websites or opinion sites in which writings are in the style of journal entries, often in reverse chronological order

journal entries, often in reverse chronological order. A well-known example is the *Huffington Post* group of political opinion blogs. They include regular columns by Arianna Huffington, businessman Gene Marks, and LGBT content producer Jincey Lumpkin, as well as opinion pieces from a wide spectrum of other celebrities and noncelebrities.

SOFT NEWS

soft news
the kind of news story that news workers feel may not have the critical importance of hard news but nevertheless would appeal to a substantial number of people in the audience

Whereas news workers generally consider hard news reporting a place for objective, accurate, and balanced reporting with little (if any) editorial commentary, they consider another news category, **soft news**, to be an area in which the reporter's opinions and biases can show through. As you may be able to tell by its name, soft news (also known as the human interest story) is the kind of tale news workers feel may not have the critical importance of hard news but nevertheless would appeal to a substantial number of people in the audience. Cooking spots, articles on the best ways to shovel snow without injuring your back, video clips highlighting local students in community plays or recitals—these are topics that news workers consider soft rather than hard news.

Information

information
the raw material that journalists use when they create news stories

One way to understand the difference between news and information—a difficult distinction to draw for some—is to say that **information** is the raw material that journalists use when they create news stories. On the most basic level, a piece of information is a fact, an item that reveals something about the world. Generally, we must bring together many pieces of information in order to draw conclusions about a person, place, thing, or incident.

All of us use pieces of information as tools in our personal and professional lives. Students gather information as part of paper-writing assignments. Accountants bring together the facts of a client's expenses and wages to fill out the client's tax return. Professors compile information to prepare (interesting, it is hoped) lectures. Similarly, journalists often stitch together facts when they create a news story.

Sometimes searching for relevant facts means speaking to individuals (as reporters might), looking at old bills (as accountants might), or reading scholarly books (as professors might). Often, however, people find the information they want in special collections of facts called databases. Journalists search motor vehicle records, collections of trial transcripts, gatherings of old newspaper articles, and city real estate files. Students, too, use databases: computerized and manual library catalogs are databases; so are dictionaries, EBSCO, Factiva, and the *Reader's Guide to Periodical Literature*.

Information is a widely used and lucrative mass media commodity—bringing together facts and packaging them in a multitude of ways. A trip to any library's reference collection reveals an extensive array of categorized facts on an enormous number of subjects that are waiting to be used for papers, dissertations, or books, or just to settle arguments.

But although a major library's collection of databases may appear quite impressive, it is merely the tip of a huge iceberg of information that mass media firms collect and offer for sale. The information industry creates and distributes much of its product for companies, not individual consumers.

Information Gathering and Distributing One major segment of the information industry aims to help businesses find, evaluate, and understand their current customers. For example, TransUnion Credit Information Company and Equifax hold collections of information about the income and debts of hundreds of millions of people worldwide. These firms are in the business of selling selected segments of that information to banks, insurance companies, and other organizations that are interested in the creditworthiness of particular individuals.

Information activities affect you directly when you are approved (or turned down) for a loan or a credit card. This part of the information business also provides lists of names to the marketers who send you postal mail or email—or phone you (often in the middle of dinner)—with "great" offers. Catalog companies often rely on information companies to help them find new customers too.

Information Research and Retrieval Another major segment of the information industry focuses on providing quick retrieval of data for people whose work requires them to get facts quickly. Consider the services provided by LexisNexis, for example. The Nexis information service, owned by publishing giant Reed Elsevier of the Netherlands, enables journalists, professors, and students—in fact, researchers of all kinds—to search for and retrieve virtually any fact in more than 2.5 billion searchable documents. Lexis, a sister service, enables attorneys and paralegals to find, analyze, and validate information from countless legal documents by keywords via computer networks. For example, through Lexis's database legal professionals can retrieve background information on public and private companies; find information about individuals; identify an organization's assets; and research judges, expert witnesses, and opposing counsel, among other things.

The subscription for services such as those offered by Reed Elsevier, Dow Jones (e.g., Factiva), and other similar firms in the information business can be costly. Information industry executives tie their high prices to the expense of collecting the data, trying to ensure their accuracy, storing them and protecting them from hackers, preparing print or computer retrieval methods, and distributing the data to clients. But the high price of information is also based on the realization that certain types of information can be extremely valuable, allowing companies to make (or save) millions of dollars. Quick access to the right information helps businesses and governments go about their work efficiently.

education
content that is purposefully crafted to teach people specific ideas about the world in specific ways

Education

When it comes to genres of media, **education** means content that is purposefully crafted to teach people specific ideas about the world in specific ways. Education is a large segment of the media marketplace. In fact, spending for "instructional materials" by elementary and high schools reached $12.8 billion for the 2013–2014 school year.[3] Much of this money was spent on textbooks, the medium that most of us conjure up when we think of instructional materials for schools. Spending for college textbooks is high, as you undoubtedly know, though costs are declining some because of physical and digital rentals. One study put the average amount spent per student in the 2016–2017 school year at $543, a drop of $64 from a year earlier.[4]

But the genre of education extends far beyond textbooks and other types of printed materials. Consider for a moment the wide variety of media that you've encountered in your long trek through school. The aforementioned spending includes not just textbooks but also workbooks, course packs, wall maps, flash cards, software, online services, and more. In addition, there is a vast amount of educational media material produced primarily

Bill Nye the Science Guy.

for home use. When you were a child, your parents might have sat you in front of the TV to view *Sesame Street* or *Reading Rainbow*. Perhaps you watched *Monsters Inside Me* or *Sex . . . With Mom and Dad* when you got a bit older. Maybe your parents gave you the Math Blaster, LeapFrog, or JumpStart computer programs for a birthday present. These are just a few of the products that media companies have explicitly designed to teach basic skills.

Advertising

advertisement
a message that explicitly aims to direct favorable attention to certain goods and services

A traditional definition of an **advertisement** is that it is a message that explicitly aims to direct favorable attention to certain goods and services. The message may have a commercial purpose or be aimed at advancing a noncommercial cause, such as the election of a political candidate or the promotion of a fundraising event.

As we will see in Chapter 4, advertising involves far more than explicit messages. People who work in the advertising industry help their clients with a range of activities from package design to coupon offers. A broad definition of advertising even includes **product placement**, which is the paid insertion of products into TV shows and movies in order to associate those products, often quietly, with certain desirable characters or activities.

product placement
the process by which a manufacturer pays—often tens of thousands of dollars and sometimes far more—a production company for the opportunity to have its product displayed in a movie or TV show

Subgenres of Advertisements No matter what the medium, advertising practitioners speak about three broad subgenres of advertisements:

- Informational ads
- Hard-sell ads
- Soft-sell ads

INFORMATIONAL ADVERTISEMENTS

informational ads
advertisements that rely primarily on the recitation of facts about a product and the product's features to convince target consumers that it is the right product for them to purchase

Informational ads rely primarily on a recitation of facts about a product and the product's features to convince target consumers that it is the right product for them to purchase. An advertisement in *Sound & Vision* magazine that carefully details the specifications and capabilities of a set of Bose speakers would be informational in nature. Similarly, a television announcement aired during PBS's *This Old House* noting the program's support by Home Depot is another example of an informational ad.

HARD-SELL ADVERTISEMENTS

hard-sell ads
messages that combine information about the product with intense attempts to get the consumer to purchase it as soon as possible

Hard-sell ads are messages that combine information about the product with intense attempts to get the consumer to purchase it as soon as possible. For example, a TV commercial in which a car salesman speaks a mile a minute about the glories of his dealership, shouts about a two-day-only sale, and recites the address of the dealership four times before the spot ends is a hard-sell ad.

SOFT-SELL ADVERTISEMENTS

soft-sell ads
advertisements that aim mostly to create good feelings about the product or service by associating it with music, personalities, or events that the creators of that product or service feel would appeal to the target audience

Soft-sell ads aim mostly to create good feelings about the product or service by associating it with music, personalities, or events that the creators of that product or service feel would appeal to the target audience. Television commercials for a wide variety of products, including soft drinks, beer, and athletic footwear, are soft-sell ads. Remember the Dove's "Campaign for Real Beauty," "The Hire" videos for BMW, or "Old Spice: The Man Your Man Could Smell Like" for Old Spice body wash? These are examples of ads that aim to create a "hip" feeling about a product that will lead consumers to want to be identified with it.

It is important to note that these three types of ads—informational, hard-sell, and soft-sell—mainly differ in the amount of stress they place on facts about the product, the intensity of the sales pitch, and the emotional connection between the consumer and the product. There are, however, circumstances in which much longer ads are created, and the advertisers can then combine informational, hard-sell, and soft-sell tactics. If you watch TV shopping channels such as HSN, you might see this mix. A hostess may provide a demonstration of a gold necklace that mixes specific information about the necklace ("beautiful 14-karat gold, 30 inches long, with a sturdy lock, as you can see") and hard-sell encouragement ("these necklaces are going so fast that if you don't call us right now, we might run out of them") with soft-sell tactics that include joking around by people on the set and an attempt to build an entertaining environment for selling.

Mixing Genres in a Convergent Media System

You have probably noticed that various forms of soft-sell advertising sometimes show up as part of entertainment-oriented TV shows. When the Lifetime cable network paraded L'Oréal products as part of the action on *Project Runway* (a soft-sell activity called product placement), that was a clear case of mixing genres. Clearly, L'Oréal executives believed that audiences would get a favorable feeling for their brand if the audiences saw their products pop up within a popular entertainment program. As we will discuss in depth in Chapter 4, hybridity involving advertising and entertainment—and other content genres—is becoming increasingly common. Of course, advertising is not the only genre that mixes with other genres. Media practitioners who work in the fields of entertainment, information, and education explore the value of this sort of hybridity in order to attract and hold audiences. Media practitioners and advertisements often borrow comedic, dramatic, festival, and gaming elements to attract and hold audiences. Writers for *Sesame Street*, for example, often deliver their educational messages in segments that resemble situation comedies, game shows, and musical variety programs.

As you probably know by now, the organizations that create material based on any of the genres, or any combination of genres, have a strong incentive to follow the logic of convergence by moving their material across media boundaries so that as many people as possible in their target audience will see it. Think of the commercials that advertisers create around the Super Bowl—say the Budweiser beer ads that tell cute stories via the entertainment genre about those iconic Clydesdale horses. Many advertisers place their commercials on popular websites such as YouTube for people to view either before or after the game. Then they try to create interest in going to those sites by getting journalists or other media creators to use their commercials in *their* stories on television, in newspapers and magazines, or on the web.

Knowing how to use genres and their formulas to create materials that are popular with carefully targeted audiences across multiple platforms is a highly valued skill in mass media industries. But there's a lot more to creating a work valued by audiences than just thinking it up. We have already discussed audience construction and research as important factors in content selection. All mass media organizations also must be concerned with five other primary business activities:

- Production
- Distribution
- Exhibition
- Audience research
- Finance

As Figure 3.6 shows, production involves creating the content. Distribution involves sending the material to exhibitors (e.g., music stores and TV stations). The

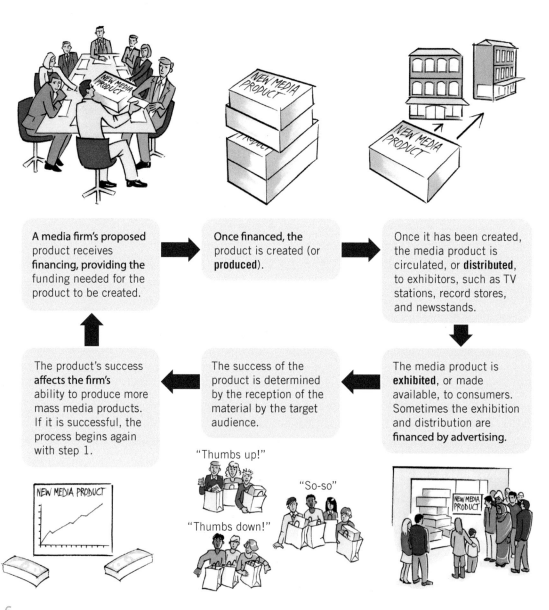

A media firm's proposed product receives **financing, providing the** funding needed for the product to be created.

Once financed, the product is created (or **produced**).

Once it has been created, the media product is circulated, or **distributed**, to exhibitors, such as TV stations, record stores, and newsstands.

The media product is **exhibited**, or made available, to consumers. Sometimes the exhibition and distribution are **financed by advertising.**

The success of the product is determined by the reception of the material by the target audience.

The product's success **affects the firm's** ability to produce more mass media products. If it is successful, the process begins again with step 1.

Figure 3.6

Organizations involved in production, distribution, and exhibition—activities central to the function of all media organizations—must first secure financing before they can proceed.

exhibitors, in turn, make the material available to consumers. Let's examine these steps, which lie at the heart of what goes on in mass media industries, one at a time.

Production of Mass Media Content

Production is the beginning of the chain of events that brings mass media content to audiences. **Production** for the mass media means the creation of materials for distribution through one or more mass media vehicles.

Media Production Firms

A **mass media production firm** is a company that creates materials for circulation through one or more mass media vehicles. The Washington Post Company, which puts together the *Washington Post*, is a production company. So are *The New Yorker*, a magazine owned by Conde Nast; Comcast's NBC Universal, which produces *NBC Nightly News*; and Bad Robot Productions, a firm that is responsible for the television series *Alias*, *Lost*, *Fringe*, *Person of Interest*, and *Westworld*, as well as some of the *Star Trek* movies.

Who Does the Work? The making of all these media products requires both administrative personnel and creative personnel. **Administrative personnel** make sure the business side of the media organization is humming along. They must thoroughly understand that the media business they are in and their daily jobs—for example, in accounting, law, and marketing—have much to do with the success of the organizations for which they work. Their work does not, however, relate directly to the creation of their firm's media materials. **Creative personnel** do that. They are the individuals who get initial ideas for the material or use their artistic talent to put the material together.

In all media industries, work on the creative side of a production firm can be done in two ways: on-staff or freelance. An **on-staff worker** has secured a full-time position at a production firm. For example, most, though not all, art directors in advertising agencies are on-staff workers. They work for the same agency all the time; the projects they work on may change, but the company that issues their paycheck remains the same. **Freelancers**, on the other hand, are workers who make a living by accepting and completing assignments for a number of different companies—sometimes several at one time. Most movie actors work as freelancers, for example; when they finish one film, they look for work on another film, which may be made by a different company. Self-employed individuals who write blogs or Instagram posts for companies are typically also freelancers. They are often called **influencers**.

Although freelancing can be highly lucrative for some (we are familiar with the names of well-paid freelance creatives such as the novelist John Grisham and the film actor Tom Cruise), historically freelancing has been a difficult road for many creatives. Even when salaries are high (and they frequently are not), many freelance creatives do not work as often as they would like because of the heavy competition for desirable assignments. Historically, this competition has given tremendous power to the production companies that hire these freelance creatives. Freelancers, from actors, to book editors, ghost writers, to cinematographers, have reported that production companies have used this power to "borrow" innovative ideas discussed in job interviews, force them to work unusually long hours, and withhold their due credits when the assignment is completed.

production
the creation of mass media materials for distribution through one or more mass media vehicles

mass media production firm
a company that creates materials for distribution through one or more mass media vehicles

administrative personnel
workers who oversee the business side of the media organization

creative personnel
individuals who get the initial ideas for the material or use their artistic talent to put the material together

on-staff worker
a worker who has secured a full-time position at a production firm

freelancers
workers who make a living by accepting and completing assignments for a number of different companies—sometimes several at one time

influencers
self-employed people who use media, typically social media such as Instagram, Facebook, and blogs—to comment on and/ or model products

talent guild

a union formed by people who work in similar crafts to help negotiate rules with major production firms in their industries regarding the ways in which freelance creatives will be treated and paid

collaborative activity

an activity in which many people work together to initiate, create, and polish the end material

Figure 3.7

Some roles involved in two types of media production. The mass media production process is almost always a collaborative process.

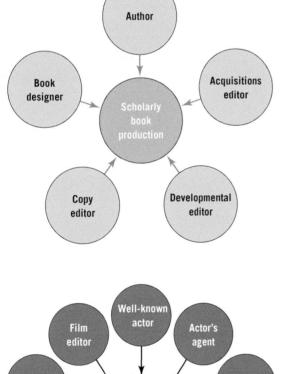

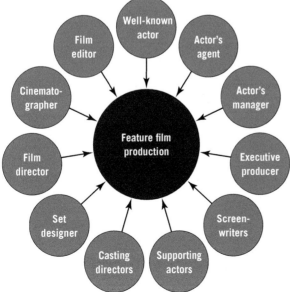

To establish a power of their own, many freelance creatives have banded together to create talent guilds. A **talent guild** is a union formed by people who work in a particular craft; consider, for example, the Writers Guild of America, the Screen Actors Guild, and the Directors Guild of America. These guilds negotiate rules with major production firms in their industries regarding the ways in which freelance creatives will be treated and paid.

The administrative and creative personnel of mass media production firms recognize that the previous successes of individual freelance creators—their positive track records—can help reduce the risk that a project will fail. In an effort to manage their risks, movie production companies typically will not allow high-budget movies to be made unless a high-profile actor (such as Matt Damon or Robert Downey Jr.) signs on.

How Does Production Take Place? The personal vision of an actor, novelist, or scholar can sometimes make it to the screen or the page. Inserting such a personal vision into a work is called authorship. Generally, however, production in media industries is a **collaborative activity**, in which many people work together to initiate, create, and polish the end material (see Figure 3.7). The collaborative nature of production holds true for every mass media product, from movies to scholarly books. Some types of production require more creative hands than others. When there are many creators, the "author" of the work may not be a person, but rather a group or company.

Compare the production of a scholarly book with that of a typical commercial movie starring a well-known actor. A professor can write the book manuscript by herself or himself and then work with a publishing firm that can arrange for editing help, as well as printing and binding, to make the finished product. That requires a collaborative effort among several individuals in one or more companies, but it is nothing like the work needed to create the major motion picture mentioned earlier. The well-known actor is chosen by an executive producer company head, with the assistance of the actor's business representatives. In addition, the film will need screenwriters to write and rewrite the script, other actors to work with the star, a casting director with assistants to choose the other actors, a set designer and assistants to plan the backdrops, a director and assistants to organize the filming, a cinematographer and assistants to photograph the scenes, an editor and assistants to put the scenes together into a finished movie, and many more collaborators. Although individual authorship of the scholarly book may be fairly clear (sometimes the author thanks the editor, sometimes not), the same cannot be said of the movie. Because so many people are involved on the creative side, it is often very difficult to argue that the final version of a Hollywood film is one person's vision.

Distribution of Mass Media Content

Most of us tend to think of production when we think of mass media industries. After all, it is the output of this production—the newspapers we read, the cable TV shows we watch—that grabs our attention, that makes us happy or angry, interested or bored. Moreover, most public discussion about mass communication tends to center around production. The latest gossip about which actor will be in which film, the angry comments a mayor makes about the violence on local TV news, the newest CD by an up-and-coming music group—these are the kinds of topics that are most often the focus of our attention when we discuss media.

However, media executives and media-literate citizens know that production is only one step in the arduous and risky process of getting a mass media idea to an audience and that distribution is just as important as production. **Distribution** is the delivery of the produced material to the point where it will be shown to its intended audience. Although the activity takes place out of public view, distributors often have a large say in marketing the products to the target audience.

distribution
the delivery of the produced material to the point where it will be shown to its intended audience

We have already mentioned that ABC acts as a distributor when it disseminates television programming to TV stations via satellite. When Philadelphia Media Network delivers its *Philadelphia Inquirer* to city newsstands, when Random House delivers the titles it has published to a university, when Disney moves its movies to the Regal Cinema Theaters, when the Ingram Content Group delivers titles of many book publishing companies to thousands of libraries across the United States, and when Sony Music sends its newest releases to Apple to be sold through Apple Music, they are all involved in distribution to exhibitors.

In 2015 Amazon opened its first brick-and-mortar bookstore. They now have seventeen, with more openings planned.

Note that these firms—Philadelphia Media Network, Disney, and Sony Music—use their own distribution divisions rather than rely on other independent distribution firms (such as Ingram in the book world) to do the job. This background ought to underscore for you the importance of successful distribution in the world of media business. Some executives argue that although "content is king," distribution ought to share the crown. The reason is simple: without a distributor, a production firm's media product would literally go nowhere. It would stack up in the warehouse or on a computer, eventually to be destroyed. To get a feel for the power in distribution, consider that your class could produce and publish books quite easily. That is, you could take any works of art members of your class created—some doodles, a love poem, notes to this book—and get them photocopied and bound at the nearest store, such as the FedEx Office Print & Ship Center. Say your publishing organization creates a roster of ten books. Say your organization splurges and prints 200 copies for each of the ten titles. For a bit more money than you'd spend in the copy shop, you could put a fancy binding on the products, so that they would look like "real" books. Even easier, you could format the documents on a computer to look like a book.

Of course, now that you have a printed and/or digital book, the trick is to sell it. You might try to get the university bookstore to carry it, but chances are the store won't. Barnes & Noble Booksellers probably won't touch your books with a ten-foot pole. It's likely, in fact, that no legitimate bookstore will carry your titles. This is not necessarily because your authors' writing is bad; your titles might actually be true works of art. The real reason that your chances of getting your books into a bookstore are so poor is that your book publishing organization doesn't have a powerful marketing team or a powerful book distributor behind them. Even if you manage to get Amazon to carry your book online (a special Amazon program does that for authors), without a track record to get potential readers' attention and without money for promoting the book, you have little chance of getting people to buy it among Amazon's millions of offerings. If, however, you could persuade a major publishing company with a widespread distribution subsidiary to add your book roster to its publication-and-distribution list, have its publicity force-pitch your book to offline bookstores, and have you interviewed by radio and print journalists, you might have a pretty good chance to get your book sold.

THINKING ABOUT MEDIA LITERACY

Think of a "hard-sell" ad you've seen. What is the product and what arguments were used to "pitch" the product? Now, think about how this same product might pitch with a "soft-sell" ad. How would the advertisements differ?

Production, then, is useless without distribution. Without a powerful distributor, the roster of products that a publishing organization's executives believe could be tremendously successful will have much less chance of achieving its potential. Some people believe that the internet reduces the importance of publication and distribution because just about anyone can post—that is, distribute—a collection of just about anything online for very little cost. But putting things on a personal website or even on a backwater page of a popular distributor such as YouTube or Facebook does not ensure that anyone but your friends will go to it. Perhaps you will get lucky, and the clip you posted to YouTube will become a popular viral video viewed by millions. In most cases, however, the key is to have the clout to place the content in a position where many people have a good chance of seeing it. That means getting the attention of a powerful distributor.

powerful distributor
a firm that can ensure the media products it carries will end up in the best locations at the best exhibitors to the best audience

What makes a **powerful distributor**? Simply put, a distributor's power is measured in terms of the firm's ability to ensure that the media products it carries will end up in the best locations of the best exhibitors to the best audience. To understand what that means, we have to look at exhibition.

Exhibition of Mass Media Content

The exhibition of mass media material is closely linked to distribution in the sense that both are steps in bringing the content to the audience. Sometimes the same company carries out both activities. Because exhibition is quite a different business from distribution, though, it often involves different firms.

exhibition
the activity of presenting mass media materials to audiences for viewing or purchase

shelf space
the amount of area or time available for presenting products to consumers

Exhibition is the activity of presenting mass media materials to audiences for viewing or purchase. When media executives speak about the importance of exhibition, they often mention shelf space. **Shelf space** is the amount of area or time available for presenting products to consumers. Think of bookstores with their long rows of shelves and display tables. As large as typical chain stores are today, production firms want to rent and sell more types of titles than will fit into even the biggest stores. As a result, store executives must decide which categories of products and which company's products within those categories are carried and which get more room than others.

Consequently, book distribution firms that rely on stores to present their products to consumers must compete furiously for shelf space. The distributors that wield the most power are those with products that the stores need to have because consumers demand them. These distributors have more ability to negotiate shelf space for new products than do distributors of goods that are not so important to the stores.

The same is true elsewhere in the media business. Magazine and book producers must compete for shelf space in bookstores, on newsstands, and in supermarket aisles. Moreover, some spots in stores and on newsstands are more valuable than others. The area toward the front of a bookstore is most valuable because all customers pass through it. Racks on a newsstand that are at eye level are more valuable than those at floor level because consumers are likely to look at the racks at eye level first. The exhibitors (i.e., the stores) often charge book or magazine distributors money for placing their products in such privileged positions.

For cable TV, movies, broadcast TV, radio, the web, mobile phones, and other media, the concept of shelf space has to be stretched just a bit, but it applies just the same. Executives think of the limited number of channels of a cable system as its shelves. Similarly, some broadcast television executives see the 24 hours in a day as their stations' shelves, because time limits what they can air. In cable, radio, and broadcast TV, certain time slots and channels (or stations) are more valuable than others. The same goes for high-traffic pages on websites such as Auto.com and the space mobile phone companies reserve for applications (apps) that come with a smartphone at the time of purchase. Even when it comes to selling via an internet distributor such as Amazon, where the "shelf" seems limitless, being the first company with items on the relevant search results among many competitors can make a big difference for revenues.

Now imagine a particular brick-and-mortar case: feel the tension that Marisol Durán, a salesperson for a newly formed independent book distribution firm, experiences as she waits to speak to a purchasing executive at the large bookstore chain Barnes & Noble. Marisol represents small publishing firms specializing in science fiction. Because of their small size, these firms don't have the money to hire their own salespeople. She knows that Barnes & Noble's shelves hold many books, but she also knows that the number of books published each year alone would take up far more space than those shelves can hold. She has been successful in placing many of the titles she carries in bookstores that specialize in the science fiction genre. She has ambitions beyond these small stores, however. A chance to catch the eyes of science fiction readers who shop at Barnes & Noble would, she believes, surely result in a strong increase in sales.

She knows, however, that she would get a better hearing at Barnes & Noble—and would place more books there—if she worked for the distribution arm of a publishing house such as Penguin Random House or Simon & Schuster, two giants of the

trade incentives
payments in cash, discounts, or publicity activities that provide a special reason for an exhibitor to highlight a product

cooperative advertising
(also known as co-op advertising) advertising paid for in part by media production firms or their distributors in order to help the exhibitor promote the product

book business. One reason is that such publishing giants can afford to advertise and promote their titles to the public better than her struggling publishers can, and such publicity can strongly affect sales.

The large distributors also may be better able than smaller ones to offer **trade incentives**—payments in cash, discounts, or publicity activities that provide a special reason for an exhibitor to highlight a product—that could influence large stores such as Barnes & Noble to carry their books. To make sure that a bookstore chain exhibits key titles at the entrances to its stores, for example, a distributor may have to offer to pay the bookstore chain a sum of money for taking up that space. Bringing the author in for special book readings and book signings and helping to pay for ads in newspapers (a practice called **cooperative advertising**) might also be part of the deal.

As this hypothetical experience suggests, linking up with a powerful distributor is of great benefit to publishers (and through them, to producers) in every mass media industry. You may think of the internet, and especially search, as a way around this problem of distribution. Though it does allow for the distribution of material with less difficulty than in the past, it by no means gets around the distribution problem. If your work is one of a million books or apps or anything in an online store, you will still have a tough time getting people to notice it and pay attention. Not surprisingly, the major publishing companies either own or are otherwise strategically linked to the major distribution organizations. In these cases, it is important to keep in mind that power over production, publication, and distribution is self-reinforcing: creative personnel with strong track records are attracted to a production-and-publishing firm, in part because it has powerful distribution. In turn, the company has powerful distribution, in part because its production and publishing arms attract creative personnel with strong track records.

THINKING ABOUT MEDIA LITERACY

Think of all the ways that you help finance the media industry. How is your consumption of various media products providing direct support to the media companies? Think about both monetary and usage behavior insights the company might use.

vertical integration
an organization's control over a media product from production through distribution to exhibition

In some industries, major firms consolidate their strength by owning not only the distribution organizations but the major exhibition firms as well. Television networks such as NBC, CBS, and ABC, for example, have production divisions that create fiction, sports, and news programs. They also own broadcast TV networks that aggregate—or "publish"—those programs into schedules and then distribute the scheduled programs to their own broadcast stations in key cities, which exhibit them. This control of the entire process from production through publication to distribution to exhibition is called **vertical integration**, and it represents yet another way in which media companies try to reduce the risk that their target audiences will even have an opportunity to choose the material that competitors create (see Figure 3.8).

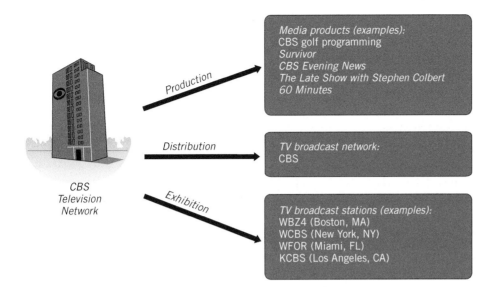

Financing Mass Media Content

As you can probably guess, the production, distribution, and exhibition of mass media materials requires a lot of money. Starting a publishing company, even a very small one, costs hundreds of thousands of dollars. Creating a one-hour program for a major broadcast or cable television network costs more than a million dollars. Starting a new magazine can cost even more. Want to buy a radio station? Despite the recent slowdown of growth in radio advertising, stations still go for tens of millions of dollars.

The cash coming into a mass media firm can be divided into two categories:

* Money to fund new production
* Money to pay for already-completed products

We'll explore each in detail.

Funding New Productions

Executives in mass media enterprises may need to raise funds to expand into new areas, or they may want to build up areas in which they are already operating. A movie exhibition chain may want to expand by building new theaters in China. A publishing firm might want to start a new unit to create oversized coffee table books. A company might want to buy a radio station. In such cases, executives may not want or be able to use the company's current revenues to cover the costs of the new venture.

A company generally has two ways to get money in anticipation of production: it can take out loans, or it can encourage investments in the company.

Taking Out Loans A **loan** is money borrowed from an organization, usually a bank, for a certain price (a percentage of the loan called an interest rate). To get a loan, executives must persuade the lending organization that their plans will realistically bring in the cash they expect so that the firm will be able to repay the amount of the loan (its principal) plus the interest in a timely way. The lender will also want to be sure that it has a claim on some of the current value (assets) of the firm—for example, the

loan
money borrowed from an
organization, usually a bank, for
a certain price (a percentage of
the loan called an interest rate)

investment banks

companies that arrange to lend millions, even tens and hundreds of millions, of dollars to companies and that also arrange stock offerings

syndicate

a group of banks that agree to share the risks and rewards of the lending deal, organized by investment banks when very large amounts of money are required

stock offerings

selling units of ownership in the company, or shares of stock, to organizations and individuals

venture capitalists

individuals or companies that invest in startup or nonpublic firms in the hope that the firms' value will increase over time

real estate of an exhibition chain or the current holdings of a radio station owner—in case the firm does not pay back the loan.

Investment banks are companies that arrange to lend millions, even tens and hundreds of millions, of dollars to companies and that also arrange stock offerings. Some investment banks specialize in particular industries, and the executives of these investment banks feel that they understand quite well the risks involved. Large investment banks hire experts in particular industries to guide the banks' lending activities in their areas of expertise. These investment bankers assess the firms that want loans and put together the terms of agreement. When very large amounts of money are involved, the investment banker will organize a **syndicate**, a group of banks that agree to share the risks and rewards of the lending deal. Because it takes on more responsibility, the lead bank (the bank that organizes the syndicate) makes more money on the deal than the others.

Encouraging Investments Whereas bankers worry that firms will not be able to pay back the money they have borrowed, executives of those firms worry about how much money the loans are costing them. That is, paying the interest on the loans requires cash that the company could use for other purposes. Consequently, executives may prefer to raise money through **stock offerings**. A share of stock is a unit of ownership in a company. All corporations, whether they are owned by only a few people or by millions of people, issue stock. When a company engages in a stock offering, it sells these units of ownership to organizations and individuals.

For example, let's say that DigitalFeast, a media organization that creates specialized restaurant and recipe sites for the web and mobile devices, wants to expand. One of its computer engineers has just devised software that executives believe will revolutionize the industry and make the firm a leader.

The three founders of the company still own all the stock; because there is no public market for the stock, the value of each founder's holdings equals the assets of the firm divided by three. The founders (who also run the firm) are concerned that taking out loans in addition to the loans they already have would make the interest payments too high for the firm to afford, given that they don't expect the new device to be profitable for at least a year. They decide to open up ownership of the company to people other than themselves.

Working with the company's accountants and with outside specialists, the company's founders determine the value of the company. That amount includes the worth of its equipment and its goodwill—that is, the value of its reputation among its clients and potential clients in the online world. The founders decide that the company should issue 6 million shares; each of the founders will keep 1 million of those shares, and DigitalFeast will offer the other 3 million at $2 each. Consequently, if the company is able to sell all of the nonpartners' shares, it will receive $6 million, which will be enough to expand the venture.

In view of its small size, DigitalFeast will probably sell its stock to **venture capitalists**. Venture capitalists are individuals or companies that invest in startup or nonpublic firms in the hope that the firms' value will increase over time. These people and firms are in the business of assuming the high risks of investing in such firms in the hope of receiving high rewards. In the case of DigitalFeast, they are assuming that the company's earnings will increase because its new device will bring in more business. That increase

Facebook made big news when it held its IPO in 2012.

in earnings will make the company more valuable, and so each share will be worth more than the amount the venture capitalists paid for it. If the company were then sold, the venture capitalists would get substantially more money than they invested.

There are other ways in which DigitalFeast can raise more money. Assume, for example, that after the sale of stock to the venture capitalists, DigitalFeast's board of directors (which now includes some of the venture capitalists) decides on an **initial public offering (IPO)** of the company's stock. The board needs to convince an investment banker that the company's future is so great that investment companies and individual investors would buy 5 million new shares of the company's stock at $10 a share. The investment bank agrees to manage (or underwrite) the offering for a fee. Because 5 million new shares will be created, the shares that already exist will represent a smaller percentage of the ownership than they did before the IPO. Still, the market value of the early stockholders' shares will go from $2 to $10 a share. DigitalFeast, meanwhile, has $50 million more to chew on.

initial public offering (IPO) the offering for sale to the general public of a predetermined number of shares of company stock that were previously owned by a limited number of individuals and the listing of the company's shares on the stock exchange

Funding When Production Is Already Complete

A primary indicator of the health of any company is its **profits**—the amount of money brought in by the completed products (the revenues) minus expenses. Even if a company is run efficiently and its expenses are low, it still needs to bring in ever-increasing amounts of revenue in order to increase its profits and satisfy its investors and lenders. In mass media firms, there are several ways to bring in revenues.

profits the amount of money brought in by the completed products (the revenues) minus expenses

Direct Sales The purchaser pays the production firm or a separate distributor or exhibitor for the item and can use it in any way she or he sees fit—keep it forever, throw it away, give it to someone else, or even resell it. In college textbook publishing, for example, most of the money comes from sales to consumers (the students).

License Fees A person or organization pays the production firm or a separate distributor or exhibitor for the use of a product, but the producer has ultimate control over the way it is used. For example, a toy company may pay Warner Bros. for the right to use the image of Bugs Bunny on toy banks for five years. Similarly, if you have Microsoft Word on your computer, what you have actually bought is a license to use it. (Remember the notice telling you that if you use the software, you are accepting the "license agreement"? One consequence is that, according to the agreement, you are prohibited from reselling the software to someone else.)

Rentals The production firm or a separate distributor or exhibitor charges for the right to employ (read, view, or hear) a mass media product for a certain period of time and then gets the product back. For example, with physical movie DVD rentals, the store or kiosk company (e.g., Redbox) typically buys the video from the production firm and tries to make a profit by renting it to you and many others. When you rent a video to stream, the online store (say Amazon) pays the production or distribution firm (depending on who has the rights to the video) a percentage of the rental fee.

Usage Fee The amount the producer or the separate distributor or exhibitor charges for a mass media product is based on the number of times the product is employed. For example, an internet database of articles may charge you for the number of articles or "page views" you print.

Subscriptions The producer or the separate distributor or exhibitor charges for regularly providing a media product or service. (Think of a magazine subscription, a subscription to a cable system or streaming service, and a subscription to a company that provides you with internet service.) Those firms use your subscription fees to create or rent content. If you subscribe to Netflix or HBO Now for streaming productions, those firms use the cash to pay firms to create programming for them. They also use it to pay rights holders of existing movies and TV shows to stream those products for an agreed-upon period.

Advertising A company buys space or time on a mass medium (a page in a magazine, thirty seconds on a radio station) in which it is allowed to display a persuasive message (an advertisement) for a product or service. We will have a good deal to say about the workings of the advertising industry in Chapter 4. What is important to remember here is that the advertising industry is the dominant support system for the mass media. If advertising did not exist, the amount you pay for magazines, newspapers, internet content, and cable television, not to mention broadcast television and radio, would skyrocket. Reliable estimates suggest, for example, that because of advertising, people on average pay less than half of what they would otherwise pay for magazines and newspapers.

The mention of magazines and newspapers brings up another important point about the sources of cash in mass media industries. Particularly in an era of convergence, companies work hard to bring in money from what economists call multiple revenue streams. Magazine and newspaper firms, for example, sell ads for their print editions as well as their web and tablet versions. They also ask consumers to pay for the print versions, and many magazines and newspapers charge for tablet access as well. Movie companies, we will see, have even longer revenue streams. They bring in money for their titles from theaters, DVDs, on-demand cable and satellite services, hotels, and other places. Local TV broadcasters, by contrast, overwhelmingly have long lived off only a single revenue stream, advertiser support; viewers do not have to pay them. This revenue stream happens to be quite an outpouring: in 2017, local TV stations took in $21.7 billion from advertisers.[5] But as competition tightens in the television industry, as costs go up, and as advertisers have the option of placing ads in other media if the local stations raise their advertising rates, the single revenue stream does not look as lucrative as it once did. That is why the stations have been demanding that cable systems pay them for carrying their signals to their customers (what is called a **retransmission fee**). The stations are also trying to make money via advertising on their websites and apps.

By now, the complexity of trying to navigate the mass media environment should be quite clear. But wait—there's more! Not only do media practitioners have to worry about production, distribution, exhibition, and finance; they also have to concern themselves with **government regulation**. Government regulation involves a wide variety of activities and laws through which elected and appointed officials at local, state, and federal levels exercise influence over media firms. The different forms of regulation are so important to what media firms can and cannot do when it comes to production, distribution, exhibition, advertising, and finance that we devote an entire chapter—Chapter 5—to them.

retransmission fee
amount a cable system or satellite firm pays to a broadcaster for the right to pick the broadcaster's signal off the air and send it to cable or satellite subscribers.

government regulation
a wide variety of activities and laws through which elected and appointed officials at local, state, and federal levels exercise influence over media firms

Media Literacy and the Business of Mass Media

At this point, you may be asking yourself two questions: How does knowing about the business of media help me to be a more aware consumer of mass media materials? And what difference might being an aware consumer make in my life? The questions speak, of course, to the important topic of media literacy, which we introduced in Chapter 1.

Think back to the billboard scenario that began this chapter. Remember that the premise was that community leaders in the neighborhood where you live had two complaints. One was that billboard advertising in the area too often featured beer and sex. The other was that digital billboards at the edge of the highway cutting through the neighborhood made it hard for people living around there to sleep at night. At the beginning of this chapter, you could mostly just list what you didn't know. Now, after reading the chapter, you ought to know enough to help your community deal with those "outdoor" firms.

- To begin with, you know that billboard companies are the exhibition point of a chain that often also involves companies that create the ad ideas. In the case of the nondigital signs, there are firms that make the posters and distribute them to the billboard owners. The digital signs are themselves expensive pieces of equipment created by high-tech firms. Using special software, the advertising companies work with the signage firms to create the look the clients want. Your community group will try to persuade the exhibitors to change their policies, but if they refuse, you now know that there may well be other firms to which you can bring your demands. You might put pressure on the ad agencies that thought up the ads, or the advertisers that are paying the agencies for the work, or the companies that manufactured and delivered the ads to the billboard firm, or the technology firms that make the digital displays. You conclude it's likely the advertisers and their agencies will be the most sensitive of this group.

- You now bring to your talk with executives a basic understanding of the advertising genre that will give you credibility with them and help you make your arguments. You know, for example, that sex and violence are often used in soft-sell advertising. The issue here is twofold: whether the practice is ethical when it is used for selling beer and whether it is ethical in areas where there are children who might consider the ads attractive and hip and so consider the combination (sex and beer) attractive and hip. The other major concern—the bright and flickering digital boards at night—raises the question of the companies' interference in the basic lives of individuals in that rather poor neighborhood. This, too, is an ethical issue that, you argue, may encourage regulation by the city government to prohibit bright digital signs if the billboard firms continue to place them near homes.

- Our discussion of the way media firms think about audiences and of the importance of segmentation to today's media should sensitize you to the issues that outdoor firms consider when they put up their billboards and that advertisers think about when they decide to place their ads on the billboards. By examining the locations of the billboards with sex and beer messages, you might be able to show the billboard firms that you know that their supposed targets—adults—are not their only targets. You might, for example, find several of the objectionable billboards within a few blocks of high schools. That can get you into an interesting discussion about the ethics of targeting that audience and lead to leverage that you can apply to the firms.

- An understanding of the billboard firms' target audiences might also be combined with your exploration of their sports, transit, and mall activities to create leverage to get rid of the objectionable boards. Your research turns up that parents from that working-class neighborhood are also major bus travelers as well as fans of the local sports teams. That is information you may introduce into discussions with billboard executives and their advertisers when you are trying to persuade them to get rid of the objectionable messages and move the garishly lit digital boards. You might add that they won't look good when the larger public learns that the outdoor firms are making large groups of fans—and relatively poor ones at that—uncomfortable on their home turf.

Even if there is still much to learn about this billboard issue as well as other aspects of media, the hope is that you have already begun to watch TV, read the newspaper, and use the web with a new awareness of what is going on. Have you begun to dissect the formats of your favorite TV shows or magazines? When you open up "junk" mail or get an ad on the web or phone, have you tried to figure out what target audiences you fit into and where the firms got your name? When you've gone into a bookstore, have you thought of the relationships among exhibition, distribution, publication, and production? Have you watched and read the news with an eye to the subgenres that journalists use and, if it is hard news, the way they present the sense of an "objective" approach to the world through their use of the verbal and visual conventions we discussed?

If not, you ought to try; it will open up new ways to view reality and the forces that create it.

CHAPTER REVIEW

Visit the Companion website at www.routledge.com/cw/turow for additional study tools and resources.

Key Terms

You can find the definitions to these key terms in the marginal glossary throughout this chapter. Test your knowledge of these terms with interactive flash cards on the *Media Today* Companion Website.

accuracy	demographics	government regulation
adequate revenue	distribution	hard news
administrative personnel	dramedy	hard-sell ads
advertisement	editorial	hybrid genres
analysis of existing data	education	hybridity
audiences	entertainment	influencers
blogs	exhibition	information
collaborative activity	focus group	informational ads
columnists	format	initial public offering (IPO)
cooperative advertising	formula	investigative reports
creative personnel	freelancers	investment banks
demographic indicators	genres	journalists

lifestyle categories	profits	subgenres
loan	psychographics	surveys
mass media production firm	research and development (R&D)	syndicate
media practitioners	retransmission fee	talent guild
objectivity	schedule	track record
on-staff worker	setting	trade incentives
patterns of action	shelf space	typical characters
powerful distributor	soft news	venture capitalists
product placement	soft-sell ads	vertical integration
production	stock offerings	

 ## Questions for Discussion and Critical Thinking

1. Understanding the target audience reduces risk for media companies in the three key stages of production, distribution, and exhibition. How would understanding the target audience help a book publisher interested in funding a series of do-it-yourself books influence decisions at each of these three stages?

2. It is said that media is in the business of "selling audiences to advertisers." Look through a magazine you read online or in print. How do the advertisements in the magazine reflect the audience the publishers are "selling" to advertisers? When you go to a movie, how do the trailers that are shown reflect an understanding of the audience in the theater?

3. The chapter describes different mass media genres (entertainment, news, information, education, advertising). Think about a news website or newspaper. Describe how it could be said to span all of the genre (or at least serve each of these roles). Does the news organization clearly identify the different genre within its product?

4. Funding is obviously key to media companies' success. There are two stages of funding: financing a new product and revenue from existing products. Think about the differences in funding requirements for a company that wants to create a hub for musicians to sell their music. How would the funding stream be different at the start of the firm's life compared to when it gets a good reputation for its work?

Activity

To be successful, media companies must "construct the audience" for their products. Think about the way that you would, or would not, fit into a particular media product's constructed audience.

Create a profile of yourself using the following descriptors:

- Demographics (age, sex, income, occupation, ethnicity)
- Psychographics (attitudes, personality types, or motivations)
- Lifestyle (activities you enjoy, hobbies, musical styles, etc.)

Now, make a list of the top three publications you read. Look up their media kits and identify the demographic and psychographic characteristics of their audiences. In what ways are you similar or different to the audiences that these publications say they are reaching? Would you say you are one of the target audiences for these publications? Why or why not?

You buy a book from a local bookstore. You go to the movies and pay at the box office (even though your date offers to do it). You listen to a new album on Spotify; that student discount encouraged you to sign up and pay monthly. You forget to pay the internet bill two months in a row—you thought your roommate was supposed to do it—but you get the notice in time not to have the service shut off.

We all pay to use certain kinds of media content. PWC consulting firm estimates that Americans in 2017 shelled out $290.5 billion on media content. A few years earlier, the PQ Media firm estimated that Americans spent $264.8 billion on media technology. "Content" means specific materials such as music and books. "Technology" refers to the devices we use to get the content. That may include the mobile phone you buy or rent, the Apple TV you use to stream Netflix programs from the internet to your television set, or the Xbox console you use to play video games and stream Amazon Fire movies. But here's a point you might initially find odd: even though we put in a lot of money for media, companies supply a huge amount of money to pay for the media we use. The media-services firm Zenith estimates that in 2018 companies will have spent $446 billion to support the media content and services we receive.[1] Well, if you think about it, you'll realize that much of the content you receive is not supported by you. You may watch several television networks and listen to many radio stations over the air for free. If you subscribe to a "consumer" magazine (that is, one not aimed at people in a specific business or trade), you might find it interesting to know that the amount people pay ("subscriptions") make up only about 32 percent of the revenues magazine firms bring in. In all these cases, companies pay for the content so that they can send messages (ads) to you to persuade you to purchase particular products and services.

It turns out, though, that the $446 billion includes more than advertising. Advertising is the company support of media that we can see. Under the hood of the converging

media world, though, are activities that also support media firms but in a more hidden and indirect way than advertising. They fall under the label "public relations." Consider a local television news reporter who is trying to think up a story for the weekend broadcast. A representative of the largest museum in the area suggests a story about the Van Gogh exhibit that has just started there. The representative provides the reporter with great video regarding the paintings and the artist. Can you see how that kind of activity is an important indirect media support? It gives the reporter a useful idea and supplies material that could have been expensive for the television station to create by itself. The museum, in turn, receives the ability to call attention to its new presentation on a major television outlet. Multiply such TV news spots by similar activities thousands and thousands of times a day across virtually every media firm, big and small. That's a lot of media support. You can see, then, that public relations (PR) and advertising are crucial support systems for the media. This chapter explores how they work, including how advertising and PR often combine in new forms under the umbrella of marketing communications. We will see that the advertising and PR industries help media platforms pay the bills while performing other important activities for companies they represent. In doing so, advertising and PR exert major influence on media content. We will see how social observers debate whether the widespread influence of advertising and public relations practitioners has had problematic consequences for the view of life the media present. Let's start with an overview of the advertising industry.

The Advertising Industry

advertising
the activity of explicitly paying for media space or time in order to direct favorable attention to certain goods or services

Advertising is the activity of explicitly paying for media space or time in order to direct favorable attention to certain goods or services. Three points about this definition deserve emphasis. First, advertisers pay for the space or time that they receive. Second, advertising clearly states its presence. When you see an ad, you know what it is for, and you often know quite easily who is sponsoring it. Third, advertising involves persuasion—the ability or power to induce an individual or

Table 4.1 US Media Ad Spending in Certain Media, 2016

Medium	Amount (in Billions)
Television	$68.
Internet	$72.5
Newspapers	$18.2
Magazines	$15.13
Radio	$17.4
Outdoor	$9.2
Cinema	$0.8

Source: PWC Global Entertainment and Media Outlook, accessed June 6, 2018.

group of individuals to undertake a course of action or embrace a point of view by means of argument, reasoning, or emotional plea.

Advertising is a large and widespread operation, and as we suggested previously, the amount of money advertisers shell out is impressive. Table 4.1 provides details about what advertisers spend on particular media. According to the Price Waterhouse consultancy firm, in 2016 advertisers in the United States spent around $68 billion in support of television programming and about $17.4 billion to fund radio broadcasting. In addition, the ad industry spent $18.2 billion on advertisements in newspapers (including their online and mobile versions), compared with the $11.7 billion that consumers shelled out to buy the papers. Advertisers funded consumer magazines (including their online and mobile versions) to the tune of about $16.7 billion, and consumers dropped a smaller $7.7 billion into the periodicals' coffers. When it came to specifically supporting internet and mobile platforms—both for the traditional media just mentioned and for "pure play" internet firms, such as those involved search (e.g., Google), social media (e.g., Facebook), and gaming (e.g., Zynga)—advertisers put out about $72 billion. Note, though, that on the internet, the ad monies disproportionately benefited two firms: According to eMarketer, in 2016 over 50 percent of the money went to properties owned by Google and Facebook.

In recent years decisions by advertisers regarding what media to fund have changed dramatically. Newspapers have lost out, whereas the pure-play internet has won many advertising dollars. In future chapters, we explore reasons for these changes. But you can imagine that when advertisers start removing their money from particular media industries in large amounts, that can ignite great anxiety among people in those industries. The plummeting advertising in newspapers, for example, has led to much speculation about the future of that business. By contrast, the huge increases in pure-play internet advertising (think of Google and Facebook as examples) have caused enormous positive excitement among entrepreneurs that the advertising industry will support their digital plans.

An Overview of the Modern Advertising Industry

The number of companies involved in advertising is huge. Just about every business advertises somewhere. Sometimes the executives of the business write the ads themselves and then place them in newspapers and magazines. Other times—and this is

Many people have found it interesting to watch the series *Mad Men*, which follows an advertising agency during the 1960s.

advertising agencies
companies that specialize in the creation of ads for placement in media that accept payment for exhibiting those ads

agency holding companies
firms that own full-service advertising agencies, specialty agencies, direct-marketing firms, research companies, and even public relations agencies

client conflicts
situations that occur when agencies serve companies that compete with one another

particularly true of larger firms—the executives turn to companies that specialize in the creation of ads and their placement in media that accept payment for exhibiting those ads. These companies are called **advertising agencies**. The companies that hire them and pay for their work are called advertisers. In the ad industry, when an agency takes on an advertiser's business, it is said to take on an account. The biggest advertising agencies are owned by large companies known as **agency holding companies**. These are umbrella firms that own two or more ad agencies, plus research firms, public relations consultancies, or other organizations that contribute to the business of selling products, services, or ideas. Such holding companies offer clients a range of services beyond advertising, including public relations. They own more than one agency under their conglomerate umbrella to be able to serve firms that compete with one another. Traditionally, companies would not think of giving business to an agency that has such **client conflicts** for fear that confidential information might be shared among employees and get to competitors. If a totally different agency network is involved, though, most advertisers don't mind—even if both agencies are controlled by one firm. They accept the claim that those parts of the two businesses are kept quite separate. As Table 4.2 shows, the top seven holding companies (which are by far the biggest) have substantial business outside the United States.

Whether or not they are owned by a holding company, the largest agencies tend to be located in the largest cities, especially New York, Chicago, and Los Angeles. But big cities are by no means the only sites for ad agencies. There are about 5,000 advertising agencies in the United States, and they are scattered throughout the country. Ad agencies range from one-site operations with just a few people to organizations with several offices and thousands of employees. The kinds of things ad agencies do also vary. We can describe them along four dimensions:

- Business-to-business agencies versus consumer agencies
- General agencies versus specialty agencies
- Traditional agencies versus direct-marketing agencies
- Agency networks versus stand-alone firms

Table 4.2 The "Big Seven" Marketing Agency Holding Companies, 2017

Holding company	Headquarters	Worldwide revenues ($)	US revenue ($)	US percentage of total revenue
WPP	London	19.7 billion	6.7 billion	34
Omnicom Group	New York	15.3 billion	8.2 billion	54
Publicis Group	Paris	10.9 billion	5.8 billion	53
Interpublic Group	New York	7.9 billion	4.7 billion	59
Dentsu	Tokyo	7.8 billion	1.8 billion	23
Accenture Interactive	New York	6.5 billion	2.9 billion	45
PWC Digital Services	New York	5.1 billion	2.3 billion	45

Source: *Advertising Age Datacenter*, http://adage.com/datacenter, accessed June 6, 2018.

BUSINESS-TO-BUSINESS AGENCIES VERSUS CONSUMER AGENCIES

Business-to-business agencies work for companies that are interested in persuading personnel in other companies to buy from them instead of from their competitors. For example, a zipper manufacturer might want to inform a pants manufacturer about its great new development in the fly business. **Consumer agencies**, by contrast, work for advertisers that want to persuade people in their nonwork roles to buy products. An agency that touts a client's cereal to children and their parents is one example. Individual agencies typically do not do both.

GENERAL AGENCIES VERSUS SPECIALTY AGENCIES

A **general ad agency** invites business from all types of advertisers, whereas a **specialty ad agency** tackles only certain types of clients. One type of specialty agency that works in both the consumer and business-to-business areas is the **digital agency**. This is a company that promotes its expertise in understanding the technology for reaching people online, for creating the ads and websites that will lead to customer responses, and for measuring those responses. A different type of specialty agency deals with health care advertising. A big source of clients is the pharmaceutical industry because firms in this industry are constantly competing to persuade physicians that their prescription products are best. In recent years, pharmaceutical firms' desire to get consumers to nudge their doctors to order new prescription drugs for them has led to a specialty called **direct-to-consumer (DTC)** pharmaceutical advertising, and ad firms focusing on that business have developed. Advertising to ethnic and racial groups is also a big specialty in the consumer area. You can find agencies that claim to have particular knowledge of how to persuade African Americans, others that tout their abilities to move Latinos to buy, others that go after Irish Americans, and still others that specialize in Asian or Russian immigrants—and the list can go on.

TRADITIONAL AGENCIES VERSUS DIRECT-MARKETING AGENCIES

A **traditional ad agency** creates and distributes persuasive messages with the aim of creating a favorable impression of the product in the minds of target consumers that will lead them to buy it in stores. **Direct-marketing agencies** have a different mandate. Their job is not just to create a favorable image that will eventually result in purchases; they also have to shape consumer mailings, telephone marketing contacts, TV commercials, and other appeals to target audiences so as to elicit purchases right then and there. Traditional advertising practitioners generally consider direct-marketing approaches more gruff, fast-talking, and even obnoxious than the traditional rhetorical tools. For their part, direct-marketing people believe that they are the only ones who really show that advertising can sell things, given that the results are immediate: either people buy the product, or they don't.

AGENCY NETWORKS VERSUS STAND-ALONE FIRMS

The biggest advertising agencies tend to be traditional, consumer-oriented companies (see Table 4.3). They often have offices in a number of cities in the United States as well as in foreign countries; the trade press calls firms such as these **agency networks**. These types of agencies are different from firms that have only one location. The agency networks typically work for large national advertisers such as Procter & Gamble (P&G), Philip Morris, General Motors, Ford, and McDonald's. Because national advertisers tend to sell many products, they will often appoint a number of

business-to-business agencies
advertising agencies that carry out work for companies that are interested in persuading personnel in other companies to buy from them instead of from their competitors

consumer agencies
advertising agencies that carry out work for advertisers that want to persuade people in their nonwork roles to buy products

general ad agency
an advertising agency that invites business from all types of advertisers

specialty ad agency
an advertising agency that tackles only certain types of clients (and accounts)

internet agency
an advertising company that promotes its expertise in understanding the technology for reaching people online, for creating the ads and websites that will lead to customer responses, and for measuring those responses

direct-to-consumer (DTC)
a type of advertising used most effectively by the pharmaceutical industry, which presents a prescription drug as a medial solution and encourages viewers to ask their physician to order the medicine if appropriate

traditional ad agency
an advertising agency that creates and distributes persuasive messages with the aim of creating a favorable impression of the product in the minds of target consumers that will lead them to buy it in stores

direct-marketing agencies
agencies that focus on consumer mailings, telephone marketing contacts, TV commercials, and other appeals to target audiences so as to elicit purchases right then and there

agency networks
advertising agencies with branch offices in a number of different cities worldwide

ad agencies to work for them, each working on a different product or a different set of products. Specialty racial and ethnic firms sometimes enter the mix. For example, in addition to relying on Saatchi and Saatchi (owned by Publicis) for general advertising of Pampers worldwide, P&G in 2017 called on Saatchi and Saatchi's Conill Advertising in Miami to pitch Pampers to US Hispanics.

Popular books, movies, magazine articles, and television shows encourage most people to think of a large and powerful "full-service" ad agency such as J. Walter Thompson or Young and Rubicam when they think about the advertising industry. In today's complex marketing world, though, even large agencies such as J. Walter Thompson work with other organizations in the industry to carry out the three basic functions of ad work: **creative persuasion**, **market research**, and **media planning and buying**. We can explain how these three functions are carried out by exploring how they fit into the three basic activities of media industries: production, distribution, and exhibition.

Production in the Advertising Industry

It is through their work with their clients that the biggest advertising agencies channel hundreds of millions, even billions, of dollars into various media—a major source of support for American media industries. But the advertising industry does not really spend its money to support media. It spends money to persuade people to buy products, services, or ideas. How does it go about doing that?

The production of persuasive advertising messages goes on with the approval, and often the direct involvement, of executives from the client/advertiser. To ensure that clients continually understand what the agency is doing for their products, agency heads appoint an **account executive** for every account. The job of the account executive is to move information between the advertiser and the agency, as well as to make sure that all production, distribution, and exhibition activities take place as planned.

creative persuasion
the set of imaginative activities involved in producing and creating advertisements

market research
research whose end goal is gathering information that will help an organization sell more products or services

media planning and buying
a function of advertising involving purchasing media space and/ or time on strategically selected outlets that are deemed best suited to carry a client's ad message

account executive
a person who moves information between the advertiser and the agency and makes sure that all production, distribution, and exhibition activities take place as planned

Table 4.3 Top 10 Agency Networks, Ranked by 2017 Worldwide Network Revenue

RANK AGENCY [COMPANY]	HEADQUARTERS	WORLDWIDE REVENUE 2017 (billions)
1 Dentsu [Dentsu]	Tokyo	$2,302.3
2 BBDO Worldwide [Omnicom]	New York	1,952.8
3 DDB Worldwide [Omnicom]	New York	1,739.8
4 TBWA Worldwide [Omnicom]	New York	1,431.7
5 McCann [Interpublic]	New York	1,417.1
6 Hakuhodo [Hakuhodo DY Holdings]	Tokyo	1,359.0
7 Y&R [WPP]	New York	1,152.5
8 J. Walter Thompson Co. [WPP]	New York	1,116.6
9 Ogilvy [WPP]	New York	990.1
10 Grey [WPP]	New York	751.2
Total revenue for world's 10 largest ad agencies		$14.2

Source: Advertising Age Data Center, accessed June 6, 2017.

Production activities involve the individuals whose work relates directly to the creation of their firm's media materials; people in the ad industry call such individuals **creatives or creative personnel**. They include copywriters (who write the words for the ads), art directors (who guide the creation of artwork), print production personnel (who supervise the final production of magazine and newspaper ads), and TV–radio production personnel (who supervise the final production of TV and radio commercials) (see Figure 4.1).

But the work of the creatives does not take place in a vacuum. Copywriters and art directors generally do not concoct a print ad or TV commercial out of just any ideas that come to them. On the contrary, they work hard to determine which ideas will lead target consumers to purchase the product. Typically, a client does not expect that an ad will be directed toward the entire population. For example, a cosmetics company would generally expect its lipstick ads to be directed to women, not men. However, for reasons having to do with the nature of the lipstick or the company's marketing strategy, company executives may want to advertise a particular lipstick to a few specific groups of women—say, women from 18 to 34 years or executive women from 18 to 34 years. Dividing society into different categories of consumers is an activity called **market segmentation**. Agency creatives must understand the segments they are aiming at before they produce their ads. In fact, both when ad agency executives are competing for new business and when they are working on products for current clients, they place a high priority on learning a lot about both the product they are seeking to represent and the audience they are trying to reach. What are the product's strengths? What do consumers think about it? What kinds of people buy it? Who are the best potential customers? Why do they—or don't they—buy the product?

creatives or creative personnel people whose work relates directly to the creation of their firm's media materials

market segmentation dividing society into different categories of consumers

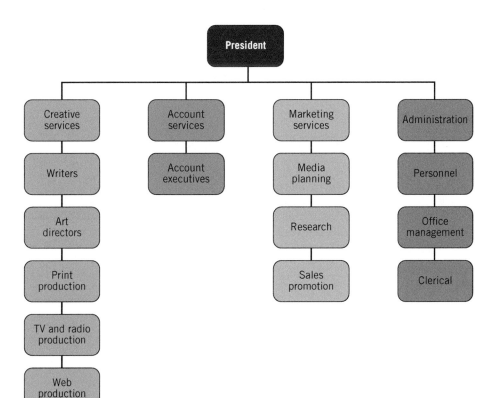

Figure 4.1
Structure of a typical advertising agency.

THINKING ABOUT MEDIA LITERACY

Location-based advertising delivered to smartphones is increasing. What are the advantages of this type of advertising to the advertiser and to the consumer? Are there any disadvantages?

Answering these questions often requires drawing on the market research function of the ad agency. Such research might involve compiling the results of previous investigations on the product or its competitors. It might involve commissioning original surveys or experiments with potential customers to check the persuasiveness of a new ad or the success of one that already has been introduced to the marketplace. It might involve joining other firms in ongoing "syndicated" studies that inquire about social trends, general product use, media habits, or other characteristics of the American population.

sales pitch
a presentation to a client, portraying the world of the client's intended audience and actions, to show how the client's product is valuable in that world

Through these and other approaches, researchers construct detailed portraits of the intended audience and its position within the society at large. Then creatives mix those portraits with their own sensibilities and apply the results to their work. Armed with these imaginings, a creative team can concoct a **sales pitch**—a message that

GLOBAL MEDIA TODAY & CULTURE

FREE MEDIA AND ADVERTISING

How much do you pay every month to have access to media content or to any social networks/platforms? When you don't pay for it and you are retrieving it from a legitimate source, it is very likely that the media content you are experiencing is paid by advertisers who are vying for your attention and the platform you are interacting with is utilizing an advertising-based business model. What is a business model? It is the result of strategic decisions made by a company to determine the best cost structure of their businesses and the revenue streams to exceed these costs, ranging, for example, from advertising to subscriptions (whenever you pay to access media content) or different combinations of the

two. Advertising remains at the center of business models of both legacy media players (such as free television networks ABC, CBS, and NBC) and the new leading entities emerging in the digital landscape (such as Facebook and Google).

Advertising is at the same time the engine of many media sectors and the tip of the marketing iceberg, a vital communication connection for nonprofit- and profit-oriented entities to reach out to their constituents—their current and potential consumers. We might not know what the marketing strategies of an entity might be, but we can infer them by watching their ads and understanding the message, their competitive positioning, and the intended target. The NFL Super Bowl is the most watched TV program in the United States, and, as a result, advertisers are willing to pay record amounts of money to insert their commercials in the program. Do you remember any commercials from the last Super Bowl you watched?

portrays the world of the intended audience, a problem in that world, and actions that show how the product can solve that problem.

The next step is to illustrate the sales pitch in stories and settings that the creatives believe the target audience will accept. Often an agency develops different campaigns for distinct audiences. Editing and casting decisions take into consideration research findings about how different audiences look at the product and the world. This approach enables agencies to create an image of the product that matches what they believe will lead various audiences to feel good about the product and to purchase it.

Creating a specific image of a product that makes it stand out in the marketplace is called **branding** it. Ad practitioners consider the creation and nurturing of these product images—these brands—to be among their most important activities. The reason is their belief that people will pay more for a well-regarded brand than for a product they do not know or about which they have a bad feeling. Think about it: Which would you rather buy from your supermarket for a party—Pepsi or Coke (whichever you prefer) or something called Pop-Soda Cola? Even if your supermarket guarantees the quality of Pop-Soda Cola and says it tastes "like the big guys," and even if it's a dollar less expensive, you might feel funny serving it to your guests. Chances are you would choose Pepsi or Coke. These are brands you trust; perhaps, after years of seeing commercials, you may even think that these products *belong* at parties.

branding
creating a specific image of a product that makes it stand out in the marketplace

Distribution in the Advertising Industry

Creating a series of ads and spending money to test them would be totally useless if the ad agency had no idea how and where to distribute them. Decisions on how to distribute ads have been affected by improvements in technology. Because of cooperation between ad agencies and media firms, now ad practitioners can actually send finished print and television ads directly to media outlets by internet or satellite. In some cases, print ads can be sent in digital form directly to the computers of the magazines or newspapers in which they will appear. From that standpoint, distribution of ads is constantly getting easier.

Because media fragmentation has dramatically increased the number of ad vehicles, however, deciding where to place advertisements is not getting easier; instead, it is becoming more and more challenging. Making these decisions is the work of an agency's **media planners**. To get an idea of the challenges they face, think of where you would place TV commercials for GEICO Insurance if that firm wanted to reach young adults. Where, too, would you place web ads that aim to convey the same message about the company to young adults?

media planners
agency personnel who make decisions about where to place advertisements

The answer is that media planners track computerized data about the number and kinds of people that various media outlets (specific magazines, radio stations, TV networks, or apps) reach. Much of this information about individual media outlets is collected in syndicated studies by audience research firms such as Comscore (for internet, television, and movie ratings), Nielsen (for television, cable, radio, and the internet), the Traffic Audit Bureau (for billboard advertising), and Simmons and MRI (for magazines). Nielsen and Comscore also carry out research that aims to track audience across media and even to the purchases they make after seeing one or more ads for certain products. The goal is to help advertisers and their agencies with what they call the **attribution challenge**: finding out which

attribution challenge
finding out which one or more of the media on which they advertised has been the most effective one for persuading people to purchase their products

one or more of the media on which they advertised has been the most effective one for persuading people to purchase their products.

While using this information, media planners sometimes also pay attention to custom research findings presented to them by individual media firms that want to impress them with further details. The custom research may add to the demographic data that syndicated research provides; for example, it might explore the religious affiliations or occupations of an audience. The research might present **psychographic data**, information that links demographic categories to the personality characteristics of an audience—for instance, whether they are "materialistic" or "confident" or people who want to lead rather than follow.

The research might also provide details about the lifestyles of the audience that could impress potential advertisers: how many vacations they took last year, what cars they drive, whether they play golf regularly. *Seventeen* magazine executives, for example, might commission research about how many of their teen readers have begun to use cosmetics or go to the movies each week or own cars. They then would present these data to potential cosmetic, movie, and car advertisers in the hope of convincing them to include *Seventeen* in their **media plan**—that is, in the list of media outlets in which they advertise their products.

Outdoor and in-store media are of increasing importance for some marketers, and an insurance company such as GEICO may be one such marketer. Outdoor media encompass a great variety of stationary billboards and signs, as well as moving media such as buses and trains. The term "**in-store media**" refers to a raft of print and audiovisual ads that people see when they walk into retail spaces. In a growing number of supermarkets, a company called MediaCart sells ads on grocery carriages. Supermarkets show videos and ads at checkout too. In stores such as Wal-Mart and Best Buy, PRN Corporation (owned by Thomson) sells ad space on checkout screens. Captivate Network, a company owned by the Gannett newspaper firm, sets up screens in office building elevators that run ads along with entertainment, weather, or news. Accent Health, a company owned by Discovery Holdings, has TV screens with CNN clips and targeted ads in more than 10,000 doctors' offices across the country. And supermarket firms fill their stores with the audio announcements of sales, shelf signs, floor mats with ads, and video screens showing ads at checkout. The locations for ads seem to be boundless. To hype its shows during 2007, CBS even had a company stamp 35 million supermarket eggs with its trademark "eye" logo, as well as the names and logos of the programs in its fall television lineup.

In evaluating a media outlet, media planners examine syndicated and custom demographic, psychographic, and lifestyle research to decide whether the audience segment they are aiming at can be found at that outlet. If it can, the planners then ask the following questions:

- What is the outlet's reach with respect to (ad planners use the term "against") the target audience? That is, what percentage of the entire target audience (say, teenage girls) will the outlet reach?
- Considering the costs of running an ad there, how efficient is the outlet in reaching that audience compared with other outlets?

In studying *Seventeen* for a makeup client, ad planners may find that it sells 22 million copies, the overwhelming percentage of which are sold to teenage girls. Moreover, *Seventeen* provides lifestyle research that contends that many of these

psychographic data
information that links demographic categories to personality characteristics of an audience

media plan
the list of media outlets in which companies advertise their products

in-store media
the print and audiovisual ads that people see when they walk into retail spaces

readers are trying makeup for the first time. Just as important, the planners learn that although the cost of buying space for a four-color, full-page ad in *Seventeen* is similar to the cost of buying such an ad in women's magazines with larger circulations, the **cost per thousand (CPM)** of teenage girls is quite a bit lower. That is because of the selectivity of the magazine: magazines such as *Glamour* reach lots of teenage girls, but an advertiser would not be able to target an edition directly to them, and so much of the ad money would be wasted. Because *Seventeen* reaches virtually only teenage girls, the CPM of the target audience is lower.

This factor makes *Seventeen* an efficient buy compared with women's magazines, but how does *Seventeen* compare with *Teen Vogue*, for example, or with MTV? Ad planners have to study their own research, their syndicated research, and the research presented to them by the magazine and cable companies to decide. They might decide to see whether one or another of the teen magazines would give them a discount for the bulk of the makeup ad money. Or they might discuss the pros and cons of splitting their ad purchases equally among major teen periodicals and teen-oriented cable networks.

Considerations such as these constantly occupy media planners. Perhaps by now you're beginning to get a strong sense of how powerful the decisions they make are to the success or failure of particular media companies. The executives of newspaper firms, magazine companies, websites, apps, television stations, and even TV networks worry constantly whether they are reaching the types of people advertisers want to reach. If market research shows they are not reaching the right targets, the firms may well change their content to try to attract the ones advertisers want to reach. During the late 2000s, for example, a few radio stations in Philadelphia learned, based on a new audience-measurement device, that they were not reaching nearly enough of the kinds of listeners advertisers wanted. A few stations drastically changed the music they played—and the DJs who introduced the music—as a result.

Exhibition in the Advertising Industry

The goal of the production and distribution of an ad is to exhibit it across a variety of media to a target audience. Once the media plan for an **ad campaign**—the entire set of advertisements using a particular theme to promote a certain product for a certain period of time—has been created, it is up to the advertisers' media buyers to carry it out. The buyers often work for separate media-buying companies. (Although Martin Agency creates and produces GEICO's ads, it works with Horizon Media to plan ad-placement strategy; Horizon does the actual buying.) Every mass media firm publishes its rates for space or time. It also makes a pitch for different target audiences that advertisers crave. For example, MTV has made "global youth" aged 18 to 34 a key target audience. Aware that advertisers were concerned about a downturn in its audience in the mid-2010s, network executives in 2018 touted a resurgence based on shows such as Jersey Shore and the *Video Music Awards*. Pointing to Nielsen data, a press release trumpeted "9 consecutive months of Primetime Growth [making MTV the] fastest growing Top 40 cable entertainment network."[2] Knowing that advertisers trying to reach young people are increasingly interested in doing so when they are engaged with social media such as Facebook, Twitter, and Instagram, MTV has worked hard to get global audiences viewing its concerts and awards shows to connect with its social media sites. The vice president of digital content stated in 2017 that her network has "a robust background creating high-quality content to exploit

cost per thousand (CPM)
the basic measurement of advertising efficiency in all media; it is used by advertisers to evaluate how much space they will buy in a given medium and what price they will pay

ad campaign
the entire set of advertisements using a particular theme to promote a certain product for a certain period of time

Thank you, Mom by P&G
506,755 likes · 26,084 talking about this

During the 2012 Olympic Games, Procter & Gamble launched a massive and memorable ad campaign titled "Thanks, Mom" in which they focused on the important role "Mom" plays in helping young athletes achieve their dreams of participating in the Olympics. In addition to the series of commercials on television, there were online and social media campaigns linked to this ad campaign.

Programatic advertising
the use of software to buy advertising on digital media as opposed to human negotiations and purchases

real time bidding auctions
auctions that take place as individuals are entering particular media locations

ad exchange
a technology platform that helps the buying and selling of media advertising inventory

across all platforms. We know original content incredibly well, but the definition of content has shifted now and is as much about 'snaps' and 'gifts' as long-form TV shows," she explained. She added that "social platforms like Snapchat provide a chance to work with up-and-coming talent and are a place to trial multiple short-form videos."[3]

Media buyers representing large advertisers, however, see audience numbers and strategies by media firms as the starting point for negotiation. They dangle the large amounts of cash that they control as they attempt to negotiate discounts from the basic rates. Media firms, for their part, know that buyers like to follow audiences across different platforms. So, for example, the AMC cable network commissions "webisodes" for its series *The Walking Dead*. Posted online, they are short video clips that reveal brief story lines behind some of the episodes and characters. A commercial often precedes them.

When it comes to buying ads to reach people on the web or mobile apps, the advertising tradition of having media buyers haggling with sellers over rates has given way to computerized procedures for buying and selling. That is because websites and apps have the ability to send ("serve") ads to individuals, they have learned a lot by tracking their activities and collecting data about them. (See Chapter 6 for a discussion of how they do that using cookies and other techniques.) Much of this activity happens in real time through a process called programmatic advertising. **Programmatic advertising** involves the use of software to buy advertising on digital media as opposed to the human negotiations and purchases described earlier. The process is complex, with many computers involved, but the essence is this: Media firms, or firms representing media firms, offer advertisers the ability to reach individuals with specific characteristics in **real-time bidding auctions**—that is, in auctions that take place as individuals are entering particular media locations. Say, for example, People.com knows that a 22-year-old woman is entering its website. People's computers send information about the user and the page it is on to an **ad exchange**, which is a technology platform that helps the buying and selling of media advertising inventory. The ad exchange auctions the right to reach the 22-year-old woman on People to the advertiser willing to pay the highest price for it. The whole process takes just milliseconds. In fact, at any second, real-time bidding to reach huge numbers of people on digital media is being auctioned around the world.

This ability to connect individuals with specific ads based upon what the company auctioning them knows about them is revolutionizing advertising. As we noted earlier in examples about the AMC and MTV cable channels, as well as about *Seventeen* magazine, advertisers typically buy space in print media and time on traditional TV (and radio) based on broad audience descriptions. They target 18- to 49-year-olds, for example, or women, or people who buy cars. The rise of programmatic advertising allows them to go after specific types of people, or even specific individuals they know, across a wide range of digital locations. How they do that requires technical description beyond what we can provide here; Chapter 6 can help with some of that, too.

The gist of it, though, is that companies have techniques to track individuals as they move across apps and websites. They can even determine that a particular person who has visited People.com and clicked on a dress ad there (but didn't buy it) is now visiting NYTimes.com, and the *New York Times* is offering advertisers the opportunity to reach her through real-time bidding. That means that the retailer selling the dress on People.com can try to reach her again with the same dress, at perhaps a reduced price. These sorts of retargeting activities happen all the time. You've undoubtedly seen them in your use of digital media.

The popularity of programmatic advertising has been rising dramatically with media firms and media buyers because of the opportunity to reach targets efficiently without human-to-human haggling. Eventually, with the right technology, the goal is to help advertisers track individuals across many media, so as to reach them when they are most ready to receive ads. One hint of the way that might happen relates to certain marketing firms' ability to track people's locations. If individuals accept giving up their location on their mobile device (and they sometimes agree without realizing they are opening themselves up to being bid on), the companies can send them ads on their mobile devices based on where they are. This sort of advertising is called **location-based advertising**, and it, too, takes place through programmatic real-time bidding. In fact, even some traditional media—broadcast television, broadcast radio, and cable distribution firms—have been experimenting with introducing various forms of programmatic bidding in their ad-selling operations. Comcast, which also owns the NBC television network and MSNBC and CNBC, has been especially interested in this computerized way to buy and sell households in real time.

This process is not without controversy, though. One major problem for the advertising industry are fraudsters who introduce large numbers of fictitious "people" into ad exchanges by making it seem that the cookies or other tags representing them come from legitimate sites. Advertisers' computers bid on those make-believe individuals and pay for the right to reach them, funneling money uselessly to gangs that often work from places where they are difficult to prosecute. One major problem for users of media—that is, for you and me—is that programmatic advertising is typically based on following what people do across websites and apps and even what they say on social media. Companies create profiles of people based on this tracking, and the profiles lead to certain people being treated differently from others—offered different products, different messages, even different prices—depending on what the advertisers have concluded about them. At the end of this chapter we will discuss the concerns people feel about these activities.

Determining an Advertisement's Success

After an ad campaign is exhibited, the ad agency's research division will probably be involved with the advertiser in evaluating the campaign's success. In the case of a direct-marketing campaign, this evaluation is easy: if the campaign led to the purchase of a certain number of products (or a certain dollar amount), it may be judged a success. In the case of a web ad, evaluation depends on the nature of the response and the expectations of the marketers. Other times, the advertiser hopes that the recipients will click on the ad to learn more or even to buy. If the ad is of the **click-through** sort, in which the reader can purchase the product directly, the ad's success can also be evaluated through direct purchases. Yet one can argue that the ad may be successful even if the people reading it do not click on it or, if they do click on it,

location-based advertising
the process of sending commercial messages to people based on their geographic location

click-through ad
a web-based advertisement that, when clicked on, takes the user to the advertiser's website

- You're the marketing head of a large consumer products firm. One of your assistants phones to tell you that a rumor sweeping through Twitter and Facebook claims that your firm's logo is a coded picture that encourages devil worship. You get your PR team together to brainstorm a response.
- As CEO of a pharmaceutical firm, you learn in a late-night phone call of a rumor that one of your company's over-the-counter products has been poisoning people in the Midwestern United States. You are sure that's not true. Although your firm has a crisis management team for emergencies of this type, you turn to a PR firm for further suggestions about how to handle the victims and their families, the press, politicians, and federal regulators.

Public relations
information, activities, and policies by which corporations and other organizations seek to create attitudes favorable to themselves and their work, and to counter adverse attitudes

What do these different scenarios have in common? One expert has put it this way: public relations involves "information, activities, and policies by which corporations and other organizations seek to create attitudes favorable to themselves and their work, and to counter adverse attitudes." That's a neat way of tying the examples together, and it also brings up another important issue: the relationship between PR and mass media. If you think about the description and the four scenarios for a few moments, you'll see that they all suggest that PR activities need not involve the technologies of mass communication. Much of the PR firm's plans for the state legislators, for example, may involve one-on-one lobbying, which is a form of interpersonal communication.

Still, in many aspects of their work, PR practitioners do turn to the mass media—beyond simply getting good publicity for a client. For one thing, their work often involves trying to counter negative media impressions of the client that were created by others. For another, media strategies typically fit into a larger PR communication strategy regarding the organization. PR work for the chemical firm, for example, may have an important mass media component, such as reaching out to reporters in the state capital with stories about the positive role the company is playing in the local economy and the care its leaders are taking with the environment. The PR people might also believe that presenting the company in a good light to the viewing public might, in turn, encourage state politicians to believe that their constituents would applaud new laws that do not harm the firm.

We've already suggested that advertising differs from PR in the mass media in two major ways, but it pays to state the differences directly here. First, advertisers pay for the space or time that they receive, whereas PR practitioners typically do not. Second, advertising clearly states its presence. When you see an ad, you know what it is for, and you often know quite easily who is sponsoring it. A PR activity, by contrast, typically hides its presence and its sponsor.

What advertising and PR have in common is that they deal in billions of dollars and play profound roles in American mass media. Whereas advertising activities supply money directly to support particular media outlets, PR activities supply ideas to media for stories. Of course, the ad agencies supply cash when they are convinced a media outlet is reaching the target audiences they want to reach for their clients. But as we will see, PR agencies also provide valuable resources when they pitch ideas to media outlets that they believe are reaching the audiences their clients want to reach. They are helping the media personnel get their work done more efficiently and quickly than would have been the case if the PR firms hadn't helped out.

The Public Relations Industry and Media

Our aim here is to describe those aspects of the PR business that play an important role in what we read, see, and hear in various media. We start by looking at the PR departments that are found in many corporations, government bodies, health care institutions, military branches, professional services firms, associations, non-profit organizations, and other public and private entities. The PR practitioners in these places often carry out three types of work: media relations, internal relations, and external relations. **Media relations** is the work most obviously related to media. Employees concerned with it typically handle calls and emails from journalists looking for information or wanting to speak to particular executives. They provide the answers and coordinate the interviews with executives. They also may teach executives the best ways to act on camera or with a journalist.

The other two corporate PR functions—external relations and internal relations—don't sound on the surface like they have much to do with media. Internal relations involves presenting the views of the company to company workers and owners—employees, union groups, and shareholders. External relations, logically, involves presenting the views of the company to people and organizations outside the firm. Many of the outside and inside activities involve interpersonal activities: face-to-face meetings with congressional staff, for example, or speeches to union members. At the same time, a fair amount of the work in both areas may well involve a variety of media outlets. For example, external relations specialists may create corporate reports and email blasts aimed at shareholders as well as news firms that reach the general public or a particular industry. Their internal relations counterparts also may use media to communicate to their large number of employees. They may do so through websites, email summaries of company developments, or (in really big companies) even video news programs about the company for employees in offices around the globe.

Just as the work of PR departments in companies often involves fueling media content of one sort or another, so PR agencies often aim to "subsidize" media firms with content that benefits their clients. The US Census Bureau found more than 7,000 public relations firms in the United States in 2006. Companies large and small hire such "outside" PR companies for various projects, ranging from special lobbying that may or may not involve the media to getting or controlling media exposure. Public relations companies often charge fees based on the number of hours that their employees work for a client. Sometimes clients make "retainer" deals with an agency, under which the company agrees to carry out a PR program at an agreed-upon rate per month.

Not all PR companies do the same things. Large firms such as Fleishman-Hillard help their clients with virtually any area of communication, including teaching their top executives how to speak on TV and in front of large groups. Many smaller PR firms, however, specialize in a particular part of their industry's work. Examples of medium-size independent agencies that specialize include HealthSTAR Communications, a health care agency; Cerrell Associates, a public affairs and environmental agency; and Integrated Corporate Relations, a company that helps firms speak to stock analysts, institutional investors, financial media, and other corporate audiences.

The biggest PR firms are widely considered to be Fleishman-Hillard, Weber Shandwick, Hill & Knowlton Strategies, Burson-Marsteller, Incepta Communication, Edelman Worldwide, BSMG Worldwide, Ogilvy PR, Porter Novelli, and Ketchum.

media relations
all dealings with reporters and other members of media organizations who might tell a story about a client

Table 4.4 Major PR Firms Owned by Large Agency Holding Companies

WPP	Omnicom Group	Interpublic	Publicis
Burson-Marsteller	Fleishman-Hillard	Weber Shandwick	Publicis Consultants Public Relations
Hill & Knowlton	Ketchum	Golin Harris	Schwartz Communications
Cohn and Wolfe	Porter Novelli	Rogers & Cowan	Hanmer MSL (India)
Ogilvy PR	Brodeur Worldwide	PMK/HBH	Genedigi (China)
Carl Byoir	Clark and Weinstock	Carmichael Lynch Spong	
GCI Health	Cone		
Dewey Square Group			

Sources: Holding company websites.

the Big Four
the largest agency holding companies, including Omnicom, WPP, Interpublic, and Publicis

All of these companies, with the exception of Edelman and Incepta, are owned by one of the agency holding companies known as **the Big Four:** Omnicom, WPP, Interpublic, and Publicis (see Table 4.4). As we noted earlier, agency holding companies are firms that own large ad agency networks; PR firms; and a multitude of branding, market research, and marketing communications firms.

Global reach is key to the activities of the biggest firms. Hill & Knowlton Strategies, part of the WPP holding company, reports on its website that it has eighty-five offices "around the globe." The company adds that

> We understand and keep up with the perpetual motion of today's global public. . . . Behind all of our insight-led ideas and communication strategies are a deep understanding of data and analytics, creativity and master storytelling. . . . We understand that our clients today have more ways to communicate, influence, and engage with their audiences than ever before. . . . We have the fullest and deepest range of services possible, which we are able to draw on in realizing our clients' objectives.[5]

Especially prominent public relations activities fall into these areas:

Corporate communications
Financial communications
Health care
Public affairs
Crisis management

The biggest firms tackle many of these categories, though not always all of them. Moreover, some companies may combine one or another category in organizing their expertise and personnel. Table 4.5 defines each of these activities and gives an example of the ways a PR agency may influence hard news and soft news in carrying it out for a client. (For a discussion of these news forms, see Chapter 2.) The examples suggest the broad range of clients these agencies serve and the wide range of topics we see and hear in various media that result from such PR activities.

Table 4.5 Examples of Ways Public Relations Agencies May Influence Media Content Through Prominent Public Relations Activities

Activity	Definition	Type of client and aim	Influence on hard news	Influence on soft news
Corporate communications	The creation and presentation of a company's overall image to its employees and to the public at large	An automobile manufacturer wants to spread the notion that it is a technologically advanced yet socially responsible company.	The firm sponsors a coast-to-coast solar-car race named after the company on college campuses and makes sure all the local TV and radio stations in the areas cover the race.	The company convinces the star of an action TV series to work with the team from his college alma mater. The company donates a car to a charity the actor chooses.
Financial communications	Helping a client's interactions with lenders, shareholders, and stock market regulators proceed smoothly	A pharmaceutical firm wants its shareholders to trust that the firm's management is doing excellent work guiding new drugs with great profit potential to market.	The company's PR firm offers a popular news magazine an exclusive look at the firm's state-of-the art drug-innovation facilities. The company places the news magazine's article and mails copies to shareholders.	The company's PR firm uses research on social media discussions to learn names of online comedians liked by young mothers who are a target audience for one of the client's key over-the-counter vitamins. The PR firm sends the comedians samples and literature about the product, and a number of them do end up integrating the brand into their jokes.
Health care	Helping hospitals, health maintenance organizations, pharmaceutical firms, and provider organizations such as the American Medical Association and the American Nursing Association in relation to government regulations, international sales; tensions with organizations that purchase their goods and services; and confused, angry, and even frightened members of the public	A major medical center wants to encourage people bordering on high obesity to visit the medical center's new weight loss clinics in different cities across the United States.	On the day the clinic chain opens, the director manages to land a *Today Show* interview in which she champions the mix of exercise and drugs that the clinic offers for severely obese people.	On the day the drug is released, the firm manages to schedule an interview on HLN and *The Tonight Show* with a well-known actress who lost fifty pounds using a new drug the clinic has been testing in clinical trials.
Public affairs	Helps companies that depend on government contracts that worry about lawmakers imposing regulations that will have negative effects on the firms	A large digital advertising firm is concerned that the public is angry at the firm for gathering information about its audiences without their explicit opt-in permission. The worry is that large numbers of people might encourage Congress to push for opt-in laws.	The company's PR firm makes the advertising firm's persuasive CEO available to editorial boards of major newspapers to lay out his belief that the audiences are happy with an opt-out approach that allows them to stop the gathering of information if they like.	The company's PR firm persuades that charismatic CEO to play the saxophone at the South by Southwest Festival in Austin, Texas, with the hope that his musicianship—and he—will get wide favorable press coverage. That, the PR firm believes, might move people to be favorable toward the firm.
Crisis management	The range of activities that help a company respond to its business partners, the general public, or the government in the event of an unforeseen disaster affecting its image or products	A petroleum company responsible for a huge oil spill in the Gulf of Mexico wants the public and the government to believe it is doing the cleanup correctly and with the residents of the area in mind.	The firm's CEO makes the rounds of the major TV news networks with news of the company's huge donation to the towns affected by the oil spill, as well as its rollout of new technologies that will make such oil spills "nearly impossible."	A popular singer whose parents live in one of the towns getting the donation agrees to appear on celebrity news programs and *Nightline* with baby birds who recently hatched in the area where the oil company paid for the cleanup.

How does this work of placing topics and products into the media get accomplished? As we did with advertising, we can answer by approaching the activities through the lenses of production, distribution, and exhibition.

Production in the Public Relations Industry

We've already noted that the term "media relations" covers all dealings with members of media organizations who might tell a story about a client. Much of that work involves hard news or soft news. In some of these dealings, journalists take the initiative—for example, when reporters want to know what is going on during a company crisis. Other dealings with the media take place at the initiative of PR practitioners who want to spread the word about their clients' activities. Your university probably uses a PR staff to spread good news about research that is being carried out and about the success of its sports teams. The goal is to make both alumni and current students so proud of the institution that they will want to donate money.

PR practitioners often spread news by building good relationships with relevant journalists and editors. That way, the PR staff will have the best chance at getting its organization's desired point of view across in a media story. Getting a desired viewpoint across usually means more than just answering incoming calls and sending out information. Most media relations work is proactive. So in addition to providing interested parties with relevant facts and information for their stories, PR staff members have to go the extra mile by doing much of the journalists' job for them—for example, thinking up, selling, and sometimes even writing sample stories.

Of course, journalists have the final word on which stories they'll choose to write or rewrite and finally run, and they are often suspicious of their PR contacts. In addition, journalists have a large number of choices among PR-initiated stories, given that so many companies are involved in media relations activities. These two circumstances create a lot of pressure on the PR practitioner.

The most basic product of a PR firm's attempt to influence the media is the **press release**—a short essay that is written in the form of an objective news story. Because the goal is to get a reporter or editor to write about a particular aspect of the client's activities, a successful press release finds a hook in the client's tale that the reporter can use. PR practitioners know that reporters will dismiss as propaganda stories that simply tout the views of the firm's executives or present the firm's accomplishments. The trick is to write a story with an angle that the journalist will see as interesting to her or his audience and that also can include other firms and other points of view. A press release that is too obviously self-serving will rarely get picked up.

Because of the importance of knowing what attracts journalists to particular stories, PR firms and PR departments of organizations often hire former journalists as their press contacts. Back in 2013, Hill & Knowlton's (H+K) LinkedIn page made the point directly:

> We have a reputation for handling complex media situations in positive circumstances as well as in times of crisis. Our media relations professionals—including former journalists, press secretaries and communications officers—have delivered results throughout the world.
>
> Using solid research and analysis, messaging, journalistic skills and close media relationships, we can deliver real business impact.[6]

press release
a short essay that is written in the form of an objective news story

In 2018, the LinkedIn description focused on the impact of H+K's journalistic skills and media relationships by stating "Our campaigns influence decision-makers, shape reputations, manage risk, engage stakeholders and impact bottom lines. . . . We're idea experts who connect. We are strategic storytellers."[7]

As these lines suggest, writing press releases is only part of a PR firm's media duties. The company must also hire practitioners who can field questions from members of the press who come to them for stories. PR practitioners are also increasingly involved in reaching out to entertainment companies to coordinate the production of audiovisual materials that present the points of view of their companies to various constituencies. A mobile phone company, for example, might send a video to high schools to describe for students the new technologies it is using to keep rates down while providing the best service. A university might create a YouTube channel to provide tours of the campus and "behind-the-scenes" looks at specific departments as well as research centers. Also important is the role of digital vehicles that encourage target audiences to interact with companies and feel friendly toward them. PR firms help clients set up Facebook pages or Twitter feeds that inform about discounts, answer questions, quash rumors, and exude a likable personality.

Smart companies shift their marketing focus to reflect changing media consumption habits. Others play digital catch-up in order to remain relevant and competitive. Either way, companies need to know how to harness the power of social media by building community around an issue or a brand, driving engagement, and building strong relationships with all audiences—and all this in a way designed to appear open, honest, and genuine.

Companies involved in consumer PR often decide to reach people in a less-than-open way—by turning out their own TV "news" stories. For example, a computer chip manufacturer might create a short video for use on local news programs that shows how cutting-edge computer chips allow typical home users to perform an enormous number of tasks faster and make these tasks more fun. The trick to getting such a spot on the air is to make it seem like a soft news story created by the TV station. PR practitioners know that they should mention their client, the chip manufacturer, only in passing and show its logo only a couple of times. Subtlety is important. Overtly pushing the company and its products would be the kiss of death for a spot; a news show would never use it.

Distribution in the Public Relations Industry

Once materials for the media part of a PR campaign have been prepared, the PR firm must distribute them to the proper publicity outlets. A **publicity outlet** is a media vehicle (e.g., a particular magazine, a specific TV interview program, or a particular radio talk show) that has in the past been open to input from PR practitioners. "Proper" in this case has two meanings: it refers to both outlets that reach the kinds of people the firm is targeting and outlets that are appropriate for the particular ideas, products, or services that the firm is trying to push.

PR practitioners keep lists of the publicity outlets in different areas that are appropriate for different types of products and for reaching different groups of people. When they are working on a particular campaign, they use these lists to determine which outlets to concentrate on and whom to contact. Sometimes only a press release will be sent. At other times, PR practitioners will be so familiar with the individuals involved that they will phone them directly. In fact, having good connections among media people, especially the press corps, is a crucial asset in the PR business.

publicity outlet
a media vehicle (e.g., a particular magazine, a specific TV interview program, or a particular radio talk show) that has in the past been open to input from public relations practitioners

Advanced distribution technologies also have become crucial to the PR industry during the past few years. PR practitioners use email and (less often) fax machines to send press releases. They pay firms to track the discussions—the buzz—about their clients in chat rooms and on blogs, Facebook, Twitter, and elsewhere, and they respond by paying people to go online and insert comments that reflect the positive spin that fits the aim of the PR campaign. (They're supposed to say they represent the firm, but they don't always do that.) PR practitioners use satellite linkups to set up interviews with TV reporters from around the country and the world for their clients. They also use satellites to send video press releases to appropriate publicity outlets. These are packages of photographs, video clips, and interviews from which a reporter can choose to create a story. A video press release for a new adventure film, for example, might contain short clips from the movie, a background piece on the special effects used to make the movie, and separate as well as combined interviews with the male and female stars. Each piece would be designed to be used as a feature story on a local television newscast. The interviews would be shot in a way that allows news people in local stations to create the impression that the discussion was created exclusively for their broadcasts.

Exhibition in the Public Relations Industry

"But," you may ask, "why do TV and print journalists use this material? Don't journalists pride themselves on their objectivity and independence?" Good question. The answer lies in the costs of news reporting in the print and electronic worlds. Costs here relate both to monetary expense and to the amount of time involved. Reporting stories totally from scratch can cost a lot of money. It can also cost reporters an enormous amount of time, time that they often do not have because of deadlines.

Imagine how many reporters the *Washington Post* would have to assign to the Departments of State and Agriculture, the Treasury, and the other Cabinet-level divisions of the US government if there were no systematic way to find out about meetings, speeches, reports, and other materials emanating from each. The paper could not afford to ferret out all that information, but it doesn't have to do so because each department's PR division provides the newspaper with its basic schedule. Moreover, in key parts of the government, such as the State Department, PR representatives summarize key issues for reporters and answer their questions.

In addition to allowing news organizations to allocate fewer journalists to government agencies, these press briefings help journalists budget their time efficiently. The briefings enable journalists to gather the basic information needed to write their daily stories. They can then spend the rest of their time following up issues raised by the briefings; each journalist hopes that his or her stories will stand out from those of other journalists who were also at the meetings.

As you can see, PR practitioners help the media get their work done. Communication scholar Oscar Gandy calls this sort of help to media organizations and their personnel **"information subsidies."** The term means that PR people's help with information is akin to advancing money and time. Faced with a beautifully done clip that is part of a video press release, a TV station's news director may genuinely believe that some of the material in that clip is interesting enough to warrant a story. She or he also knows that the low cost of putting that spot on the air will offset the extra expenses of a locally produced story.

information subsidies
the time and money that PR people provide media practitioners that helps the latter get their work done

The danger of information subsidies from a client's standpoint is that they may not be used. News organizations receive many more offerings from PR firms than they have room for, and journalists can often be quite selective. The most successful—and most expensive—PR practitioners work hard to establish strong relationships with members of the press to help grease the path to coverage. In the mid-1990s, the *New York Times* reported that Sard Verbinnen, the head of the PR agency with that name, would get pieces in the news by currying favor with journalists: giving an "exclusive" about a deal or an interview with a chief executive to one newspaper and then offering a behind-the-scenes look at a transaction to a reporter of another paper that did not get the original exclusive. By doing that, he would be able to call on both sources to help him with coverage when he needed it.

For Verbinnen or anyone else, though, coverage doesn't always work out the way the PR practitioner wants it to. Good journalists do their own independent investigations of material suggested by a press release or some other PR initiative. Consequently, what begins as an attempt to present a favorable image of a firm or a person may backfire if the reporter finds material that contradicts the original report.

The Rise of Marketing Communications

As we have seen, PR is potentially very useful but also unpredictable when it comes to getting a company, person, or product specific and favorable mass media coverage aimed at a particular audience. In contrast, advertising can provide quite predictable media coverage (because the advertiser pays for time or space), but it can be quite a bit more expensive than PR work and may not be as persuasive as PR stories that appear as news.

During the past several years, the awareness that advertising and PR can complement each other has led executives to attempt to coordinate the two types of activities to get the best of both worlds. Some have dubbed this approach **integrated marketing communications (IMC)**, or often simply **marketing communications**. The goal is to blend (integrate) historically different ways to communicate to an organization's various audiences and markets. Under the best of circumstances, integration means creating a campaign that sends different yet consistent messages around particular themes to present and potential consumers of a firm's products, as well as to its employees, to the companies that sell to it and buy from it, and to government regulators. In addition to traditional advertising and PR, IMC often brings three related activities into its mix: branded entertainment, direct marketing, and relationship marketing. Let's take a look at each.

Branded Entertainment

Branded entertainment involves associating a company or product with media activities in ways that are not as obviously intrusive as advertisements. The word "branded" refers to linking the firm or product's name (and personality) with an activity that the target audience enjoys. The three most common forms of branded entertainment are event marketing, event sponsorship, and product placement.

Event marketing involves creating compelling circumstances that command attention in ways that are relevant to the product or firm. These activities typically take place at sports and entertainment venues by way of mobile trailers or road shows

integrated marketing communications (IMC) or marketing communications a blending of historically different ways to communicate to an organization's various audiences and markets

branded entertainment the act of linking the firm or product's name (and personality) with an activity that the target audience enjoys

event marketing creating compelling circumstances that command attention in ways that are relevant to the product or firm. These activities typically take place at sports and entertainment venues by way of mobile trailers or road shows that publicize products and on college campuses, in malls, and in bars

Note the placement of company logos throughout the hockey arena of the L.A. Kings indicating their sponsorship of the arena and/or the team.

event sponsorship
situation in which companies pay money to be associated with particular activities that their target audiences enjoy or value. Examples include sports, concerts, and charities

barter
process by which products used in movies and TV shows are provided by the manufacturer to the producers for free in exchange for the publicity

product integration
the act of building plot lines or discussions for talk shows and reality TV around specific brands

that publicize products and on college campuses, in malls, and in bars. Some of the activities are termed "grassroots." That is, companies pay nonprofessionals (say, moms who like their products) to set up parties or other meetings that promote the items. These are activities that bring the products in front of people in unusual ways. Other activities are called "guerrilla" events. An example is when the Red Bull energy drink firm sponsored Red Bull Stratos, "a scientific mission to prove that humans could survive accelerating through the sound barrier in free fall and land back on earth safely." That culminated in the Red Bull–enabled skydive in October 2012 by Austrian Felix Baumgartner, who became the first person to break the sound barrier without engine power by jumping from a capsule twenty-four miles above the Earth. The company received huge publicity that even included a Red Bull Stratos exhibit in the Smithsonian Air and Space Museum.[8] PQ Media estimates that companies spent $12.99 billion on event marketing to the general public in the United States during 2014.

Event Sponsorship In event marketing, the product is the focus of the activity. By contrast, **event sponsorship** occurs when companies pay money to be associated with particular activities that their target audiences enjoy or value. It happens a lot with sports, concerts, and charities. A notable concert sponsorship was by the Doritos brand of chips owned by Frito-Lay, which is in turn owned by Pepsi-Cola. The brand shelled out $2.5 million for a single Lady Gaga performance in Austin's 2014 SXSW festival. Part of the deal involved the singer giving up time in her act to describe an oddball Doritos #BoldMissions promotion that required all attendees to complete various acts of "boldness"—for example, getting unusual haircuts or surrendering a suitcase at the airport for two days—in order to get into the show.[9] PQ Media estimates that firms spent $15.25 billion on event sponsorship in the United States during 2014.

Product Placement Product placement takes place when a firm manages to insert its brand in a positive way into fiction or nonfiction content. Think of AT&T, Ford, and Coca-Cola on the TV series *American Idol* or the appearances of particular car models in movies, TV shows, and video games that you've seen. Traditionally, products used in movies and TV shows were provided by the manufacturer to the producers for free in exchange for the publicity. That is called **barter**, and it still represents the largest percentage of product placement. But in recent years, paid product placement has been increasing, though observers say it still takes place less often than barter. Some marketers have paid producers of so-called reality shows and talk shows to build plot lines or discussions around their brands. The activity is called **product integration**, and it is increasing, particularly online. If you saw the hit Universal Picture's movie *The Fate of the Furious*, which hit theaters in 2017, you may have noticed that Dodge vehicles played a big role. That was purposeful, part of a long-term promotional relationship Dodge has had with the popular set of Universal films revolving around a group that (improbably) uses superhuman driving abilities while it fights crime. In a press release, a Dodge executive noted that "Fast Dodge cars, adrenaline-filled action and family have fueled the *Fast & Furious* franchise from the beginning." The "co-branding" of car and film took place in 2017 across a variety of media, including social media, websites, apps, and various licensed products. In that way and others, Dodge hoped to make the most from its investment in the picture, and Universal hoped to benefit from the high level of Dodge publicity.[10]

Direct Marketing

Direct marketing uses media vehicles created by the marketer (phone messages, email, postal mailings) to send persuasive messages asking that the consumers who receive them respond to the marketer. Think of any of the late-night TV commercials you've watched that urge you to phone them via an 800 number or a web ad that asks you to click to buy a product or service. Nowadays, most direct marketing involves **databases**. These are lists of customers and potential customers that can be used to determine what those people might purchase in the future. The marketer contacts the people on these lists with advertising or PR messages. The practice of using these computerized lists is called **database marketing**.

Although the use of lists in marketing dates back to at least the 1800s, the past few decades have seen a huge growth in the use of computers to store information about people and their habits. This growth in marketers' ability to cross-link and retrieve huge amounts of information about people took place at the same time that the introduction of toll-free numbers, more efficient mailing techniques, and fast delivery firms made shopping from home easier than ever in the decades before the internet. These changes led to a huge increase in targeted persuasion through direct marketing.

Relationship Marketing

Relationship marketing involves a determination by the firm to maintain long-term contact with its customers. This can be done by regular mailings of custom magazines, brochures, letters, or emails or through frequent user programs that encourage repeat purchases and keep the person connected to the firm. It can also be done by sponsoring influencers. They have credibility with target audiences and can build interest in the company's products. Some influencers are celebrities. Others are noted experts from particular industries. The largest number, though are internet content creators who use vehicles such as Instagram, Pinterest, Facebook, and other forms of social media to discuss their areas of interest and the products linked to them. They typically post comments related to their areas of interest. That might be childrearing, women's fashion, finance, movies—a range of life's topics.

A company may look for a celebrity or industry expert who seems to authentically fit with the firms' products as well as the product's target audience. The company then pays that person to use the products publicly and perhaps comment about them. The situation with internet influencers is similar, though more complex. A firm will use a variety of search tools (and even search companies) to find people whose writings relate to the kinds of products the company produces and who have large numbers of followers. The firm will then send its products to the writer with the hope the person will write favorably about those items. Often firms will create more formal ties with influencers that appear to have particularly valuable

direct marketing
marketing that uses media vehicles created by the marketer (phone messages, email, postal mailings) to send persuasive messages asking that the consumers who receive them respond to the marketer

databases
lists of customers and potential customers that can be used to determine what those people might purchase in the future

database marketing
practice of constructing computerized lists of customers and potential customers that can be used to determine what those people might purchase in the future. The marketer then contacts the people on these lists with advertising or PR messages

relationship marketing
a firm's process of maintaining long-term contact with its customers

relationships with their followers. That might involve payments to mention the company and its products in the influencer's writings. In recent years the Federal Trade Commission has insisted that this sort of activity—the reception of payment or free products—must trigger a mention of that gift when the influencer writes about the product. Influencers seem to have learned to do that without alienating their followers, so many firms continue to value their help in getting past people's resistance to traditional ads.

THINKING ABOUT MEDIA LITERACY

Corporate social responsibility may be, above all else, a strategic business practice. Consider an initiative or program funded by a large corporation (such as Google Green) and think about how the initiative affects the business and its customers, regulators, or others that can affect the company's success.

Advertising, Public Relations, and Convergence

Nowadays, the interconnection of advertising PR and marketing communications is often so tight that so-called advertising practitioners perform PR and marketing communications activities, and vice versa. In fact, some practitioners have dropped those traditional descriptions in favor of three terms that describe how they cause persuasive messages to enter the media stream. **Paid media** refers to situations when they pay platforms (TV networks, magazines) a fee in order to place their messages; the term essentially refers to traditional advertising. **Owned media** refers to platforms that the practitioners' clients own in order to present their messages in favor of a product or service. Pampers.com is an example of Procter & Gamble's owned media for its diaper division. **Earned media** refers to situations when the practitioners persuade platforms to present their clients' messages without directly charging them because the company's message is interesting or useful to the platforms' audiences. In traditional terms, PR practitioners are continually trying to get earned

By this point in the chapter you should be getting a pretty good feel for the idea that advertising, PR, and marketing communications together exert a substantial impact on the media. Although PR activities tend to relate to hard and soft news, the same firms that carry out PR also often have divisions that work the entertainment beat for their clients. The *Mission Impossible* movie series that linked BMW cars and motorcycles to Tom Cruise's daring escapades provides a good example of the way advertising and marketing communications work together. One can imagine, in fact, how the PR practitioners could parlay the long-term linkup into a spot on a celebrity TV show such as *Entertainment Tonight*. The show's producers might well want to interview the show's star, and he might casually insert references to both vehicles into the conversation. Or perhaps the *ET* people might like the idea of directly describing the ways in which parts of the *MI* plots are crafted with the BMW in mind.

With the word "convergence" in this section's heading in mind, you might realize multiple media are often involved as a result of the earned-, paid-, and owned-media work that advertising agencies, PR agencies, and marketing communications specialists perform for their clients. When a PR practitioner puts out a press release, he or she does it with the hope that the story will be picked up by many media outlets.

paid media
situations when platforms ask companies for a fee in order to place their messages owned media

owned media
platforms that companies themselves own in order to present their messages in favor of a product or service

earned media
situations when platforms present a company's messages without directly charging it because they feel the company's message is interesting or useful to the platforms' audiences

Often the practitioner prepares an audiovisual version along with a print version so that television stations can use the story. And, of course the material will show up on the company's websites and on its Facebook and Instagram pages—and people might be drawn to it through Twitter posts and ads on Facebook and Twitter aimed at the kinds of people who would be interested in that aspect of the client's activities. Carried out with skill, stories that benefit the client can nowadays take advantage of media convergence so as to reach substantial percentages of the target audiences at least once—and often more than that.

THINKING ABOUT MEDIA LITERACY

Your new book has just been published. What might go into your publishing company's media campaign to promote your book? Consider all of the types of strategic communications (advertising and PR work) that might go into the campaign. For example, what information subsidies might be generated and where would they be sent?

Media Literacy Issues Related to Advertising and PR

More generally, if this chapter has done its job, you might now be impressed by the power of advertisers' sponsorship decisions to support certain media firms and doom others. And you might be impressed by the ability of advertising, PR, and marketing communications practitioners to spread content to target audiences across a multitude of media outlets.

But what about people who are members of the larger society? What should citizens who want to live in a democratic, peaceful, thriving world think about the relationship between these businesses and media? This is an important question, if only because advertising, PR, and IMC—what might be called the persuasion industries—are all around us. Many scholars suggest that we really ought to think deeply about them. A few writers even contend that the future of world civilization depends on redefining society's relationship to these media support systems. That may sound like an extravagant claim about industries that sell cars and candy bars. But is it really that far-fetched? See what you think as we review three issues that center on these industries, the mass media, and society: advertising and commercialism, truth and hidden influence, and the social impact of targeting. As we will see, all three issues are quite interrelated.

Advertising and Commercialism

"**Commercialism**," a term often associated with advertising and its impact on American life, refers to a situation in which the buying and selling of goods and services is a highly promoted value. Many people say that the United States is a nation in which commercialism runs rampant. Everywhere we turn, we see a sales pitch. Defenders of commercialism insist that Americans never would have achieved the high standard of living that many now have—or acquired the products that they take for granted—were it not for the industrial competition that commercialism has encouraged. Detractors of commercialism question this notion of progress. They insist that many difficulties come along with making commercialism a central tenet of American society. The most common problem, they say, is leading people to purchase things that they don't really need.

commercialism
a situation in which the buying and selling of goods and services is a highly promoted value

hidden curriculum
a body of knowledge that people
unconsciously absorb when
consuming ads

From the time Americans are very young, the critics say, they are presented with a daily barrage of ads. These ads are important not primarily because they aim to sell individual products or services; sometimes they succeed at that, and sometimes they don't. Rather, the importance of the advertising barrage is that it is part of what some observers call a **hidden curriculum**—a body of knowledge that people unconsciously absorb when consuming ads. Advertising critics argue that what advertising teaches—and what Americans accept as a basic lesson from the ad "course" they receive—is that society is merely a huge marketplace and that buying products and defining oneself through them is an essential aspect of life.

Supporters of advertising say that even if this hidden curriculum exists in as powerful a manner as its critics suggest, it is not harmful. People need to feel good about themselves, and advertising provides a vehicle—products—for doing that. Critics respond, however, that commercialism has dire side effects. They especially highlight the exploitation of children and the destruction of the global environment.

The Exploitation of Children Media critics contend that advertising to children is ethically unacceptable. They point out that children aged 2 through 12 years are often treated just like any other consumers. Ad people know that children influence their parents' spending and, as they get older, also have their own purchasing power from gifts and allowances. The critics cite scholarly research showing that the youngest children (those under 4 or 5 years) often don't have the skills to be critical of advertisers' claims—and often can't tell an advertisement from other types of content. As for the older kids, the critics contend that by getting children hyped for toys, foods, and other products that their parents must approve, the advertisers may be encouraging family arguments. In fact, marketers and media firms that invite children into a separate channel to advertise to them are quietly setting themselves up in opposition to the children's parents—a situation that, the critics argue, is morally highly questionable.

Destruction of the Global Environment Some critics argue that when so many people are taught that the continual purchase of new products is the key to the good life, their resulting activities place an enormous burden on the Earth's resources. The energy used to create the products they buy, the energy (and pollution) created by the use of the products, the garbage problems that are created when people throw away things that they could still use but that aren't fashionable—all these activities make the Earth a more and more difficult place to inhabit. Supporters of advertisers counter that these problems are not really so bad, that people are living better now than ever before in history. The critics reply that the ecological disasters caused by commercialism are just beginning. As the billions of people in developing countries such as China buy into the commercialist philosophy of countries such as the United States, the pressure on the Earth's environment will mount to unacceptable levels. Advertising critics such as Sut Jhally have argued that this predicament will literally lead to the end of the Earth's ability to sustain human beings.

Truth and Hidden Influence in Public Relations

Advertising is the industry that most scholars mention when discussing commercialism. Our examples of PR demonstrate that a lot of what PR practitioners do promotes commercialism as well. Scholars tend to focus on PR when they raise the issue of truth and hidden influence. They argue that when a company deliberately hides the sponsor or power behind a media message (as PR practitioners typically do), the action very much represents a problem of truth. Leading an audience to get the wrong impression of a story by encouraging it to believe that the story had one author rather than another—for instance, a TV station rather than the pharmaceutical firm that supplied the video and gave the station the idea for the story—is very close to promoting a lie.

Critics of advertising, PR, and marketing communications—which, again, together might be called the persuasion industries—argue that their practitioners can never really be truthful because their business is to portray people, products, and organizations purposefully in ways that do not reveal problems. Advertising, PR, and IMC practitioners respond that there is nothing wrong with emphasizing the positive aspects of something, as long as what is emphasized is not demonstrably wrong. Moreover, often companies use IMC to promote genuinely pro-social activities in which they engage. Consider, for example, the activities of an automobile maker that stress environmental sustainability through reducing the use of water in manufacturing and waste in landfills. Shouldn't companies promoting such activities toot their horns and gain customers as well as encourage more firms to do the same?

Their critics reply that it is possible to create an ad or PR campaign that deceives even when the text in the ad is legally truthful. A PR gloss on a sustainability campaign might well ignore problems with the firms' approaches that would cast a less pretty picture than the company would like. And think about all the ads you see in which men are attracted to women—or women are attracted to men—who use certain products. Technically, these ads are truthful because they never contend that using these products will automatically make you alluring. Still, the critics argue, there is a fundamental deception in photographs that imply over and over that material goods will make you sexually attractive.

A pioneering professor of PR, Scott Cutlip, worried about the industry's problem with the truth. He admonished,

Reality says . . . that the public relations [practitioner] should be seen as the advocate . . . not as a dedicated purveyor of truth to serve the public interest. Many [practitioners] serve as advocates of institutions and causes in the same way that lawyers serve clients, to put the best possible face on the facts they can, regardless of merit or truth.

He added that because of this, "as many PR practitioners shade the truth and deal in obfuscation as they purvey accurate, useful information to the public via the news media."[11]

Executives in the persuasion industries usually shrug off such complaints. They argue that not being able to suggest that a product will bring psychological benefits or that a company has a warm personality would seriously hamper their ability to create successful advertising and PR campaigns. When it comes to ethics, they focus instead on circumstances that can hurt them legally or economically. Can the government hold them legally liable for deception in an ad or PR campaign? Are competitors making incorrect statements about their products that are likely to hurt sales? Will unscrupulous practices by competitors lessen the credibility of their industry and prompt government investigations?

To make the rules clear and to deter government regulators from intruding on their business, industry leaders have turned to self-regulation. That means they have

Social media have increasingly hosted sponsored content or ads that generate revenue for the platform and for individual creators. These can be sophisticated (and controversial) examples of native advertising.

created professional associations that develop norms for the industry and write them into codes of good practice. The American Association of Advertising Agencies and the American Advertising Federation, for example, both circulate similar standards that their members promise to follow. Among their many prohibitions are misleading price claims and misleading rumors about competitors. In a similar vein, the Direct Marketing Association compiles lists of "deceptive and misleading practices" that its members should avoid. The Public Relations Society of America also has a code of "professional standards" that includes such topics as safeguarding "the confidences of present and former clients," not engaging "in any practice which tends to corrupt the integrity of channels of communication or the processes of government," and "not intentionally" communicating "false and misleading information."[12]

Some critics contend that PR and advertising firms violate these rules every day. Moreover, no society can force a nonmember to even pay lip service to its rules. Attempts to enforce complaints by one member against another do exist. If, for example, one advertiser believes that another advertiser is harming its products by broadcasting misleading or inaccurate commercials, the advertiser can complain to the National Advertising Division (NAD) of the Council of Better Business Bureaus. The NAD will investigate. If it finds the advertiser's work misleading, the charge is reviewed by the National Advertising Review Board, which consists of industry practitioners. That industry body will act as a referee and make a report on its conclusion available to the public. It will also suggest how the commercial might be changed. For the sake of self-regulation, advertisers typically agree to follow these suggestions.

Although critics of advertising point out that industry disputes over accuracy are only the tip of the iceberg of problems with the truthfulness of information, they acknowledge that at least an ad is out in the open for its audience to see. A person who sees an advertisement almost always knows that it is an ad and so can be sensitive to claims and images that may be exaggerated or are unsupportable. PR, in contrast, is by its very nature an activity that hides its creators from public view. That, say its critics, makes it almost impossible to examine its products for accuracy as one might examine an ad. In fact, as we noted previously, this is one of the persuasive advantages over advertising that PR practitioners cite. People naturally suspect an ad, they say, whereas in the case of PR, they don't even know it is taking place.

The negative social effects of PR's hidden nature can be considerable. As we have seen, many media activities today are influenced by the information subsidies that various types of PR agencies supply. These subsidies can be as seemingly harmless as products placed by companies in entertainment or as clearly outrageous as fake atrocity stories orchestrated to sway the news media, the public, and Congress to support a war. In all cases, though, PR practitioners are manipulating mass media content to their clients' commercial and political benefit without letting the public know about it.

People who don't consider the impact of PR on news and entertainment may believe what they see because they trust the news or entertainment organization that they think is the source. They may act against their best interests because they don't realize that the real source of the story is quite different from the one that they believe instigated and interpreted the story. At the same time, people who are aware of the power of PR over the mass media typically will still not be able to figure out whether a PR organization is behind a particular story or how or why. The result of this inability to know may be a cynical view that everything in the media is tainted by PR and therefore is not what it seems. In either case, the hidden nature of PR may have an unfortunate, even corrosive, effect on the way people understand those parts of society that are outside their immediate reach.

Targeting by Advertising and Public Relations Firms

The past two decades have seen tremendous growth in the ways advertisers and PR practitioners create, combine, and use lists to reach target audiences. Americans have told pollsters in growing numbers that they worry that too much information about their lives and personal preferences is being exchanged without their knowledge. It also seems clear to direct marketers that people believe that they are receiving too much junk mail and too many telemarketing calls. Moreover, both pollsters and academics predict that the growth of online services will increase worries about privacy as more ways of collecting personal information are created.

Another possible consequence of targeting that deserves mention involves marketing and media firms surrounding people with content that speaks so much to their own particular interests that those people learn little—and care little—about parts of society that do not relate directly to those interests.

Critics, including this book's author, point out that the ultimate aim of 21st-century marketing is to reach consumers with specific messages about how products and services tie in to their personal lifestyles. Target-minded media help advertisers and PR practitioners do this by building what we might call "primary media communities." These are not real-life communities where people live. Rather, they are ideas of connection with certain types of people that are formed when viewers or readers feel that a magazine, radio station, or other medium harmonizes with their personal beliefs and helps them understand their position in the larger world.

Some media are going a step beyond trying to attract certain types of people. They make an active effort to exclude people who do not fit the desired profile. This makes the community more "pure" and thereby more efficient for advertisers. **Tailoring** is the capacity to aim media content and ads at particular individuals. With just a little effort (habit, actually), people can listen to radio stations, read magazines, watch cable programs, surf the web, and participate in loyalty programs that parade their self-images and clusters of concerns. With seemingly no effort at all, they receive offers from marketers that complement their lifestyles. And with just a bit of cash, they can pay for technologies that further tailor information to their interests—through highly personalized news delivery, for example.

Nurse Jackie, a Showtime original series based around a drug-addicted and troubled nurse, targeted an audience that is more accepting of, relates to, or is interested in this type of character—specifically 25- to 54-year-olds. Showtime presented new episodes from 2009 through 2015.

tailoring
the capacity to aim media content and ads at particular individuals

THINKING ABOUT MEDIA LITERACY

Think about the ethical issues with PR. Do you believe a PR firm has more responsibility to the public to be completely honest about a client, or do they have more responsibility to construct a favorable story about a client (which might not reveal everything)?

Customized audiovisual materials are still pretty expensive, so PR and advertising practitioners mostly reserve them for upscale audiences. The high cost of introducing interactive television that can customize programming for large populations has caused the process to take longer than some media firms would like. But the competition to develop personalizable interactive technologies has not faded. The momentum toward creating targeted spaces for increasingly narrow niches of consumers is both national and global.

All signs point to a 21st century in which media firms can efficiently attract all sorts of marketers by offering three things. One is **selectability**—the ability to reach an individual with entertainment, news, information, and advertising based on knowledge of the individual's background, interests, and habits. The second is **accountability to advertisers**—the ability to trace an individual's response to a particular ad. The third is **interactivity**—the ability to cultivate a rapport with, as well as the loyalty of, individual consumers. Some companies, to be sure, want to get their brands out to the broad population as quickly as possible and will continue to find mass market media useful. They will support the presence of billboards, supermarket signs, and the few TV broadcasts that still draw mass audiences, such as the Super Bowl, the World Series, and the Miss America Pageant. This kind of programming helps create immediate national awareness for a new car model, athletic shoe, or computer.

But even this material will be targeted in the future. For example, Warner Bros. Television might try to reach as many people as possible to offset the high production costs of a TV movie about nuclear disaster that involves major battle scenes with impressive computer-generated special effects. Yet it might achieve this by PR activities aimed at targeting people's personal TV navigators with tailored plot synopses—one for people who are interested in science and a different one for people who like the lead actor. At present, it is cheaper to customize news and information programs than to customize top-of-the-line entertainment. For instance, NBC might tailor its election coverage to viewers with different interests. Consumers who care about foreign affairs, agricultural topics, or environmental issues might be able to choose the network feed that features detailed coverage of election results in their special-interest area.

Over and over, some media critics predict, different versions of news will present different social distinctions to different people. And even when the content is the same (as in the nuclear disaster movie), producers will aim different PR and ad campaigns to different types of people or different media communities, thus encouraging the perception that the viewing experience in America is an enormously splintered one. The net result will be to push separation over collectivity.

These critics argue that it will take time, possibly decades, for the full effects of the emerging media world to take shape. Even when the new media environment does crystallize, consumers will still seek media that are not specifically aimed at them. Increasingly, though, the easiest path will be to go with the customized flow of media and marketing paraphernalia. For you and me—individual readers and viewers—this segmentation and targeting portends terrific things. If we can afford to pay, or if we're important to PR or advertising sponsors who will pick up the tab, we will be able to receive all the news, information, and entertainment we like. Who would not welcome media and sponsors that offer to surround us with exactly what we want when we want it?

A critical view of the situation would argue that although this may benefit us as individuals, it could potentially have a harmful effect on society. Customized media driven by target-oriented advertising and PR allow—even encourage—individuals to live in their own personally constructed worlds, separate from people and issues that they don't care about and don't want to be bothered with. This kind of segmentation of the population diminishes the chance that individuals who identify with certain

selectability
ability to reach an individual with entertainment, news, information, and advertising based on knowledge of the individual's background, interests, and habits

accountability to advertisers
the ability to trace an individual's response to a particular ad

interactivity
the ability to cultivate a rapport with, as well as the loyalty of, individual consumers

groups will even have an opportunity to learn about others. In a society in which immigration is increasing ethnic variation and tensions, the goal should not be to use the media to disconnect people. Rather, the media should encourage people to do the hard work necessary to become aware of other cultures' interests; to enjoy various backgrounds collectively; and to seek out media interactions to celebrate, argue, and learn with a wide spectrum of groups in the society.

The problem, say media critics, is that the advertising and PR industries are working with media firms to go in the opposite direction. Their goal is to ease people into media environments that comfortably mirror their own interests so that they can be persuaded more easily. Media practitioners see nothing wrong with this approach. Media analyst Sut Jhally is among those who disagree. He argues that the tendency of the persuasion industries to play to people's self-interests rather than the larger society's interests is quite predictable. "The market," he says, "appeals to the worst in us . . . and discourages what is best in us." As you move through the media world, it's useful to keep both perspectives in mind.[13]

CHAPTER REVIEW

Visit the Companion Website at www.routledge.com/cw/turow for additional study tools and resources.

Key Terms

You can find the definitions to these key terms in the marginal glossary throughout this chapter. Test your knowledge of these terms with interactive flash cards on the *Media Today* Companion Website.

account executive
accountability to advertisers
ad campaign
ad exchange
advertising
advertising agencies
agency holding companies
agency networks
barter
the Big Four
branded entertainment
branding
business-to-business
    agencies
click-through ad
client conflicts
commercialism
consumer agencies
cost per thousand (CPM)
creative persuasion
creatives or creative personnel

database marketing
databases
direct-to-consumer (DTC)
direct-marketing agencies
earned media
event marketing
event sponsorship
general ad agency
hidden curriculum
in-store media
information subsidies
influencers
integrated marketing
    communications (IMC) or
    marketing communications
interactivity
internet agency
location-based advertising
market research
market segmentation
media plan

media planners
media planning and buying
media relations
native advertising
owned media
paid media
press release
product integration
programmatic advertising
psychographic data
publicity
publicity outlet
public relations
real-time bidding auctions
relationship marketing
sales pitch
selectability
specialty ad agency
tailoring
traditional ad agency

Questions for Discussion and Critical Thinking

1. Imagine an advertising campaign for a brand of athletic shoes. How might the company present different attributes of their product depending on different target audiences. Think of three different types of consumers of athletic shoes. What would effective persuasive arguments the advertising creative might employ to target each?

2. Do you think it is useful to distinguish, as this chapter does, between publicity and public relations? Why or why not?

3. Increasingly complex algorithms are used to target specific advertising or strategic messaging to people based on what they search for, where they buy products, and other online behaviors. What are your feelings about this kind of "data mining" for the purposes of targeting you as a consumer? What impacts might this have for a company's advertising strategies? What public relations scenarios might arise that would have to be addressed by the company?

4. The PR office for a movie studio will generate "information subsidies" about an upcoming release. What kinds of information subsidies might they generate, and how will different elements that may influence the public's perception of the movie (for example, newspapers, network TV morning shows, and websites) use that information? Why is the information called "subsidies" to these organizations?

Activity

In early 2018, Facebook became embroiled in major public anger due to the use of data of users and their friends by a firm called Cambridge Analytica. The company had received an app called "This Is Your Digital Life" from a data scientist at Cambridge University (no relation to the company) that ran on Facebook. People who used the app filled out a survey and agreed to let Cambridge Analytica see their Facebook profile. Unknown to them, though, Facebook's technology allowed the app to collect the personal information of all the people they were connected to on Facebook. Cambridge Analytica in this way was able collect data on millions of people.

The UK paper *The Observer*, its related news outlet theguardian.com, and *The New York Times* broke the story simultaneously. Cambridge Analytica took much anger over its activities, and it ultimately went out of business. Facebook, a much larger organization with billions of users, also became a target of ire because it allowed an app to so easily take information about so many of its users without their permission.

Drawing on your school library's resources, identify various "stakeholders" that Facebook had to address after the initial news reports of what Cambridge Analytica did came out. How did these stakeholders react, and what did Facebook do in response? What, if anything, did Facebook do proactively to try to ease stakehoders' concerns about its future ability to treat its visitors ethically? How would use judge "success" in these activities from Facebook's standpoint? To what extent do you think Facebook did or did not succeed?

Controls on Media Content

Government Regulation, Self-Regulation, and Ethics

5

CHAPTER OBJECTIVES

1   Explain the reasons for and the theories underlying media regulation.

2   Identify and describe the different types of media regulation.

3   Analyze the struggles between citizens and regulatory agencies in the search for information.

4   Discuss the ways in which media organizations self-regulate.

5   Identify and evaluate ethical dilemmas facing media practitioners today.

6   Harness your media literacy skills to comprehend how media regulation affects you as a customer and citizen.

"Trump Gambles and Loses on AT&T" read a *New York Times* editorial on June 12, 2018.[1] The headline summed up a contention by the newspaper that the president had tried—and ultimately failed—to halt a huge media merger for political reasons. In 2016 AT&T indicated its desire to purchase Time Warner for $85.4 billion, and Time Warner agreed. Then-candidate Trump said that his administration would try to stop it. When Trump became president, the Justice Department sued AT&T to do just that. AT&T then took the department to court, and now (in June 2018) a judge had ruled against the department and said the merger could go ahead.

Certainly, there were many people other than Donald Trump who expressed reasons to oppose the merger. They pointed out that AT&T was the United States' leading pay-TV provider (Comcast was second), with 25 million subscribers to its cable and DirectTV satellite operations. It was also the nation's number-two wireless carrier, next to Verizon. In Time Warner it would be hooking up with a firm that controlled some of the most popular and high-profile television networks (HBO, TBS, CNN) and content-creation organizations with popular creations ranging from *Game of Thrones* to Harry Potter movies to *Superman* comics and other output. Critics of the deal worried that AT&T would raise the price other cable and satellite firms would have to pay for this programming so that customers would find it attractive to turn to AT&T's own mobile phone, cable, and satellite services in search of low prices. Such tactics, critics contended, amounted to competition that would hurt the public.

The *Times*' editorial board was among the critics. The board didn't believe the merger should have been banned outright. "In antitrust lingo," the board wrote, "this deal represents a classic example of vertical integration: The companies have a 'vertical' relationship where one company . . . supplies the other"—that is, where Time Warner's content-creation firms supply AT&T's cable operations and DirectTV. "However," the editorial continued, although one company supplies the other, "the two companies main businesses do not actually compete with each other and so a merger would not reduce the number of competitors in any particular market." If they did compete, the merger would be termed "horizontal integration," a type of acquisition that policymakers traditionally have considered more damaging to the public

> "What progress we are making. In the Middle Ages they would have burned me. Now they are content with burning my books."

SIGMUND FREUD (1856–1939), JEWISH AUSTRIAN PSYCHIATRIST, 1933

interests than vertical integration. Nevertheless, the *Times*' board worried that AT&T would use its Time Warner assets to create unfair competition and raise prices for many of its competitors' customers. The editorial wished the judge had set prohibitions against that sort of activity when approving the merger, much as he had done when approving a similar merger between Comcast and NBC-Universal in 2011—but he didn't.

Instead, the editorial stated, the judge focused angrily on what seemed to be a clear attempt by President Trump to halt the AT&T–Time Warner merger, not because it was against the public interest, but because President Trump was angry at Time Warner's news network for reporting negatively on him. Traditionally, the US Justice Department evaluates mergers on criteria of vertical integration and horizontal integration. The attorneys representing the department could have asked the judge to force the parties to accept various guidelines for competition, including on price, if they wanted the merger to go through. In this case, the *Times* (and, it seems, the judge) believed talk by the president and his advisors pointed to the Justice Department trying to scuttle the deal completely in order to please the president. As a result, the department's lawyers never raised any arguments that would encourage guidelines for competition if the judge allowed the deal to go through.

The *Times*' editorial highlighted the important role government regulation and the courts play in setting up the playing field in which media firms big and small operate. The editorial also underscored the importance of making decisions based on well-understood rules, not "the whims of partisans," such as those the *Times* alleged of the president and his loyalists. The aim of this chapter is to explain the most important of government rules that shape activities so you can understand the crucial role the government plays setting the boundaries for what goes on in US media industries.

Why Do Media Firms Care About What Government Does?

When we talk about the regulation of mass media, we mean the laws and guidelines that influence the way media companies produce, distribute, or exhibit materials for audiences. Government regulation of mass media covers a wide range of territory. It can mean regulation by federal, state, county, or city government. And, as we saw earlier, sometimes the courts get involved in deciding whether one or another regulation is legally acceptable.

"Wait!" you may hear yourself saying to this page, "I remember from high school history classes that the US Constitution says we should have freedom of the press. That means that there should be no government restrictions on the work of content creators. How, then, can you say that government regulation has such an effect on media firms?" This is a good and important question. A short answer is that the value of a free press has turned out to be less straightforward than it may seem. Sometimes the constitutional value of free press conflicts with another constitutional value. For example, the Constitution guarantees an author's ownership of a creative work for a period of time. If you have created a video or poem, does your ownership of the work mean that you have the right to stop a website from publishing it without your permission? Or does the website have a free-press right to do so? Sometimes freedom of the press conflicts with an important social value. If a person is using his app or website to spread ugly, untrue, and potentially hurtful rumors about you, do you have the right to halt that even though the person has freedom of the press? At other times, conflicting parties argue that freedom of the press is on their side. Say your firm runs an internet news site and makes money through advertising on the site. Should a company that provides households in Chicago with internet service be allowed to stop people from reaching your firm's website unless the firm pays the internet service provider money?

These are just three kinds of situations where courts or elected officials (or both) have had to make decisions about how to interpret freedom of the press for one party when it may interfere with the press freedom, or other freedoms, of another party. Attorneys who specialize in media law—perhaps you might be interested in becoming one—spend their entire professional lives trying to understand how to argue for clients in situations where the free-press rights of one group clash with the free-press rights or other social rights of other groups. Large media companies and organizations representing media industries also hire lobbyists to argue that laws they favor are best for society as well as for their industry and don't contradict the Constitution.

The aim of this chapter is to give you a broad sense of the way three key arguments—over how to define freedom of the press, what a good media system means, and how much government should guide it—have shaped media laws in the United States. As we've already suggested, the story must start with the US Constitution, which is the basis for the authority of this country's government and courts. The legal foundation for government's regulation of the press is the First Amendment to the Constitution, which is one of a group of ten amendments collectively known as the Bill of Rights. Let's look at what it says and what it means.

The First Amendment

The First Amendment to the Constitution reads,

> Congress shall make no law respecting an establishment of religion, or pro-hibiting the free exercise thereof; or abridging the freedom of speech, or of the press; or the right of the people peaceably to assemble, and to petition the Government for a redress of grievances.

The First Amendment's statement that "Congress shall make no law . . . abridging the freedom of speech, or of the press" seems to rule out any type of government interference in journalistic organizations ("the press") and even in media that present content other than news. The country's founders were determined that in the new nation no one would need the government's permission to communicate ideas to a wide public.

As we have noted, the reality of lawmaking has been quite different, however. Over the decades, the federal government has been involved in regulating media firms, which raises continuing debate about the precise meaning of the First Amendment. The US Supreme Court has repeatedly sorted out fights between government agencies that seek to curtail mass media content and companies interested in protecting and extending it. Consider these questions:

What Does the First Amendment Mean by "No Law," and Where Does It Apply?
Since the time the First Amendment was passed, lawmakers and lawyers have under-stood that its phrase "make no law" means that the federal branches of government cannot make laws abridging press freedoms. But here's a question: Does the First Amendment apply to the states as well? The issue is an important one. Imagine you are the publisher of a newspaper that prints controversial views about politicians throughout the United States. You would like to be sure that the Constitution pro-tects your work, no matter which politicians object to it. If the legislature of the state in which you work has the right to stop you from publishing your views, your news-paper would likely go out of business.

In 1925 this question was resolved by the Supreme Court in the case of *Gitlow v. New York*. Socialist agitator Benjamin Gitlow published a circular called the *Left Wing Manifesto*, calling for an uprising to overthrow the government. This upset local authorities, and Gitlow was convicted of "criminal anarchy," a wrongdoing in New York State. Gitlow then appealed his case to the US Supreme Court. His lawyers argued that the Constitution (and therefore the First Amendment) should override any state law that contradicts it. The US Supreme Court agreed with Gitlow and his lawyers, ruling that the First Amendment's phrase "Congress shall make no law" should be interpreted as "government and its agencies shall make no law," regardless of the location or level of government.

What Does the First Amendment Mean by "the Press"? When the founders wrote that "Congress shall make no law . . . abridging the freedom of speech, or of the press," how did they define the term "press"? The founders could not have possibly imagined the complex world of media messages and channels in which we currently live. So which segments of the media are included under the First Amendment's definition of the press?

If only newspaper companies fell under the protection of the First Amendment, then book publishers, magazine firms, television stations, movie companies, web-sites, and advertising firms would be subject to government interference. This, in

GLOBAL MEDIA TODAY & CULTURE

PUBLIC BROADCASTING: PBS VS. BBC

There are ongoing debates on the role of public broadcasting in the United States, discussing to what extent it should be funded by taxpayers or even still exist in the 21st century. What do you think?

An international comparison could contribute to these conversations. In the United States the Public Broadcasting Service (PBS) and National Public Radio (NPR) were created as a result of the Public Broadcasting Act of 1967. The rationale was to facilitate the development of high-quality programming that also had an educational intent, without the constraints of commercial economic forces. Previously, the only major players in broadcasting (radio and TV) were private networks funded by advertising, which also after the development of public broadcasting have retained their primacy in the competitive landscape.

On the other side of the Atlantic, however, we can historically observe the opposite evolution in the UK media landscape. The British Broadcasting Corporation (BBC) was created in the 1920s as a public service broadcaster, as a radio network first and television later, funded by license fees paid by British consumers. The country opened up to commercial broadcasting only in the 1950s following the deregulation of the Television Act of 1954, while public broadcasting has remained central in the local media landscape. The BBC plays an essential role in the UK media landscape, offering independent news coverage on domestic and international events and entertainment programs for all ages on different media platforms, including the internet.

You might want to do some reading—and viewing—to compare PBS and the BBC. As a point of reference, it is worth noting that the structure of most of the media landscapes in the world is similar to the UK, comprising a leading public television broadcaster and a variety of privately owned, profit-oriented operators.

turn, might place a chill on the creation of entertainment and fiction, given that companies might fear getting in trouble with federal and state governments. But more than 150 years after the writing of the Constitution, the Supreme Court agreed with the notion that entertainment and nonprint media make up "the press" along with print news media. It may seem difficult to understand today, but as late as 1919, the court ruled that films were not a protected form of expression because they were entertainment, not the kind of serious information that would make up "the press."

In 1952 the Supreme Court overturned this view. This decision was part of a trend that began around the middle of the 20th century. The court's justices adopted an increasingly broad view of "the press" that included factually truthful advertising and many forms of entertainment in film, television, and radio, as well as print media. The justices also agreed that when media firms circulate incorrect facts about individuals or organizations that are created by mistake or even sloppiness (though not by a clear desire to harm those described), the errors are protected under the First Amendment. That protection, the court emphasized in 1967, applies to errors in entertainment as well as in news. In explaining, Justice William Brennan quoted

Walt Whitman's *Leaves of Grass* was written in the morally and socially conservative Victorian era. This work celebrating love, sensuality, and sexuality was met with great opposition—including a call from a Boston district attorney to the publisher of the work to remove certain poems from the collection and to stop distribution of the work. The book was banned by many of the larger, more popular book distributors. Nevertheless, the first printing sold out quickly, and Whitman went on to find a new publisher that wouldn't cave into such demands.

a previous court ruling that both forms of content "must be protected if the freedoms of expression are to have the 'breathing space' that they 'need . . . to survive.'"[2]

What Does the First Amendment Mean by "Abridging"? The term "abridge" means "to cut short" or "to curtail." In fact, the Supreme Court has often approved government restrictions on speech or the press that place limits on the time, place, and manner of an expression. Such restrictions are legal as long as those limits

- are applicable to everyone,
- are without political bias,
- serve a significant governmental interest, and
- leave ample alternative ways for the communication to take place.

The issue of restriction has come up a lot in the area of outdoor advertising. Over the decades, communities upset about both the clutter that billboards bring and the content of some of them—sexual images and unwholesome products—have tried to create laws regulating them. Based on the preceding points, courts have ruled that any laws restricting outdoor advertising have to apply to all businesses and cannot reflect any prejudice toward any particular lawful business. Following this logic, federal courts have ruled that liquor ads cannot be singled out for a ban on highways on the presumption that teen drivers would be influenced by them. The reasoning is that free speech should be protected as long as there are other ways to warn teenagers about the dangers of drinking and driving.

Anti-cigarette activists argue that outdoor cigarette advertising ought to be an exception to this approach. At this point, cigarette companies have stopped using large billboards as part of a "voluntary" agreement with the federal government to limit commercial messages for the product that, although it harms people, can still be bought legally.

More Allowable Government Control Over Media Content

So far we have seen that the US Supreme Court has tackled questions about whether and how much the First Amendment applies to entertainment, news, and advertising. We have also seen that the court has laid out broad rules that the government must follow if it wants to abridge certain kinds of speech. As it turns out, the Supreme Court has gone even further than those broad rules of abridgment. It has ruled over the decades that the government has a right to abridge media "speech" more on certain topics and in certain situations than others.

We can divide these types of governmental media regulation into three categories:

- Regulation of content before it is distributed
- Regulation of content after it has been distributed
- Economic regulation

Let's look at each of these three types separately.

Regulating Content Before Distribution

When the government restricts speech before it is made or distributed, it is engaging in **prior restraint**. Since the 1930s, the US Supreme Court has consistently ruled that the practice of regulating or restricting speech before it is made violates both the spirit and the letter of the First Amendment. At the same time, however, the court has held that in some rare and specific circumstances, prior restraint is in the interest of the public good. Table 5.1 sketches four types of content situations that the court says may in some circumstances warrant restriction in advance: education, national security, clear and present danger to public safety, and commercial speech. Three other such areas are obscenity, military operations, and copyright. Let's take a look at these in some detail.

prior restraint
government restriction of speech before it is made

Obscenity When was the last time you saw something you considered truly **obscene**? Well, if you did see obscene material, you should know that the Supreme Court has ruled that such matter is not protected by the First Amendment. The government can exercise prior restraint and not allow the material to be distributed. This sounds like a major power of the government that it could exercise every day, even against some HBO pay-cable programs (such as *Real Sex*) that you, your friends, or your parents may not consider obscene. But over the decades the Supreme Court has set the bar for determining obscenity so high that, in practice, this sort of prior restraint rarely takes place today.

obscene
offensive to accepted standards of decency or modesty

The term "obscene" means offensive to accepted standards of decency or modesty. One difficulty in determining whether something is obscene, of course, is that different people may have different standards of acceptability. Books such as

Table 5.1 Additional Examples of Types of Content for Which the Supreme Court Allows Prior Restraint

Content category	Definition	Example	Note
Education	The right of primary and secondary school administrators to dictate school-newspaper policy and refuse to allow articles to appear	A school principal's objection to publishing a story about a pregnant student	The Supreme Court held that when the school newspaper is part of the school's educational mission, it is not entitled to First Amendment protections "even though the government could not censor similar speech outside the school."
National security	Information that, if revealed, would pose a clear and present danger to the ability of the United States to defend itself against enemies	Information on government plans during wartime	The Supreme Court has emphasized that this prior restraint should be used rarely: "Paramount among the responsibilities of a free press is the duty to prevent any part of the government from deceiving the people and sending them off to distant lands to die."
Clear and present danger to public safety	A situation in which media content itself poses a threat to the physical welfare of citizens	A Ku Klux Klan video that urges members to commit physical violence against African Americans at a particular date, place, and time	The Supreme Court has emphasized that this prior restraint should be used rarely: when the danger is close in time, likely, and lawless in approach.
Commercial speech	Messages designed to sell products or services	A soup company's television commercial that uses marbles at the bottom of a soup bowl to make it look as if it contains big pieces of meat and vegetables	Many public advocacy groups argue that the government should exercise prior restraint on commercials and product placements of high-calorie foods and drinks in TV programs with large audiences of children.

D. H. Lawrence's *Lady Chatterley's Lover* and Walt Whitman's *Leaves of Grass* may not be acceptable to some in society but may be considered genuine works of art by others. (Did your high school assign J. D. Salinger's *Catcher in the Rye*? Some school systems classify it as obscene, whereas others assign it as a classic.) Of course, the same holds with respect to images on television and websites.

Further complicating these disagreements about obscenity is the dilemma that the public's collective standards of what is obscene and what is not obscene change and shift almost constantly. Communities that deemed a book or film obscene in the 1970s might not agree with that assessment today. In 1957 the US Supreme Court ruled that explicit depictions of sex need not be obscene. It noted that "sex, a great and mysterious motive force in human life, has indisputably been a subject of absorbing interest to mankind through the ages; it is one of the vital problems of human interest and public concern." So when is explicit sex obscene to the court? "Obscene material," it wrote, "is material which deals with sex in a manner appealing to prurient interests."[3]

All right, does that make it clear when something is obscene? Well, not really. You see, the court made a number of additional specifications about the definition of obscenity that make giving something that label quite difficult. For example, the work has to portray in a *clearly offensive manner*—in pictures or writing—certain sexual conduct specifically described as unallowable by state law. The court also said that the media product—such as a television episode or entire film—must be considered in its entirety, not just an excerpt. So, for example, the company circulating the material in question might argue that a particular sex scene may indeed be quite explicit but that it is necessary to explain the character's personality as it evolves through the movie. And if that doesn't make labeling something as obscene difficult enough, the court added that the standard of "appealing to prurient interests" must be community based. It stipulates that an *average person*, applying current standards of the community, would have to find that the work as an entirety reflects an obsessive interest in sex. Finally, it states that a *reasonable person* has to agree that the work lacks serious literary, artistic, scientific, or political usefulness.

These criteria make it quite difficult for the government to make the case for prior restraint on the basis of obscenity, even if content is pornographic—that is, sexually explicit. There are, it is important to note, other ways to control certain kinds of sexual content, even if they do not meet these tests of obscenity. Materials can still be restricted under import regulations, postal regulations, zoning ordinances, and other laws. For example, child abuse laws have been used to bar materials that feature nude children.

Military Operations The regulation and control of news during times of war have taken place since the Civil War. At times, media personnel have been required to submit their scripts and stories for governmental review before distribution.

During World War I, Congress passed the Espionage Act (1917) and the Sedition Act (1918), which together formalized wartime censorship of the press by preventing "disloyal" publications from being mailed via the US Postal Service. During World War II, the Espionage Act was again put into effect—allowing the government to control broadcasting from 1941 until 1945. During this time, the Office of Censorship had the power to censor international communication at its "absolute discretion." With a staff of more than 10,000 censors, the office routinely examined mail, cables, newspapers, magazines, films, and radio broadcasts. Its operations constituted the most extensive government censorship of the media in US history and one of the most vivid examples of the use of executive emergency powers.

In cases in which the United States is involved in a military operation but has not officially declared war, the government may seek to control access to information, rather than officially censoring that content. When US troops were sent to the Caribbean island of Grenada in 1983, the Pentagon took control of all transportation to and from the island and refused to transport reporters to the island to cover the conflict. Journalists protested this military news "blackout." In 1989, when US troops were sent to Panama, the Pentagon instituted a system of **pool reporters**—selected members of the media who get access to a news event and share facts, stories, images, and firsthand knowledge of that event with others. Journalists were skeptical about the system, and as it turned out, their skepticism was well founded. Reporters in the press pool were held in a briefing room at a military post and were given briefings that consisted of little more than history lessons on the relationship between the United States and Panama. As a consequence, journalists soured on the idea of a specially chosen pool of reporters, and the practice faded.

pool reporters
selected members of the media who are present at a news event and share facts, stories, images, and firsthand knowledge of that event with others

THINKING ABOUT MEDIA LITERACY

Consider the four examples of when "prior restraint" has been upheld by the Supreme Court. Do you agree with the court's arguments? What might be an argument for denying prior restraint?

In the Iraq War that began in 2004, as well as in the parallel, continuing Afghanistan conflict, the military allowed **embeds**—reporters who received permission to travel with a military unit across the battlefield. The Defense Department required all embeds to agree not to break military information embargos, not to report on ongoing missions without clearance, and not to reveal deployment levels below large numbers such as troop corps and carrier battle groups. Nevertheless, some news outlets such as CNN and the United Kingdom's ITN did reveal certain information about the fighting that the military would have liked to keep secret, and they were periodically threatened with losing the right to have embeds. Despite the restrictions, many of the embeds in Iraq were able to report on the battlefield in great detail; one book calls the initial US invasion of Iraq "the most covered war in history."[4] According to one reporter who studied the embed approach, journalists who were embedded in Iraq "experienced a freedom to do their jobs that journalists had not had since the Vietnam War."[5]

embeds
reporters who receive permission from the military to travel with a military unit across the battlefield

Critics pointed out that a disadvantage of the embed approach was the tendency for such journalists to be highly sympathetic to the troops with whom they lived and on whom they depended for survival. These critics argued that self-censorship was sometimes the result. To address these criticisms, the military allowed other journalists to work as unilaterals—to travel through the war zone by themselves.

Copyright When we speak about **copyright**, we mean the legal protection of a creator's right to a work. According to the US Constitution, the purpose of copyright is "to promote the progress of science and the useful arts." The framers of the Constitution believed that only if people could profit from their work would they want to create materials that could ultimately benefit the nation as a whole. At the same time, the

copyright
the legal protection of a creator's right to a work

framers wanted lawmakers to strike a balance between the rights of authors to gain personally from their work and the right of the society to draw on the information.

The hesitancy of government agencies to stop the press from circulating content does not apply to copyright violations, for two reasons. The first is that authors ought to be able to control how their work—their intellectual property—is used. The second is that authors should be paid fairly for the use of their work.

Copyright Act of 1976
a law that recognizes the rights of an individual creator (in any medium) from the time he or she has created a work and that protects a creative work for the lifetime of that author plus seventy years

The **Copyright Act of 1976** lays out the basic rules as they exist in the United States today. The law, as later modified (in 1978 and again in 1998), recognizes the rights of an individual creator (in any medium) from the time he or she has created a work and protects a creative work for the lifetime of its author plus seventy years. Copyright for a work of corporate authorship lasts 120 years after creation or 95 years after creation, whichever comes earlier.

As an example, let us say that Hector, an English student, writes a poem. From the moment Hector finishes the poem, he holds an automatic copyright on the poem for his lifetime plus seventy years. He may, if he decides, send the poem to the US Copyright Office to register it for a small fee. Even if he does not do this, however, he is protected as long as he can prove that he wrote the poem before anyone else did. In order to prove when a work was created, some people mail a copy of the work to themselves and do not open it. The cancellation by the post office serves as proof of the date the material was sent. Let's say that Hector does this with his poem.

Hector is proud of his poem, and he also sends it to his friend Paloma, a former classmate in a summer poetry workshop. Now let's say that Paloma is envious of Hector's poem. She submits the poem to an online literary journal as her own, and the journal accepts it, pays her a small honorarium, and publishes it under her name, not Hector's. At this point, Paloma has violated US copyright law, and she can be prosecuted if Hector pursues the case, because she falsely passed herself off as the poem's true author.

But even if Paloma had not lied about the poem's authorship—let's say she submitted it to the journal under Hector's name to surprise him—Paloma (and the journal) probably would not be allowed to publish the poem, or even parts of it. Apart from not asking Hector's permission to publish the poem, Paloma has also violated the second proposition of copyright law—that authors must be paid fairly for the use of their works. Hector might in the future want to earn money from publishing the entire poem or parts of it. Sometimes, even a line of a poem or a song may be considered crucial to the work's value. As you can see, Paloma and the editors of the literary journal would have to think hard before they printed all or part of Hector's poem without getting his permission.

The copyright rules for musical compositions are similar to those for poems. If a magazine or website wants to publish selected words or music from a tune by Paul

THINKING ABOUT MEDIA LITERACY

In general, reporters are supposed to maintain a professional and personal distance from the people they write about. Embedded reporters, or embeds, travel with the troops during wartime, facing the same dangers as the troops and relying on the troops for their safety. As a result, some embeds develop strong ties to the troops they travel with. How might this situation influence a reporter when he or she is covering a story about a botched invasion or a soldier accidentally killed by friendly fire? Why might a reporter be reluctant to write stories that might portray troops in a negative light?

THINKING ABOUT MEDIA LITERACY

Think back to times when your teacher used photographs, clips, or short segments from films as material for class discussion. Keeping in mind the basic tenets of fair use, how does this exception benefit students and teachers in these classes? What challenges might teachers face if fair use did not allow them to use these materials? How is the concept of fair use important to you as a student as well as to your teachers?

McCartney, it needs the permission of his publisher. Copying parts of copyrighted musical material from someone else who has paid for it is also illegal. For decades, although businesses paid attention to this law, individuals ignored it. Friends would often lend albums to their friends so that they could copy them onto tapes or CDs. If recording industry executives minded, they generally didn't make noise about it. One reason might be that the taped copies were not as good in sound quality as the originals. As we will see when we discuss the recording industry in Chapter 10, their perspective has changed drastically. With the advent of perfect digital copies and the ability to share them over the internet, recording industry officials started hauling into court people who shared copyrighted music without the publisher's permission. We will review the pros and cons of this activity in Chapter 10, but here it is relevant to note what those officials have not emphasized: even copying part of a song without permission can make one a copyright violator. The same is true regarding movies, which, as we will see in Chapter 12, have also become a target for illegal uploading and sharing.

Fair Use

Although Congress has generally supported the right of copyright holders over the desire of individuals to copy their material, one exception involves writers, documentary producers, artists, or academics who want to quote from copyrighted material in order to carry out critical analyses. A poet, artist, novelist, or movie studio might charge an exorbitant rate for use of their works, and this might make it impossible for a scholar to share critical responses to it. To get around these problems, the law provides exceptions via **fair use regulations**. Generally, these regulations indicate that under certain conditions, a person or company may use small portions of a copyrighted work without asking permission. Nonprofit, educational purposes have more leeway than for-profit ventures.

Another important consideration in fair use decisions is the commercial damage that copying may cause to the copyright material. The less potential damage, the greater chance it will be considered fair use. A third criterion in favor of fair use is the transformative use of the copyrighted material. A use is considered **transformative** when it presents the work in a way that adds interpretations to it so that some people might see it in a new light. So, for example, an online magazine essay on World War II movies that links to short snippets of such flicks to show how views of the war have changed over time would likely be considered fair use. By these criteria, when scholarly critiques of popular culture quote from copyrighted materials to make their points, this is almost surely fair use.

Despite fair use regulations, college copy shops must contact publishers and get permission when they want to use entire articles in "course packs" for classes. You may not know it, but photocopying a work for your own pleasure is normally not

fair use regulations
provisions under which a person or company may use small portions of copyrighted work without asking permission

transformative
when use of copyrighted material presents the work in a way that adds interpretation to it so that some people might see it in a new light

Defining a work as a parody can be legally risky. Many observers saw the "Blue Harvest" episode of *Family Guy* as a parody of *Star Wars*, but the program's producers still sought the copyright holder's permission to make sure there would be no lawsuit.

parody
a work that imitates another work for laughs in a way that comments on the original work

defamation
a highly disreputable or false statement about a living person or an organization that causes injury to the reputation that a substantial group of people hold for that person or entity

fair use. One curious exception to fair use guidelines relates to the videotape recorder. The Supreme Court ruled in 1984 that viewers may record copyrighted TV shows for their personal, noncommercial use. A majority of the justices reasoned that taping was legal because people used the tapes for *time shifting*—that is, taping for later viewing what they would have watched anyway.

Today, time shifting is a way of life for many people who record TV shows and movies on digital video recorders (DVRs). Although the practice is legal, it has brought interesting headaches to media companies and their advertisers, given that people view the programs they copy but not the commercials that support them. Even greater headaches have come with the rise of digital technologies that make it simple for people to copy all sorts of copyrighted materials (including music and movies) in circumstances that do not fall within the fair use rules. Some copyright owners call these behaviors "piracy" and demand that audiences stop doing it. The activities raise important legal and ethical issues that we will explore in chapters to come.

Parodies

A **parody** is a work that imitates another work for laughs in a way that comments on the original work. A number of major court cases have ruled that when artists add new perspectives to copyrighted material, in the process critiquing it and encouraging people to see it in different ways, that is fully legal. Supreme Court Justice David Souter even suggested that parodies have stronger rights than other kinds of fair use material, in that the creator of a parody "may quite legitimately aim at destroying [the original] commercially as well as artistically." [6] The problem with parodies from a legal standpoint, though, is that the line between fair use and copyright violation is sometimes hard to figure out.

For one thing, not all comically altered versions of songs are fair use. Weird Al is a performer who has based his professional career on writing and recording parodies of popular songs. Pieces such as "Word Crimes" (which parodies "Blurred Lines" by Robin Thicke), "My Bologna" (a take on the Knack's "My Sharona"), "Eat It," "Like a Surgeon," and "Smells Like Nirvana" have given him long-term popularity with a huge number of fans around the globe, as well as ignited controversy over his lampooning lyrics. Yet Weird Al is actually pretty conservative regarding his parodic creations. His lawyers may have pointed out to him that although his lyrics are funny, they don't really criticize the originals; nor does his musical take on the originals vary much from them. Perhaps as a result, Weird Al notes that he always seeks permission from the artists and writers of the songs before he puts his spin on them. "The parodies are all in good fun and good taste," he says, "and most of the artists normally take it that way. I prefer to have them on my team and I like to sleep well at night." [7]

Regulating Content After Distribution

There are some types of content where courts have stated that authorities must wait until after distribution to press charges of illegal activity. The two biggies in this area are defamation and invasion of privacy.

Defamation An act of **defamation** is a highly disreputable or false statement about a living person or an organization that causes injury to the reputation that a substantial group of people hold for that person or entity. One hopes that will never happen to you, but can you imagine if it did? Let's say someone you know (and who doesn't like you) is a columnist for the local newspaper website. In the course of arguing that several people who lost their jobs during the recession deserved it, he describes a person who everyone in your community recognizes as you. He asserts that when you left a job two years ago, it wasn't because of the bad financial situation of the company (as you claimed), but because you stole money from one of the employees. The "real fact" about your job loss circulates, people bring it up in conversation, and as you decide to look for a new job, you worry it is inhibiting local employers from seriously considering you. What recourse do you have against the person and the newspaper that published that horrible stuff?

If, in a panic, you read up on the subject of defamation, you will find there are two forms: slander and libel. Traditionally, **slander** has been seen as spoken communication considered harmful to a person's reputation. **Libel** has traditionally been seen as written communication that is considered harmful to a person's reputation. In the 19th century the courts treated slander and libel differently. They considered written defamation the more serious offense. The reasoning was that libel lasted longer, was more widely circulated, and seemed to be more planned than slander (a spoken comment might be made in a flash of anger). The distinction between spoken and written defamation fell apart in the 20th century, with the rise of sound media. Now even spoken communication is circulated broadly and can be planned ahead of time (as, for example, through use of a script). As experts in media law have noted, it's no longer useful to distinguish between oral and written forms of communication. Table 5.2 contains "red flag" words and expressions that courts have generally considered **libel per se**—that is, libel on their face. But some words, expressions, and statements that seem on their face to be innocent and not injurious may be considered libel in their actual contexts; they are called **libel per quod**. For example, saying that Bradley is married to Marisol doesn't sound libelous, but if you know that Bradley is married to Nadia, being married to Marisol would make him a bigamist. And that statement is libelous.

It is also important to recognize that there are two categories of libel plaintiffs: public figures and private persons. A **public figure** may be an elected or appointed official (a politician) or someone who has stepped (willingly or unwillingly) into a public spotlight (e.g., movie stars and TV stars, famous athletes, or other persons who draw attention to themselves). A **private person** may be well known in the community, but he or she has no authority or responsibility for the conduct

slander
spoken communication that is considered harmful to a person's reputation

libel
written communication that is considered harmful to a person's reputation

libel per se
written communication that is considered obvious libel

libel per quod
words, expressions, and statements that, at face value, seem to be innocent and not injurious but that may be considered libelous in their actual context

public figure
a person who is an elected or appointed official (a politician) or someone who has stepped (willingly or unwillingly) into a public role

private person
an individual who may be well known in the community but who has no authority or responsibility for the conduct of government affairs and has not thrust himself or herself into the middle of an important public role

Table 5.2 Libel Per Se

Listed here are some "red flag" words and expressions that courts have generally considered libelous per se:

ignoramus	rascal	amoral
bankrupt	slacker	unprofessional
thief	sneaky	incompetent
cheat	unethical	illegitimate
traitor	unprincipled	hypocritical
drunk	corrupt	cheating
blockhead		

of governmental affairs and has not thrust himself or herself into the middle of an important public spotlight. The distinction between private and public individuals is important because it is much more difficult for a public figure to win the kind of libel claim we have fictitiously noted for you.

The difficulty for public figures claiming libel was made particularly clear in a 1964 Supreme Court decision regarding the case of *New York Times v. Sullivan*. The case profoundly altered libel law and set legal precedent that is still in effect today. On March 29, 1960, a full-page advertisement titled "Heed Their Rising Voices" was placed in the *New York Times* by the Committee to Defend Martin Luther King Jr. and the Struggle for Freedom in the South. The ad criticized police and public officials in several cities for tactics used to disrupt the civil rights movement and sought contributions toward bail for the Rev. Martin Luther King Jr. and other movement leaders. The accusations made in the advertisement were true for the most part, but the copy contained several rather minor factual errors. L. B. Sullivan, police commissioner in Montgomery, Alabama, sued the *New York Times* for libel, claiming that the ad had defamed him indirectly. He won $500,000 for damages in the state courts of Alabama, but the US Supreme Court overturned the damage award, reasoning that Alabama's libel laws violated the *New York Times*' First Amendment rights.

actual malice
reckless disregard for truth or knowledge of falsity

simple malice
hatred or ill will toward another person

In issuing its opinion, the Supreme Court said that the US Constitution protected false and defamatory statements made about *public officials* if the false statements were not published with actual malice. The court defined **actual malice** as reckless disregard for truth or knowledge of falsity. Note that actual malice considers a defendant's attitude toward truth, not the defendant's attitude toward the plaintiff. This differs from **simple malice**, which means hatred or ill will toward another person.

Because actual malice is difficult to prove, this ruling makes it difficult for a public official to win a libel suit. Additionally, the Supreme Court has broadened the actual malice protection to include public figures as well as public officials. The court's reasoning is simple: the actual malice test sets a high bar, but it does so to protect the First Amendment rights of the media. At the same time, it allows media outlets to pursue legitimate news stories without the constant fear of being sued by the subjects of news stories. In the end, concern for the First Amendment takes precedence over libel laws as they relate to media.

simple negligence
lack of reasonable care

Supreme Court decisions have also made it hard for a person who is neither a public figure nor a public official to sue a media firm for libel. The court has ruled that the First Amendment requires proof of **simple negligence**—lack of reasonable care—even when private persons sue the mass media for libel. So in our hypothetical situation, for you to win a libel suit against the columnist and the newspaper (which can pay you more money for your lost employment opportunities than can the columnist), you would have to prove that neither the columnist nor the paper's editors tried to check the column's "facts" with your employer and that the columnist didn't camouflage your identity well in the piece.

Invasion of Privacy Now that you have a feel for what it means to be defamed, how about getting a feel for the law you would turn to if a media firm invaded your privacy? Here's one way that could happen: Suppose a TV station is creating a news report about the growing use of heroin by middle-class residents of your city. To illustrate the idea that "average" citizens are increasingly involved in the problem, the producer films footage of people walking down the streets of the city; you happen to be one of them.

Turning on the local news one evening, you see a report that shows you quite clearly walking down the street just as the narrator notes that average residents are becoming hooked on heroin. You are angry at the TV station. What rights do you have?

Before answering directly, let's step back a bit to look at the larger topic. **Privacy**—the right to be protected from unwanted intrusions or disclosures—is a broad area of the law when it comes to media industries. Almost every state recognizes some right of privacy, either by statute or under common law. Most state laws attempt to strike a balance between the individual's right to privacy and the public interest in freedom of the press. However, these rights often clash.

The law regarding privacy is aimed at protecting what the law has come to call a person's "reasonable expectations of privacy." Only a person can claim a right of privacy; corporations, organizations, and other entities cannot. In view of what we previously said about public figures when it comes to defamation, you'd be right to expect that public figures have a limited claim to a right of privacy. Past and present government officials, political candidates, entertainers, and sports figures are generally considered to be public figures. According to the law, they have voluntarily exposed themselves to scrutiny and have waived their right of privacy, at least regarding media coverage of matters that might have an impact on their ability to perform their public duties.

Although private individuals can usually claim the right to be protected from unwarranted intrusions or disclosures, that right is not absolute. For example, if a person who is normally not considered a public figure is thrust into the spotlight because of her participation in a newsworthy event—say, a state lottery—her claims to a right of privacy may be limited. Table 5.3 presents brief definitions and examples of four areas of privacy that particularly affect how news organizations can go about

privacy
the right to be protected from unwanted intrusions or disclosures

Table 5.3 Invasion-of-Privacy Activities Media Firms Sometimes Carry Out When Creating Content

Activity	Definition	Example	Note
False light	Publishing material that falsely suggests an individual is involved in an illegal or unethical situation	To illustrate the idea that "average" citizens are increasingly involved in using heroin, a TV news producer tapes footage of people walking down the streets of the city. You happen to be one of them when the narrator states that average citizens are hooked on heroin.	Courts do not particularly favor false light cases because very often they conflict with freedom of speech. A plaintiff is required to prove "by clear and convincing evidence" that the defendant knew of the statement's falsity or acted in reckless disregard of its truth or falsity. In this case, the producer could argue viewers would understand the crowd scene was used to make a broad point and not to focus on any individual in it.
Appropriation	The unauthorized use of a person's name or likeness in an advertisement, poster, public relations promotion, or other commercial context	A magazine publishes photographs of living cancer survivors without their permission.	Judges have allowed the use of such images without permission for newsworthy purposes—that is, for stories tied to a timely event. But when the story stops being "news," the photo's subject can claim appropriation.

(continued)

Table 5.3 Invasion-of-Privacy Activities Media Firms Sometimes Carry Out When Creating Content *(Continued)*

Activity	Definition	Example	Note
Intrusion	When a person or organization intentionally invades a person's solitude, private area, or affairs	A reporter records a phone conversation with a subject in a state where permission is required to record.	The intrusion can be physical (e.g., sneaking into a person's office) or nonphysical (e.g., putting an electronic listening device outside the office but in a position to hear what is going on inside).
Public disclosure	Truthful information concerning the private life of a person that a media source reveals and that both would be highly offensive to a reasonable person and is not of legitimate public concern	A newspaper reveals private, sensational facts about a person's sexual activity and economic status.	First Amendment considerations have tended to grant media businesses the right to reveal information about individuals. How the information was obtained and its newsworthiness often determine liability in cases of public disclosure. If a journalistic organization obtains information unlawfully—whether or not the information is truthful—the organization may be held liable for invasion of privacy under the rules of public disclosure.

false light
invading a person's privacy by implying something untrue about him or her

appropriation
an invasion of privacy that takes place via the unauthorized use of a person's name or likeness in an advertisement, poster, public relations promotion, or other commercial context

intrusion
an invasion of privacy that takes place when a person or organization intentionally invades a person's solitude, private space, or affairs

public disclosure
an invasion of privacy that occurs when truthful information concerning the private life of a person (which would be highly offensive to a reasonable person and is not of legitimate public concern) is revealed by a media source

doing their work: **false light**, **appropriation**, **intrusion**, and **public disclosure**. If you've been following the logic of the legal thinking until now, you will not be surprised that courts have made it difficult to win suits against journalists in these four areas. Just as concerns for the First Amendment have given mass media firms a great deal of latitude when it comes to libel, First Amendment considerations have tended to grant media businesses the right to reveal information about individuals in one way or another. In short, you'd have a tough time winning a suit against the producer of that TV program about heroin use.

Databases and Privacy Concerns

Separate from these four areas is another world of media activities that some call an invasion of privacy but others simply call business. It involves media firms' collection of many types of data about individuals for marketing purposes. This area of data-privacy regulation is still emerging. It's a great example of how government decisions and indecisions about what media firms should be able to do can have major effects on the way media industries take shape. We'll be discussing different aspects of this struggle in forthcoming chapters. Here let's sketch out the major sides of the controversy.

On one side are media firms and marketers who want to take advantage of new digital technologies to reach specific audiences with their media products and advertising—and make money doing it. To do that, they have developed techniques to learn loads of information about the individuals who visit them or might visit them, either by name or anonymously. One popular way is by silently tracking what you do on your computer, on your tablet, or on your phone. For example, when you visit a website via a web browser on these devices, the site may place a hidden text file called a cookie in the browser. Every time you visit the site, the cookie identifies you, probably by an identification number, unless you gave the site your name. This action allows the company to record your movements through the site. Over time, the company that created the cookie develops a profile of your interests that it can bring together with other profiles to offer to advertisers. There is an active trade in cookies with particular characteristics, and technologies to target individuals with specific backgrounds—from age to income to lifestyles and much more—are developing quickly. (The same basic approach takes place in apps, though there, companies use special tags instead of cookies.) internet publishers can now offer to advertisers the ability to reach certain types of people—say, women searching for baby carriages—in real time, as they are entering their sites. Moreover, those publishers and advertisers may use computer techniques called **predictive analytics** to draw conclusions about the nature and value of particular shoppers. Predictive analytics is a term that encompasses a gamut of statistical techniques that look for patterns in facts about individuals and, based on those patterns, make calculations about how the individuals will act. So, for example, a supermarket chain might use such techniques to explore a family's grocery-buying activities and come up with a score that indicates whether the family's purchases will yield profits for the chain over the next two years. That score could then affect the discounts the chain sends the family.

Chapter 6 looks in greater detail at targeting activities in digital advertising. The point of bringing it up here is that whereas media and marketing practitioners laud its possibilities as the major future business model for the media system, organizations critical of these uses of databases want the government to limit them strictly, pointing to many possibilities for harm. Take health data: A company might use a person's online comments about diabetes or clicks on a diabetes site, for example, as a consideration against giving the person a job (because of the possible medical costs). A college may track tagged photos of applicants to decide whether their behavior in the photos befits the standards of the school. Finance companies may use data that evaluate how well your Facebook friends pay back their loans to decide whether to give you a loan and how much to charge. More broadly, a marketer may use online data it buys about you to decide whether and how to advertise toward you and whether to give you discounts (and, if so, how much).

Organizations that represent marketers typically don't respond to these criticisms directly, but they do argue that there is already sufficient protection for the public. They note that a law called Gramm-Leach-Bliley prevents banks and credit card companies from selling certain kinds of sensitive data about Americans. Similarly, a law called the Health Insurance Portability and Accountability Act (HIPAA) stops health providers from sharing your personal medical information with marketers. The Children's Online Privacy Protection Act (COPPA) requires online publishers and advertisers to get parents' permission if they want to collect information from children younger than 13 years of age. Moreover, they add, the Federal Trade Commission does suggest strongly that websites and apps have privacy policies that lay out what those sites do with their users' data.

The critics respond that there are plenty of ways to find out health, financial, and family information without breaking these laws. What you look at when you are on a medical website isn't protected by HIPAA, for example. The critics also point to research that people generally don't read privacy policies, and the ones who do don't understand them. The privacy advocates want clearer and stronger limitations on what information organizations and individuals can track and store about people without their explicit permission. This is a long-term, major media boxing match, with a diverse assortment of media companies and advocacy groups making various pleadings to various government entities at the state and federal levels.

predictive analytics
a term that encompasses a gamut of statistical techniques that look for patterns in facts about individuals and, based on those patterns, make calculations about how the individuals will act

In the absence of strong federal regulation, California may be setting an example for states to act. In 2018 its legislature passed a law that goes into effect in January 2020 that gives people the right to know what information companies are collecting about them, how they are using the data, and with whom they are sharing this information. It also gives consumers the right to tell companies to delete their information, as well as to not sell or share their data. Significantly, businesses must give individuals who indicate they don't want to be tracked the same quality of service as those who allow tracking. The law also makes it more difficult to share or sell data on children younger than 16—which is older than the federal age of 12. Some optimistic privacy activists believe that companies will end up compromising on a federal law similar to California's. The reason is that executives worry several states will follow California's example and create a patchwork of different privacy regulations that will be hard for firms to navigate. Also nudging federal lawmakers toward a stronger privacy regime, the optimists say, are major privacy lapses by Facebook that came to light in 2017 and 2018. They believe the incidents angered enough federal lawmakers to create a likelihood of more protective internet privacy laws in the next few years. We will see.

Economic Regulation

Media firms and advocacy organizations regularly keep an eye on government actions that define and limit media activities, such as defamation and privacy invasion. They know that laws and court decisions will affect how companies can make money and what audiences read, see, and hear. But regulations regarding content make up only one part of the influence government has over media industries. **Economic regulations** make up another important government leverage. These are rules the government sets about how firms are allowed to compete with one another—in essence, about what constitutes "fair play" when it comes to doing business in the media space. Economic regulation of media organizations greatly affects the ways in which those organizations finance, produce, distribute, and exhibit their products. The discussion about AT&T and Time Warner at the start of this chapter reflects two of the most common types of media economic regulation: antitrust laws and direct regulation by government agencies. Let's deal with these two topics systematically.

Antitrust Laws One way to expand the marketplace of ideas without directly making rules about content is to limit excessive market control by mass media corporations. Excessive market control is behavior by one company or a few companies that makes it nearly impossible for new companies to enter the marketplace and compete. For example, in the process we called horizontal integration, a production company might gain this kind of power by buying up competitors and making sure that exhibitors do not deal with any new competitors. Distributors and exhibitors might do the same thing: a few bookstore chains might swallow up their retail competition to the point that all publishers must deal primarily with them. When it comes to mass media, excessive control over the market might directly affect consumers or advertisers, or both.

Control of the market by one firm is called a **monopoly**. Control by a select few firms is called an **oligopoly**. Great concern over train and steel monopolies and oligopolies in the late 1800s led US legislators to begin to take special actions with respect to these activities in order to maintain competition. These laws came to be known broadly as **antitrust policies**, and in the following decades they were carried out in three ways:

economic regulations
rules set by the government about how firms are allowed to compete with one another

monopoly
control of the market by a single firm

oligopoly
control of the market by a select few firms

antitrust policies
policies put in place to maintain competition in the US economy, carried out through the passing of laws, through enforcement of the laws by the US Department of Justice and state attorneys general, and through federal court decisions that determine how far the government ought to go in encouraging competition and forcing companies to break themselves into a number of smaller companies

- Through the passage of laws
- Through enforcement of the laws by the US Department of Justice and by state attorneys general
- Through federal court decisions that (as we saw in the AT&T case) determine how far the government ought to go in encouraging competition and forcing companies to break themselves up into a number of smaller companies

Over the years, regulators and the courts have ruled that certain activities by firms involved in mass communication represent excessive market control. Typically, these activities have involved the use of vertical integration by a few firms to control an industry. We will note the most important of these cases when we deal with particular industries in the chapters to come.

Direct Regulation by Government Agencies The **Federal Trade Commission (FTC)** and the **Federal Communications Commission (FCC)** are the two most important federal agencies involved in regulating the mass media (see Figure 5.1).

Federal Trade Commission (FTC)
a federal agency whose mission is to ensure that the nation's markets function competitively; its coverage can include any mass media—print or electronic—as long as the issue involved is related to the smooth functioning of the marketplace and consumer protection in that sphere

Federal Communications Commission (FCC)
a federal agency specifically mandated by Congress to govern interstate and international communication by television, radio, wire, satellite, and cable

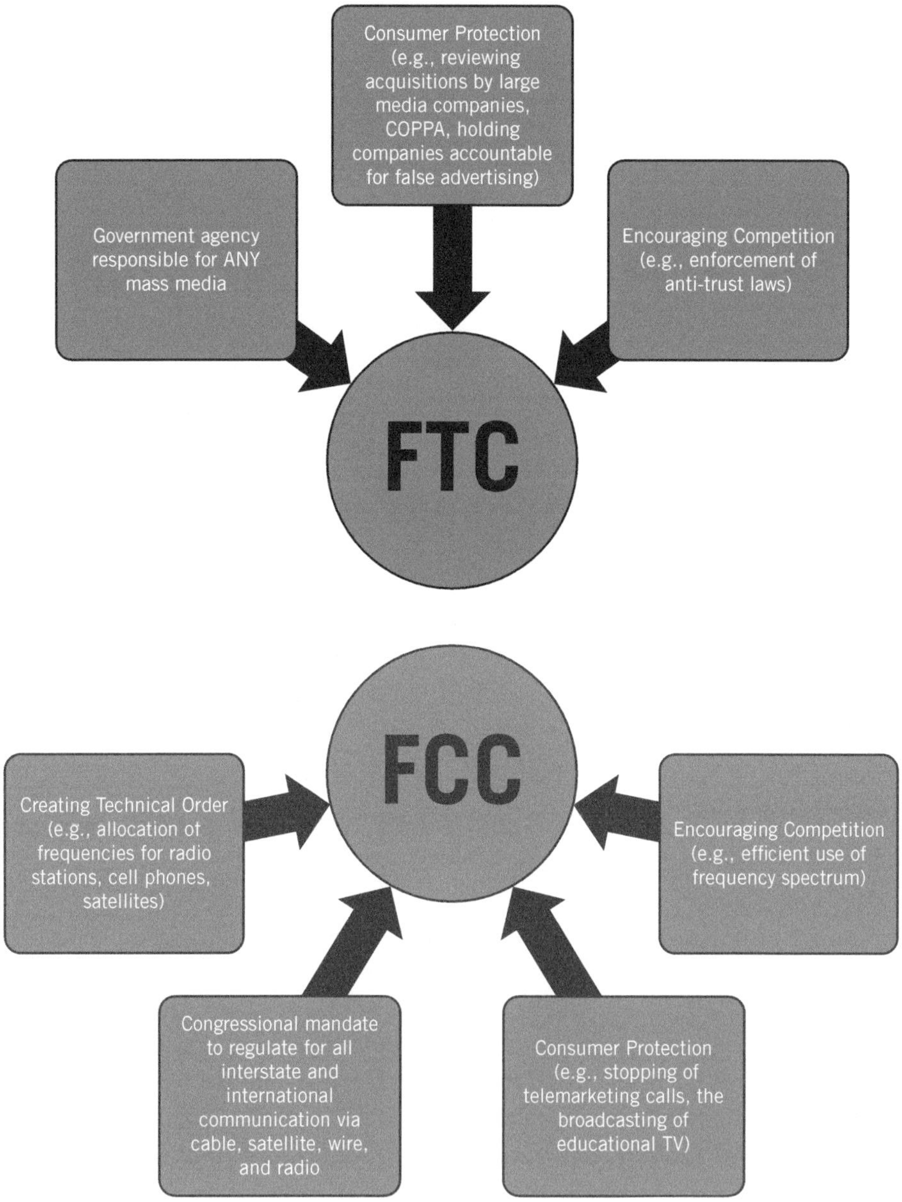

Figure 5.1
Comparison of the roles of the FCC and FTC in the regulation of media.

The first thing to remember when comparing the two agencies is that the FTC's coverage can include any of the mass media—print or electronic—as long as the issue involved is related to the smooth functioning of the marketplace and consumer protection in that sphere. By contrast, the FCC is specifically mandated by Congress to govern interstate and international communications by television, radio, wire, satellite, and cable.

The FTC describes its overall mission as carrying out three responsibilities that very much relate to media today: creating technical order, encouraging competition, and consumer protection. These three responsibilities can also be said to apply to the FCC in its domain. Let's briefly take a look at them.

Creating Technical Order

Many of the FCC's most important activities are aimed at simply creating technical order in an electronic environment that could become chaotic without some kind of regulation. It is through the FCC that radio stations get licenses that allow them to broadcast on specific wavelengths (the numbers we associate with the stations—e.g., 105.1 FM). The FCC is also in charge of allocating the frequency spectrum among various other technologies, including satellites and cellular phones. Although some of these technical activities have nothing to do with mass media, many of them do. Most major news organizations use satellites and cell phones for their work. Many consumers pay to get TV programming via satellite. Increasingly, too, consumers are getting news, information, and advertisements through their mobile phones. FCC decisions about how to allocate spectrum space help define which and how many companies can afford to get into this business in different parts of the country. That, in turn, affects the number of companies consumers have to choose from and how much they will have to pay.

Encouraging Competition

Encouraging competition, to the FCC, means promoting efficient use of the frequency spectrum. To the commission, that means eliminating regulations that discourage innovation and "allocating frequencies in a manner to facilitate entry into the market of new competitors," as well as "the introduction of new applications and technologies" for the frequencies it oversees.[8] Examples would be allowing satellite radio services, enacting regulations that allow mobile wireless firms to use new faster technologies, allowing the auction of spectrum space with the idea that companies bidding the most for it will use it in innovative ways, and regulating interstate cable television company activities. The FCC had its hands full in the area of cable regulation during 2015 as it considered Comcast's proposed acquisition of Time Warner Cable (TWC). Comcast, the largest cable firm as well as the largest US media company, sought the acquisition's approval from both the FCC and the US Department of Justice. Comcast executives understood that because TWC is the second-largest cable firm, both the Justice Department and the FCC would have to rule that the combination of the two firms (a case of horizontal integration) would not raise prices for consumers or lessen competition in the television industry. Comcast Vice President David Cohen stated that absorbing TWC would give his company the revenues to do good things for his subscribers: "This transaction is all about increasing competition and creating more consumer benefit as a result of gaining additional scale," he insisted. By contrast, many media activists, law professors, lawmakers, and program-channel executives opposed the deal. They argued it would give Comcast too much power to dictate prices people pay for programming channels and internet service. It would also, they say, give Comcast overwhelming clout in negotiating what it pays cable channels such as CNN, AMC, HBO, and others for carrying them on cable. In April 2015 Comcast's leadership determined that business as well as public pressures against the deal were so strong that the government was not inclined to let the merger go through, and it withdrew from the deal.[9] In 2016 a cable firm that was smaller than Comcast, Charter Communications, offered to buy TWC. The FCC and Justice Department, seeing no public-interest problems with this merger, let it go through.

At the FTC, in the meantime, encouraging competition means enforcing federal antitrust laws. Again, these are laws designed to prevent one or a few companies from controlling such a large percentage of an industry that they can dictate high prices and so harm the consumer. As with the FCC, FTC decisions in this area generate controversy.

Consider the FTC's decision to review the announcement by Google in 2009 that it would like to purchase the firm AdMob for $750 million. AdMob tracks people's mobile phones and serves ads to them based on their location and data about their web use. The FTC contacted Google for more information about the deal, possibly out of concern that it might deter future competition in the mobile space. Reinforcing this perspective was a joint letter sent to the commission by two advocacy groups, Consumer Watchdog and the Center for Digital Democracy. They argued that Google was buying its way to dominance in the mobile advertising industry by diminishing the competition "to the detriment of consumers." According to a press release by the organizations, the letter asserted, "The mobile sector is the next frontier of the digital revolution. Without vigorous competition and strong privacy guarantees this vital and growing segment of the online economy will be stifled." The two groups added that the deal raised substantial privacy concerns because both companies involved in the deal gather tremendous amounts of data about consumers.[10] As it turned out, the groups were disappointed. The FTC approved the AdMob deal, considering it not anticompetitive. Today AdMob is an important part of Google's advertising business. As you can see, the struggle between various societal forces that are for and against various forms of consolidation and data use in media industries goes on continuously.

Consumer Protection

Both the FCC and the FTC pay attention to consumer protection as it relates to mass media. Of course, consumer protection can mean many things, so this area can be especially controversial. At the FCC, consumer protection has meant stopping marketers from using unsolicited prerecorded telemarketing calls ("robocalls"), making sure broadcasters and cable systems do not allow commercials that are louder than the programs around them, making rules about wireless 911 emergency phone lines, and promoting hearing aid compatibility for wireless telephones.

More controversially, the FCC has tried to make sure broadcasters use their spectrum "in the public interest"—in ways that are not always aimed at making the most money. You might be surprised that the commission has this sort of influence. It is the case that the basic principles of freedom of speech and of the press apply in electronic media just as they do in print media. Yet from the early days of broadcasting, Congress viewed it as different from print because the available wavelengths for radio and TV signals were limited (or scarce). According to Congress, this wavelength scarcity justified the creation of an agency such as the FCC to oversee the distribution of frequencies and to ensure competition of ideas over the airwaves.

Congress's notion of wavelength scarcity applies to broadcasting only—not to cable or satellite television. This limitation has sometimes put Congress and the FCC in the strange position of announcing content regulations for broadcasters that do not apply to hundreds of cable and satellite channels. For example, in 1996 the FCC announced that each week broadcast TV stations must air three hours of educational television programs aimed at children aged 16 and under that serve their "intellectual, cognitive, social, and emotional needs." Broadcasters complain that it is unfair that they alone, not cable or satellite networks, are required to spend the time and money on such programming. They also say that the requirement is outdated in an era of specialized children's channels such as Nickelodeon and the Disney Channel. Supporters of the rule argue that broadcasters should have greater obligations than other media firms because broadcasters are using valuable public airwaves that reach virtually everyone. The rule's supporters also claim that broadcasters do not always air programs that match the spirit of the FCC rule. In the case of Univision, the country's largest Spanish-language broadcaster, the commission agreed. In 2007 it forced Univision to pay a record $24 million fine for airing telenovelas (soap operas) that simply included children in plots during the time it claimed it was fulfilling the children's educational requirement from 2004 to 2006.[11]

The FTC's consumer protection work covers a wide territory, from combating deceptive advertising to protecting children's privacy on the web. As we have noted, the FTC was placed in charge of implementing and administering COPPA. To implement the act, the FTC had to create rules that specified exactly what websites were covered by the act, exactly what rules should apply to them, and when the rules would go into effect. To administer the act, the FTC had to create a system for monitoring websites on a regular basis to make sure that they were adhering to COPPA.

The FTC also sues firms that it contends have engaged in false advertising that has harmed consumers. For example, it brought charges against the Skechers footwear company, saying that it deceived consumers with weight-loss and toning claims related to Shape-ups shoes and other toning products. At issue were ads (many starring the celebrity Kim Kardashian) urging consumers, "Shape up while you walk" and "Get in shape without setting foot in a gym." In 2012 the commission announced that Skechers had agreed to pay $40 million to settle the charges, though it didn't admit wrongdoing. Skechers' settlement with the FTC was part of a broader agreement with attorneys general from nearly all fifty states; consumers who bought the sneakers could request compensation.[12]

Media Self-Regulation

As you might imagine, advertising executives do not welcome actions of this sort from the government. Media executives in general don't welcome government interference. Even competitors within a media industry are not always happy when the FTC or FCC—or any government agency—responds to a problem by forcing other firms to act in certain ways. They worry that once the government gets involved in one company's activities, regulators may begin to exert unwanted influence on what other companies do too. Executives therefore often believe that it is best to create self-regulation regimes. **Self-regulation regimes** are sets of codes and agreements among companies in an industry to ensure that employees carry out their work in what industry officials agree is an ethical manner.

It's important to recognize that pressures toward self-regulation don't always originate from the government. Some of the pressures come from other places outside the industry. Some even come from within the media industry itself. Three major external sources of influence are members of the public, public advocacy organizations, and advertisers. Two sources from within the industry are professional groups and concerned leaders. Let's briefly look at these.

External Pressures on Media to Self-Regulate

Pressure from Members of the Public When individuals are disturbed about media content, they may contact the production, distribution, or exhibition firms involved to express their displeasure and demand alterations in the content. Pick any topic—from racism to religion, from politicians to businesspeople—and you will probably find that some sector of society is concerned about the portrayal of that topic in the mass media. People who see the mass media as a series of windows on the world often want to see the people, behaviors, and values that they hold dear portrayed fairly in the media products they use.

As we noted in Chapter 2, media executives understand that they must think of their audiences as consumers who buy their products or whom they sell to advertisers. The complaining individual might be successful in getting the content changed or even removed if he or she convinces the media executives that they might otherwise lose a substantial portion of their target market. But an individual's concern will garner little attention if it is clear that the person does not belong in the target audience. The editors from *Cosmopolitan* magazine, which aims at 20-something single women, for example, are not likely to follow the advice of an elderly sounding woman from rural Kansas who phones to protest what she feels are demeaning portrayals of women on covers of the magazine that she sees in the supermarket. Yet the magazine staff might well act favorably if a *Cosmo* subscriber writes with a suggestion for a new column that would attract more of the upscale single women they want as readers.

Pressure From Advocacy Organizations Individuals who are particularly outraged about certain media portrayals may try to find others who share their concerns. They might join or start **advocacy organizations or pressure groups**, which work to change the nature of certain kinds of mass media materials.

Some advocacy organizations are specific to media. For example, the Center for Media Education concentrates on children and television, the Committee for Accuracy in Middle East Reporting in America (CAMERA) is devoted to promoting its view of accurate coverage of Israel in the media, and the Center for the Study of Commercialism criticizes advertising and marketing. Other advocacy organizations pay attention to media as part of more general concerns. For example, People for the American Way supports politically liberal approaches to social problems, GLAAD (formerly the Gay & Lesbian Alliance Against Defamation) advocates for fair representations of lesbian, gay, bisexual, and transgender people in the media, and the conservative American Family Association monitors all aspects of society for attacks on its preferred image of the family.

self-regulation regimes
codes and agreements among companies in an industry to ensure that employees carry out their work in what industry officials agree is an ethical manner

advocacy organizations or pressure groups
collections of people who work to change the nature of certain kinds of mass media materials

Representatives of these organizations may try to meet with the heads of media firms, start letter-writing campaigns, or attempt to embarrass media firms by attracting press coverage about an issue. If their target is an advertiser-supported medium, they may threaten to boycott the products of sponsors. They also may appeal to government officials for help.

Pressure From Advertisers Advertisers are a powerful force in pressuring the media to make changes in their content. Many advertisers like to buy space or time for their commercial messages within media content that reflects well on their products. Companies such as Unilever and Procter & Gamble, which spend enormous amounts of money on advertising, sometimes have the clout to persuade media firms to tone down certain kinds of portrayals that don't fit their brand image.

Consider, for example, efforts by marketers to generate more "family-friendly" programming to sponsor during prime time on television networks. In 1998 such advertising giants as Johnson & Johnson, AT&T, Bristol-Myers Squibb, Coca-Cola, Ford Motor Company, General Motors, Gillette, IBM, Kellogg's, McDonald's, Procter & Gamble, and Unilever United States became concerned that the increased level of sex and violence on TV was angering many of their customers. These elements of TV programming were also making it difficult for them to reach both parents and children at the same time.

In response, the marketers created the Family Friendly Programming Forum. It seeks to stimulate the production of shows meant to appeal to broader, multigenerational audiences and suitable to run between 8:00 and 10:00 p.m. (Eastern and Pacific times). "We want to sit and watch TV with our families and not be embarrassed," explained Steve Johnston, vice president for advertising and brand management at Nationwide Mutual Enterprises in Columbus, Ohio.[13]

Critics of this coalition fear that it wants to create programs that romanticize a kind of fictional nuclear family. The advertisers insist, however, that it is possible to be both contemporary and family friendly. "We have to be realistic; families may not be gathered around one TV anymore, and they're not your traditional families," said

Disney-owned ABC Family rebranded the channel as Freeform in 2016 to attract a younger audience. The network's shows like *Pretty Little Liars* often feature LGBTQ characters, sex, violence, and other topics many criticize as not being family friendly.

Susan Frank, executive vice president and general manager of the Odyssey Network in Studio City, California, a cable channel owned by Hallmark Cards that focuses on family-oriented programming. "But there are times you can bring family members together with content that's thought-provoking, done in a good, quality way," she added. "You have to be relevant to the way people live today."[14]

By 2009 the Family Friendly Programming Forum had come directly under the wing of the Association of National Advertisers (ANA) and changed its name to the ANA Alliance for Family Entertainment. The name change indicated a broadened mission to reflect the changing media environment and "to ensuring there are programming choices on broadcast/cable networks, internet, mobile devices and gaming platforms, wherever consumers look for family entertainment." To emphasize that it was building on past successes, the alliance noted on its website that it had "played a significant role in bringing 20 primetime programs to air, including hits *The Gilmore Girls*, *Chuck*, *Everybody Hates Chris*, and *Friday Night Lights*."[15] Although this project has itself created controversy, it does show how powerful advertisers can respond to concerns they perceive in their target audience and act to influence media.

Internal Pressures on Media to Self-Regulate

To maintain their credibility with the public at large (and their target audiences in particular) and to avoid pressures from government and other outside entities interfering with their firms' activities, media executives set up self-regulation policies and codes. This internal self-regulation can take a number of forms, including editorial standards and ombudspersons at the level of individual organizations and professional codes of ethics, journalism reviews, and content ratings at the industry level.

Editorial Standards Most media organizations have established **editorial standards**—written statements of policy and conduct. In the case of the network television industry, these policies are maintained and enforced by a department known as Standards and Practices, which makes difficult decisions regarding the acceptability of language in scripts, themes in plot lines, and images used in visual portrayals. At the local television station level, policy and conduct are most often guided by **policy books**, which help to lay down guidelines for fairness, accuracy, and appropriateness of station content, among other things.

Newspapers and magazines are most often guided by two kinds of editorial standards. The first kind of standards, **operating policies**, spell out guidelines for everyday operations, such as conflicts of interest, acceptable advertising content, boundaries of deceptive information-gathering practices, and payment to sources for news stories, among other things. The second kind, **editorial policies**, identify company positions on specific issues, such as which presidential candidate the paper supports and whether the paper is in support of certain governmental policies.

Ombudspersons An **ombudsperson** is hired by a media organization to deal with readers, viewers, or listeners who have a complaint to report or an issue to discuss. Although an ombudsperson is employed directly by a media organization, his or her role is to act as an impartial intermediary between the organization and the public.

Professional Codes of Ethics One of the oldest approaches to self-regulation is the professional **code of ethics**. This is a formal list of guidelines and standards that tell the members of the profession—in this case, media practitioners—what they should and should not do. These codes are designed to establish internal standards of professionalism and are often administered by societies or associations that represent an industry's interests to the outside world. Examples of such organizations are the Society of Professional Journalists, the American Society of Newspaper Editors, the Radio-Television News Directors Association, the American Advertising Federation, and the Public Relations Society of America. Each has an established code of ethics, and you can find these codes online.

Journalism Reviews **Journalism reviews**—publications that report on and analyze examples of ethical and unethical journalism—are yet another internal force that helps the media self-regulate. These reviews include publications such as *Quill* and *Columbia Journalism Review*. What you'll see are vehicles that explore the realities of the news business and stand up for the values of journalism and for the rights of journalists around the world.

Content Ratings and Advisories Another way in which media organizations regulate themselves is through the adoption of ratings systems. Most prominent are those of the film, television, and video game industries. The Motion Picture Association of America (MPAA) created the first of these three voluntary ratings systems in 1968; it was revised in 1990. Film ratings are determined by a full-time Ratings Board, located in Los Angeles, California. The board is made up of eight to thirteen people

editorial standards
Take a look at them online. established by media organizations as a form of self-regulation

policy books
guidelines for fairness, accuracy, and appropriateness of station content and the like adopted by media organizations in the interest of self-regulation

operating policies
policies, most often used by print media organizations, that spell out guidelines for everyday operations, such as conflicts of interest, acceptable advertising content, boundaries of deceptive information-gathering practices, payment to sources for news stories, and so on

editorial policies
policies, most often used by print media organizations, that identify company positions on specific issues, such as which presidential candidate the paper supports and whether the paper is in support of certain governmental policies

ombudsperson
an individual who is hired by a media organization to deal with readers, viewers, or listeners who have a complaint to report or an issue to discuss

journalism reviews
publications that report on and analyze examples of ethical and unethical journalism

code of ethics
a formal list of guidelines and standards designed to establish standards of professionalism within an industry

who are not specially qualified in any way, other than the fact that they all have "parenthood experience." When a film is submitted to the Ratings Board, each member estimates what most parents would consider to be an appropriate rating for the film. The criteria the board considers are theme, violence, language, nudity, sensuality, and drug abuse, among other elements. After a group discussion, the board votes on the film's rating, which is decided by a majority vote.

The Ratings Board process sounds quite rational, but movie executives and members of the public have complained that the decisions to rate films PG, R, or NC-17 are often quite subjective and based on the particular, sometimes eccentric, judgments of the committee members. A film about the movie ratings process, *This Film Is Not Yet Rated* (2006), emphasizes these limitations to a process the movie industry likes to portray as rational, systematic, and predictable. This movie's release seems not to have deterred the industry from using the ratings as its primary form of self-regulation. The success of the approach has led other industries to copy it.

The video game and television industries are cases in point. They model their ratings after the MPAA approach. Games' ratings are set by the Entertainment Software Rating Board (ESRB), an organization of industry leaders created in the early 1990s as a result of threatened federal intervention because of public outcry over violence and sex in certain video games. Like the movie ratings, the ESRB ratings are determined by a specially chosen panel of "regular" people. Table 5.4 and Table 5.5 present the ratings categories for movies and video games along with their meaning.

You undoubtedly have seen some of the letters during the course of your leisure activities. You also may be familiar with the categories the television industry uses to help parents sort through the huge volume of material available through their cable or satellite feeds. Also modeled after the movie ratings, these guidelines consist of six categories (see Table 5.6). Rather than using "regular" people, the networks and producers of each show determine the show's parental guidelines. A monitoring board formed by the National Association of Broadcasters works to achieve accuracy and consistency in applying the parental guidelines by examining programs with inappropriate guidelines and reviewing programs that have been publicly criticized.

Table 5.4 The Entertainment Software Ratings Board Ratings Categories

- EC: *Early childhood*. May be suitable for children aged 3 and older. Contains no material that parents would find inappropriate.

- E: *Everyone*. May be suitable for persons aged 6 and older. These titles will appeal to people of many ages and tastes. They may contain minimal cartoon, fantasy, or mild violence and/or infrequent use of mild language. This rating was formerly known as Kids to Adult (K-A).

- E10+: *Everyone 10 and older*. May be suitable for ages 10 and older. Titles in this category may contain more cartoon, fantasy, or mild violence; mild language; and/or minimal suggestive themes.

- T: *Teen*. May be suitable for ages 13 and older. Titles in this category may contain violence, suggestive themes, crude humor, minimal blood, simulated gambling, and/or infrequent use of strong language.

- M: *Mature*. May be suitable for persons aged 17 and older. Titles in this category may contain intense violence, blood and gore, sexual content, and/or strong language.

- AO: *Adults only*. Should be played only by persons 18 years or older. Titles in this category may include prolonged scenes of intense violence and/or graphic sexual content and nudity.

Table 5.5 The Motion Picture Association of America Ratings Categories

- G: *General audience—all ages admitted.* This is a film that contains nothing in theme, language, nudity and sex, violence, and so on that would be offensive to parents whose younger children view the film.

- PG: *Parental guidance suggested—some material may not be suitable for children.* This is a film that needs to be examined or inquired into by parents before they let their children attend.

- PG-13: *Parents strongly cautioned—some material may be inappropriate for children under 13.* This is a film that goes beyond the boundaries of the PG rating in theme, violence, nudity, sensuality, language, or other content but that does not quite fit within the restricted R category.

- R: *Restricted—anyone under 17 requires accompanying parent or adult guardian.* This is a film that definitely contains some adult material, possibly including hard language, tough violence, nudity within sensual scenes, drug abuse, or a combination of these and other elements.

- NC-17: *No one under 17 admitted.* This is a film that most parents will consider patently too adult for their youngsters under 17. No children will be admitted.

Table 5.6 The National Association of Broadcasters Ratings Categories

- TV-Y: *All children.* This program is designed to be appropriate for all children, including children aged 2 to 6.

- TV-Y7: *Directed to older children.* This program is designed for children aged 7 and above.

- TV-G: *General audience.* Most parents would find this program suitable for all ages. It contains little or no violence, no strong language, and little or no sexual dialogue or situations.

- TV-PG: *Parental guidance suggested.* This program contains material that parents may find unsuitable for younger children. The theme itself may call for parental guidance and/or the program may contain one or more of the following: moderate violence (V), some sexual situations (S), infrequent coarse language (L), or some suggestive dialogue (D).

- TV-14: *Parents strongly cautioned.* This program contains some material that many parents would find unsuitable for children under 14 years of age. This program contains one or more of the following: intense violence (V), intense sexual situations (S), strong coarse language (L), or intensely suggestive dialogue (D).

- TV-MA: *Mature audience only.* This program is specifically designed to be viewed by adults and therefore may be unsuitable for children under 17. This program contains one or more of the following: graphic violence (V), explicit sexual activity (S), or crude indecent language (L).

These ratings do seem to have done what their industries wanted them to do: stop lawmakers from threatening companies with some sort of punishment if they didn't calm large sectors of the public about their products. Still, the ratings are controversial in some circles. Some people believe they are merely a fig leaf to cover the huge amount of objectionable material these industries produce and promote. Others take

a very different view. They point out that mainstream exhibitors such as movie theaters, stores, and websites hesitate to carry products with ratings that are for adults only. These critics believe that the difficulty of getting "objectionable" materials in front of the public means that works with controversial yet important themes and images will not be made—or, if made, will not get the attention they deserve.

They point to the documentary film *Bully* (2011) as an example. The producers created it with the goal of getting schoolchildren to see the terrible nature of bullying and its consequences for young people. After being exposed to the coarse language of the bullies in the movie, though, the Ratings Board gave it an NC-17 rating, and so major movie theater chains refused to show it. It was only when 17 year old Katy Butler launched a petition to change the rating and the film's distributor, the Weinstein Company, launched a public relations blitz pointing out the folly of this decision that executives of the largest chains changed their minds and scheduled *Bully* in their theaters. The MPAA eventually changed the rating to PG-13.

The initial ratings of the documentary *Bully* (NC-17 and R) would have made it much more difficult for the intended audience of the film (adolescents 17 years old and younger) to see it because they would have to be attended by an adult guardian. Katy Butler, a 17-year-old student from Michigan, launched a campaign to have the MPAA lower the rating so that teens would be able to see the movie without a guardian. She managed to secure a petition with more than 200,000 signatures.

ethics
a system of principles about what is right that guides a person's actions

The Role of Ethics

Ethics is a system of notions about right and wrong that guides a person's actions. Let's look a bit more carefully at the topic of ethics and the way it relates to business requirements.

Making Ethical Decisions

Every day you find yourself in situations in which ethical decisions need to be made, whether those situations involve the mass media or not. How do you make these decisions? What sort of moral reasoning process should you follow—not only as a media consumer but also, and more importantly, as a good citizen?

Bob Steele, a scholar affiliated with the Poynter Institute, outlines a model that media literates and professionals alike can use to evaluate and examine their decisions and to make good ethical decisions. Steele is concerned specifically with journalism, but the ethical thinking process that he suggests can work for all sorts of media practitioners and consumers. Steele says to ask yourself these ten questions:[16]

1. What do I know? What do I need to know?
2. What are my ethical concerns?
3. What is my journalistic (or informational, entertainment, advertising, or educational) purpose?

4. What organizational policies and professional guidelines should I consider?
5. How can I include other people, with different perspectives and diverse ideas, in the decision-making process?
6. Who are the stakeholders—those affected by my decision? What are their motivations? Which are legitimate?
7. What if the roles were reversed? How would I feel if I were in the shoes of one of the stakeholders?
8. What are the possible consequences of my actions in the short term and in the long term?
9. What are my alternatives to maximize my truth-telling responsibility and minimize harm?
10. Can I clearly and fully justify my thinking and my decision to my colleagues, to the stakeholders, and to the public?

Ethical Duties to Various Constituencies

When combined with larger philosophies of ethics, Bob Steele's questions can help media practitioners think about their day-to-day responsibilities and prepare for events that raise grave ethical dilemmas. Ethical dilemmas often come about because we are torn over an issue, pulled in a number of directions. The perspective that media ethics scholars Clifford Christians, Mark Fackler, and Kim Rotzoll contribute to this topic can help bring a sharper focus to the issues Steele raises when it comes to knotty ethical situations. In order to reach a responsible decision, these scholars write, an individual must clarify which parties will be influenced by a decision and which ones the person feels particularly obligated to support.[17]

Imagine, for example, that you are a movie theater executive who must make the decision of whether to carry *Bully* with an NC-17 rating. How would you use Steele's previously listed questions to think through your decision? Where would you stand before and after the petition and the Weinstein public relations blitz—and why? What considerations would guide your decisions? Christians and his colleagues stress that as you make this decision—or carry out the production, distribution, or exhibition of any media product—you should realize you have obligations to five parties, or constituencies. These five parties are you, the audience, the employer, the profession, and society. To these five, we will add one more: the people to whom we've made promises, such as publics and (in the case of journalists) sources.

- *Duty to self.* As a media practitioner, you clearly feel a duty to make sure your actions do not harm you. In fact, a key goal of your work is to make yourself look good—to shine in your job—and to act in ways that allow you to feel ethically correct.
- *Duty to audience.* As a media practitioner, you also have a duty to make sure that what you do takes the nature and expectations of the audience into consideration.
- *Duty to the employer.* The company that pays your salary is also an important consideration. At the very least, a practitioner owes the firm good work—a product that meets the expectations that caused the person to be hired in the first place.
- *Duty to the profession.* Most practitioners feel an allegiance to their profession. Movie scriptwriters feel an obligation to keep up the reputation and pay of the people who ply that craft. Similarly, reporters feel a responsibility to help other

journalists who are in trouble and to make sure that their profession is taken seriously by editors and publishers.

- *Duty to promise holders.* If you made promises to people during the course of covering a news story, putting a movie together, or making an ad, you may (and should) feel an obligation to those people when you move forward with your work. If a source requested anonymity, you can't divulge the source's name even if your editor thinks the article would be better if it were there. If you promised a young TV talk show host the first interview about your new film, you are obligated to give that show the first interview, even though Jimmy Fallon wants you first.
- *Duty to society.* Many practitioners also feel an obligation to society at large. You live in a real world, with neighbors, children, stores, churches, and governments. If you produce recordings, edit movies, write sitcoms, or illustrate children's books, you may feel that what you produce should have a positive social impact. At least, you may say, what you produce should not have a negative social impact.

Forming Ethical Standards for the Mass Media

If you think about these ethical systems, about Bob Steele's ten questions, and about the constituencies that Clifford Christians and his colleagues discuss, you will see that ethical standards for the mass media often involve at least three levels:

- The personal level
- The professional level
- The societal level

Most media practitioners find that they cannot exist on one level only. How their standards develop at each level has to do with their values and ideals. From these two sources come their principles—the basis for their ethical actions at every level.

values
those things that reflect our presuppositions about social life and human nature

ideals
notions of excellence or goals that are thought to bring about greater harmony to ourselves and to others

principles
those guidelines we derive from values and ideals that are precursors to codified rules

Values reflect our presuppositions about social life and human nature. They cover a broad range of possibilities, such as aesthetic values (how harmonious or pleasing something is), professional values (innovation and promptness), logical values (consistency and competency), sociocultural values (thrift and hard work), and moral values (honesty and nonviolence).

Ideals are notions of excellence or goals that are thought to bring about greater harmony to ourselves and to others. For example, American culture respects ideals such as tolerance, compassion, loyalty, forgiveness, peace, justice, fairness, and respect for persons. In addition to these human ideals, there are institutional or organizational ideals, such as profit, efficiency, productivity, quality, and stability.

Principles are those guidelines we derive from values and ideals and are precursors to codified rules. They are usually stated in positive (prescriptive) or negative (proscriptive) terms. Consider, for example, the motto "never corrupt the integrity of media channels"—a principle derived from the professional value of truth telling in public relations—or the statement "always maximize profit"—a principle derived from belief in the efficacy of the free enterprise system. The ideals, values, and principles of media practitioners, organizations, and industries will differ according to the differing goals and loyalties of each.

Media Literacy, Regulation, and Ethics

The high risks involved in today's highly competitive media environment often make decisions that may seem straightforward—such as allowing the exhibition of *Bully*—complex. The high risks also create pressure on individuals to conform to organizational activities that, although legal, might be considered unethical. An individual's duty to the media organization may conflict with his or her duty to society; an individual's personal values may conflict with the organization's values.

For example, consider the use of graphic violence in TV dramas, in local TV news programs, in ads, and in music recordings. Many of the distributors and exhibitors of the material—and even its creators—may personally abhor some elements of what they are doing. In their business lives, though, they may feel they have to use those elements. Why? Because they "work"—that is, they seem to sell the product to the right audience in a manner that supports the organization and brings paychecks to its members. A well-paid writer of TV movies once yelled at me for asking him questions that implied respect for his craft. "I write junk!" he shouted. He added that he knew he used violence and sex as props to advance his plots and that he wrote according to the most blatant pop-cultural formulas. He said, "I do it because I have a family to support and a big mortgage to pay off for this house in Brentwood! I do it, but I know it's junk. Don't forget that!"

Whereas this writer may condemn his own scripts as contributing to the violent and mediocre nature of popular culture, the producers of the programs that were based on these scripts might argue that they were handsome creations that explore issues of good and evil in ways that are accessible to large audiences.

There also may be ambiguity regarding how to apply ethical principles. Ethical criteria may seem straightforward, but they are not always so. Take the principle of not misleading people—a notion that most people would agree is a basic ethical principle. Consider a famous case from the 1970s in light of this principle: The Campbell Soup Company's ad agency put marbles in the bottom of a bowl of soup in an ad to emphasize the soup's chunkiness by making it look as if it contained many big pieces of meat and vegetables. Responding to complaints from competitors, the FTC forced the company to withdraw the ad. But one can ask, was that really misleading? Campbell's argued that the company was trying to emphasize a genuine feature of its soup that the camera couldn't easily reflect without the marbles. The FTC disagreed, but that doesn't mean that Campbell's employees felt that they were acting unethically—do you believe they were?

Sometimes, though, executives do acknowledge that business competition leads them to act unethically. One way to guard themselves and their competitors from improper behavior is by encouraging rules that prohibit it. From one point of view, then, media laws and regulations can be seen as a way to formally enforce agreed-upon norms of behavior. The First Amendment is a proposition that reflects ethical values regarding the government's relation to media, information, and the public. Similarly, antitrust laws, laws against deceptive advertising, and self-regulatory ratings voice norms about how media firms and media practitioners ought to behave.

Why are codes of ethics developed? How do they help media organizations and the people who work in them? What are some ethical standards that are not only good media practice but also required legally?

THINKING ABOUT MEDIA LITERACY

Review the examples of "invasion of privacy" activities. Have you or anyone you know been subjected to one of these situations by a media outlet? How about on a social media site? Are expectations for privacy different in the context of commercially published media material and "socially" published postings? What are your feelings, as some pundits claim, that social media has caused the death of privacy?

Media Regulations and the Savvy Citizen

Thinking about the rules that guide the media is crucial for a media-literate consumer. You can undoubtedly think of many examples of anger directed at the media. Activists who believe in a woman's right to choose abortion might be deeply offended by the portrayals of teen pregnancies in a TV movie shown by one of the networks. They might feel that doing nothing about these portrayals invites further support of the antiabortion position by the producers when they work on other shows. They also might believe that the portrayals will reinforce in the audience unfortunate images of and actions toward teen abortions in society. So they might mobilize to prevent the network from showing the film again and to force the network to air a film or series that is more sympathetic toward teenagers who choose abortions.

However, at the same time that the pro-choice activists are voicing their complaints, groups that find any portrayal of abortion to be reprehensible might make totally opposite demands of the network. They might argue that such portrayals encourage children and others to think that abortion is acceptable in society and that this erodes family values—the very values that define American society. Consequently, they might demand that the network never portray any abortions.

Three points about these opposing groups and their demands deserve attention here. One point is the similarity in their approach: although they are far apart ideologically, their concern about the media comes not so much from a worry about how the members of their immediate groups will react to the movie as from concern about how members of society who are less informed on the subject—especially children—will relate to the material. This type of concern is common among media activists. Arguments with media firms are often based on fear about the media's effects on other segments of society.

A second point is that the two groups are divided on the question of what is ethically correct for the media to do in this case. One side has notions of ethically proper images that involve certain positive portrayals of abortion. The other side considers any depiction of abortion as playing a legitimate part in mainstream society to be unethical.

Finally, it should be clear that this is an ethical conflict that cannot be resolved by government regulation. As we have seen, the First Amendment protects the creators of media materials, including most forms of entertainment, from government interference. The First Amendment would apply in the abortion fight. In other circumstances, however, other laws might take precedence, and a concerned citizen would need to understand when it is appropriate to

ABC's *Scandal* shocked viewers when it premiered an episode where one of its main characters gets an abortion after discovering she's pregnant.

ask the government to intervene. We have seen, for example, that in the case of libel of a nonpublic figure in a TV entertainment program, the person who was insulted likely would be allowed to have her or his day in court.

Knowing the laws that relate to particular media in particular circumstances is critical to understanding the rights and responsibilities that apply to you, media firms, and government when it comes to materials you like or don't like. In many cases, you will find that no governmental law will help you to force certain media organizations to act in what you believe is an ethical manner. You will also find out that there are few easily agreed-upon media ethics in a nation as complex and varied as the United States. Of course, people who care about media ethics should not give up trying to persuade media organizations to alter their notions of proper behavior. However, persuading media organizations to do things involves much more than simply insisting on the ethical value of one person's or one group's suggestions; as we have seen, there may be others who insist on the ethical value of totally opposite actions. So it is also necessary to understand the following: controversial proposals likely will not be accepted by media organizations as a result of social debate unless the party making the proposal is able to exercise economic and political power.

CHAPTER REVIEW

 Visit the Companion Website at www.routledge.com/cw/turow for additional study tools and resources.

 ## Key Terms

You can find the definitions to these key terms in the marginal glossary throughout this chapter. Test your knowledge of these terms with interactive flash cards on the *Media Today* Companion Website.

actual malice
advocacy organizations or
    pressure groups
antitrust policies
appropriation
code of ethics
copyright
Copyright Act of 1976
defamation
economic regulations
editorial policies
editorial standards
embeds
ethics
fair use regulations
false light

Federal Communications
    Commission (FCC)
Federal Trade Commission (FTC)
ideals
intrusion
journalism reviews
libel
libel per quod
libel per se
monopoly
obscene
oligopoly
ombudsperson
operating policies
parody
policy books

pool reporters
predictive analytics
principles
prior restraint
privacy
private person
public disclosure
public figure
self-regulation regimes
simple malice
simple negligence
slander
transformative
values

 ## Questions for Discussion and Critical Thinking

1. Ethical standards operate on three levels: the personal, the professional, and the societal. Consider this situation: a reporter is anonymously given a document that reveals apparent fraud in the spending at a local nonprofit that serves homeless people. Think about the personal, professional, and societal implications if the reporter does not thoroughly investigate the claims the document makes before publishing a story. Which of Steele's "Ten Questions" would you consider to be the most important to answer before publishing the story?

2. The FCC and the FTC are both involved in the regulation of media industries. Think about how the FCC and the FTC differ in their regulatory charge and how they are similar in their regulatory objectives.

3. According to a list created by the Fort Lewis College Library, the following are "Common Reasons for Banning Books." Look over the list and consider a book you've read that might have triggered a call for banning based on these reasons. What arguments would you have made about the book to counter an attempt to ban, or would you have supported the banning of the book?

(Source: "Common Reasons for Banning Books," Fort Lewis College, John F. Reed Library. Banned Books, Censorship & Free Speech. November 15, 2013.)

- Racial issues: encourages racism
- Blasphemous dialogue: uses words such as "God" or "Jesus" as profanity

- Sexual situations or dialogue
- Violence or negativity: content that includes violence or is deemed too negative or depressing
- Presence of witchcraft: books that include magic or witchcraft themes
- Political bias: support or examine extreme political philosophies such as fascism and anarchism
- Age inappropriate: book's content and age level at which it is aimed deemed inappropriate

4. The definition of copyright from Copyright.com states, "Copyright protection exists from the moment a work is created in a fixed, tangible form of expression. The copyright immediately becomes the property of the author who created the work." And fair use is described as being "intended to allow the use of copyright-protected works for commentary, parody, news reporting, research and education."

Consider a situation where someone uploads an adorable cat video on YouTube. Are you in violation of copyright if you post it to your own YouTube channel? Could you use the video and do a voice-over that makes fun of cat videos? What if you use the video in a college course you are teaching about digital culture? How about if you use the video in a subscription website you created where customers learn about movie-making techniques?

Activity

Think about the types of information that are routinely posted on social media sites. People "tag" others by posting photos of them, people comment on others' posts, people post material on their walls about other people, and so forth. In addition, review sites invite comments by people about their experiences with a restaurant or reaction to a movie.

In this chapter we've discussed a variety of laws that regulate information *after it has been distributed*. For the most part, these laws cover the type of content that is created, produced, and distributed by mass communication organizations using the industrial processes that we've been exploring. However, given the wide adoption of social media, we might ask whether the laws that cover the mass media might also start to be applied to the types of information that is posted in social sites and in reviews.

Let's take privacy as one example. Here are four areas of privacy law:

- False light: material that misrepresents or distorts information that puts someone in a false light (e.g., arrangement of photos that gives a false impression)
- Appropriation: using someone's name or likeness in an unauthorized manner for commercial purposes
- Public disclosure: publication of private facts about someone that are not of public concern
- Intrusion: physical or nonphysical invasion into a person's solitude, private area, or affairs

1. For each of these areas of privacy, think about things you've seen on a social media site you frequent, that you've posted yourself or that have been posted about you, or that you can imagine someone else posting. Give one or two examples that demonstrate how that posting might violate the privacy rights of the person involved.
2. Do you think the privacy laws that govern how mass media organizations handle information should also apply to social media posts? Why or why not?

Now, consider review sites. What if someone had a bad experience with a restaurant meal and decides to post multiple negative reviews that exaggerate the poor quality of their meal. These reviews cause the restaurant to lose traffic and therefore money. What recourse does the restaurant owner have?

iPod 2001

iPod 2 2002

The Media Industries
The Forces Driving Convergence in Media Industries

The first part of this book covered the big picture of today's media industries. It looked at the components of those industries and analyzed how they relate to the ideas of "mass communication," "mass media," and the interrelationship of media with culture. It described the interactive nature of digital media and how companies today often encourage members of the audience to act as consumers and producers of digital media. The first part also surveyed ways that researchers have studied the impacts of media on society and individuals. It outlined ways to look at content genres across the media industries and explored the advertising and public relations structures that fund the media, and it laid out US laws that guide them.

The second part of this book shifts gears. Now that you have a bird's-eye view of the system and the parts that make it work, we will focus on key media industries within that system. Those industries create the content (and the culture) that we associate with media today. Think about what your world would be like without books, newspapers, magazines, recorded music, radio, movies, television, and video games. Think, too, what it would be like without the internet, which we often take for granted when we use it to bring the content of books, newspapers, video games, and more to us in digital forms. Decisions about the production, distribution, and exhibition of these different media materials take place in particular industries. The people who work in them typically see the industries as separate, with distinct histories within the larger media system described in the first section of the book. So, for example, to understand who chooses the books we see in stores and online and why, we have to explore the book industry. To trace the considerations that lead to the films shown in local movie theaters, we need to take a look at the movie industry. That's the kind of thinking we will be doing in the next several chapters.

An aim of this part of the book is to stress the importance of convergence in media industries and to sketch the considerations that cause convergence to happen even while the media practitioners see themselves as working within particular industries. You probably recall from Chapter 1 that media convergence is the presentation across several media of content traditionally associated with one medium, such as when you can watch a film on a movie screen, a television set, a laptop, and a cell phone. You may remember that in Chapter 1 we described three elements—corporations, content, and computers—that need to be brought together if convergence as a mass communication process is to occur. That is, convergence in the mass media requires corporations serving content via networked computers to their audiences. Today, the corporation–content–computer relationship is commonplace, and media convergence is skyrocketing. Take a look at any computer-related device—your laptop, tablet, smartphone, or video game console, for example—and you'll undoubtedly find the capability to download movies, music, magazine articles, books, and much more content that you could also find on other devices.

But why does convergence take place? Why do people in the book and newspaper industries see a need to move the content they produce to e-readers? Why do movie companies move their films from theaters to hotels, airplanes, and DVDs? One answer—to make money—may seem obvious. But that begs another question. What developments are taking place in industries that make it possible to make money through the movement of materials across traditional media boundaries?

It turns out that convergence is being propelled by five developments that stand at the heart of today's media industries:

- The spread of digital media
- The importance of distribution windows
- Audience fragmentation and segmentation
- Globalization
- Conglomeration

Understanding these developments is critical to understanding the changes taking place in all media industries today. They all have different histories. The importance of distribution windows, audience fragmentation and segmentation, globalization, and conglomeration came into being even before the spread of digital media. Digital media, however, have encouraged and extended these processes. In turn, the processes, as well as the further spread of digital media, have encouraged convergence. These developments will show up in the following chapters on particular media industries. There we will discuss not only why it is *possible* to move materials across media boundaries but also why it is often *necessary*. Here we will sketch the five developments briefly as a foundation for the following chapters so that you will understand them and their importance when you encounter them later.

The Spread of Digital Media

We start with the spread of digital media because today these media stand at the core of so many convergent activities. **Digital media** are devices with computer processors that allow access to textual, audio, and/or visual content. As we've noted, among the most popular digital media are smartphones, video game machines, and tablets, as well as laptop or desktop computers. One key aspect of the spread of these and other digital media is their link to the internet. If content is placed on the web, it then becomes rather easy to use that content on many different devices.

An important reason for the acceleration of convergence, then, is the technical ability to carry it out as a result of the spread of the internet among the US population. The internet accelerates the spread of convergence. In 2018 the Pew Research Center found that roughly two-thirds of US households had a computer with fairly fast ("broadband") internet connections. At the same time, Pew found that people without broadband computer connections were going online, typically via their smartphones. When Pew asked adults that year whether they use the internet, 97 percent said they do.[1] At this point, you might be marveling at how digitization has created enormous opportunities for companies.

But digitization also has created major challenges for firms involved in the production, distribution, and exhibition of media materials. One challenge is that all these new devices bring the potential for lots more competition among publishers. To executives in the 21st century, a publisher is a person or organization that produces, markets, and distributes content. For example, on the web both the *New York Times* newspaper and the CBS television network are publishers. The more important point, though, is that on the web those two large media firms compete with untold numbers of other news and entertainment producers-distributors. Because of the low costs of making digital documents and distributing them on the web, almost anyone can be a publisher today.

The competition among producers and distributors of media material also extends to exhibitors. Recall from Chapter 1 that exhibitors present distributed materials to targeted audiences for them to choose. Before the digital media era, for many types of media materials, competition among exhibitors within a particular area was fairly limited. As an example, a neighborhood might have just one or two video stores, one newspaper home-delivery firm, a few newspaper and magazine stands and pay boxes, a couple of bookstores, and a cable system

digital media
devices with computer processors that allow access to textual, audio, and/or visual material

Digital media *are* now commonplace, among both the old and especially the younger generations. Tablets, iPods, and portable video game consoles make it possible to engage with digital media both in the home and outside the home, thanks to 3G and 4G technology and the growing abundance of wireless hotspots.

that competes with one or two TV satellite operators. With the rise of the web, all that has changed. Now the video stores (if they still exist) compete directly with digital streaming-movie sites such as Netflix and Amazon. The bookstore (if it remains in business) must compete with Amazon and Barnes & Noble online. The newspaper vendors must worry that people who live in the area will access local, national, and even international newspapers on the web. And the cable and satellite operators, apart from competing with one another, must face sites such as Netflix, Hulu, Hulu Plus, Amazon Prime, and YouTube that offer many of the same programs.

The Importance of Distribution Windows

windows

the various exhibition points distributors use to generate revenues for a product—for example, a movie theater, a newspaper, or a cable network

The mention of Netflix, Hulu, and Amazon Prime brings up the importance of distribution **windows**. The term "windows" refers to the various exhibition points distributors use to generate revenues for a product—for example, a movie theater, a newspaper, or a cable network. The concept of windows predates the rise of digital media. Companies have long used the idea of windows in the analog (non-digital) media world to bring in revenues from different places for the same materials. This approach is not too different from the British TV firm ITV's way of selling its hit series *Downton Abbey* in the United States during 2011 and 2012. It sold the first window—the Public Broadcasting Service (PBS)—the rights to show every new

Figure P.1

An example of distribution windows for a movie. Contracts between the distributor and the exhibitors determine the order of windows and time between them.

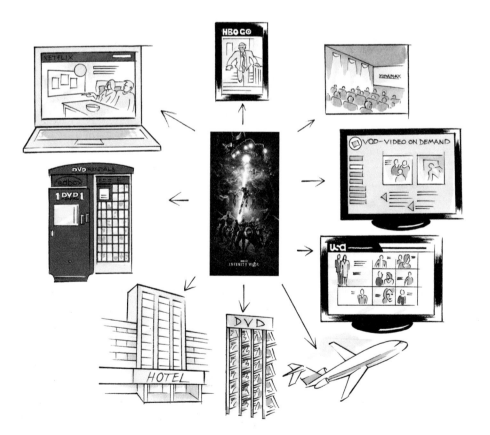

season's program episode by episode. After every season of the series ended, ITV yanked repeat episodes off PBS and made money from the season's episodes through other windows: physical stores (with the episodes packaged as a DVD set), online stores (as a DVD set), and rental locations such as video stores and digital streaming sites.

As the *Downton Abbey* example indicates, media producers try to increase revenues by moving their content across a number of windows. Different media industries have tended to approach this activity in different ways. In the television and film businesses, where production costs are quite high, the challenge of covering costs has forced production organizations to design their output with an eye toward moving it across mass media boundaries.

When companies make theatrical films, their windows are quite a bit more varied than that of TV producers. Blockbuster movies such as the *Mission Impossible* and *Jurassic World* franchises likely move through a gauntlet of platforms, including movie theaters, store-bought DVDs, Redbox video machines, pay-per-view sites such as FiOS and Amazon Prime (which has some "free" movies and some for rent), hotel pay-per-view channels, video-on-demand cable and satellite channels, airline flights, premium subscription cable/satellite networks (and streaming sites) such as HBO and Showtime, subscription streaming sites such as Netflix, and (rarely nowadays) finally, broadcast networks and local stations (see Figure P.1).

In the digital world, distributors' desire to have as many windows as possible for their products has encouraged the growth in convergence—that is, the movement of the same content across different digital media.

Why do distributors want more and more windows? As you might suspect, the answer has to do with money. Of course, the use of all these windows to cover costs and make a good profit assumes that people will want to view the movies and TV shows across the various windows. When we get to the chapters on print media—books, newspapers, and magazines—we will see that making money from windows, especially digital windows, is not at all a sure thing. The rush is to use the convergence of media by exhibiting through as many digital windows as possible or be left out of the new world.

Audience Fragmentation and Segmentation

The previous section explored the challenges and opportunities of using convergence to exploit new windows with the aim of increasing a media firm's revenues and extending the value of its brands. At the same time, media producers, distributors, and exhibitors must also confront another major development: the growth of audience fragmentation and segmentation. As with windows, audience fragmentation and segmentation preceded the rise of digital media. And as with windows, the process influences more than media convergence. So we will now describe audience fragmentation and segmentation and examine their role in media today and especially in the growth of convergence.

Audience segmentation is a direct result of channel fragmentation. As we discussed in Chapter 1, the term **channel fragmentation** refers to the great increase in the number of mass media outlets that has taken place during the past two decades. This fragmentation started well before the web. It was particularly startling in the

channel fragmentation
the great increase in the number of mass media outlets that has taken place during the past two decades

case of television. In 1975 a family in Philadelphia could receive television signals only over the air, which meant they had access to seven channels. During the 1980s cable television companies began to spread across the city, and during the 1990s satellite TV firms came in. Today, most households subscribe to a cable or satellite service and receive well over 100 channels. This is the pattern throughout the United States.

Although channel fragmentation preceded the internet, the internet rise accelerated the trend. To understand how the web has multiplied TV fragmentation substantially, consider the number of places you can find short and long video clips online. The same holds true with any medium that has digital competition. Local newspapers now must share space with journalistic services that are thousands of miles away. Traditional magazine firms confront competition with a multitude of web outlets that cover the same subjects. The steep rise of digital media clearly encourages the movement of material that might have been locally available only in print or video to find homes in many digital spaces.

As with channel fragmentation, audience erosion by no means started with the internet. The most important erosion of magazine and newspaper audiences began as a result of the introduction of television in the late 1940s. Erosion of AM radio audiences began with the introduction of FM radio in the 1960s. Since the 1980s, media and advertising practitioners have noted that the audiences for all media are eroding at an increasing pace. Much of that erosion is due to the dramatic splintering of audiences for broadcast television. From the late 1940s until the early 1980s, fully 90 percent of all those watching television were tuned in to ABC, CBS, or NBC, according to Nielsen. By around 2000, though, the three networks' "share" had slid to about 51 percent—that's a 39 percent drop. According to Nielsen, the missing population could be found at the relatively new Fox network (which had about 13 percent of the audience); at the smaller, newer broadcast networks (e.g., CW and Univision); and playing DVDs and video games.

The spread of digital media in the 21st century—and the nearly limitless number of websites and apps a person can access through many media—makes audience fragmentation a bigger issue now more than ever. Instead of trying to attract everybody, today's media executives typically respond to the situation by focusing on a specific audience. They are trying to define and hold an audience niche—to earn the loyalty of specific portions of the population, while other companies in the fragmenting media world try to attract other groups. As media executives think about their desired audiences more and more carefully, they engage in what is known as audience segmentation.

audience segmentation
producers and distributors try to reach different types of people with content tailored specifically for them

The term "**audience segmentation**" refers to the practice by which producers and distributors try to reach different types of people with messages tailored specifically for them (see Figure P.2). No individual media materials can attract all of the approximately 316 million individuals in the United States. Instead, these materials reach segments, or parts, of society. These segments vary greatly in terms of the number of people involved and the time it takes for most of them to receive the material. NCIS is an example of a television program that reaches more than ten million viewers virtually instantaneously. Conversely, the unexpected death of pop icon Prince in 2016 showed how huge audiences can build over time—although many heard the "breaking news" on television, many more learned about it in news programs, newspapers, and web reports.

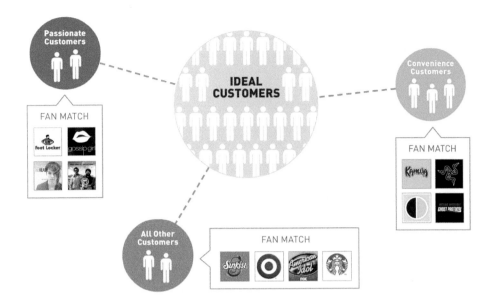

Figure P.2
An example of audience
segmentation from LoudDoor.
It categorizes members of a
company's "ideal customers"
based on the companies the
customer chose to become a fan
of on Facebook. (Courtesy of
LoudDoor, www.louddoor.com.)

Increasingly, though, the pursuit of relatively small audiences by firms involved in the production, distribution, and exhibition of messages is purposeful and profitable. **Targeting** occurs when a mass media organization sets its sights on having as its audience one or more of the social segments it has identified in the population. Consider, for example, a magazine company that for decades has put out a periodical aimed at women in general. Women, of course, constitute an audience segment—quite a large one (women make up a bit more than half of the US population). Greater audience segmentation on the part of the publisher might involve deciding to create two websites: one goes after specific types of women aged 18 to 35 who are mothers, and the other is set up to attract women aged 40 to 54 whose children have left home. One form of targeting would involve advertising to women who fit that profile in the hope that they will visit the website and keep coming back. An additional approach would be to publish articles on topics clearly aimed at one group or another so that those articles show up high on organic search-engine results when people of that group search for the topic. That would lead women to the magazine, and maybe they would return.

Why would a media company want to reduce its audience by segmenting and targeting in a particular way? The answer is that decisions to segment and target are based on business considerations. Why and how executives engage in segmentation and targeting differ according to whether their media outlet is supported primarily by advertising funds. Recall from Chapter 2 that some media companies rely mostly on advertising for their revenues. Other companies get support from a balanced combination of advertising and subscriptions. Still others get most of their support from individual purchases or subscriptions. If a marketer sees that particular segments are well off economically or are more likely than other segments to purchase its products, the marketer will target more lucrative segments and pay less attention to the others.

targeting
when a mass media organization
sets its sights on having as its
audience one or more of the
social segments it has identified
in the population

Globalization

In the face of media fragmentation, audience erosion, and the need to move materials to more digital windows in order to increase revenues, US production and

Digital technology is now a truly global phenomenon, reaching all corners of the world, such as these Hmong people. Even tribes and peoples who live primarily pastoral existences are increasingly connected via the internet and digital technology. They are therefore potential targets for advertising and other media phenomena.

globalization
the movement of media content around the world

coproduction
a deal between two firms for the funding of media material

distribution executives are looking to the global marketplace as a way to solve their revenue problems. Digital media allow for that to happen more quickly and efficiently. That fueling of **globalization**, like the other developments we've discussed so far, fuels convergence.

It's not as if US mass media firms have been ignoring the rest of the world until now. On the contrary, the movie, recording, radio, television, book, and magazine industries have all to some extent been distributing their products internationally for a long time. However, during the first three-quarters of the 20th century, "going global" meant taking materials that had already generated profits in the United States and adding to those profits by selling them elsewhere.

Today, a new mind-set about the world outside the United States' borders is at work. Its logic is as follows: Media fragmentation and audience erosion make it difficult for mass media distributors to reach the huge audiences they would like in the United States. When producers use audience segmentation to attract advertisers or cultivate consumer loyalty, they inevitably lower the number of American consumers who will view those products. Global consumers are a way to make the audience larger. In this way, media executives view countries around the world as part of the initial marketplace for these mass media materials. Moreover, the internet provides the opportunity for US-based media firms to reach people globally. It allows these firms to take advantage of convergence by presenting these audiences with news, movies, digital books, music, games, and more.

For media critics, there are two questions about this global approach that particularly stand out. First, these critics ask, "Who's to say that there are audience segments outside the United States that have tastes similar to those of Americans?" Second, they ask, "Don't those parts of the world that have strong and growing consumer economies—Europe, Asia, and Central and South America—have their own mass media firms that create materials aimed at their own consumers?" As we will see in the chapters to come, companies in different media industries answer these questions differently. Recording companies, for example, have decided that they can't, in fact, take it for granted that people throughout the world share American tastes. Tastes in music are often vastly different within each country, let alone worldwide. But the costs of producing a CD or selling digital copies through Apple Music or another web music store are so relatively low that it is often quite profitable to pursue audience segments within a country. Consequently, even the biggest firms have split themselves into different subsidiaries that concentrate on different parts of the world and funnel the profits back to the home office. The US movie industry, by contrast, derives a lot of its revenues from sending the same movies around the world. At the same time, the major US film producers have been getting more involved than ever in international coproductions. A **coproduction** is a deal between two firms for the funding of media material. So, for example, US firms Universal Pictures and Atlas Entertainment collaborated with Legendary Entertainment East of China and China

Film Group to finance *The Great Wall*, a movie starring Matt Damon. The companies varied in their investments; two of them (Universal and China Film) picked up distribution rights. The film lost money (an estimated $75 million) even after going through all its exhibition windows. Some of the partners lost more than others, depending on their investments and the deals they struck.

Looking at global possibilities, then, mass media executives see both opportunities and risks, particularly because convergence potentially provides the space for companies to reach across the world for audiences, advertisers, and the meeting of the two. Moreover, as convergence allows for increased global media competition, the companies involved may push for even more convergence—that is, for the movement of more content across a larger number of digital technologies. But although competition across a wide swath of media, both analog and digital, may sound great to consumers, many executives get nervous that their firms will lose out if too many products fight for audience attention. Other—typically large—companies can do more because their ownership of content and exhibition windows around the world and in the United States allows them to reach huge audiences (and advertisers) internationally on both digital and nondigital media. These companies represent the rise (and power) of conglomeration.

Conglomeration

In the media world, **conglomeration** refers to the activities involved in becoming and acting like a mass media conglomerate. A **mass media conglomerate** is a company that holds several mass media firms in different media industries under its corporate umbrella. Mass media conglomerates are not new. What is relatively new is the approach that their corporate leaders are taking.

Until the 1980s, the executives who ran media conglomerates typically did not require the different parts of their firm to work with one another. To them, the value of owning magazines, TV stations, music labels, and the like lay in the ability of each business to generate profits separately for the parent firm. Things began to change in the 1980s for a number of reasons. One reason was simply that top media executives and financiers got caught up in the greedy merger-and-acquisition mania that swept through corporate America during that decade. An even more intense period of combinations took place during the mid-1990s, with multibillion-dollar linkages between such companies as Time and Warner and then between AOL and Time and Warner; Twentieth Century Fox and News Corporation; Sony and Columbia; Disney and ABC; and CBS and Viacom.

To justify the high costs of these mergers, the chief executives of these companies describe the media world evolving in a way that requires them to have holdings in several mass media industries if their companies are to remain major players in the 21st century. They believe the danger for a media firm otherwise is that its competitors will prevent it from accessing the distribution and exhibition outlets that it needs if it is to carry out its revenue-generating mission. True, they can make agreements with other firms that allow them to use outlets owned by those other firms on the condition that those firms also can use *their* outlets. But ultimately, they believe, a company's destiny in the new media world will be determined by its ability to own, alone or with others, the distribution and exhibition outlets that it needs in order

conglomeration
the activities involved in becoming and acting like a company's becoming a mass media conglomerate

mass media conglomerate
a company that holds several mass media firms in different media industries under its corporate umbrella

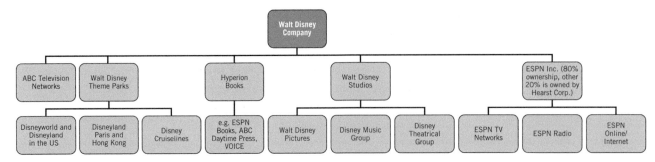

Figure P.3

The Walt Disney Company's various divisions allow for much horizontal integration. Can you see how and think of some examples?

to reach its audiences. Perhaps ten or fifteen companies from around the world will achieve this power. Executives of large firms want their companies to be among them.

Recall that we have used the term "vertical integration" to describe an organization's control of a media product from the production of content through its distribution and exhibition. Vertical integration is now in the TV industry and, to a certain extent, in the video game industry. In circumstances in which vertical integration hasn't been legalized (as was the case in the movie and broadcast TV industries until recently), companies have tried to grab control of two of the three stages—production and/or distribution and/or exhibition—to keep their industry clout.

What the leaders of media conglomerates urge today is horizontal integration in addition to as much vertical integration as possible. **Horizontal integration** (see Figure P.3) has two aspects. First, it involves the ownership of production facilities, distribution channels, and/or exhibition outlets in different, even potentially competing, companies across a number of media industries. Second, it involves bringing those parts together (integrating them) so that each can profit from the expertise of the others. A term that is similar to horizontal integration and that became a buzzword among media executives is "synergy." **Synergy** describes a situation in which the whole is greater than the sum of its parts. It is synergy at work when DC Comics, owned by AT&T's Warner Media, provides the characters (including Batman) for WarnerMedia's Warner Bros. movies, which in turn provide the inspiration for *Batman* clothing and when all of these elements get publicity through the following:

- WarnerMedia's CW broadcast network (which it owns with CBS)
- WarnerMedia's TNT, TBS, and CNN cable networks
- All of WarnerMedia's and AT&T's websites and mobile apps—as well as those managed by the DirectTV satellite firm, which AT&T owns
- The expressed enthusiasm by the target audience on *Batman* Facebook fan pages
- *Batman* feeds on Twitter
- The encouragement of more media attention to *Batman* as a result of real-time monitoring of these activities by DC Comics and its public relations agency

As you can see from some of the examples (and you undoubtedly have been thinking of some of your own), convergence is a major aspect of these synergistic activities. As we noted earlier, all media companies have as a goal crossing digital media in order to be accessible to their target audiences whenever and wherever they want their content. Because of their wealth and multimedia capabilities, media

horizontal integration
the ownership of production facilities, distribution channels, and/or exhibition outlets in a number of media industries and the integration of those elements so that each can profit from the expertise of the others

synergy
a situation in which the whole is greater than the sum of its parts; the ability of mass media organizations to channel content into a wide variety of mass media on a global scale through control over production, distribution, and exhibition in as many of those media as possible

conglomerates pursue this goal as well, but with the kind of money that links tens and even hundreds of millions of people with techniques of audience segmentation, windows, and globalization across a panoply of media.

Media companies often need help from other firms in order to compete globally across media boundaries. To get that help, they can join up with larger firms or turn to one or more of the thousands of smaller firms eager to extend their niches in the global media environment. Called **joint ventures**, these alliances involve companies agreeing to work together or to share investments. As noted earlier, the CW broadcast network is a joint venture. So is Hulu, which is owned by Disney (via its Direct-to-Consumer and International subsidiary) and Comcast (through NBC Universal).

joint ventures
alliances formed between a large media firm and one or more of the thousands of smaller firms that are eager to extend their niches in the global media environment; the companies either work together or share investments

Moving Forward

The bottom line is that companies are moving forward with convergence quickly because they are aware of its importance for competition in today's media world. In fact, the distribution of materials across media boundaries nationally and globally has become so much a part of what media firms do that we all take this activity for granted. As we have seen, the movement of much content across media is becoming more common, at least partly because it is technologically easier via digital media. It is also taking place because the fragmentation of channels and the segmentation of audiences encourage attempts to make target audiences cumulatively larger through distribution windows across media industries, through globalization of distribution, and through the kind of conglomeration that gives companies a lot of clout in analog and digital distribution of the content within their countries and around the world.

These activities will show up in the forthcoming chapters on individual media industries. As we'll see, the five drivers of media convergence have provoked concern both from within the media system and from critics outside it. Perhaps some anxious thoughts about the possible impact of globalization or conglomeration crossed your mind as you read the previous pages. We may well discuss your worries in future chapters, or we may bring up other issues relating to convergence. The exploration of particular media industries today is a fascinating, many-sided activity. Let's get started.

 ## Key Terms

audience segmentation	digital media	mass media conglomerate
channel fragmentation	globalization	synergy
conglomeration	horizontal integration	targeting
coproduction	joint ventures	windows

The Internet Industry

6

CHAPTER OBJECTIVES

1   Discuss the history of the internet and the devices that link to it.

2   Understand the internet as a technology.

3   Describe the internet industry, its relationship to convergence, and its impact on media organizations and their consumers.

4   Analyze concerns that observers hold about internet privacy issues.

In 2017 a Forrester consulting firm survey found that 90 percent of Americans aged between 18 and 29 watch some form of TV over the internet. Forrester also concluded from the survey that that 18- to 29-year-olds make up the only age group in the United States that prefers "streaming" across a range of mobile devices over offline TV viewing.[1] This doesn't mean that 18- to 29-year-olds stay away from cable and broadcast networks. It means much of that viewing—as well as the viewing of native internet programming sources such as Netflix and Hulu—is done through streaming.

Do you fit this description? Perhaps you also use social media—Twitter, Facebook, even Snapchat—to converse with others about the shows you're viewing online or on the traditional box. Or you may also find yourself using your phone or tablet to find out the score of a game while you watch a drama series on your laptop. Ad agency researchers have found that distraction from TV screens by smartphones and tablets may be fairly severe.[2] But the number of digital media devices associated with television keeps going up.

The internet stands at the center of this convergence of technologies around television content. The internet is also central to so many other aspects of media convergence—for example, watching movies on your "smart TV," reading books on your e-reader, browsing magazines and newspapers on your tablet, listening to music on your phone,

> "The internet, like the steam engine, is a technological breakthrough that changed the world."

PETER SINGER, PROFESSOR OF BIOETHICS AT PRINCETON UNIVERSITY

playing a video game with faraway strangers, and seeing ads on all of them. As you can imagine, and as we'll see in the following chapters, the people who work in industries that produce, distribute, and exhibit materials for these media are quite aware of the importance of the internet for their livelihoods. Much of their work takes place with the internet in mind.

The internet is so important to media today that to understand books, newspapers, magazines, recorded music, radio, the movies, television, and video games (the subjects of the forthcoming chapters), it's crucial that we first understand the internet. Our goal here is to answer three basic questions: Exactly what is the internet? Where did it come from? How does it work? We will see that an entire industry has built up around the internet. The internet industry is involved in producing, distributing, and exhibiting its own content, as well as connecting with other media industries that want to distribute and exhibit their own content via the "Net."

The Rise of the Internet

The **internet** is a global system of interconnected private, public, academic, business, and government computer networks that use a standard set of commands to link billions of users worldwide. ARPANet, as it was first known, was conceived by the Advanced Research Projects Agency (ARPA) of the Department of Defense in 1969. The aim was to create a network that would allow a research computer at one university or military installation to "talk to" research computers at other universities or military installations, even if part of the system was destroyed by war or disaster. The system of data transfer was fundamentally different from the way telephone conversations made their way from one person to another. In a standard landline phone conversation, the entire flow of voice "data"—the electrical impulses representing what each person says—is continuous. Every phone call, therefore, continuously takes up a wire connection until the people hang up, even if there is silence on the line for seconds or minutes.

The unique aspect of the new system was that it allowed for a transmission line to carry more than one data "conversation" at a time. It did that by breaking down messages into segments called **packets** and sending the packets through parts of the network that had the fewest other packets moving through them at

Internet
a global system of interconnected private, public, academic, business, and government computer networks that use a standard set of commands to link billions of users worldwide

packets
segments of messages that contain digital instructions that allow them to reassemble properly at the same time at the destination

Figure 6.1

Who's not online?

% of US adults who do not use the internet (2018)

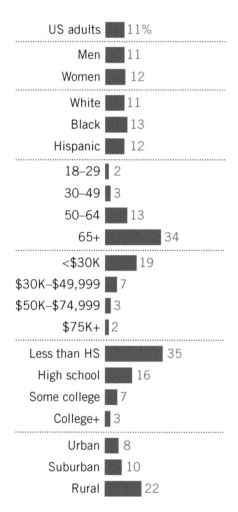

US adults	11%
Men	11
Women	12
White	11
Black	13
Hispanic	12
18–29	2
30–49	3
50–64	13
65+	34
<$30K	19
$30K–$49,999	7
$50K–$74,999	3
$75K+	2
Less than HS	35
High school	16
Some college	7
College+	3
Urban	8
Suburban	10
Rural	22

Note: Whites and blacks include only non-Hispanics.
Source: Survey conducted Jan. 3-10, 2018.

PEW RESEARCH CENTER

Source: www.pewresearch.org/fact-tank/2018/03/05/some-americans-dont-use-the-internet-who-are-they/ft_18-03-01_notonline_demos/, accessed June 18, 2018.

a particular moment. The packets contained digital instructions that allowed them to be reassembled properly at the same time at the destination. Because packets could be routed or rerouted in more than one direction in the process of looking for the most efficient paths of a network, ARPANet could continue to function even if parts of it were destroyed in the event of a military attack or other disaster.

But some computer scientists had even more ambitious ideas. They didn't want the internet to be simply a vehicle for transferring messages or documents between individuals. Instead, they wanted to create a way for large groups of people to access and work on the same files. They also wanted to be able to direct people to those documents through **hyperlinks**, or specially coded words or pictures that, when clicked, connect the user to a particular file, even to a specific relevant part of a document. Researchers at the Center for European Nuclear Research (CERN) in Geneva, Switzerland, made this linking possible in 1989. Tim Berners-Lee and Sam Walker from the United Kingdom and Robert Cailliau from Belgium created **Hypertext Markup Language (HTML)**, a computer language system that allowed people to access a system of interlinked documents through the internet. The CERN researchers built this system to work via the internet, and they called it the World Wide Web. A key aspect of this web was that users could go to the materials by typing in a specific World Wide Web address or by clicking on a link in a document that contained the address, which would automatically connect them to that place.

internet messages at the time had to be transmitted in text form. Sending graphical images was possible, but the images had to be decoded by the receiver before viewing. That situation changed in 1993, when computer scientists at the University of Illinois created the web browser, a graphical way to access the World Wide Web. They called it Mosaic. With its successor browsers—for example, Apple's Safari, Microsoft Edge, Google Chrome, or Mozilla Firefox—a computer user today can easily view complex drawings or photographs.

By the mid-1990s, the internet had moved far beyond its original military and academic purposes to become a vast societal communication system. Scientists figured out ways to attach devices such as desktop and laptop computers to the internet with both indoor wired and wireless connections. They also figured out ways to connect the internet to outdoor mobile devices—first basic mobile phones, then more powerful smartphones, and then e-readers and tablets. Much of the activity in cyberspace (i.e., in the online world of computer networks) still involved mediated interpersonal communication or individuals interacting one-on-one with other individuals through written words, voice, and video (see Chapter 1). But much of that activity, as well as other parts of the online world, involved commercial attempts to profit from reaching various audiences. Companies sprang up to create sites on the web, to determine who was coming to these sites, and to encourage advertising on them. The digital world of the internet, in short, had become a new mass medium.

Take a look at the timeline in Figure 6.2. It charts key points in the evolution of the internet and the devices (especially mobile ones) that connect to it. Relatively new as these technologies are, they have become quite popular and widespread. In 2018 the Pew Research Center found that 89 percent of adult Americans (those 18 years and older) said they "use the internet." Many people also have a number of ways to connect. It found that 77 percent say they go online daily, including 26 percent who do it "almost constantly." When it comes to being almost-constantly connected, 18- to 29-year-olds beat other age groups, with 39 percent saying that. By contrast, 8 percent of Americans 65 and older say they are online that often.

At the other end of the connectivity continuum—the 11 percent who say they don't go online—Figure 6.1 contains Pew data that show people who don't use the internet are overrepresented among Americans who are over age 65, who have less than a high school education, and who live in rural areas. Some of these people—a third, Pew learned—say they have no interest in going online or don't think it's relevant to their lives. Another third finds the internet too difficult to use (including 8 percent who say they are too old to learn). The last third of those who don't go online contains people who say cost is a barrier (19 percent), live in areas where a decent connection is tough to get, or give another reason for not linking up. The social cost of not being able to connect to the internet for any reason is a topic worth discussing. Moreover, we ought to consider that "going online" can mean very different experiences and opportunities. The ability to use several internet-connected devices—a laptop, tablet, and high-end smartphone, for example—and high internet speeds may provide a person with more social and economic opportunities than someone who has to rely on one device—say, a low-end smartphone with a very slow connection. Nevertheless, it is noteworthy that by Pew's counting, the percentage of US adults who do not use the internet has declined from nearly one out of two in 2000 to about one out of ten just eighteen years later.

hyperlinks

highlighted words or pictures on the internet that, when clicked, will connect the user to a particular file, even to a specific relevant part of a document

Hypertext Markup Language (HTML)

a computer language system that allowed people to access a system of interlinked documents through the internet. HTML is used to define the structure, content, and layout of a page by using what are called tags.

THINKING ABOUT MEDIA LITERACY

Tim Berners-Lee, one of the main people credited with creating the World Wide Web, is quoted as saying, "The original idea of the web was that it should be a collaborative space where you can communicate through sharing information." Do you think the current online environment is a realization of that original idea? Why or why not?

The Pew Research Center continually surveys the US population regarding its internet use, knowledge, and habits.[3] Its research in 2018 shows that 95 percent of young people aged 13 to 17 own a smartphone—that is, a device that makes calls and also connects to the internet; we'll use a more elaborate definition later in the chapter. As Figure 6.3 shows, fully 85 percent of them say they use Google's video viewing and sharing service YouTube, 72 percent use Facebook's photo captioning and sharing service Instagram, and 69 percent use the message-sharing facility Snapchat. Pew found there are demographic differences among teen use. For example, 70 percent of teens living in households earning less than $30,000 a year say they use Facebook, compared with 36 percent whose family income is $75,000 or more a year. Although 22 percent of lower-income teens say Facebook is the social media platform they use "most often," only 4 percent of teens from higher-income households say that. Gender brings out interesting

1930s	1940s	1950s	1960s	1970s
1931: Emanuel Goldberg and Robert Luther in Germany receive a US patent for a "Statistical Machine," an early document search engine that uses photoelectric cells and pattern recognition to search for specific words on microfilm documents.	**1945:** Scientist Vannevar Bush publishes the article "As We May Think" in *The Atlantic* magazine predicting the invention of technology that would allow ideas in different parts of text to link to one another. **1946:** University of Pennsylvania engineers create ENIAC, the Electronic Numerical Integrator and Computer.	**1958:** President Eisenhower requests funds to create the US Defense Advanced Research Projects Agency (ARPA).	**1962:** Len Kleinrock writes an MIT dissertation on "packet switching." **1965:** Larry Roberts at MIT sets up an experiment in which two computers communicate to each other using packet-switching technology. **1966:** ARPANET project begins in Cambridge, Massachusetts; Larry Roberts is in charge. **1969:** ARPANET connects computers at four US universities. The first ARPANET message is sent between UCLA and Stanford University.	**1971:** Ray Tomlinson creates the first email program, along with the @ sign to signify "at." **1973:** ARPANET establishes connections to two universities in the UK and Norway. **1976:** Steve Jobs and Steve Wozniak found Apple computers.

Figure 6.2
Timeline of the internet industry

differences, too: Girls are more likely than boys to say Snapchat is the site they use most often (42 percent vs. 29 percent). Boys, by contrast, are more likely than girls to choose YouTube as their favorite social media place (39 percent vs. 25 percent). Generally, though, the story is that all teens find the internet to be central parts of their lives. As the Pew report notes, "45 percent of teens now say they are online on a near-constant basis."[4]

1980s

1981: IBM announces the first personal computer (PC). Microsoft creates the PC's disk operating system (DOS).

1983: Paul Mockapetris and Jon Postel create the domain name system for the internet.
1987: 25 million PCs are sold in the United States and the first Cisco routers are shipped.

1990s

1990: ARPANet formally ends. Tim Berners-Lee creates the World Wide Web.

1993: Carnegie Mellon University offers the first campus-wide wireless access to the internet.
1993: Marc Andreessen and Eric Bina invent Mosaic, the first widely used web browser, at the University of Illinois, Urbana-Champaign.
1995: Microsoft releases Windows 95.

1996: The *New York Times* establishes a website.
1998: Sergey Brin and Larry Page incorporate Google.
1998: US Congress passes the Children's Online Privacy Protection Act.

2000s

2001: Apple introduces the first iTunes media player and library application.
2001: The European Council adopts the first treaty addressing criminal offenses committed over the internet.
2003: The RIAA sues 261 individuals for allegedly distributing copyrighted music files over peer-to-peer networks.
2004: Mark Zuckerberg and fellow Harvard students create the Facebook social networking site.

2006: Jack Dorsey, Evan Williams, Biz Stone, and Noah Glass launch Twitter.
2006: Google, Inc., acquires YouTube for $1.65 billion in a stock-for-stock transaction.

2007: Search engine giant Google surpasses software giant Microsoft in having the most visited website.

2010s

2010: Kevin Systrom and Mike Krieger create Instagram.
2011: Over one-third (35%) of American adults own a smartphone.

2011: Evan Spiegel and Bobby Murphy create Snapchat while students at Stanford University.

2012: Facebook purchases Instagram for $1 billion.
2015: Nearly two-thirds of Americans (64%) own a smartphone, and one in five rely solely on smartphones to access the internet.
2016: Internet Society celebrates 25th Anniversary.
2017: The FCC repeals 2015 net neutrality rules, saying a restoration of the Federal Trade Commission's authority over internet service providers would benefit consumers.
2018: Cambridge Analytica, a data analytics firm, accesses information of millions of Facebook users, opening Facebook to an investigation by the FTC about privacy protections.

Figure 6.3

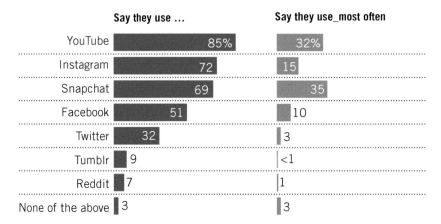

YouTube, Instagram and Snapchat are the most popular online platforms among teens

% of US teens who ...

Note: Figures in first column add to more than 100% because multiple response were allowed. Question about most-used site was asked only of respondents who use multiple sites; results have been recalculated to include those who use only one site. Respondents who did not give an answer are not shown.
Source: Survey conducted March 7-April 10, 2018.
"Teenss Social Media & Technology 2018"

PEW RESEARCH CENTER

Source: www.pewinternet.org/2018/05/31/teens-social-media-technology-2018/, accessed June 18, 2018.

Production, Distribution, and Exhibition on the Internet

As we discussed in Chapter 1, it is helpful to think of the activities of production, distribution, and exhibition when trying to understand media activities. On the internet, the firm that owns the site is not necessarily the firm that creates its content. Often, companies and individuals create content for locations they don't control. An example is a video production firm paid to create a travel video for Frommers.com. Very different would be an individual who makes a travel video during a recent trip to Spain and posts it on YouTube and Facebook. Creative products made by individuals who visit sites are often called **user-generated content (UGC)**. The *Huffington Post* is an example of a popular current events website that uses a lot of UGC to fill its space and attract users. Although it does that, the parent firm TheHuffingtonPost.com still plays an important role in production: it formats the material and finds relevant photos, for example.

Apart from this shared production role, TheHuffingtonPost.com also acts as a distributor by placing and marketing *The Huffington Post* online. Websites in general fulfil this role as distributors. NYTimes.com, for example, is a major distributor of the material produced by the *New York Times* newspaper. This is also the case with Amazon.com, which produces and distributes its retail website online. Google

user-generated content (UGC) creative products, such as videos and music, generated by people on websites and apps.

produces and distributes its search engine to people who tell their browser to go to it. And Instagram produces and distributes its software that allows people to create mini-sites within its site that their friends can access in various ways.

THINKING ABOUT MEDIA LITERACY

The statistics from Pew Research Center studies have these stunning data:

"70 percent of teens living in households earning less than $30,000 a year say they use Facebook, compared with 36 percent whose family income is $75,000 or more a year."

What do you make of this statistic? Is it surprising? What do you think might explain such a huge difference in use of Facebook in teens from different household income levels?

But who is the exhibitor in this situation? Recall from Chapter 1 that an exhibitor is a company that provides the public with access to the material it accepts from a distributor. From one standpoint, we can say that the sites themselves exhibit the materials to their visitors, much as customers visit physical stores that show their products. Another, perhaps better, view is that the internet exhibitor is the **internet service provider (ISP)**, the firm that provides the technology through which the person can access the internet. There's a fair chance that much of college students' contact with the online world is through their school. In that case, the school typically picks up the tab for your email and your connections to the college's online resources (such as the library catalog), as well as to the internet. Outside of colleges, the firms that carry out this role tend to be cable companies such as Comcast and Charter Communications, packagers of internet services such as Windstream, and phone companies such as AT&T and Verizon.

> **Internet service provider (ISP)**
> a company that sells access to the internet

Most ISPs today provide their customers with the ability to connect via **Wi-Fi**. Wi-Fi is a radio technology (called IEEE 802.11) that engineers designed in the late 1990s to provide secure, reliable, fast wireless connectivity. Many consumer devices use Wi-Fi—personal computers can network to each other and connect to the internet, mobile computers can connect to the internet from any Wi-Fi hotspot, and digital cameras can transfer images wirelessly. There are four types of Wi-Fi—b, g, n, and ac—and each provides faster connection to the web router (see Figure 6.4). Because Wi-Fi frequencies don't travel more than a few hundred yards, it takes many Wi-Fi transmitters to cover an area such as a college campus.

> **Wi-Fi**
> a radio technology (called IEEE 802.11) that engineers designed in the late 1990s to provide secure, reliable, fast wireless connectivity

Some ISPs have rules about how much downloading from the internet you can do before you have to pay them more money. Someone who regularly streams movies to a cell phone, for example, may be charged a substantial extra charge. A cable company may not charge more, but it may "throttle" the data speeds, or slow down the service. ISP executives explain that they do this because people who download or stream movies and other products that take up a lot of electronic space—bandwidth—often clog the ISP's system and make it difficult for other customers to have their packets delivered efficiently.

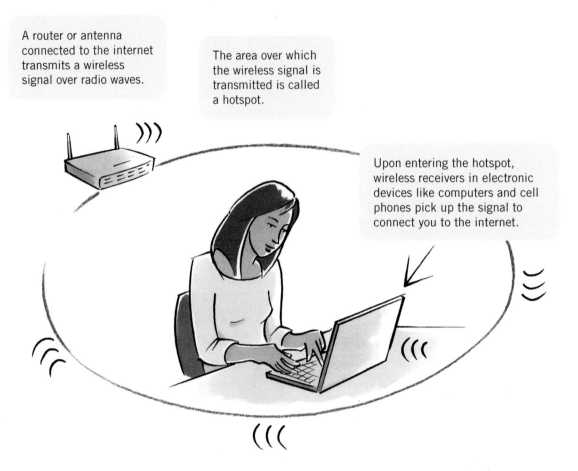

A router or antenna connected to the internet transmits a wireless signal over radio waves.

The area over which the wireless signal is transmitted is called a hotspot.

Upon entering the hotspot, wireless receivers in electronic devices like computers and cell phones pick up the signal to connect you to the internet.

Figure 6.4
How Wi-Fi works. Wi-Fi technology allows an internet connection to be broadcast and received using radio waves. Technology in computers, video game consoles, smartphones, MP3 players, tablets, and other wireless-enabled devices can pick up the signals to connect to the internet when they are within range of a wireless network. The area in which one can connect to a wireless network is known as a hotspot.

The Net Neutrality Controversy

It is important to note, though, that so far no ISPs have stopped their customers from going to a site they type into the Uniform Resource Locator (URL) box.

There have been cases where a branch of the federal government called the National Intellectual Property Rights Center has seized a site's domain name after getting a judge's warrant for violating counterfeiting, pirating, or other criminal laws. In that situation, no ISP can access the site. Under ordinary conditions, though, you may think that any place you want to go on the web is open to you. That is why the notion of the ISP as exhibitor may not seem as important to the producer and distributor as does a cable provider or a newsstand, where the owners decide what material to accept and what to reject for presentation to the public. Some companies do restrict their workers' ability to use the firms' computers to visit sites that the companies feel will waste workers' time (e.g., game sites and Facebook) or embarrass other employees (e.g., pornography sites). Imagine, though, if the ISP for your home computer decided that it would allow only certain websites to reach its clients but not others. The ISP might do this in order to get websites to pay to "exhibit" the sites in people's homes. Or the ISP may tell certain websites that it might slow them down (thus encouraging users to go to other sites) unless they pay fees to get the fastest speeds.

GLOBAL MEDIA TODAY & CULTURE

FAANG IN YOUR DAILY LIFE

YouTube has become ubiquitous. You can use it to access movies, premium paid content, and a music streaming service, in addition to news, viral videos, and regular UGC.

The leading players in consumer-facing digital landscape—Facebook, Apple, Amazon, Netflix, and Google—are ubiquitous and increasingly involved in our daily lives. In the financial community these entities are referred to with the acronym *FAANG* (from the initial letters of these companies). They currently represent five of the most popular and best-performing tech stocks in the market, and although some of them are relatively new as publicly traded companies, they have among the highest market capitalizations—an estimate of their value—in the entire world. They are also increasingly funding and distributing media content through their platforms, presenting it to media audiences, domestically and globally.

Facebook, a leading global player in the social media landscape, is also funding original content and through acquisitions has become a leading company in the media landscape. So is Apple, in addition to its primacy in consumer electronics and computer software. Also Amazon, the leading online retailer and cloud computing conglomerate, has entered the media landscape through its Prime service, funding and distributing entertainment content. Netflix is a leading video-on-demand platform, increasingly extending its global reach and funding original productions in addition to licensing third-party media content, whereas Google, originally starting out as the leading search engine, has morphed into a diversified player offering internet-related services and products, including media content—for example, via their company platform YouTube. It is very likely that you interact with at least one of these companies on a daily basis. Which of the FAANG companies do you utilize the most? What does it mean for you to have them so involved in your daily life?

As a consumer, you may think this is a terrible idea because it might make it difficult or impossible to reach certain sites. But some ISP executives argue that they should have the right to charge some sites for "exhibition" because the sites use up enormous amounts of bandwidth (by providing videos, for example) that they have to provide to their customers and for which they do not get compensated. Website executives and consumer advocates respond that the ISPs do get money back by charging their customers for access. Moreover, they argue that the internet has become so important to society that to restrict or diminish the use of it could have unfortunate consequences for what people know and what they can share with one another.

This is the argument used by people in favor of **net neutrality**. Net (or network) neutrality is the proposition that ISPs should treat all traffic on the internet equally. President Barack Obama picked up this argument and in 2014 recommended the Federal Communications Commission (FCC) categorize broadband internet service as a "telecommunications service" in order to preserve net neutrality. Calling the internet a telecommunications service means that it has features of a common carrier—like the water or phone company or a railroad that transports goods. Just as the phone company cannot refuse to allow you to make a phone call, slow your particular call, or charge you more than it charges your friend for the same call,

net (or network) neutrality proposition that ISPs should treat all traffic on the internet equally

so—the logic goes—an ISP should not be allowed to do that with its system. In 2015 the FCC agreed with that logic and ruled in favor of net neutrality by reclassifying broadband access as a telecommunications service and applying its "common carrier" designation to ISPs. The FCC chair under President Donald Trump's administration, however, reversed that rule, claiming that it was unnecessary infringement on media competition. Critics worried that this would mark the undoing of net neutrality, and some members of Congress tried to make it a law. As of this writing, it hasn't happened, and public advocates are watching the internet industry warily to see if one or another ISP would charge apps or websites to speed their traffic.

Social Media Sites and Search Engines

Let's leave the topic of exhibition and return to our discussion of producers and distributors of content on the web. You'll recall we mentioned NYTimes.com, TheHuffingtonPost.com, Amazon, Google, and Facebook. These five firms reflect three different kinds of content businesses that exist online. The *New York Times* is an example of a firm from another industry that, seeing the need for digital convergence, has brought its business online. TheHuffingtonPost.com and Amazon represent firms that started on the web but that are carrying out activities that resemble offline firms. (The *Huffington Post* acts somewhat like an offline newspaper, whereas Amazon acts somewhat like a big offline retail catalog. We will discuss these newspaper and catalog forms and their relation to the internet in forthcoming chapters.) As a search engine and a social media site, respectively, Google and Facebook are examples of businesses that don't exist outside the internet environment, even though other media industries (such as newspapers and retail advertising) make great use of them.

> **social media site (social networking site or SNS)**
> an online location where people can interact with others around information, entertainment, and news of their own choosing and, often, of their own making

A **social media site** (sometimes called a social networking site or SNS) is an online location where people can interact with others around information, entertainment, and news of their own choosing and, often, of their own making. Facebook, Instagram, Twitter, and LinkedIn are popular social media locations that offer people quite different approaches to interacting. Twitter requires users to communicate via messages of no more than 240 characters, though they can add links, photos, or videos. LinkedIn invites people to connect around business networks. Facebook and Instagram see themselves as ways in which friends can stay connected with each other on a continuing basis. All four social media locations also offer companies ways to maintain an important presence. If you've been to a fan page on Facebook or followed a company on Twitter, you know how popular those places can be.

> **search engine**
> websites that allow users to find sites relevant to topics of interest to them
>
> **web crawlers (web spiders)**
> programs used by search engines that search the internet to retrieve and catalog the content of websites

Whereas people go to social media to find people and companies on those sites, they go to search engines to find people, products, services, and ideas—just about anything—on the internet. *Merriam-Webster's Collegiate Dictionary* defines a **search engine** as "computer software used to search data (as text or a database) for specified information." The search engine developed out of the need for people using the web to find sites relevant to topics of interest to them. You undoubtedly have gone to Google, Bing, Safari, or another search program to find out about a person, location, or fact. Search engines work by using **web crawlers** (also known as **web spiders**), programs that automatically browse the World Wide Web to create copies of all the visited pages. The search engine software then catalogs or "indexes" the downloaded pages so that a person searching for a word in them will find it quickly. Depending on the search engine, the spiders index more or less of the web, but they never catalog the entire web. Not only would it take too much time (and the crawlers have to keep doing their jobs over and over again to update their findings), but there are also some parts of the web that they cannot crawl because they are refused entry.

When you type in search terms, you activate a complex set of mathematically based rules, called an **algorithm**, that comes up with sites that relate to your search terms. Algorithms are the "secret sauce" of search engines. It is quite well known, though, that Google's approach to search

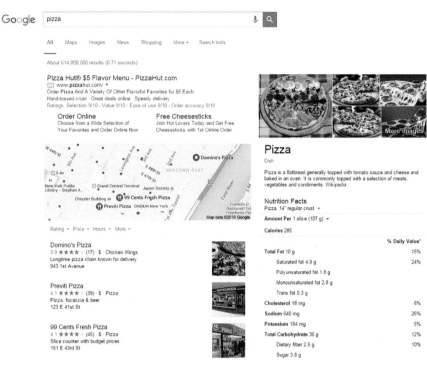

Google search for pizza in New York City. The first listed result is an advertisement for Pizza Hut, followed by a map listing nearby pizza places. Google and the Google logo are registered trademarks of Google, Inc., used with permission.

involves a particular definition of popularity: the number of websites that are linked to a site that uses the search term. The search engine will also take into consideration what Google knows about you based on previous searches, your location, and information you gave Google if you signed into the site. So, for example, if you type "pizza" into a Google search box, the links that appear will probably be for pizza stores near your house. After those, you might get a Wikipedia article about the history of pizza.

The main list of sites that you get in response to typing "pizza" in the Google search box is called Google's **natural or organic search results**. That means that the sites come up based on Google's algorithm without any influence from a pizza restaurant or any other advertiser. Bing, Duckduckgo, and most other major search engines work this way too because they want to maintain their credibility in the eyes of their users. The way these search companies survive is by sending advertising to their users. If natural results were intermingled with ads, users might have a tough time knowing whether a link was placed higher because it was really relevant or because a company paid for its placement there.

natural or organic search results
websites that come up based on a search engine's algorithm without any influence from advertisers

Although it may seem that search engines and social media sites are quite different from one another, during the past few years companies in both areas have begun to realize that they may well end up in similar businesses. The reason for this is the emergence of what they call **social search**, a search carried out to find what people in a person's social circle say about an item. Let's say you are deciding whether to go to a new *Batman* movie called (for this example) *Batman's Cape*. You could go to Google or Bing and type in the movie's name along with the word "review" to find out what critics have said about the film. Or you could go to Facebook and type "*Batman's Cape*" into the search box, and out would come comments that your Facebook friends have made about the film. These comments might be more relevant to you than anonymous Google reviews. In fact, the utility of this sort of search led Google to integrate

social search
a search that is carried out to find what people in a person's social circle say about an item

its social network, Google+, into members' search findings when they are signed into the network. Google+ shut down in 2018, but Bing integrates comments from people's friends into their search results.

Funding Online Content

Search engines and social media sites are very competitive with each other for a basic reason: they survive through advertising revenues, and they must convince advertisers to place money on their sites rather than other sites. In fact, very many sites support their production and distribution of content by attracting audiences to advertising messages. There are, however, other ways companies approach making money on the web. Some companies see their sites as helping to build good images for themselves and their products so that they will be able to later sell their products online and/or offline. Some companies build their sites to sell products directly to people who visit. Still others display content aimed at making money by attracting audiences through subscriptions. Sometimes, firms approach sites with more than one of these goals. Let's take a look at each.

Sites Involved in Image Making

The idea behind using a site for image-making activities is typically to encourage fans of a product or service to purchase the product or service offline. Kraft Foods' Jell-O website, for example, is a site that provides recipes based on various forms of the product. The site also allows people to watch Jell-O commercials and learn about Jell-O products. The site further urges people to use various forms of the product with other Kraft products (e.g., Cool Whip). Jell-O also hosts a fan page on Facebook. None of these activities directly makes any money for Kraft. Instead, they cultivate a friendly, healthful, family-oriented image for Kraft Foods that they hope will yield purchases in supermarkets and other physical stores.

Sites Selling Products or Services

If you have ever bought anything online (and a large majority of internet-enabled individuals have), you are familiar with websites that sell products or services. This selling method has much in common with an old-fashioned catalog, except that online you sometimes have an opportunity to see a video of the products in operation. Amazon sells virtually entirely online; at this writing it has only a few permanent physical stores, though it does own the mostly brick-and-mortar Whole Foods grocery chain. Although Amazon, Amazon-owned Zappos, and Apple Music are internet-first retailers that do extremely well, it should come as no surprise that the most popular brick-and-mortar stores are among the most popular online stores. For example, Walmart, JCPenney, and Home Depot draw millions to their websites.

Content Sites Selling Subscriptions

Netflix is a site that charges a subscription fee for access to movies and TV shows. Subscription fees also work for specialized business magazines and databases because companies may be willing to pay for their employees to access important information related to their industries. For example, the legal database Lexis charges for entry to and use of its site. Along these lines, the trade magazine *Advertising Age* requires a subscription to get into parts of its site with especially desirable information about the advertising industry.

Generally, though, the idea of a publisher charging people subscriptions to see the content of a site hasn't worked very well on the web. It seems that people who are spending hundreds, even thousands, of dollars for hardware and monthly payments to receive the internet have come, over the decades, to expect that media content will be free or very low cost. Moreover, the competition among websites means that people can find adequate (or even the same) news, information, and entertainment for free rather than for a fee.

The *New York Times* and many other newspapers with online content use multilevel subscription services. Initial access might be free, but further features involve in-app purchases.

Nevertheless, as sites such as LinkedIn, Netflix, Spotify, and Hulu can attest, companies do try to find ways to make subscriptions work. The *Wall Street Journal*, the *Financial Times*, and the *New York Times* newspapers also have created subscription models for their websites. Netflix and the *Wall Street Journal* charge a flat subscription fee, perhaps after a trial period. The approach LinkedIn, Spotify, Hulu, the *Financial Times*, the *New York Times*, and others use involves multilevel (or *tiered*) content offerings: The site will allow users to have some materials without charge, perhaps at the price of receiving advertisements. If the users want other materials, or if they want to get the materials without ads, they will have to pay. Other online publishers have adopted a hybrid "freemium" (free + premium) business model. It provides a basic or limited version of a service or type of content for free but also offers users the option to pay for additional content, additional features, or fewer advertisements.

Unfortunately for many online publishers, though, charging for content seems to draw significant numbers of paying customers only on prominent sites. Over the past decade, many newspapers and magazines that have tried subscription models have abandoned this approach for all but archives of their periodicals. Instead, they have turned to advertising as the way to support their online ventures.

Selling Advertisements

As with so much of the media we have explored in previous chapters, and as we will see in forthcoming chapters, a huge part of the web is supported by advertising. Advertising of all types brought in $88 billion to internet businesses in 2018, a growth rate of 17 percent from the previous year at a time when most traditional media were growing slowly or losing money.[5]

The pitch that websites make to advertisers is that they attract the best potential customers for their products. Because the online world is so diverse, they argue, advertisers can find sites that reach people with very specific interests. They also provide advertisers with technology that, they claim, can actually ensure that certain ads will be seen by some people on their sites and that other ads will be seen by different people.

Web marketers argue that this ability to target individuals makes online advertising more "customizable" than any other mass medium in history. One way to customize an advertising message is by **keyword advertising**, an approach used by search engines. Say you type the words "cat food" into a search box. Not only will the search engine find websites about cat food, but it will also show you ads for companies interested in reaching people who search for cat food. Related to keyword advertising is **contextual advertising**, in which software determines what a person is reading and

keyword advertising
when software uses the words in the search box to send the person ads for products that advertisers consider related to the topic

contextual advertising
when software determines what a person is reading and sends the person ads for products that advertisers consider related to the topic

sends the person ads for products that advertisers consider related to the topic. Say you are reading an article about cat food that the search engine found for you. There may be advertisers who want to reach people who read articles about cats and even about cat food, and so the website you are on will send you that sort of ad.

Because tailoring messages in this way requires information about particular members of the audience, website owners engage in online data gathering to find out as much as they can about the individuals who visit their domains. Creating a description of someone based on collected data is called **profiling**. One straightforward method a firm can use to get data for profiling is to ask people to register to get access to a site. When you sign up for Facebook, for example, the company asks you to fill out your name, gender, age, and email address. As you continue the sign-up process, the company asks for your high school, college, and employer's name. That information may not be reliable because you could make up everything except your email address (the Facebook computer tries to check that the email address is correct). A second profiling method that sites use (and which yields different sorts of data) is to ask people what topics they want to learn about through the site. The *New York Times*, for example, allows you to choose news and entertainment categories as guides to the material it sends you.

A third method of profiling yields still other kinds of data: the computer tracks your choices as you move through a particular website or across websites. These choices are stored on your computer in a tiny hidden text file called a **cookie**. Note that the cookie doesn't know your name or address, or even your email address, unless you told its owner or the company went through special means to get it. But each time you visit the site, the cookie identifies you by a number and allows the company to record your mouse clicks, or **clickstream**, through the site. Over time, the company that created the cookie develops a profile of your interests that it can bring together with other profiles to offer to advertisers. The company can track your behavior within its site, and many advertising networks track your behavior with their cookies across sites. The process of following your behavior and then sending you material tailored to what was learned about you is called **behavioral targeting**.

profiling
creating a description of someone based on collected data

cookie
information that a website puts on your computer's hard drive so that it can remember something about you at a later time; more technically, it is information for future use that is stored by the server on the client side of a client/server communication

clickstream
computer jargon used to describe user movement through websites

behavioral targeting
the process of following people's behavior and then sending them material tailored to what was learned about them

THINKING ABOUT MEDIA LITERACY

Many websites generate traffic, and gain popularity, through UGC. YouTube, for example, features videos created and uploaded by people for sharing with their friends and others. Most videos have an advertisement lead-in that you must watch (or click out of) before you can see the video. Who do you think makes the money on that advertisement? Is this an effective financing model for YouTube? What are your views on "must-view" advertising? Who should receive the advertising income?

data mining
the process of gathering and storing information about many individuals—often millions—to be used in audience profiling and interactive marketing

Other methods such as web bugs (code objects embedded in HTML code) can be used to track the internet protocol (IP) addresses of computers that visit a particular website, or even to learn when and from where a particular email was opened. The process of gathering and storing information about many individuals—often millions—to be used in audience profiling and interactive marketing is called **data mining**. In addition to the three forms of online data gathering just mentioned, data miners try to find offline information about individuals—for example, drivers' license records, mortgage information, and credit ratings—that they can link by

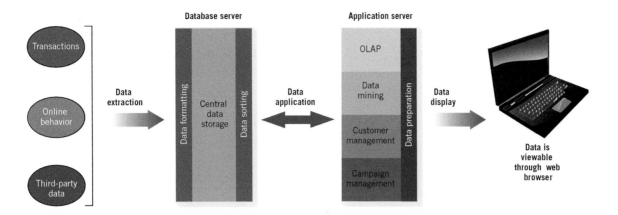

Figure 6.5

The data mining process in action. This figure illustrates how information on individuals is "extracted" from various sources and analyzed. The database server stores the information for the application server, which takes the information and sorts it to make profiles (a process called data mining), to create lists of types of profiles (data management) and to create web ad campaigns and other online targeting activities. OLAP stands for "online analytical processing," an activity that analyzes new and old data about an individual in real time.

computer to other data in the website's collection. Companies also have a means to match cookies from different sources that relate to the same person.

Because of the wide interest in data gathering on the web, an entire data mining industry has grown up around these activities. You may have heard the term **big data** used in connection with data mining. When industry practitioners use the term, they typically mean data about audiences that can be described by high levels of **the 3Vs**: volume, variety, and velocity. Volume refers to the large number of data points collected about individuals and populations. These can come from business records, internet clickstream logs, social networks, and even real-time data sensors such as cameras in stores. Variety refers to the different forms of data that are collected. The large number of data points may reflect a wide spectrum of information—what people's backgrounds are, where they go on the internet, what they buy online, who their online friends are, and more. Velocity refers to the speed at which the information comes to the firm gathering it. Decades ago, new information about audiences often came monthly or weekly. Nowadays, the interactional nature of digital media allows enormous amounts of new information about populations to come to firms in virtually real time.

The goal of the data mining industry is to help web companies sort through the many pieces of information they have on the individuals who come to their sites so that the producers of the sites can profitably use mass customization in editorial and advertising content. Figure 6.5 illustrates this data mining process in action. Such data mining helps websites get advertisers. And even sites that don't rely on ads want to know about the people who visit. They believe that very specific audience data can help them better customize their content and more persuasively encourage people to buy their products or services. Then there are other types of firms that collect and analyze information about people who travel the web so that they can use the information to make money from advertisers and publishers. One such type of company is an **ad network**—or a collection of many websites that a company knits together in order to sell ads on them. The ad-serving company then shares its revenues with the sites on which it places the ads. Another way advertisers can get in front of target audiences on the web is by using **ad exchanges**.

big data
information about audiences that can be described by high levels of the 3Vs

the 3Vs: volume, variety, and velocity of data
volume refers to the large number of data points collected about individuals and populations. Variety refers to the different forms of data that are collected. Velocity refers to the speed at which the information comes to the firm gathering it

ad network
a collection of many websites that a company knits together in order to sell ads on them

ad exchanges
electronic auctions in which various publishers and ad networks offer advertisers the ability to reach specific types of people, often at exactly the moment those people are entering certain sites

Apps on smartphones have gone far beyond the basic calendar, music, and email functionality. More and more apps are being released every day, ranging from no cost to about $1,000 as technology allows for more sophisticated capabilities from the palm of your hand. They include surveillance technology and specialized apps for professionals, such as DDS GP for dentists and CyberTuner (for tuning pianos, which costs $999.99).

applications ("apps")
software that uses the internet, but not the web system, to bring material to audiences

feature phone
a mobile telephone that carries extras unrelated to calling ("features" such as texting, calendars, cameras, and media players) but does not have the sophisticated web-browsing, app-importing operating system of a smartphone

These are electronic auctions in which various publishers and ad networks offer advertisers the ability to reach specific types of people (e.g., women aged 18 to 24 or men who are considering the purchase of a BMW), often at exactly the moment those people are entering certain sites.

People are so used to going on the web (i.e., accessing information through browsers such as Google Chrome, internet Explorer, Firefox, and Safari) that they typically believe that the web *is* the internet. As we have seen, though, the web is a system of linked data that works *through* the internet. There are other types of internet activities—such as certain types of email (e.g., accessed through Outlook) and audio messaging—that use the internet but not the web. For companies involved in producing, distributing, and exhibiting materials ("media content") for audiences, the most important distinction is between web-centered and app-centered businesses. A web-centered business involves reaching out to target audiences through web browsers. For example, the web-centered business of the *New York Times* can be found at its website address, NYTimes.com. An app-centered business involves reaching people not through the web but through **applications** or "**apps.**" An app is software that uses the internet, but not the web system, to bring material to audiences. A person must download the app to get the material. If you have a smartphone or a tablet, you probably can download an app for the *New York Times* that will present its materials to you in ways that may be different from the ways they look on the website.

As these examples suggest, media firms traditionally have used web browsers rather than apps to reach people on desktop and laptop computers. (The internet industry does not consider laptops to be mobile devices even though you can boogie with a laptop while accessing the web on many of them.) When it comes to mobile devices, media firms often build their businesses around apps. At the same time, web browsers play an important part in companies' approaches to audiences in the mobile world as well. Let's take a short definitional detour to explain.

The term "mobile device" describes a growing number of instruments that fall under two broad categories: phones and tablets. When it comes to phones, Americans tend to use either a **feature phone** or a **smartphone**. A smartphone is a mobile telephone that uses a special computer operating system to offer connections to the internet through a web browser, as well as through special applications (apps) that are compatible with that operating system. The most common smartphone operating systems are Google's Android and Apple's iOS. Feature phones do not have these complex operating systems, and although they often carry a variety of extras unrelated to calling ("features" such as texting, calendars, cameras, and media players), many do not have web browsers, and most do not allow the importation and use of apps.

Because of their ability to connect to the web and download apps, smartphones are more expensive to buy than feature phones, and they are often more expensive to keep. Feature phone owners often pay extra for text messaging, but smartphone owners often pay a lot more because connecting to the web and apps requires payment for monthly data plans, as well as for the ability to make voice calls. Apps often cost money too, and people download many of those. One 2017 survey found that US mobile users reported an average of more than 90 apps on their phone, whereas they actually used 38 per month.[6]

In January 2018, according to the Pew Research Center, 75 percent of Americans had a smartphone.[7] Pew also reported that in January 2018 53 percent of US adults owned a tablet and 22 percent had an electronic reader (an e-reader).[8] As the costs of smartphones and tablets decrease, the proportion of Americans who use this technology is likely to grow larger and larger. Many technology experts predict that some of the most important developments in media during the next decade will center on mobile devices. Businesses are certainly paying a lot of attention. During the past several years, two major developments have marked the spread of mobile devices. One is that some publishers are making sure that the sites they present to mobile owners are different from those that show up on desktop and laptop computers. The other is the creation of apps designed specifically for the devices.

Not all publishers show mobile users a different view of the web. Some companies, however, do change the look and functionality of their websites to make them easy to load on a phone and tablet, where the speed of the device's computer processor and the size of the screen (especially in the case of phones) might not work well with the graphics-intensive websites that they have created for desktops and laptops. For example, if you went to Facebook on the iPhone's Safari browser in 2018, Facebook directed you to m.Facebook.com, to a page that aimed to optimize its look on mobile and "browse faster."

Another increasingly common reason for customizing a website for mobile involves making sure the content you receive relates directly to what the publisher believes are your needs on a device that often moves with you and can make phone calls. Google's search engine takes this approach. Type the word "pizza" into the Google search engine on a laptop during 2018 and you were likely to find a list of local restaurants serving the food; click on one and you will see ratings, its addresses, a map with a "directions" button, times open (and busy), a link to its website and menu, and a phone number. The mobile version showed all that but, understandably, also has a button for phoning.

Apps provide another popular approach to getting specific information in the mobile realm. Going on the web via a mobile device is still a more common activity than using mobile apps, but Apple noted in June 2017 that from the start of the Apple App Store in July 2008 visitors have downloaded 180 billion apps to their various Apple mobile technologies—the iPhone, iPod touch, and iPad.[9] These apps run the gamut from electronic book (e-book) readers to games, banking instruments, meditation timers, running programs, and much more. Many of the publishers of these apps also have websites with similar material, but many do not. Apps have built-in features that load immediately, and they update information through an internet channel that does not use a web browser. Unlike with a website, that download can stay in the app even when you disconnect from the internet. For example, after you download a book-reading app from your mobile device's store, you may be able to read books from the app, regardless of whether you are connected to your cellular network or to a Wi-Fi network. But your app would need to connect to the internet to purchase a new book or make changes in the book reader.

From everything we have discussed, you can see that, in the mobile industry, publishers are often also both content creators (when they do create the content they carry) and distributors of the content to the point of its public exhibition. As in the online industry, exhibition is carried out in the mobile web and app space by the ISP. But other digital players may also take on the role of exhibitors. When a website or

smartphone
a mobile telephone that uses a special computer operating system to offer connections to the internet through a web browser, as well as through special applications (apps) that are compatible with that operating system

app sells items to visitors (as Amazon's mobile website and the Apple App Store do), it is acting as an exhibitor as well as a distributor.

In view of the increasing popularity of mobile apps and the mobile web in so many circumstances, it should not be surprising that advertising is increasingly part of the mobile industry. Newspapers and magazines, which for generations have made revenues only in print, are connecting to readers on the mobile web and via apps and trying to find sponsors to help them pay for it. Although ads have not historically been a common feature of the book industry, Amazon decided to buck that tradition by inviting ads on its e-reader for those who want to pay less for the device. Other digital-only publishers such as Google, Yahoo!, Facebook, Twitter, and AOL are trying to turn rapidly expanding mobile usage into an important source of advertising money.

THINKING ABOUT MEDIA LITERACY

After reading through this discussion on net neutrality, where do you stand on the issue? Do you think that ISPs have a valid point in their arguments? Why or why not?

As more and more people use online SNSs, such as Facebook, advertisers are increasingly interested in finding ways to reach out to potential customers and to learn more about their web browsing and online behavior that might help them better reach those people. In addition, because many people aren't necessarily thinking about their privacy when they are interacting with these media, they often reveal information about their appearance (e.g., posting photos) and their location and other information that might be abused by criminals, such as identity thieves.

Advertising companies are using the same kinds of data mining activities on the mobile web that they use in the online space—behavioral targeting via cookies through publishers, ad networks, and exchanges. Apps don't accept cookies, but publishers and ad networks can identify individual mobile devices by specific identification numbers that the creators of the mobile operating systems placed there specifically for that purpose. Through those IDs and other tagging technologies, marketers can track individuals' visits to apps, as well as if and when they clicked on ads in the apps. Marketing technology firms have also developed ways to track people's movements from app to app and even from one device to another. For advertisers and their agencies, the holy grail of advertising is to be able to track an individual across all sorts of digital devices, from laptops to tablets, TV sets, retail checkout machines, and more.

Media Ethics: Confronting Internet Privacy

As we will see in forthcoming chapters, executives from various media industries see these targeting capabilities as extremely helpful for bringing in advertising money in their highly competitive business environments. Critics, however, worry that the 21st-century media world might also cause trouble by trampling on people's privacy. They point out that the phenomenal growth of digital media, as well as the convergence that has come along with it, has made so much of what we do every day a two-way experience. It is interactive. In one direction we bring news, information, advertising, email, retail forms, bank information, tweets, Facebook and Instagram updates, and more into our devices. In the other direction, we respond by clicking on links, writing blogs, transferring money, filling out retail forms, creating tweets, creating Facebook and Instagram updates, and more. All these activities describe our lives, the critics point out, and they contain information—about who we are, what we do, our likes and dislikes—that we might not want others to know.

That, say concerned individuals and organizations, is a major problem we have to think through as a society. They argue that we are moving into a new era when it comes to information. It is an era, they say, in which governments will be able to find out far more about citizens than the citizens want them to know. And it is an era in which companies will be able to find out far more about their customers than those customers realize or want them to know. In the new age of digital convergence, critics say, more and more devices are two way, and so people must be aware of companies' secret use of their data.

The first stirrings of concern began in the 1970s, when companies began to use computers to combine enormous amounts of information from public and private records about virtually everyone in the nation and sell this information to marketers. Among the largest of these companies are Experian, Equifax, Acxiom, and Choicepoint. Many marketers use these firms' universal databases (called that because they hold information on almost everyone) to find people whose profiles make them potential customers.

But privacy really took off as a media issue with the rise of marketing on the World Wide Web in the mid-1990s. Recall our discussion of interactive marketing and cookie technology earlier in this chapter. Interactive media firms see the ability to track clickstreams as a great way to find out what users want and how best to serve them. It is important to point out that placing a cookie in a person's computer does not allow a marketer to learn the name, postal address, or any other so-called **personally identifiable information (PII)** about the person who owns the computer. Many online marketers contend that this anonymity makes following people online and creating cookie profiles about them perfectly acceptable. Critics of this viewpoint, though, point out that many ad networks and websites can easily determine PII by relating a cookie to the name or email address used when the person registered on a site. When no registration information is available, a marketer can encourage a person with a cookie to sign up for a sweepstakes. The personal information provided then can get linked to the cookie data. Critics add that even when marketers and websites don't have PII, they still surround individuals with ads and other content that are tailored to their understanding of what that individual is like. Based on profiles they have created without people's knowledge or permission, they are creating views of the world for people and giving certain people discounts that they don't give others.

Rarely will media executives argue publicly that people should have no right to stop firms from collecting information about them. Under government pressures, many often concede that members of the public should have the right to know that material about them is being collected. Media executives emphasize, however, that in today's competitive media world, being able to show advertisers that a medium can deliver specific, desirable types of people is crucial for media companies' survival. Supporters of data collection also use the argument that this invasion of privacy has its positive side. They argue that the more marketers know about people, the more they will be able to send individuals materials that these individuals will find relevant to their lives. The result, they say, is that people will be unlikely to complain that they receive junk mail. Nowadays, most web marketers say that they understand people's

personally identifiable information (PII)
the name, postal address, or any other information that allows tracking down the specific person who owns a device

desire to keep certain information private. They also insist, however, that many individuals are willing to give up information about themselves if, in return, they get something that they consider valuable. Many privacy advocates agree that people should have the right to decide whether they want to give up private information as part of a transaction. They disagree with the web marketers on the way in which consumers should be informed about the data that will be collected about them—which often occurs without their knowledge.

Privacy advocates want members of the public to have to opt in when it comes to giving out information. That is, marketers should not be permitted to collect information about a person unless that person explicitly indicates that it is all right for them to do so (say, by checking a box online). Some American advocates point to privacy developments in the European Union (EU). The EU's **General Data Protection Regulation (the GDPR)** went into full effect in 2018. With large fines as penalties, it requires firms that use people's data to clearly disclose what they do and under many circumstances to get their permission before the firms are allowed to collect the data. US marketers that interact with EU residents have to obey the GDRP, but when it comes to US regulations, they contend that getting **opt-in** permission is too difficult because people either are too lazy to give it or are concerned about their privacy when the question is put to them in that manner. The marketers prefer an **opt-out approach**. That means they will be permitted to collect personal information from consumers as long as they inform people of what they are doing and give them the opportunity to check a "no" box or otherwise refuse to allow it.

Note that these privacy issues are not related only to the web. What people do on mobile devices is already of interest to many advertisers; some government agencies might want to see these data as well. The same is the case with what and how people play video games. In fact, as home-based television viewing becomes a two-way activity (we'll discuss this in Chapter 13), getting data about what individuals do with the medium will also interest marketers and, possibly, certain branches of government. As these types of surveillance continue to take place, various advocacy groups will argue against them and ask for legal safeguards against the misuse and abuse of people's data. Clearly, the fight over US consumer privacy in the digital age will continue.

General Data Protection Regulation (the GDPR)
a European Union law with large fines as penalties that requires firms that use people's data to clearly disclose what they do and under many circumstances to get their permission before the firms are allowed to collect the data

opt-in approach
the view that marketers should not be permitted to collect information about a person unless the person explicitly indicates that it is all right for them to do so

opt-out approach
the view that marketers should be permitted to collect personal information from consumers as long as they inform people of what they are doing and give them the opportunity to refuse

---

THINKING ABOUT MEDIA LITERACY

Behavioral targeting allows websites and advertisers to send content to you based on your past online activities. Although the preceding paragraphs suggest the advantages to advertisers, can you think of advantages this targeting offers to web users? What about disadvantages?

Determining Your Own Point of View as a Critical Consumer of Media

As you consider the preceding paragraphs, you may end up deciding that what is happening with people's data is fine. Or you might decide that important changes should be made. You may also feel strongly (pro or con) regarding the windows, globalization, and conglomeration activities we described in the introduction to Part II.

More and more, these activities are taking hold in all media industries, and they are beginning to affect all our lives profoundly. Think about where you stand on these issues when you read about individual industries in the rest of the book. Remember that today every mass media industry is part of the big, cross-media picture.

CHAPTER REVIEW

 Visit the Companion Website at www.routledge.com/cw/turow for additional study tools and resources.

 ## Key Terms

You can find the definitions to these key terms in the marginal glossary throughout this chapter. Test your knowledge of these terms with interactive flash cards on the *Media Today* Companion Website.

ad exchanges
ad network
algorithm
applications (apps)
behavioral targeting
big data
clickstream
contextual advertising
cookie
data mining
feature phone
General Data Protection
    Regulation (GDPR)

hyperlinks
Hypertext Markup Language
    (HTML)
internet
internet service provider (ISP)
keyword advertising
mobile application (mobile app)
natural or organic search
    results
net neutrality controversy
opt-in approach
opt-out approach
packets

personally identifiable
    information (PII)
profiling
search engine
smartphone
social media site (social
    networking site or SNS)
social search
user-generated content (UGC)
the 3Vs
web crawlers (web spiders)
wireless fidelity (Wi-Fi)

 ## Questions for Discussion and Critical Thinking

1. Stewart Brand is credited with saying in the very early days of internet development that "Information wants to be free." What is your interpretation of this saying? Think about it in both monetary and philosophical terms. How is the current digital environment fulfilling Brand's statement? How is it not?

2. Freemium-based payment models are becoming more prevalent. What do you think of freemiums? What arguments can consumers make in favor of and against freemium payments? What advantages and disadvantages do they have for the companies that use that payment model?

3. Most, if not all, "print legacy" media companies have fully embraced digital delivery. Mobile devices provide access to the internet, but they also run apps that have

specific functions or provide information for publications. Think about the difference between, for example, reading the *New York Times* in print form, on its website, and browsing it through its mobile app. What is different about these ways to access the *New York Times*'s content?

4. Your use of the internet, including your activities in social media sites and apps, is compiled into a profile used by advertisers and marketers to target their messages. Consider what your own digital profile would consist of. How well do you think your online use represents who you are? What are your feelings about being targeted with advertising based on your previous web browsing/ online purchasing data?

Activity

The internet is referred to as a "disruptive technology" because of the impact it has had on how people use media and how media organizations produce, distribute, and exhibit their products. But it is not the only technology with the potential to "disrupt" the products and practices of media companies. Two others are augmented reality and virtual reality.

Augmented reality: A layer of information is placed on top of what you are viewing, using digital glasses or a mobile device and app, empowering users to access and transmit real-time digital information (e.g., Google Lens).

Virtual reality: An immersive experience (using immersive headsets like Oculus Rift) that simulates a world and sight, sound, and feel, with real-time manipulation of objects in a 3D space.

The Book Industry

7

CHAPTER OBJECTIVES

1   Understand today's books in terms of the development of books over the centuries.

2   Differentiate among the different types of books within the book publishing industry.

3   Explain the roles of production, distribution, and exhibition as they pertain to the book publishing industry.

4   Realize and evaluate the effects of new digital technologies on the book publishing industry.

5   Analyze ethical pitfalls present in the book publishing industry.

My daughter gave me a Barnes & Noble bookstore gift card as a birthday present in 2017, and I decided to use it to buy my wife a cookbook she had mentioned. I went to the Barnes & Noble website and found the cookbook selling at almost $14 below the price that the Barnes & Noble store about five miles from my house wanted. Even with shipping costs, it was substantially cheaper. I phoned the physical store and asked them if they would match their own website's price. They said no, that their prices were separate from the website's and that they didn't match them. Startled, I blurted something like, "This is the 21st century, and yours is a 20th-century approach to pricing." The store clerk was unmoved. I ended up buying the book online.

Barnes & Noble, a major bookseller founded in 1873, undoubtedly had reasons for its pricing policy, but observers of the company were skeptical that the firm could continue its current path in the face of huge competition from Amazon, the giant online bookseller. (Amazon's price for the cookbook was slightly lower than Barnes & Noble's online price when I compared them at the same time.) CNN *Money* wrote in late 2015 that "the bookseller's recent performance is scarier than a Stephen King novel."[1] It noted that Barnes & Noble had five quarters in which earned revenue was lower than the previous year. The *Money* article noted that the chain was making efforts to move forward. It hired a new CEO. It sold its college bookstore business. It was trying to turn around plummeting interest in the Nook reader—a key mark of convergence between physical books and the new digital universe. By 2019, B&N had begun to allow the shoppers in its physical store to pay the online prices in some cases. But the firm clearly needed help. A venture capital firm that also owns a large UK bookstore chain bought it.

> "If I rely on just the bookstore sales, I won't make a living. Putting [my book] online does not put my livelihood at risk; you make a living finding new ways to do business."

CORY DOCTOROW, SCIENCE FICTION WRITER AND BLOGGER

Barnes & Noble's situation reflects the tumultuous changes taking place in one of the oldest mass media industries. The book you are reading now is a product of one area of the transforming book industry: the college textbook segment. *Media Today* is available via the Kindle. Moreover, if you think of the "extra" materials that come with the print version of the book—the website and the bolded vocabulary terms you can download to your mobile device, for example—you will realize that in this area, too, book publishers in the converging media environment are also going beyond the printed page in various ways. Their biggest long-term concerns involve figuring out how to compete in a digital world, in which paper is only one way to deliver the information in books.

For one of the oldest communication media—books are older than newspapers—and for an industry that has typically been pretty set in its ways, that is a tall order. It's by no means an impossible one, though, as we will see. If you are involved in the task, probably the first thing you would have to do is ask two basic questions: What are the essential features of a book that could have drawn readers over the centuries? And what are the essential elements of today's book industry that would encourage or discourage bold new movements into the digital age?

The History of the Book

We should begin by making one point clear: despite the startling growth of e-book readers during the past several years, people still read paper books in far greater numbers than electronic ones. As we will see later in this chapter, there are those in the industry who present evidence that e-books have actually begun to diminish in popularity. Others present evidence to draw the opposite conclusion.[2] That professional observers of the book industry are arguing strongly about the direction of this new form of book reading suggests an air of uncertainty about the future of their industry. Adding to the growth and sense of instability are digital audiobooks, as people use mobile devices to listen to books as they move through the world. Public libraries are certainly feeling the change in a big way. Libraries are increasingly letting patrons download e-books and digital audiobooks. According to Overdrive, which provides the technology for doing that, libraries worldwide in 2018 hit 1 billion checkouts.[3] Are audiobooks diminishing an important number of people's interest in actually reading books? That's another big question hovering over the industry.

The strong presence of e-books and audiobooks is convincing some in the book industry that a great transformation is upon them. Others aren't so sure. Both sides are certainly not the first people in history who had to confront changing technologies when it came to the book. The history of the book is, at its heart, a story of humans trying to use technology to record and circulate ideas. Although the book as we know it can be traced back only about 500 years, the idea of the book is much older. Scholars consider the papyrus roll in Egypt around 3000 BCE to be an early ancestor of the modern book. Papyrus was made from a reed-like plant in the Nile Valley, and it resembled paper. Scribes laid out sheets of papyrus, copied a text on one side of the sheets, and then rolled up the finished manuscript. The Greeks adopted the papyrus roll from the Egyptians and stored their rolls in great libraries. In fact, the Greeks considered the book so important that they began to use it, rather than memorizing poems and speeches (called the oral tradition), as the main way to make ideas "public"—or available to large numbers of people. Greek writers of the era refer to a market in books and to prices paid for them. Large libraries maintained scriptoria where many books were copied by hand.

These manuscripts in the scriptoria don't sound at all like the books we know, do they? Take a look at the book timeline (Figure 7.1), and you'll realize just how long it took for the idea of a book as we know it to emerge. Study the timeline carefully, and you'll probably notice three important themes:

1. The modern book did not arrive in a flash as a result of one inventor's grand change.

Instead, pieces of what we know as the printed book developed slowly and came together at certain important stages. For example, Johannes Gutenberg's invention of the printing press in 1440 was certainly a milestone because it allowed far more copies of a particular book to be created than was possible when copies were written by hand. But Gutenberg's amazing step forward drew on innovations made centuries earlier. He didn't wake up one morning and say, "Hey, I think I'll develop a printing press."

Rather, as the timeline makes clear, people in China had already developed the ink that Gutenberg needed for his technology, and traders had brought the recipe to Europe. Similarly, Asians had also pioneered the process of carving on wooden blocks, inking them, and "printing" what was on the blocks onto a variety of materials. Gutenberg knew of these developments. He also knew that although the communication of meaning in China took place through pictures, European languages such as Latin conveyed meaning through individual letters of an alphabet. Gutenberg's genius, then, was in deciding the "blocks" needed to be letters. Doing that, he created movable type. The machine that he invented to hold the type, allow it to be inked, and then allow the inked type to be pressed on the paper became what we know as the printing press. Even the printing press wasn't a totally original invention. He borrowed the design from a wine press.

Other parts of the book timeline also reflect this idea that the technology evolved rather than appeared suddenly. It is a theme we will see in the history of other media industries.

2. The book as a medium of communication developed as a result of social and legal responses to the technology during different periods.

It is impossible to separate the decisions of those who wrote, created, and sold books from the beliefs of their time, the reading ability of the population, and the government actions of the historical period. It is no accident that one of the first titles Gutenberg printed was the Bible. Because the Bible was by far the most important book of his era, he knew he could sell it at a relatively high price to the relatively small number of typically wealthy people who could read. As the timeline indicates, though, the ability to use printing presses to print any book led leaders in different parts of Europe to proclaim laws laying out the subjects that were appropriate for books and even taking care to allow only those they trusted to print books.

The timeline also notes that a crucial social development for the growth of book publishing in the United States during 19th century was the spread of literacy. Book publishers recognized this development and responded by creating and circulating books to match the increasing numbers of readers and the growing diversity of their interests. Different from the days of Henry VIII in England, in the 19th century, American publishers chose many titles to publish because of a *lack* of laws: until the end of the century, the US government had not joined an international copyright convention. Companies in the States therefore felt free to print books by popular British

| **3000 BCE** | **1400s** | **1500s** | **1600s** | **1700s** |

3000 BCE: Ancient Egyptians invent the papyrus roll.

2500–3000 BCE: Lampblack ink, or "India ink," is introduced in China.
100 CE: Early Christians popularize the codex.

200s CE: Woodblock printing appears in China.

1440 CE: Gutenberg develops the printing press.

1487: Pope Innocent issued the first Papal Bull on printing, establishing prepublication censorship of books.

1529: King Henry VIII establishes licensing system.

1637: Licensing procedures are further restricted to consolidate British royal power.
1638: First printing press in US.

1710: The Copyright Act of 1709 is the first to establish copyright regulations.

Figure 7.1
Timeline of the book industry.

novelists such as Walter Scott and Charles Dickens without paying them. Among American publishers, a huge competition took place to put out the novels of those Brits quickly and cheaply, resulting in innovative methods of printing and selling books that remained even after the United States accepted the copyright claims of other countries.

3. The book as a medium of communication existed long before the existence of the book industry.

Again, take a look at the timeline, and you'll note that the United States did not develop a book industry until the middle of the 19th century. Before that time, the printing, marketing, and actual selling of books were carried out by individual printers, often with the help of family members and maybe an apprentice—a trainee who worked to learn the trade in exchange for housing and a small salary.

1800s	**1850s**	**1900s**	**1950s**	**2000s**

1800s: With the widespread mechanization of printing, publishers are established as separate entities from booksellers.
Early 1800s: Books continue to be printed by small, family-owned businesses.
1820s–eearly 20th c: The US sees a growth of canals and railroads, leading to a demand for reading material for long journeys.

1825–1875: US book business becomes an industry.
1820s–1870s: Increased democracy and educational opportunities lead to increased literacy in America.
1843: Creation of the Hoe steam-powered rotary printing press.

1840s–1924: There is a great influx of immigrants to America.

1850s: The number of US authors who are successful grows. This literary period is sometimes called the "American Renaissance."

1870s: Rise of domestic novels in the US.

1891: US joins International Copyright Convention.
1904: Offset lithography is developed.
1926: Book of the Month Club is founded.
1927: Bennett Cerf and Donald Klopfer start the Random House publishing company.
1929: Beginning of the Great Depression.
1939: Inspired by the example of cheap Penguin Books in the UK, Pocket Books produces the first mass-market paperback books in the US.

1960s–1980s: Growing conglomerate interest in book publishing.
1971: Project Gutenberg (a volunteer-led project that digitizes and archives cultural works) is founded.
1984: The first desktop publishing program for the pathbreaking Apple MacIntosh personal computer, MacPublisher, is introduced.
1996: Google cofounders Sergey Brin and Larry Page create a web crawler to index books—the precursor to Google's PageRank algorithm and Google Books.
1993–2004: Independent bookstores decrease by over 50% in the US, from 4,700 to 2,000.

2004: Google begins scanning millions of books with the goal of offering electronic access and sale.
2007: Amazon.com introduces the Kindle electronic book reader.

2009: Amazon announces that it sold more Kindle e-books for Christmas than physical books.
2010: Introduction of the iPad.
2011: Kindle Owners' Lending Library launches.
2011: Borders Books goes out of business.
2014: E-books make up 30% of all book sales in the US
2009–2014: Independent bookstores begin to make a resurgence, growing from 1,651 stores in the US in 2009 to 2,094 in 2014.
2015: Amazon gets physical with the opening of a full-service bookstore in a Seattle shopping mall, with others planned around the country.
2017: Penguin Random House pays Barack and Michelle Obama $65 million in a joint deal for their memoirs.
2018: Sales of audiobooks rise 37.1% over 2017 sales figures with e-book sales down 2.8%

The invention of the steam-powered press, techniques to create inexpensive wood-based paper, and a large and growing population of literate citizens encouraged new approaches to publishing. The tremendous social changes during this period made the sale of large numbers of copies realistic. With transportation and communication becoming easier, a publisher could expect to sell copies over a wider territory than previously had been possible. Large companies with departments specializing in different types of books aimed at different markets began to emerge. During the decades to come, a variety of social, legal, and economic responses to publisher "bigness" would lead to the presence of a small number of conglomerates as the leading forces within several sectors of the American book industry.

THINKING ABOUT MEDIA LITERACY

The content that goes into a book is now being packaged and delivered in a variety of ways (other than ink on paper bound between two covers). How would you describe what a "book" is if it is no longer just the printed object it was in the past?

One could write books about each of these historical themes, and people have. The goal of bringing them up in a text about media today is to help you understand that knowing the past is useful for interpreting the present. What happened in the past has shaped the media industries that currently surround us. Just as important, the industry processes that the themes describe apply to the present as well as to years ago. We have already noted in this chapter's introduction that contemporary books are evolving in new digital forms (theme 1). In the following pages we will explore that topic further. We will also see that the book business is responding to new social and legal developments (theme 2) and that the book industry is transforming even as we study it (theme 3). Being familiar with historical versions of these themes may well help you better understand—and even predict—how they will work in the 21st century. So let's get to it.

Textbooks for undergraduates and graduate students often contain pedagogical elements, such as review questions, chapter summaries, and marginal glossaries, and link to further resources available online via a website that has been created to complement the text.

The Book Industry Today

Book publishing is a big and generally healthy business with sales totaling $36.8 billion in 2017.[4] The people who work in the industry make a variety of distinctions among types of books. The most general distinction is between professional and educational books, on the one hand, and consumer books on the other. **Audiobooks**, however, are a type that can include professional and educational as well as consumer books. Let's get a bird's-eye view of each category.

Educational and Professional Books

Educational and professional books focus on training. Most professional and educational books are marked by their use of **pedagogy** (or particular teaching approaches), which includes features such as learning objectives, chapter recaps, questions for discussion, and the like. Although a good deal of what professional and educational publishers turn out look like traditional books, the publishers are the first to acknowledge that a growing proportion of the publications flowing from their firms aren't books in the traditional sense. An example is what educators call "digital basal materials"—these are basic teaching tools for children in early grades, but they are electronic rather than on paper. Industry observers also point to math workbooks, corporate training manuals, college course packs, online versions of textbooks, and text-related videos. Because some of the materials are not standard books (or even books at all, as we understand the term), some writers on the topic have come to refer to this area broadly as "educational and training media," suggesting that a new converging industry is developing with books as a part of it. Other experts still consider the area to be part of book publishing because the nonbook products are often closely connected to traditional books in the learning environment. People who work in the industry recognize three types of educational and training books: **K–12 books and materials, higher-education books and materials,** and **professional books**.

Consumer Books

Unlike the publishers of professional and educational books, publishers of **consumer books** are aiming their products at the general public. They target readers in their private lives, outside their roles as students and highly trained workers. Informal teaching is certainly a significant part of consumer publishing in areas as varied as religion (the Bible), science (*A Brief History of Time*), history (*Guns, Germs and Steel*), cooking (*Rachel Ray Express Lane Meals*), and ethics (*The Book of Virtues*). Noneducational genres are also a major part of consumer book publishing; these include everything from romance novels to joke books to travel books. Publishing personnel use these subject classifications and many more when they create titles.

When it comes to defining the major categories of the consumer book publishing business, though, publishers identify them quite differently. Using terms originated by the Association of American Publishers (AAP), people involved in publishing talk about the following categories:

- Trade
- Mass market paperback
- Religious
- Professional
- Book club
- Mail-order
- University press
- Subscription reference

Rather than describing the subject matter of books, all the AAP categories (with the exception of religion) refer to the way in which books are distributed or produced. Table 7.1 presents the distribution of consumer spending on the major categories by the AAP member publishers plus an estimation of others, totaling about 1,800. Overall, those are the ones who have tended to charge more for e-books than the nonlegacy bound publishers. Let's explore the categories one at a time.

Trade Books **Trade books**—general-interest titles, including both fiction and nonfiction books—are typically sold to consumers through retail bookstores (both traditional and web-based) and to libraries.

---

audiobook
a recording in which someone reads a printed book or a version of it

pedagogy
the use of features such as learning objectives, chapter recaps, and questions for discussion; this is characteristic of educational books

K–12 books and materials
books and materials created for students in kindergarten through the twelfth grade

higher-education books and materials
books and materials that focus on teaching students in college and post-college learning

professional books
books that help people who are working keep up-to-date in their areas, as well as rise to the next level of knowledge

consumer books
books that are aimed at the general public

trade books
general-interest titles, including both fiction and nonfiction books, that are typically sold to consumers through retail bookstores (both traditional and web-based) and to libraries

Table 7.1 AAP Publishers' Revenues by Book Types, 2018, in Billions of Dollars

Type of Book	2018
Adult Trade	5.1
Children's/YA	2.1
Religious	0.6
Professional	0.6
K–12 Instructional	2.7
Higher Ed Course Material	3.3
University Press	0.05

Source: Susanna Hinds, AAP StatShot: Trade Book Publisher Revenue Increased by 4.6% in 2018,

AAP, February 11, 2019, https://newsroom.publishers.org/aap-statshot-trade-book-publisher-revenue-increased-by-46-in-2018/

Publishing personnel further distinguish between adult and juvenile trade books. In turn, among juvenile books they distinguish between children's (below age 13) and young adult (13 and older). In 2018, adult trade books brought in $5.1 billion and juvenile trade books $2.1 billion. Hardbound versions of trade books made $3.1 billion for the publishers in 2018.[5]

Paperbacks Employees also distinguish between trade books that are hardbound and those that are paperbound. **Trade paperbacks** are books that are essentially the same size as hardbound versions but with paper covers. **Mass market paperbacks** are pocket-size paperback books smaller than trade paperbacks. Mass market paperbacks made up 11 percent of US consumers' spending on books in 2014. They are designed to be sold primarily in so-called **mass market outlets**—newsstands, drugstores, discount stores, and supermarkets. Many types of books come in this format, but bestsellers (after being published in trade and trade paperback formats), romance novels, and science fiction tales are among the most common. Mass market books have had a rough road in recent years. NPD BookScan, which tracks about 80 percent of print sales, found that mass market titles accounted for 13 percent of total print units sold in 2013 but that the number dropped to 9 percent in 2015. People in the trade believe that a number of reasons account for the drop, including a shift of many mass market readers to e-books, the decisions by major chains that sell many such books (exhibitors such as Walmart, Costco, and Target) to cut back on space for them in favor of higher-margin products, and consolidation among the distributors who circulate the books to such stores. The smaller number of distributors has meant they have more power over a higher percentage of mass market titles that go on the shelves—and they have chosen not to take a chance on titles and mostly rack ones that have a high chance of selling well.[6]

Religious Books **Religious books** are essentially trade books that contain specifically religious content. They are sold in general bookstores as well as in special religious bookshops. The success of this category seems to vary with the level of interest in the topic. The category includes sales of the Bible, the best-selling book of all time. It also includes Rick Warren's *The Purpose-Driven Life*, which its publisher Zondervan

trade paperbacks
standard-size books that have flexible covers

mass market paperbacks
smaller, pocket-size paperback books

mass market outlets
venues where mass market paperbacks are generally sold, including newsstands, drugstores, discount stores, and supermarkets

religious books
trade books that contain specifically religious content

(owned by News Corp's HarperCollins) contends is the best-selling nonfiction book in history (apart from the Bible), with more than 30 million copies sold worldwide.[7]

University Press This area covers titles published for those involved in primary research in academic, corporate, or government settings. University presses are typically not-for-profit divisions of universities, colleges, museums, or research institutions, and they publish mostly scholarly materials—that is, books that are read by professors and graduate students. These are not the best of times for university presses. Their main outlets, libraries, are seeing their book-buying budgets shrink because of the rising costs of electronic databases and journals. The situation has forced many university presses to reduce output.

University press books
titles published by universities, colleges, museums, or research institutions for those involved in primary research in academic, corporate, or government settings

---

THINKING ABOUT MEDIA LITERACY

Name the different formats available for consuming book "content." For the producer of the content, what are the various elements that must go into the production? For the consumer, what are the advantages and disadvantages of each? What is your own preference for engaging with a book? Why?

Variety and Specialization in Book Publishing

No matter how obscure a subject is, there is probably a book about it. In fact, there may even be a publisher specializing in the topic. Many publishers have imprints that focus on particular types of books. An imprint is a name or brand that the publisher places on the bottom of a book's spine as well as on the main title page. It signifies a publishing firm or one its divisions. Random House is an imprint of the large Penguin Random House, Inc., publishing company. But Penguin Random House also has many other imprints that deal with particular topics or aim at particular audiences. Fodor's, for example, is its travel imprint. ESPN is its sports imprint. One World is an imprint devoted to works, typically reflecting many cultures, that "challenge the status quo, subvert dominant narratives," and "represent voices from across the spectrum of humanity."

With imprints in mind, take a virtual stroll through your nearest university library's catalog, through Amazon's online bookstore, or through the "subject" section of *Books in Print*, a reference volume that you can find in print or online in any library or bookstore. Even though you've been dealing with books all your life, a close examination of the breadth of titles is likely to surprise you. Are you interested in maritime issues? *Literary Marketplace*, a standard reference volume on book publishing, lists forty-five imprints in the United States that deal with the subject. Among the other specialties noted, forty-seven US firms mention Hindu religion, thirty-one list wine and spirits, twenty-four claim veterinary science, and twenty-three note real estate.

Financing Book Publishing

These examples only begin to suggest the immensity of the book publishing business in the United States. Estimates of the number of book publishers in the United States vary enormously, from Literary Marketplace's 2,132 to 80,000.[8] For this edition, we will use the US Census Bureau's count of the number of firms in the country's

book publishing industry.⁹ In 2015, the bureau found about 2,280 book publishers. A relative few—around 70—were large enough to have 500+ employees. The greatest number—around 1,432—had between 1 and 4 employees.

Part of the reason for this huge number is that publishing a basic book really doesn't cost that much, although some titles (such as this textbook) can be very expensive to put together. For a few thousand dollars, a person can put out a handsome product to sell in fairly large numbers. The low entry costs allow zealous entrepreneurs or people who are committed to disseminating certain ideas to get in on the activity. Moreover, new printing technologies allow publishers to make a profit turning out copies of books in small numbers or even "on demand"—that is, only when someone pays for the book. (In the past, the nature of printing efficiencies meant that a publisher had to go through the expense of producing and storing lots of copies of a title so that the copies could be priced competitively.)

Sometimes small publishing ventures can yield bonanzas in terms of readership and revenue. A great recent example is the erotic (and controversial) *Fifty Shades* series of four titles: *Fifty Shades of Grey* (published in 2011), *Fifty Shades Darker* (published in 2012), *Fifty Shades Freed* (published in 2012), and *Grey* (published in 2015). Written by a British woman named E. L. James, the book began as a contribution to a fan fiction site centering on the *Twilight* book and movie series. Believing her writing had potential as a stand-alone book, James refashioned and extended her story and published it through Writers' Coffee Shop, a small publisher in Australia that released it as an e-book and a print-on-demand paperback. Because the publisher had a small marketing budget, it relied on blogs about books for early publicity. Then it seems word-of-mouth recommendations, Facebook sharing, and rave reviews on blogs aimed at women pushed the title to enormous popularity. It has more than 16,000 reader reviews on the social networking site Goodreads, and it sold out in many bookstores. The series had sold over 125 million copies worldwide by the time the fourth book entered the market.¹⁰ It also set the record as the fastest-selling paperback series of all time, beating the Harry Potter titles.

THINKING ABOUT MEDIA LITERACY

Think about the literary agent and the acquisitions editor roles. How are their jobs different? How are they similar? Who does each work for? If you were an author, what would your responsibility be to each? What would you expect from them?

Such success for small publishers is highly unusual. Although many small publishers are founded every year, a handful of companies still dominate the most lucrative areas of the book publishing business. For example, three names—Merriam-Webster, Random House, and American Heritage—regularly dominate the field of English-language dictionaries, with a combined 90 percent or greater share. In the broader book publishing arena, five publishers tend to dominate. They are Penguin Random House, Simon & Schuster, Hachette Book Group, HarperCollins, and Macmillan.

Each puts out books under many different imprints, and their books are high profile. The big five accounted for all but one of Nielsen BookScan's[11] Adult Fiction Top 15 in 2016, ten of Nielsen BookScan's Top 15 Adult Nonfiction, and six of Nielsen BookScan's Juvenile Top 20.[12] Although they are clearly not always dominant (for example, Scholastic and a couple of small publishers are also powerful in the children's book area), they consistently set the pace for what is popular in the American (and often the international) book market. Here is a brief snapshot of who owns each firm along with its well-known imprints:

- **Penguin Random House**: Until July 2013, Penguin Group and Random House were two among the six trade publishers in the United States. That month, the British company Pearson, which owned Penguin, and the German company Bertelsmann, which owned Random House, combined their adult and children's divisions, with Bertelsmann owning the largest share. The resulting company has nearly 250 imprints, including Random House, Knopf, Random House Children's Books, and Doubleday.
- **Simon & Schuster**: Owned by the CBS Corporation, Simon & Schuster publishes through imprints that include Pocket, Free Press, and Scribner.
- **Hachette Book Group, USA**: Formerly the book publishing firm owned by the Time Warner conglomerate, Hachette Book Group (HBG) now belongs to Hachette Livre, the second-largest publisher in the world. Hachette Livre is itself a wholly owned subsidiary of the French conglomerate Lagardere Group. Little Brown and Company, one of HBG's subsidiaries, has a number of important imprints, including Little Brown and Back Bay Books. Among other HBG imprints are FaithWords, 5-Spot, and Grand Central Publishing.
- **HarperCollins**: Owned by Rupert Murdoch's News Corp, HarperCollins owns imprints that publish books in different parts of the world. Among the well-known imprints are William Morrow, Zondervan, HarperTeen, and Walden Pond Press.
- **Macmillan**: Owned by the German firm Holtzbrinck, Macmillan is a collection of trade and scholarly publishers. Among the well-known publishers in its trade stable are St. Martin's Press (which itself has five imprints), Henry Holt, and Farrar Straus & Giroux.

The power of these firms raises a logical question: If producing a book is often relatively inexpensive, how is it that only a few companies dominate parts of the industry? The answer is that some parts of book publishing can be extremely expensive, and the greatest expenses are typically related to aspects other than the physical creation of the book.

The overwhelming majority of publishers do not own the basic machinery of bookmaking—a printing press and a machine that places bindings on finished pages. Typically, publishers contract out these services to firms that specialize in these activities. Publishers also contract out **composition** services, the work involved in inserting into a manuscript the codes and conventions that tell the page-making program or the printing press how the material should look on the page.

Color photographs and special layouts can be expensive. To sell the book at a reasonable price, the publisher has to sell many thousands of copies simply to make back the manufacturing costs. Still, the ability to contract out such services at reasonable costs is what makes the mere entry into book publishing so easy.

composition
the work involved in inserting into a manuscript the codes and conventions that tell the page-making program or the printing press how the material should look on the page

At its heart, though, book publishing is not really about writing or editing or printing. It is about finding, preparing, marketing, distributing, and exhibiting titles in ways that will get particular audiences to notice them and buy them. This process takes place in different ways in different sectors of the industry. Much more money is required in some sectors than in others to compete at the top level. As a result, in these sectors, the wealthiest companies can take the lead and keep it. To give you a sense of what book publishing means, we'll focus on comparing adult hardcover trade publishing and university press publishing from the standpoint of production, distribution, and exhibition.

Production in the Book Publishing Industry

As we've noted, the production of books involves finding them and preparing them for the marketplace. The same basic activities take place at every kind of book publisher.

acquisitions editor
a person who recruits and signs new authors and titles for the company's list of books

Production in Trade Publishing

An **acquisitions editor** recruits and signs new authors and titles for the company's list of books. In major firms, because of the cost of running the company, acquisitions editors must find and produce a certain number of new titles that have a certain sales potential. The titles can come as completed manuscripts or as proposals for manuscripts. A contract is drawn up that promises payments to the author. Sometimes the payments are in the form of a flat fee for producing

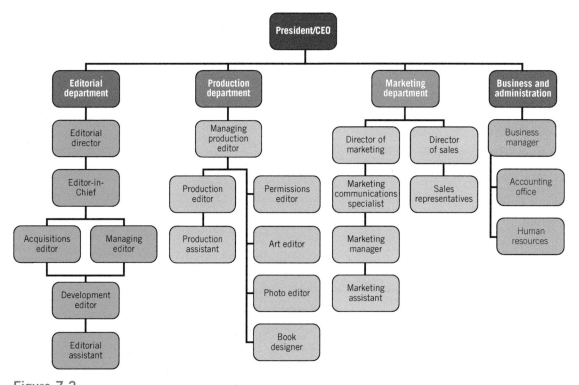

Figure 7.2
The organizational structure of a typical book publishing house.

the work. Often the payments are in the form of **royalties**—shares of the sales income, usually based on the number of copies sold. After the acquisitions editor receives a completed manuscript, permission to go ahead with publication must typically be granted by an executive committee (sometimes called a publication board) of the firm. Once the go-ahead is received, the manuscript goes to a developmental editor. That person reads and edits the work carefully to make sure that it is clear and internally consistent. After the author addresses the developmental editor's suggestions, the manuscript is transmitted from the developmental editor to a production editor in the production department. The production editor then arranges all of the technical aspects of the book—from copyediting to design to pagination—until the book is in final page-proof form (see Figure 7.2).

This process sounds straightforward, but it can be quite complex. Probably the hardest step is the first, and it belongs to the acquisitions editor—identifying the "right" manuscript. You might not think that finding manuscripts would be a big deal; we all know people who are eager to get their ideas into print. Yet acquisitions editors have to deal with two major considerations when they sift through proposals. First, they have to find topics that match the personality of their imprint, and second, they have to find authors who can write about those topics and whose books can make profits for the firm. Getting the topic and the author together is the really hard part, the editors will tell you. Not surprisingly, acquisitions editors have developed strategies to overcome this challenge and reduce their risk of failure. These strategies require the editor to be familiar with the sales goals of the firm, with the intended audience, and with the way in which books are marketed to that audience.

Adult hardcover trade acquisitions editors rarely read unsolicited manuscripts or proposals for manuscripts unless these are brought to them by known literary agents. A **literary agent** is a person who, on behalf of a client, markets the client's manuscripts to editors, publishers, and other buyers, based on knowledge of the target market and the specific content of the manuscript. Agents understand the personalities of different imprints, and they make their pitches to the ones best suited to particular authors. This system saves editors enormous amounts of work, although some authors undoubtedly fall through the cracks because of it. If an agent succeeds in placing a work, the agent receives a commission, typically 10 percent of all income related to the book that is received by the author.

Trade presses usually sell their titles through bookstores. Consumers find out about them by browsing through the shelves, reading reviews in newspapers and magazines, or noting discussions with the author in print or on TV.

In hardcover trade publishing, achieving success with a book means selling at least 50,000 copies. Achieving **bestseller** status means selling more than 75,000 hardcover copies or 100,000 paperback copies. And beyond the bestseller looms the realm of the **blockbuster**, which is a book that sells well over 100,000 hardcover copies—constituting an immense success. Major trade presses spend enormous amounts of money on marketing and publicity departments that have the expertise and resources to take books that have the potential to be bestsellers or blockbusters and help them sell the requisite number of copies. The acquisitions editor's job is to find books with that potential.

royalties
shares of a book's sales income that are paid to an author, usually based on the number of copies sold

literary agent
a person who, on behalf of a client, markets the client's manuscripts to editors, publishers, and other buyers, based on knowledge of the target market and the specific content of the manuscript

bestseller
a title that sells more than 75,000 hardcover copies or 100,000 paperback copies

blockbuster
a book that sells well over 100,000 hardcover copies

Production at a University Press

Publishing at a university press is very different from adult hardcover trade publishing in this respect. In university press publishing, a "hit" realistically means selling several thousand copies. A title reaches hit status if it commands respect from professors, who then tell their students and university libraries to buy it.

Scholarly and trade publishers take different approaches to recruiting and acquiring authors whose books may or may not be hits. To reduce the risk that academics will not like their books, editors at scholarly presses try to get manuscripts by well-known professors from well-known universities. Because acquiring books only from these professors would not yield enough titles for their lists, the editors go after the next best thing: young professors on their way up the academic ladder. To find them, the editors often turn to consultants: well-known academics that have a reputation for being able to spot innovative new work in their field that their colleagues are likely to appreciate. Sometimes these academics get paid for their services. In addition to the help of consultants, many academic editors will read unsolicited manuscripts sent to them by professors from around the country in the hope of finding something good.

In contrast to the way trade books are sold, university presses usually publicize their books at academic conferences and by mail. Academic associations rent space at their conventions to booksellers. Salespeople set out titles that they think the professors and graduate students who are attending the convention might like and then discuss the books with interested passersby. In addition, the marketing departments of these publishing companies send brochures specifically to academics who specialize in a book's topic; the brochures contain descriptions of the author and the topic along with blurbs by other professors who like the work.

Book Production in the Electronic Age

During the past few years, big and small book publishers have been active in creating books for the electronic market—placing titles for sale online at the same or a lower price than hard-copy versions. Some observers have wondered what the rush is about. In 2007 Daniel O'Brien, a book analyst for Forrester Research, called electronic books a solution in search of a problem. "Our research with consumers indicates very little interest in reading on a screen," he told the *New York Times*. "Maybe someday, but not in a five-year time frame. Books are pretty elegant." But Jack Romanos, president of Simon & Schuster, one of the first traditional publishers to begin selling electronic books, argued that "the logic of electronic books is pretty hard to refute—we see it as an incremental increase in sales as a new form of books for adults and especially for the next generation of readers."

Portable reading devices, which can be as simple as a standard ePub reader or as sophisticated as a tablet, are typically web-enabled. That makes it possible for owners to sample books, purchase them, or borrow them electronically from libraries.

It turns out that Romanos was far more correct. With the release of various Kindles by Amazon, Nooks by Barnes & Noble, the iPad, Kobo, and other portable devices, sales of e-books have soared. In 2010, in fact, one analyst suggested that sales of hardbound fiction and mass market paperback fiction had dropped because people were purchasing the books on e-readers. In fact, e-books were accounting for as much as 50 percent of new bestseller sales. By 2014 e-books were accounting for 23 percent of Simon & Schuster's sales.[13] Since then, surveys of about 1,800 publishers by the AAP have shown e-book sales dropping. The AAP saw, for example, a 4.7 percent decline in e-books from 2016 to 2017; the drop between 2017 and 2018 was 3.6 percent. Marissa Bluestone of the AAP pointed out that actually 2017's drop was "significantly less than the double-digit declines experienced in 2015 and 2016." The survey message: e-books are in trouble.

But other discussions of what is going on argue that the data showing a decline involve the e-books of "traditional" or "legacy" publishers, the types of companies surveyed by the AAP. They have tended to price e-books at about $8 a unit. They note that an entirely different stratum of book publishers (some call them "nonlegacy" or "indie" publishing) has settled on a $3 e-book price that has been continuing to drive increasing

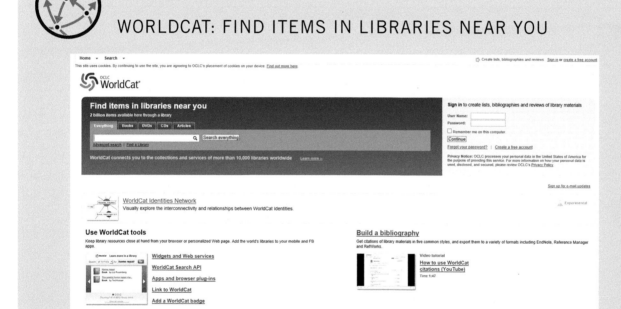

GLOBAL MEDIA TODAY & CULTURE

WORLDCAT: FIND ITEMS IN LIBRARIES NEAR YOU

How often do you visit a library? What are the libraries you prefer, the ones at your university or the ones in your home town? Over the centuries libraries have occupied and retained a central role in preserving and disseminating knowledge around the world. Think about the great library of Alexandria, in Egypt, which had a central relevance in the ancient world, and the current role of the Library of Congress in the United States. How is the digital revolution affecting the role of libraries around the world? For one, it makes it possible to share information among them, and it generates the preconditions, for example, to create worldwide catalogs.

What is *WorldCat*? It is a worldwide online catalog of library content managed by the Online Computer Library Center (OCLC) that you can explore following this link: www.worldcat.org. It tracks the catalogs of thousands of libraries around the world, so if you are a reader, you can locate the nearest library that has the book you are looking for, based on the information you will share on your location. If you are an author, you can learn where in the world a library has your book in its catalog (and might be surprised in the process). The global search for an earlier edition of this book *Media Today*, for example, reveals that more than 700 libraries worldwide have this title in their catalogs, ranging from the University of KwaZulu Natal Library in South Africa to the library of Victoria University in Melbourne, Australia.

sales. The largest of these alternative sellers, Amazon's Kindle Direct Publishing, claims to have helped more than a thousand authors earn at least $100,000 in royalties since its founding in 2007. Amazon doesn't regularly disclose its e-book sales, but observers suggest that a new arena of book publishing is developing around individual authors who in past years would have tried to publish via mass market paperback imprints. Now they are reaching out independently to electronic readers via exhibitors such as Amazon with lower prices (and perhaps lower visibility) than with the legacy publishers but with an opportunity to keep more of the revenue than with the traditional model.[14]

It may well be that electronic book publishing is, to quote the editor-in-chief of *Publishers Weekly*, "the next major thing after Gutenberg." Still, don't hold your breath waiting for the disappearance of the book. Even the just-quoted editor was adamant that books won't go away.

Reducing the Risks of Failure During the Production Process

Concerns about what kinds of books to make and in what formats come up all the time as authors, agents, and editors struggle to make books and, in turn, see those books make money. Book publishers use a number of strategies to reduce the risk of failure, including the following:

- Conducting prepublication research
- Making use of authors with positive track records
- Offering authors advances on royalties

Let's look at each of these strategies individually.

Conducting Prepublication Research You might wonder whether companies involved in publishing university press and trade books conduct **prepublication research** to gauge a title's chances of success with their likely audiences. In fact, they do, but they do it in a rather informal way. Editors may meet with people who are representative of their audience and ask them questions about the book being developed. In scholarly publishing, editors often pay a few professors to read the manuscript and comment on its prospects for success. Going a lot further in research, such as testing each title with large numbers of likely consumers to gauge their reactions, might raise the expense of publishing the book so much that to make a profit, it would have to be priced at an unrealistically high level. About the only systematic research that publishing executives carry out regularly is seeing how previous books on a topic sold. That information gives them an indication of whether going ahead with the book is worth the company's money.

Making Use of Track Records Of course, some authors have already proven their worth: they have **track records**, or histories of successes, in the book marketplace. Editors naturally like to sign these authors because doing so lowers the risk of failure. The authors' names are so well known in their area of publishing that their new titles almost sell themselves.

In academic publishing, prestige tends to be the best tool for successfully snagging an author with a substantial track record. Typically, the acquisitions editor who wants to snag such authors must work for one of the most prestigious scholarly presses—Harvard, Yale, Cambridge, Oxford, MIT, Chicago, and a few others. So the most prestigious presses continue to collect the most prestigious academic authors and thus to dominate the scholarly sector.

prepublication research
research conducted in order to gauge a title's chances of success with its likely audience

track records
the previous successes or failures of a product, person, or organization

In adult trade publishing, almost anything goes with regard to authors with positive track records or authors who, for other reasons, are expected to have high sales. The authors who garner large advances and are successful in sales are often those with some specific characteristics:

- Previously hugely successful (e.g., John Grisham, Stephen King, Patricia Cornwell)
- Controversial (e.g. inflammatory political consultant Roger Stone)
- Well known outside of book publishing (e.g., Kim Kardashian, Amy Schumer)

Offering Advances on Royalties Offering authors an **advance on royalties**—a payment of money before the book is published that the publisher anticipates the author will earn through royalties on the book—to sign a contract is not as common in academic publishing as in trade publishing. One possible reason is that academic titles do not sell that many copies. Another is that the firms can lure academic writers without advances, as they are called. Trade book authors note that even when book advances sound substantial, they get eaten up by the cost of conducting research and simply living while writing full-time. Take a reported six-figure advance, the president of the Authors Guild told the *New York Times* in 2009:

> That may mean $100,000, minus 15 percent agent's commission and self-employment tax, and if we're comparing it to a salary let us recall (a) that it does not include any fringes like a desk, let alone health insurance, and (b) that the book might take two years to write and three years to get published. . . . So a six-figure advance, while in my experience gratefully received, is not necessarily enough, in itself, for most adults to live on.[15]

advance on royalties
a payment of money before the book is published that is based on what the publisher anticipates the author will earn from royalties on the book

The amount of money that trade publishers offer in order to lure star authors—or people they suspect will be stars—can be impressive. In 2014 St. Martin's Press (a division of Macmillan Publishers) paid over $1 million for a debut novel by *New York Times* reporter Stephanie Clifford, while Random House paid $5 million to land the second novel by Abraham Verghese.[16] More spectacularly, in 2006 Simon & Schuster offered Houston televangelist Joel Osteen $10 million for the right to publish his 2007 book, *Become a Better You*. The reason? His book *Your Best Life Now: 7 Steps to Living at Your Potential*, published by small publisher FaithWords, had sold millions of copies since its release in 2004. Probably at least as important was that its audience bought audiobooks, calendars, and other spinoffs that seemed to suggest the pastor's writing career had legs. He also has television and radio gigs that continually keep him in the eye of the people who might buy his books.

Those who are involved with such deals clearly believe that they are worth the cost. An industry veteran suggested in 2014 that "for the Big Five, especially, highly sought projects have become essential," as *Publishers Weekly* put it. Because most current and backlist titles aren't selling as well as they once did, the executive explained, potential blockbuster books "are more important" than ever, the competition over them is fierce, and so the advances offered are huge. But, said a Simon & Schuster editor to *Publishers Weekly*, "We don't throw caution to the wind." In addition to considering whether the book will sell enough in hardcover to justify the advance, the publishing firm considers the title's future attraction to paperback and foreign publishers—in return for the advance, the hardback publisher typically gets the opportunity to sell the paperback and foreign rights to other publishers. In the case of an attractive title, the hardback publisher might make back a substantial portion of the advance through the sale of these rights. As the advance to Osteen suggests, the largest advances typically go to authors whose involvement in other media can help them sell copies. A title based on a popular movie or one that is written by a popular sports figure will similarly have the instant recognition among certain audiences that will help it move off the shelves.

Of course, not all titles succeed, no matter what strategies the publishers might have taken to reduce the risk of failure. *Publishers Weekly* lists standard reasons that books with hopes for great sales end in disappointment: "one too many sequels, a book where a magazine article would do, a celebrity whose day has come and gone." When a string of similar books sells strongly at the outset but ends with disappointing sales, acquisitions editors generalize about the kinds of titles in which people have temporarily or permanently lost interest. It also works the other way. When one or two books on a topic take off, editors begin to think a trend is at work, and they look for books that relate to the same or similar topics. The large number of sudoku puzzle books that have poured into stores in recent years is one example. Another example in recent years, perhaps stranger and more tentative, is a seeming mini-trend of books that try to promote atheism. *Publishers Weekly* pointed out in 2007 that at the same time that religious books were selling well, three titles against religion had also been garnering large numbers of readers: Christopher Hitchens's *God Is Not Great: How Religion Poisons Everything* (published by Twelve), Richard Dawkins's *The God Delusion* (Houghton Mifflin), and Sam Harris's *Letter to a Christian Nation* (Knopf). A *Publishers Weekly* reporter noted that "these brainy, skeptical takes on God and religion have quickly ascended to the top of national bestseller lists" and in interviewing editors found that they saw the topic as a reaction to fundamentalism among substantial segments of US society. To the editors, that meant room for more and a chance for substantial sales. As a Houghton Mifflin editor said, "If another great book came along tomorrow that I felt really advanced the issue, I'd snap it up."

Distribution in the Book Industry

Ideas that are not well conceived or well executed and trends that have passed their peak can explain the failure of titles in every sector of book publishing, from juvenile hardback to mail-order. At the same time, though, acquisitions editors and other executives in all areas of the industry realize that distribution can play an important part in making or breaking a title.

The Role of Wholesalers in the Distribution Process

The biggest trade publishers—Penguin Random House, Simon & Schuster, HarperCollins—distribute books themselves to the largest bookstore chains (Barnes & Noble and Books-A-Million) and a few others, such as the huge online bookseller Amazon. Otherwise, these publishers and others rely on three huge wholesalers—Baker & Taylor, Ingram, and Brodart—to distribute their books to bookstores and libraries. These wholesalers stock enormous numbers of titles from a great number of publishers in massive warehouses. This system allows librarians and book dealers to obtain a variety of books more quickly than if they had to order from individual presses.

The process works this way: A wholesaler purchases copies of a book from a publisher at a discount and then resells them to a retailer (the exhibitor) at a somewhat higher price. Both the wholesaler and the publisher share the risks in their relationship. When a wholesaler purchases a certain number of copies of a title, it is committing itself to devoting valuable warehouse space to that title and to fulfilling orders for the book. The publisher, though, is not off the hook when the wholesaler receives the title. In the book industry, copies of the book that don't sell can ordinarily be returned to the publisher for credit toward other titles (see Figure 7.3). As a result of this returns policy, publishing executives must be realistic regarding the **print run**, or the number of copies printed.

print run
the number of copies of a book that are printed

Assessing a Title's Popularity

Throughout the distribution process, wholesalers keep a careful eye on indicators that help them gauge how popular a book will be. Doing that allows them to decide how many copies should take up valuable space in their warehouses.

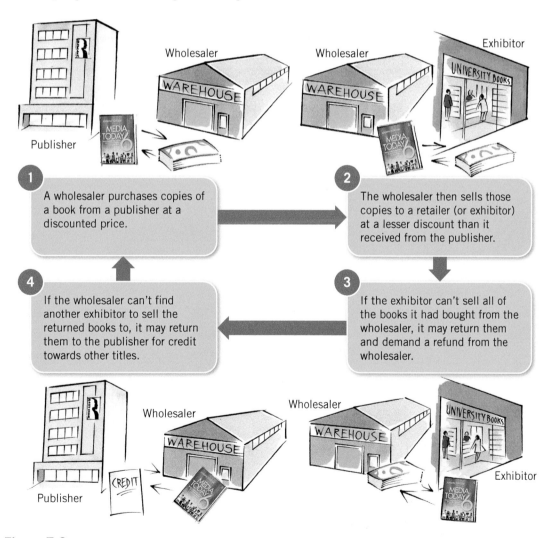

Figure 7.3
The role of the wholesaler. The wholesaler plays a crucial role in the book publishing process.

Popularity Indicator 1: The Size of the Print Run The size of the print run signals to wholesalers how popular a publisher expects a book to be. That indication helps wholesalers decide how many copies of the title to stock. Looking at the publishing imprint also helps. Wholesalers associate certain imprints with certain levels of marketing power, as well as with certain types of books. Imprints, therefore, telegraph expected sales. A distributor is more likely to stock up on a title with the Penguin Random House imprint than to take a large quantity of a title from Pantheon or Schocken, even though Penguin Random House owns those imprints.

Popularity Indicator 2: The Content of Reviews Review media are also vehicles for estimating the popularity of a forthcoming title. Review media are periodicals such as *Kirkus* and *Choice* that receive early versions of books from their publishers. Review magazine staff members read the books and predict their popularity among different audiences.

Popularity Indicator 3: The Scope of the Marketing Plan Finally, the publisher's marketing plan serves as a hint to wholesalers about a title's future. The marketing plan describes the specific ways in which the publisher will get the word out about the title to its target audience. Although the marketing plan of a small university press will probably be limited to a few mailings to appropriate libraries and academics, a trade publisher with high expectations for a title will typically do much more. The firm's publicity department might inform distributors that it will advertise the title in magazines and newspapers that deliver an audience similar to the one expected for the book.

In addition, publicists may promise to send the author on a book tour that will draw a lot of attention to the title. A **book tour** is a series of appearances that an author makes in various cities to promote a title and stimulate sales. The publicist tries to make sure that in each city the author will discuss the book with TV personalities, radio talk show hosts, and newspaper columnists. In addition, publicists might arrange for the author to appear in bookstores to talk about the book and sign copies for customers. The belief in book publishing is that a vigorous and well-put-together book tour can spike the sales of a title substantially.

book tour
a series of appearances that an author makes in various cities in order to promote a title and stimulate sales

Exhibition in the Book Publishing Industry

The concern that trade publishers and distributors feel about printing and circulating the appropriate number of copies is shared by the companies that sell the books to the public. When it comes to book exhibitors, you probably think of bookstores. Of course, there are many different kinds of bookstores. There are the nationwide chains, such as Barnes & Noble and Books-A-Million. University bookstores are often quite big and sometimes part of a chain (e.g., Follett or a spinoff of Barnes & Noble). They distinguish themselves by carrying textbooks and academic books that general bookstores typically would not stock. Then there are the "independents"—companies that are based in a particular area and have, at most, a few locations, though often only one. A large independent is Powell's Books, based in Portland, Oregon. Powell's

Powell's Books claims to be the world's largest independent bookstore. It regularly holds signings and events to promote new books.

stocks a huge number and variety of new and used books. Other independents, such as the Seattle Mystery Bookshop, are small and specialize in particular storytelling or nonfiction genres.

An important sign of exhibition in the 21st century is that all the types of exhibition establishments can be found online as well as offline. This online presence, along with the growth of electronic publishing, is changing exhibition in the book industry, just as it is changing production and distribution. To illustrate, let's look at exhibition of consumer books and textbooks.

Exhibition of Consumer Books

Think about where you went the last time you bought a hardback title for yourself or a friend. Did you purchase it from a physical bookstore with real doors and shelves (sometimes called **brick-and-mortar stores**) or from an online bookseller? If you bought it from a bookstore, do you remember if it was a chain bookstore or an independent bookseller? Traditionally, the independent bookstore was the place where Americans went to buy hardback trade books. In the mid-1990s bookstore chains overtook them, and many independents are now struggling to survive.

The brick-and-mortar bookstore chains, meanwhile, are themselves struggling to compete with a type of company that hardly existed in the 1990s: the online-only bookseller, especially Amazon. In 2016 Amazon accounted for 42 percent of all traditionally published book sales, ahead of Barnes & Noble, which held a 24 percent share of the market. Independent bookstores made up 6 percent.[17]

One particular difficulty for brick-and-mortar book exhibitors is that they often cannot compete on price with online retailers, especially as Amazon often charges less for popular titles than brick-and-mortar bookstores. Moreover, customers who pay an annual membership fee or buy a certain dollar value of books get free shipping. Plus, as we saw in the beginning of this chapter, Amazon often charges far less for the electronic edition of titles it suspects will be popular than for the hardcover versions of those books.

These activities deter many readers from purchasing books from their local bookstores. Instead, the brick-and-mortar stores—in the book industry and other industries—have noticed people using their places for window shopping. They look at the window or amble down the aisles and take note of interesting books. Then they buy them online.

As you can imagine, such activities do not encourage a healthy bottom line for traditional retailers. The bankruptcy of the large bookstore chain Borders in 2011 was one indication of the precarious health of brick-and-mortar retailers. Borders had not developed a robust enough online footprint to compete with Amazon in that retail space. Barnes & Noble has tried to keep its foot in the brick-and-mortar world while also trying to develop a major presence with the online sale of physical books and e-books. It did sell about 165 million books in the United States during 2016. That may sound impressive, but Amazon sold 275 million. There is no question that online bookselling has outstripped physical bookstore-chain outlets as the dominant way people buy consumer books.[18] Independents have moved to the internet too. With its online presence, Powell's calls itself the "largest independent used and new bookstore in the world." Powell's online book emporium highlights new and used books, and the company contends it is doing

brick-and-mortar stores stores that have a physical presence in the offline world

quite well, even though it doesn't always compete with Amazon and Barnes & Noble on price.

This major disruption and transformation of the publishing industry as a result of technological and social changes should remind you of the processes described in themes 2 and 3, presented earlier. The switch has not affected all parts of publishing as greatly or in the same way. It seems that juvenile titles remain comfortably in the printed world. Much more than adults, books for children and teens sell in print rather than in electronic form. Perhaps parents still want to buy picture books that their daughters and sons can hold, perhaps to give them the sense of the feel of a traditional book, perhaps because the color of most e-books still doesn't match that of a beautiful traditional picture book. Teenagers also seem to read paperbacks more than they read books on tablets.[19] That may be a matter of the tablet's price. And, of course, over time these views and habits may change.

Exhibition in Textbook Publishing

Textbooks represent another type of book that is clearly having some success in digital form. To understand why textbooks are different from consumer books, you have to consider who buys them and how they are bought. K–12 texts and college texts are quite different in terms of exhibition. The "exhibition" area for K–12 texts is not primarily the schools; it is special evaluation boards that inspect various titles to determine their appropriateness for children in their area. In many states, this evaluation takes place at the state level. California and Texas are the largest states with centralized selection, and board decisions can influence whether a textbook publisher has a chance of selling thousands upon thousands of copies. As you might imagine, textbook company executives pay a lot of attention to the likes and dislikes of members of the selection boards in these states. The executives often instruct their authors to make sure they write in ways that will appeal to the selection boards of California and Texas.

This activity, in turn, has bred resentment among teachers and parents in states that buy fewer books. They have expressed anger that the attitudes of a few people should have so much influence over what American children learn. You may not have known it when you were in grades K through 12, but K–12 textbooks are controversial commodities.

At the college level, instructors choose the titles they want to use and require students to buy them (sound familiar?). Presumably, if the students don't like a text, their feedback will encourage their teacher to look for a replacement. College textbook publishers regularly send professors free copies of new textbooks in the hope they will like what they see better than whatever they are currently using and will order the new book for their classes. Acquisitions editors must be alert for new trends in teaching that would suggest new text ideas, even while they encourage authors of current books to update their titles with new editions.

New editions of texts have two purposes. Most obviously, a new edition includes facts or ideas that have come to light or have been incorporated into the course as it is usually taught since the earlier edition went to press. (The changes in media that take place between this book's updates are often quite dramatic.) But there is also a strong marketing motive for new editions. Textbook publishers know that many students sell their texts after they use them and that the books then go on sale in the used-book market. The result is that publishing revenues from an edition plummet after the first year because students purchase used copies. The production of a new edition every three years or so is an attempt to derail this process, because students cannot get the updated version from used-book vendors. Revised versions of popular titles keep textbook publishers in business.

College students often complain about the high price of textbooks. During the last several years, a number of advocacy groups and politicians have taken up their cause, asserting that they are indeed paying too much and that publishers are encouraging professors to order too many extra materials—workbooks and online materials, for example—with the texts. Publishers reply that although their prices are high, the used-book market means that many students pay far less than the

original price and that the extra (or "bundled") materials are useful to instructors and students. Nevertheless, during the past several years a number of states have taken action. In 2006 Connecticut passed a law requiring publishers to disclose textbook prices to college faculty, presumably so that the faculty would consider costs in their decisions. In 2005 Virginia passed a law discouraging faculty from asking students to buy new editions that are minimally different from older ones that can be bought on the used-book market.

Enter the digital revolution. Although the price of online textbooks is often similar to their physical counterparts, many students now rent digital books for the semester instead of paying substantially more to own them. In addition, a number of school districts around the United States have experimented with giving their students Apple iPads loaded with their textbooks instead of giving hard copies of the books. This way, the districts can get updates of the books more cheaply every year; the kids can use the tablets for their work at school and at home; and the children's backs aren't strained terribly by the weight of heavy textbooks that they would otherwise lug home every day.

More and more classrooms throughout the country are providing students with tablets and digital media through which they can interact with their textbooks and other educational materials.

Convergence and Conglomeration in the Book Industry

The emergence of electronic copies of paper book titles along with the soaring popularity of reader technologies such as the Amazon Kindle, the Apple iPad, the Barnes & Noble Nook, and the Microsoft Surface point to the active presence of convergence in the book industry. These activities also reflect the blurring of media boundaries, of course. We have noted other types of boundary blurring as well, especially when it comes to trade books. Publishers promote trade book titles across a variety of media, from television shows to magazines and newspapers to the web.

The footprints of media conglomerates show up here, too. You might have noticed when reading the chapter the mention that one of the largest book publishers, Simon & Schuster, is owned by CBS Corporation. You might not be surprised, then, that synergy is sometimes at work here: Simon & Schuster is the primary publisher for books related to various program franchises owned by parent CBS, such as *Mission: Impossible*, *Star Trek*, and *CSI*. Consider some joint ventures that reflect common ownership: The National Amusements movie theater chain controls both CBS and Viacom, so National Amusements makes sure that many Viacom products stay in the corporate family. For example, Simon & Schuster has published books that tie into Viacom's Nickelodeon and Nick Jr. cable programs.

As Chapters 1 and 6 noted, convergence that is often tied to corporate synergies or joint ventures goes to the heart of how publishers believe they must operate in today's media world. Mass media executives today increasingly believe that to reach their target audiences, they must pursue these audiences across media boundaries. We should therefore expect not only more multimedia promotion of books but also more books that are *presold*. A **presold title** is one that publishers expect will sell well to specific audiences because it ties into material that is already popular with those audiences across other media. For example, a book by Oprah Winfrey or highlighted on her cable channel is presold to fans of her channel and magazine.

Many book lovers are nervous about this fixation on presold books and books that can be easily publicized across media boundaries. They worry that the books with the highest profile in bookstores and in the media are those that are reflections of popular characters or plot lines from other media—television, radio, magazines, the movies, or the web. Our age is one in which the most powerful media conglomerates own the largest book companies. These cross-media relationships are not likely to change. In fact, for reasons we suggested in Chapter 6, cross-media activities may accelerate in the name of synergy. As a media-literate person, you might want to ask the following questions as you move through the book world:

- To what extent are the books that are getting most of the media attention today generated as a result of an author's or a character's popularity in another medium?
- Are we seeing an increase in cooperative activities between movie companies and book publishers owned by the same conglomerate? That is, are movie companies mostly using the publishers to sell books that publicize the movies, and are book companies trying to come up with titles that can become films?

An optimist would answer, "Surely not." She or he would point out that many publishers publish trade books that have no connection to TV or movies and have no interest in making a TV show or movie of these books. A pessimist would concede this point but would emphasize that increasingly the titles that get the most publicity both in and out of the bookstore are those that fit the cross-media, conglomerate profile. As this chapter has shown, the history of the book is a long and complex one. Books have changed through the ages, with the currents of culture and interests of those who have the power to produce them. This long view is useful to take when you think about the future of the book.

Ethical Issues in Book Production

The process of finding and developing ideas and authors for books is filled with ethical pitfalls for authors, agents, and publishers. One of the biggest issues is that of stealing ideas. **Plagiarism**—using parts of another person's work without citing or otherwise crediting the original author—unfortunately seems to be much more common than many in publishing would like to believe. Sometimes such an act is clearly illegal, as when an author lifts sentences or paragraphs from copyrighted material. Plagiarism is not illegal when the author uses material that has not been protected by copyright; however, it remains a serious breach of ethics.

presold title
a book that publishers expect will sell well to specific audiences because it ties into material that is already popular with those audiences across other media

plagiarism
using parts of another person's work without citing or otherwise crediting the original author

THINKING ABOUT MEDIA LITERACY

Using the "track record" is one of the key determinants of a book's likelihood to be published. How is this a positive for the reading public? Are there negative consequences of a reliance on "track record"?

Ethical Issues for Authors Literary scholars and critics have concluded that many writers have been guilty of plagiarism, although the issue rarely makes the front pages. One that did get a lot of attention was the case of Harvard student Kaavya Viswanathan. In 2006 the Little Brown publishing company released her first novel, *How Opal Mehta Got Kissed, Got Wild, and Got a Life*. Soon afterward, her publisher asked bookstores to remove the book from their shelves, having confirmed accusations that she had used paragraphs from two other novels without citing them. One of the most prominent authors to be accused of plagiarism in recent years was Alex Haley, the author of *Roots*, the best-selling book that became one of the most-viewed television miniseries of all time. In 1978 Harold Courlander sued Haley for extensively lifting material for *Roots* from his book *The African*. That book itself had done quite well when it appeared in 1967: it sold 300,000 copies and was translated into several languages.

Haley eventually agreed to settle. Courlander received $650,000 just before the judge was to issue a ruling. Yet until Haley's death, he continued to claim that the numerous similarities between the books were unintentional and minor, even though a lot of evidence introduced in court indicated that he had used *The African* substantially in writing *Roots*. Courlander himself felt that the basic issue of copying never really made it onto the public agenda. He later noted that although he had felt vindicated at the time of the court settlement, public interest in the incident quickly disappeared. Haley, he added, "was a very persuasive public speaker" who dismissed questions about the settlement. "Nobody really raised the issue of literary ethics, and he continued to receive honorary degrees—it didn't slow him up. This troubled me."

An ethical issue swirling around nonfiction authors involves making up facts. In recent years a number of American writers—in newspapers and magazines as well as books—have betrayed their readers in this way. An example is Jonah Lehrer, who as a 32-year-old rising star at the *New Yorker* magazine, admitted that he had concocted a quote by the songwriter Bob Dylan for his book *Imagine*. According to an expert on Dylan's life and music, who accused Lehrer of making up the quote when he didn't recognize it from any of his research on Dylan, Lehrer also used quotes from Dylan in ways that did not at all reflect the contexts in which they had been said. Houghton Mifflin Harcourt, the publisher of *Imagine*, took the drastic and expensive step of withdrawing the book from publication. That included recalling all printed copies of the book from exhibitors and distributors. Nevertheless, *Imagine* had already sold more than 200,000 copies in hardcover and e-book.[20]

Ethical Issues for Editors and Literary Agents Editors and literary agents, as well as authors, also confront major ethical issues. Let's say you're an editor, and you get a manuscript chapter out of the blue from an unknown author. She proposes a nonfiction book about how mothers who travel frequently on business balance home and work. You don't know the writer, and you don't intend to use her. You do, however, like the topic, and you can think of at least two authors who have written for you who would do a great job with such a book. What do you do? Should you go ahead with using the idea? Is it ethical to take one person's ideas for a book and pay someone else to write it?

THINKING ABOUT MEDIA LITERACY

Think about shopping for a book in an online versus a "brick-and-mortar" bookstore. How is exhibition different in each? As a customer, how does the experience between the two differ? What is your preference?

Or let's say you are a literary agent just starting out on your own. You already represent a few authors, but you need to bring in more money. You know that among literary agents the rule is that you charge a percentage of an author's earnings, but you do not demand a fee for simply representing an author. The reason is that agents who accept fees have been known to represent authors simply to get their money, not because the agents really think the authors will succeed in finding a publisher. You also know, however, that there are many aspiring writers out there who would love to have your input, even for a fee. You tell yourself you can be honest with them. Should you do it?

As we have seen, this concern is only one of the many issues people in the book publishing industry must contend with every day. It's a challenging business facing a challenging present and future. If you care about ideas and stories, the shape of the book industry in the 21st century should certainly be on your radar.

CHAPTER REVIEW

 Visit the Companion Website at www.routledge.com/cw/turow for additional study tools and resources.

 ## Key Terms

You can find the definitions to these key terms in the marginal glossary throughout this chapter. Test your knowledge of these terms with interactive flash cards on the *Media Today* Companion Website.

acquisitions editor	higher-education books and materials	print run
advance on royalties	K–12 books and materials	professional books
audiobook	literary agent	religious books
bestseller	mass market outlets	royalties
blockbuster	mass market paperbacks	track records
book tour	pedagogy	trade books
brick-and-mortar stores	plagiarism	trade paperbacks
composition	prepublication research	University press books
consumer books	presold title	

Questions for Discussion and Critical Thinking

1. The text raised an ethical issue for editors regarding hearing an idea for a book from an untested writer and giving the idea to one of the authors you've worked with before. Think through the issues. What arguments would you make that would cause you to contract with another known writer? What, if any, legal issues might arise? Think through the repercussions of giving the idea from one author to another.

2. According to publisher Steven Piersanti, "A book has less than a 1% chance of being stocked in an average bookstore" (http://outthinkgroup.com/the-10-awful-truths-about-book-publishing/). If that is the case, what options are there for authors? What advantages and disadvantages are there for authors seeking these other routes to exhibiting their publications?

3. After reading over the chapter on the book industry, what do you think are the most important considerations for an author when embarking on a book project? Do you think it is easier or more difficult for a first-time author to get their work out to the public?

4. In the past publishers sent their authors' books to book reviewers in hopes of getting the word out about a new title. Now, sites like Amazon and Goodreads make it easy for anyone to give their opinion about a book. Compare the difference between these types of "reviews" and how they help, or hinder, a book's marketing.

 ## Activity

Imagine you are a consultant working with a book publishing company that would like to make a major investment in one of the following (fictional) companies. Given all you've read in this chapter, which of the following would be your recommendation for investment? Why? For the ones you don't recommend, what is your reasoning?

Of the different possible acquisitions, which would be your number-one recommendation for purchase and why?

A. Applewood Books: *specializes in publishing exacting re-creations of historic books, including complex reprints of books published by methods and using materials that duplicate antique publishing techniques*
B. Kiddie Lit Bookstores: *chain of bookstore "experiences" for parents and kids*
C. Green Leaves Pulp and Paper: *mission of Green Leaves Pulp and Paper is to be the leading national source for environmentally responsible, economically sound paper*
D. Tablet Application Developer: *a software company dedicated to the development of software for iPads and other tablets*
E. Eating Well Publishing: *specializes in publishing illustrated nonfiction books on cooking, baking, gourmet dining, fine wines, and related topics*
F. Bookalodium: *an e-commerce site designed to compete with Amazon in the online e-book sales and social recommendation market*

In composing your answer, consider the statistics about the book publishing industry from the AAP 2017 annual report at https://publishingperspectives.com/2018/07/us-statshot-publisher-survey-2017-estimates-revenue/.

The News Industry

8

CHAPTER OBJECTIVES

1   Describe key developments in US news history.

2   Explain the production, distribution, and exhibition processes of various types of news outlets.

3   Recognize and discuss the challenges faced by the news industry today and some approaches to dealing with them.

4   Apply your media literacy skills and ethical compass to evaluate activities of the news industry and their impact on your everyday life.

The Pew Research organization conducts regular surveys about what Americans know and think about news. Pew contacts thousands of people who are representative of the nation and asks them how they get various sorts of news and what they think of the news they get. The result is a fascinating snapshot of the population's relation to news in the changing media landscape. It's noteworthy the way over 50 percent of Americans say they are at least "somewhat" close followers of international, national, local, and neighborhood news. Far smaller percentages claim to be news junkies, though. Only 17 percent say they follow international news "very closely," though, whereas 40 percent contend they are close followers of national news, with 33 percent and 30 percent saying that about local and neighborhood news, respectively.

How do the people find out these things? The short answer is, obviously, in lots of ways—from talking with other people ("word of mouth") to television, radio, newspapers, magazines, and the internet. Pew's research especially highlights Americans' increased reliance on digital technologies for the news they receive. In 2017, for example, 65 percent of Americans said they often (31 percent) or sometimes (34 percent) use a desktop or laptop computer to access news. Higher percentages said they use a mobile device (a phone or tablet) often (45 percent) or sometimes (29 percent). In fact, 65 percent said they prefer getting news from mobile media over desktops or laptops.

In view of the controversies ignited by President Donald Trump about what he called the "fake news" media, it's interesting that 75 percent of Americans told Pew they believe the "national news media" cover national news very (21 percent) or somewhat (54 percent) fairly. Seventy-two percent said they trust the national media "a lot" (20 percent) or "somewhat" (52 percent)—percentages that were substantially higher than their trust of national news from friends and social media. Moreover, 75 percent agreed that news media "keep politicians from doing things that shouldn't be done"—the notion that media are society's watchdogs—whereas a much smaller 28 percent agreed that news organs "keep politicians from doing their jobs." Although the numbers indicating trust of the media are high, you might be inclined to see the hole rather than the bagel. That is, you might legitimately point out that in all these cases around one in four Americans does not believe the media are doing a creditable or trustworthy job regarding the topics mentioned. That is certainly an area of concern, and we will return to it. Our first order of business, however, is to present a framework for understanding production, distribution, and exhibition of content in the news industry. As we will see, convergence is at the heart of much of what takes place, and convergence is both the blessing and the curse of executives who are trying to make money in what has become a very challenging landscape for doing that.

The newspaper has been the center of the news business for several hundred years. Although, as the Pew data suggest, Americans use digital media to get a lot of their news, the newspaper still plays an important role. Alex Williams makes this point well in a recent doctoral dissertation. He points out that in 2016 Nielsen estimated that more than 169 million adults in the United States, or 69 percent of the population, read a newspaper in the past month whether it be in print, on a website or in a mobile app. The same survey estimated that 51 percent of monthly newspaper readers engaged only with the print version of the newspaper. Williams compares this audience size of 169 million to Twitter, "which has been praised as [a] major instrument for news dissemination." Twitter stated in 2017 that the company had 68 million users in the United States that logged in to their account during June of that year. Williams then turns to television, an important news medium. Nielsen estimated in 2017 that the combined average prime-time viewership of Fox News, CNN, and MSNBC was 5.1 million total viewers. These are certainly large numbers, but they don't dwarf the newspaper numbers. So, Williams concludes, "while the relative sizes of these audiences are constantly changing, newspapers clearly remain a vital source of information for the American public." At the same time, he agrees with a 2012 statement by Pew that the newspaper business is in crisis, a crisis that "is an advertising problem, not an audience problem."

What does this statement by Pew mean? In what sense is the newspaper business in a crisis, why, and why does Pew state it is an advertising, not an audience, problem? Is it still an advertising, not audience, problem in the late 2010s? (Hint: It's both.) The aim of this chapter is to provide a snapshot of the newspaper industry at this scary point in its history and to address the following questions: What historical influences shaped the newspaper business as we know it? How do print and online newspapers work today—and why are online versions bringing in so much less revenue than their print counterparts? What are newspaper firms trying to keep print going and make their digital versions profitable? And if these attempts fail, are there socially useful alternatives to the traditional newspaper industry?

The Development of the Newspaper

Newspapers traditionally are printed products created on a regular (weekly or daily) basis and released in multiple copies. By this definition, newspapers did not exist before Johannes Gutenberg invented the printing press in the middle 1400s (see Chapter 7). And although Gutenberg's printing press made it possible for newspapers to be produced, having the technical means to do so did not immediately result in an explosion of newspaper publishing (see the timeline in Figure 8.1).

In England, regular newspapers weren't even produced during most of the 1600s. England's ruling monarchs feared newspapers and greatly restricted their production. These rulers felt that if newspapers were to report on happenings in the land, they might provoke political discussions that could lead to revolution. Newspapers published in Europe tended to mix political news with business news. Merchants were the main audience because they needed to know what was going on politically and economically throughout Europe and in the "New World" that was being colonized by European nations. In the late 1600s, England's ruling monarchs were forced to yield power to a feisty Parliament, and the nation began to flex its naval and trading muscles—and newspapers become a regular feature in the country.

Recall the three themes about media history that we introduced when we discussed books in Chapter 7. You may be able to see elements of that first theme here, in connection with newspapers:

1. The modern newspaper did not arrive in a flash as a result of one inventor's grand change.

Look online for a photo of *The Daily Courant*, the first regularly published English-language newspaper, from the 1600s. It doesn't much look like the newspapers you know, does it? It took hundreds of years for the printed newspaper as we recognize it to come into being. You'll probably agree that the photo beside it of a *New York World* front page from the early 1900s appears closer to a contemporary daily paper. Explore the newspaper timeline, and you'll follow the chain of technological innovations that affected the nature of the newspaper across the centuries. Critical changes in the paper's look came about with the development of methods for creating headlines across the page, ways to reproduce photographs, ways to include color pictures and photos, and far more. Critical changes in the ability to reach more people came as a result of the steam-powered press, the rotary press, and computerized printing technologies. Then there are the technologies that helped bring the information—the news—to newspapers from outside their offices, including the telegraph, the telephone, the computer, and more.

But the newspaper we know is not just a product of technology. It's the result of people pushing the technology in certain directions in order to make money telling stories to others in the society. It's a point that leads to theme 2.

2. The newspaper as a medium of communication developed as a result of social and legal responses to the technology during different periods.

If you read through the timeline with this theme in mind, a number of fascinating incidents will pop out and connect. From Peter Zenger, to American colonists' anger over the British "tax" on knowledge, to the Constitution's First Amendment, we witness the rise of a belief in an **adversarial press**—a press that has the ability to argue with the government. On a different front, we see how the rise of literacy, the example of union papers of the 1820s, and the success of British papers aimed at the "common man" combined with fast printing-press technology and cheap paper to encourage the growth of a new kind of newspaper—the penny press—beginning in the 1830s. It was the penny press that really marked the start of newspapers in the United States aimed at virtually anyone. With that came new definitions of news; wire services to help report it from around the world; and new ways to use technologies such as the telegraph, the camera, and the telephone to report news.

Along with these developments came the development of a newspaper industry. And here's where theme 3 becomes relevant.

3. The newspaper as a medium of communication existed long before the existence of the newspaper industry.

As the timeline indicates, it wasn't until the 19th century that American society witnessed the development of a newspaper *industry*—that is, a set of organizations that interact regularly to produce, distribute, and exhibit that journalistic product. Before the penny press, the entire process of writing the articles, printing the paper, and even delivering it to readers was typically carried out by a publisher, his family, and perhaps an assistant. Sometimes the post office helped with the delivery. But with the success of the penny press came the growth of a news organization, with reporters covering particular topics, editors checking their work before publication, and business departments devoted to increasing circulation and bringing in advertising.

Follow the timeline into the late 19th century, and you'll see how big-city newspapers became big business as their circulations swelled and advertisers paid handsomely to reach their readers. But take another look at the timeline, this time from 1900 onward. You'll notice that other media—movies, radio, television, and the internet—rose over the decades with content that competed with newspapers. Each of these media brought news in new forms. Movies brought the sights and sounds of events into theaters. Radio brought narrated news and live events in the home. Television added moving pictures to what radio had initiated. The internet allowed all this along with unmatched portability: you can get news on your mobile device virtually anywhere. Moreover, you can react to news streams near-instantly and even create your own.

Over time, these new ways to access news took a toll on newspapers. A long-term decline in daily newspaper readership that began in the 1950s sped up in the 2000s, as younger consumers migrated to web-based news sources such as blogs and news collection (or aggregation) sites such as Google News, Facebook's news feeds, and Twitter. Many advertisers followed those people to the web, and newspapers consequently lost advertising money as well.

And so we arrive at the present—to a newspaper industry with a long and generally profitable history undergoing a major transition. Influenced by the rise of digital technologies and convergence, the current developments will likely transform the newspaper industry for the 21st century as profoundly as the late 19th-century events noted in the timeline shaped mass-circulation, advertising-dependent dailies for the

THINKING ABOUT MEDIA LITERACY

With all the discussion about "fake news" and these statistics about the news audience's level of trust, think about your own views on the news. What is your level of trust in the news? What makes your trust rise or fall?

1700   **1750**   **1800**   **1840**   **1860**

Late 1600s: Newspapers become a regular feature in Britain.

1735: In a landmark case, John Peter Zenger is acquitted of seditious libel for printing facts in his newspaper that reflected badly on the royal governor. The American jury found that, unlike in English law, truth could be used as a defense against libel.

1760s–1770s: Britain imposes a series of paper taxes, from the Stamp Act to the Townshend Acts, to finance war with the French.

1780s–1820s: Daily newspapers tend to be supported by political parties and to be read by merchants and politicians.

1791: The First Amendment to the US Constitution, which explicitly protects the press, is adopted.

1814 A steam-powered printing press invented by Frederick Koenig in Germany is used for the first time by *The Times* of London.

1820s: A decade in which early labor unions create newspapers read by their members.

1820s–early 20th c: The US sees a growth of canals and railroads.

1831: William Lloyd Garrison starts *The Liberator*, a weekly anti-slavery newspaper, in New England championing the nonviolent abolition of slavery through moral persuasion.

1833: Benjamin Day starts *The New York* Sun daily for a penny per issue.

1840s–1850s: Increased newspaper circulation leads to the widespread use of Hoe's Rotary (or "type-revolving") press.

1840s: The *New York Herald*, a penny newspaper, is especially innovative in appealing to different segments of the population within the same issue through the use of separate sections.

1847: Frederick Douglass, a former slave, publishes the *North Star* in Rochester, New York, inspired by Garrison's *The Liberator*.

1840s–1860s: The byline (which tells who wrote the story) emerges, as does the date line (which tells where and when the reporter wrote it).

1846: Seven New York City newspapers establish the Associated Press as a cooperative news gathering organization.

1860s: The "inverted pyramid" style of reporting evolves with the widespread use of the telegraph during and after the Civil War.

1860s: Reporters speed their words to the printing presses via carrier pigeon, Pony Express, the railroad and eventually the telegraph.

1870s–1900: The number of English-language general circulation dailies increases from 489 in 1870 to 1,967 in 1900.

1880s–1910: A new business philosophy in newspapers develops: using advertising instead of circulation revenues for their profits.

1890s: The term "yellow journalism" is used for a newspaper characterized by irresponsible, fickle, and sensational news gathering and exhibition.

Figure 8.1
Timeline of the news industry.

1860s	1900	2000	2010

1890s: Full-color presses, first used in Paris, are adapted in the United States and used especially for Sunday comics.

1898: Rise of sensationalistic coverage of the Spanish-American War, led by publishers Joseph Pulitzer and William Randolph Hearst, who are competing for circulation in New York.

1920s: Rise of the tabloids: the most popular of this sort of newspaper was the *New York Daily News*, which dubbed itself "New York's picture newspaper."

1920s: An ethic of objectivity develops among professional journalists, who increasingly create formal rules and codes.

1930s: In the midst of the Depression, powerful newspaper chains—that is, companies that own a number of papers around the nation—become established.

1930s: The Great Depression and the rise of the radio adversely affect the newspaper industry, as many advertisers switched to radio.

1950s: By the late 1950s, most US homes (86%) have at least one television set.

1990s–present: Young readers migrate to free web and app news sources such as blogs and link-collection (or *aggregation*) sites (for example, Google News). This development speeds up newspaper circulation declines.

2008–present: Six large newspaper companies file for bankruptcy protection under Chapter 11 of the US Bankruptcy Code.

2009: The *Seattle Post-Intelligencer* moves to an online-only format to save money.

Late 2000s: A global recession along with huge debts on the part of certain newspaper chains lead to major decreases in total newspaper revenues during 2008 and 2009.

2009: The *Rocky Mountain News* of Denver, Colorado, prints its final issue just two months shy of its 150th anniversary.

2010: ProPublica, an independent nonprofit news organization, becomes the first online news source to win a Pulitzer Prize.

2013: Jeff Bezos, the founder of Amazon.com, pays $250 million for *The Washington Post*, ending 80 years of local ownership of the paper by the Meyer-Graham family.

2014: Annual newspaper advertising revenue in the US is $16.4 billion, down dramatically from $46.7 billion in 2004.

2014: Using new "automation technology," the Associated Press begins to release computer-generated rather than reporter-generated stories about company earnings.

2015: Gannett and several other big media companies spin off their newspaper divisions.

2016: According to Gallup only 32% of Americans say they have a great deal or fair amount of trust in the mass media "to report the news fully, accurately and fairly," the lowest level in Gallup polling history.

2018: Pew Research Center finds 20% of US adults say they get news via social media. The percentage tops the number saying they get their news from newspapers (16%) for the first time. Television remains the most popular medium for news (49%).

20th century. The changes are affecting some types of newspapers more immediately and dramatically than others. To grasp the ways in which convergence and the digital world are affecting newspapers' production, distribution, and exhibition activities, it is first important to understand the types of papers that exist, the companies that run them, and the support they receive from advertisers. This will also make it clear that the newspaper industry today is quite varied, and it is important to get a sense of that variety before generalizing about the future of "the newspaper."

An Overview of the Contemporary Newspaper Industry

Perhaps the broadest way to think about newspapers in the United States is to divide them into **dailies** (newspapers that are published on newsprint every day, sometimes with the exception of Sunday) and **weeklies** (newspapers that are published on newsprint once or twice a week). Daily newspapers tend to present a mix of local, national and international news together with lifestyle and entertainment features. Weeklies are often given out for free, and they place a large emphasis on arts and culture—and sometimes on brash reporting about local issues. In 2016 there were 1,286 dailies in the United States. That may sound like a lot, but it's a drop of 462 papers from 1970 and 194 from 2000. As for weeklies, the trade publisher Editor and Publisher (E&P) tracks "community weekly newspapers." These aim to reach people in a geographic area—a city, town, suburb, or rural locale—with print products fewer than four times a week. E&P found 6,033 of these weeklies in January 2018; that was from 6,049 just a year earlier.

Daily Newspapers

The circulation of printed daily newspapers has moved downward over the past quarter-century, even though the nation's adult population has grown by more than a third. In 2017 circulation hovered at 30.9 million. That was a drop from 43.4 million in 2012 and from 55.2 million in 2005.[1] Of the three dailies distributed across the country—the *Wall Street Journal*, the *New York Times*, and *USA Today*—only the first has seen a long-time print circulation rise. Since 2001, the *Wall Street Journal* climbed substantially in average daily (Monday through Friday) print circulation, from around 560,000 in 2001 to 1.5 million in 2017. The *New York Times*, though, fell from around 1.1 million in 2001 to about 598,000 in 2017. *USA Today* dropped even more sharply, with 2.1 million print copies circulating daily in 2001 and 958,000 in 2017. This downward trend has also affected the hundred largest local newspapers in the country. One source calculated in 2017 that print circulation "has dropped by over a quarter at many [of those] papers in as little as three years."[2] At the same time, those papers did get many paid subscribers to their digital platforms in 2017—2.2 million for the *New York Times*, 1.08 million for the *Wall Street Journal*, and 341,000 for *USA Today*'s online properties.[3] Counting criteria established by the Alliance for Audited Media in 2010 allow them to add the digital to the print circulation in order to come up with a total average circulation number. Clearly that allowed the *New York Times* and *Wall Street Journal* to tout great circulation gains—*USA Today*, not so much.

Newspapers aimed at particular localities also have often seen print circulation drops, sometimes quite big ones. In San Francisco, for example, the *San Francisco*

dailies
newspapers that are published on newsprint every day, sometimes with the exception of Sunday

weeklies
newspapers that are published on newsprint once or twice a week

Chronicle decreased from around 500,000 paid weekday and Sunday subscribers in the early 2000s to 220,000 Sunday and 163,000 weekday subscribers in 2017. At the same time, SFGate, the *San Francisco Chronicle's* free website, was drawing 34.4 million unique individuals per month, whereas SFChronicle.com, its site aimed at print and digital subscribers, was reaching 2.8 million.[4] When the *San Francisco Chronicle's* circulation started plummeting around 2005, observers pointed out that enthusiasm for the web was widespread earlier in San Francisco than in many parts of the country, and they saw the declines there as a leading indicator. It underscored for newspaper-industry watchers that the poor state of the economy is not the only, or even the primary, factor threatening the business of many newspapers in the early 2010s. It is, rather, the availability of so many other news sources, particularly digital ones.

Daily Newspaper Chains It's important to note that, with only a few exceptions, daily newspapers tend not to have competition from other printed dailies. (The major exceptions are free papers known as *Metro* in Boston, New York, and Philadelphia; similar products in other cities tend not to be competition because they are owned by the city's own daily newspaper firm.) Moreover, many of the top one hundred papers are owned by four companies: Tronc (weird name, isn't it—formerly known as Tribune Publishing), which owns the *Chicago Tribune*, among other properties; McClatchy, with papers that include those in Fort Worth and Miami; Digital First Media, with dailies in Torrance and San Jose, California; and Gannett Company, the largest newspaper chain by total paid print circulation. It owns, for example, the Hackensack, New Jersey, *Record*, and the Lafayette, Indiana *Journal and Courier*, as well as the nationally circulated *USA Today*.

The logic of chain ownership has traditionally been quite strong. A daily newspaper that was the only one in its area could pretty well dictate prices to local advertisers—car dealers, department stores, movie theaters—that wanted to reach high percentages of the population on a regular basis. Historically, daily newspapers' margins of profit were quite high, far higher than most other industries. In recent years, newspaper executives and their investors have begun to worry that this logic no longer holds. Losses in readership and increased competition for local advertising by websites, the free newspapers in some cities, and other local media have led investors to downgrade the monetary value of some of the biggest newspaper companies. In 2008 and 2009, a national mortgage crisis that left many people without homes, a weak job market, and reduced consumer spending drove many of the large newspaper firms into a tailspin, as advertising plummeted and circulation went down. A number of newspaper chains that had borrowed lots of money now found it hard to pay their debts. With online competition growing every day, analysts began to wonder whether the newspaper industry could rebound.

The result was that many newspaper companies were struggling to stay afloat, and publicly traded newspaper companies experienced sharp drops—as much as 90 percent—in their stock value. Both these companies and privately held firms laid off reporters and closed bureaus in state and national capitals. The Tribune Company, parent to the *Chicago Tribune* and *Los Angeles Times*, among other papers, declared bankruptcy and struggled through the 2010s to right itself. The Hearst Corporation stopped publishing a print edition of the *Seattle Post-Intelligencer*. It kept a web version alive but still cut 80 percent of the newsroom staff. The E. W. Scripps Company fully closed Denver's *Rocky Mountain News* in 2009. McClatchy Company, parent company of the *Miami Herald* and *Kansas City Star*, among many other papers, cut its work force by 4,000, or one-third of its previous full-time workers. In 2014 some of the biggest media conglomerates with strong newspaper holdings—Gannett, E. W. Scripps, Journal Communications, and Tribune Company—decided to spin off their newspaper holdings into separate companies. Observers saw one reason behind these deals was a concern that the newspaper divisions of firms were dragging down otherwise healthy profits the conglomerates were making from broadcasting, cable, and other media.

Weekly Newspapers

Weekly newspapers have also been buffeted by the enormous circulation challenges that daily newspapers have been experiencing. The trade publication E&P has a list of "community weekly newspapers" in the United States. These aim to reach a geographic area—a city, town, suburb, or rural locale—with print products (and often internet sites) less than four times a week. E&P found in 2014 that about 18.5 million people paid for a weekly paper and about 23.5 million got them free, a total circulation of about 42 million.[5] It reported that in late 2017, about 16 million paid and about 28.6 million got the papers free, for a total of about 45.4 million.[6] The total circulation is up, but note the drop in paid circulation. That means that more of those weeklies bring in money only from advertising.

Community weekly newspapers often take hold in place that cannot support a daily paper. There are, in addition, other types of newspapers that come out on a weekly basis. **Ethnic weeklies** target racial/ethnic groups. *The Los Angeles Sentinel*, for example, is a weekly founded in 1933 that describes itself as "the largest subscriber paid African American owned newspaper on the West Coast."[7] **Shoppers** are typically aimed at people in particular neighborhoods who might shop at local merchants and are designed primarily to deliver coupons and advertisements, but they may also carry some news or feature content. An historically innovative type of city paper has been the **alternative (or Alt-)weekly**. This is a paper written for a young, urban audience with an eye on political and cultural commentary, as well as investigations into controversial local topics; the *Chicago Reader* is an example. Because these papers are distributed free and depend on advertising to survive, the decisions of many advertisers to reach people via the internet has hurt alt-weeklies. In 2017 the UK's *Guardian* newspaper estimated there were about 100, and the *Guardian* noted that some of the best ones had ceased publication (Baltimore's *City Paper*, for example) or gone to online-only status (New York's famed *Village Voice*).[8]

ethnic weeklies
newspapers that target ethnic and/or racial groups

shoppers
free, nondaily newspapers, typically aimed at people in particular neighborhoods who might shop at local merchants and designed primarily to deliver coupons and advertisements, though they may also carry some news or feature content

alternative weekly
a paper written for a young, urban audience with an eye on political and cultural commentary

Weekly "alternative" papers focus on local news and events. *The Village Voice* of New York City is a famed example. It stopped its print edition in 2017 but continues online.

The Variety of Newspapers

As the newspaper categories suggest, the variety that exists among daily and weekly papers is fascinating. When was the last time you read the *Arctic Sentry*, a weekly military paper in Fairbanks, Alaska, that claims a circulation of about 3,000? Are you a lawyer in Philadelphia? If so, you might know that the five-times-a-week *Legal Intelligencer* in Philadelphia counts 5,500 subscribers. If you're a resident of New Orleans, perhaps you will be interested in the *Gambit Weekly*, a self-described locally owned "alternative weekly" that distributes 50,000 copies to 400 locations throughout the area? Did you say you're a college student? Oncampusadvertising, a company that places ads in college newspapers, states that their "readership survey illustrates that

50 percent [to] 70 percent of college students regularly read their college newspaper" in its print version.[9]

The African American press includes about 200 newspapers. With the exception of a few papers such as the *Philadelphia Tribune*, which is published five days a week, almost all appear weekly. Among foreign-language newspapers, Spanish newspapers are the most common. Latino papers range from the seven-days-a-week *El Nuevo Herald* in Miami (circulation 48,000) to the twice-monthly *El Veterano* published in Vineland, New Jersey. Spanish, though, is only the tip of the iceberg of foreign-language newspapers in the United States. Daily or nondaily newspapers target speakers of Mandarin, Vietnamese, Russian, Yiddish, and Ukrainian, among other languages.

It is important to note that "circulation" (the number of paying subscribers) is not the same as readership (the number of people who actually go through the paper). Some copies tend to be shared by a few or even many people, and newspapers try to convince advertisers their readership is quite a bit higher than their circulation. The amount of sharing is called the **pass-along rate**. So, for example, the National Newspaper Association cites circulation figures of its member papers as 65.5 million copies per week and contends that the pass-along rate is about 2.3 people per copy, for a total circulation of about 150 million.[10] You probably realize that most newspapers also try to enlarge their distribution numbers beyond physical copies through digital forms—for example, the number of individuals who use their websites, mobile apps, Facebook pages, and Twitter feeds.

pass-along rate
the amount of sharing between people of a newspaper copy

GLOBAL MEDIA TODAY & CULTURE

YELLOW JOURNALISM

You may have heard of the term *yellow journalism*, but what does it mean? (Hint: It has nothing to do with painting.) Toward the end of the 19th century, the lucrative (at the time) newspaper business became increasingly competitive, and rival entrepreneurs expanded the content provided by their publications with the intent to vie for the attention of an increasing number of readers and the advertisers. In particular in New York City, Joseph Pulitzer and William Hearst engaged in a prolonged battle over the rights to publish a Sunday comic strip based on the fictional character "The Yellow Kid," in a no-holds-barred contest.

The term *yellow journalism* was coined at that time to symbolize the lengths to which publishers would go to increase their circulations to the detriment of ethical journalism practices and reporting. Sensational reporting and highly partisan approaches were, in fact, the norm. The excesses of *yellow journalism* led to self-regulation and the establishment of journalism schools across the country to protect the craft of journalism. To what extent do you think yellow journalism exists today, and to what extent do you think political actors acuse news sources of that (with the newer term *fake news*) for the actors' own benefit?

Financing the Newspaper Business

No matter what their size, topic, or language, newspapers need to make money. They can generate revenues in two ways: from advertising or from circulation. Advertising is by far the dominant source of money. Historically, printed daily newspapers have received about 75 to 80 percent of their revenues—and weekly newspapers about 90 percent of their revenues—in this way. Weeklies are still largely supported by advertising. The percentage of revenues dailies receive from advertising in print and digital combined has dropped to around 66 percent, however. The reason is that although circulation money is holding somewhat steady (many newspapers have increased their subscription fees even as circulation has decreased), advertising money has dropped significantly, so the percentage received from circulation is higher today. Individual papers have had higher or lower percentages, depending on the ad environment.

In early 2018 the *New York Times* received about 63 percent of its revenues from circulation—much higher than its publicly traded peers. According to Pew, in 2017 those daily newspapers had the opposite funding stream from the *New York Times*. They took in about 40 percent from paying subscribers. Even that 40 percent figure was high by historical standards. As late as 2005 US daily newspapers were getting only 20 percent of their revenues from paying readers, whereas most of the rest—80 percent—was coming from sponsored messages. *The New York Times* wasn't much different. The past decade has seen advertising plummet, though, as sponsors have moved their money to apps and websites that target the same audiences as the papers. Revenues from both advertising and circulation are still extremely important, however. Let's take a bit a deeper look at each.

Advertising

freestanding inserts (FSIs)
preprinted sheets that advertise particular products, services, or retailers

cost per thousand readers or cost per mil (CPM)
the basic measurement of advertising efficiency in all media; it is by taking the cost of the advertising, dividing it by the audience number, and multiplying the total by 1,000

You've undoubtedly seen a lot of advertisements in physical newspapers. Advertising can show up next to the actual stories (the most common way) or as inserts, often called **freestanding inserts (FSIs)**. These are preprinted sheets that advertise particular products, services, or retailers. When advertisers buy space in newspapers, a major way they evaluate the purchase is by looking at the **cost per thousand readers** (often abbreviated **CPM**, for **cost per mil**, "mil" being Greek for thousand). This is the basic measurement of advertising efficiency in all media; it is used by advertisers to evaluate how much space they will buy in a given newspaper or other medium and what price they will pay. If a full-page ad in a particular newspaper that reaches 100,000 people costs $10,000, the CPM is $100. Because advertisers often compare media in terms of CPM, even firms that have the only daily newspapers in their cities worry about coming up with ad prices that can compete with radio and TV or even local ads inserted into national magazines.

CPM is a concept that works for internet advertising, too. On the web and on apps, it typically stands for costs per thousand impressions. That means the amount of money a sponsor must pay to have its ads load on the browsers of 1,000 people coming to the newspaper site or on the newspaper app of 1,000 people. The approaches newspapers take to internet advertisements and data parallel the ones discussed in Chapter 6. The forms of the ads vary widely, from basic "banners" (bars or rectangles with commercial messages), to "rich media" (banners or boxes that show animations or streaming video and sometimes allow the user to interact with them), to "native" ads (commercial messages that look like the editorial matter of the site or app—see Chapter 4).

According to Pew, daily newspapers together brought in about $27.7 billion in print and in digital during 2017. That sounds like a lot of money, and it is. But consider that in 2005 the revenue brought in was $60.1 billion, and it decreased every year afterward even as newspapers were building their digital domains. To understand what's going on, you need to know that the term "advertising" as it applies to newspapers really refers to three different areas: retail advertising from companies with local outlets, classified ads, and national ads. Figure 8.2, with data from the PWC consulting firm, can help you compare these forms of advertising in relation to one another and over time from 2013 through 2017. Unfortunately, PWC's data only separate classified, national, and retail ad revenues for the print side. It lumps "digital advertising" into one category. Still, the differences between the three forms are instructive of what types of advertisers are putting their money in print.

Retail Advertising Local retail advertising is carried out by establishments located in the same geographic area as the newspaper in which the ad is placed. Think of ads from computer electronics stores, department stores, hospitals, car dealerships, restaurants, realtors, and movie theaters. Some of these advertisers may be parts of national chains, but the purpose of the ads is to persuade people to shop in the local outlets. Retail advertising is the most important of the three main areas of newspaper advertising. In 2017 it made up 59 percent of papers' print advertising revenues. The problem for the newspaper industry is that although the amount of money brought in from retail businesses that year was $6.2 billion, just four years earlier, it was $10.4 billion—about the same of the entire amount of advertising revenues the industry earned in print during 2017.

	2013	2014	2015	2016	2017p
— *Newspaper in USA*†					
— *Advertising*					
Digital advertising	4,402	4,588	4,731	4,925	5,086
— *Print advertising*					
Classified	4,350	4019	3,617	3,264	2,899
National	2,906	2,712	2,465	2,251	2,016
Retail	10,356	9,606	8,681	7,828	7,014
Total	17613	16,336	14,763	13,343	11,929
Total	22,015	20,924	19,494	18,268	17,014
— *Circulation*					
Digital	424	523	596	691	798
Print	10,446	10,657	10,760	10,999	11,142
Total	10,870	11,181	11,356	11,691	11 940
Total	32,885	32,105	30,850	29,959	28,955

Figure 8.2
Newspaper print advertising categories and associated revenue.

†At average $US 2017 exchange rates. p stands for projected revenues.

Note: Numbers shown are rounded. Totals may not equal the sum of their parts due to rounding.

classified ad
short announcement for a product or service that is typically grouped with announcements for other products or services of the same kind

Classified Advertising The second most lucrative type of newspaper advertisement is the classified ad. A **classified ad** is a short announcement for a product or service that is typically grouped with announcements for other products or services of the same kind. Newspapers typically sell classified ad space by the line to people who want to offer everything from houses to beds to bikes. In recent years, the amount of money daily newspapers have generated through classified ads has plummeted—from about $4.4 billion and 24 percent of daily print newspaper advertising to 2.9 billion and 24 percent in 2017. Consider, too, that in 2003 classified ads drew $16 billion and made up 36 percent of daily newspaper print advertising. The huge drops have a lot to do with the rise of online real estate, auto, and general classified sites, especially free (or very cheap) ones such as Craigslist. They provide users with continually updated information, interactivity, and immediate responsiveness that papers cannot possibly match.

national ads
advertisements placed by large national and multinational firms that do business in a newspaper's geographic area

National Advertising **National ads** are advertisements placed by large national and multinational firms that do business in a newspaper's geographic area. Airline and cruise line ads are often national purchases. Political advertisements and movie ads also often fit the "national" tag. The distinction between retail and national ads may not always be clear. Sometimes what appear to be retail ads are actually national ads. The reason is that national marketers often provide co-op advertising money to retailers that carry their products. In co-op advertising, manufacturers or distributors of products provide money to exhibitors in order to help the exhibitor with the cost of promoting a particular product. A soup manufacturer, for example, might provide a local supermarket chain with an allowance to purchase ads that highlight the manufacturer's soups. The money may be used to buy time on local radio and TV, as well as ads in local newspapers.

Since at least 2003, national advertising has represented between 17 and 19 percent of daily newspaper advertising. As with retail and classified advertising, though, the actual amounts represented by those numbers declined sharply in the late 2000s. In 2003 national ads revenue amounted to $7.8 billion, in 2013 it amounted to $2.9 billion, but by 2017 it dropped further to $2 billion.

Circulation

If you were a newspaper executive, you would probably find the retail, classified, and national advertising trends in the industry—and the lower digital CPMs—depressing and scary. But there's more: as if the problem of advertising was not enough, circulation presents another major revenue challenge for newspapers. We have already noted that a downturn in readership of printed copies has caused alarm among newspaper executives. Although newspaper income from circulation is typically far less than that from advertising, it is still critical because advertisers typically buy space in newspapers because of circulation numbers.

Two particular circulation issues concern many daily newspaper executives. One is whether young people will stop reading printed papers because they are so heavily involved in electronic media. The other is whether young people or anyone else will pay for digital newspapers in amounts that will allow newspapers to survive as the printed version decreases in importance and the amount of advertising they receive online is not enough to support staffs of professional journalists.

Executives see the question about young people as critical. They believe that newspaper publishers' inability to attract new young readers is a major factor in the circulation declines. Consider Nielsen's finding that whereas in 1999 42 percent of those aged 18 to 24 reported being a daily newspaper reader, only 16 percent said that in 2015. Similarly, whereas in 1999 63 percent of those aged 45 to 54 said they read newspapers daily, the proportion dropped to 28 percent in 2015. Frankly, though, even a higher percentage of Americans age 65+ admit to not reading the paper daily nowadays compared to the late 1980s, though the percentage who say they do so is higher than the percentage for younger Americans: 72 percent of those ages 55 to 64 in 1999 and 50 percent in 2015.[11] One analysis of these declining numbers concluded that "the decline in overall readership can be attributed to the migration of readers to other media offering around-the-clock news coverage, including cable news networks and internet news sources" such as search engines, blogs, and social networking sites such as Facebook and Twitter. The analyst didn't mention that people may well go to their own local newspaper's website. That would be good for the newspaper, if it could make money from their visit through subscriptions and advertising.

In fact, many newspaper websites attract large numbers of readers, and newspaper executives want to spread the message that when advertisers consider circulation, they should include online subscribers as well. And, in fact, Pew estimated an average of 12.5 million unique individuals came monthly to websites of the most popular US print newspapers in 2017.[12] Beginning in 2011, the organization that tracks readership for the industry, the Alliance for Audited Media, began to include

All the major newspapers in the country (and around the world) have an online version of their paper, allowing readers (or "users") to engage more interactively with the content of the site and even the reporters.

paying online subscribers in the total circulation. But it is important to note that the advertising money that newspapers collect from activities online, though growing, represents a small percentage of the ad revenues they bring in. According to PWC, daily newspaper companies made about $5 billion from online advertisers in 2017. That sounds like a lot until you recognize it's 42 percent of the $11.9 billion worth of ads in their printed pages. You might think that there is really no problem here—as advertisers move their ads to the internet, the nearly $12 billion that they have been investing in the newspaper's printed page will simply move over to its electronic one.

But it doesn't work that way. Advertisers have been leaving newspapers to put money on the web, but they often have been doing it in places other than those newspapers. Often they desert the papers because the other places are cheaper or because they can reach more younger people than the ones who read the papers' sites. As for the advertisers who do come to the newspapers' sites, they insist on paying far less per 1,000 readers than they would pay in the print edition. They can do that because the competition for ads online among websites is so fierce that it has driven down prices drastically. The upshot is that even when newspapers attract more people online than they do offline, the amount of money they make advertising to them is far lower.

If you've been putting yourself in the place of a newspaper executive, you realize that you cannot simply give up on print, despite the consistently lower number of readers and advertising figures. Print simply brings in too high a percentage of the company revenue to dismiss it. You also then undoubtedly understand the dual dilemma facing the business: (1) to keep drawing advertising and circulation profits from the declining print product while (2) building digital products that are on track to replace print as the future of the business. As we will see, most still have not figured out how to solve either problem, though new ideas keep coming. Print strategies involve trying to create products that are both attractive to readers and efficient in terms of distribution. Digital strategies involve trying to rethink the presentation and delivery of news, as well as who should pay for it. Both strategies affect the agenda of the news that newspaper firms are offering their audiences. Let's look at them through our familiar categories of production, distribution, and exhibition.

Production in the Newspaper Industry

In discussing the production of newspapers, we will focus on two general areas. One involves the creation of the content that goes into the papers, and the other involves the actual technical process of putting together a newspaper.

Creating Newspaper Content

The way a newspaper's content is created differs between dailies and weeklies and between newspapers with large circulations and those with small ones. We can, however, generalize about the basic approach to creating content (see Figure 8.3). The newspaper's publisher is in charge of the entire company's operation, which includes financial issues (getting advertising, increasing circulation), production issues, and editorial issues. "Editorial" in this case has two meanings. In a narrow sense, it means

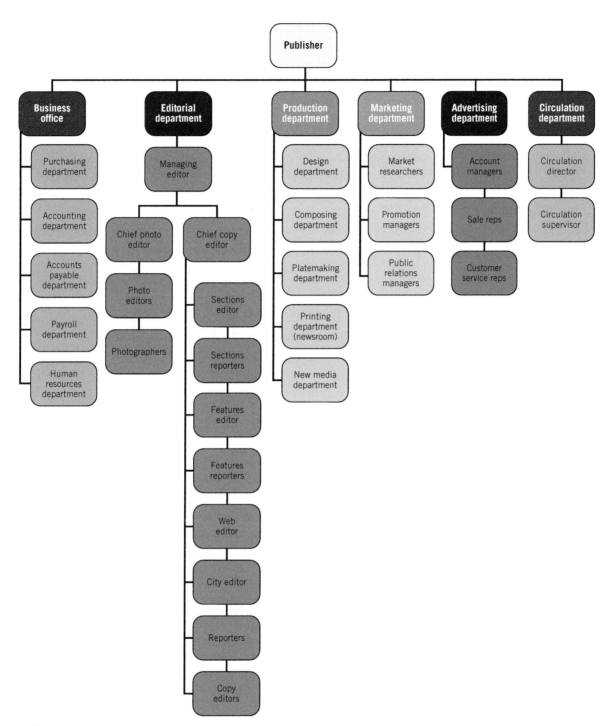

Figure 8.3

The organizational structure of a typical newspaper

the creation of opinion pieces by the firm's editorial writers. More broadly, it means all nonadvertising matter in the paper.

The publisher sets an **advertising–editorial ratio**, which determines the balance between the amount of space available for advertisements and the amount of space available for editorial matter in one issue of a newspaper. A typical daily newspaper carries 60 percent advertising and 40 percent editorial content. Weeklies have

advertising–editorial ratio
set by the publisher, this ratio determines the balance between the amount of space available for advertisements and the amount of space available for editorial matter in one issue of a newspaper

news hole
the number of pages left over and available for editorial matter (based on the number of pages needed for advertisements)

editor
the executive in charge of all the operations required to fill the news hole

managing editor
individual who coordinates the work of the sections (or departments) within the newspaper

general assignment reporters
newspaper reporters who cover a variety of topics within their department

beat
a specific, long-term assignment that covers a single topic area

freelancers
workers who make a living by accepting and completing creative assignments from a number of different newspapers—sometimes several at one time

wire services
organizations that, for a fee, supply newspapers with a continual stream of hard news and feature stories about international, national, and even state topics via high-speed telephone, cable, and/or internet connections

syndicates
companies that sell soft news, editorial matter, cartoons, and photographs to newspapers for use

a higher percentage of advertising; some are virtually all advertising. For any particular issue of the paper, the number of pages left over and available for editorial matter (based on the number of pages needed for advertisements) is called the **news hole**. The executive in charge of all the operations required to fill the news hole is called the **editor**. He or she is aided by a **managing editor**, who coordinates the work of the sections (or departments) of the paper, if there are any.

In a daily urban newspaper, typical departments might be sports, lifestyles, entertainment/leisure, business, TV, city news, a "neighborhoods" section, and real estate. Each department has one or more reporters assigned to it, and the editor may tell them what topics to cover and when and where. Reporters who cover a variety of topics within their department are called **general assignment reporters**.

If the newspaper's editor and publisher consider a department especially important, they may give the editor the money and personnel to assign reporters to particular places or topics—for example, city hall and crime in the city news department, college athletics in the sports department, or movie reviewing in the entertainment/ leisure department. Such specific long-term assignments are called **beats**.

Hiring individuals for this work can be expensive. Some newspaper chains save money by using "shared services." That often means assigning people to work across newspapers for copy editing and page design. Moreover, a fair amount of a paper's editorial matter will not be written by members of the newspaper's staff. Sometimes an editor may hire individuals who accept creative assignments from a number of different newspapers to write such pieces as music or book reviews; these people are called **freelancers**. If the paper is owned by a group—Gannett or McClatchy, for example—that group may have its own news service that provides stories created by other papers in the chain. A substantial number of stories also will come from **wire services** such as the Associated Press and Reuters. These services, for a fee, supply via high-speed telephone, cable, and/or internet connections a continual stream of hard news and feature stories about international, national, and even state topics for which the newspaper may have no reporters. Special wire editors and others continually check the stream of stories that "come over the wires" for likely material.

Syndicates also provide important materials for newspapers. A syndicate is a company that sells soft news, editorial matter, cartoons, and photographs to newspapers for use. There are hundreds of syndicates that supply a variety of content for different departments and different audiences, including the following:

- The Washington Post Writers Group, the syndication arm of the *Washington Post*, circulates the work of columnists such as George Will, Fareed Zakaria, Michelle Singletary, and Robert Samuelson.
- Creators Syndicate sells editorial cartoons.
- The Universal Press Syndicate offers a wide range of choices, including many comic strips (for example, *Garfield, Nancy, Ziggy*), Ann Coulter's political essays, the "Dear Abby" advice column, and "The Last Word in Astrology."

As you might imagine, syndicates supply some of the most popular parts of a paper.

For every issue, editors from all departments draw on all these sources to make up the paper. Under the watchful eye of editors, reporters on beats and those assigned to particular stories carry out their assignments. When it comes to the print version, everyone knows the paper's **deadline**—the time when the final version of their work has to be in. The news staff enters the stories into computers, which are linked to the managing editor and copy editors, as well as to others on the paper. **Copy editors** read the stories the reporters write and edit them for length, accuracy, style, and grammar. Headlines are written, and photographs and design work to accompany the stories are selected. Computer-ready syndicated material is chosen and added to the mix. The newspaper is ready to be printed.

Until around 2005, that was it: the work cycle of a newspaper centered on the time at which one or more editions had to be printed. When newspaper organizations began putting their material online, they still followed this approach. To a large extent what readers saw on the web was a reproduction of the printed product. Updates rarely happened, and editors were hesitant to put a story online that would reveal happenings that would override or contradict the printed product. That reluctance changed rather quickly, as newspaper executives realized that they were now competing with local and national television sites, including all-news channels, that were constantly updating stories and presenting new ones. Newspaper executives decided they had to do that as well, and so many newspaper websites have become round-the-clock—or **24/7**—operations. Today, stories are just as likely to premiere online as in the printed edition.

Moreover, the difference between the online and offline reporting staff is blurring. For certain topics not covered in the printed version—say, technology or certain local neighborhoods—the newspaper might hire special staff for the website. In general, though, the expectation today is that reporters will create for both the print and online products. That often means that they have to learn new skills that go beyond straightforward reportage. Creating for the online "paper" sometimes means preparing a photographic or videographic version of the written material. In many cases, it also means writing a web log, or **blog**, which is a sort of diary or journal that may describe the events surrounding the coverage and that invites reader responses.

As you might imagine, this is a lot of work, and reporters have complained that the need to produce ever more materials for analog and digital forms does more than make them tired. The piling on of new reportorial tasks, they say, makes them focus so much on getting out the product in different ways that they have little time to conduct time-consuming legwork and thinking that will help them get below the surface of stories. They also resent that their work is sometimes evaluated by the number of readers who clicked on their articles—something that obviously cannot happen in print. Publishers and editors, though perhaps sympathetic, state that an expectation of intense cross-media activity and reader "engagement" (based on clicks and time spent with material) is the direction in which the news world is moving.

If you've been to a newspaper website, you have probably noticed that the contents do not stop with the staff's takes on the day's news. Increasingly, newspaper websites aim to encourage their audiences—oddly called **users** on the web—to engage with the site in numerous ways. On many sites, for example, you can email a reporter whose story you have read; join a "community" of readers to discuss particular news topics; register approval of a story by "liking" or "sharing" it; respond to a story in the comment section that accompanies it; create a blog around any topic you like; search the week's news by using key words of your choosing; browse an archive of

deadline
the time when the final version of reporters' work has to be in

copy editors
the individuals who edit stories written by reporters; they edit for length, accuracy, style, and grammar and write headlines to accompany the stories

24/7
around-the-clock news organizations that constantly update stories and present new ones

blog
a sort of diary or journal that may describe the events surrounding the coverage and that invites reader responses

users
the audience of newspaper websites

newspaper issues that may go back decades and beyond; watch video reviews, product demonstrations, or news stories from the paper's staff or one of the wire services; click on an article so that the computer will read it to you; and (of course and importantly for the sites) click on ads.

The Technology of Publishing the Paper

Despite this seeming cornucopia of material in the digital version of the daily or weekly newspaper, many people still do read the printed version or both. Creating a website for them to read on a 24/7 schedule is a challenging and expensive activity. It requires information technology professionals who tie the journalists into a world involving the creation of sites with many layers and the storage of huge amounts of material. Interestingly, much of the printed product starts out digital too. Computers and related digital technologies are the mainstays of contemporary newspapers. Reporters now can go anywhere with portable computers and send stories to the home department in a form that can be immediately read and printed. Digital cameras, which translate the visual world directly into computer code, allow images to be instantly entered into the computers.

Key to the activity is a process called **pagination**—the ability to compose and display completed pages, with pictures and graphics, on screen. In large daily and weekly newspapers, the technology enables the editors to transmit these images to the plates of the company's printing presses. Smaller papers use similar, though much less expensive, approaches. With personal computers, editors can use desktop publishing software to create the paper's layout. They can then take the results to a local printing shop, where the material can be printed relatively inexpensively. The costs of the operation are low enough that classified notices and ads from local merchants can support these small papers.

pagination
the process by which newspaper pages are composed and displayed as completed pages, with pictures and graphics, on screen

Distribution in the Newspaper Industry

Newspaper distribution means bringing the finished issue to the point of exhibition. For a newspaper, that might be a person's house, a newsstand, a supermarket, or a vending machine—or a computer or mobile device. Populating a news website on a 24/7 schedule—that is, distributing material to it—is at least as challenging as creating the material. The company's information technology professionals must coordinate the serving of textual, graphical, and video stories to users who use their computers or mobile devices (tablets or smartphones) to access the newspaper's website or the newspaper's special apps for the iPhone and Android systems. They must distribute links to their paper's digital stories to people who request email or Twitter updates. They must ensure the serving of ads to those users (often with the help of separate ad-serving companies). And they must run software that learns about users (in part to help sell ads) by getting them to register and by tracking their activities on the sites.

Distributing physical newspapers is enormously challenging as well. Newspaper firms, especially dailies, typically distribute their own products. The task is carried out by the circulation department's personnel, under the authority of the business manager and publisher.

newspaper distribution
bringing the finished issue to the point of exhibition

Determining Where to Market the Newspaper

The most basic question the circulation department must confront has to do with the geographic area in which it will market the paper. Many considerations go into making the decision. Among them are these factors:

• The location of consumers that major advertisers would like to reach
• The location of present and future printing plants
• The competition of other papers
• The loyalty to the paper, if any, that people in different areas seem to have

Any or all of these considerations can change, of course. New major advertisers may be found, new printing plants can be built in certain places and not others, and marketing can try to encourage loyalty to the paper and beat the competition. The newspaper's businesspeople, however, must examine the costs and benefits of every decision. The solutions they arrive at must necessarily vary with the newspaper's circumstances.

Executives at the *New York Times*, for example, have decided that their audience is an upper-income, educated class of readers that reaches far beyond the borders of New York City. As a result, they distribute a digital version of the paper by satellite to printing plants throughout the United States every day. The *New York Times* contracts with local companies to print and distribute the paper in those areas. As the *New York Times'* self-assurance regarding selling digital-only increases, though, the paper may encourage print readers outside the New York metropolitan area to drop the higher-priced physical paper in favor of the internet one. Not only is it less expensive for the readers but fewer physical subscriptions outside its dominant area will mean the *New York Times* will reduce the circulation costs it must pay to the faraway printers.

Most daily newspapers do not have the lofty nation and international circulation goals of the *New York Times*, but their executives do have to decide on the limits of their marketing territory. In deciding on those limits, they may lose out on some ads from chain stores that have branches in the outlying areas that they have excluded. On the other hand, the paper won't incur the substantial costs of marketing and delivering papers beyond its primary territory.

Alternative Distribution and Marketing Tactics In recent years, some newspaper groups have been having their cake and eating it too when it comes to winning chain store ads and not incurring the high costs of "fringe" circulation. Their tactic has been to buy dailies that serve adjacent communities. The groups then offer advertisers, particularly national and regional retailers, a single buy for the larger geographic area. The newspaper groups also save substantial amounts of money by combining some of their existing production facilities and staff. At the same time, each individual paper keeps its traditional coverage area and the loyalty of the readers in that area. The Newsday Media Group takes that approach. In addition to *Newsday*, a Long Island daily, and its website, it publishes the commuter paper *AMNewYork* and a number of penny-saver papers in the region that are called *Hometown Shopper*.[13]

Exhibition of print newspapers hasn't changed all that much in recent years, despite the exploding trend of online papers. For people who prefer to purchase individual copies of a newspaper, they are still sold on newsstands and in vending machines.

Exhibition in the Newspaper Industry

An online newspaper has a distribution site; see the *Washington Post*'s website, www.washingtonpost.com, for an example. Like other online news outlets, it is distributed through exhibitors—typically cable and telephone companies—to computers, smartphones, and other devices wherever users can and want to access it. In the physical world, the exhibition point of a newspaper is more specific and depends on its type. Free weeklies are often placed in special boxes in stores or on streets, with placards inviting people to take a copy. Weeklies and dailies that cost money can, of course, also be found in stores and in coin-operated boxes on streets as well as on newsstands.

However, circulation executives for paid weeklies and dailies typically prefer the exhibition point for their papers to be their readers' homes or places of work, as opposed to a newsstand. The reason is that delivery to a home or office implies a subscription to the paper, a paid-in-advance commitment to receive the product. Such commitments help the paper's businesspeople sell advertising in the paper by enabling them to guarantee that advertisers can reach a fixed number of consumers in particular locations.

Achieving Total Market Coverage

Historically, paid-subscription daily or weekly newspapers could guarantee to advertisers that their ads would reach virtually every home in a newspaper's coverage area. However, because of the nationwide decrease in the percentage of homes receiving newspapers, the major dailies or weeklies in a region can no longer automatically provide advertisers with what people in the industry call **total market coverage (TMC)**. One way to get around this problem is to produce a paper that is distributed without charge to every household in the community. A competitor to the daily newspaper in a particular area can carry out this activity, or the daily newspaper firm itself can create a TMC spinoff. An example of the latter is New England Newspapers (NEN), Inc., which publishes the daily *The Berkshire Eagle* in Massachusetts with a total paid (subscribers and single-copy) circulation of 20,235. NEN also publishes the *Berkshire Eager Shopper*, a weekly that it says "is delivered free to 56,300 residences throughout Berkshire County, featuring classified, specials offers, supermarket circulars, and more to a broad audience including subscribers and non-subscribers."[14]

Other companies offering TMC to advertisers are **direct mail firms**, which mail ads directly to homes. Companies that specialize in delivering circulars that might otherwise be newspaper inserts are called **marriage mail outfits**; they produce sheets and brochures from several advertisers that are bundled together (hence the term "marriage") and sent via the post office to every address in a particular area. With this approach, names are not nearly as important as reaching every house or apartment. In fact, the required postal cards accompanying the ads are often addressed simply to "current resident." Retailers have found that marriage mail is an efficient way to get their FSIs out to entire neighborhoods when local newspapers cannot offer that kind of service or when they are more expensive. But there is little, if any, nonadvertising matter in the package. Moreover, the pieces have a tendency of scattering in the wind. Some would say that what we have here is quintessential junk mail.

total market coverage (TMC)
reaching nearly all households in a newspaper's market area

direct mail firms
advertising firms that mail advertisements directly to consumers' homes

marriage mail outfits
advertising firms that specialize in delivering circular advertisements that might otherwise be inserts as FSIs in newspapers; they produce sheets and brochures from several advertisers that are bundled together

A Key Industry Issue: Building Readership

Despite such tactics for reaching large proportions of their target areas, publishers and editors are extremely concerned with the recent downturn in newspaper readership trends. They know that physical newspapers charge more per 1,000 readers for advertising than their websites do and bring in far more advertising revenue than their web versions. In the foreseeable future, their organizations could not survive without a healthy print edition. As a result, many newspapers are pursuing two types of approaches to building readership. One group of approaches might be called analog strategies, which involve the physical paper. The other might be termed digital strategies, which involve the website and other digital-convergent ways that the paper can intersect with the lives of its readers. We will look at each group separately.

Building Print Readership

One question is basic: What does a physical newspaper have to look like to attract more people, now and in the future? Newspaper executives have been working hard to develop answers. Here are a number of approaches that they have tried, together and separately.

More Attractive and Colorful Layouts Most papers have switched to color presses and embarked on major redesigns aimed at stopping readers in their tracks and getting them to want to read every issue. Other features designed to be reader-friendly include fewer stories on the front page, more liberal use of white space, quick news summaries and notes about "what's inside," and more use of charts and pictures to convey information. Individual stories, too, have gotten shorter. The aim is to create a quick and not-too-taxing read.

Sections Designed to Attract Crucial Audiences Newspapers aim to create a collection of articles that are relevant to the audiences that newspaper companies care about. For many papers, that means the people aged 20-something to 40-something (and hopefully relatively well-off) whom most major national and local advertisers covet. To find out what those target audiences want, publishers employ research firms to conduct surveys and focus groups. The idea is to concentrate on news that people can "use"—that is, news that is clearly relevant to their lives.

Emphasizing Localism Many newspaper executives have concluded that it is reporting on the communities in which their readers live that gives them a leg up on competition from other media firms, especially online news sources. Newspaper consultant George Hayes put it bluntly: "One should never underestimate the importance of being local! Newspapers own that." Being local can mean many things. It may mean publishing news about local school events, photos of county fair winners, and letters to the editor that discuss community affairs. It may mean polling readers through surveys or focus groups to find out what they think are the most important issues in local, state, or national election campaigns. It may mean covering problems in the area and editorializing with vigor about ways to solve

The *Philadelphia Inquirer* has diversified its local news output over the years.

them. Newspapers are using these and other techniques to encourage people in their areas to see them as related to their lives on a regular basis. In Oklahoma, for example, the *Tulsa World's* marketing department has held activities that brought in new revenue and highlighted the paper's connections to the community. The paper set up a garage sale and a senior living fair, as well as a cooking show. It also talked about holding a high school football awards event.[15]

Even papers in the biggest US cities, which have tended to emphasize national and international coverage more than the goings-on in neighborhoods, have begun to increase their attention to local news. In some places, this means increasing the attention that city and regional stories get on the front page. That has been happening at the *Philadelphia Inquirer*, whose parent is now the nonprofit Philadelphia Foundation. In many papers it means expanding or adding sections that relate to the goings-on in neighborhoods. Those sections are typically distributed once a week to the places that they cover. That specificity allows advertisers to target segments of the newspaper's market without paying for advertising in the entire distribution of the paper. One criticism of such sections, though, is that they tend to focus on affluent suburbs because those are the places that attract advertisers.[16]

Related to this desire to reach out to various segments of readership are some major newspaper publishers' investments in, or outright purchase of, weekly and smaller daily papers in the markets that surround them. Some of these papers are useful to have because they represent direct competition for advertising. Other properties that executives consider useful include free commuter dailies, ethnic publications, and alternative weeklies. These fill a different but still important niche: with lower rates, they attract smaller advertisers who would not advertise in the larger daily.

THINKING ABOUT MEDIA LITERACY

Pick up a copy of your local newspaper and then look at the newspaper's website. What differences do you see in who advertises in each? What observations can you make about who the target audience might be for the different advertisers?

Building Digital Readership

To make and keep their sites attractive to readers, newspapers have continually updated the print and audiovisual materials mentioned earlier. Many offer users the ability to download audio stories automatically to their MP3 players. This activity is called podcasting; the programs are called **podcasts**. Also common on newspaper sites are blogs created by reporters who work for the newspaper. They write on a regular basis about the subject they cover in ways that shed light on both the topic and the journalism process. Comment sections invite responses from readers. The overall aim of the blogs, comment sections, and podcasts is to encourage users to pull toward them parts of the newspaper that they like. Each of the activities comes

podcasts
audio recordings that can be downloaded to MP3 players

with advertising, and newspapers have been busy trying to figure out how to efficiently serve ads to people based on both their registration material and their activities online (e.g., their interest in the automotive section or the style section). The hope is that advertisers looking for people with those interests and backgrounds will pay a premium to reach them.

Even as newspaper firms struggle to build the amount of advertising they sell online, on mobile phones, and on tablets, they have even greater challenges convincing their audience to pay for their journalistic products. In the early days of the web, the mid-1990s, newspaper executives concluded that people wouldn't pay to read news online because they would always find a site to offer it without charge. They therefore tried to finance websites through only advertising. As you know, online advertising doesn't bring in nearly enough money to support a traditional news organization, and news executives worry that in the future, digital sites might have to carry the costs of most of the news-gathering activities. During the past few years, they therefore have tried to find ways to charge people for using their sites. This barrier is called a **paywall**. Most online newspapers don't erect a complete paywall for fear of driving away audiences and advertisers. Instead, they allow people access to parts of their sites or to a certain number of articles per month for free, and they require payment from individuals who want to go beyond those limitations. The goal is to keep the number of visitors high while also developing a good flow of online subscription money. Often access to the newspapers' mobile apps comes with the online payments.

The most prominent US newspapers to successfully adopt limited paywalls are the *Wall Street Journal* and the *New York Times*. Gannett is one of the newspaper chains instituting these forced payments in local newspapers around the country. It's important to stress, though, that limited paywalls by no means solve newspapers' struggle to make ends meet in the digital world. The payments do not make up enough for the low price of online newspaper ads for most newspapers to survive online only without drastically cutting their news-gathering staff. The *New York Times* contends it is solving this problem, as its paid digital circulation numbers climb along with some of its digital advertising initiatives. Other newspaper publishers also hope this problem will be solved in the years to come, as they try (in the words of one analyst) to "find the optimal balance between free, free with a paywall, and all-paid circulation, and advertising pricing models."[17]

The Future of Newspapers Versus the Future of Journalism

That ability to make money is at the heart of the concerns that knowledgeable observers have about the newspaper's future. Some of them believe that the print version is doomed to disappear and that the digital versions of most will not be able to make enough advertising money to support the staff that is required to put out an acceptable product. One controversial writer, the media consultant Henry Blodget, wrote bluntly on his blog in 2007 that "newspapers are screwed." More sober, but still pessimistic, was the 2007 assessment by the famously savvy investor Warren Buffett. Buffett, who has had a long connection with the newspaper business (he owns the *Omaha World Herald*, for example), wrote that "fundamentals are definitely eroding in the newspaper industry, and the skid will almost certainly continue." He went on to state that

> the economic potential of a newspaper internet site—given the many alternative sources of information and entertainment that are free and only a click away, is at best a small fraction of that existing in the past for a print newspaper facing no competition.

Buffett and Blodget made those pronouncements before the major recession that began in 2008. That economic downturn underscored the dilemma as physical advertising went south and as the growth of online newspaper advertising slowed considerably. As we have seen, revenues did not improve when the economy started rebounding. In 2010 Buffett reflected on this development when he told Politico that "Newspapers are going to go downhill. Most newspapers, the transition to the internet so far hasn't worked in digital."[18]

Now and in the foreseeable future, then, what you will see when you look at the traditional industry and its products is a search for business models that will ensure the industry's viability. Some people see parts of that "legacy" industry still having potential. For all his naysaying, Warren Buffett's Berkshire Hathaway conglomerate did not sell the *Omaha World-Herald* or other papers when they hit a particularly rough economic patch in 2017. His firm, BH Media, did order their local papers to make major budget cuts, which resulted in many job losses. It also signed a deal with another Nebraska newspaper group to manage the *Omaha World-Herald* with the hope of increasing the efficiency of the paper's operations. Regarding the cutbacks and job slashes, the *Columbia Journalism Review (CJR)* commented that "Warren Buffett's newspapers deploy familiar playbook as fortunes dim."

Executives observe sadly that there aren't really many great bright spots in the newspaper industry. Pessimism reigns, especially with respect to local papers. As the *CJR* notes, "as local newspapers have closed across the country, more and more communities are left with no daily local news outlet at all." For example, Oneida, Chippewa, and Rusk are among the counties in the state of Wisconsin without any daily newspapers. In fact, the editor for the *New York Times* said in 2018 that "the biggest crisis in journalism is not Donald Trump's attacks on *The Washington Post* and *The New York Times*." It is, he suggested, "the decline of local newspapers."[19] Making the point more specifically, the *CJR* argues that "rural America isn't the only place local news is disappearing. It's also drying up in urban centers around the country," as important weeklies such as the *Boston Phoenix* close and dailies such as *The Denver Post* shed reporters to the point where their coverage of important areas of government and society is spotty or nonexistent.

Many newspapers would like members of the public to believe that the health of journalism—and of democratic ideals—rests with the survival of the newspaper organizations we know today. Cheerleaders for this venture argue that without it, American society will suffer greatly. Where, they ask, will the great investigative reports come from? Where will the great editorials about local issues appear? Certainly, they argue, neither bloggers nor volunteer reporters can play the role that newspapers have taken on for 200 years in keeping people in touch with their society, communities, and democracy.

Many people who present such arguments involving the future of democracy seem to hope that these ideals might well induce enough guilt to make some Americans shell out money to support their physical and digital big-city newspapers, however begrudgingly. Other advocates for the importance of newspapers in the nation's life argue that in the absence of enough paid circulation and advertising money, new funding streams need to be created to ensure the papers' survival. Some hope that charitable foundations will increasingly support certain forms of reporting, as some already are doing. They endorse government subsidies of one sort or another that encourage great reporting but take care not to allow government influence regarding journalistic decisions.

Other supporters of journalism present a different perspective. They point out, as we learned in Chapter 2, that the profession of journalism is not tied to the newspaper. There may be ways, they argue, to encourage the best forms of news making that do not come from traditional newspaper companies. In 2018 journalistic exploits of digital firms such as Buzzfeed, Axios, Vox, and Vice were grabbing the attention of people who cared about the future of news. So were innovative journalistic works by National Public Radio and ProPublica, an investigative journalism nonprofit that often collaborates with traditional newspapers. Observers cautioned that these activities are mostly still not profit generating. Moreover, they often do not cover the local governmental issues that small papers were sometimes so important in presenting. Yet the developments suggest there may be ways to encourage professional journalism that do not come from traditional newspaper companies. Some newspaper companies may still turn out to have the most persuasive solutions for keeping you and me abreast of what we need to know of the world. If so, we should pay for them. As for those that cannot survive, we should see their predicaments as an encouragement to rethink as a society what professional journalism means, why we should care about it, and how it should be supported.

THINKING ABOUT MEDIA LITERACY

The news "cycle" has changed dramatically from a daily set deadline to the 24/7 deadline. Think about the advantages and disadvantages of each. If you were a reporter, what would your preference be: a newspaper's daily deadline or the constantly updatable news online?

Ethics and New Models of Journalism

Some newspaper workers reading the preceding paragraph may have a response about competition they face, competition that they say is unethical and destructive not only to the newspaper industry but to the journalism profession as a whole. Their argument is that a significant reason for newspapers' difficulties earning sufficient revenues in digital media relates to two unscrupulous activities that non-newspaper websites carry out. One activity involves those entities' use of newspapers' work without paying them. The other involves the creation of "content farms" that edge out newspapers' work and pay journalists low wages.

The first activity—use of newspapers' work without paying them—has caused complex tensions among executives at major newspapers. They have noticed that many sites—including Facebook and Google—present users' descriptions of what the newspapers have written that morning, with links to those papers. The sites' argument is that they are just advising readers of what is available in those papers and that the readers will then click to go to those sites. Newspaper executives do appreciate the attention, and they hope people will click on the links and read the articles so the papers will get revenues from the ads that appear with the news. At the same time, newspaper executives know that only a small percentage of readers actually click on the links; mainly, the linking sites are receiving the benefit of the enormous resources that went into creating the material.

This frustration is also shared by the news agencies that get much of their incomes from subscribing newspapers. In 2017 nine European press agencies, including Agence France-Presse and Press Association, argued that governments should force Facebook and Google to pay for using news content. "Facebook has become the biggest media [sic] in the world," they stated in an ad published in the French daily newspaper *Le Monde*. "Yet neither Facebook nor Google have a newsroom. . . . They do not have journalists in Syria risking their lives, nor a bureau in Zimbabwe investigating (former president Robert) Mugabe's departure, nor editors to check and verify information sent in by reporters on the ground."[20]

Neither Google nor Facebook has agreed to pay them, and the argument continues to fester. But both firms have every now and then sent friendly overtures to newspaper organizations, offering changes to the way they present their content that might encourage or increase readership. In 2018, for example, Google said that it would change its search algorithm to make sure that its users who subscribe to particular newspapers via a new Google tool would get articles from those papers higher in their search results than links to other papers. As Bloomberg noted, "the initiative marks the latest olive branch from Silicon Valley in its evolving relationship with media companies."[21] But cynics might say that, in view of past activities, what Google giveth, Google also can taketh away. Newspaper executives are wary of placing their faith on the kindness of major internet distributors.

The second activity—content farms or content mills—involves another way of destroying newspapers' playing field, say executives. A content farm is an unfavorable way of describing a company that turns out thousands of pieces of "news" a day with the aim of catching peoples' interest on search engines. Among the largest are Leaf Group and Dotdash. The firm has multiple websites covering different areas of life—for example, cuteness (animal videos, craft tips, DIY tutorials), sapling (a site with personal finance advice), and leaf (eating and fashion). They work this way: Computers in those firms keep constant track of the words people are using when they search on Google and Bing. When they note topics that are "trending"—that is, that seem to be increasingly popular—Leaf puts out the word that articles and videos need to be quickly written about those topics. The articles and the headings for the articles are written to show up high on the "organic" search results—those lists of links that show up in the center of the page after you hit the search button. Their high position means that people who search for the topics are likely to click on those links—which then gives the content farm an opportunity to serve them ads for sponsors looking for people with those interests and put a cookie in their browser. (See Chapter 2 for an explanation of how this works.)

Marketers and others in the digital publishing arena are often impressed with their activities. The trade website Digiday called Dotdash "Publisher of the Year' in 2018. But newspaper executives are often not so kind. They argue that rushing articles onto the web based on trending search topics inevitably leads to superficial writing. They note that many of the articles merely stitch together facts and ideas the writers find by searching on the web. There is little, if any, original research. In the meantime, good journalistic pieces on the topics that lie in newspapers' digital archives—articles that the content-farm writers may have used to write their pieces—show up farther down the list because they haven't been written or positioned in the crafty ways the content farms use. That hurts the newspaper's ability to attract advertisers, the papers' employees argue. Moreover, they continue, the content farms are pushing further down the salaries of journalists because although some of the people who prepare the content-farm works are full-time employees, many are freelancers who get paid a small amount for every piece they prepare. Sadly, among these freelancers are recent journalism graduates who can't find newspaper jobs and former newspaper reporters laid off in the bad economy.

The companies that carry out these activities argue that they are performing a service and making money legally. Some also add, with the CEO of Dotdash, that they do produce quality work. Newspaper executives, they say, are simply complaining when they must learn to adjust to this publishing competition that will not go away.[22]

THINKING ABOUT MEDIA LITERACY

There is a saying in newsrooms that in reporting, it is important to "make the local global and the global local." What do you think is meant by that saying? How would this kind of reporting appeal to readers?

CHAPTER REVIEW

Visit the Companion Website at www.routledge.com/cw/turow for additional study tools and resources.

 Key Terms

You can find the definitions to these key terms in the marginal glossary throughout this chapter. Test your knowledge of these terms with interactive flash cards on the *Media Today* Companion Website.

24/7	direct mail firms	pagination
adversarial press	editor	pass-along rate
advertising–editorial ratio	ethnic weeklies	paywall
alternative weekly	freelancers	podcasts
beat	freestanding inserts (FSI)	shoppers
blog	general assignment reporters	syndicates
classified ad	managing editor	total market coverage (TMC)
copy editors	marriage mail outfits	users
cost per thousand readers or cost per mil (CPM)	mobile feed	weeklies
	national ads	wire services
dailies	newspaper distribution	
deadline	newspapers	

 Questions for Discussion and Critical Thinking

1. List all of the various ways one can learn about current events on any given day. The combination of sources and channels for receiving news is probably more complex than you thought. In what ways does the variety of news delivery and exhibition options complicate the news gathering and reporting work for journalists?

2. The demographics of newspaper readership are skewing older. Attracting and keeping younger audiences is critical to the future viability of news organizations. If you were giving advice to leaders of a news organization about how to attract and keep *your* attention as a news consumer, what would you advise?

3. The *advertising–editorial ratio*, which "determines the balance between the amount of space available for advertisements and the amount of space available

for editorial matter in one issue of a newspaper" determines the "news hole." What are the implications of fewer advertisements on newspaper pages? What impact does this have on the community that the newspaper covers?

4. Many news consumers say their preferred method for getting news is through social media, mainly postings from people in their own network. Think about the role of the editor in a news organization. In what ways are the newsroom editor's and the social media poster's roles the same? How might the criteria for what constitutes "newsworthiness" differ between an editor and a poster? Does it matter? What are your own feelings about user comments? Do they add to your understanding of a news event or not?

Activity

Does the area where you live have a daily newspaper? If yes, conduct research on whether the forces described in this chapter have affected the newspaper's operations. Drawing on public records, including reports in the newspaper itself, how has the newspaper been doing during the past decade? Have its print and digital revenues from advertising decreased or increased? Has its circulation declined or increased in the print and digital sides? What about the number of reporters working for the paper? Has that gone down or up during the past several years?

Another way to approach this topic is by looking at the print paper itself. Using actual or microfilm copies from the library, compare a number of days of the newspaper from ten years ago, five years ago, and today. What differences do you note in the number of pages of the paper as well as in the number and types of ads? Can you note differences in the kinds of topics covered by the paper? For example, is there a greater emphasis today on local news compared to five and ten years ago?

It might be interesting to share your findings, or the findings of the class, with longtime editors or other executives of the paper in order to hear their explanation of the changes and the reasons for them.

9 The Magazine Industry

CHAPTER OBJECTIVES

1   Connect the importance of understanding magazine history to understanding magazines today.

2   Describe the physical and digital production, distribution, and exhibition of different types of magazines.

3   Explain the view that magazines are brands that need to follow their readers across a variety of converging platforms.

4   Analyze ethical issues regarding the influence of advertising on magazine content.

"Is it chaotic and anxiety-producing and nerve-racking? Of course it is," said one *Time* magazine writer to a writer for *New York* magazine. "Welcome to a career in media in 2018."

The topic was the confusion, even uncertainty, that came with the 2017 purchase of Time Inc. by the magazine conglomerate Meredith. Based in Des Moines, Iowa, Meredith owns a stable of popular lifestyle periodicals, including *Family Circle*, *Better Homes and Gardens*, and *Rachel Ray Every Day*. Time Inc. is a storied magazine firm with titles that include *Time*, *Fortune*, *Sports Illustrated*, *Travel + Leisure*, *Life*, *InStyle*, *People*, *Golf*, *Real Simple*, *Entertainment Weekly*, and more. The company's slide began in 2014 when Time Warner executives spun it off as an independent company. As the *New York Times* reported, the magazine "company failed to keep pace as the industrywide transformation from print to digital rendered old methods of magazine-making obsolete and publishing companies crumbled under the pressure of declines in print advertising and circulation."

Meredith remained relatively strong, though, as it focused on using its lifestyle-oriented titles in print and digital as environments that not only would draw readers but would also help advertisers sell products and services related to those lifestyles. Meredith executives clearly saw that *Travel + Leisure*, *Life*, *InStyle*, *People*, *Golf*, *Real Simple*, and *Entertainment Weekly* could be molded to their approach to audiences and advertisers. But they believed that *Time*, *Fortune*, and *Sports Illustrated*—historically the crown jewels of Time Inc. and known for timely, often searching stories—were not their cup of tea and announced they were for sale. Consequently, said *New York*'s writer, "in a media landscape in which chaos has long been the norm, the past few months have been a whirlwind for reporters, editors, and business staff at a group of magazines that defined a

> "Most women's magazines simply try to mold women into bigger and better consumers."
>
> **GLORIA STEINEM, WRITER**

sort of middlebrow American sensibility for much of the past century." Staffers and outsiders argued for strategic approaches where *Time* and *Fortune*—and perhaps even *Sports Illustrated*—would fit nicely into the Meredith magazine portfolio. Company executives, though, suggested otherwise, implying the trio was too elitist, too New Meredith did ultimately sell the three. "I think there is a sense that we wished that Meredith would have given it a try with us," said a staffer. "But it seems like they just want to basically be a glorified catalog company."

The Time Inc. employee clearly meant the phrase "glorified catalog company" to be an insult regarding Meredith. What does it mean? Is it part of the survival strategy of the traditional magazine industry? Where, in general, are magazines headed? Will the digital magazines lead to the death of the paper ones, or will paper and digital titles with the same names actually serve different purposes? And will digital magazines try to make themselves distinct from other digital products—for example, newspapers, videos, and blogs? If so, how?

In this chapter we will explore how the industry is trying to shape answers to these questions. Doing that means examining the very meaning of the word "magazine" and its relevance in our age of convergence. As you probably expect by this point in the book, we'll start our exploration with a bit of history to understand the forces that shaped what we know today as the magazine and the magazine industry.

The Development of Magazines

The word "magazine" is French; it means storehouse. When you think of it, that is, at the core, what defines magazines. They are collections of materials (stories, ads, poems, and other items) that their editors believe will interest their audience. If you look at the photos of historical magazines that accompany the timeline (Figure 9.1), you'll note how different early magazines were from the ones of today. You'll also notice that slowly, over the centuries and decades, the magazines began to look like the ones we read today. Study the timeline, and the ways that happened will come into focus. So will magazine versions of the themes we have seen in the book and newspaper chapters.

1. The modern magazine did not arrive in a flash as a result of one inventor's grand change.

As we said, the pictures begin to tell that story, and the timeline's details help fill it in. Follow the chain of technological innovations that influenced the look of the magazines. As with the newspaper, magazines through the early 19th century were

| 1700s | 1750s | 1800s | 1850s |

1700s: Magazines published regularly in England.

1741: First magazines appear in the United States.

1810: Fewer than 100 magazines in print in the United States.

1825–1860: The transformation of magazines into commercial operations.

1830s: Some editors are paid well enough to be able to work full time at their editorial duties.

1860: *Godey's Lady's Book,* founded in 1830, reaches a circulation of 150,000 readers and becomes the most widely circulated magazine before the Civil War.

1879: The Postal Act of 1879, intended to create distinctions between different classes of mail, lowered postage rates for magazines, making them more affordable and easily circulated.

1883: Cyrus H. K. Curtis launches *Ladies' Home Journal* with his wife, Louisa Knapp Curtis, as editor.

1893: Frank Munsey drops the price of *Munsey's Magazine* to ten cents and the subscription cost to one dollar. That causes the circulation to skyrocket.

Late 19th century: Magazines increase their reliance on advertisements as a source of revenue.

Figure 9.1
Timeline of the magazine industry.

produced in a decidedly nonindustrial manner, by a hand-powered press. Although the type was often impressive, it was tight and rarely relieved by drawings or designs. The 19th century saw critical developments in the magazine's look with respect to

1900s

1950s

2000s

1903: *Ladies' Home Journal* becomes the best-selling magazine in the United States, selling 1 million copies per month.

1908: Curtis Publishing's *Saturday Evening Post*, America's best-selling magazine, sells more than 1 million copies a week.

1920s: The rise of upscale and topical magazines such as *The New Yorker* and *Business Week* as alternatives to mass circulation magazines.
1922: *Reader's Digest* is founded by DeWitt and Lila Wallace.
1925: *The New Yorker* is founded and quickly becomes a preeminent forum for long-form journalism and fiction.

1950s: Magazines must compete with television.

1950s–1970s: Gay rights organizations like the Mattachine Society and the Daughters of Bilitis begin to publish alternative magazines (the *Mattachine Review* and *The Ladder*) advocating for the civil and political rights of gay and lesbian Americans.
1960s: The era of mass circulation magazines ends, and a new era of specialized, audience-targeted magazines begins.

1990s to the present: Conglomerates rule the consumer magazine industry.
Early 1990s: Young third-wave feminists begin to publish "zines": creative, collage-driven, Xeroxed handmade magazines that promote feminist causes.
1994: *HotWired* (sister publication of *Wired* magazine) launches as the first commercial web magazine.

2010: Apple releases the iPad.

2011: Apple requires magazines offering apps on iTunes to adopt Apple's new subscription system for magazines and newspapers, Newsstand, and share any resulting revenues with Apple.
2012: In response to an online petition by a 14-year-old reader, *Seventeen* magazine pledges not to digitally alter the body sizes or face shapes of the young women it features.
2015: Two gunmen open fire in the Paris headquarters of *Charlie Hebdo,* a French satirical weekly magazine, killing 12 and prompting worldwide debate over freedom of expression, violence and the limits of satire.

2015: Apple ends its Newsstand app and launches News, a new content-aggregation app that allows magazines and other publishers to deliver their content directly to users.
2018: The magazine app, Flipboard, founded in 2010, hits a record of 145 million users and 11,000 publishers contributing content to the app.
2018: Iowa-based publishing company, Meredith, becomes the largest publisher in the US after its acquisition of Time Inc.
2019: After 80 years of publication, *Glamour's* last print issue will be January's, moving to online only with its February edition.

both the covers and the internal layouts. There was more white space, and there were more illustrations and different fonts—in fact, this meant the development of a discipline of magazine designers. These design changes also affected the look and placement of advertisements. Ads existed virtually from the beginning of magazines, but they did not take up a lot of space and tended to be placed at the back of issues. The 20th century saw more ads than ever, and they appeared throughout the issues.

Why did this flood of design changes and advertisements happen? It wasn't just because of the good ideas of individual publishers and printing-press inventors. The answer ties into theme 2.

2. The magazine as a medium of communication developed as a result of social and legal responses to the technology during different periods.

As the timeline indicates, in 1825 fewer than 100 magazines were being published in the United States. The number changed drastically over the next fifty years. The spread of literacy, the spread of railroads across the nation, and postal laws that substantially lowered the cost of mailing magazines encouraged entrepreneurs to try their hands at the business. In addition, the great expansion of American business after the Civil War's end in 1865 had a major positive impact. As more and more factories sprang up across the United States, the large number of items being produced increased the competition among manufacturers of similar goods. One result was the creation of **brands**—products with distinctive names and identities that make them stand out from their competitors. But to make money on a particular brand of soap, or any other mass-produced item, a manufacturer had to make sure that hordes of people recognized the brand and bought it.

brand
a name and image associated with a particular product

THINKING ABOUT MEDIA LITERACY

What are some of the techniques used by brands to advertise their products to different customer types? What does an advertiser need to know about a particular publication before deciding which to use for an advertising placement?

In earlier decades, readers' subscriptions covered a large percentage of the publishers' costs. However, magazine owner Frank Munsey showed how advertising could pay most of the costs of producing the magazine. His low subscription prices for *Munsey's* magazine attracted a large number of readers, which in turn attracted advertisers who wanted to reach those readers. Munsey charged the advertisers for reaching his audience, and he proved quite successful. It wasn't long before Munsey's approach caught on industry-wide. For the first time, magazine publishers aimed to attract hundreds of thousands, even millions, of customers in order to deliver them to advertisers. And so we transition to theme 3.

3. The magazine as a medium of communication existed long before the existence of the magazine industry.

As the timeline shows, it was the explosive growth of magazines after the Civil War and into the 20th century that marked the beginning of a magazine industry in the

United States. Large firms developed with staffs of editors, illustrators, and writers, as well as marketing and circulation specialists. The magazine publishers established important relationships with major advertising clients and their advertising agencies. The industry had its major ups and downs. Notably, the shift of advertisers to television marked the beginning of the end of America's mass-circulation magazines, despite their large readerships.

It took the magazine industry a few years to adjust to the drop in advertising brought about by television, but by the early 1970s, executives had developed a new approach to their business. Although some magazines already were tailored to particular ethnic, religious, occupational, and hobby groups, new magazines tried to go beyond those categories and tap into the newer, narrower interests and lifestyles of the relatively affluent in US society—target audiences that advertisers especially wanted. This potential for great profits drew giant firms that soon dominated the magazine industry by the early part of the 21st century. Leading consumer magazine groups were Time Inc., Meredith, Hearst Magazines (e.g., *Good Housekeeping*, *Cosmopolitan*), and Conde Nast (*Vogue*, *Vanity Fair*).

But if the 1990s were a time of strong revenues and confidence, the 2000s and beyond are, as noted earlier, a time of worry and sober concern about the future. Let's look at the current profile of the industry.

An Overview of the Modern Magazine Industry

According to *Publishing Executive* magazine, the bookstore chains Barnes & Noble and Books-A-Million display the largest number of magazine titles in the United States. Barnes & Noble reported that it carried 5,065 individual titles between March 2015 and March 2016. Even those titles don't come close to representing all printed magazines. One industry count identified over 8,600 titles sold in the United States and Canada during 2016—and it's not clear these include all the magazines found in academic and public libraries.[1] What is clear is that the world of printed magazines includes a wide variation of topics and circulation sizes. Consider, for example, that the list of titles a major magazine association presents includes titles as different as *AARP The Magazine* (monthly 2018 estimated circulation 38 million), *The Family Handyman* (monthly estimated circulation 4.9 million), and *Yoga Journal* (monthly estimated circulation 1.8 million).

That's quite a variety, and it's only the tip of the iceberg when it comes to magazine diversity in the United States. We can note an important trait these products share: they are collections of essays or reports—articles—that their publishers gather together. A few years ago, we might have added two other traits. One is that their companies release them on a regular (or periodic) schedule—in these cases, a monthly basis. The other is that their articles are printed on paper stapled to a cover. These traits no longer apply. Although the four magazines just listed as examples certainly exist on paper, as paper products do come out periodically, they also may appear on websites and apps in continually changing forms. *Yoga Journal* online (www.yogajournal.com), for example, is a kaleidoscope of photos and instructions about poses and meditations with blogs and videos that are updated on a very different schedule than *Yoga Journal*'s paper incarnation.

Convergence is certainly alive and growing in the magazine industry, as we will see. Because of convergence, though, people who work in the magazine industry often have a hard time describing what a magazine is today.

There is a magazine for just about every topic that comes to mind. Even though magazines broadly fit into one of the five topics discussed, they also fit into many subcategories. Some are devoted to specific topics, such as vegetarian cooking.

Five Major Types of Magazines

Recognizing the importance of convergence, the Magazine Publishers Association changed its name to the Association of Magazine Media. The new title recognizes that even though members' magazines started on paper, magazines now exist in many digital forms. Nowhere on the association's site, though, is there a definition of "magazine." The association's members seem content to accept that everyone knows a magazine when they see it. Yet within the industry, general agreement exists that if a periodical fits into one of the following five general-topic categories, it is to be considered a magazine:

- Business or trade magazines
- Consumer magazines
- Literary reviews and academic journals
- Newsletters
- Comic books

Let's see what each of these categories includes.

Business-to-Business Magazines/Trade Magazines

business-to-business (b-to-b) magazine or trade magazine
a magazine that focuses on topics related to a particular occupation, profession, or industry

A **business-to-business (b-to-b) magazine**, also called a **trade magazine**, focuses on topics related to a particular occupation, profession, or industry. Published by a private firm or by a business association, it is written to reach people who are involved with that occupation, profession, or industry.

Standard Rate and Data Service (SRDS), a firm that collects information about magazine audiences and ad rates and sells it to advertisers and ad agencies, devotes an entire reference directory to business magazines. The directory divides business specializations into more than 200 categories. Examples are advertising and marketing; automotive; banking; building; ceramics; computers; engineering and construction; health care; and hotels, motels, clubs, and resorts.

In addition to reaching their readers via paper, trade magazines now almost always have quite elaborate websites. These often carry daily updates or other articles that the print edition does not contain. The sites may also have areas that present data or special research papers that require visitors to pay a special fee (beyond the magazine subscription) to gain entry. In fact, some entrepreneurs within particular industries have reversed the traditional model: instead of focusing on paper magazines and using the website as secondary, they concentrate their resources on the web and other digital versions. Often they allow some free access and charge for deeper use of the sites. They may or may not also support a paper version.

MediaPost, a trade publisher for marketing and media practitioners, uses this model. Go to MediaPost.com, and you can subscribe to its monthly print magazines, *OMMA* magazine and *MEDIA* magazine. You can also read the magazines' articles for free online, and you can read a huge number of other articles that stay digital. The digital and the printed versions are all supported by advertising. The company also makes money by mounting well-attended conferences for digital media and digital marketing practitioners. MediaPost charges hefty entry fees for the conferences and gets support from firms that want to advertise to the attendees. That is a common activity among trade magazine firms.

Consumer Magazines

Consumer magazines are aimed at people in their private, nonbusiness lives. The printed versions are sold by subscription (sent through the US Postal Service [USPS]) and on newsstands and magazine racks in stores. They almost always have websites, and many have apps for the iPad and other tablets. They are called **consumer magazines** because their readers buy and consume products and services that are sold through retail outlets and that may be advertised in those magazines. Think of a magazine that you or your friends read for fun—for example, *InStyle*, *Men's Health*, *People*, *Time*, *Essence*, *Cosmopolitan*, *Vanity Fair*, *Wired*, or *Maxim*. It's likely to be considered a consumer magazine. Table 9.1 lists the top ten by circulation in March 2015 in terms of new criteria set forth by the Association of Magazine Media. As a representative of major magazine companies, one of the association's goals is to persuade advertisers that many people are still paying attention to magazines. The association also wants advertisers and others to recognize that convergence is the heart of what is happening in the magazine industry. It therefore presents research firms' estimates of the magazines' circulation. It's important to note that the "estimated circulation" figures include both people who have paid to receive the magazine and those who have not. Advertisers may or may not agree with those numbers. Interestingly, though, it presents the estimates in four different ways: the average number of separate individuals (in thousands) who read the print or digital editions in a month, the average number

consumer magazines
magazines aimed at the general public

Table 9.1 Top Ten "Magazine Media 360°" for September 2018 (Numbers Are in Millions)

Magazine brand	Print + digital edition	Web (desktop/laptop)	Mobile web	Video	Total 360°
People Magazine	36,859	6,745	6,745	6,745	6,745
ESPN The Magazine	16,672	21,902	50,919	39,510	129,004
WebMD Magazine	9,921	9,921	9,921	9,921	9,921
AARP the Magazine	38,878	2,735	5,333	33	46,979
Time	17,967	5,036	16,435	3,258	42,696
Allrecipes	7,999	8,372	31,336	2,768	50,476
Better Homes and Gardens	33,016	1,921	5,601	160	40,699
Good Housekeeping	18,639	2,665	13,689	1,607	36,600
National Geographic	31,680	2,184	2,694	168	36,726
Cosmopolitan	14,847	2,322	16,289	2,975	36,433

Source: Association for Magazine Media, https://asme.magazine.org/sites/default/files/Sept%20360%C2%B0%20BAR%20Month%20%26%20YTD_0.pdf and https://asme.magazine.org/magazine-media-360/top-ten-lists, accessed March 14, 2019.

of unique individuals (in thousands) who have visited the magazine's website on a desktop or laptop at least once during the month, the number of unique individuals (in thousands) who have visited the magazine's website on a mobile device, and the number of unique viewers who have watched a video from the magazine publisher at least once during the month. If you think about the table for a bit, you will recognize that the numbers in the columns surely overlap. That is, a person who reads a print edition of a magazine may well read the online (web) edition as well as a mobile version. That person may even view some of the magazine's videos. A skeptic might argue that the numbers in the table wildly inflate the audiences for the top ten magazines. The 360-degree "total" is an even greater inflation of those numbers, because it is a total of the overlapping audiences. Nevertheless, the table is an interesting exercise in pointing out the various platforms on which today's readers find consumer magazines.

Literary Reviews and Academic Journals

This category includes hundreds of publications with small circulation figures—in the thousands compared to consumer magazines' tens of thousands and far more. **Literary reviews** (periodicals about literature and related topics) and **academic journals** (periodicals about scholarly topics, with articles typically edited and written by professors and/or other university-affiliated researchers) are generally nonprofit; funded by scholarly associations, universities, or foundations; and sold by subscription to individuals and libraries through the mail. Examples are the *Journal of Communication* (a scholarly journal from the International Communication Association), *The Gettysburg Review* (a literary review of short fiction, poetry, essays, and art), *Foreign Affairs* (a journal of opinion from the Council on Foreign Relations), and *Harvard Lampoon* (the oldest humor magazine in America).

Many literary reviews and academic journals have websites where visitors can learn about the publication, subscribe to it, and perhaps download a digital version of an article for a fee. If the academic journals are owned by major publishers such as Elsevier, Oxford, Routledge, and Sage, they are also likely to be included in electronic journal collections that the publishers sell to libraries. So, for example, if you go into your college's electronic library and search for *Journal of Communication*, you may well find decades of its issues accessible via your computer.

Newsletters

A **newsletter** is a small-circulation periodical that is composed in a simple style. It typically runs four to eight pages when printed. The rather plain look of a newsletter often matches not only its need to suppress costs (because of its usually small circulation) but also its editorial purpose: to convey needed information in a straightforward way.

When we hear the term "newsletter," many of us may think of the information bulletin of a church or school. We are less likely to know about the large number of newsletters used in business. They often center on specific areas of an industry, and they are published frequently—usually weekly or biweekly. They address decision makers and provide statistical trends and news about a targeted area of business. Executives pay a lot of money for those newsletters, from a few hundred to a few thousand dollars per subscription.

literary reviews
periodicals about literature and related topics

academic journals
periodicals about scholarly topics, with articles typically edited and written by professors and/or other university-affiliated researchers

newsletter
a small-circulation periodical, typically four to eight pages long, that is composed and printed in a simple style

Today, most newsletters are circulated via the web, email, or both. It's quicker than postal mail and saves lots of money on postage. Subscribers can easily print out electronic newsletters to read, if they wish. Earlier we discussed MediaPost as a trade magazine publisher. If you go to Mediapost.com, you will see that the company also describes itself as "an integrated publishing and content company whose mission is to provide a complete array of resources for media, marketing and advertising professionals." Among those resources is a "portfolio of daily and weekly email newsletters." There are over fifty of them, and they provide news in the categories of online media (e.g., *Online Media Daily*), traditional media (*MediaDailyNews*), and marketing (*Marketing Daily*). You might find one or more of the newsletters useful. There is no subscription fee; they are supported by advertising and by MediaPost's various conferences.

Comic Books

A **comic book** is a periodical that tells a story through pictures as well as words. Comic books were developed in the 1930s, as publishers of cheap ("pulp") magazines that presented detective, romance, action, and supernatural science stories tried to take advantage of the popularity of newspaper comic strips to boost sagging sales. They put their material into comic-strip form and sold it in a complete story unit as a comic book.

Today, comic books run a wide gamut. Archie Comics publishes traditional titles, aiming at girls and boys aged 6 to 11 years—*Archie*, *Betty and Veronica*, *Sabrina the Teenage Witch*, and the like. Companies like Marvel and DC Comics typically go after older audiences via superhero-centered titles such as *Spider-Man, The Avengers, X-Men, Superman, Batman,* and *Wonder Woman.* Other publishers such as Image Comics and Dark Horse also appeal to a cross-section of audiences with genre work such as horror, science fiction, and manga. Titles such as *Invincible, Spawn, Lone Wolf and Cub*, and *Incognegro: Renaissance* cut across ages and demographics. A **graphic novel** often refers to an illustrated story that aims to be longer and more developed than a comic book.

For decades, comic book characters have flown across media, including toys, T-shirts, lunch boxes, TV shows, video games, movies, and more. Movies seem to be the holy grail of adventure-oriented comic book companies. Success in that realm has been enjoyed by the two largest comic-book firms in terms of overall circulation: Marvel Comics Group and DC Comics. Warner Media (a subsidiary of AT&T) owns DC Comics, which is one reason flicks about Batman and Superman appear under the Warner Bros. movie banner. Marvel Comics is a subsidiary of Marvel Entertainment, which the Walt Disney Company bought in 2010. Spider-Man and The Avengers are Marvel characters that have become the hubs of hit movies. Image Comics has seen similar multimedia success as its creator-owned agreements allow authors and artists to freely market their properties for adaptation. In 2010 AMC debuted a television series of *The Walking Dead* to critical and commercial acclaim. Comic books have proven to be a lucrative trove of properties that can be adapted for other media, leading to licensing agreements with many popular brands or adaptations of comic work. Companies such as IDW Publishing have worked to produce material specifically for

comic book
a periodical that tells a story through pictures as well as words

graphic novel
an illustrated story that aims to be longer and more developed than a comic book

Comic books like *The Amazing Spider-Man* have become less a staple in the magazine industry and developed into a large part of the movie and TV industry.

this purpose, as well as licensing characters from popular toys and television shows for comic book adaptation. A separate arm, named IDW Entertainment, is, according to its website, "charged with developing, financing, producing and distributing entertainment content ranging from series and features to interactive experiences and digital content from sister company IDW Publishing's extensive IP catalog of comic books and graphic novels, as well as from third party content."[2]

Financing Magazine Publishing

In recent years, the advertising market has been tough for magazines, though the money advertisers spend on the digital versions has helped the industry. From $14.4 billion in 2010, advertising support for print versions of consumer magazines dropped to an estimated $11.5 billion in 2016. During that period digital ad money rose from $1.1 billion to $5.2 billion, so that overall the industry was up about $2.3 billion. In the trade magazine sector, digital ad money was also helpful in preventing a slide backwards. From 2010 to 2014, print ad revenues dropped from $3.7 billion to an estimated $2.7 billion. But digital ad payments went up from about half a billion dollars to an estimated $1.6 billion—enough to lift the trade sector's 2016 advertising revenues by $600 million. Of course, some magazine firms suffered more than others from advertisers' reduced investment in print, and some firms benefited more than others from the infusion of ad money into the digital magazine realm.[3]

As you might imagine, some magazines make a lot more money than others. On a very basic level, magazines that reach more people tend to garner more revenues. The Association of Magazine Media stated in 2015 that "the top 25 magazines reach more adults and teens than the top 25 primetime TV shows." Table 9.2 lists the magazine industry's major patrons: the advertisers who spend the most money on magazine advertisements. The Magazine Media Association estimates a magazine's revenue from an advertiser by looking at the number of ad pages it ran in the magazine, figuring the cost the magazine charges per page, and multiplying that by the

Table 9.2 Top Ten Magazine Advertisers by Total Ad Dollars Spent

Rank	Company	2016 US ad $ in millions
1	L'Oréal SA	683.73
2	Pfizer	454.01
3	Procter & Gamble	418.97
4	Kraft Heinz	331.47
5	Johnson & Johnson	296.2
6	LVMH Moet Hennessy Louis Vuitton SA	231.54
7	Unilever	219.73
8	Allergan, PLC	209.09
9	Berkshire Hathaway	193.65
10	Merck	192.34

Source: MPA; Kantar Media; Publishers Information Bureau vis Statista. Retrieved July 13, 2018, from https://proxy.library.upenn.edu:3875/statistics/238609/leading-magazine-advertisers-in-the-united-states/. The dollars spent are based on the rate card. See text.

number of pages. As an indicator of the per-page charges, the association turns to the rate card. That is the formal statement of advertising space charges that a magazine presents to advertisers. In actuality, though, many large advertisers have the clout to bargain with magazine executives so that the price they pay is lower than the numbers on the card. The amounts in Table 9.2 are therefore rough estimates. The actual amounts paid are likely lower.

Beyond money from advertising, magazines bring in money from readers. Unfortunately for industry executives, 2007–2015 saw circulation losses each year on the part of trade and consumer magazines. Not only did that loss reduce the amount of money brought in from single copies and subscriptions, it also meant advertisers were able to reach fewer people through magazines. Single-copy purchases particularly took a hit on the consumer side. When it comes to consumer magazines, buying single copies can be quite a bit more expensive than subscribing. A single copy of *InStyle*, for example, cost $5.99 in 2019, whereas an entire one-year print and digital subscription (12 issues) could be had for $11 through Amazon—$0.92 an issue. When it comes to trade magazines, prices swing from high to zero. The show-business weekly *Variety* charged $139 for an annual subscription for print (48 issues) and digital access to the print coverage (including archives and databases) in 2019. At the same time, a large number of trade magazine readers receive trade periodicals that are free.

Controlled Circulation Magazines

Why the free trade magazines? Advertisers are so interested in paying to reach people who work in certain industries that trade publishers can support the production and distribution of these magazines at no cost to readers. This type of magazine is called a **controlled circulation magazine**. Consider, for example, *Medical Economics*, a magazine for doctors about the business of medicine. Its circulation is "controlled" in the sense that the publisher—rather than the reader—decides who gets it. *Medical Economics* creates a list of doctors whom advertisers would likely consider useful targets and mails issues to those people only. Postal rules require publishers to ask readers annually if they want to continue receiving the material.

One type of consumer magazine that often has controlled circulation is the **custom magazine**. It is typically created for a company with the goal of reaching out to the company's customers or other people (such as government officials) it wants to impress. *American Way*, given out on American Airlines flights, is one example of a custom magazine. Another example is the custom magazine you may have seen in a hotel after coming from the airport. Hawthorn Creative in Portsmouth, New Hampshire, is a company that creates those handsome, photograph-filled works that you often see in your room. The publisher encourages clients to think about convergence. "Diverse distribution," it notes, "is key to [reaching] consumers at those moments that influence their buying decisions. Our effective distribution strategies engage your consumers throughout various channels—websites, social platforms, consumer review forums, video, and more—to make your brand ever present during the purchasing process."[4]

controlled circulation magazine
a magazine whose production and mailing are supported not by charging readers, but (typically) through advertising revenues; the publisher, rather than the reader, decides who gets the magazine

custom magazine
a controlled circulation magazine that is typically created for a company with the goal of reaching out to a specific audience that the company wants to impress

---

THINKING ABOUT MEDIA LITERACY

Consider the following statement: Magazines are in the business of delivering audiences to advertisers. What do you think? Is this a good business to be in? As a member of the audience, how do you feel about being "delivered" to advertisers?

paid circulation magazines
a magazine that supports its production and mailing by charging readers money, either for a subscription or for a single copy

circulation
the number of units of the magazine sold or distributed free to individuals in one publishing cycle

media kits
databases compiled by magazines that tell potential advertisers attractive key facts about their readers

segments
portions of a magazine's readership that an advertiser wants to reach

Paid Circulation Magazines

The overwhelming majority of consumer periodicals are **paid circulation magazines**—in which readers of a magazine purchase either a subscription or a single copy. Competition for advertising among consumer magazines is intense—as such, a magazine can't raise its ad rates enough to cover its production and distribution costs. As a result, consumer magazines must rely on a dual revenue stream—from both advertisers and readers.

Advertisers who are considering buying space in business or consumer magazines carry out research on the magazine's readers before they put down their money. The most basic information is **circulation**—the number of units of the magazine sold or distributed free to individuals in one publishing cycle. Publishers can hire a company such as the Alliance for Audited Media (AAM) or BPA Worldwide to inspect ("audit") their shipments on a regular basis and certify that the number of copies they claim to circulate is, in fact, the number they do circulate. Small publications often can't pay for these audits, and they may use a "sworn circulation" number that they hope potential advertisers will take seriously. These audits apply to both controlled and paid circulation periodicals. For example, the circulation of controlled circulation *Medical Economics* (about 191,000) is audited by BPA, whereas the paid circulation of *Pharmaceutical Representative* magazine (about 70,000) is sworn.[5]

Beyond offering an attractive and accurate circulation figure, in order to survive, a magazine firm must prove to potential advertisers that its readers are of the kind that the advertisers want. Often, that means paying research companies to obtain information about readers that might lure sponsors. Publishers invest money in their own databases about readers, as well as in custom and syndicated research. Magazine firms include this research when they produce and circulate **media kits** to entice advertisers. These kits are collections of statements and data aimed at supporting the proposition that their readers are better buys than other magazines' readers. For example, *Seventeen*'s 2017 online media kit presents a circulation chart to support the claim that it is "the most vital young women's magazine." The magazine uses data to support the point that it reaches one in six females. The kit also provides data from research firm Gfk MRI to argue that the magazine in print and on Seventeen.com delivers a "large and vital" female market with a lot of buying potential.

Market Segmentation

Time's media kit notes that the magazine can target print ads to certain demographics and regions of the country. In fact, many consumer and trade magazines offer advertisers the possibility of paying for certain **segments** of the readership. During the printing process, certain ads (and even special articles) are bound into copies that go to certain segments of people, and other ads and articles are printed in copies that go to other segments of people. Printing different ads based on audience characteristics is expensive, and small-circulation titles are usually unable to offer it. But publishers of small titles probably don't need to bear the costs of segmentation anyway because they are already niche-oriented.

Large-circulation magazines, however, do have a particular incentive to break their readership into segments: to allow advertisers to zero in on readers by geography or demographic type. *Time*, which bills itself as the "most influential, most authoritative and largest circulation newsmagazine," reports that the AAM confirms subscription and single-copy sales of 3 million for its weekly US national print edition. *Time* also offers advertisers the ability to place ads that go to people in only certain parts of the country, as well as that target only executive and professional subscribers.[6]

Reader's Digest guarantees a full (subscription and single-copy sale) circulation of 3 million with an average age of 57. It notes that "regional and demographic are available upon request," including a large-print edition (for people with poor eyesight). The much younger-oriented *Men's Health* doesn't break up its 1.8 million readership in the United States. The media kit notes, though, that it has thirty-five editions worldwide, inviting international segmentation under the *Men's Health* brand. When it comes to *Men's Health* in the United States, the magazine emphasizes that its audience is "an attractive market" for advertisers—a relatively young median age of 43.6 and a relatively high median income of $84,642, willing to pay for subscriptions—compared with other men's magazines. The *Men's Health* media kit also claims its readers emphasize lifestyle-related psychological characteristics called psychographics that will attract advertisers. It cites MRI research indicating that *Men's Health* readers are more likely than most adults to be tech-savvy or tech-mobile men; natural leaders; driven and ambitious; trendsetters or style-conscious; and adventure seekers, risk takers, or explorers. Emphasis on high income, loyalty, and favorable psychographic or lifestyle characteristics is a tack virtually all magazines use in their media kits.

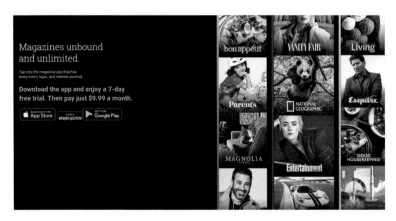

As tablets and smartphones continue to grow in availability and popularity, more and more magazines are turning to digital publications that include more interactive features such as videos, quizzes, apps, and more.

Digital Circulation

The PricewaterhouseCoopers consultancy reflected a rather pessimistic outlook for digital media's ability to help the magazine industry. It noted that in 2018 that "[p]rint consumer magazine revenue in the US is continuing to fall, but digital has so far not proved the saviour that it was once pitched as."[7] Magazine executives clearly hope that prediction is wrong.

Just about every magazine today has a website plus a variety of other digital opportunities for its audience to keep in touch with the magazine—and for advertisers to reach them. For example, using Comscore data, *Time* claims a digital desktop audience of 6.7 million people who make $100,000 or more and a mobile audience of 12.1 million in that income category. *Men's Health* touts MensHealth.com as "the premier online destination for guys interested in living a performance-driven life" "a direct route to the hearts, souls, and wallets of millions of American men." Men's Health Digital is "a multi-platform digital resource consisting of MensHealth.com and 28 mobile apps." As you might imagine in this convergence age, the emphasis is on a variety of interactive and social tools across platforms: "mobile, video, community, downloads, photo slideshows, interactive tools, newsletters, articles, and any other format that allows them access [to] time and topic information—when they want it, and how they want it." The media kit touts 6.9 million "uniques" (that is, unique visitors) per month to the website, with 36.5 million page views. It also claims 8.9 million Facebook fans, 4.7 million Twitter followers, and about a million Instagram followers. The 2018 media kit says the average digital visitor's household income is $93,539, the median age is 39.4, and 71 percent of visitors are employed full time. That makes the digital audience is a bit younger and wealthier than *Men's Health*'s overall readership.

GLOBAL MEDIA TODAY & CULTURE

THE NEWSWEEK CASE: FROM ANALOG TO DIGITAL AND BACK

On October 18, 2012, *Newsweek* announced it would discontinue by the end of the year its printed edition to focus on a digital version only, after eighty years of publication, which had reported on events shaping the world such as the Great Depression, World War II, and the first moon landing. The magazine had navigated the changes in readership, technology, and society throughout the 20th century, but seemed unprepared to successfully deal with the disruptive changes in readership, platforms, and content ushered in by the digital revolution.

The decision of this very prestigious weekly magazine, an iconic brand in print media, followed difficult years of declining readership affecting its finances and leading to changes of its ownership. *Newsweek* going only digital sent shockwaves around the magazine industry, signaling the seemingly irreversible shift from analog to digital of the entire print landscape, apparently unable to compete with new platforms and business models introduced by the new digital technology.

Interestingly enough, however, the decision was reversed in March 2014, and the print edition of *Newsweek* was relaunched by new ownership—again—of the magazine. New and legacy players, digital and analog platforms appear to coexist and compete during these transitional times in the 21st-century media. Different demographics, expectations, and interactions with the content proposed are dictating changes in the way magazines operate and compete. Do you read print versions of any magazine? Have you read *Newsweek* recently? What kind of content would you expect from this magazine? What other platforms are you using?

Don't think that the move to convergence across several platforms takes place only with audiences that are relatively well-off and young. *Reader's Digest* reaches a relatively old audience, but its media kit emphasizes how advertisers can reach its 11.8 million monthly uniques with targeting, native advertising, and "channel sponsorships" (for example, on the RD Health Connect channel) across the publication's many cross-media incarnations. These include *Reader's Digest* on tablets, phones, social media, digital audio, digital video, email, and more.

Production in the Magazine Industry

The creation of *Reader's Digest*, *Men's Health*, and *Seventeen* is overseen by publishers. In the magazine industry, the term "publisher" refers not just to the company making the magazine but also to a person who works there. A **magazine publisher** is the chief executive of a magazine and is in charge of its financial health. Under the publisher are the business departments (in charge of advertising and circulation), the technical production department, and the editorial department. The editorial

magazine publisher
the chief executive of a magazine, who is in charge of its financial health

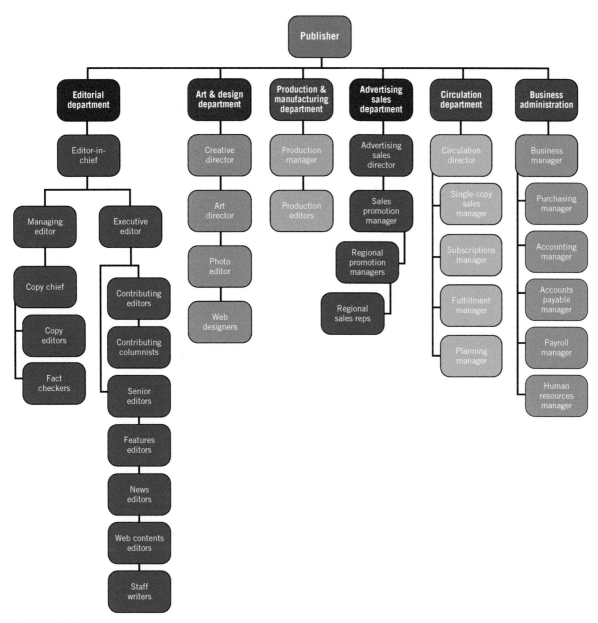

Figure 9.2
Organizational structure of a typical magazine.

department is in charge of developing the content for the publication. The magazine's editor-in-chief works for the publisher; several editors may, in turn, work for the editor-in-chief (see Figure 9.2).

Magazine publishers work with their editors to build their magazines around distinct topics that will attract segments of readers. In turn, the publishers expect that their magazines will pull in advertisers who need to reach those population segments with the best medium possible.

Magazine Production Goals

What magazine makes the best medium possible for an advertiser? To both advertisers and publishers, the answer is a magazine with these characteristics:

- Draws an attractive audience
- Draws an audience that is loyal to the content and personality of the magazine—its "brand"
- Provides an environment conducive to the sale of the advertisers' products
- Provides this audience and environment at an efficient price
- Provides a way for advertisers to associate with the magazine's brand and audience beyond the magazine's pages to a variety of platforms.

Let's look at these features one at a time.

Drawing an Attractive Audience Typically, magazine publishers want to reach what they call **upscale readers**. These are upper-middle-class or upper-class people with substantial disposable income—that is, money beyond the amount needed for basic expenses that they can spend on special or expensive items. Because so many periodicals reach these sorts of people, a magazine has to be distinctive enough to draw particular upscale readers whose social characteristics and lifestyles fit a profile that interests enough advertisers to support the magazine.

To make the case that they have a distinctly attractive audience, magazine firms turn to syndicated and custom research. We've already seen how *Men's Health* and *Seventeen* emphasize their readers' ability to spend. Similarly, seeking to position itself as the place for car ads, *Autoweek* draws on information from MRI to boast to potential advertisers that its readers are influential. Moreover, the magazine encourages marketers to pay to reach special "active core readers of our *Autoweek* content" who "pride themselves on being the first to know about product launches, innovations and other insider information."

Drawing a Loyal Audience In today's competitive media environment, it is not enough for a magazine to have a distinctly attractive audience on its rolls. Any number of magazines (or other media) may make similarly alluring claims. A magazine's business executives therefore must convince advertisers that the magazine is edited so effectively that the people who receive it read it consistently and thoroughly—presumably so thoroughly that they pay attention to the ads. *AutoWeek*, for example, asserts there are 9.12 readers per copy, that its subscribers spend an average of 33 minutes reading each issue, and that 65 percent of subscribers have done so for ten or more years. *Parade* magazine states in its 2018 media kit that "our readers love a dose of entertainment coverage, supplemented by inspiring stories and health content designed to make life and community connections more meaningful."

upscale readers
upper-middle-class or upper-class people with substantial disposable income (money beyond the amount needed for basic expenses)

THINKING ABOUT MEDIA LITERACY

Do you consider a comic book to be in the category of magazines? Why or why not?

Creating a Conducive Environment As the *AutoWeek* and *Parade* statements suggest, publishers understand that from an advertiser's standpoint, a magazine is, above all, a platform for persuasive messages. That is, advertisers want to convince audiences that certain products and services are worth buying. Advertisers particularly like magazines with articles and photos that create a conducive environment for their products or services.

It is no accident that in *Redbook*, *Woman's Day*, and other women's service magazines, you're likely to find ads for foods in the recipe section. In fact, publishers and editors often develop new magazine sections to attract advertisers that would find these sections appealing. In the digital realm, magazines offer applications (apps) for mobile phones that bring particular aspects of the magazine features to the fan. *InStyle* magazine offers an app that shows mobile videos from fashion shows. Advertisers that want to be associated with such activities can sponsor the apps or advertise within them.

Setting an Efficient Price Publishers know that they must present advertisers with a competitively low cost per thousand (or cost per mil, CPM) readers if they want to get or keep business. Of course, a CPM is truly low only if the consumers that the magazine reaches are the consumers that the advertiser is targeting.

Say, for example, that you represent an advertiser that wants to use *Time* to reach upper-class executives who are interested in world affairs. If you advertise in the general edition of *Time* magazine, you might get a relatively low CPM (say $15) when all the readers are considered. When you consider only upper-class executives who read the magazine, however, your CPM actually may be much higher because you are paying to reach so many people that you do not want. It is more efficient to use one of the special *Time* editions that target highly paid executives. In fact, *Time*'s printing technology is set up so that your ad can target people based on their executive status and their geography—executives living in the northeastern United States, for example. The CPM may be higher than the CPM for *Time*'s general audience, but you will get the specific audience you want.

CPM is still an important consideration for magazines in the digital environment. Although media kits typically reveal the advertising rates for the physical magazine, they rarely do so for the digital platforms, even though they often provide information about the people who interact with the website, mobile apps, and other incarnations of the periodical. What the media kits do detail are the acceptable formats of ads on the magazine's digital properties, from the sizes in pixels of various banner ads to the kinds of animation that may be linked to them and the approach advertisers need to take to insert audio in the ads. (In a *Men's Health* ad, for example, sound must be initiated by the individual visiting the site.) Many online magazines offer video "articles," and they sometimes sell ads before, during, and/or after the presentations; these "in-video ads" are called pre-rolls, mid-rolls, and post-rolls, respectively. Commercials in videos are generally more expensive than banner ads because more advertisers want them, and fewer sites offer them than offer the banners. Consequently, video ads will typically have higher CPM.

Producing the Magazine as a Branded Event

An increasingly important way that a major magazine company tries to keep advertisers and get new ones is to position every title not just as paper-bound reading material but as a personality—a brand—with which readers want to engage in many areas of their lives. In doing this, magazines have become central actors in the movement of materials across media boundaries that we discussed in Chapter 2. We've already seen that a major way in which they interact with their audience is through digital media. Another is by expanding into other media and staging events. In both, the magazines invite strong advertising participation. Let's look at examples.

Forbes has a hugely international output in both traditional and nontraditional media.

Forbes, a business-oriented consumer magazine, described its convergent approach to media in 2018 by saying, "We reach diverse audiences across all platforms." The company publishes *Forbes*, *Forbes Asia*, and *Forbes Europe* magazines, as well as Forbes.com. It also creates what it calls "brand extensions"—ForbesLive conferences, real estate deals, education programs, license agreements to use its technologies, and more. Its 2018 media kit sums up its mission this way: "With a wide editorial lens and iconic status in the lexicon of American media, Forbes is not just a business magazine and website, but a media brand that documents and promotes innovation across a broad range of platforms and industries." It adds that "With a footprint of 115 million touchpoints each month across several platforms and industries, we provide our audience of influential leaders, consumers and millennials with critical business insight and unparalleled access to the world's most powerful people." In that connection, the company touts that it is the most shared publisher on the LinkedIn social-business site and more generally has 41.5 million social followers. In addition to standard advertising, its digital platforms encourage firms to use Forbes BrandVoice, a native advertising vehicle that allows firms to create articles of their own choosing that fit the *Forbes* environment. (For more on native advertising, see Chapter 4.) Describing BrandVoice, *Forbes*' media kit states "that through multiplatform integrations, high levels of discoverability, targeting, transparency and expert consultancy at every stage, we ensure your stories, insights and points of view consistently reach and resonate with the right audience. Forbes' publishing expertise and tools will make you a better content marketer."

It is clear that faced with slowing circulation and competition from so many digital sources, consumer magazine publishers are trying to reach audiences in as many places as possible, in ways that help advertisers persuade them. The same could be said regarding trade magazines. Many of the trade publishers also have begun to place increased emphasis on setting up trade fairs and conferences, as well as digital trade sites, to make money.

Magazine events are by no means confined to this elite level. Look at any magazine's media kit, and you'll see how executives try to help their advertisers reach their readers beyond the page and website. For example, *Entertainment Weekly* magazine has an Entertainment Weekly Radio talk and news program on Sirius XM satellite radio. And, of course, the characters and logos of comic books and graphic novels show up in video games, toys, and clothes, as well as movies and television programs.

Distribution in the Magazine Industry

magazine distribution
the channel through which a magazine reaches its exhibition point

Magazine distribution refers to the channel through which the magazine reaches its exhibition point, the place where the reader sees it (see Figure 9.3). We've already seen that magazines are now available in digital form as well as in print. The distribution activities among these forms are quite different, but executives see both realms as part of the larger goal of encouraging target audiences to see magazines as brands relevant to their lives that they want to access wherever they go.

Magazines are sent via mail to subscribers.

Magazines are sent to retail outlets for single-copy sales.

A Magazine Industry HQ

Magazines are distributed digitally through various web/mobile sources.

Figure 9.3

Magazine distribution. Although for print products, distribution methods (subscription or single-copy sales) have remained the same over time, digital distribution has revolutionized the magazine industry and accounts for an increasingly large amount of revenue for magazine publishers.

When it comes to print materials, trade magazines are typically sent to subscribers through the mail. Comic book companies distribute their products by themselves or through wholesalers to special stores that stock them. They are also increasingly migrating to web-based or mobile app portals that allow customers to both access back-issue content and purchase new content a la carte. Distribution for consumer magazines takes place in two ways. First, consumer magazines are distributed through the mail to readers who have a **subscription**—a long-term order for a magazine that is paid for in advance, for a predetermined period of time or number of issues. Second, independent distribution companies deliver consumer magazines to retail outlets where **single-copy sales**, or the sale of copies one issue at a time, take place (see Figure 9.3).

Each of these avenues has its benefits and obstacles. From the standpoint of a small publisher, the mail is a useful distribution channel because the USPS must accept all comers; therefore, a magazine from a major firm will not have precedence over a magazine from a minor firm. But small publishers are also angered that the USPS has raised rates for magazines that send out relatively few copies, but not for magazines that send out large numbers of copies that are bundled by ZIP codes. This "bulk-rate" approach privileges big mailers over small ones and makes it difficult for magazine publishers with small circulations to stay profitable.

subscription
a long-term order for a magazine that is paid for in advance, for a predetermined period of time or number of issues

single-copy sales
the number of copies of a magazine sold not by subscription, but one issue at a time

---

THINKING ABOUT MEDIA LITERACY

Think about the fact that *Men's Health* magazine has "35 editions worldwide, inviting international segmentation under the Men's Health brand." How might the content in the edition sold in the United Arab Emirates differ from the edition sold in Italy? What factors would go into the advertising and the magazine's editorial decision making? Be specific.

To create, build, and maintain circulation, small magazine firms may have to rely on rented lists to contact new potential readers. They also may turn to a direct-mail subscription firm such as Publishers Clearing House that advertises many magazines to consumers. However, subscription firms charge the magazines about 90 percent of the price the subscriber pays, meaning the magazine benefits from the new reader only as a target for its advertisers. Some magazines may nevertheless find these firms helpful in enlarging their circulation in order to attract sponsors. Although large magazine companies sometimes take the sweepstakes route, they can do a lot on their own to increase circulation. With their own expensively produced databases of potential readers, they can mail highly targeted ads that entice desirable readers to subscribe; that way, they get to keep the subscription money for themselves. Large magazine firms are also able to put a lot of money and effort into one of the most difficult aspects of their business—getting readers to renew their subscriptions—a process that can take several mailings and a lot of money.

Although creating, building, and maintaining a magazine's circulation by mail is difficult, doing it through magazine distributors is even harder. These national distribution firms reach a few hundred regional wholesalers, who in turn service well over 100,000 local retailers—typically supermarkets, drugstores, convenience stores, and newsstands. In retail, the field is complex and highly competitive, with the largest magazine racks carrying only about 200 titles. For this and other reasons, only a small number of magazines (notably *Woman's World*, *First for Women*, and *US Weekly*) use single-copy sales as their main strategy. At the same time, single-copy sales can bring in more per-copy revenues than subscriptions, which are often sold at substantial discounts off the cover price. Display on the newsstand and in the supermarket is an important way to introduce the magazine to new readers, who might use cards inside the periodical to become subscribers.

The distributor, the wholesaler, and the retailer are able to make money because they pay a discount off the cover price when they purchase the magazine. The total discount that a publisher typically gives up is about 50 percent. That is, if an issue's cover price is $4, the distributor, wholesaler, and retailer together make $2 on each issue. But as in the book publishing industry, the publisher typically takes responsibility for unsold copies. If a wholesaler gets too many copies and returns proof of the unsold ones, the publisher refunds the money to the national distributor (which credits the wholesaler and retailer) and absorbs the loss.

When it comes to websites and other digital activities, distribution means sending content through internet service providers (ISPs), which act as exhibitors. To the dismay of many magazine publishers, major phone manufacturers or operating-system creators—notably Apple and Google—have also gotten into the distribution space. They create "app" marketplaces on their devices and require that all applications that phone users don't access through the phone's web browser be routed through their marketplace. In doing so, they act as wholesale distributors between the publisher and the exhibitor. If you've ever downloaded a paid-for video game to a handheld device, you have participated in an app marketplace.

Apple, Google, and Facebook also have setups that distribute specific articles to individuals based on their interests. Apple, for example, has a News app that works across all its devices. Users can read news articles with it based on publishers, websites, and topics they select. The app, Apple tells publishers, "makes it easy for anyone, from major news organizations and magazines to blogs and independent publications, to distribute interactive and engaging articles in News." It adds that "Apple News comes with a built-in advertising platform that helps you earn revenue from the content you publish. Campaign management, targeting, creative and reporting capabilities give you the tools you need to drive your business." If the publishing firm sells ads itself, Apple lets it keep all the revenue. If Apple sells ads that show up on the publisher's digital pages, the publisher keeps 70 percent of the revenue.[8]

Exhibition in the Magazine Industry

If you access the internet via a browser, you probably take your ability to download content for granted. That is the result of the pressure for net neutrality that federal regulators have placed on ISPs; see Chapter 6. In the case of magazine apps for the mobile environment, net neutrality considerations don't exist. Nevertheless, ISPs haven't interfered with the magazine-app marketplace. The main limitation they place is on gigabytes. If you stream or download many movies, you may reach a service cap that slows your service drastically and makes it difficult to access your magazine via apps or a browser unless you pay extra.

Although publishers don't have to deal much with exhibitors online, the situation is quite different in the print realm.[9] The challenge for a publisher is to persuade (and pay) a distributor to place the publisher's title on a rack in a store and for people to then purchase single copies in numbers that make the retailer and distributor want to keep putting the title out there. Accomplishing that task has been getting increasingly difficult since around 2008. Back then, more than 20 percent of the circulation of audited consumer magazines came from single-copy sales. By 2018, the number had dropped to around just 6 percent.[10] Industry analysts suggest that Americans are purchasing fewer single copies partly because they get so much content online and partly because they go to supermarkets (traditionally a major site for single-copy purchases) less frequently than in the past. With the drop in sales, stores are reducing the number of racks for magazines. Moreover, only the most popular magazines tend to make it into stores because only two wholesalers supply most of the stores, and to make the most money on the limited space, they place mostly the bestselling titles. Meredith and Hearst, in fact, control nearly half of all the (declining) newsstand sales in the United States.

Many consumer magazines have traditionally relied on single copies to recruit new subscribers. With the steep decline in single-copy sales, they have to find new ways to get potential readers to see the value of a long-term relationship with their magazines. One approach has been to present targeted offers to Amazon's subscribing ("Prime") customers when they go to Amazon's home page.

It's easy to see how a magazine can get lost in a display if the distributor is not able to pay a good slotting fee for its product.

Media Ethics and the Magazine Industry

Now that we have a good grasp on how the magazine business works, let's step back as citizens and explore one of the key ethical complaints that social critics have lodged against the industry. This key ethical complaint has to do with a central feature of magazines: advertising. As you know, a great deal of what we have said about the US magazine business throughout this chapter comes down to attempts to attract advertisers. This fact of industry life raises another concern of media critics: the influence of advertisers on magazine content.

As the executives of consumer and business magazines feel increasing competition from other media and other periodicals, the possibility of routine advertiser influence on editorial matter looms large. Some publishers and editors may not consider this a problem. After all, they will point out, advertisers have always had a profound influence on the magazine industry because they underwrite most of the production costs. As a result, the very basic decisions about target readers—whom to attract and whom to ignore—are typically made with commercial sponsors in mind. Similarly, as we have noted, decisions about what types of sections to place in a new periodical or to add to a mature one are made with an eye toward potential advertisers. Recipe columns draw food ads. Travel columns draw travel ads. The list goes on.

Magazine publishers and editors have consistently recognized that this kind of sponsor influence is the unavoidable price of doing business in a commercial world. One long-standing principle of magazine editing, however, is that ads must be clearly separated and differentiated from other content, such as through use of a different layout and a different font. US postal regulations require that ads that don't clearly look different from editorial matter be labeled "Advertisement."

Situations in which advertisers are mentioned or shown as part of the editorial content of the magazine are more difficult. Some companies, such as Time Inc, have had explicit policies that keep the business and advertising activities of its magazines away from the editorial activities. They call this separation the "church–state divide," with editorial being the church and business being the state. The partition is supposed to ensure that editors do not worry about offending advertisers, because they do not deal at all with people from the ad department. Nevertheless, for obvious reasons, most magazine editors do not go out of their way to antagonize regular sponsors, and this can sometimes lead to ethical problems. Should, for example, a women's magazine run articles about the dangers of smoking if its major advertisers are cigarette firms?

Research on the relationship between smoking ads and the lack of articles about smoking in women's magazines suggests that cigarettes have quietly "bought" protection from bad publicity by paying for ad space. Publishers counter that because cigarettes are legal, they have a right to carry these ads. Besides, publishers say, cigarette companies often purchase expensive space, such as the back cover, that is difficult to sell on a regular basis.

Publishers and their editors often face other difficult decisions relating to advertisers. For example, say you are running a controlled circulation magazine, and a potentially large advertiser agrees to purchase space on condition that the advertiser's activities will be regularly mentioned in the editorial matter of the periodical. What do you do? If your magazine needs (or covets) the money, would you say to yourself that the advertiser would probably be mentioned in the magazine anyway, so it's fine to agree? The American Business Press code of ethics states that such activities are prohibited. Trading ads for editorial coverage certainly occurs in the business press, but because this practice is rarely admitted, no one really knows how often it takes place.

THINKING ABOUT MEDIA LITERACY

As you can see from the list Table 9.2, three of the top-spending advertisers are health and drug industry advertisers (Pfizer, Allergan, Merck.) Imagine you were the editor of a lifestyle magazine and a writer sends an article about the rising cost of prescription drugs and what an impact it is having on people. It is an excellent article, but you know that Pfizer is a major advertiser in your magazine. What ethical issues would arise? How would you deal with them?

What about consumer magazines? How vulnerable are they to mixing advertising and editorial matter and to making themselves merely the instruments of the highest bidders? Magazine specialists J. William Click and Russell Baird years ago quoted a former editor of *Good Housekeeping* as contending that although "to set out deliberately to antagonize advertisers would be senseless . . . when there was reason to investigate and expose, there was no hesitation." Click and Baird also note that "editorial integrity is much easier to maintain if the [magazine] is in solid financial condition and does not desperately need to woo advertisers."[11] The problem is that as magazines compete for narrower audiences than ever before and as publishers worry about losing advertisers to a bad economy and other media, they worry more about their financial stability.

An article about breaking into the magazine industry quoted the advertising production manager of *Entrepreneur* as encouraging editorial people to cooperate with the advertising staff. Speaking to aspiring publishers, he said,

> You'll want to work hard to develop a strong relationship between your advertising and editorial production departments. One of the reasons we're so successful is that we've always worked well with our editorial team to develop the give and take that's necessary to make both sides of the business happy and successful.

Many people in the magazine industry would cringe at these sorts of relationships. But with even the largest magazines struggling, signs are emerging that the lines between the business and editorial departments are beginning to blur in some magazines, that the publishers of some magazines are actively encouraging "partnerships" with advertisers they feel reflect their audiences' lifestyles. The practice of seeing magazines as brands that set up events and internet sites sometimes encourages dimmed lines between the editorial department and advertisers. An example is when a fashion magazine mounts a show of the latest dresses, and the bulk of the clothes going down the runway are made by the companies sponsoring the event.

This blurring of the lines between editorial and advertising is a topic magazine executives don't like to discuss. Every now and then, though, the realities of advertiser power come through in talks at industry conferences and in trade magazine interviews. A few years ago, for example, a marketing executive for Hachette magazines, which then owned *Car and Driver* (now Hearst does), was quite clear about his desire not to alienate advertisers in videos about cars on the magazine's website. He said that although the published written review would still pull no punches, the online magazine would likely eliminate the negative aspects of the review from the video to make sponsors (likely the car company) comfortable. "If the editorial staff has said that the vehicle is overweight, we'll never say it's light," he said. Instead, "we'll focus on other aspects of the vehicle on behalf of the consumer."

This type of concern with making sure potential advertisers are not worried about editorial matter seems common. Some magazine firms are going even further, particularly in their digital versions. Not only are they trying not to offend advertisers; they are trying to attract marketers by offering to present marketers' products in ways that link them to the magazine's brand and even make them appear part of the magazine's editorial matter. Recall that this activity is called native advertising: the process of placing material in a magazine that looks and reads like something that came from the editorial department but was actually created in service of a sponsor. If you want to see an example, go to Forbes.com and look for articles that are tagged Forbes BrandVoice. If you had travelled to the Forbes.com home page on July 14, 2018, you could have seen a BrandVoice's tag in thin caps under the name of the author of an article titled "Six Things Companies Can Do to Help Women Rise to the Top."[12] Apart from that label—elaborated with the subheading KMPG—and the vague label of the author as a "brand contributor," it would have been hard to tell that it wasn't an article from a Forbes journalist. Read the article, though, and you see at the bottom that the "brand contributor" is the chair and CEO of KPMG, a major consulting firm. Moreover, a search for the article in Google brought up the link as a Forbes.com piece (*www. forbes.com/ . . . /six-things-companies-can-do-to-help-women-rise-to-the-to.*) without any indication of BrandVoice. Critics complain that it is wrong to place such an article amid the regular flow of Forbes's journalistic writing—and that the articles are designed to look like regular Forbes material in search engines. The publisher responds that it is being open about sponsorship and that BrandVoice plays a positive role in "connecting marketers to the Forbes audience." As you might imagine, the presence of native advertising on Forbes.com and in many other magazines, print and digital, has created great arguments between those who think it is a terrible breach of ethics with long-term negative consequences for the credibility of the industry and those who believe it is an honest way to keep the magazine industry financially afloat.

Meredith takes a different approach from Forbes, but with the same aims. It has been quite open about using what it calls "the equity and influence of our trusted [magazine] brands" to help its advertisers—what it calls its "partners"—"acquire and build stronger, more meaningful customer relationships."[13] The company uses a variety of techniques to do that, including target marketing using lots of data about its readers and custom-produced content by its own creative agency (called The Foundry) that fit the style of the magazines in which they appear. In addition to these native ads, Meredith offers to help brands create collections of articles from its magazines that the brands can then associate with their own products. It will, it says

> [curate] content from Meredith's trusted [magazine] brands to best fit your strategy and deliver cost-effective solutions. Available for use across multiple channels, including online, email, mobile, social and print, we offer broad rights to our extensive libraries of 10,000 recipes and 5,000+ articles, slide-shows, videos and high-quality images.

This overarching company concern with meeting advertisers' needs with stories that match customer lifestyles may be why Meredith chose not to keep *Time*, *Sports Illus-trated*, and *Fortune*, which take more hard-hitting approaches to news. Meredith's consumption- and advertiser-oriented approach may also be why the *Time* staffer quoted at the start of this chapter suggested Meredith "may want to basically be a glorified catalog company."

The magazine industry is an enormously varied business that runs the gamut from widely read consumer periodicals to narrowly read newsletters. There are huge differences in types of readership and sources of financial support. Perhaps the one major similarity among magazine practitioners is that all are being buffeted by the changes taking place in the broad media environment. New electronic media present both challenges and opportunities. Though always intense, competition for readers is becoming more intense. In decades past, such challenges have led to profound changes in several parts of the industry. There are signs that advertisers have a grow-ing influence on content in some areas of consumer magazines. It will be interesting to see how the magazine industry adapts to the 21st-century media world and how that affects what we get from magazines and how we get it.

CHAPTER REVIEW

 Visit the Companion Website at www.routledge.com/cw/turow for additional study tools and resources.

 Key Terms

You can find the definitions to these key terms in the marginal glossary throughout this chapter. Test your knowledge of these terms with interactive flash cards on the Media Today Companion Website.

academic journals	controlled circulation magazine	native advertising
brand	custom magazine	newsletter
business-to-business (b-to-b) magazine or trade magazine	graphic novel	paid circulation magazines
	literary reviews	segments
circulation	magazine distribution	single-copy sales
comic book	magazine publisher	subscription
consumer magazines	media kits	upscale readers

Questions for Discussion and Critical Thinking

1. Consider the experience of reading a printed magazine and browsing through its online version. What are some of the advantages of the print magazine in terms of user experience? What can be done with a print edition that can't be done online? Now, think about the features that can be presented online that won't work in a print edition. If you could only have one or the other, which would you choose and why?

2. Go to the website for one of the magazines you like to follow. Describe some of the features, design elements, and advertisements that give you clues as to which audience segment(s) the magazine hopes to appeal. Find the magazine's media kit on its website (it's usually at the bottom and will say something like "media kit" or "advertise with us"). Look at the demographics of its readership—do the numbers indicate you made a correct assessment of audience segment?

3. An annual subscription to the consumer fashion magazine *Vogue* costs $19.99. An annual subscription to the business magazine *Women's Wear Daily* (*WWD*) is $149.00. An advertiser wanting to place a four-color, full-page ad in *Vogue* will pay almost $190,000. A full-page color ad in *WWD* is around $38,000. *Vogue* has a circulation of 1.2 million. *WWD*'s circulation is 61,000. What do these figures tell you about the business models for each of the publications?

4. In the newspaper industry, a distinct wall exists between the editorial and the advertising sides of the organization in order to maintain journalistic integrity. Does this same "wall" exist in magazine publications? What examples have you seen of the more symbiotic relationship between advertising and editorial content in magazines?

Activity

Production and financing are two key parts of the media industry. Let's use the example of *Rolling Stone* magazine to examine these two aspects.

Production: First, go to the rollingstone.com website. What aspects of the site might be duplicated in the print version and what are unique to the site? What expectations might a subscriber have to what they will be able to do/see/hear on the website that they wouldn't have in the print magazine? How might these expectations affect the work of the journalists, editors, and designers on the magazine staff?

Finance: As has been discussed, advertising and circulation are the two key means of financing magazines. Examine the website and identify the different types of paid content placement you find there. Reflect on the difference between the types of paid content online versus in print. If you were an advertiser, what would you see as the advantages of one platform over the other?

Now, look at the options for subscribing to *Rolling Stone* as stated on the magazine's website.

Print + Digital Editions (for new subscribers)
1 year for $59.95

Print only (for new subscribers)
1 year for $49.95

<magazine vendor>	<no. of issues>	<real price>	<unit price>
MagazinesUSA	26	$9.95	$0.38
Bluedolphin	26	$19.95	$0.77
MagMall	26	$20.00	$0.77
Magazineline	12	$49.95	$4.16

What observations can you make about these subscription rates?

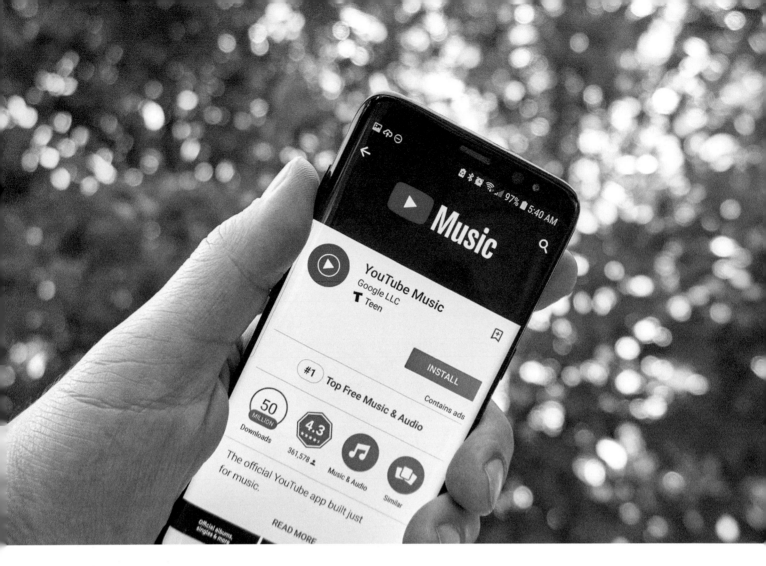

The Recording Industry

10

CHAPTER OBJECTIVES

1 Sketch the history of the recording industry.

2 Describe the enormous changes taking place in the industry as a result of digital technologies and convergence.

3 Explain how a recording is developed, from the time an artist creates a song to the time the recording ends up in your collection.

4 Explain the ways in which artists and recording companies make money.

5 Decide where you stand on the major ethical issues facing the recording industry today.

Are you part of the recording industry's value gap? If you go to YouTube to stream music videos—and especially if you upload music videos to YouTube—you may well be. The Recording Industry Association of America (RIAA) called the value gap "the biggest threat to the future sustainability of the music industry."[3] The music industry and the recording industry are very much intertwined. The RIAA and related bodies around the world are clamoring for government action.

It's likely you have never heard of the value gap, and you may be wondering how you could pose a threat to a huge industry whose products seem to circulating all over the place, and making money while doing it. That may seem especially true about YouTube, as well—the ads surrounding many of the popular videos you view certainly seem to be bringing in lots of money, especially when you click on them. So what's the problem?

The problem is twofold, say recording executives. The first part has to do with people or organizations who upload music to ad-supported video streaming services such as YouTube without getting permission of the copyright holder. The second part has to do with the video streaming services. The industry claims that they, and especially YouTube, make large amounts of money by placing ads (often high-priced video ads) around the uploaded music videos but—because they assume that the uploader has gotten permission to put up the music video—feel no responsibility to pay the copyright holder. Moreover, because of the way the law is structured in the United States and elsewhere, YouTube and its ilk also have no legal responsibility to kick the video off their platforms unless the copyright holder asks for that specific stream to be yanked. The copyright holders argue that searching for every illegally uploaded video is an onerous job that the video streaming services could accomplish quite efficiently, if they wanted to do it. In the meantime, they argue, whereas the subscription-based audio streaming firm Spotify pays back to the recording industry an estimated $20 per user annually, YouTube pays back only $1 per user annually.

The clearest way to solve the problem, argue recording executives, is for laws to be changed that require video streamers such as YouTube to negotiate licenses with copyright holders for everything that exists on their platforms. That, of course, might lead the sites and apps to

> "Creating music takes courage. As songwriters and composers, we all face that blank page every day and go exploring."

—PAUL WILLIAMS[1]

> "Keep in mind when brothas start flexing the verbal skillz, it always reflects what's going on politically, socially, and economicaly."

—MUSICIAN DAVEY D[2]

charge their users for at least some of what they stream, and it might fundamentally change the freewheeling attractiveness of destinations such as YouTube. As recording industry executives in the United States and elsewhere try to persuade legislators toward their point of view, the rhetoric reflects an awareness that the industry has gone through a painful transition. It has shifted from a business model based on physical products—records—to one based predominantly around the internet and digits. An international recording industry body phrased the story this way:

> The music industry has transformed itself into a predominantly digital, growing industry. To achieve this, record companies have worked tirelessly to adapt, innovate and invest, to drive a new digital age for music. However, for this positive development to be sustainable, there must be a fair digital marketplace where all the participants play by the same fair rules.[4]

The aim of this chapter is to explore the "new" recording industry that is still taking shape. We will investigate where the industry is now and where it seems to be going. As you might imagine, we will be aided in the exploration by our good old categories of production, distribution, and exhibition. And we will start by providing a historical perspective (via the three themes and timeline) of how the industry got to where it is.[5]

The Rise of Records

As late as 1880 or 1890, people growing up in a middle-class US household had no recorded music in their homes in the sense that we understand it today. That's not to say that homes didn't have music. For one thing, family members often played musical instruments. Pianos were especially popular in middle-class homes. Many family members learned to play, and there was a vigorous and growing industry that published sheet music and sold it in music stores around the country.

How did people know which of the latest sheet-music compositions to buy? Sometimes, the salesperson at the store would play the piece so that the customer could hear it. Other times, people heard the songs they wanted to buy at concerts of musicians and singers. If audience members at these concerts liked a particular piece, they might purchase a copy from the sheet-music proprietor. As the timeline notes, two particularly important touring sources for popular new songs were the minstrel show and the vaudeville show. The first was popular around the mid-19th century, whereas the second enjoyed its run from the late 19th century through the 1920s.

People who couldn't play sheet music could enjoy other forms of music in their homes, even before the advent of records. Wind-up music boxes were a popular way of providing in-home music. Inside these music boxes were metal rolls with specially arranged pegs on them. As the rolls turned, the pegs struck steel combs. When the combs were struck, they played notes, and so the music box played a song. By around 1890 people were buying much larger music boxes that used interchangeable disks to hit the metal bars so that one music box could play many songs.

Another popular "music machine" was the player piano, which used a perforated roll of paper and an air-powered mechanism to get the keys to hit the strings. Some player pianos reproduced not only the notes recorded on the paper roll but also other characteristics of the original performance, such as the pressure applied to individual keys and the loudness of notes. Note that none of these devices reproduced the actual sounds of a live performance. Enter the record player, or phonograph. Well, it wasn't nearly that simple, as you probably expect if you remember the first theme in connection with the book, newspaper, and magazine industries. Here it is in relation to records:

1. Sound (or audio) recordings did not arrive in a flash as a result of one inventor's grand change.

Explore the timeline (Figure 10.1), and you'll see that although Thomas Edison recorded "Mary Had a Little Lamb" in 1877, it took years for what he initially described as a "toy, which has no commercial value," to become a technology that could accurately record sound in a commercially profitable manner. Notice the role of Emile Berliner, who introduced the flat disk, which could be produced more efficiently than cylinders. Berliner's gramophone had drawbacks that took a while to fix, and it wasn't until around the 1920s that the flat disk became the standard for audio recordings.

Explore the timeline some more, and you will note that the quality of sound and reproduction in audio recordings continued changing for the better throughout the 20th century. A key development was the invention of electric amplification in the 1920s. Before its introduction, record producers needed loud instruments and voices to pick up and preserve the sound in the record. Electric amplification allowed records to capture the soft, subtle sounds of voices and instruments that had previously been too soft to pick up. The timeline shows how increasing the amount of audio material on a record as well as its quality became an important goal for recording engineers.

Why did engineers have this goal? The answer may seem obvious: "it's good to make things better." Actually, the reason is more complex than that, which leads us to the second theme:

2. Audio recording as a medium of communication developed as a result of social and legal responses to the technology during different periods.

Go down the timeline, and you'll see how the developments in audio recordings often resulted from competition among record manufacturers, as well as among the firms that made the machines to play them. They believed that their audiences wanted higher-quality sound from their products along with increasing amounts of play and durability. Sometimes the companies came up with a variety of technologies to "solve" the problem. When it came to length of recording, Columbia Records came up with the large, "long-playing record"—a platter that turned at 33 1/3 revolutions per minute (RPM), and RCA around the same time put out the 45 RPM record. Both found their places in the industry. The former became "albums" of symphonies and multiple songs, for example, and the latter became popular in the form of "singles," with one song on each side. At the same time, manufacturers of the equipment to play the music continually tried to outdo one another in claiming advantages for their devices. New formats such as the audio cassette player-recorder led to the ability to listen to recorded music in cars and on the run for up to about an hour at a time. The invention of the CD and the digital music player extended this mobility and (with the digital player) miniaturized it. The digital technologies also allowed playing music for hours at a time, far exceeding previous technologies.

It bears noting that courts have disallowed some forms of audio transfer because they violate copyright—see the timeline's item about Napster. Also note that despite the impeccable quality of digital reproduction, sound engineers sometimes sacrificed audio quality for storability and accessibility. They did so to make their products downloadable to people with relatively slow broadband and relatively small amounts of memory for song files in their devices. An example is the MP3 format for digital audio, which compresses the audio material to accommodate efficient internet downloading. This efficient use of space comes at the cost of some richness in the reproduced music.

By now it should be pretty obvious that the developments noted previously and listed in the timeline were not the work of individuals working alone. They were the work of companies within an industry. Unlike the book, newspaper, and magazine industries we have examined in previous chapters, the audio recording industry developed not long after the invention of the first records. Edison, Berliner, and the people they worked and competed with built the beginnings of that industry. Several of the names you see on recordings today—RCA, Columbia, and Decca, for example—hark back to companies of those early years. Follow the corporate activities

The Capitol Records building in Los Angeles, California. Capitol Records is owned by Universal Music Group and has been releasing records since 1942.

noted previously—the competition between RCA and CBS over a longer-playing record, for example—and you can see this new formulation of theme 3.

3. The recording industry developed and changed as a result of struggles to control audio recordings and their relation to audiences.

1875s	1900s	1925s

1877: Thomas Edison invents the first phonograph.

Before 1880: Much sheet music publishing in the US was conducted by music stores or "serious" music publishers.
1885: Chichester Bell (cousin to Alexander Graham Bell) and Charles Tainter introduce the Graphophone, which improves upon the phonograph by using a wax-covered cylinder for recording rather than the phonograph's more fragile tinfoil surface.

1887: Emile Berliner patents the gramophone, the first recording device to use flat disks rather than cylinders.

1906: The Victor Talking Machine Company, led by a former colleague of Berliner, introduces the Victrola, an easy-to-use gramophone that is also a piece of furniture.
1910: Record sales hit 30 million.
1912: Edison's company begins producing discs, which replace cylinders entirely by 1929.
1914: The American Society of Composers, Authors, and Publishers (known as ASCAP) is founded as the first US performing rights organization by composer Victor Herbert in New York City.
1916: Sheet music sales fall dramatically.
1920s: A number of firms (most prominently Bell Telephone) work to develop "electronic recordings," which Victor Talking Machine and Columbia Phonograph release in 1926.
1920s: The development of commercial radio threatens record sales.

1929: Victor Talking Machine Company merges with the Radio Corporation of America, owner of the NBC radio networks.
1930s: The Great Depression hits the recording industry hard.
Late 1930s and
1940s: Record sales rebound as a result of swing bands and celebrity musicians.
1948: CBS introduces the LP (long-playing) record.

Figure 10.1
Timeline of the music industry.

The timeline takes you through decades of attempts by record companies to develop ways to reach out to audiences with both technologies and content that would lead them to purchase records. Music publishers (e.g., Chappell) and performance rights organizations (e.g., ASCAP and BMI) have been critical to the development of the industry. A music publisher ensures that the writers of music and

1950s

1950s: The rise of television leads radio stations to emphasize recorded music as a way to save money (rather than to have live bands) and to make up for types of programming (dramas, situation comedies, adventure serials) that have gone to TV.

1950s and 1960s: Improvements in technology encourage the purchasing of recorded music, driven by teen-oriented rock 'n' roll radio.

1960s: Audiotape technology gives musicians more freedom in creating music. It also encourages manufacturers to create lightweight players that play music cartridges.

1963: Phillips releases the first compact cassette tape and recorder.

1975s

1981: Warner Cable starts the MTV (Music Television) cable network.

1983: The compact disc is introduced in the United States.

1999: Napster peer-to-peer (P2P) file-sharing service is launched.

2000s

2001: Apple releases its iPod.

2003: Apple allows users to purchase songs on iTunes, its online music store.

2003: The Recording Industry Association of America (RIAA) files 261 lawsuits against people it claims have illegally downloaded and distributed copyrighted music.

2003: Nielsen SoundScan, a sister company of Billboard, the influential industry trade magazine, begins to track digital music downloads for the first time.

2011: Digital recordings make up a bit more than 50 percent of the unit sales of recordings in the US

2014: Streaming music sales outpace CD sales for the first time.

2014: Billboard begins to track on-demand streaming (via sources like Spotify and Google Play) as a component of its Billboard 200 chart, which tracks the top 200 albums of the week.

2015: Jay-Z and other celebrity musicians announce the launch of Tidal, a more artist-led service than others that offers higher-quality sound. Apple debuts Apple Music, a subscription streaming service to make up for the downturn in its sales of individual songs and albums on iTunes.

2017: A Citigroup report states that music artists received only 12% of the $43 billion industry in 2017.

2017: Wixen Music Publishing sues Spotify for $1.6 billion for using their music catalog without proper licensing or compensation, the latest of several lawsuits for the streaming service. The suit is settled a year later.

2018: 32% of consumers worldwide illegally download music through stream ripping, according to IFPI (International Federation of Phonographic Industry).

lyrics get paid when artists use their compositions on records, on media (e.g., radio, television, and the internet), and in concerts. In return the publisher receives part of the artists' royalties—sometimes as much as 50 percent. A performance rights organization signs up artists who want to make sure they receive the royalties they deserve from radio stations, movies, or other outlets that use their compositions. These organizations keep part of the royalties as well; the rest go through the publisher to the composers and songwriters.

The timeline also shows that the recording industry and the radio industry have become intertwined. Recording artists have provided the sound of many radio shows, and radio has helped sell their records. Companies big and small have targeted various audiences by social categories (e.g., "race music"), supposed location ("country" or "hillbilly" music), age (teen music), and music genre (classical, jazz). A few firms emerged that controlled much of the industry's product.

If you follow the timeline to the near-present, you will realize that winning the struggle to control doesn't always mean success. Despite the power of many recording industry companies such as Fisher, RCA, and Sony to create technologies that define how people hear and buy audio recordings, that clout is by no means absolute. Sometimes executives have struggled to control developments they had not intended and could not control. Consider the creation by home-technology firms of products that could copy the record companies' products. The ability to transfer music from records to home tape recorders marked the beginning of the challenge to the record companies' control over their material. It's true that record-to-tape and tape-to-tape transfers could not make perfect reproductions because features of the analog sound (see Chapter 1) inevitably did not copy impeccably. With the invention of the digital compact disc (the CD) and the personal computer, though, it became quite possible to make perfect digital copies (see Chapter 1).

In the contemporary environment of convergence that we have discussed throughout this book, the digitization of music has meant not only that audiences can hear the same sound performances on many different devices but also that recording firms can promote their products by having them, or parts of them, hyped on many different devices. Yet from an industry standpoint there has been a major downside to these remarkable convergent technologies: the technologies have led to wholesale copying as audience members have found ways to share files across media without paying for them. Such activities have also led to the industry furor about uploading video music performances to YouTube that we discussed at the start of this chapter.

So what is this industry like now? What new activities are emerging to consider the digital challenges facing the recording companies and their artists in relation to production, distribution, and exhibition? Let's take a look.

An Overview of the Modern Recording Industry

A broad look at the recording industry in the United States makes three things about the industry very clear:

1. Its ownership is international.
2. Its production is dispersed.
3. Its distribution is concentrated.

Let's look at each of these areas individually.

International Ownership

To get an idea of the international nature of the recording business, consider that only one of the three largest recording companies—Universal Music Group, Sony Music Entertainment, and Warner Music Group—is based in the United States. Universal is owned by Vivendi, a French conglomerate. Sony Music is owned by the Sony Corporation of Japan. Warner is owned by a New York–based conglomerate called Access Industries (owned by a Ukraine-born, US-educated British citizen—talk about international), which has chemical and telecommunications as well as media holdings. The country of origin of each of these firms, however, does not typically dictate the kind of music it tries to circulate in the United States.

"Think globally; act locally" is a phrase that is very apt for executives in the recording industry. Twenty or thirty years ago, their perspective was quite different. At that time the major firms (often called "the majors") concentrated on taking American and British hits and making them into worldwide mega-hits. Now, although many top American and, to a lesser extent, British artists still sell well globally, the real action and money seem to be in finding top local and regional talent.

Dispersed Production

A person scanning the talent recording music might well notice that the recording industry is dispersed at the production end. In this context, fragmentation means that there are thousands of companies turning out recordings they would like to sell. These recording firms are called independents because they are not owned by the major companies mentioned previously, which are also the major distributors in the industry. Although the United States has always had many small firms producing recordings, the number of independents has soared in the past decade. In fact, independent record distributors as a group have become the fourth-largest distributor of recorded music in the United States, after Sony.

One reason for the rise of independent firms is that newly affordable, powerful personal digital recording technology has enabled small companies to produce high-quality sound. The availability of this technology has led to a flood of independent recordings. Many small production firms circulate their products to stores or sell them directly on the web or at concerts instead of hooking up with the major distributors. Some independents are actually quite large operations. Epitaph Records is a standout example. Guitarist Brett Gurewitz of the band Bad Religion started the company in the 1980s to sell his group's records. Over time, Gurewitz turned Epitaph into a broader business. He signed several other groups, mostly creators of punk and pop punk, to his label and helped them find ways to distribute their work. One of the label's big successes was with the band The Offspring. Epitaph released the group's 1994 album *Smash*, which sold more than 11 million copies. That made it one of the best-selling independent label albums of all time.[6]

Concentration of Distribution

Such huge successes by independents are highly unusual. The major recording companies are the distributors of choice because of the immense power they bring to the marketplace. Because they represent many popular artists, they have access to radio stations, cable systems, stores, and popular websites for promoting acts that small distributors might not have. Being large organizations, they are able to spend a lot of money to push artists their executives believe have promise. They are also able to poach bands from independent labels that have begun to achieve popularity

Table 10.1 2017 Global Revenues of the Three Majors, Independents, and Self-Distributing Artists

Company	Revenues (US billions $)	% of industry revenue
Universal Music Group	5.1	30
Sony Music	3.6	21
Warner Music	3.1	18
Independent Distributors	4.8	28
Self-distributing artists	.5	3
Total	17.1	100

Source: https://musicindustryblog.wordpress.com/2018/04/19/global-recorded-music-revenues-grew-by-1-4-billion-in-2017/. accessed July 17, 2018

by promising to use great marketing muscle to bring the bands the kind of fame and fortune their independent label supposedly could not. Not long after The Offspring achieved its Smash hit, for example, it left Epitaph and signed a multirecord contract with Sony Music's Columbia Records division.

Table 10.1 shows that worldwide during 2017, the three majors captured 69 percent of the recording industry's global revenues. All independent labels together garnered 28 percent of the revenues. The table also points to a small but growing feature of the recorded music scene, self-distributing artists. These are artists such as Avenue D and Children of Zeus that generate sales by distributing physical and digital materials themselves. They do it by placing the items on their own websites, as well as offering digital recordings to outlets such as Spotify on their own websites and via music platforms such as TuneCore and Bandcamp. Bandcamp offers artists the ability to set their own prices for access to their content. For example, they can set the price for listening to their music, including no charge. The focus is on the artist controlling his or her product. "When you buy something on Bandcamp," the website tells visitors, "whether it's digital music, vinyl, or a t-shirt, ticket or cassette, 80–85 percent of your money goes to the artist, and we pay out daily. The remainder goes to payment processor fees and Bandcamp's revenue share, which is 10–15 percent on digital items, and 10 percent on physical goods."[7]

Despite the growth of self-distributing artists, the distribution power of the majors is strong, as the table indicates. If you go to the part of the Universal Music Group, Sony Music, or Warner Music website that describes the company (the "Overview" or even just the home page's description), you'll see pride in this clout. The companies insist that their size and their strong international presence give them a stature and credibility that make them the distributors of choice. It's no wonder that when some performers who are signed to independent distributors begin to make it big, they move to one of the majors.

THINKING ABOUT MEDIA LITERACY

Music is easy to get for free. But is it free? Think about how you listen to music. Even if you didn't buy a physical object (like a CD or vinyl), how is the music outlet that provides the music to you financing their business?

Features of the Recording Industry Audience

According to the RIAA, in 2017, men and women, who each make up about half the population, were represented about equally as music buyers. Compared to their presence in the internet population among people age 13 and older, whites were just a bit overrepresented as buyers of physical and digital music, whereas African Americans and Asians were just slightly underrepresented. Latinos, too, were slightly underrepresented. When it placed adults into age groupings, the RIAA reports that younger groups buy music in any format in percentages that are a few points higher than their percentages in the internet (13+) population. People 55 years and older, though, tended to buy music in percentages smaller than their proportion in the population. The difference is particularly stark with regard to paid digital purchasing of music. Whereas people 55+ make up 26 percent of the internet population, they make up only 11 percent of buyers of music via digital means.

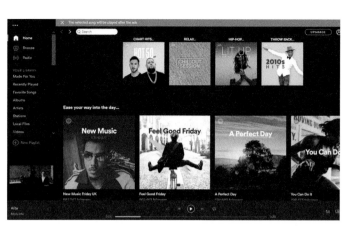

Without a Spotify Premium subscription, music streaming is interrupted by video or audio advertisements, which cannot be skipped.

US Sales: The Importance of Digital Downloading and Streaming

Despite lack of interest by older people in buying digital, that area is booming. In fact, during the past few years, the US music industry has seen a remarkable turn toward the digital and away from physical products such as CDs and vinyl records. The shift to digital took a major turn in 2011, when for the first time the percentage of digital recordings sold was higher—even though just a teeny bit higher—than the percentage of physical sales: 50.3 percent to 49.7 percent. By 2017, physical had plummeted to 18 percent of total industry sales of about $8.5 billion, with digital 82 percent of that amount.

The term digital actually refers to several ways people can purchase digital music. All typically involve a form of **downloading**, which means that the company sends the song as a digital file to the buyer's smartphone, computer, and/or tablet. Paying to own downloaded songs used to be the most common way recording companies sold music via digital platforms. Now, streaming is. **Streaming** is the process in which an audio file is delivered to a computer-like device from a website so that it can be heard while it is coming into the device but cannot be saved. **Ringtones** are also ways some companies make money. They are bits of songs (or even new musical compositions) that people download to their mobile phones and that play when someone calls them. A decade or so ago, they were a substantial digital moneymaker, but their revenue contribution is near-negligible now, according to the RIAA. Also declining is the permanent downloading of recordings, both albums and singles. An **album** is a collection of a dozen or more individual songs, whereas a single contains only one or two songs. **Singles** are the building blocks of radio formats, and the airplay of these singles is often how the public first learns about an artist. However, artists and labels make their money from album sales, and the recording companies often do not price physical singles so that they are worthwhile purchases relative to the albums. As a result, in 2017 sales of physical singles (typically in CD form) were negligible compared with sales of albums; they constituted only less than 1 percent of sales. By contrast, on Apple Music and other sites, digital singles are often far less expensive than albums—$1.29,

downloading
transfer of data or programs from a server or host computer to one's own computer or digital device

streaming
process in which an audio file is delivered to a computer-like device from a website so that it can be heard while it is coming into the device but cannot be saved or stored

ringtones
bits of songs (or even new musical compositions) that people download to their mobile phones so that they play when someone calls them

album
a collection of a dozen or more individual songs

single
a product that contains only one or two individual musical recordings

Table 10.2 US Digital and Physical Recorded Estimated US Dollar Retail Value

Format	2016 ($B)	2016 (%)	2017 ($B)	2017 (%)
Streaming	4.0	53	5.7	67
Permanent Downloads	1.8	24	1.3	15
Ringtones and Ringbacks	.1	1	.03	—
Physical shipments	1.6	21	1.5	18
Totals	7.5	99	8.5	100

Source: "2017 Year End Industry Revenue Statistics," RIAA, www.riaa.com/wp-content/uploads/2018/03/RIAA-Year-End-2017-News-and-Notes.pdf, accessed July 18, 2018.

89 cents, or even 69 cents compared with several dollars. In that space, buyers go after their favorite songs. Nevertheless, the number of single units downloaded dropped substantially between 2016 and 2017, even more than the strong drop in album sales.

The reason for the drop, the table suggests, is that the real growth is in music streaming. You probably know that firms such as Apple Music and Amazon Music sell subscriptions for streaming. For example, you pay around $100 a year and can stream as many songs as you want, and you can download them to your smartphone. Other paid streaming services (e.g., SoundCloud and Spotify) have hybrid models: free if you listen to ads, but you pay for music without ads). Then there are ad-supported streaming firms. Companies such as Pandora and IHeartRadio give users the opportunity to listen to pre-chosen music streams based on certain genres—for example, hip-hop or classical—for free if they listen to commercials. Because the approach is much like a radio station, the activity has come to be known as **internet radio**. The growth of subscription and ad-supported streaming has been remarkable. From 2016 to 2017, the number of paid subscriptions in the United States has risen from about 23 million to about 35 million, with the amount people paid increasing from $2.5 billion to $4.1 billion as a result. The amount of money flowing into ad-supported streaming firms also skyrocketed over the two years, from $571 million to $921. Music executives see streaming as the future of the recording industry. That is why they want to clear up what they call the "value gap" we discussed at the beginning of this chapter.

Internet radio
pre-chosen music streams based around certain genres—for example, hip-hop or classical—provided free to listeners and paid for by commercial advertisements, much like a radio station

Diverse Music Genres

The recording industry releases music in many genres targeted to different slices of the music-buying public. According to Nielsen Music in 2017, for the first time R&B/hip-hop became the top genre in the United States, taking into account digital downloads and physical sales. In fact, nine of the top ten songs came from that genre, including hits by Migos, Post Malone, and Cardi B. For the very top artists, the numbers of song units people listen to are astounding. In the United States alone, for example, rapper Drake's albums saw what Nielsen calls total music "consumption" of 4.8 billion units. That is a combination of physical album purchases, track-equivalent albums downloaded (where ten downloaded tracks equals one album), and streaming-equivalent albums (where 1,500 streams equals one album). Another rapper veteran, Kendrick Lamar, had a total music consumption of 2.7 billion units in the United States for one album, *Damn*. As Nielsen notes, streaming had the most influence on these huge numbers.

It should be noted that these equivalent metrics, set by *Billboard* magazine with record label input, are a big deal because they affect the lists that rank the most popular artists, records, and genres. In 2018, with streaming skyrocketing, *Billboard* decided to create two different measures: one for songs streamed by paying subscribers and one for songs streamed by sites that are free to users but show ads. The measures, which Billboard created after months of industry lobbying, are 1,250 for paid streams and 3,750 for free streams. The idea is that three times as many free clicks equals a paid one.

Table 10.3 notes the percentages of total streams, paid downloads, and physical sales the top genres received. Figure 10.2 lists the genres in order of their popularity

Table 10.3 Share of Total Volume by Top Recording Genres

Genre	% of Total Volume
R&B/Hip-Hop	24.5
Rock	20.8
Pop	12.7
Country	7.7
Latin	5,9
Electronic/Dance	3.5
Christian/Gospel	2.7
Holiday/Seasonal	1.7
Children	1.3
Jazz	1.0
Classical	1.0

Source: "2017 Year-End Music Report, U.S.," Nielsen, www.nielsen.com/content/dam/corporate/us/en/reports-downloads/2018-reports/2017-year-end-music-report-us.pdf, accessed July 18, 2018. Total Volume = Albums + TEA + SEA (audio and video). See text for details. Copyrighted information ©2018, of The Nielsen Company, licensed for use herein.

SHARE OF TOTAL AUDIO CONSUMPTION BY FORMAT

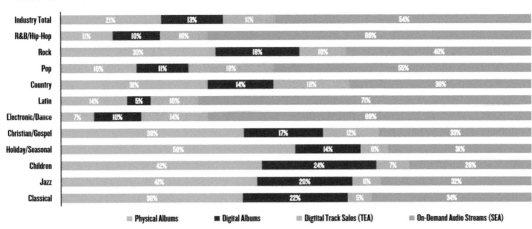

Read as: 33% of Rock consumption comes from Physical Album sales

Figure 10.2

Source: "2017 Year-End Music Report, U.S.," Nielsen, www.nielsen.com/content/dam/corporate/us/en/reports-downloads/2018-reports/2017-year-end-music-report-us.pdf, accessed July 18, 2018. Copyrighted information ©2018, of The Nielsen Company, licensed for use herein.

and notes whether audiences tend to access them by physical or digital means. The table shows that rock held the second spot, followed by pop and country music. Note the purchase of physical albums made up a minority format among all the genres but holiday/seasonal. There were stark differences, though. With R&B/hip-hop, pop, Latin, and electronic dance, physical sales represented 16 percent or less of the units "consumed"; with children's, Christian gospel, jazz, and classical, the percentage of physical sales exceeded 37 percent and more. Perhaps the difference had to do with the age of the listeners and/or the conviction by some music aficionados that physical recordings (especially those on vinyl) exceed the reproductive quality of digital downloads and streaming.

So we know what kinds of musical recordings have moved more quickly than others. But how do those products get to their audiences in the first place? What happens between the time someone gets an idea for a song and the moment the recording of that song is sold? To answer this basic but difficult question, we turn to issues of production, distribution, and exhibition.

Production and the Recording Industry

Chances are you know someone who is in a band. Maybe the band plays at local college bars, and the members practice when they are not working at day jobs

GLOBAL MEDIA TODAY & CULTURE

THE INTERNATIONAL MUSIC PHENOMENON OF K-POP

Do you like the Korean boy band BTS? On September 24, 2018, this band delivered a speech at the 73rd session of the United Nations General Assembly urging young people around the world to believe in themselves, echoing the theme of their album *Love Yourself* released one year earlier. The occasion was the inaugural ceremony of UNICEF's global partnership Generation Unlimited, a new initiative aimed at providing quality education and training for young people around the world. BTS is one of most popular bands in the K-Pop music movement, part of a larger phenomenon named *Hallyu* [Korean Wave], representing media entertainment produced in South Korea becoming increasingly popular around the world.

Korean band BTS at the 2019 Grammy Awards.

K-Pop bands have specific, distinctive traits. They are developed by the local star system with a global audience in mind: Their members undergo rigorous training to develop and polish their talent in order to create shows that, although centered in music, offer an entertainment spectacle combining attractive visual images with their specific pop sound, oftentimes integrating both Korean and English in their lyrics.

The fact that the K-Pop band BTS addressed the United Nations is a sign of their global popularity and of the magnitude of the soft power dimension achieved by the Korean Wave in the global communication landscape. The international success of K-Pop, originating outside the mainstream Atlantic corridor between the United States and Europe, brings to the fore the complexities of the global music landscape and the variety of popular cultural artifacts produced and distributed worldwide.

to pay the bills. Perhaps the band's members have even recorded a demonstration (or "demo") song at a local studio and given you a copy. They are working hard while they wait for their big break: a contract with a record company, which they know will bring them fortune and fame in Hollywood. Will they still take your phone calls when they become big stars?

Across the country, many aspiring recording artists are waiting for their big break. Most of these artists never record a professional album and eventually move on to other, more lucrative lines of work. The age-old advice to struggling artists—"Don't quit your day job"—is especially true in the record business.

Artists Looking for Labels, Labels Looking for Artists

Realistically, artists know that they are much more likely to start their recording careers with small independent firms willing to take a chance on them. Still, many struggling bands dream about being "discovered" by a label of one of the major record production and distribution companies. A **label** is a division of a recording firm that releases a certain type of music and reflects a certain personality. It is very much like an imprint in the book industry. For example, among Universal's many labels are Island Def Jam (for rap and hip-hop), Verve (for jazz and blues), MCA Nashville (for country), and Mercury Records (for classical).

The point person in a recording company for signing new artists is the label's **A&R** person. A&R stands for **artist and repertoire**, a term that dates back to the time when record executives saw themselves as shaping artists by choosing the collection of songs (the repertoire) that an artist played or sang. Today, the function of the A&R person is to screen new acts for a firm and determine whether to sign those acts. Like baseball scouts looking for the next Cy Young Award winner, A&R people are constantly searching for new acts for their label (see Figure 10.3).

label
a division of a recording firm that releases a certain type of music and reflects a certain personality

A&R (artist and repertoire)
recording firm executives who screen new acts for a firm and determine whether to sign those acts

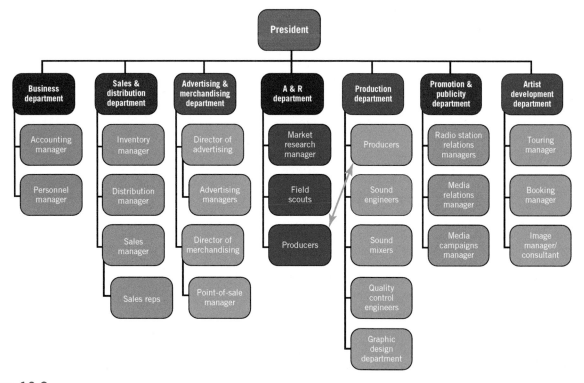

Figure 10.3
Organization of a typical recording company.

Suppose your friends, after years of paying their dues in nightclubs throughout the state, are approached by the A&R person for Universal's Interscope record label (which distributes work by Lady Gaga, 50 Cent, and Eminem, among many others). Somehow, the record company executive learned about the band—perhaps through hearing a demo record or attending a performance at a local bar—and wants to sign it to a record deal. At this point, certain relationships come into play. Negotiating the terms and conditions of these relationships is very important. Many struggling artists, unfamiliar with the business side of the artistic process and desperate to make it in the recording industry, have entered into bad, one-sided agreements. Billy Joel, 'N Sync, Janet Jackson, and Tupac Shakur are only a few of the well-known musical acts who have fallen into this trap.

Many artists on their way up realize the necessity of hiring a competent manager to coordinate the development of their career; to help arrange business opportunities for them; and to handle the receipt, disbursement, and accounting of their revenues. In return for these services, the manager earns a percentage—typically 10 to 25 percent—of all the revenue the artist earns. Of course, artists try to hire a manager who will further their career, preferably one who knows the intricacies of the music business and most of the important people in the business. Despite artists' understandable wish for a manager who will act exclusively on their behalf, good managers often handle several artists at once.

Other business relationships for the band quickly follow. Most acts hire an attorney and an accountant to assist their manager in handling their often complex business affairs. Artists may also join a union such as the American Federation of Musicians (AFM) or the American Federation of Television and Radio Artists (AFTRA), which provide access to television and motion picture work, represent the artists' interests with various media industries, and offer benefits such as group health insurance. Joining a royalty-collecting association, such as the American Society of Composers, Authors and Publishers (ASCAP) or Broadcast Music, Inc. (BMI), is also important. But of all these contractual relationships, the most important one is the one the artist develops with a record label. Simply put, the music industry today revolves around the issuance of recorded music and the joint effort of the artist and the company to sell as many records as possible.

Finding Music to Record

Artists, of course, need music to perform. Many popular artists today perform music that they have written themselves. Yet at some point in their careers, virtually all artists record music that someone else wrote. There are several ways for an artist or group to find music. Music publishing companies maintain catalogs of songs, and many record stores still sell printed copies of music, usually intended to be played on a guitar or piano. When an artist uses any song in these libraries commercially, songwriters and their publishing companies expect to be paid a share of the money the production firm receives; this payment is called a **royalty**.

royalty
the share of money paid to a songwriter or music composer out of the money that the production firm receives from the sale or exhibition of a work

Royalties

There are important legal steps that songwriters must take, such as filing their songs with the US copyright authorities, in order to ensure that they make money from a song they have written even if they do not sing it themselves. But it is difficult for the owner of a song to keep track of where and how the song is performed. For example, songwriters are entitled to compensation whenever a radio station plays their songs, a band performs their work at a nightclub, or a record company releases their songs.

The industry distinguishes between two types of royalties for the creators of music and the words to the music: performance royalties and mechanical royalties. **Performance royalties** are paid to composers, their publishers, and their record labels when their material is used (live or recorded) in front of audiences via stage acts, jukeboxes, radio, television, or online radio. If performers or organizations want to use the music, they must obtain a "performing rights license" from music societies. Agencies such as ASCAP and BMI exist to make sure that publishers and songwriters are compensated for the use of their work. These agencies take over the daunting task of verifying compliance with the law on behalf of the rights holder. ASCAP is the largest of the performing rights organizations and represents around 650,000 songwriters, composers, and publishers. Though the airing of one covered song on a radio station may result in a royalty payment to ASCAP or its agents of only a fraction of a penny, these small amounts add up. ASCAP licenses over 11.5 million songs and scores to businesses that play them publicly, keeps 12 percent of the fees, and the rest goes to its members as royalties. According to its annual report, in 2018 ASCAP distributed a bit over $1 billion on behalf of its member songwriters and publishers. ASCAP uses formulas derived from surveys that rank the popularity of each songwriter's songs during the year to determine each member's share of the revenue after expenses and distributes that share to each member.[8]

Mechanical royalties are collected as a result of the sale of physical media (e.g., CDs) and the sale or download of digital recordings, including albums, individual tracks, and ringtones. In the United States any artist has a right to record a musical work as long as the creators have already given permission to someone to make a public recording of that work. If you write the melody for a song and your friend writes the lyrics, you have the right to tell the singer Taylor Swift she cannot perform it or make a record of it. But if you have already allowed Katy Perry to release a track of the song, you have to allow Taylor to do it—though Taylor must have a mechanical license. (You can still refuse to allow Taylor to perform it onstage.) Both Taylor Swift and Katy Perry must pay you according to a royalty rate set by the US government.

The Harry Fox Agency is the dominant US organization that issues mechanical licenses and collects and disperses mechanical royalties. The licenses are valid only for physical or digital sound recordings distributed to the public for private use (i.e., not for use in stage shows or on radio) in the United States. If you go to HarryFox. com to learn more about mechanical royalties, you will find that the subject can get quite complex. The same is true regarding performance royalties; check out ASCAP. com, for example. A large part of this domain is the province of entertainment attorneys. Their job (for a fee) is to help composers and lyricists, as well as performing artists and record labels, navigate the terrain legally and profitably.

performance royalties
money paid to composers, their publishers, and their record labels when their material is used (live or recorded) in front of audiences via stage acts, jukeboxes, radio, television, or online radio

mechanical royalties
money collected as a result of the sale of physical media (e.g., CDs) and the sale or download of digital recordings, including albums, individual tracks, and ringtones

THINKING ABOUT MEDIA LITERACY

Some musicians choose to make their music available for free through sites such as Soundcloud or Jamendo. Why do you think artists might choose to go this route? If they aren't financing their music through sales of their songs, what is their financial model? If you were a musician, what would be your own argument for, and against, providing free music downloads?

Producing a Record

The firm that has signed a contract to record an artist's album will often line up a producer to oversee the recording of the album and its final sound. The producer, like the artist, is generally compensated on a royalty basis. A typical royalty percentage for a good producer is 2 to 4 percent of the total retail sales of the album.

The producer is responsible for obtaining copyright clearances, lining up session musicians if needed, staying on budget, and delivering a high-quality master tape to the record company. An important first task for a producer is to book a good place to record. Studios with good equipment and good engineers can be found all over the world, and producers carefully select a studio where the artist will be comfortable and productive. It may come as no surprise to you that many major albums are produced in quiet, out-of-the way places where the artists are unlikely to be disturbed.

A producer also works to keep the project on budget. Each extra day in the studio can cost thousands of dollars. Record companies can financially penalize the recording artist for cost overruns by taking the money out of the artist's royalties. After the recording sessions have been completed, the producer and artist finish mixing the songs on the album. They pay special attention to making the songs fit the specific technical requirements of the label, such as the length of each song, and also to identifying any potential singles on the album.

Chance the Rapper is a highly successful rap artist who never signed to a record label. Instead, he self-produces and makes all his music available freely online; he makes money through touring and merchandise.

Self-Producing Music for Sale

For the many struggling singers and musicians who don't have a contract with a recording firm, there is another route. Because of the difficulty of getting noticed even by independent companies, some artists decide to produce their own CDs and then sell them at performances and maybe even in some stores. As we noted earlier, they also may place tracks of their music online for people to hear and perhaps even purchase. The good news is that recording studio rates have been halved in the past few years. Some artists don't even bother with studios. It is possible to make a perfectly acceptable recording in someone's basement, and people often do. Moreover, because of intense competition in the CD manufacturing business and the movement toward digital downloads, the cost of making CDs has plummeted too.

Compensating Artists

After artists have worked on a recording, they typically want to get paid. Artists are compensated for their performance on recorded music in one of two ways. If they help to make an album but are not central to it, they are paid an hourly fee. In accordance with the rules of their union, these studio musicians or singers are remunerated with at least the industry scale. Many studio musicians and singers are quite comfortable with their predictable payments. Artists who are in great demand as backup talent for albums receive far more than scale and can make a very good living.

The central artists on the recording, in contrast, are generally not paid by the hour. They receive royalties for their work. Many artists believe that they can hit the jackpot if their recordings sell well and so prefer royalties over flat fees. A typical recording industry contract gives an artist or group 10 to 15 percent of the retail price of an album. Yet the road from laying down music tracks to making money from them can be quite rocky. Specifics about how many singles or albums—physical or digital—a musician must sell to break even are hard to come by and may vary greatly by the individual artist and his or her recording contract. Two points seem clear, though: making money is not easy, and the flow of money varies depending on the music format. Moreover, if money from recordings must be divided among members of a band, that makes the individual taking even smaller.

Widespread evidence and discussions by industry practitioners suggest how difficult it is to make a good living recording music. Independent labels generally have even more restrictive artistic contracts than the majors do. Contracts with independent labels are for a longer period than those with the majors, and they provide lower royalty rates than those of the majors, require the artists to share the copyright on songs with the labels, and may even demand a share of the artists' merchandising monies. Independent-label executives claim that such contract stipulations are necessary because a label incurs large financial risks when it subsidizes a new artist. Recording companies can spend hundreds of thousands of dollars breaking a new artist in, and many new artists, despite the best efforts of both sides, never contribute to the overall profitability of the record company. In addition, the executives argue, independent firms have to pay a percentage of their income to the firms that distribute their product.

The hope of making it truly big is always there for the artists, however. If they become superstars, their power relationship with the record label equalizes. For artists with proven market demand, their agents and lawyers can negotiate generous deals. At the height of his popularity, Michael Jackson reportedly received a royalty rate of 20 percent from one of Sony Music's labels.

Distribution in the Recording Industry

And who says you need a CD at the start? Many musicians load their work onto sites such as YouTube with the hope they'll get noticed. MySpace is, of course, a distribution venue, but you don't have to pay anything to get on it. You can sell your music from it, and although the site may take a cut of the sale, the amount is far less than a label takes. If a group called the Morning Light can produce its music in a basement and release its songs on YouTube, Myspace, or Facebook just a click away from Bruno Mars, why would any group choose to sign with a label?

THINKING ABOUT MEDIA LITERACY

In the past, being "signed" by a record label was the surest way for a musician to get their music heard. What were the advantages of a deal with a record label? What disadvantages might there be in being signed to a label?

It's a good question, particularly if you pay attention to stories such as Ingrid Michaelson's. Her experience makes the online model of distribution seem extremely attractive. An aspiring singer/songwriter/pianist and part-time teacher of theater to

Ingrid Michaelson has had great success with a small management company rather than a major record label.

kids, Michaelson was 24 when in 2005 she set up a page on Myspace with the aim of networking with musicians and potential fans. Within a year, her soft vocals and romantic piano had attracted a management company that specializes in finding little-known acts for TV shows, advertisers, movie companies, and video games. The firm placed three of her songs on ABC's popular *Grey's Anatomy*, and the exposure sent one of her songs, "The Way I Am," to number 13 on the iTunes pop music chart. She had to pay 15 to 20 percent of her music royalties to the management company, but not having a label allowed her to keep most of what was left. The *Wall Street Journal* pointed out,

Because Ms. Michaelson doesn't have a record-label contract, she stands to make substantially more from online sales of her music. For each 99-cent sale on Apple Music, Ms. Michaelson grosses 63 cents, compared with perhaps 10 or 15 cents that typical major-label artists receive via their label.

By mid-2007, she had sold about 60,000 copies of her songs on iTunes and other digital stores. She used some of that money to press (and sell) her own CDs, arrange distribution for them, make T-shirts for concerts, and hire a marketing company to produce promotional podcasts.

What, then, does a label bring to an artist's career? The short answer is sustained cross-media exposure. Getting the ears of powerful concert promoters, radio program executives, and cable gatekeepers who select music for large, though targeted, audiences is a task that requires a strong organization with much experience. A management company can help an artist, but record labels insist that they have the ability to push her further. The manager for several bands, including Death Cab for Cutie, adds that an unsigned artist risks losing momentum. "There's a lot more components to an artist's career than being featured prominently on a show, just as there's more to it than having one hit on the radio," he stated. Someone agreeing would point out that because Michaelson had no record label or distributor, her first two CDs, *Slow the Rain* and *Girls and Boys*, which she put out herself in 2004 and 2006, respectively, weren't carried by many traditional music stores, even as she was becoming quite well known.

And, in fact, in 2007 Michaelson signed a deal with a new independent label, Original Signal Recordings, to act as the marketing and distribution arm for Michaelson's label. Through Original Signal, the marketing of Michaelson's music took a more mainstream turn. Original Signal re-released *Girls and Boys* in ways that would get reviews from critics. Moreover, it helped place one of the songs from the album, *Girls and Boys*, in an Old Navy commercial. The 30-second ad gave Michaelson more than sixty-five appearances in prime-time, including seventeen season premieres. Michaelson later created her own label, Cable 24 Records, but continued her work with other independent labels to market her voice into the mainstream. For example, the release of her 2016 album, *It Doesn't Have to Make Sense*, was coordinated by the Mom + Pop Music label based in New York.[9]

As in other mass media industries, having good distribution avenues does not ensure that a recording will be a hit. Without the strong ability to place recordings where people will hear them and want to buy them, though, the chances that a recording will be a hit diminish considerably. And having a hit with a major label builds on itself. Go to YouTube's home page for music to see the popularity of artists with major labels at work. Although you will certainly note performers distributed by independent labels, you are much more likely to find performers who have one of the majors behind them, such as Justin Bieber, Rihanna, Chris Brown, Nicki Minaj, and Katy Perry.

Distribution does not simply mean being able to send recordings to an exhibition location—for example, a local Walmart or Apple Music. The real distribution power of the "big three" and the other major producers-distributors lies in their ability to generate buzz among an artist's potential fans that will induce brick-and-mortar and digital retailers to carry his or her records and display them properly. The task is an imposing one. The statistics must be frightening to anyone who is hoping to hit it big without the big three, which together still control around 63 percent of US music sales and an average of 69 percent of global music sales—though their influence varies by country. Powerful distributors have the benefit of big promotional teams, liaisons with radio stations, and money for cooperative advertising. Let's take a look.

The Importance of Convergence in Promotion

As we've suggested, more than anything else distributors contribute marketing expertise to building a recording artist's career. Much of that involves promotion, and much of *that* takes advantage of convergence and even encourages it. Let's first define **promotion**. Promotion involves using a variety of media to lead target audiences to learn about, or hear, a recording in order to encourage them to purchase it. It also may include cooperative advertising, which means that the recording firm provides a retailer with a portion of the money the retailer needs in order to buy space in local newspapers or time on local radio and TV stations. All this may sound easy, but in the competitive media environment, it is extremely difficult. Recording firms have particular difficulty motivating people to buy the albums of new groups because people need to hear music before they buy it. Attractive cover art is nice, but it is hard to visually "window shop" for a new album. You really have to hear the music first.

The recording industry is therefore dependent on other media to inform audiences about new products. Physical stores that sell recordings also allow you to sample albums, but often the choices are limited to the ones that recording firms have paid the stores to promote. With the rise of Facebook and other social media, people share favorite artists and tracks with friends. Record companies often hope that these and other vehicles for hearing tracks will encourage people to fan sites, where they will get more tastes of the artists' music. Leading audiences to the artists' sites and getting buzz going often involves taking advantage of the convergent ability of digital media and their relationships with nondigital media. Promotional work takes advantage of analog media companies' common practice of also having digital outlets. Record promoters create publicity for a recording artist—for example, an interview, album review, or charity work—with the knowledge it can go digital and analog. The paper magazine *Billboard*, for example, has an active website as well as apps for smartphones and tablets. Similarly, radio stations have websites and apps that not only stream the broadcast fare but also often pay special attention to artists who would interest the stations' audiences. Record promoters can encourage the convergence of these media in ways that help the media firms (they get to play new music or interview the musicians) and publicize the product.

promotion
the process of scheduling publicity appearances for a recording artist, with the goal of generating excitement about the artist and thereby sales of his or her album

As you might imagine, creative record promoters put a lot of effort into media convergence in the interest of their artists' output. Think of the many labels owned by the majors, as well as the many independents and their labels—and then think of the many artists the labels represent—and you can see how music promotion is a real engine of cross-media convergence. The work may include uploading videos and audio files to YouTube and Facebook fan sites while generating excitement on a local radio station about an artist's concert tour that will come through the station's area. In return for the on-air promotion of a group and its rock concert, for example, a radio station might receive free tickets to give away, exclusive radio interview rights when the artist hits town, and the on-air mention of the YouTube and Facebook pages to increase fan excitement.

The Recording Industry and the Radio Industry Despite the internet's rise, over-the-air radio is still very important for the music industry. In fact, according to Nielsen, it is the dominant way people discover new songs that they then buy or choose on streaming services.[10] Particular genres of music especially need radio. According to Nielsen Music, "Country traditionally trails other genres in terms of overall streaming consumption and audience penetration." So, Nielsen notes, "when a country singer is able to get 'crossover' radio airplay on rock and pop stations, it encourages people [to] showcase the Country music genre to new audiences." That happened when Sam Hunt enjoyed crossover radio success with his song "Body like a Back Road." It led to an unusually high streaming for a country track—434 million times.[11]

To get radio airplay, recording-industry promotion executives focus particularly on radio program directors, because they are the ones who choose the particular pieces from albums (the cuts) that get airplay on the station. The relationship between the two groups is quite symbiotic; that is, each lives off the other. Both are in the business of targeting a large but fairly narrow audience by age, gender, ethnicity, or race with a particular genre of music. A hit recording keeps listeners tuned in to a radio station and helps the station in its battle to win ratings, and airplay on the radio station converts listeners to buyers, fulfilling the goals of the record company and its artists.

Still, the needs of recording company promoters sometimes conflict with those of the programmers. Many radio stations are conservative about adding new music. Program directors give preference to existing artists because those artists have a track record of success and because listeners are familiar with their sound. New artists are very much an uncertainty, and gambling on new material from unknowns might hurt the station's ratings. Music promoters also face the problem of competition. In any given week, a station may add only one new song to its playlist, whereas the various record labels may have a dozen new songs that they believe fit the station's format.

Faced with the daunting task of deciding which of the many new songs that come out each week to add to their playlists, radio station programmers supplement their own impressions of the quality of music with outside data. Several firms, including Nielsen, now electronically monitor radio stations across the country, verify the identity of songs played on those stations, and report these data to subscribers. Nielsen also records the sales of music at participating retail stores and online, plus tracking on-demand and programmed audio and video streams. Each week Nielsen metrics are used to compile lists of record sales across the country. Based on such data, various trade publications compile weekly lists of the top-selling or most-played songs.

Radio programming executives often look at these lists to help them make decisions about airplay. Station program directors also monitor their own station's request line to see whether typical listeners want to hear more of a new song. Some conduct phone surveys of listeners in which they play bits of songs and ask whether they would want to hear them on the station.

Knowing that radio stations use various pieces of data to make decisions on airplay, record executives have to work hard to get the airplay in certain markets and on particular stations that will convince program directors on the largest stations to insert a song into a playlist rotation. There are many ethical ways of doing that, but the enormous pressure to succeed in radio has also led to unethical tactics. There are reports, for example, that record company representatives have organized campaigns to flood stations with requests for a particular song. An even more unsavory activity aimed at placing songs on radio stations is **payola**—the payment of money by a promotion executive to a station program director to ensure that the program director includes certain music on the playlist. In the late 1950s the federal government made payola illegal. In view of the millions of dollars at stake in the recording industry, though, you shouldn't be surprised that prosecutions for this kind of improper influence continue. Stories consistently circulate that newer versions of payola, in the form of drugs or other noncash favors, are given to radio executives or consultants in return for adding new songs to their stations' playlists.

payola
an activity in which promotion personnel pay money to radio personnel to ensure that the latter will devote airtime to artists that the former's recording companies represent

Video, Television, and Movie Promotions

Until now, we have discussed the convergence of media around recordings' audio sounds. But you are probably quite aware that promotion of music doesn't stop with sound alone. During the past three decades, music videos have played an important role in driving rock, pop, and rap sales. Recording companies often help artists produce these videos because of the proven ability of a sizzling video to lead consumers to buy and stream music. We have already noted that people in search of music can find much of it on YouTube and other websites; often the material is in the form of music videos. Much of this material can also be accessed on mobile devices such as tablets and smartphones—further examples of convergence.

Universal Music and Sony wanted to ensure that artists they represent are present in music videos throughout the digital universe, so they joined with the Abu Dhabi Media company in 2009 to create a music video player called VEVO. You could access VEVO through its website, apps for phones and tablets, and apps for the Xbox video game machine, among other devices. VEVO said that it "powers music videos on artist pages across Facebook, as well as syndicates to dozens of online sites, including AOL, BET, CBS Interactive Music Group (including Last.fm, Metro Lyrics and MP3.com), Disney Interactive, Fuse.tv, Univision, Viacom Media Networks, Wenner Media and Yahoo! Music. By 2018, the owners decided that all this work wasn't bringing in enough benefit. They shut down their website and apps and decided instead to concentrate on showcasing VEVO artists on YouTube."[12]

The ability to get music this way, if only for a decade, may make theatrical films and cable-television videos seem like positively old-fashioned ways of promoting music. Nevertheless, those remain important vehicles for introducing specific audiences to particular types of music. Movies often hype new and old songs. Examples are "Happy" by Pharrell Williams in *Despicable Me 2* (2014), "Let It Go," sung by Idina Menzel (and written by Kristen-Anderson Lopez and Robert Lopez) in *Frozen* (2014), "Orinoco Flow (Sail Away)" by Enya in *The Girl With the Dragon Tattoo* (2011), and "The Times They Are A-Changin'" by Bob Dylan in *Watchmen* (2009). And there are the music video presentations on cable television. Think of Black Entertainment Television (BET) and some of MTV's various youth-oriented channels.

As Ingrid Michaelson's experience shows, television series have also become important venues for new music, particularly by new performers. For TV producers who want to reach young adults, introducing indie artists is less expensive than paying huge amounts for stars, and it may signal to the audience that the program is in tune with the newest sounds. Advertising agencies are beginning to imitate TV series' use of new songs in this way for commercials. Although these sorts of programs and commercials may not be a place for major labels to introduce big releases from hit acts, the venues may be good for relative newbies. Moreover, the indie acts that make it to TV series are getting the kind of promotion that may well make the major labels take a look at them and decide that the publicity makes them ready to move to higher levels of popularity.

Concert Tours

Presenting live concerts across the country is a time-honored way to promote an album. In fact, in a digital world where songs are often given away free as promotions, the way artists (and, increasingly, their labels) make money is through concert tours; the songs act as vehicles to publicize the tours. That's true even for stars such as Taylor Swift, who makes most of her earnings through concerts. You may know that Taylor Swift's *Reputation* album was the bestselling album of 2017 in the US. According to the International Federation of the Phonographic Industry (IFPI), it was the second global bestselling album of 2017 with sales of 4.5 million physical and album-equivalent copies. But total sales of the album in 2017 and beyond were only the beginning. A few months after *Reputation*'s release Swift embarked on a multinational Reputation tour, which broke attendance records from the start. It made $54 million in the first five concert cities and by its end was expected to yield $400 million.[13]

Performing is second nature for most groups; after all, many groups start out by playing local gigs in their hometown. A good manager tries to book a new group as the opening act in a tour by an established superstar, thus quickly introducing the new group to the established superstar's large audience. One often overlooked fact is that although tours have the potential to generate lots of money, the expenses also are often quite high. Experienced help has to be hired, and trucks and buses must be rented. Schedules have to be reasonable so as not to wear out the artists. Millions of dollars can be lost if a major artist comes down with pneumonia and has to cancel performances. One technique for reducing the financial uncertainty of a major tour is to find a national sponsor, such as a beverage company.

At each stop along the tour, the artist seeks to build support for his or her records. The artist may visit local radio stations in an attempt to influence their decisions on airplay and help generate a large crowd at the arena. T-shirts, sweatshirts, and other memorabilia are given away free by promoters and sold at the concerts; so are albums. The total take from concert paraphernalia can be surprisingly high. Recording artists often make a substantial percentage of their income from such sales.

A promotion company may help make some of the arrangements and share in the risks and potential rewards of putting on a concert. The largest such firm is Live Nation Entertainment, which mounts or publicizes over 22,000 events a year.[14] Live Nation owns or operates large and small event locations in the United States and abroad. Competing firms are the Anschutz Entertainment Group (AEG) and

Comcast Spectacor. The challenge for artists working with these or another firm is to make sure the arena chosen is the right size and configuration for the nature of the act. The promoter carefully prices concert tickets so that the venue will be 60 percent full at the very least. After all, it costs virtually the same amount to perform for a small audience as to perform for a large audience, but empty seats generate no revenue.

In recent years, Universal Music Group (UMG), Sony Music, and Warner Music have dived into concert merchandising in a bid to find new revenue avenues as sales of recorded music have declined. The majors recognize that increasing proportions of many artists' incomes are coming from concerts rather than purchased records, and the distributors want to be involved. UMG says on its website that Bravado, its merchandising company, "is the only global, 360 degree full service merchandise company that develops and markets high-quality licensed merchandise to a worldwide audience. . . . Product is sold on live tours, via selected retail outlets and through web-based stores." And Warner Music Group states that its Warner Music Artists Services

is powered by a team of experts in everything from tour and VIP execution to consumer analytics and web development, Warner Music Artist Services is uniquely positioned to evolve what it means to run an integrated artist branding campaign. With a comprehensive suite of services covering all direct-to-fan and merchandise capabilities, the division is built to move fast and experiment more in a constantly shifting music industry that rewards those who lead by example.

Although many artists are party to these sorts of all-encompassing deals, they warn that a label can take too much of the revenues from concerts and merchandise, leaving a group much poorer in the process. A 2011 article on the issue had the title "Your Favorite Rapper Is Poor: The Ins and Outs of 360 Deals & Artist Development."[15] The consensus in the industry is that although labels can certainly be helpful in increasing the overall revenues of an artist, the artist and manager must aggressively negotiate the best deal possible.

THINKING ABOUT MEDIA LITERACY

The tracking of audience "metrics" (statistics about who is listening to what music where) is complicated. See if you can come up with at least ten different measures of where a particular artist's music might be played that would have to be considered if you wanted a complete picture of their reach.

Exhibition in the Recording Industry

After all the work of making the record and all the work of distributing it is completed, recordings are laid out for members of the public to choose. As we've already suggested, recordings make it into the hands of the public through two major paths: digital and physical. As you probably have gathered from the chapter so far (and may have noticed in your everyday life), the landscapes of both paths have been changing dramatically over the past few years. Let's investigate a bit.

Digital Downloads

It's useful to start with the digital exhibition mode because we've already described it during the discussion of various vehicles for recorded music. Although internet service providers play the critical role of exhibitor in the sense of allowing the public to access online stores, online merchants that provide digital downloads can also be considered exhibitors in that they offer the distributors' materials to the public.

A theme that you've probably noticed in this chapter is that digital sales have become critical to the health of the recording industry. In 2017 the revenues from digital sales of singles, albums, and ringtones, as well as from streaming, equaled about $7 billion, compared to about $1.5 billion from physical sales of albums and singles. That is a major change from just a couple of decades ago, when almost all the sales were physical. The past several years has seen major changes, too. As late as 2014 the recording industry made more money through permanent downloads than it did through paid and ad-supported subscriptions. Not long afterwards streaming took the lead.

Both streaming and permanent downloads have advantages. The good thing about subscription streaming is that you can choose to listen to almost any album or single you want, or any recording genre you want—without paying more than the subscription fee. Ad-supported streaming places restrictions on your choices—you might be able to listen to an artist's work but not an entire album, for example. Nevertheless, streaming gives you a lot of freedom of choice at relatively low cost, which is probably why it has become popular. Spotify, in particular, has grown sharply. It had 75 million subscribers worldwide in mid-2018 compared to 30 million in early 2016. (Its major competitor, Apple Music, had 44 million subscribers.) Spotify also reports that 99 million people listen to its ad-supported (free) option.[16]

There are two major downsides to streaming, though. One is that you need a good internet connection to link up to the streaming site or app, which may not always be the case if you are traveling. The way around that problem if you have subscription streaming is to download songs for offline play if you know you will be in an internet-challenged location. But that possibility raises the other negative about streaming: if you stop paying the monthly subscription fee, you lose access to all the recordings you downloaded.

Some people might not care about that eventuality. Their perspective is that they simply want to listen to music, not own it. Other people do want to keep the recordings and play them on any device they choose. An added benefit to buying music over streaming is that it gets more money into the hands of the artists and labels; you're more directly supporting music creation.[17] Apple Music, Amazon Music, and Google Play Music are the dominant vehicles for doing that. They all have pretty much the same huge catalogs of available recorded materials. Some indie products may not be available or easily uncovered there, however. Bandcamp's download site is set up for people whose interests tend toward purchasing music that is relatively obscure.

Although the record labels benefit from the sales of digital recordings, there are those in the industry who believe that the huge drops in purchases after around 2014 indicate that part of the business is dying and that streaming is taking over.[18] In fact, rumors swirled in 2018 that Apple was planning to completely phase out the sale of digital music from its iTunes Store. If that happens, it will be interesting to see how Amazon, Google, Bandcamp, and other exhibitors who sell downloads respond.

THINKING ABOUT MEDIA LITERACY

Consider the role of the A&R person at a label. What factors would they need to consider when scouting artists? Why do you think recording labels have A&R positions? How is A&R work for music similar to acquisitions editors in the book publishing world?

Physical Sales

And then there are the physical recordings. Many people still buy them, though as we noted, they are a decreasing way in which people access music. As noted earlier, in 2017 they accounted for $1.5 billion of the US industry's coffers. That was more than the sales of permanent digital downloads that year. Still, revenues were miserable compared to 2007, when physical sales, which made up most of the industry's sales, were $8 billion. For decades, the record store on the street or in the mall was probably the best-known place to buy music, but physical stores such as Walmart did a brisk record business as well. According to market-research firm Almighty Music Marketing, in 2003 there were about 16,400 outlets in the United States for buying music in physical format, mostly CDs. The rise of Amazon's online CD store, which often had the lowest prices, made life tougher for physical stores. With the closing of the large chains Tower Records in 2006 and Virgin Megastores in 2009, and the decimation of other sellers as a result of the Great Recession around 2008, physical places to buy records dropped enormously. By 2014 there were 9,200. That number includes large general retail chains such as Target and Walmart, and recently they have been scaling down their physical-store music offerings, too.

The past few years, though, have seen a small uptick in the number of independent record stores around the United States. In 2017 they numbered 2,400. These tended to be small merchants who were riding the wave of a renaissance in the sale of analog vinyl recordings that has surprised producers and exhibitors. Though still a sliver of the marketplace, vinyl albums have risen from annual sales of fewer than 1 million in 2005 to more than 13 million, according to Nielsen Music research cited by the Associated Press. Although many people buy vinyl albums online, those small independent brick-and-mortar stores sell many of them. They even celebrate an annual Record Store Day across the country with music events and special releases timed by labels to the event. One retailing executive argued that the physical places can offer a segment of music aficionados what online retailers cannot: "personality, face-to-face interactions, and a sense of community around the ritual of enjoying music."[19]

Nevertheless, there is no getting around the fact that companies that stream music are the exhibitors of choice for most Americans. A stark illustration of this development involves rapper Drake's fifth album, *Scorpion*. During the first three days after its release in 2018 it logged a record-breaking number of streams for even a week—435 million. In fact, when in the week after the CD's release the *New York Times* tried to track down copies in sixteen stores that sell new music across Manhattan, Brooklyn, and Queens, it "proved challenging." Only six stores had them, and prices ranged from $17.99 to $20.99. The *New York Times* pointed noted that a monthly subscription to Spotify or Apple Music costs $9.99. In fact, according to Nielsen, in the four days after the Scorpion CD came out, it sold only 8,000 physical copies. That, observed the *New York Times*, is a relatively microscopic figure that's a powerful reminder of how little some artists need physical sales to drive their success.[20]

Ethical Issues in the Recording Industry

If you listen to certain forms of popular music and to discussions of popular music, you're probably aware that the lyrics can sometimes be quite controversial, particularly when it comes to positive presentations of violence, misogyny, and the use of the "n" word when it comes to African Americans. Critics' discussions of all three of these issues converge on hip-hop. As one writer noted, "Since the 1980s, hip-hop artists have been accused of objectifying women, demeaning women, and promoting violence and sexual abuse against women." Individual incidents generate headlines—for example, rapper Rick Ross's inclusion of a drug-rape lyric in his song U.O.E.N.O, Kanye West holding a woman's decapitated head in the music video for the song "Monster," and Lil Wayne singing "beat the pussy up like Emmett Till," who was a black lynching victim. Yet even casual listening to recent hit rap songs reveals an undercurrent of sexism and also (especially with gangsta rap) violence.

Many music listeners find these words and the images that go with them offensive. Too, parents worry about the lyrics of the songs their kids stream. Neither is

C. Delores Tucker's fight to "clean up" rap music resulted in Time Warner getting rid of Interscope Records.

a new concern. For decades, recording companies, artists, and stores have been pelted with complaints from parents and teachers around the country that their children are purchasing music with lyrics unsuitable for the children's—and that they say offend even older people's—ears.

Many of their concerns came to a head during the 1980s when Tipper Gore, the wife of then-US senator Al Gore, joined with other wives of influential Washington politicians and businessmen to form the Parents Music Resource Center (PMRC). The PMRC had a number of goals. It aimed to lobby the music industry to place warnings about lyrics on album covers. It wanted explicit album covers kept under the counter. It demanded a records ratings system similar to that used for films and a ratings system for concerts. The group also suggested that companies reassess the contracts of those performers who engage in violence and explicit sexual behavior onstage, and it proposed a media watch by citizens and record companies that would pressure broadcasters not to air songs that the group considered problematic.

The anger succeeded in leading major recording companies to put parental advisory labels on albums that warned parents about objectionable lyrics. The nation's leading retailer, Walmart, has in fact refused to stock albums with controversial lyrics. As a result, some recording firms have resorted to distributing two versions of an album: one with safer, censored lyrics and the original one that the musician intended to distribute.

The rise of gangsta rap in the late 1980s raised more concerns about violent or sexually explicit lyrics in censored and uncensored albums. Others objected to the depiction of women in many rap songs, as well as in other musical genres. In the mid-1990s, civil rights activist C. Delores Tucker launched a highly visible campaign to clean up rap music. She focused on Time Warner, whose subsidiary Interscope was home to hard-core rappers Snoop Dogg and Tupac Shakur. In 1995 Tucker and her allies succeeded in forcing Time Warner to get rid of Interscope. But Time Warner simply sold Interscope to Polygram (now Universal Music Group), and the label continued to turn out songs that Tucker and others reviled by immensely popular artists such as 50 Cent and Eminem. A dozen years later, the battle reached another crescendo, with Al Sharpton and other public figures objecting particularly to racial epithets (particularly the n-word) and sexual profanities (the omnipresent b-word) in the music.

Some people have lauded these calls for reining in rappers and other songwriters who use what they consider immoral lyrics. They have argued that popular music speaks to an enormous number of impressionable young people and teaches them about romance and love and relationships. Bleeping out a word here and there on the radio or a censored album doesn't erase many of the objectionable words and ideas in the songs, they have argued. In 2006 the filmmaker Byron Hurt released *Beyond Beats and Rhymes*, a documentary critical of rap that, in the words of a *Time* magazine writer, was notable "not just for its hard critique but for the fact that most of the people doing the criticizing were not dowdy church ladies but members of the hip-hop generation who deplore rap's recent fixation on the sensational."

Many of rap's defenders have responded that rap is not the only form of music that contains violence and sexism (listen to some forms of rock and country), but that it seems to get an outsized amount of the blame. They also argue that outsiders should not impose their values on an important field of artistic endeavor. Rappers, they have said, reflect views that many African Americans have about their surroundings; such hard-edged views need to be heard and understood, they argue. They continue that in order to understand the violence and misogyny in hip-hop, "it is necessary to look at it as the product of a set of historical, political, and economic circumstances and to study the role it has served as voice for those subjugated by systematic political and economic oppression." In fact, "if the issue of violence in rap music is to be effectively addressed, the root of the problem—disparity in resources and opportunities for urban minorities—must be aggressively dealt with."[21]

The difficulty with this view, respond the critics, is that it sees the solution to problematic hip-hop content in major social changes. The difficulty of instituting such changes suggests that the presence of misogyny and violence in rap music will continue for the foreseeable future. That, they say, harms the images of African Americans and injects insulting coarseness into American music. The argument continues. Where do you stand?

CHAPTER REVIEW

 Visit the Companion Website at www.routledge.com/cw/turow for additional study tools and resources.

 ## Key Terms

You can find the definitions to these key terms in the marginal glossary throughout this chapter. Test your knowledge of these terms with interactive flash cards on the *Media Today* Companion Website.

album	label	promotion
A&R (artist and repertoire)	mechanical royalties	ringtones
counterfeiting	payola	royalty
digital locker	peer-to-peer (P2P) computing	single
downloading	performance royalties	streaming
internet radio	piracy	

 ## Questions for Discussion and Critical Thinking

1.
   - The American Federation of Musicians is an organization that supports the interests of professional musicians.
   - The Music Business Association's membership consists of organizations involved in the sale of music (record stores and music outlets).
   - The RIAA is "the trade organization that supports and promotes the creative and financial vitality of the major music companies."

   Think about where the interests and concerns of each of these three music industry organizations intersect. Where might the issues differ between these three membership groups? What roles do industry associations like these play?

2. Music packaged in a CD or album is generally played in the order of the tracks. With services like Pandora or Spotify, songs are listened to individually, not necessarily in track order. How might this change how songs are written? Does an album "tell a story" through the deliberate placement of tracks? Is that story lost when songs are listened to separately? Reflect on how the creative process in music production has changed from an album to individual tracks.

3. In 1985 the RIAA worked with the National Parent Teacher Association to create the Parent Advisory Label program. One of the tenets of the program is "that contemporary cultural morals and standards should be used in determining whether parents or guardians would find the sound recording suitable for children." Consider this statement in the context of its creation in 1985 and now, thirty-three years later. How would you determine "contemporary cultural morals and standards"? Why?

4. Think about the media through which you can listen to music (CD, digital stream, vinyl, radio, etc.). To what extent and how do the different media change the way you enjoy and pay attention to the music? Is there a difference in the music experience when listening with earbuds versus over the air? How is listening to music on a Pandora "station" different than listening to an album? What is your own preference for experiencing music, and why?

Activity

The financial models for musicians have changed drastically. Under the studio model, royalties and contracts provided the paycheck. Now the various ways in which music can be distributed and consumed have different financial arrangements for musicians. The Future of Music Coalition has a series of quizzes for musicians to help them understand royalties and copyright. Go to futureofmusic.org/music-and-money-quizzes and take any (or all) of the four quizzes that will expand as well as test your understanding of music's complicated copyright and royalties issues. After completing the quizzes, reflect on the ways musicians are protected (or not) by existing copyright laws and how the revenue streams for musicians' work flow to the artist. What would you want to see changed if you were a musician? How do you feel about these issues as a consumer of musicians' work?

The Radio Industry

11

CHAPTER OBJECTIVES

1   Sketch the history of the radio industry.

2   Explain the relationship between advertising and programming.

3   Detail the role of market research in the radio industry.

4   Examine critically the issues surrounding the consolidation of radio station ownership.

5   Discuss ways in which new digital technologies are challenging traditional radio.

In this age of media convergence, what is radio?

Consider this quote from a magazine writer: "When my daughter, who is 17, wants to hear a song, she doesn't turn to radio. Nor does she go to Spotify or Pandora. YouTube is her on-demand streaming service."

For the moment, set aside whether you like the daughter's choice; we'll deal with that later in the chapter. Instead, think about what the writer (her mother) doesn't count as radio: Spotify, Pandora, and YouTube. Do you agree that these shouldn't be called radio?

Technically, she is correct. As we will see, radio in American society has historically meant audio signals transmitted ("broadcast") over the air by organizations ("stations") licensed for that activity by the Federal Communications Commission (FCC) and publicly accessible via devices called radio receivers. By that definition, satellite-delivered music can be considered part of the radio industry. But neither Spotify nor Pandora nor Apple Music, which are unlicensed by the FCC and offer music to listeners over the internet, would be considered radio. Similarly, YouTube, which is internet-based and often includes video as well as audio, would not fit the classic definition of radio either.

But the traditional definition begins to fall apart when you realize that Spotify, Pandora, YouTube, Apple Music, and similar companies compete with traditional radio-industry actors for advertisers and audiences. Thinking of internet audio and broadcast radio as part of one industry also makes sense when you realize that broadcast radio companies regularly reach out to listeners via the web and other digital platforms such as mobile phones and tablets. Recognizing this, some analysts include radio companies' digital activities as part of the radio industry. Yet many of these analysts exclude Spotify, Pandora, and other similar services because, they say, these are internet audio companies unrelated to traditional radio firms.

From the perspective that guides this book, this exclusion is a mistake. As we know, all media industries today are struggling with convergence. Radio is no exception, and it makes little sense to exclude threats to the traditional radio business when, at heart, they are extending the radio model into new technologies. Before the 1990s radio meant over-the-air audio signals picked up by a special receiver. But in the age of convergence, the defining feature of the industry

is the streaming audio it presents to audiences via various technologies. **Streaming audio** is the flow of sounds (usually music) to listeners in such a way that the sounds are meant to disappear after they are heard. This approach is quite different from the traditional business of the recording industry (Chapter 10), where the goal was to get people to pay to keep individual songs or specific collections of songs. Today, though, getting people to stream songs and entire albums is a major strategy of the recording industry; see Chapter 10 about that, too. Seen from this perspective, the various old and new platforms for radio—traditional broadcast, the desktop, laptop, smartphone, tablet, even smart TV—are merely competitive ways to deliver the same audio streams that are central to the ways people enjoy recordings.

But you may ask, "Doesn't calling all streaming audio 'radio' give the word a meaning that is quite different from its original meaning?" The answer is yes, but in doing this, we—and many who work in the industry—are not treating the radio industry differently from the other media industries we have described. As we have seen, digital "books," "newspapers," "magazines," and "records" are quite different from their pre-digital versions, but they still carry the tags of the original media platforms. In this sense, when we say a person reading something on a Kindle is reading a "book," or a person reading the *New York Times* on a tablet is reading a newspaper, or a person listening to Pandora is experiencing internet radio, we are using traditional media labels as metaphors. That is, the labels are figures of speech that imply comparisons to other things.

This is certainly not the first time people's understanding of the radio business has shifted. "Radio" as we understand it today is quite different from how people understood it one hundred years ago, sixty years ago, and even thirty years ago. To learn how we got from there to Pandora and consider what those developments mean for the future radio industry, let's turn to our timeline and three key historical themes.

The Rise of Radio

The word "radio" seems to have been coined by a French physicist, Edouard Branly, in 1897. He was interested in helping developers of the new "wireless" technology detect the sounds they were radiating into the air.[1] Linking a form of the

streaming audio
the flow of sounds (usually music) to listeners in such a way that the sounds are meant to disappear after they are heard

verb "to radiate" with a word to indicate flow, he concocted the word "radioconductor." The "radio" part of that term stuck in both the French and English languages. Over time, wireless activity became known in the United States as radio broadcasting. To Americans, the word "broadcasting" evoked an image of radiation, but one different from Branly's. Used this way, broadcasting is a metaphor. It was originally an agricultural term referring to the scattering of seeds on a field.

The technology of radio broadcasting in the late 19th century could transmit only click-like sounds. To appreciate why this was still important, consider it in relation to the development of the telegraph. After Samuel Morse developed the telegraph in 1842, scientists began to look to send messages over the air using electric waves or frequencies. In 1895 Italian Guglielmo Marconi succeeded in sending messages wirelessly over long distances using the code of dots and dashes that Morse had developed. Because the Italian government showed no interest in Marconi's find, he took it to England, where people quickly saw its value to the far-flung British Empire. The Marconi Company was formed to equip the commercial and military ships of England, the United States, and other countries with wireless telegraphy for communicating with one another and with shore points around the world.

Clearly, what the Marconi Company was doing has little to do with the radio industry as we know it today. This point brings us to our first historical theme:

1. Radio, as we know it, did not arrive in a flash as a result of one inventor's grand change.

Take a look at the timeline (Figure 11.1), and you'll see the way inventions and their uses progressed to the point where radio as a technology involved the public transmission of voices and music that people could receive in their homes on receivers they bought. Even when radio first "talked," it was not for the general public but for the business of shipping and for use by the Navy. So on Christmas Eve in 1906, when the inventor Reginald Fessenden first broadcast music and speech, his radio "audience" was composed of the wireless operators on ships in various parts of the Atlantic Ocean. In another way, too, Fessenden's broadcast was not characteristic of modern radio: his audience could hear the broadcast only through earphones. It was not until a year later that Lee de Forest's Audion vacuum tube made it possible for people to listen to the radio in groups through speakers.

De Forest envisioned stations sending out continuous music, news, and other material. But as you can see in the timeline, in the United States it took more than two decades to develop the kind of radio programming de Forest imagined. This early approach to radio was quite different from the one we know today. It was more like broadcast network television in airing a diversity of genres: light talk shows in the morning; soap operas during the late morning and afternoon; children's programs after school; news after dinner; and then musical variety shows, dramas, and situation comedies in the evening.

How did we get from this model to the contemporary idea of what radio means? Follow the timeline, and you'll see that the rise of television during the 1950s, along with the rise of FM in the 1960s, forced radio companies to change their approaches to their business. Instead of full-service programming aimed at everyone in an area, stations began to target particular types of people by age (e.g., teenagers) and by interests (e.g., country music, news). As the introduction noted and the timeline illustrates, the rise of companies using converging digital technologies to compete with radio has forced executives to think yet again about what their stations should do and how they should reach out to their audiences.

This story of the transformation of radio over the decades is very much tied to our second historical theme.

2. Radio as a medium of communication developed as a result of social, legal, and organizational responses to the technology during different periods.

We've already noted that it took a while for the radio system to develop programming aimed at the general public and that competition with television then forced radio firms to develop more targeted approaches to their stations' programming. We've also indicated that those approaches are now undergoing change because of competition stemming from digital convergence. If you follow these developments across the timeline with the second historical theme in mind, you will see how the technology and the content of the radio system were shaped—and continue to be shaped—by social and legal debates about what radio should be and who should control it.

You will see, for example, that when the United States entered World War I in 1917, the US Navy took control of domestic radio and developed it in ways that would most benefit the military. After the war, the navy sought congressional permission to retain control over radio for reasons of national security. Its argument was that if enemies of the United States got control of radio stations, they could disseminate propaganda that could be damaging to the interests of the country.

However, American tradition dictates that mass media should not be under government control. Allowing the US Navy to dictate radio's use would mean that a government agency could potentially control the ideas presented to large segments of the population—a controversial proposition. Both business and government leaders therefore believed that the best way to develop radio's great potential was to move it from the public to the private sector.

As a result of this debate, Congress decreed in 1919 that broadcasting was to be a privately sponsored enterprise, open to any citizen who paid for a license. But radio's split from government had a catch. To ensure that dominant control of radio would remain in friendly hands, the government forced the British and Italian Marconi Company to sell its interests to the American company General Electric (GE). The US Navy then encouraged a number of American firms that owned major broadcast patents (notably American Telephone and Telegraph [AT&T], GE, and Westinghouse) to form a **patent trust**, or a company owned by a number of firms and formed to share their patents in order to prevent other firms from entering their industry unless the trust allows them to use the patents. They called this trust the Radio Corporation of America (RCA) and gave it the power to force anyone interested in setting up a radio station to pay for a radio patent. RCA, in turn, imposed conditions for the use of the airwaves. The trust quickly became the most powerful force in developing the airwaves.

US courts broke up this radio monopoly within a decade, separating RCA from GE, AT&T, and Westinghouse, but not before it had shaped the new medium in ways that are still with us. Following are the three most important consequences of this decision:

*   The development of advertising as a means to support radio
*   The creation of networks to spread advertiser-sponsored programming around the country
*   The creation of a federal regulatory body (first the Federal Radio Commission and then the FCC) to decide which firms best serve the "public interest"

patent trust
a company owned by a number of firms that is formed to share their patents in order to prevent other firms from entering their industry unless the trust allows them to use the patents

1875s

1900s

1925s

1895: Italian inventor and engineer Guglielmo Marconi succeeds in sending wireless messages over long distance using Morse code.
1896: Marconi patents the first radio transmitter.

1900: Reginald Fessenden manages to broadcast speech and music with Marconi's device.
1907: US inventor Lee de Forest patents the Audion vacuum tube.

1912: Congress passes Radio Act of 1912.
1917–1919: During World War I, the US Navy takes control of domestic radio for military purposes.
1919: Congress decrees that broadcasting is to be a privately sponsored enterprise.
1919: AT&T, Westinghouse, GE, and United Fruit Company form the Radio Corporation of America.

1920: Westinghouse Corporation founds KDKA radio station in Pittsburgh with the purpose of providing programming over the air so people will buy Westinghouse radio sets. The station is the nation's first commercial broadcast station.
1920s–1930s: Varied entertainment genres develop in radio.

1920s–1930s: News slowly develops into an important part of radio.

1922 AT&T allows the Queensboro Realty Company to pay $50 each for five "talks" on AT&T's New York City radio station, WEAF—the first radio commercials.

1926: The earliest radio network, the National Broadcasting Company (NBC), is formed.
1927: The Radio Act of 1927 creates the Federal Radio Commission (FRC) to issue radio licenses and bring order to the nation's radio airwaves.
1927: United Independent Broadcasters is reorganized into Columbia Broadcasting System (CBS).
1933–1939: Columbia University engineer Edwin Armstrong invents frequency modulation (FM) radio.
1934: The Federal Communications Act of 1934 turns the Federal Radio Commission into a larger Federal Communications Commission (FCC). The act also holds that the spectrum on which radio waves are broadcast constitute a public resource, and in return for the use of this resource, the FCC retains the right to make certain demands of broadcasters.
Late 1940s: NBC, CBS, and ABC begin to shift the profits of their radio networks into building television networks.
1945: NBC Blue is sold and becomes the American Broadcasting Company (ABC).
1947: The transistor is invented as a smaller and more efficient replacement for the Audion vacuum tube.

Figure 11.1
Timeline of the radio industry.

1950s

1975s

2000s

1950s: Audiences and advertisers leave network radio for television. Local radio stations begin to program specific types of music to reach audiences.

1965: The FCC passes a rule that prohibits companies from simulcasting more than 50% of their AM broadcasts on their FM stations.

1970s onward: Radio stations increasingly tailor their programming for audiences of particular social categories.

1979: Sony releases the Walkman, a portable cassette player.

1993: Carl Malamud creates the first internet talk radio station.

1996: Congress passes the Telecommunications Act of 1996, eliminating the cap on nationwide radio station ownership and deregulating the market substantially.

1999: Napster's creation encourages the sharing of songs via the internet.

1990–2000: The first satellite radio companies, Satellite CD Radio (the precursor to Sirius Satellite Radio) and XM Satellite Radio, develop, raising money to launch satellites into orbit shortly after the year 2000.

2000: Pandora streaming radio founded.

2000: The US Copyright Office rules that webcasters must pay recording artists for their songs.

2001: Rhapsody Music, the first streaming music service that allowed users access to a large digital music library for a monthly fee, allows people to choose their music.

2008–present: A number of associations concerned with protecting various music-publishing and online interests come to a voluntary agreement about royalties for internet streaming and downloads to a limited number of devices.

2007: Sirius and XM Satellite Radio merge into a single entity, SiriusXM Radio.

2008: Clear Channel creates iHeartRadio, an internet radio platform that aggregates content from hundreds of stations nationwide.

2015: There are 15,455 licensed radio stations in the US.

2015: Eight years after the merger, SiriusXM radio claims a larger audience than any other radio broadcasting company in America, with 28.4 million subscribers.

2015: Spotify, the internet streaming music service, hits 20 million paid subscribers and 75 million active users.

2018: Flat advertising revenues and large debt force iHeartMedia to file for Chapter 11 bankruptcy.

Old radio showing the AM and FM frequency bands in megahertz and kilohertz.

frequency modulation (FM)
a means of radio broadcasting, utilizing the band between 88 and 108 megahertz; FM signals are marked by high levels of clarity but rarely travel more than eighty miles from the site of their transmission

amplitude modulation (AM)
a means of radio broadcasting, utilizing the band between 540 and 1,700 megahertz; AM signals are prone to frequent static interference, but their high-powered signals allow them to travel great distances, especially at night

Radio advertising and variations on the idea of radio networks are still with us, as we will see. So is the FCC, but its power over radio has decreased over the past few decades. This is primarily because the industry has convinced the commission, the executive branch of the federal government (which oversees it), and Congress (which can write laws that determine its powers) that the industry's direction is best decided through competition from within the radio industry (resulting from the large number of radio stations in the United States—over 12,000), as well as from competition that radio stations experience from other media.

These historical responses to social and legal debates that shaped the number of stations and what people heard on them clearly also shaped the radio industry, as the third theme notes:

3. The radio industry developed and changed as a result of struggles to control audio channels and their relations to audiences.

The radio industry has changed enormously from its beginnings with RCA. Follow the timeline, and you'll note the rise of the National Broadcast Company (NBC), Mutual Broadcasting Network, the CBS Radio Network, and later the several station "groups" (including CBS) that now dominate the radio landscape. These developments and others involved attempts by companies to take advantage of perceived opportunities. Sometimes companies have tried to block developments they do not believe are in their interests. This happened with FM radio, which stands for **frequency modulation**—an invention of engineer Edwin Armstrong during the 1930s. From the start, leading radio executives realized that the static-free sound of FM was far superior to the sound produced by the **amplitude modulation**, or AM, technology upon which existing radio transmitters and sets were based. But for technical reasons, the FM technology could not simply be used to improve AM radio. FM would have to either replace AM or coexist with it. Broadcasters worried that their huge investment in AM would be threatened if they developed FM as a substitute. They also worried that the development of a whole new set of FM stations would reduce their profits by dividing both audiences and advertising money. For these reasons, radio executives tried hard to influence the FCC to derail the development of FM radio.

FM radio did emerge, though years later than its supporters wanted. By the 1960s the FCC was not handing out new AM licenses, and the amount of money needed to buy an existing AM station soared. In the face of these developments, new business interests saw opportunities in FM radio and pressured the FCC to encourage the growth of FM by passing a nonduplication rule. The FCC passed this rule in 1965, stating that an owner of both an AM and an FM station could not play the same material on both stations more than 50 percent of the time. The rule had the effect supporters of FM wanted. FM stations, looking for things to play and not having many commercials, developed music-based formats that played long cuts or even entire albums—an approach that AM stations resisted. Many listeners migrated to FM; they liked the music and the static-free sound. In 1972 FM had 28 percent of the radio audience in the top 40 radio markets, with AM taking 72 percent. By 1990 these figures were reversed.

The FM example shows how powerful forces within the radio industry could use their leverage to delay a technology they believed would transform their industry in a way they didn't want. During the 1990s radio broadcasters applied pressure to Congress to allow changes in the industry that they *did* want. Before that time, the FCC did not allow broadcasters to own more than one FM and one AM station in a given area. However, the industry convinced legislators who crafted the Telecommunications Act of 1996 to do away with such restrictions. The new law allowed broadcast companies to snatch up several AM and FM properties in the same market. This sparked the creation of large radio conglomerates, most notably Clear Channel Communications (now called iHeartMedia), which controlled large proportions of radio advertising in markets across the country.

The rise of radio conglomerates has sparked the criticism that much of broadcast (also called over-the-air and terrestrial) radio is repetitive, boring, and clogged with commercials. This criticism is being voiced at a time when digital media—such as satellite radio, internet-linked computers, smart speakers, mobile phones, and related technologies—are opening up new ways for people to get audio programming that radio has long provided. Once again, radio executives stand between an old and new world. They have a lot invested in traditional broadcast radio, but their audience numbers are declining. So they are trying to understand how to adapt to and compete with the new technologies. Let's take a look at the established and emerging worlds of radio. We start with today's terrestrial radio world and then examine digital competition to the radio industry and the industry's response to it.

An Overview of the Terrestrial Radio Industry

It's certainly a world with a lot of stations. In summer 2018 there were 15,499 radio stations in the United States.[2] Despite increased competition from digital media for advertising and audiences, the number of stations has grown—in 2008 this count was 13,977. At the same time, the ownership of the stations in and around big cities has become concentrated. As we have seen, the federal government has greatly relaxed its limitations on the number of stations one party can own. The law allows ownership based on a sliding scale that depends on the number of stations in the area. Station groups hold up to eight stations in large markets and up to five stations in smaller markets as long as the company stations don't number more than 50 percent of those in the market. The law places no limit on the total number companies can own across multiple markets.[3] As a result, most large-market stations are now part of station groups owned by companies such as iHeartMedia, Cumulus, Citadel, and Entercom.

Consider Philadelphia, Pennsylvania, as an example. There are thirty-seven stations that reach the city with strong signals. Of these, Entercom owns eight, iHeartMedia owns six, and the Beasley Broadcast Group owns seven (including one in nearby Wilmington, Delaware). That means that four firms own twenty-one (57 percent) of the stations that target the city. Moreover, these stations are among the most popular, so the four firms likely gather more than 57 percent of the listeners and more than 57 percent of the advertising.[4]

THINKING ABOUT MEDIA LITERACY

Consider your own radio listening habits. What stations do you listen to most frequently? What is it that the station offers you that is different from other methods of getting that material (news, music)? If you had to pay to listen to a particular station, would you? Why or why not?

Where and When People Listen to the Radio

Nielsen is a company that makes money supplying radio ratings to the industry and its advertisers. It notes in a 2018 report that

> AM/FM radio continues to reach more people each week than any other medium in the United States at 228.5 million adults 18+ compared with 216.5 million for TV (live, DVR, and time-shifted), 203.8 million for apps/web on a smartphone, and 127.6 million for video on a smartphone. Looking at the audio landscape, broadcast radio's weekly reach of 228.5 million also outpaces the 68.5 million for streaming audio, 35.7 million using satellite radio, and 21.9 million consuming podcasts.[5]

To reinforce the point, it adds that "each week more Americans tune into AM/FM radio than watch television, or use smartphones, tablets, or computers."

Since the 1950s radio's strength in the face of competition from other media has had to do with its portability—people have been able to use radio outside the home, where they have historically had less access to the medium's audiovisual competition. According to Nielsen, listening at home has been on a long-term decline. Whereas 53 percent of all radio listening (as measured in quarter hours) took place at home in 1986, that percentage had dropped to less than a third by 2017. Listening to terrestrial radio has become a predominantly "away-from-home" (in cars, at work, on the beach, in the park) activity.[6]

What Nielsen means by "listening" is tuning in at least once for five minutes during a quarter hour during a week. A somewhat tougher gauge of attention to radio is the *number* of quarter hours during a week in which a listener has spent five minutes or more with a radio station. Using that measure, the time spent listening (TSL) has gone down substantially over the past few years. Studies by Arbitron (the radio research company later bought by Nielsen) show that in March 2007 Americans spent nineteen hours and forty-six minutes per week listening to radio. In June 2018, that number was thirteen hours.[7] Older people tend to listen more, as Figure 11.2 shows. The decline has been taking place for both in-home and out-of-home listening, as other technologies that carry music—most prominently websites and apps—take terrestrial radio's place.[8]

AM Versus FM Technology

You already know that terrestrial radio stations broadcast using one of two technologies, AM or FM. The two technologies operate on different ranges of frequencies (called bands) and utilize two different means of broadcasting their signal (see Figure 11.3). There are about 4,633 AM stations and 10,866 FM stations in the

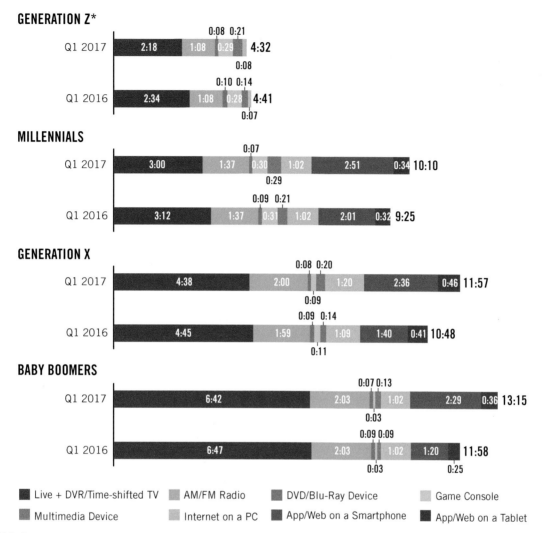

Figure 11.2
Source: The Nielsen Total Audience Report Q1 2017, p. 7, accessed July 26, 2018. Copyrighted information ©2017, of The Nielsen Company, licensed for use herein.

United States.[9] Since the 1970s listeners clearly have preferred FM because its sound is clearer than AM, with less static. In 1981 AM stations attracted 41 percent of the listeners per average quarter hour; in 2011 they managed to grab only 15.6 percent of listeners in an average quarter hour.[10]

Commercial Radio Stations Versus Noncommercial Radio Stations

In addition to distinguishing radio stations according to their positions in the AM or FM band, we can characterize them by the way they get the money they need to stay in business. In terms of funding, there are two types of radio stations:

- Commercial stations
- Noncommercial stations

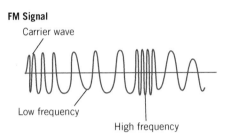

AM Signal

Carrier wave

Low amplitude

High amplitude

FM Signal

Carrier wave

Low frequency

High frequency

Figure 11.3

Both AM and FM radio stations transmit a carrier wave that is changed, or "modulated," to carry audio signals such as music or voice. With AM radio, the amplitude, or strength, of the carrier wave's vibration fluctuates with the sound. With FM radio, the strength of the carrier wave remains constant, and instead it is the frequency, or number of vibrations within the wave, that changes based on the sound.

commercial stations
radio stations that support themselves financially by selling time on their airwaves to advertisers

noncommercial stations
radio stations that do not receive financial support from advertisers

billboards
the mention of a sponsor's name or products at the start or end of an aired program, acknowledged in return for money

The vast majority of stations in the United States—about 11,000—are **commercial stations**. As the name implies, these stations support themselves financially by selling time on their airwaves to advertisers. **Noncommercial stations** do not receive financial support from advertisers in the traditional sense of airing commercials. Most noncommercial stations are located at the very left of the FM band (between 88 and 92 MHz) because these frequencies have been reserved by the government exclusively for noncommercial use. If your college or university owns a station, it may very well broadcast here. Because the FCC does not permit these stations to sell products directly, the stations support themselves through donations from listeners, private foundations, and corporations—the latter in return for mentioning the firm or its products in announcements at the beginning and end of their programs. These announcements, called **billboards**, often sound suspiciously like the commercials these stations aren't allowed by law to run. National Public Radio is a network that uses billboards.

Radio Market Size

Radio stations can be grouped according to the size of the market they serve (see Table 11.1). Listeners in small cities such as Laramie, Wyoming, or Kenai, Alaska, may have only a handful of stations available to them. Despite the availability of frequencies, many rural towns cannot attract the advertising or noncommercial support to field even a single radio station. Contrast this

Table 11.1 Top Fifteen Radio Markets by Population, Fall 2017

Rank	Market location	Fall 2012 population*
1	New York	16,285,500
2	Los Angeles	11,465,400
3	Chicago	7,945,800
4	San Francisco	6,710,000
5	Dallas–Fort Worth	6,063,100
6	Houston–Galveston	5,822,000
7	Washington, DC	4,921,100
8	Atlanta	4,823,200
9	Philadelphia	4,593,500
10	Boston	4,294,800
11	Miami–Fort Lauderdale–Hollywood	4,070,400
12	Seattle–Tacoma	3,63,400
13	Detroit	3,813,700
14	Phoenix	3,662,700
15	Minneapolis–St. Paul	2,957,900

Source: Nielsen, "Radio Market Survey Population, Rankings, & Information," Nielsen, Fall 2017, www.nielsen.com/content/dam/corporate/us/en/docs/nielsen-audio/market_populations_and_rankings_2017.pdf accessed July 26, 2018. Copyrighted information ©2017, of The Nielsen Company, licensed for use herein.

situation with that of major markets such as New York City and Los Angeles, where more than sixty stations compete for residents' ears. Despite the large number of stations fighting for listeners, a frequency in a large city can be worth hundreds of millions of dollars.

THINKING ABOUT MEDIA LITERACY

Radio relies, as do other media industries, on advertising to finance their business. What are some of the methods radio stations use to draw in listeners? Are they effective?

How can so many stations survive in a major urban environment? The answer lies in the second major reason that radio has so far been able to compete in the new media world: segmentation, specifically format segmentation and audience segmentation. To understand what these activities mean and how they guide the radio industry, let's turn to the categories of production, distribution, and exhibition.

Production in the Radio Industry

Research suggests that despite the large number of signals they may be able to receive, people tend to be loyal to no more than two or three radio stations. Think about the stations that you listen to at different times during the day. Most likely you listen to a station that plays music. Perhaps you listen to a "talk station," where listeners can phone in and speak their mind, or to an all-news station or an all-sports station.

Let's focus on the music station for the moment. What does that station create, or "produce"? Unless the station is broadcasting a special concert, it almost certainly does not produce the music. Today, virtually all radio stations rely on recordings for their musical repertoire. Those recordings were created elsewhere; typically, they are CDs or digital files made by recording companies.

Radio Formats

If you think about it, you'll realize that what music-oriented radio stations produce is an overall sound: a flow of songs punctuated by the comments of the DJs, the commercials, the station identification, the news, the weather, and sports. Radio industry practitioners call this flow of on-air sounds a **format**, or the "personality" of the radio station. As such, it attracts certain kinds of listeners and not others. In the highly competitive media environment, radio practitioners have found that the way to prosper is not to be all things to all people. In both commercial and noncommercial radio, profits come from breaking the audience into different groups (segments) and then attracting a lucrative segment. For commercial broadcasters, a lucrative segment is one that many advertisers want to reach. For noncommercial broadcasters, a lucrative segment is a population group that has the money to help support the station or that corporate donors want to impress.

The fragmentation of the radio industry spurred the creation of many different radio formats, as radio executives struggled for ways to reduce their risk of failure amid enormous competition. They hoped that the formats they created would help them home in on audiences that would be large and desirable enough for local and national advertisers (or donors) to support. As Table 11.2 indicates, country music

format
the personality of a station, designed to attract a particular audience segment

Table 11.2 Most Popular Formats Among US Radio Stations, 2018

Rank	Format	#Stations
1	Country	2,137
2	News/Talk	1,314
3	Classic Hits	984
4	Spanish	843
5	Sports	736
6	Top 40	593
7	Adult Contemporary	587
8	Classic Rock	517
9	Hot Adult Contemporary	452
10	Religion (Teaching, Variety)	351
11	Oldies	299
12	Rock	282
13	Contemporary Christian	201
13	Black Gospel	200
14	Urban Adult Contemporary	167
15	Ethnic	165
16	R&B	157
17	Adult Standards	145
18	Southern Gospel	133
19	Alternative Rock	118
20	Soft Adult Contemporary	114
21	Modern Rock	112
22	R&B Adult/Oldies	73
23	Variety	62
24	Jazz	23
25	Gospel	19
26	Rhythmic Adult Contemporary	19
27	Easy Listening	15
28	Classical	10
29	Modern Adult Contemporary	6
30	Pre-Teen	0
31	Other/Format Not Available	46

Source: Radio Advertising Bureau, www.rab.com/whyradio/reportresults.cfm, accessed July 27, 2018; thanks to Annette at RAB.

formats were represented in the largest number of stations at the start of 2017, at 2,126. According to Nielsen, news/talk actually garnered the highest share of audience listening per average quarter hour (AQH) through the day. It captured 9.9 percent of the radio audience in 2017, whereas country lassoed second with 7.7 percent ant adult contemporary was third with 7.6 percent, per AQH. Other common formats had lower shares of the national audience.[11]

Determining a Station's Format A music radio station's format is governed by four factors:

- Music style
- Music time period
- Music activity level
- Music sophistication

Music style refers strictly to the type of music a radio station plays, regardless of how the music is packaged for airplay. **Music time period** refers to the time of the music's release.

"Current" music generally refers to music released within the last year, "contemporary" music generally refers to music released within the past ten to fifteen years, "oldies" generally refers to music released between the mid-1950s and the mid-1970s, and "nostalgia" generally refers to music released prior to the mid-1950s.

Music activity level is a measure of the music's dynamic impact, ranging from soft and mellow to loud and hard-driving. The names of some music styles include built-in descriptions of the music's activity level, such as "hard rock" or "smooth jazz." **Music sophistication** reflects the simplicity or complexity of the musical structure and lyrical content of the music played. This factor often determines the composition of a station's audience, and it is also reflected in the presentation of the station's on-air staff.

Types of Formats By some counts there are more than forty different formats. One guide to formats for radio practitioners lists thirty-eight of them,[12] but many formats have variations to reach specific demographic segments. For example, the tag "country" is broad, considering that some stations narrow the kinds of country music they play to suit particular target tastes. Some stations play contemporary country, whereas others play "classic" country songs (usually twenty-five years old), and some brand them themselves even more specifically as "bluegrass country." Moreover, new formats are created each year.

Selecting the Right Format Because the format is the basis for attracting a target audience, radio station executives spend a lot of time developing it —often hiring **format consultants** to analyze the competition and choose a format that will attract the most lucrative audience niche possible. Most of the formats are based on music, but the bottom-line issue is a station's ability to gather a distinct audience for sponsors, not the aesthetics or diversity of its sound. People in the industry often use the term **narrowcasting** to describe the activity of going after specific slices of the radio audience that are especially attractive to advertisers. One well-known radio consultant explained that a radio station's need for distinct listeners was the reason behind narrowcasting: "As the [audience] pie gets thinner and thinner [because of the large number of competing stations], it's not so much whether you have ten thousand listeners at any given time. . . [but] what's the difference between [stations] A, B, C, and D."

music style
the aspect of a radio station's format that refers to the type of music the station plays

music time period
the aspect of a radio station's format that refers to the release date of the music that the station plays (e.g., "contemporary," "oldies")

music activity level
the aspect of a radio station's format that refers to the played music's dynamic impact (e.g., "soft rock," "smooth jazz")

music sophistication
the aspect of a radio station's format that refers to the simplicity or complexity of the musical structure and lyrical content of the music played

format consultants
individuals hired by a radio station to analyze the competition and select a format that will attract the most lucrative audience niche possible

narrowcasting
going after specific slices of the radio audience that are especially attractive to advertisers

THINKING ABOUT MEDIA LITERACY

Radio stations' "curation" of music is one of the ways they try to draw in listeners (and thereby attract advertisers). How important do you think curation is to the contemporary radio industry? Many music websites and apps allow users to perform this same curation function for themselves and to share these curated streams with their social networks. What are the differences in these two curation activities? How does the curation of music at a radio station differ from that done by your friend?

Determining Listening Patterns

listening patterns
the habits that describe people's use of radio

Listening patterns describe people's habits of radio use. Radio industry executives suggest that the following five propositions about listening patterns help them effectively segment audiences:

- Individuals tend to listen to only three radio stations at any particular period in their lives, with the most "preferred" of those stations taking up 65 to 70 percent of their listening time.
- In the United States, there tends to be a large and widening divide between the music preferences of black, white, and Hispanic people.
- Men and women often have separate musical interests.
- People who are ten years apart in age tend to belong to different "music generations" with different tastes.
- Music preferences can be useful tools for identifying people with distinct styles of living.

Format consultants argue, for example, that they can construct formats that will divide the African American audience by age and lifestyle. Several cities have urban/adult contemporary stations that combine the features of both adult contemporary and urban contemporary stations. They try to reach an older African American audience by playing both current songs and the "soft" tunes that were popular in these listeners' youths. In a similar vein, the news/talk format can be further divided into distinct subformats such as all news, sports talk, motivational talk, and political talk.

Consultants point out that it is the combination of a radio station's cues—the kind of music or talk, the presence of announcers and their speech patterns, the presence or absence of jingles and other identifiers (called interstitials in the business)—that keep listeners of particular genders, ages, races, and ethnicities coming back.

Working With Formats

Once station management chooses a target audience and a format for a local station with the help of consultants, the station's personnel are typically responsible for working with the format—producing it and making it attractive to the target audience on a daily basis (see Figure 11.4).

The general manager is in charge of the entire station operation. He or she represents the owners of the station and is responsible for its activities. The station's sound is controlled by the chief engineer, the news director, and the program director. The chief engineer makes sure that the station's sound goes over the air reliably and, with the help of the compliance manager, that the station's equipment complies with the technical rules of the FCC. The news director supervises news that is read over the air, perhaps assisted by reporters. In preparation for delivering the news

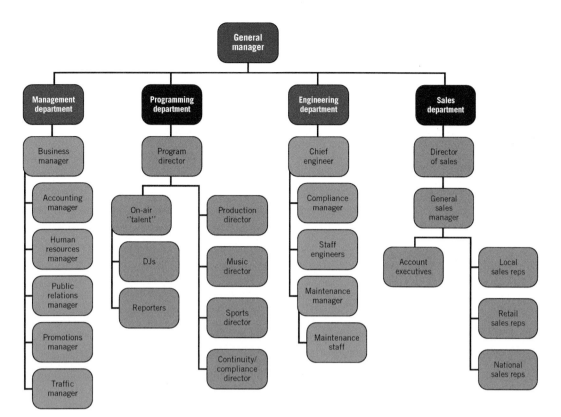

Figure 11.4
Organizational structure of a typical radio station.

over the air, these workers scan the news wires for relevant stories and conduct brief interviews with local officials in order to supplement their stories.

The program director works to ensure that the station's programming is consistent with the format and popular with the target audience and controls the station's on-air functions. Almost everything a listener hears over the air is the responsibility of the program director. The on-air personalities, or DJs, work for the program director. The program director is often assisted by a music director and a promotions manager. In many cases, these individuals also handle a shift on the air.

The average on-air personality (also known as **on-air talent**) works a four- or five-hour shift. Although this may sound like cushy work, it isn't. Running a format requires being able to handle many different, time-sensitive tasks simultaneously. During his or her hours on the air, a DJ may play up to seventy-five records and an equal number of commercials. In addition, the personality will answer select listener phone calls, manage on-air contests or promotions, and update the weather forecast or sports scores. Keeping all these format elements in order while sounding upbeat on the air requires a fair amount of technical skill. Using computers, station employees carefully ensure that when a song ends a new one smoothly begins. Otherwise, the station will transmit **dead air**—that is, nothing. Silence is a big taboo in radio because the mandate is to keep the target audience interested. Figuring out how to fill time attractively is a big challenge for a DJ. After their shift in the on-air studio, many disc jockeys move to a production studio, where they create items like commercials or comedy bits for later airing.

Wendy Williams, most popular for her role as a celebrity gossip "shock jockette," had a radio show on WBLS, a popular hip-hop station in New York City. Other well-known personalities, such as Steve Harvey, also had programs. Williams left broadcast radio in 2009 to host her own television talk show, *The Wendy Williams Show*.

on-air talent
term referring to radio workers whose voices and personalities are broadcast over the radio's airwaves

dead air
the silence on the airwaves that is produced when a radio station fails to transmit sound

playlist
the roster or lineup of songs that a radio station can play on the air during a given period of time

Producing the Playlist

Let's assume you have been named the program director of a new Top 40 station. What do you play to attract your target audience of young people in their teens and twenties? Your DJs need a playlist to guide them. The **playlist** is the roster of songs the DJs can put on the air (see Figure 11.5). The first step in creating a playlist is to find the appropriate songs that reflect the format. Most stations designate 600 to 700 songs that quickly signal their station's personality to listeners and that they play in rotation. In addition, stations that play contemporary music regularly highlight new songs by adding 50 to 100 songs to the rotation list each week. Sometimes an artist is so well known that his or her songs will be added automatically, or a new song just sounds so good that it is immediately added to the playlist. But more often than not, adding a song requires careful thought. Program directors tend to believe listeners are fickle and will tune out of a station if it plays a song they don't want to hear. Ideas about kinds of music the target audience wants are crucial. So, for example, the

Rank	Title	Artist
KISS FM playlist for March 8, 2010		
1	Nothin on You	B.o.B.
2	Tik Tok	Kesha
3	Carry Out	Timbaland Feat/Justin Timberlake
4	Rude Boy	Rihanna
5	Tie Me Down	New Boyz/Ray J
6	Telephone	Lady Gaga/Beyoncé
7	Solo	Iyaz
8	Imma Bee	Black Eyed Peas
9	Bad Romance	Lady Gaga
10	In My Head	Jason Derulo
11	Today Was a Fairytale	Taylor Swift
12	What Do You Want from Me	Adam Lambert
13	Bedrock	Young Money/Lloyd
14	Sexy Chick	David Guetta/Akon
15	We Are the World 2010	Various
16	According to You	Orianthi
17	Young Forever	Jay-z/Mr. Hudson
18	Blah Blah Blah	Kesha/3 Oh! 3
19	Lalala	Lmfao
20	Empire State of Mind	Jay-z/Alicia Keys

Figure 11.5

A sample playlist. This excerpted playlist from KISS 102.7—Los Angeles, California's number-one hit radio station—represents some of the songs that KISS can play for a certain period of time.

programming director of a Chicago classic hits station noted in 2018 that "Eighties is now the No. 1 decade for the format if you look at the top 500 played."[13] In 2008 the seventies might have been "classic" to the target middle-aged audience because that was the music period they remember fondly.

When in doubt, programmers use research.

Conducting Research to Compile the Playlist

Research can take many forms. Stations test the general music rotation by contracting with a company to phone a sample of known listeners or inviting them to an online location. The company carries out a callout music evaluation, which is sometimes called a **burn music test**. This test involves playing many of the playlist's songs for the people—or asking the surveyed people to go to a website and click on the songs—to determine which ones still draw interest and which have lost their popularity (or "burned out"). When it comes to adding new songs, executives may look at what successful stations in other cities are playing. Executives may check trade periodicals such as *Billboard*. They may go on the internet to see what people are talking about, downloading, watching on YouTube, or getting from Pandora. They also may survey listeners in person or online from time to time and ask them about their preferences. In these surveys, the station may ask a listener to rate certain songs. Only songs that test well with the audience will receive substantial airplay.

Research can also shape the overall direction of a station. Stations or a research firm they hire may conduct **focus groups**, gathering and interviewing groups of area residents (usually eight to ten per group) who fit the profile of the station's target audience. The individuals may be asked for their thoughts on various local radio stations and what they like and dislike about a certain station personality. These sessions are designed to capture the spontaneous reactions of the participants. One company that carries out focus groups for radio stations argues that they can "serve as a quick indicator of how well marketing or programming changes are taking hold and whether fine tuning adjustments are necessary." The company acknowledges that "[w]hile the small sample is not designed to be extrapolated to the general population, face-to-face discussions with listeners can help us generate ideas, questions, and issues worth further investigation."[14]

Maintaining the Format and Retaining the Target Audience

No matter what their format, programmers work hard to please the largest possible segment of the station's target audience. To hold the interest of those who fall within the target audience but rarely listen to a particular station—that is, **fringe listeners**—the programmer wants to play only the most appropriate songs. Otherwise, when these fringe listeners tune in, they will quickly tune out again because the station is playing something they do not know or like. But the **core audience**—listeners who spend a lot of time listening to a radio station—quickly tire of hearing the same songs over and over again. A programmer must therefore carefully balance the desires of the station's fringe listeners and those of its core audience.

To strike this balance, most radio stations create an hourly **format clock** (also called a **format wheel**). This circular chart divides one hour of the station's format into different, timed "show" elements (see Figure 11.6). The clock helps the programmer maintain stability while making sure that key service elements show up at specific times. For example, a radio station may schedule news at the top of the hour, followed by

burn music test
surveying people to determine which songs still draw interest and which have lost their popularity (or "burned out")

focus groups
assemblages of eight to ten carefully chosen people who are asked to discuss their habits and opinions about one or more topics

fringe listeners
listeners who fall within the target audience but rarely listen to a particular station

core audience
listeners who spend a lot of time listening to a radio station

format clock (format wheel)
a circular chart that divides one hour of a radio station's format into different timed program elements

Figure 11.6

A sample format clock (available here: https://en.wikipedia.org/wiki/Broadcast_clock#/media/File:Broadcast_Clock.png)

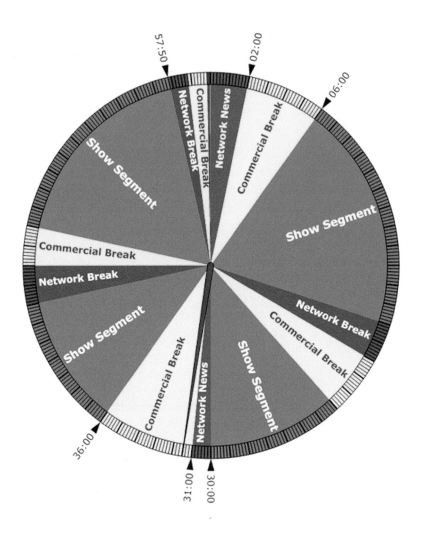

drive time

early weekday mornings and late afternoons—when people are driving to and from work—when radio stations expect to capture their largest audience

a hit song. By FCC requirements, and to help listeners remember which station they are hearing, the clock instructs DJs to broadcast the station's call letters and frequency often. Stations also may use jingles to improve their listeners' retention of the station's identity. Perhaps most important from the station owner's viewpoint, the clock dictates when on-air personalities play those vital commercials.

The clock also provides the framework for the scheduling and placement of music. Many stations use complex music-scheduling software to make sure that individual songs are properly spaced and balanced. The clock guarantees that the most popular records are repeated more often, whereas less popular records air less frequently.

The programming approach may vary somewhat during different times of the day. In radio, **drive time**—or the period when people are driving to and from work during early weekday mornings and late afternoons—is when radio stations expect to capture their largest audience. Given the large audience, advertising rates are also at their highest during these time slots. The morning shift is especially important for the station, and finding the right person or team to handle a station's early morning shift is often a great challenge. It is a strong belief within the radio business that a good morning personality will keep listeners tuned in to the station for the rest of the day. Funny morning personalities can therefore command large salaries.

Because so much listenership (and advertising money) rides on drive time, program directors cannot afford much risk in terms of what is aired. During times when there are fewer listeners—like late at night or on weekends—program directors can be more adventurous, using these hours of lower listenership to introduce new music. Through its request line, a station can hear from members of its audience about whether they like a new song or not. This feedback might affect whether the program director will slot it during drive time.

Companies that own several stations with similar formats—for example, country music or adult contemporary—often take a group approach to programming. They conduct music tests with people from across the country, and they apply their results to all the stations. Moreover, these large radio firms—for example, iHeartMedia and Cumulus—often hire on-air talent to present the music for all or some of their stations from a central location. The same DJ presents the same music to listeners in several cities while giving the impression that the program is local. In fact, a local service may cut into the program feed at precise moments to provide the traffic or weather. The aim, of course, is to save as much money as possible on local programming executives and on-air personalities.

It is interesting to note that most on-air personalities have little input into what music they play. Program directors and their general managers believe that the stakes are too high and the risk too great to allow a single DJ to decide what music to play based on his or her mood. In contemporary radio, a carefully crafted format must be consistent throughout the broadcast day.

Distribution in the Radio Industry

In large cities more so than in small and rural ones, the sound that a station broadcasts every day may be mostly locally produced and so locally distributed. When a station group programs the DJs or talk show hosts centrally, production and distribution obviously originate from afar. But even when much of a station's live programming originates locally, there may be interest in broadcasting live programming from elsewhere—for example, concerts by famous rock acts or programs with famous talk show hosts—in order to attract the right kind of listeners to the station. Yet paying to create these programs is often far beyond the means of an individual radio station. As such, most stations depend on outside suppliers to supplement their local programming.

The Role of Networks, Syndicators, and Format Networks

Traditionally, outside suppliers have fallen into two categories: networks and syndicators. A **network** provides a regular schedule of programming materials to its affiliate radio stations for broadcast. A **syndicator** typically makes a licensing deal for one show (or one series of shows) at a time. In recent years these distinctions have been disappearing. As an example, the *Rush Limbaugh Show* is a popular talk program distributed by Premiere Networks (a subsidiary of iHeartMedia). Stations may carry only a few Premiere talk programs (e.g., Sean Hannity, Glenn Beck, and Ryan Seacrest) or its many talk, music, or sports programs offered during different times of the week.

The ultimate in network programming is the growing phenomenon of round-the-clock **format networks**. Westwood One (owned by Cumulus Media) is a major provider of such networks. It offers numerous "format streams" to help a radio station owner create a sound for its market. "Explore our programming options," says the Westwood One website to potential clients, and it offers streams of classic hits,

network
a company that distributes programs simultaneously to radio stations that agree to carry a substantial amount of its material on an ongoing basis; typically, a network provides a regular schedule of programming material to its affiliate stations for broadcast

syndicator
a company that licenses programming to radio stations on a market-by-market basis

format networks
programming firms that provide subscribing radio stations with all the programming they need to fill their airwaves twenty-four hours a day, seven days a week; often the station needs only to insert local commercial spots into the programming

rock, variety hits, adult contemporary, country, and urban/R&B. Under each category, Westwood One presents subformats for sale. So, if a radio station is interested in country music, executives can choose among different subformats. It describes the Hot Country stream as emphasizing "popular, current songs and mixes in top-testing songs from the 1990s and 2000s. Hot Country draws a young, active segment of the Country audience. The music is wrapped with clever imaging, engaging air personalities and fun, large-scale promotions." Westwood One even presents a format clock with each stream. The firm provides a subscribing station with all the programming it needs, and the station can insert local commercials, news, and weather when needed. A station affiliated with one of these networks no longer needs to have a fully staffed programming department, which means saving perhaps hundreds of thousands of dollars annually. These stations can still hire a person to deliver local news and weather so as to give listeners a sense that they are linked to the community.

These different forms of program suppliers typically circulate their material to stations via satellite. Sometimes the supplier charges the station. For example, Premiere often demands money from stations for carrying the highly popular *Rush Limbaugh Show*. Generally, though, stations don't pay to receive syndicated programming. Instead, programs are put on the air through **barter**. This means that the syndicator provides the show and keeps a number of minutes for the sale of commercials to advertisers. Such a company therefore makes most of its money by selling time on its programs to advertisers that want to reach the listeners of certain types of radio stations around the United States. They also may give the local station some of the advertising time available during the programming. In Philadelphia, for example, the station that airs Salem Radio Network's *The Dennis Prager Show* makes money during the first six minutes of the hour by running its own commercials during the news. During the fifty-four minutes of *The Dennis Prager Show*, there are sixteen minutes of commercials. The Salem Radio Network makes money running commercials across the stations during five of those minutes. The remaining eleven minutes make up commercial time that the station can sell to local or national advertisers.[15]

Even noncommercial stations use networks. The largest of these networks, National Public Radio (NPR), distributes cultural and informational programming to its member stations across the country. It is probably best known for its news programs such as *All Things Considered* and *Talk of the Nation*. Another large noncommercial network is American Public Media (APM), which distributes such well-known programs as *Marketplace*, *On Being*, and *Prairie Home Companion*. Because noncommercial networks are prohibited from soliciting advertisements, these networks help defray their costs by getting foundations or companies to support a program in return for being mentioned on the air, as well as by charging a fee to their affiliated stations. Foundations and companies are attracted by the chance to parade their names in front of the typically well-educated, prosperous, and influential audiences that NPR and APM deliver.

barter
practice in which a syndicator provides the radio program and keeps a number of minutes for the sale of commercials to advertisers

THINKING ABOUT MEDIA LITERACY

Think about the large radio corporations, for example, iHeartMedia. If you were a radio executive, why is the ownership of hundreds of stations across the country a wise business decision? If you were a radio industry critic, what would your argument be against this type of widespread ownership by one corporation?

Exhibition in the Radio Industry

From the standpoint of the radio station's owner, the purpose of producing a format and/or buying one from a distributor (a network) is to make money at the exhibition point—the moment at which the format is actually broadcast from the station.

Advertising's Role in Radio Exhibition

For the general manager and the program director, the success or failure of their product depends on whether the station's sales team can sell enough advertising to bring the station adequate profits. Four kinds of advertising come into radio stations:

- Local advertising
- National spot advertising
- Network advertising
- Digital advertising

In **local advertising**, airtime is purchased from a local station by local advertisers (a neighborhood car dealership, for example). In **national spot advertising**, local time is bought by national advertisers or their representatives (Ford or American Airlines, for example). The word "spot" distinguishes this kind of sponsorship from **network advertising**, in which sponsors (perhaps also Ford and American Airlines) purchase airtime not from the station but from a network that serves the station. National advertisers use spots to target certain cities with particular ads. Buying network ads is often more efficient when the aim is to reach a particular radio audience across the country. According to the research firm SNL Kagan, local advertising made up 59 percent ($10.3 billion) of the $17.6 billion in revenue that radio stations brought in during 2017.[16]

Whereas 14 percent ($2.5 billion) came from national spots, 10.7 percent ($1.1 billion) came from network advertising during that year. A bit more—also around 10 percent ($1.3 billion)—came from digital advertising, a relatively new income stream for radio. Digital advertising includes all revenue coming from the radio station's website or app. That may include money from selling ads on the site as well as from audio ads amidst music streaming from the site. It may also include e-commerce sales by various stations. That leads us to consider the money brought in through what industry practitioners call off-air revenue. The term stands for revenue generated from businesses in the physical world that radio stations have been building. These include running live concerts that attract stations' listeners and that make money through gate receipts, signage, concessions (hot dogs and drinks), sponsorships, and merchandising (for example, coffee mugs and T-shirts with the guest artist's— or radio station's—name on them). This revenue stream added up to a solid $2.4 billion in 2017, 14 percent of the total radio station revenue for the period.

From the numbers presented here, you can see that advertising purchased by local firms is especially critical; it made up 59 percent in 2017, according to Kagan. A radio station's local market represents advertising dollars that the station can collect from businesses in the area. To gain this revenue, the station's sales manager and staff must convince local businesses and organizations to advertise on the station.

The sales manager works with the traffic manager to coordinate the placement of commercials. The traffic manager ensures that advertisements are scheduled and broadcast correctly. For example, it is considered bad practice to schedule

local advertising
advertising money that comes from companies within listening range of the radio station

national spot advertising
form of advertising in which airtime is purchased from a local radio station by national advertisers or their representatives

network advertising
form of radio advertising in which national advertisers or their representatives purchase airtime not from local radio stations but from the network that serves the radio station

commercials from directly competing companies, say the local Pepsi and Coke distributors, right after each other.

Learning Who Listens

Advertisers need to be convinced that they will benefit from paying for time on a radio station. The most basic question they ask is, how many people are listening? Answering that question with certainty is nearly impossible. Newspaper and magazine companies can actually count the individual copies of the paper or magazine sold to people. For electronic media, however, the product being delivered is by definition untouchable; it is sent out free over the air. As a result, the people who choose to listen to the product must be counted. Because it is nearly impossible to ask all the people in a community what radio station they listened to this morning, radio stations pay research firms to ask this question of a sample of the population designed to represent the entire community.

Conducting Market Research to Determine Ratings

The largest firm that conducts radio audience measurement is Nielsen. The area in which Nielsen surveys people about a station is called the station's market. Des Moines, Iowa; Los Angeles, California; and Madison, Wisconsin, are radio markets of different sizes. On a regular basis, Nielsen selects a sample of listeners in more than 225 radio markets to participate in its survey. Nielsen then repeatedly tries to contact its selected sample. For example, say Nielsen reaches you at your home and asks you to participate. Given your interest in the mass media, you agree. The Nielsen representative asks you to fill out a diary listing all your radio listening for a week and then to return the diary online. The company pays you a token fee—usually a few dollars—for your participation.

The diary contains space for a week's worth of responses, and you fill it out every time you listen to the radio. You promptly submit it through the company's website at the end of the week. Nielsen says it uses the diary findings in twelve-week bunches to produce local ratings reports, which it delivers to client stations and advertisers quarterly or twice a year, depending on the market.

The firm now has an accurate survey, right? Not so fast. This technique of audience measurement has some drawbacks. First, the research firm may have had difficulty getting a random sample of everyone in the area to participate. For example, people such as college students or seasonal workers move frequently or are hard to find, so they are often underrepresented in the survey sample. In addition, evidence suggests that people with busy lifestyles are less likely to participate than those who have more time on their hands. Therefore, the assumption that the sample is representative of the community is often invalid.

In addition, many of the people who do make it into the survey drop out or fail to fill out the diary completely. Though Nielsen designs the diary to be taken with the participant throughout the day, many participants do not do so. So at the end of a day or week, these participants must try to remember their station choices and re-create their listening activity before they write it down in the diary. Even listeners who try to participate conscientiously may accidentally record incorrect information. If you are like many people, you sometimes jump between stations while you are in your car. Would you be able to record which ones you heard?

Recognizing these problems, Nielsen has rolled out a device called a **portable people meter (PPM)** for tracking radio listening both at home and on the street. At this

portable people meter (PPM)
Nielsen's electronic device for tracking radio listening both at home and on the street

point, the company is using it in forty-eight of the largest US markets—for example, New York, Philadelphia, Houston, and Cleveland—though it says it hopes to eventually replace the diary in all US markets. The PPM is a mobile phone–sized device that consumers wear throughout the day. It works by detecting identification codes that can be embedded in the audio portion of any transmission. The PPM can determine what consumers listen to on the radio; what they watch on broadcast, cable, and satellite TV; what media they stream on the internet; and what they hear in stores and entertainment venues. But this approach also has flaws. For example, the PPM may pick up radio stations' codes as the person carrying it is walking through a store, even if the person is not listening to their transmissions. There have also been cases where the audio codes for a particular station are not strong enough to be picked up by the PPM.

As radio stations have begun to stream their music online, Nielsen has developed a service called **streaming audio measurement**. It brings together data it collects from people's apps or web players (along with third-party information about those people) with data it gets from its diaries and PPMs. The result, Nielsen claims, is "seamless audio measurement that provides an integrated view of the audience, regardless of platform."[17]

Although it's likely no radio executive believes Nielsen data are fully accurate, most local stations and advertisers use the diary-based Nielsen rating results because they are the best available. When ratings are reported to subscribing stations, employees await the news with trepidation. Ratings are to station employees what report cards are to students: rows of raw numbers that summarize many months of effort. One **rating point** equals 1 percent of the population in a market. Because typically there are dozens of stations broadcasting in major markets, the ratings for individual stations are often quite small. Stations are considered successful if they manage to garner even four or five rating points. Yet the raw number is often not the only thing of interest to a radio advertiser. The extent to which the advertiser's target audience—in demographic and lifestyle terms—is cost-efficiently being reached is often more important. For example, a concert promoter may want to know which station in town attracts the greatest share of the young adult audience so that she can effectively buy advertising to attract a rock band's core audience.

Nielsen results give radio executives and advertisers information on such basic categories as listener gender, race, and age. These characteristics form the basis for discussions between a radio station's sales force and potential advertisers about the appropriateness of the station's target audience compared with those of other stations. To gather evidence about other audience characteristics that might also attract advertisers, many radio stations subscribe to Scarborough Research surveys. Nielsen-owned Scarborough conducts telephone surveys of a market's population and asks people questions about various aspects of their lives—from purchasing habits to hobbies to radio listening preferences. Radio stations' sales forces often link these data with Nielsen data. They then use the findings to try to convince certain local advertisers that their station can deliver the most appropriate audience. This doesn't always work, however, because Scarborough studies and others like them have their own drawbacks.

streaming audio measurement
brings together data it collects from people's apps or web players (along with third-party information about those people) with data it gets from its diaries and PPMs

rating point
one rating point equals 1 percent of the population in a market

Singer Shawn Mendes performs onstage at the iHeartRadio Music Festival in Las Vegas, Nevada. The annual music festival is promoted by the iHeartRadio network of more than 800 radio stations, offering contests for listeners to attend for free.

radio promotion
a radio contest or event in which
prizes are given out

Sometimes advertisers purchase time on a radio station primarily because they believe that the format is suitable for their product or message and because the sales staff has arranged to tie them to a **radio promotion** (a contest or event in which prizes are given out) that will both highlight the advertiser and result in concrete responses from listeners to the advertiser. Almost everyone knows of a radio station that has given away cash prizes, trips, or concert tickets. The prizes are geared toward the demographic and lifestyle categories of the listening population that the station's management wants to attract.

A station whose ratings are up will often try to raise its advertising rates to reflect its increased popularity. Some station employees may directly benefit from the ratings report because their salaries are tied to ratings. But the celebration cannot last too long because a new ratings report card is always being prepared. Most large radio markets, such as Chicago, are surveyed year-round by Nielsen.

THINKING ABOUT MEDIA LITERACY

Consider the methods used by the radio industry to track usage (diaries, PPM). As a listener, would you think these methods fairly track your usage? If you were a consultant to the radio industry, what advice would you give about how to track radio listenership?

When Stations Fare Poorly in the Ratings

When stations have fared poorly in the ratings, managers may institute immediate changes. Sometimes managers blame internal factors such as a poor choice of recorded music. They also may blame factors outside the station's control. For example, many music-intensive stations have poorer ratings during severe winters because listeners flock to competing news/talk stations for updates on school closings and icy roadways. In that case, a program director of a Top 40 station, for example, will recognize that the ratings fluctuation was due to unusual circumstances and may decide to make no changes in the hope that listeners will return to their normal habits with the approach of milder spring weather.

Often, however, poor ratings lead to personnel changes. A careful analysis of Nielsen data may indicate that a particular time slot is not performing as well as the program director and station manager expected. In this case, the on-air personality during that period is likely to be replaced. When a station has a history of poor ratings and revenue performance, station owners might decide to try a new station format in an effort to grab a larger target audience and more advertisers. Overnight, a station that is known for playing classical music may start playing country tunes. With these wholesale makeovers, it is not unusual for all employees associated with the station's old format to lose their jobs.

Although management may consider it deadly to stick with an unprofitable format, instituting a new format on a radio station also has risks. Listeners of the old format are likely to feel abandoned and angry, and it may be tough to get the new target audience to find the station. Attempts to attract new listeners through publicity stunts and advertisements on billboards, on TV, and in newspapers can be quite expensive. And if the new format doesn't work, management may be in a worse situation than it was before the change. Nevertheless, the formats of certain stations do change fairly frequently; their managers believe that the benefits of responding to the shifting interests of audiences and advertisers outweigh the costs and risks of change.

Radio and the New Digital World

Radio executives today find themselves in a world fraught with far more problems than those posed by new format trends. The most obvious change is that after decades of revenue growth, the financial strength of the terrestrial radio industry has plummeted. Recall that in 2017, advertisers spent about $17.6 billion on terrestrial radio, including local, network spot, network, digital, and off-air revenues. That may sound like a lot, but it was far less than the $20.1 billion they spent in 2006. During the past few years radio revenues have been creeping up rather than going down. Note, though, that $3.6 billion of the 2017 amount came from digital sales and off-air revenues. These are sources of income that hardly existed in 2006, and they indicate that the traditional way radio stations make money—over-the-air advertising—has been decreasing even as radio stations' coffers are slowly increasing every year.

As noted earlier, radio station executives recognize that the drop in revenues reflects a realization by advertisers that the time audiences, especially young audiences, spend with radio is decreasing. The main reason for this decline is that many people have taken advantage of digital convergence to shift toward digital sources of music. They download songs from certain internet sites, listen to streaming songs from other sites, and share their favorites with friends. Others turn to satellite radio. Let's look at each area.

Satellite Radio

Satellite radio is a technology through which a consumer can receive streaming channels of music and/or talk through a special receiver (see Figure 11.7). Even though it is connected to the word "radio," the activity has little to do with the technology of broadcasting as it developed over the past century. In 2008 the two competing players in the satellite radio market, Sirius and XM, merged to become SiriusXM Radio. SiriusXM makes money from subscriptions (which cost about $20 a month, though many people who buy new cars get promotional rates for a year or two), as well as through advertising on some of the hundreds of channels it offers that feature a wide variety of formats. SiriusXM produces the programs, sometimes in joint ventures with other firms. (The 24/7 "Business Radio on SiriusXM," for example, is produced by the University of Pennsylvania's Wharton School.) The channels are uploaded to satellites and can be picked up in most places around the country by receivers sold at stores such as Best Buy. In addition, SiriusXM has made deals with major car companies to offer their receivers as original equipment. Some of the equipment is portable, making it possible to listen at home and while outdoors, as well as in the car.

In the years leading up to the merger of Sirius and XM, observers worried that the combination could create a behemoth that would set prices and squeeze consumers. Yet by the start of 2018, SiriusXM had 32.7 million subscribers[18]—not a small number, but not the large proportion of the population that some had predicted. The company was trying some creative new approaches to gain adherents, including "family-friendly" packages that would allow a family with more than one car to pay less than the full price for two subscriptions. SiriusXM also streams its channels

1. SiriusXM produces live and taped programming, ranging broadly from Alanis Morissette to sports and news.

2. The programming is beamed to satellites from dishes operated by each company.

3. The satellites broadcast the signal back to Earth, where it's picked up directly by receiver units. The signal is also received and rebroadcast by repeater stations in metropolitan areas. SiriusXM uses three satellites, two of which are always over the country.

4. A receiver buffers the broadcast for a few seconds, so if it loses the satellite signal it can use one from a repeater station, helping ensure a continuous broadcast. Overpasses and tall buildings are particular problems.

Figure 11.7
How satellite radio works.

GLOBAL MEDIA TODAY & CULTURE

TENCENT MUSIC

Do you regularly listen to any radio networks? Is this your preferred way to listen to music? Or are you subscribing to new music platforms such as Spotify or Pandora? If you do, you might have heard of a company in the streaming music services market competing with the two leading platforms just mentioned: *Tencent Music*. It is a Chinese-based corporation, whose daily number of users is estimated in the hundreds of million. Just like the old radio stations, it provides access to music having reached deals with all the major record labels. Unlike the free analog radio networks, however, it charges listeners to have access to its music catalog, and in addition it offers features made available in the new digital environment, such as social entertainment services comprising, for example, online karaoke.

It is part of a large Chinese conglomerate with operations in different internet-based businesses, such as online payment platforms (Tenpay), social networks (Qzone), instant messaging (QQ), and interactive services (Weixin/WeChat). They are also active in media entertainment, as online game developers and operators, and in particular in animation and sports, and they manage an internet radio app as well (Nextradio). In China they dominate the domestic market with exclusive deals with the leading international record conglomerates, and they are proposing new ways to access what used to be offered by the radio networks operating in the old analog landscape, adding new digital interactive features while combining music and social media.

online for subscribers who pay extra for that; nonsubscribers can also listen to some channels online. Radio industry analysts now believe that although satellite radio may have an enduring role to play in the US media system, it is not a fundamental threat to broadcast radio. SiriusXM executives probably also realized that they had to broaden their activities in the highly competitive digital environment. In late 2018 they announced their intention to buy Pandora for $3.5 billion. At the time Pandora claimed more than 70 million monthly listeners, both paid music streamers and those who received music in exchange for ads.[19]

Online Radio

Online radio could more appropriately be called **audio streaming** because it involves the flow of music or other audio signals to a computer via the packet-switching technologies that are at the core of the internet. As we noted earlier, unlike a song downloaded from the web, streaming music is not designed to be saved by the computer through which it is playing, unless a special recording device captures it and translates it into a saveable format (e.g., MP3). Thousands of websites offer streaming music. When they provide it, they pay royalty fees to rights organizations representing the publishers and artists. Many of these sites earn money when a listener clicks to buy a song from a digital music store linked to the site. Often the sites also make money through advertising. We can distinguish between two broad types: *streaming by category or interest* and *streaming on demand*.

audio streaming
practice in which an audio file is delivered to a computer-like device from a website so that it can be heard while it is coming into the device but cannot be saved or stored

Streaming by Category or Interest Companies that adopt this strategy offer music based around genres the listener chooses (e.g., rock, hip-hop, jazz) or around personalization, offering the specific types of music the listener seems to like. Personalization of music is a growing, if complex, activity. You may be familiar with the way the popular music streaming site Pandora carries out this activity. Pandora (which Sirius XM bought in 2019) describes itself as "a hand-curated listening experience that's uniquely yours." It supports itself through a "freemium" model: you can get it free, but you will receive ads. If you pay a monthly fee, the ads go away, and you will get higher-quality audio.

Pandora calls itself "hand-curated" because it attempts personalization by first systematically analyzing the musical tracks of songs ("melody, harmony, instrumentation, rhythm, vocals, lyrics . . . and more"). When you first use the site, it asks you to note a favorite artist, song, or genre, and Pandora's computers work to construct a flow of sounds (it actually has comedy tracks as well as music) that its formulas predict you will appreciate. People disagree on how well it works, and other streaming services are trying machine learning to accomplish this task. The service asks listeners to give its computer program feedback (thumbs up, thumbs down) to help the computer adjust the choices. If you find the personalization doesn't work, you can still turn to Pandora's genre stations and go with the flow.

Streaming on Demand Many listeners don't want computers choosing their streams. They want to pick individual tracks and albums by themselves. Pandora offers this option as Pandora Premium: for extra money per month, you can choose to stream any song or album, not just music genres. Spotify and Tidal offer this type of service as well.

Another form of streaming on demand involves music videos. Spotify has moved into this area. Also popular is VEVO, which is owned by Universal Music Group, Sony Music Entertainment, Abu Dhabi Media, and Google. VEVO describes itself as "the world's leading all-premium music video and entertainment platform." With "all-premium," VEVO is distinguishing itself from another streaming-on-demand music powerhouse, YouTube, which Google owns. Many artists have "official" YouTube channels where visitors will typically find music videos as well as fan-related paraphernalia. As it turns out, Google and VEVO have a strong relationship beyond just ownership. Google makes deals to place VEVO videos on many websites in exchange for being able to serve ads with the videos. Google and VEVO then share the advertising revenue. You can also find VEVO videos on YouTube.

Most online radio firms—whether they stream by category or on demand—allow listeners who pay for the service to receive it on a number of platforms, including laptops, desktops, smartphones, tablets, and some car audio systems. They also trumpet the ability of subscribers to share what they are hearing with friends. Spotify, for example, is equipped to feed your listening activity directly to your Facebook friends. (Spotify requires you to register via Facebook; you may or may not like this idea.) On-demand firms also allow people to save the lists of streams they have created. Say, for example, you are interested in movie scores in Marvel films. By clicking through Spotify you could create a list of music that, as a group, represents your understanding of Warner Bros. movie scores. You could then "publish" this list on Spotify so that any subscriber, by clicking on a link, could hear all the pieces you've strung together.

Traditional Radio's Responses to Digital Music

You may have noticed that the preceding examples given for online radio— streaming by category and streaming on demand—are services not owned by companies that own terrestrial radio companies. VEVO is a product of the recording industry's attempts to find ways to profit from convergence in the age of digital music. Google and Spotify are based solely in the internet world; Wall Street analysts call these businesses "pure-plays," indicating that they are not related to traditional (or "legacy") media.

But legacy media firms—in this case, terrestrial radio companies—are not asleep when it comes to digital competition. So far, they see satellite radio as only a minor annoyance to their business, but they know that online radio is a much bigger competitive force. One optimistic mantra that some radio executives repeat is that people like the "curation" function of traditional radio. That is, people rely on their favorite stations to tell them about new music. Then they go online to find those songs—to illegally download them or to legally stream or purchase them.

One way terrestrial radio companies have tried to keep people listening is by using what they call HD radio to multiply the number of stations they use for this curation function. **HD**, or **hybrid digital/analog radio**, is a system in which digital signals of AM and FM stations are sent along with the traditional analog station sounds on the same frequencies allocated to the analog stations. The technology was developed by the company iBiquity Digital in 1991 and was approved for use by the FCC in 2002. HD stations simulcast programs digitally, providing listeners with better audio quality than traditional radio, as well as side channels that allow for additional programming. HD radio programming is free, but people who want to listen must have a special receiver to get the signals. By 2018, 211 AM and 1,980 FM stations were broadcasting an HD radio signal. With car manufacturers including HD radio in their new cars, some in the industry see HD as part of the features they must use to convince listeners and advertisers to stay with them.

Yet as we have just seen, the idea that over-the-air radio—AM, FM, or HD—has a special function doesn't hold up. The internet's new music distribution and exhibition platforms perform many of the same functions that contemporary AM and FM stations do and are available when people want them. Online radio offers many vehicles for curation, including ways to learn what your friends are hearing when they are hearing it. Online radio outlets help guide listeners through the thicket of songs that they feel they should know about or might want to learn about. In fact, internet radio sites often present a lot of information about the music they are playing, including biographies of the artists and discographies (i.e., lists of the records they have put out).

The one advantage that broadcast radio has retained is its presence in virtually all automobiles. Americans report that fully one-quarter of their music listening takes place in the car, and much of that is still captured by traditional radio stations. The relative lack of in-car competition may represent only short-term relief, however. With virtually all new cars connecting to mobile devices, it is increasingly the case that many people have the choice to stream sound virtually anywhere, including from behind the steering wheel.

Astute radio executives realize that the changes in music-listening habits we see are only beginning. They know that their revenue growth from programming is due

HD (hybrid digital/analog) radio a system in which digital signals of AM and FM stations are sent along with the traditional analog station sounds on the same frequencies allocated to the analog stations

not to their over-the-air ads but to their digital revenues. They are determined to find a way to join the online world rather than fight it. Therefore, broadcast radio executives are moving rapidly to work with internet radio. Just about every radio station's management realizes that it has to have a website. The site streams what the terrestrial radio station is playing, but it goes beyond that to engage the user with the personality that the station aims to project.

Consider the website of Power99FM, one of five iHeartMedia radio stations in Philadelphia. This station focuses on "hip hop and R&B," to quote the site. The website is filled with songs, music videos, and in-studio performances that reflect the radio station's theme. Listeners can go to the site to find out about the station's upcoming events (for example, "Jay Z and Beyoncé Pre-Show party at Xfinity Live") and contests (e.g., "Win Tickets to See Drake + Migos"). Surrounding all this content is a large promotional and advertising environment, with advertising for local and national companies. In addition, the site connects to iheartradio.com, iHeartMedia's platform for the websites of its 350+ stations. "Tell us all the genres you like," the site says. "We'll suggest stations just For You." It links to podcasts on a myriad of topics. And, working with the Napster streaming service, it offers a subscription deal that allows you to stream albums and individual songs.

The websites of stations owned by Entercom Radio, Citadel, and other firms have many of the same features as the iHeartMedia sites. In many ways, all these "radio" services, digital and terrestrial, offer people a way to find and organize music they want to hear. An odd but for some people useful extension of this approach is Last.FM, owned by CBS Interactive. It bills itself as a vehicle to help music lovers keep track of what they listen to, get new ideas for listening, and find music soulmates. The site pulls in music from services such as Spotify, Tidal, and Deezer. Its software follows the songs that individuals choose and uses their listening data and those of others "to organize and recommend music to people, [as well as] to create personalized music and event recommendations" for them. Like iHeartMedia's internet activities, advertising supports most of the service, though in some countries outside the United States, Germany, and the United Kingdom, it charges members a small amount per month. Unlike iHeartMedia, CBS clearly wants to make its internet service a stand-alone product. The parent company of CBS Interactive sold its radio division to Entercom in 2017 but kept Last.FM. CBS's decision to stay in this part of the audio business reflects views in and out of the radio industry that organizing music for people in ways that draw advertisers can take place through paths different from AM and FM radio.

You might expect that creating strategies to succeed with all these complex audio-media activities might make executives' heads spin. It's certainly a risky business in an uncertain business environment. Both Cumulus Media (in 2017) and iHeartMedia (in 2018) filed for Chapter 11 bankruptcy, a term named after a section of the US Bankruptcy code. That is when a business is unable to pay its debts, but rather than go out of business convinces the court to allow it to stay in operation while it reorganizes its operations and pays off at least some portion of what it owes its creditors. In IHeartMedia's case, reorganization meant creating a new structure where 94 percent of its stock went to its to major creditors, with the goal of paying them back in the long run through rising share values of the new firm. (Nonmajor creditors collectively received 5 percent of the company and shareholders of the old iHeartMedia had to contend with only 1 percent of the new one.)[20] Despite a tough revenue environment, in late 2018 iHeartRadio was claiming that its new plan was "moving along as anticipated."[21]

Media Ethics and the Construction of Radio Audiences

Our excursion through the radio business provides an opportunity to explore an issue that relates particularly to radio but also is relevant to many parts of the media system: the issue of how the industry "constructs" its audience. Recall from Chapter 3 that media companies construct audiences in the sense that they attach demographic, lifestyle, and psychographic labels to people based on research and then often act as if these labels reflect the truth about the people who read and hear their materials. The problem is that all attempts to describe who people are and what they want conflict with the reality that individuals are complex and that any descriptions of them will inevitably not provide a "full" picture even if the facts presented are correct. From a media-literate standpoint, the best way to look at audience research is to ask three questions:

- How do the methods used in audience research affect the kinds of facts collected about the people who use a medium?
- How do these facts, in turn, lead to certain ideas or pictures of those people?
- How do these ideas and pictures affect the extent to which, and the way in which, advertisers want to spend money to reach them?

These might not seem like questions that relate to media ethics, but they sometimes are. For example, research firms may use methods that underrepresent certain social groups. As a result, advertisers might not try to reach those groups, and so media firms might not try to create materials with them in mind. Just this sort of problem happened with Arbitron's PPM, which we discussed earlier. When the company rolled out the technology to replace the diary in a few cities during the mid-2000s, the ratings for stations programming to African Americans and Latinos dropped drastically. A station in Philadelphia changed its format away from certain African American sounds after the findings were released. But soon executives at stations targeting African American and Latino audiences began to complain that Arbitron had not included enough people with those characteristics in its PPM samples. This resulted in the ratings for their radio stations dropping drastically. There were angry protests, and an industry group called the Media Ratings Council threatened not to certify the PPMs in various cities if Arbitron didn't fix its samples. Arbitron executives agreed to make their panels more representative.

The Media Ratings Council does perform an important service for the advertising industry in making sure the sampling procedures of research firms meet statisticians' standards. In this case, the council's intervention helped keep certain formats alive for African American and Latino audiences in particular areas. But sometimes, even though the statistical approaches are acceptable, the very method of audience research and the very categories of questions asked of the audience may lead to findings that make claims that either overplay or underplay the medium's importance in society.

Take radio's use of diaries as an example. Apart from major cities, radio station ratings—and trends in radio listening—are still based on the sheets Nielsen asks individuals to fill out at certain times during the year. The chart requires participants to note the stations they listen to by the quarter hour. Radio executives readily admit that the diary is a highly flawed measurement. Because so much listening is carried out in a car, it is unlikely that most people fill out the diary as they are listening—that

Online radio and podcasts are ever-growing mediums, but 94 percent of Americans still tune in to a network-affiliated show every month, across age groups.[22]

is, while driving. Nielsen considers that most people fill them out at the end of the listening day or even a few days afterward. It's likely that people write down only the stations that they typically like. Yet most claims about radio station ratings, about time spent listening, and about radio's popularity in society come from those ratings.

Compared to the diary, the introduction of the PPM created an entirely different sense about how people listened to radio. Nielsen found, for example, that individuals with PPMs listened to more stations—and for a shorter time per station—than people who wrote diaries. Were the people different, or did the methods determine the results? It's quite likely the different methods led to the different findings. In fact, the PPM has its own built-in bias toward reporting that people tune in to more stations than they actually care to hear. It works by picking up a special coded sound that indicates a specific radio station to the PPM. That may lead to the PPM indicating a person carrying it has listened to a station even though the person merely passed by a place where the station was playing. The opposite problem also sometimes occurs: People with the PPM may listen to a station that for technical reasons doesn't emit a strong-enough coded signal to register on the meter. In that situation, the station would get a lower audience than it should.

A final bit of radio ratings bias we'll mention has to do with the industry's definition of a quarter hour of listening. Nielsen tells diary participants that to put an entry in the diary that says they listened for a quarter hour (the minimum amount), they must have listened for at least five minutes. So a person who listens for five minutes at the top of the hour, for five minutes 20 minutes later, and for five minutes 10 minutes after that would check off listening in three quarter-hour boxes. Nielsen would report these fifteen total minutes as forty-five minutes spent with radio. This may not be a listening pattern that is common, but it underscores the flaw that the quarter hour injects into the system. Interestingly, with the PPM, Nielsen has minute-by-minute data but continues to use fifteen minutes as the minimum time period. When asked why, a Nielsen executive answered that the industry prefers that unit of measurement. One reason may be that it overstates radio listening in ways that help the radio stations that, after all, pay Nielsen for the service. (The Nielsen executive didn't disagree when the possibility was presented to her.)

All these activities that influence ratings affect the ideas that radio executives hold about how people use the medium, how long they spend with it, and the kinds of formats that will be successful in this environment. More broadly, they influence the "facts" about radio that industry officials present to the larger society—to policymakers, academics, and other citizens who are trying to make sense of how radio as a business fits into the new media world. To release data that claim, for example, that teenagers and young people still have high "time spent listening" to radio without placing enormous warnings around the findings (for people who don't know the methods that created the data) is ethically suspect. When told that, contrary to Nielsen data, many college students say in class that they hardly listen to radio for any length of time, a radio station executive in the same city responded that young people simply won't admit listening because radio is not a cool medium.

Which listening pattern is correct—what the students report in class or the radio ratings? This review of audience construction suggests the answer is far from clear. It's an issue to consider when you think about audience research in all media industries.

CHAPTER REVIEW

Visit the Companion Website at www.routledge.com/cw/turow for additional study tools and resources.

Key Terms

You can find the definitions to these key terms in the marginal glossary throughout this chapter. Test your knowledge of these terms with interactive flash cards on the *Media Today* Companion Website.

amplitude modulation (AM)
audio streaming
barter
billboards
burn music test
commercial stations
core audience
dead air
drive time
focus groups
format
format clock (format wheel)
format consultants

format networks
frequency modulation (FM)
fringe listeners
HD (hybrid digital/analog) radio
listening patterns
local advertising
music activity level
music sophistication
music style
music time period
narrowcasting
national spot advertising
network

network advertising
noncommercial stations
on-air talent
patent trust
playlist
portable people meter (PPM)
radio promotion
rating point
streaming audio
streaming audio measurement
syndicator

Questions for Discussion and Critical Thinking

1. According to the 2018 Nielsen report "Audio Today: How America Listens," "data comparing adults 18+, AM/FM radio continues to reach more people each week than any other medium in the U.S. at 228.5 million consumers, compared with 216.5 million for TV (live, DVR and time-shifted), 203.8 million for app/web on a smartphone, and 127.6 million for video on a smartphone. Looking at the audio landscape, broadcast radio's weekly reach of 228.5 million also outpaces the 68.5 million for streaming audio, 35.7 million using satellite radio and 21.9 million consuming podcasts." Are you surprised by this? Why or why not?

2. Commercial radio relies, as do other media, on advertising to fund its ongoing operation. What methods do radio stations use to deliver targeted audiences to advertisers?

3. Prior to the 1996 Telecommunications Act, media companies were restricted from owning newspaper, television, and radio stations in the same market. After the act was passed and the caps on cross-media ownership were eliminated, there was a surge of media consolidation. Think about both the positive and the negative impacts of allowing one media company to own multiple media outlets in a community. What is the effect on media consumers? How does this help, or hurt, media businesses? How does this help, or hurt, advertisers?

4. In the chapter on the music industry the variety of ways in which music can be found and listened to were outlined. Where does radio fit into this music media environment? Can you make an argument for why it might be the most endangered of the media? What about an argument for why it is a strong and profitable medium?

Activity

There are many ways that the evolving digital environment has disrupted, and enhanced, media consumption. For this activity, consider two of these disruptions: social media engagement and "second screen" experience. The first presumes consumers want to engage with the media company and with each other. The second refers to the use of a media device to enhance the media experience the consumer is having on a different device. Think about your favorite radio station and explore how, or if, they are developing methods for providing social media and second screen engagement for their audience. What advice would you give them if you were asked to consult on how better to engage their audiences?

The Movie Industry

CHAPTER OBJECTIVES

1 Explain the history of movies in the United States and how it affects the industry today.

2 Analyze the production, distribution, and exhibition processes for theatrical motion pictures in the United States and recognize the major players in each realm.

3 Describe how movies are financed and how they make money through various exhibition arrangements.

4 Analyze the relationship between movie distributors and theaters.

5 Explain the impact of new technologies and globalization on the movie industry.

6 Consider the impact of American movie culture on world culture.

You may not see the movies as a place to go for a "date." (A lot of people say they don't really date anymore, anyway.) Still, the website wikiHow (to do anything) actually has an article called "How to Act on a Movie Date." It's been looked at over 660,000 times. "Movie dates," it begins, "are a great way to spend time together without the added pressure of making deep conversation. To make your date even more of a breeze, here are a few guidelines on how you should act as well as strategies for initiating kissing." The list that follows includes such helpful hints as "don't forget to brush your teeth" and "if you plan to kiss, you and your date might want to head to the back."

For dates or not, movie theaters still do attract teens and young adults in larger numbers than any other age group. But theatergoing is by no means limited to teens and young adults. Check out the Saturday and Sunday afternoon theater hordes around malls, and you'll see a lot of children and their parents. Married adults with older kids attend movie theaters fairly often, and senior citizens frequent early evening shows.

But movie theaters are just the beginning—or a stop along the way—of a march across media platforms that many movies take in the digital age. As we will see in the pages that follow, convergence has become a critical part of the movie industry. If you missed the theatrical showing of a film, you will probably be able to watch it on a multitude of digital windows, from pay-per-view on your big-screen TV to your smartphone.

It may seem odd that in the 21st century we talk about "movies" as a separate category of audiovisual experience—different, for example, from "television shows" and "videos"—even when we often don't see them in movie

> "The words 'Kiss Kiss Bang Bang'—which I saw on an Italian movie poster—are perhaps the briefest statement imaginable of the basic appeal of the movies."
>
> **PAULINE KAEL, MOVIE CRITIC**

theaters. The industry works hard to maintain this distinction even as it pushes convergence to the point where the theater is only the start of a movie's movement through the media system. To many in the audience, "the movies" means "Hollywood." Hollywood, in turn, represents a place and level of excitement and star power not to be matched by other audiovisual industries.

This chapter goes beyond the glitz and glamour of movies to sketch what popular media presentations of the industry rarely explain: how the motion picture industry actually works. What companies are involved in production, distribution, and exhibition? Where does the money come from to support these activities? To what extent is convergence changing the way motion picture executives do their jobs? To what extent is convergence changing the nature of "movies"? And how do executives try to keep the distinctiveness of movies in the age of audiovisual convergence?

To begin answering these questions, we have to first understand how the notion of "the movies" and Hollywood took hold in American society and in the American imagination. Our timeline and our themes begin with magicians in the late 18th century.

The Rise of Motion Pictures

Magicians were the master showmen of Europe and the United States in the 1800s. What most people in their audiences didn't know was how important projected images were in their acts. As early as the 1790s, magicians used slides to project mystical pictures onto smoke rising from canisters in their darkened theaters. This "magic lantern" presentation grew more sophisticated through the 1800s. It makes sense, then, that magicians were particularly interested in the experiments that inventors in the latter part of the century were conducting in creating and projecting moving pictures. All of these inventors' devices involved preparing a series of drawings of objects in which each drawing was slightly different from the one before it. When the drawings were made to move quickly (say, if they were pasted next to one another on the side of a revolving drum), it appeared to the viewer that the objects were moving.

While some inventors were trying to make still drawings appear to move, others were developing the same idea using photographic images. One particularly important figure was Eadweard Muybridge, who immigrated to the United States from England. In 1878, Leland Stanford, an entrepreneur, politician, and horse breeder, recruited Muybridge to settle a $25,000 bet that he had made; he had bet that all four feet of a galloping horse were sometimes off the ground at the same time. Muybridge set up twenty-four cameras close to one another at a racetrack to take photos as a horse ran by. Stanford got his money; the photographs showed all four feet off the ground.

If none of this sounds like the modern movie to you, welcome to historical theme 1. You might well have anticipated it from previous chapters:

1. The movies, as we know them, did not arrive in a flash as a result of one inventor's grand change.

"OK, but what does Muybridge have to do with movies?" you may ask. The answer is that Muybridge's work got inventors to think that motion picture photography might be possible. The next trick was to be able to take twenty-four photographs with one camera rather than with twenty-four different cameras. Explore the timeline (Figure 12.1), and you'll notice a succession of innovations by several people that led to what we today call the motion picture. It would be wrong to say that one person invented the movies. Thomas Edison played a large part in developing the motion-picture camera and projector, as the timeline shows, but so did his assistant William Dickson, as well as inventors Thomas Armat and C. Francis Jenkins, Louis and Auguste Lumière of France, and Robert Paul, a competitor in England.

These people and more struggled over the technology that pointed movies in a particular direction: reels of developed photographic film projected on a screen in front of large audiences. It didn't have to be that way. Edison initially conceived of making money from the motion picture by showing it in a small box that one person could peer inside for a nickel. The Lumière brothers explored a more lucrative path in 1894, demonstrating that popular interest could be whipped up, and lots of money could be, made by projecting movies to many people simultaneously. Edison came to accept this approach as well.

Both Thomas Edison and the Lumières saw the motion picture as a storytelling medium. Noteworthy early Lumière titles were *Workers Leaving the Lumière Factory*, *The Arrival of a Train at La Ciotat Station*, and *The Sprinkler Sprinkled*. Early Edison films included *The Kiss*, *Aunt Sallie's Wonderful Bustle*, *Automobile Parade*, and *An Artist's Dream*. But neither Edison nor the Lumières created their products by themselves from start to finish. They, and those who came after them, saw moviemaking as a collective activity. Individual innovators did emerge who had the creativity to guide collective storytelling in the new medium. Frenchman George Méliès; Americans Edwin S. Porter and D. W. Griffith; and Russians Sergei Eisenstein, Lev Kuleshov, and Dziga Vertov are among those who developed the styles of plotting, acting, and especially editing that defined what movies became for generations to come. As talented as these people were, they had to work with many others to complete their "photoplays."

THINKING ABOUT MEDIA LITERACY

Edison's nickelodeon allowed one person at a time to view the movie through a peephole. Eventually, projection onto large screens became the industry norm for showing movies to audiences. What spurred the industry's move from an individual experience to a large audience experience? Now, think about how many times you've watched a movie by yourself on your phone. How is that experience different from that of watching with a mass of people in a large movie theater?

1600s | **1800s** | **1875s** | **1900s**

Late 1600s: Magicians and other performers use the magic lantern, an early projection system, in shows.

Early 1800s: Inventors create devices that make still drawings appear to move.

1878: In California, photographer Eadweard Muybridge becomes the first successful photographer to capture motion, recording a galloping horse using multiple cameras.

1889–1891: Under the direction of his employer Thomas Edison, William Dickson invents a moving picture device called a Kinetoscope.

1894: Edison invites people to use Kinetoscopes for a fee in New York City.

1895: Louis and August Lumière patent a combination movie camera and projector.
1896: Edison buys the rights to a projector invented by Thomas Armat and Charles Francis Jenkins and calls it the Edison Vitascope.

Early 1900s: Popularity of movie theaters (nickelodeons) grows in the United States, particularly among immigrants.

1902: Georges Méliès produces *Le Voyage dans la Lune* (*A Trip to the Moon*), a silent movie that becomes the earliest example of science fiction in film.
1903: Edwin S. Porter produces *The Life of an American Fireman* and *The Great Train Robbery*.
1908: The Edison Company encourages formation of the Motion Picture Patents Company (MPPC) (also known as the Movie Trust, the Edison Trust, or simply the Trust).
1915: The US Supreme Court rules that the MPPC violates antitrust laws and must cease its activities.
1915: The US Supreme Court rules that movies are "entertainment" and so are not protected by the First Amendment's free speech guarantees.
1920s: Several of the major Hollywood production and distribution firms—MGM, Warner Bros., Paramount, and Twentieth Century Fox—also own (or are owned by) large theater chains.
1920s: The major Hollywood production and distribution firms—Paramount, MGM, Twentieth Century Fox, Warner Bros., Columbia, and Universal—develop the "studio system," which features long-term contracts for film stars, high production values, and centralized creative control by studios.

1922: The major studios form the Motion Picture Producers and Distributors of America.

Figure 12.1
Timeline of the movie industry.

If you go online to view movies associated with any of these artists or with the early movie companies such as Edison, Biograph, or Vitagraph, you will probably conclude that what you see has little to do with what you think of as movies today. The reason has to do with theme 2:

2. The movie as a medium of communication developed as a result of social, legal, and organizational responses to the technology during different periods.

1925s	**1950s**	**1975s**	**2010s**

1927: Warner Bros. studios risks a lot of money experimenting with sound in movies and releases *The Jazz Singer*.

1948: The U.S. Justice Department settles an antitrust suit against Paramount, Warner, MGM, RKO, and Fox. Called the Paramount Consent Decree (after the primary defendant in the case) the settlement forces the firms to split off their production and distribution divisions from the theaters where the films are exhibited. The agreement opens the major studios to competition with some independent production and distribution firms who now have access to theaters they could not enter when the major studios owned them.

Early 1950s: The major movie studios refuse to sell old movies to television or to make programs for TV.
1952: The US Supreme Court overturns its 1915 ruling and states that movies are entitled to First Amendment protection, marking the beginning of the decline of American film censorship.
1954: The Walt Disney movie studio sells a TV series, *Disneyland*, to the ABC television network.
1955: Warner Bros. becomes the first major movie studio to create an original series, *Cheyenne*, for a television network, ABC.
1960: 87% of US households own at least one television set, up considerably from just 9% of households in 1950.

1971: The video cassette recorder (VCR) is introduced.

1973: *Westworld* becomes the first feature film to use computer-generated imagery (CGI).
1970s and 1980s: The spread of cable television in American life creates a new venue for movies after their theatrical release.

1980s and 1990s: Warner Bros., Twentieth Century Fox, Paramount, Universal, and Columbia become part of major international multimedia conglomerates.
1994: The amount of box office money the US-based major studios receive from outside the US exceeds the amount they receive within the US for the first time.
1995: Pixar's *Toy Story* becomes the first computer-animated feature film.

Early 2000s: Documentary films rise in popularity as a commercial genre.
2009: Paramount releases *Avatar* in 3D, which becomes the highest-grossing film of all time, earning over $2.8 billion gross worldwide.

2012: Major studios Paramount and Universal Studios mark their 100th anniversary in the industry.
2015: *Jurassic World* sets a record for the biggest global box office weekend in history, pulling in $524.1 million in a single weekend.
2016: AMC Entertainment, owned by Dalian Wanda Group, acquires Carmike Cinemas. They now control one out of five US movie theaters.
2017: Domestic theater attendance fell to its lowest point since 1992, but global box office revenue is up.
2018: For the first time, streaming services Netflix and Amazon won Oscars for their productions.

Let's start with the social and organizational responses to the movie technology that the film pioneers developed. The technology allowed the creation of what were called "silent movies." It may seem obvious to say that films were called "silent" because they carried no sound. Actually, though, the film producers and exhibitors ensured that the viewing experience wasn't at all silent. Movie theaters hired musicians (individual piano players or even entire orchestras) to accompany the theater's presentation of a film. Some movie companies even sent musical scores to theaters exhibiting their silent films.

In telling stories without spoken dialogue, the film companies had to create ways to help the audience understand what was taking place. They inserted cards into the movies that explained the context and told viewers what people were saying. The music could also give clues as to the comedic or dramatic nature of a scene. To further emphasize the plot, actors often exaggerated their emotions to points beyond what we would consider reasonable today. Above all, the photoplay creators helped audiences know what was going on by drawing on historically popular genres of American storytelling. When movies told tales of the Wizard of Oz and Joan of Arc, many in the audience already knew what to expect. More generally, the genres of romance, adventure, and comedy had already been popular in prior media such as books and magazines. Silent movies built on that knowledge and familiarity.

Still, there were some in society who didn't like the stories that movie companies were telling in order to draw audiences. As the timeline testifies, public fears arose that the vivid nature of the new medium might lead some in the audience to copy immoral or illegal activities—how to rob a bank or how to immodestly consort with the opposite sex. These social responses to the movie companies' uses of the technologies shaped the way the companies used the medium. The Supreme Court's 1919 ruling that movies were not protected by the First Amendment to the Constitution encouraged states and even cities to censor films or to force their creators to edit them. The cost of coping with many different government-required edits of movies around the country led movie companies toward self-regulation. By the mid-1930s, creators' ideas of what an American movie could be were guided by a mixture of considerations that involved a sense of what large audiences would pay to see and what the social norms would allow.

Despite the importance of these pressures, the development of the movies—and of Americans' understanding of movies in their lives—did not develop primarily as a result of tensions with governments and advocacy groups around content. Rather, they developed as a result of power struggles among various companies for dominance over changing movie technologies and paths to the audience. This point ties directly to the third historical theme:

3. The movie industry developed and changed as a result of struggles to control its distribution channels to audiences.

The timeline charts the movement from the era in which the founding companies tried to control their industry through patents to the rise of firms that challenged them and, by 1920, replaced them. These new firms located most of their production facilities in the Los Angeles area, and the movie industry became identified with the community of Hollywood. Instead of controlling their business through technology patents, the five Hollywood "majors" (Metro-Goldwyn-Mayer, Warner Bros., Columbia, Twentieth Century Fox, and Universal) chose two broad methods for controlling competition and creating movies efficiently. One was vertical integration—the control of production, distribution, and exhibition. The most powerful studios not only made movies and distributed them but also owned the most important theaters in major cities. The studio system was the other method the majors used to control their industry. It involved the star system as well as A and B movie units. The **star system** was designed to find and cultivate actors under long-term contracts, with the intention of developing those actors into famous "stars" who would enhance the profitability of the studio's films. "**A" films** were expensively made productions featuring glamorous, highly paid stars; think of *Gone with the Wind*. **B" films** were made more quickly, with much smaller budgets. The Ma and Pa Kettle series of comedy movies from that era is an example.

The ability of the five major movie companies to create the audiovisual stories that most audiences watched at least weekly from the 1920s through the early 1950s gave them enormous cultural power. The studio system heralded the glitz, romance, drama, and adventures of the movies—and of the stars in the movies—so that "Hollywood" and "the movies" became synonymous with these qualities.

The movie industry has changed quite often. One critical pivot point was when the financially precarious Warner Bros. took the financial risk of experimenting with sound in movies. The hallmark film of this effort, 1927's *The Jazz Singer*, started a revolution in moviemaking. From that point onward, movies would be defined by the way sound—speech, audio effects, and music—worked together with action to make the moving pictures move audiences.

Keep going down the timeline, and you'll see more changes in the shape of the movie industry. With the Paramount Consent Decree of the late 1940s, the government forced the breakup of the vertical integration that gave just a few companies a grip over their industry. A few years later, the growing popularity of television drew audiences away from movie theaters and further eroded the power of the major studios. Movies changed from products that people saw regularly on a weekly or even twice-weekly basis to special events that the studios promoted as reasons to get out of the house. The "B" series pictures that had sustained Hollywood essentially left the theaters. But the movie companies did find a new home for the form: television.

Follow the timeline further, and you'll see how a stream of new technologies—cable television, the videocassette recorder, the DVD player, and the internet—posed new challenges for the industry. The movie industry today is far different from the industry of *The Jazz Singer* days or of the days that made the great films you can see on the TCM cable channel. Yet the industry has managed to keep its association with glitz, stars, and high-profile entertainment.

How does "Hollywood" work today? Let's find out.

star system
an operation designed to find and cultivate actors under long-term contracts, with the intention of developing those actors into famous "stars" who would enhance the profitability of the studio's films

A films
expensively made productions featuring glamorous, highly paid stars

B films
lower-budget films that were made quickly

Movie poster for *Gone with the Wind*, 1940.

An Overview of the Modern Motion Picture Industry

The most appropriate name for the enterprise that we're dealing with in this chapter is the theatrical motion picture industry, so called because the business is set up in such a way that much of its output (movies) initially goes to theaters. The great majority of **theatrical films** distributed in the United States appear in nontheatrical locations only *after* they have completed their runs in movie theaters in the United States and abroad. These movies are typically made available quite broadly. They are for rental or sale; shown in hotels, airplanes, and homes on pay-per-view systems; shown on cable, satellite, and broadcast TV; downloaded or streamed from the internet to computers, TV sets, and mobile phones; and more. The revenues that come from these nontheatrical activities can be substantial. Still, the term *the movie industry* continues to refer to the industry that produces films that will typically first be exhibited ("featured") in theaters.

According to the Motion Picture Association of America (MPAA), in 2017 North Americans (in the United States and Canada) purchased about 1.24 billion tickets to see theatrical films. The number of tickets sold has bounced around a bit during this decade, from highs of 1.34 billion in 2010 and 2013. Spending, though, has gone up fairly consistently from $10.6 billion in 2010's **box office receipts**—the sum of money taken in for admission. In 2017 North Americans spent $11.1 billion on movie tickets, at an average price of $8.97 per ticket. The average ticket price has gone up sharply over the past few years from $6.41 in 2005. That is principally because more and more people are paying more than the regular ticket price to see movies in 3D and widescreen IMAX. You might still feel that the $8.97 is low in comparison to what you pay to see a film, but keep in mind that this price includes discounts for senior citizens and children. Moreover, prices in some parts of the country are a good deal lower than those in other areas. In Times Square, New York City, for example, adult moviegoers typically pay $15 per person or more to see a non-3D, non-IMAX presentation of a new movie. Across the river in some parts of Queens or Brooklyn, the price might be a couple of dollars lower.

theatrical films
films created to be shown first in traditional movie theaters

box office receipts
the sum of money taken in for admission at movie theaters around the country

THINKING ABOUT MEDIA LITERACY

If ticket sales make up the smallest percentage of movie theaters' revenue, what sorts of activities and services are they providing to generate more income? Think about all of the things that happen at a movie theater now and make a list of the revenue-generating opportunities.

Going to the movies continues to be most common among young people. People 12 to 24 years old buy 23 percent of the tickets even though they make up only 17 percent of the nation's population. People aged 25 to 39 buy 26 percent of the tickets, which is five percentage points higher than their percentage in the population. In contrast, Americans aged 60 and older, who make up about 22 percent of the population, account for only 16 percent of tickets.[1]

From 2008 to 2017, between 557 and 777 movies a year made it to the approximately 40,000 movie screens in US theaters. The number of releases has gotten high in recent years; 2017 saw 777 releases, according to the MPAA. Executives tend to pay most attention to the movies that bring in more than $200 million at the US box office; they call such films **blockbusters**. There aren't very many

blockbusters
films that bring in more than $200 million at the US box office

blockbusters each year, but they tend to bring in a high percentage of the money that theatrical films as a whole make at the box office. In 2017 two movies made more than $500 million in US and Canadian theaters, nine films made between $200 and $500 million, and fourteen films brought in between $124 and $200 million. Together, the top ten movies of 2017 brought in $3.5 billion, which constituted about 32 percent of the total $11.1 billion at the domestic box office[2] (see Table 12.1 for the Top twenty-five films).

Table 12.1 Top Twenty-Five Films by US/Canada Box Office Earned in 2017

Rank	Title	Distributor	Box Office [USD MM]	Rating	3D
1	Star Wars: The Last Jedi*	Disney	517.2	PG13	✓
2	Beauty and the Beast	Disney	504.0	PG	✓
3	Wonder Woman	Warner Bros.	412.6	PG13	✓
4	Guardians of the Galaxy Vol. 2	Disney	398.8	PG13	✓
5	Spider-Man: Homecoming	Sony	334.2	PG13	✓
6	It	Warner Bros.	327.5	R	
7	Thor: Ragnarok*	Disney	311.2	PG13	✓
8	Despicable Me 3	Universal	264.6	PG	
9	Logan	20th Century Fox	226.3	R	
10	The Fate of the Furious	Universal	226.0	PG13	✓
11	Justice League*	Warner Bros.	225.5	PG13	✓
12	Dunkirk	Warner Bros.	188.4	PG13	
13	Coco*	Disney	179.8	PG	✓
14	The Lego Batman Movie	Warner Bros.	175.8	PG	✓
15	Get Out	Universal	175.7	R	
16	The Boss Baby	20th Century Fox	175.0	PG	✓
17	Pirate of the Caribbean: Dead Men Tell No Tales	Disney	172.6	PG13	✓
18	Kong: Skull Island	Warner Bros.	168.1	PG13	✓
19	Hidden Figures**	20th Century Fox	167.6	PG	
20	Jumanji: Welcome to the Jungle*	Sony	167.1	PG13	✓
21	Cars 3	Disney	152.9	G	✓
22	War for the Planet of the Apes	20th Century Fox	146.9	PG13	✓
23	Split	Universal	138.3	PG13	
24	Transformers: The Last Knight	Paramount	130.2	PG13	✓
25	Rogue One: A Star Wars Story**	Disney	123.9	PG13	✓

Source: "2017 Theatrical Home Entertainment Market Environment," MPAA, April 2018, www.mpaa.org/research-docs/2017-theatrical-home-entertainment-market-environment-theme-report/, accessed August 2, 2018

Source: Comscore—Box Office Essentials, CARA [Rating]

*Film still in theaters in 2018; total reflects box office earned from Jan. 1–Dec. 31, 2017

**Film released in theaters in 2016; total reflects box office earned from Jan. 1–Dec. 31, 2017

multiplex
a modern, air-conditioned building that houses between eight and fifteen screens and has the capacity to exhibit a number of different films at the same time

megaplex
a modern, air-conditioned building that houses sixteen or more screens and has the capacity to exhibit a number of different films at the same time

Movie executives pay attention to more than just US and Canadian theaters, though. What they call the "international" (that is, not North America) marketplace becomes crucial to making profits on movies. Around the world, moviegoing has been encouraged by the building of modern, air-conditioned **multiplexes**, or theaters with eight to fifteen screens, and **megaplexes**, or theaters with more than sixteen screens. As a result, box office receipts in the international sector have grown substantially faster than US box office revenues in recent years. Today, the dominant Hollywood movie firms are Warner Bros., Disney (which incorporated Twentieth Century Fox in 2018), Sony Pictures (Columbia), Paramount, and Universal. During 2017 these Hollywood studios (including Fox) took in $29.5 billion from international box office sales. That amounted to 72 percent of their global (US plus international) box office take.[3]

The decisions made in Hollywood radiate outward, influencing the films that people around the world see in their neighborhood theaters and on DVDs and TV sets. Consequently, a large part of the movie business focuses on getting films and people together in theaters. What does the "Hollywood" way of doing business look like? Let's start with production.

Production in the Motion Picture Industry

People tend to think that when they see the symbols for Disney, Universal Pictures, Warner Bros., Columbia, and Paramount at the start of films, this means that those companies produced the movies. In many cases, however, they didn't.

The Role of the Majors

the majors
the five most powerful companies in Hollywood because of their distribution power

The five companies that people most associate with Hollywood are called **the majors**, and they are the most powerful companies in the movie business. Despite their prominence and power, however, these firms create only a small fraction (often one-third or less) of the movies to which their names are attached. Their names appear on screen because of their role as distributors, but more often than not, the films have been produced by other companies. (Confusingly, the logos of some of those firms—say, Amblin or Relativity—also appear at the beginning of films.)

Distinguishing Between Production and Distribution

film production firms
companies involved in coming up with story ideas, finding scriptwriters, hiring the personnel needed to make the movie, and making sure the work is carried out on time and on budget

film distribution firms
companies responsible for finding theaters in which to show the movies around the world and for promoting the films to the public

The distinction between production and distribution in the movie industry is critical to understanding the film business. **Film production firms** are involved in coming up with story ideas, finding scriptwriters, hiring the personnel needed to make the movie, and making sure the work is carried out on time and on budget. **Film distribution firms**, in contrast, are responsible for finding theaters in which to show the movies around the world and for promoting the films to the public. Distribution firms often contribute money toward the production firms' costs of making the film.

When you see the phrase "a Universal release," for example, you should be aware that this does not necessarily mean that the company's studio arm has fully financed and produced the movie. Although the Universal studio does fully produce movies that its distribution division circulates to theaters, most of the films that it deals with as a distributor come from separate production firms. For example, Vertigo Entertainment and Amblin Entertainment produced and arranged funding for *The Turning*, which Universal released in early 2020.

The Role of Independent Producers

Why don't the majors produce all the movies they distribute? The reason is straightforward: for a distribution firm to maintain a strong relationship with theaters, it has to provide a strong roster of films to help fill theater seats. If a distributor offers theaters fewer than fifteen or twenty movies a year, theaters will not take the distributor seriously, and the distributor will not be an influential force in the movie industry. Yet movies are both very expensive and very risky to make. They typically cost tens of millions of dollars each, and many of them lose money. A firm such as Universal cannot afford to risk the amount of cash that would be required to fully fund many films. Consequently, Universal's own studio generates only five to ten films itself per year, and the company picks up the rest of its distribution roster from **independent producers**—that is, from production firms not owned by distributors.

Consider the 2007 movie *3:10 to Yuma*, which was released by the independent distributor Lionsgate. According to *Variety* it was mostly financed by its executive producer, Ryan Kavanaugh, and his company, Relativity Media, with Lionsgate acting as an investor of $42.5 million on the $87.5 million-plus project.[4] Relativity financed several other high-profile movies such as *The Fighter, Limitless*, and *Act of Valor*. The precariousness of this business revealed itself by 2014, when the firm reported that it owed more than twice the amount of money that it had as assets. The result was that Relativity reneged on debts (through a process called Chapter 11 bankruptcy) and went through major restructuring.

independent producers
production firms that are not owned by a distributor

The Process of Making a Movie

The process by which a movie goes from an idea in someone's head to a film that the distributor can ship to theaters is time consuming and expensive (see Figure 12.2). Production company executives will also say that overseeing the filming and editing of their movies is only a small part of what their company does. Other important steps involve getting the idea, getting the talent, and raising the money. Only after these steps have been performed can the activities involved in the actual making of the movie take place. Let's look briefly at each stage in this process.

Getting the Idea An idea for a movie can come from virtually anywhere. Producers have gotten ideas for movies from television shows, comic books, toys, short stories, and newspaper articles. Scriptwriters and books (including history books) have traditionally been the most common sources, however.

Scriptwriters are individuals who create plays for the movies, with scenes and dialogue. Their plot ideas often come to production firms via writers' **talent agents**—individuals who represent various creative personnel (e.g., actors, directors, authors, and screenwriters) and aim to link them with production firms in exchange for a percentage of the creators' revenues from the finished product. An agent's job is to gain a reputation around Hollywood for having good creative and business ideas so that when he or she knocks on a producer's door with a suggestion, the producer will listen. Agents try to learn what powerful executives think is popular and will be popular. They also know what kinds of films certain producers like to make.

An established writer's idea for a film will sometimes be only a few lines that go to the heart of the plot—for example, "A small wooden box arrives on the doorstep of a troubled married couple, who open it and become instantly wealthy. Little do they realize that opening the box also kills someone they do not know." The presentation of the idea to the producer is called a **pitch**. If the producer likes the idea

scriptwriters
individuals who create plays for the movies, with scenes and dialogue

talent agents
individuals who represent various creative personnel (e.g., actors, directors, authors, and screenwriters) and aim to link them with production firms in exchange for a percentage of the creators' revenues from the finished product

pitch
the initial presentation of a movie idea to a producer

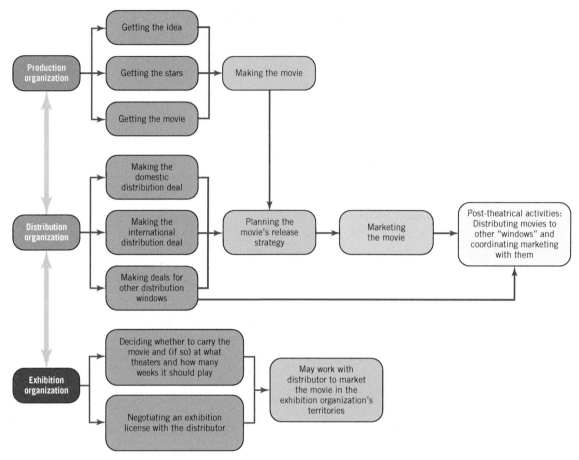

Figure 12.2
Producing a movie and releasing it to theaters.

treatment
detailed outline of an initial
pitch to executives of a
production or distribution firm;
if the executives approve of the
treatment, they will probably
order a script to be written

on spec
writing a script for a film without
a contract to do so, with the hope
that when the script is passed
along to various production firms
by the scriptwriter's agent, it will
be bid for and purchased

(the preceding example actually came from an episode of the classic TV series *The Twilight Zone*), the writer might be paid to write a detailed outline, which is called a **treatment**. If the producer likes the treatment, the next step might be payment for a full script. Less-established writers may write an entire script without getting paid, which is called writing a script **on spec**. The writer's agent will pass around a spec script to various production firms in the hope that they will bid for it. Attractive scripts can fetch hundreds of thousands of dollars or more, but most are never purchased. Even when they are purchased, the process of making them into a movie—if that happens—can take a long time. For example, J. J. Abrams and Billy Ray sold the script for the horror film *Overlord* to Paramount in 2007. The movie did not appear in theaters until late 2018.[5]

The second traditional source for film ideas—books—became especially popular in the late 1990s. Producers had long looked for successful books with stories that fit the types and budgets of films that they expected to make. Now they were furiously trying to beat one another to new books, or even books that had not yet been published, with stories that seemed to suggest a cinematic gold mine. *The Horse Whisperer* was an early example of the stampede to come. In 1994, while the book was still in manuscript form, the writer's agent orchestrated an auction of film rights that netted the author $3 million. The amounts involved in such purchases can go much higher than that. According to the trade magazine *Variety*, producer Dino de Laurentis plunked down $10 million in 1999 for film rights to Thomas Harris's sequel to the successful book and movie *Silence of the Lambs* before the sequel even hit the bookstores. This was a shrewd move—the movie that resulted from that investment, *Hannibal*, was a major hit of 2001. Books are still a healthy source of movie ideas. Think of the hit *Twilight* vampire series, which started as books; it was handled by an independent distributor, Summit Entertainment. Summit's success with these teen vampire films made it attractive to another large independent producer, Lionsgate, which bought it in 2012. That was right before the last installment of *Twilight*, and Lionsgate used the release to hype the first installment of its own teen series, *The Hunger Games*, in those theaters.

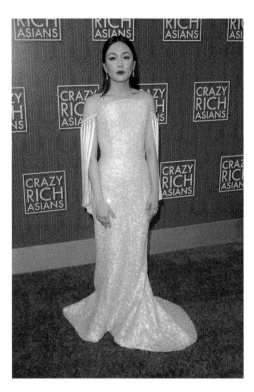

When top production executives approve the making of a movie, they green-light it. A project will have the chance of being given a **green light** only if it fits a movie production firm's ideas about what will succeed in the marketplace. Production company heads have ideas about segments of the market that it is useful to target with particular types of films. Teens and young adults, for example, are thought to like horror films (e.g., *Halloween*). Women are thought to like romantic comedies (e.g., *Second Act*, *Trainwreck*), whereas men are typed as preferring adventure movies (imagine *Fast & Furious 52*) or gross-out comedies (e.g., *The Hangover 2*, *Hot Tub Time Machine*). People over age 45 are often the targets for small-budget films (sometimes British-made) that have a subtle comedic or deeply dramatic sensibility. Think of *The Grand Budapest Hotel* or *Silver Linings Playbook*. Of course, many women and men attend the movies together, so executives often try to leaven movies targeted to one type of audience with some material that another type would like. An adventure film will often have a strong romantic component, for example.

Kevin Kwan's book *Crazy Rich Asians* saw huge success when it was adapted for the big screen in 2018. Constance Wu (in the photo) was among the stars.

green light
a term used to describe production and distribution executives' approval of the making of a particular film

The rising importance of the non-US market to Hollywood has meant that when executives green-light a film, they evaluate its potential around the world. Historically, most US-made comedies have not "traveled" well, so a budget for a comedy typically has to be low enough to be profitable from US revenues alone. Adventure films do tend to travel well, but they can be very expensive. As a result, action movies tend to emphasize violence and hair-raising stunts that usually require little knowledge of English to understand. Some of these films have been produced by a US firm (though often filmed elsewhere), and others have been coproductions that blend the investment and production talents of a US-based firm with those of a firm of another country.

China, in particular, is of interest to US producers and distributors, because of its huge population and growing theatergoing audience. Apart from the basic idea of integrating Chinese and American ideas to create stories attractive to both nations, Chinese regulations about whether and when movies from other countries can be shown theatrically make coproductions sound especially smart. The reason is that the Chinese government allows somewhat freer distribution and the ability for the US firm to enjoy a higher proportion of the box office revenue than when there is no partnership. Yet to get the distribution perks of a US–China production, the story has to have "considerable Chinese cultural elements," with a considerable proportion of Chinese staff as well. The meshing hasn't worked so far. *The Hollywood Reporter* noted in 2018 that

> despite many attempts, big and small, and seemingly endless industry panel discussions dedicated to the topic, there are virtually no U.S.-China co-productions

that have succeeded financially in both territories. The landscape is littered with examples of promising projects that faltered or failed. Remember *The Flowers of War?* Zhang Yimou's World War II period epic starring Christian Bale and Chinese star Ni Ni was a hit at home, grossing $95 million in China but wilted stateside, earning a mere $311,000. 2011's *Inseparable*, a mystery drama starring Kevin Spacey and Daniel Wu, didn't even secure a U.S. release. And Legendary Entertainment's *The Great Wall*, billed as the film that would usher in a new era of big-budget, mutually beneficial collaboration between Hollywood and Beijing, ended up a disaster for all concerned. After the pricey Yimou-directed tentpole [that is, expensive, blockbuster-style motion picture] starring Matt Damon bombed in North America and underwhelmed in China, losing at least $75 million [even including post-theatrical windows], the viability of such partnerships has never been more in doubt.[6]

It's safe to say, though, that US producers will continue to try scripts that could work in China, if only because of that market's size.

Getting the Talent When a production firm purchases a script or the right to use a book, its executives typically have certain actors and directors in mind. Sometimes, a major actor may get control of a property with the idea of starring in a film based on it. The actor's agent may go even further in dealing with production firms interested in the project: the agent may take a number of people from his or her roster of clients—actors, a well-known director, a highly regarded cinematographer—and tell production firms that the deal comes in a package. To many observers of the film industry, the fact that a number of talent agencies have the power to organize such major film deals with production firms is evidence that talent agencies are among Hollywood's most powerful players.

The money to pay actors and other creative personnel must, of course, come from the overall budget. The salary requirements of the most popular stars (some make more than $20 million a picture) mean that only the major studios and a few other production companies can afford to hire these stars. Sometimes a production firm will make a deal with a famous actor or director in which the actor or director takes a lower base salary but gets a percentage of the money that the production firm receives from the distributor—known as a **back-end deal** or **percentage of the gross**. Stars often negotiate variations on such deals to help their careers and help movies get made. For the 2008 Warner Bros. comedy *Yes Man*, for example, Jim Carrey gave up his up-front salary (usually $22 million) to become a one-third investor in the film. He also agreed to start receiving a back-end percentage only once the studio recouped the $53 million Warner said the film cost. The deal paid off handsomely. *Yes Man* grossed about $223 million worldwide. Especially with later non-theatrical revenues, Carrey stood to earn more than his regular salary.[7]

Some industry insiders have suggested that the high salaries stars are demanding are leading producers to hold off on hiring established, experienced actors in secondary roles in favor of more affordable relative newcomers. Rules about actors' minimum pay and working conditions have been established through deals between the Screen Actors Guild and the major production firms. Similar arrangements for screenwriters have been made by the Writers Guild of America. These **guilds** are unions established by writers, directors, actors, and other crew members to protect their mutual interests and maintain standards.

back-end deal (percentage of the gross)
a deal in which a production firm convinces a famous actor or director to take a lower salary in exchange for getting a percentage of the money that the production firm receives from the distributor

guilds
unions established by writers, directors, actors, and other crew members to protect their mutual interests and maintain standards

The guilds provide less highly paid workers with a collective voice. Sometimes that results in a strike. This happened in 2007 and 2008, when the Writers Guild of America could not come to terms with the Alliance of Motion Picture and Television Producers about how much pay the writers should receive from the major studios for work that appears on the internet. The strike of more than 10,000 Writers Guild members crippled Hollywood. It ended production on TV dramas and comedies, caused the Golden Globe Awards to be canceled, and delayed a number of movie productions.

Getting the Money Getting a well-known actor to agree to play the lead in a movie can help a production firm get the cash it needs to make the film. Getting the money is often the hardest part of making a motion picture. The amount it costs to make a movie varies, from way more than $100 million dollars (for movies such as *Fate of the Furious*, *Black Panther*, and *Wonder Woman*) to between $50 and $100 million (*War Room*, *Get Out*, *The Greatest Showman*) to less than $50 million (*It*, *Creed*). The word in Hollywood is that it is the most expensive movies that tend to become mega-hits. Still, a moderately inexpensive film can also reap great benefits for its production firm. *The Gallows*, a 2015 film, cost about $100,000 to make. In the United States alone, it brought in $23 million in box office returns, and its global gross hit about $43 million.[8]

A film's budget isn't typically created based on the producer's calculations of what is necessary to tell the story. Instead, a story is often chosen and developed to fit the budget that executives of a production firm can manage. Consequently, a production firm's executives decide what kinds of monetary risks they want to take (or can take). They then go about choosing a story—or tailoring one—to fit the budget they have. Take, as an example, the 2008 Cloverfield horror brand. Bad Robot, the production firm, doesn't make only horror films. Still, founder J. J. Abrams and Paramount Pictures, his distributor, saw something compelling in the story of six New Yorkers running away from a huge monster that attacks the city when they are having a party in which one of them is due to leave for Japan. When *Cloverfield* did very well (its global box office was $171 million on a production budget of $25 million), Bad Robot and Paramount decided to pursue the genre by putting out films that didn't extend the plot or characters of *Cloverfield* but copied the same combination of dread and humor. Their work led to *10 Cloverfield Lane* in 2016 and *The Cloverfield Paradox* in 2018.[9]

When millions and millions of dollars are hanging in the balance, giving a film the green light is not easy. Not only must executives believe in the script, the director, and the stars but they also must have the money to make the film and a company to distribute it. If the production firm is part of a major studio, the chief executive officer of the studio typically discusses the proposed film with the production and distribution chiefs. Once the film and its budget are approved, the studio as a whole (encompassing both the production and distribution divisions) provides the money. It is the distribution division, however, that works to make the money back—and more—through a percentage of the box office receipts.

Independent firms have a harder time than large studios getting the money to make a film. If the independent firm has had previous successes, it may be fortunate enough to have a multipicture distribution deal with a major that includes some financing. However, the independent may still have to use its own funds or funds borrowed from banks to make up the rest of the film's budget. The banks, of course, are hoping that the movie will make back its costs for the production firm so that they can retrieve their money with interest.

The most consistently successful independent production outfits are so tightly linked to particular distributors that they are virtually extensions of the distribution firm's own output. When it was independent, the Pixar animation firm had a distribution deal with Disney. Pixar films became so important to Disney's slate that eventually Disney decided to buy the company. More recently, Morgan Creek Productions has had a steady output deal with Universal.

Production companies that don't have long-term deals with distributors have to work a lot harder to find cash and a distributor. Sometimes wealthy investors will put up the money in the hope that they will get lucky and the film will be a hit. Sometimes an independent production firm with a record of successes (a positive track record) will be able to convince a major bank to provide a revolving credit agreement for several pictures. When a production firm is seeking a loan for part of a film's budget, the loan will be easier to get if the production firm can show that an established star has been signed for the film and that an established distribution firm has agreed to take it on and to advance it money.

distribution rights
the rights to circulate a particular movie in different parts of the world

A popular way for independent producers to get the money for film projects is to sell **distribution rights**: the rights to circulate a particular movie in different parts of the world. For example, a production firm's executives might get $2 million from an Asian firm that wants the rights to distribute the film to theaters (and perhaps home video rights) in Southeast Asia. Another distributor may bid $2 million for distribution rights in Australia and New Zealand. A third distributor might buy North American theatrical and home video rights. By accumulating these territory deals, often before the film is fully made, the production firm can show banks that a substantial portion of the film's budget is already in hand. Through the internet Movie Database, you can check out the many regional distributors involved in circulating (and financing) *The Wrestler*, a 2008 release produced by Wild Bunch, Protozoa Pictures, and Saturn Films.[10] The film turned out to be a hit in many territories. That kind of financing, however, is a difficult puzzle to put together, and in the late 2000s the economic downturn and the popularity of local films in different regions of the world made it quite difficult for independent production firms to gather substantial parts of their budgets from international sales.

Getting to the Actual Making of the Movie As you can see, a lot of work has to be done on a movie project before the actual moviemaking even begins. The moviemaking process involves a large number of people with widely different talents. To get an idea of how many people are involved, first take a look at Figure 12.3. Then watch all the credits at the end of the next movie you attend. Alternatively, look up any movie on a site such as the internet Movie Database and look at the cast and crew listings. Pay particular attention to the different jobs that are involved. Experienced personnel scout locations for certain scenes in the movie and try to minimize problems that might occur while filming there. Casting directors help the director choose many of the actors. Set designers, production designers, costume designers, makeup experts, and computer graphics personnel help create the physical shape of the space in which the actors work. Stand-ins and stunt people help actors with boring or dangerous parts of the work. The cinematographer and the film crew create the look of the film as it will appear on screen. Recording engineers make sure the sounds of the movie are appropriate (much of the dialogue will have to be re-recorded in a studio for clarity). A wide variety of personnel handle the equipment, the soundstage work, the salaries, the food, and all the other duties connected with a large project. The editor decides (usually with the director) which versions ("shots") of different scenes should end up in the final version of the film.

Because of the large number of resources involved, every extra day of filming can be an enormous drain on the production firm's budget. Keeping the production on

Understanding film and television credits

The reason film credits can be so long is that filmmaking draws on the efforts of numerous people over an extended period. The process of taking a film or television show from idea to audiences involves several key phases and a wide assortment of skills. Based on a typical live action film, following are a few examples of workers involved in a film. Many of these workers are involved on all or multiple phases of the production.

1. DEVELOPMENT
Coming up with an idea, writing a script, and pitching it.

Agents	Business managers	Investors	Personal assistants	Screenwriters
Assistants to the producers	Consultants	Lawyers	Producers	Studio executives
	Executive producers	Line producers	Publicists	

2. PREPRODUCTION
Developing, planning, and visualizing the idea. Preparing a budget, hiring crew members, and making a schedule.

Art department assistants	Choreographers	Costume supervisors	Location assistants	Props masters
Art department coordinators	Concept artists	Costumers	Location managers	Set decorators
Art directors	Construction coordinators	Dialogue coaches	Paint foremen	Set designers
Artists	Construction electricians	Directors	Production assistants	Set dressers
Assistant directors	Construction first aid	Directors' assistants	Production designers	Set staff assistants
Carpenters	Construction foremen	Directors of photography	Production managers	Storyboard artists
Casting directors	Construction grips	Financial executives	Props builders	Stunt coordinators
	Construction workers	Illustrators		Tailors/seamstresses
	Costume designers			Wardrobe

3. PRODUCTION
Shooting scenes, working with cast, locations, and reviewing footage.

Accounting clerks	Electricians	Payroll accountants	Property workers	Stills photographers
Actors	Extras	Picture car coordinators	Script supervisors	Stunt performers
Animal handlers	Extras casting coordinators	Picture car drivers	Set strike workers	Swing gang workers
Assistant accountants	First aid workers	Picture editors	Sound editors	Teachers/welfare workers
Assistant directors	Gaffers (lighting)	Production accountants	Sound technicians	Technical advisors
Boom operators	Grips (set operations)	Production coordinators	Special effects coordinators	Transportation coordinators
Camera loaders	Hair stylists	Production sound mixers	Special effects supervisors	Transportation captains
Camera operators	Makeup artists	Property masters	Special effects technicians	
Caterers	Office coordinators		Standby painters	
Cinematographers	On-set dressers			
Drivers				

4. POSTPRODUCTION
Editing the film, adding titles, music, and special effects.

Audio recording engineers	Dubbing editors	Film and video editors	Musicians	Special effects technicians
Composers	Editing room assistants	Lab technicians	Projectionists	
			Sound designers	

5. DISTRIBUTION
Taking the finished product and bringing it to theaters, home video, television, online, and other venues for audiences to see it.

Accountants	Distribution executives	Licensing executives	Partnership developers	Sales staff
Advertising executives	Financial managers	Marketers	Publicists	

Figure 12.3
Understanding film and TV credits.

line producer
the individual who makes sure
the equipment and personnel are
there when they are needed

completion bond companies
insurance companies that, for
a large fee, pay any costs that
exceed an agreed-upon amount
for a film

schedule is the role of the director, who controls the pace of filming, along with the **line producer**, who makes sure the equipment and personnel are there when they are needed. Some moneylenders, worried about spiraling costs, require production firms to hire **completion bond companies**. These are insurance companies that, for a large fee, will pay any costs that exceed an agreed-upon amount for a film. When a completion bond company signs on to a movie, especially one that is in danger of going over budget, it often sends its own executives to the sites where filming is taking place. By contract, those executives have the right to take control of some of the film's activities to keep it on budget.

Theatrical Distribution in the Movie Industry

When you're putting tens of millions of dollars into a movie, you want it to have a chance to reach the intended audience so that your firm can make its money back and hopefully turn a profit. As we've seen, helping a movie get that chance is the job of the distribution company. The most powerful companies in the movie business have distribution arms with a reputation of being able to place films in theaters in the United States and around the world. The major distribution firms have offices around the world, and the mandate for their personnel is twofold: to get the films they distribute into theaters and to market these films effectively to target audiences.

Finding Movies to Distribute

The first order of business for a distributor is to get movies to distribute. You might suspect that the major distributors would have it easy, given that they are linked to studios that create their own films. Certainly, they have a simpler time of it than independent distributors. Executives in those firms have to scour the world for the rights to films that will attract the audiences they know how to reach. But even the majors cannot afford to circulate only films that their studios make. They distribute several films from their own studio each year and get the rest from other places.

In rare instances, the majors have sometimes collaborated with each other to finance and distribute particularly expensive films in order to lower their risk of losing enormous amounts of money if those films fail. For example, Warner Bros. and Sony worked together to fund the 2009 movie *Terminator: Salvation*, which cost $200 million to produce, plus the cost of marketing. The deal was that Warner Bros. would distribute the movie in the United States, and Sony would have international distribution rights.[11] Because the firms expected the film would earn more outside the United States, Sony invested more money in the picture than Warner Bros. Sometimes the politics of the deal influence what firm distributes where. That happened with the 2016 movie *Central Intelligence*. The cost wasn't exorbitant; it ended up at around $50 million, plus marketing fees. What seems to have happened was that the script by Ike Barinholtz and David Stassen had been bought by Universal Pictures with the intention of making a buddy movie with Ed Helms and Will Ferrell, with Rawson Marshall Thurber (best known for the hit comedies *Dodgeball* and *We're the Millers*) selected to direct. But then Universal executives changed their mind and decided not to go ahead with the film. Thurber, unhappy, then convinced executives at New Line Cinema (a distribution arm of Warner Bros.) to buy the script from Universal.[12] New Line, it turned out, was looking for a possible buddy franchise. In

GLOBAL MEDIA TODAY & CULTURE

HOLLYWOOD, BOLLYWOOD, AND NOLLYWOOD

Hollywood is a district of Los Angeles, California. For more than a century it has become synonymous with the American movie industry, revolving around the Hollywood studios (of which only one, Paramount Pictures, is physically located in Hollywood, whereas the others are all headquartered in other districts and cities in Southern California). It successfully distributes feature-length motion pictures and TV series worldwide, and it has been leading the global entertainment landscape for decades.

Yet the global entertainment landscape is a mosaic of international players producing and distributing media content competing locally and globally, and Hollywood is not the only production and distribution hub in the international marketplace. For example, Bollywood and Nollywood release annually a larger number of feature-length motion pictures than Hollywood does. *Bollywood* is the nickname of the Indian movie industry, in particular, its Hindi cinema (combining the names of Bombay—the former name of the city of Mumbai—and Hollywood), and it has been producing for decades movies in its own distinctive style, oftentimes featuring dance and music. Similarly, *Nollywood* represents the Nigerian film industry, one of the most vibrant in the African context, annually distributing a large number of feature-length motion pictures, especially for the video-cassette home entertainment market.

Their distribution outside their respective regions, however, has not generated an interest on the part of international audiences comparable to Hollywood's productions. Why do you think Hollywood has a global appeal, more than Bollywood and Nollywood? Have you ever watched a movie from Bollywood or Nollywood, or any movie in a foreign language? If not, make a point to do it. It could be an illuminating experience.

the renegotiated deal, Warner Bros. become the film's domestic distributor through New Line, while Universal kept international. With the move, the film was recast; it now starred Dwayne Johnson and Kevin Hart.

Releasing Movies

Once a distributor has set its slate of motion pictures and these pictures are completed (or nearing completion), the challenge is to choose a release date and a release pattern. The **release date** is the day on which the film will open in theaters. In setting a film's release date and release pattern, executives take into consideration the kind of film it is, how popular its actors are, its target audience, and the other films on their slate. They also try to figure out when their competitors' movies will be released.

release date
date on which the film will open in theaters

Typically, executives schedule the release of potential blockbusters in the United States during the summer or between Thanksgiving and Christmas. These are periods when students are off from school and when many adults spend extra time with their families. Because different societies may have different moviegoing habits, a film's release date may be different around the world. In recent years, though, movie distributors have tended to release blockbuster films at the same time in many different countries—a practice known as a **day-and-date release**. Some executives believe that this practice discourages pirates from distributing the film online illegally because

day-and-date release
a simultaneous release date for a movie in different countries

every area gets the theatrical release at the same time. More important, perhaps, is the belief that new technologies allow distributors to efficiently promote a movie across the world at the same time.

Release Patterns In addition to the release date, distribution executives must agree on the pattern in which the movie will be released in theaters around the country. Two basic release patterns are now common in the United States:

- A **wide release**, the most common pattern, typically involves opening a film in more than 600 theaters simultaneously. **Saturation releases** involve opening the film in more than 2,000 theaters simultaneously. Putting a film in thousands of theaters beginning the same weekend is increasingly common because it creates hype for potential blockbusters around the country (and the world) at the same time. In 2018 Disney's *Ant-Man and the Wasp*, Sony's *Equalizer 2*, and Paramount's *Mission: Impossible—Fallout* all opened in wide or even saturation release.

- A **limited release** involves the initial distribution of a movie in far fewer theaters in a relatively small number of areas. Executives are likely to choose this approach for films that they feel have potentially wide appeal but that need time for media reviews and other discussions of the film to emerge and ignite interest among the target audience. They typically start with fewer than 600 screens. Their hope is to increase the number of theaters showing the film as the movie's popularity builds, thus encouraging the snowballing of attendance. In 2018 the independent distributor Bleeker Street released the drama *Disobedience* (starring Rachel Weisz and Rachel McAdams) in a US platform release.

Of course, the number of movie theaters available to show a film is also an important consideration in determining release dates and release patterns. Theater-chain executives have their own ideas about what pictures they want in what locations, and they negotiate with the distributors regarding what pictures they will take and for how long. By law, movie distributors are not allowed to force exhibitors to book blocks of their films—a practice known as **block booking**. Paramount, for example, is prohibited from telling the Regal Cinemas theater chain that it can have a particular film only if it takes three other motion pictures. Over the decades, though, the major distributors and the major theater chains have developed ways to accommodate each other's needs.

Marketing Movies

One reason that theater chains like dealing with the major distributors is that the majors have sophisticated marketing operations. To help reduce the risk of failure, distributors often conduct two types of research before a film is released. **Title testing** involves conducting interviews with filmgoers in shopping malls and other public places to determine the most alluring name for an upcoming picture. **Previewing** is a type of concept testing that takes place after a film is completed but before it is formally released: theatergoers see a preliminary (**rough cut**) version of a movie and answer survey questions about what they like or don't like about it, and the reactions may be used to re-edit parts of the film. The original sad ending of *Fatal Attraction*, for example, was changed to make it happier after it received negative audience reactions during previews.

---

wide release
the opening of a film in more than 600 theaters simultaneously, usually accompanied by a large publicity campaign to entice people to see the film; the most common release pattern in the United States

saturation release
the initial release of a film in more than 2,000 theaters simultaneously

limited release
the release of a film to only a handful of carefully selected theaters around the country

block booking
when movie distributors force exhibitors to book blocks of their films

title testing
conducting interviews with filmgoers in shopping malls and other public places to determine the most alluring name for an upcoming picture

previewing
a type of concept testing that takes place after a film is completed but before it is formally released

rough cut
a preliminary version of a movie

You are undoubtedly familiar with **publicity** and advertising for movies—this can take the form of lavish parties for a film's cast on the day of the movie's premiere, with the press in attendance; interviews with the film's actors on TV programs such as *The Late Show with Stephen Colbert* and *Entertainment Tonight*; previews of the film on YouTube and Facebook; comments posted about the film on Twitter; and free preview tickets given to college students before a film formally opens. The aim of publicity is to get favorable "buzz" going about the movie among its target audiences. The aim of advertising is to turn that buzz into actual moviegoing by telling people that the movie is playing near them and urging them to see it.

The flurry of publicity and advertising for a film is usually intense and short, taking place before and around the time the movie is released to the theaters. Although marketing can build anticipation among moviegoers, after the first weekend of its release, **word of mouth**—the discussions that people who see the movie have with their friends in person and on social media sites such as Facebook—determines whether more people will go to see it. The life of a film in theaters is no more than a few months. The greatest proportion of the money received from a film comes in during the first few weeks; in fact, executives believe that they can predict the total amount of money a movie will make by looking at how it does during that short period.

Distribution executives often order **tracking studies**—research on the public's awareness of and interest in a film—beginning two weeks before the film's release and continuing through the film's first month of release. Three times during each of those weeks, a company called National Research Group surveys a random sample of Americans by phone. National's operators read a list of current or soon-to-be-released films to people who say they have recently seen theatrical movies. For every film on the list, the people are asked if they are aware of it and if they want to see it. The film's marketers may use the results, which are broken down by age and gender categories, to determine whether revisions in their publicity, advertising, or even release plans are needed.

All this activity requires a lot of money. For major domestic releases in the early 21st century, marketing costs amounted to around half of the film's **negative cost**—the total cost of making and editing the movie. According to *Variety*, the negative cost of *3:10 to Yuma* came to roughly $178 million, to which distributor Lionsgate added $27.5 million for costs of actually distributing the film to theaters and marketing it to the public.[13] However, in the case of expensive films the majors hope will be global blockbusters, the cost of conducting advertising and publicity campaigns worldwide is so high that it comes close to the negative cost. Consider 2014's *Captain America: The Winter Soldier*. One reason you've probably heard of it even if you haven't seen it is that Disney, the distributor, spent $143.8 million to release and market it worldwide. Those charges add about 85 percent of the movie's negative cost, $170 million, to the cost of the film. 2014's *Transformers: Age of Extinction* wasn't that different. Paramount spent $210 million to make the film and $161.5 million (an additional 78 percent of the negative cost) to release and market it.[14]

Captain America and *Transformers* certainly brought in a lot of money from tickets in the wake of their 2014 releases. In *Captain America*'s case global box office was about $714.5 million. In the case of Optimus Prime and colleagues, the ticket take was around $1.1 billion. But not all the money made at the box office comes back to the distributor. Let's look at the exhibitor's side of the story.

publicity
the process of creating and maintaining favorable "buzz" about a movie among its target audiences

word of mouth
the discussions that people who see the movie have with their friends in person and on social media sites such as Facebook

tracking studies
research on the public's awareness of and interest in a film, beginning two weeks before the film's release and continuing through the film's first month of release

negative cost
the total cost of making and editing the movie

Theatrical Exhibition in the Motion Picture Industry

Just as a few major distributors control a large proportion of US theatrical activity, so the largest movie chains control a large percentage of the screens on which the films are shown. Recall that in 1948 the federal government and the major studios signed a settlement that prohibited the major film distributors (several of which are still majors today) from owning theaters. As a result, from the 1950s onward, large chains developed outside the ownership orbits of Hollywood moviemakers. The chains with the largest numbers of screens are AMC, Regal, Cinemark, Carmike, Cineplex Entertainment, and Marcus Theaters. According to the National Association of Theater Owners, these six companies control 56 percent of the 40,837 screens in the United States.

The Relationship Between Distributors and Theater Chains

Negotiations over what movies to choose and how much to pay have long been part of the relationship between exhibitors and distributors. Just as distributors have to set up a slate of films to show to the public, exhibitors must have pictures that will fill the seats of their theaters. Theater executives who book movies want popular films to come out on a schedule that allows the chains to maximize the use of their theaters on a year-round basis. This desire has created tensions with the major distributors, who have traditionally tried to release most of their films during the summer and during the Thanksgiving and Christmas vacation periods. Nevertheless, because distributors and exhibitors need each other, distributors try to adjust some of their release strategies to accommodate theaters' needs, and theaters try to help distributors get screens for hoped-for blockbusters during times of the year when every studio, it seems, wants to have a place in theaters.

The relationship typically works in the following way: A theater chain often has booking divisions in different areas of the United States, depending on where it concentrates its screens. AMC, for example, has three booking divisions—one handling the Northeast, one the South, and one the West. Each division has a number of **bookers**. Say you work as a booker for a chain of movie theaters in a particular region of the United States. Movie distributors inform you, months in advance, of what films they intend to release and when. That information allows you to begin thinking about the kinds of movies you might have in your theaters at different times of the year. As a particular film's release date gets closer, the distributor sends you publicity material about the film, and you also have the opportunity to see uncompleted versions. Based on this information and what you know about other movies that are coming out around the same time, you make an estimate of how well you believe the film will do at the box office compared with the others.

The distributor of the movie, for its part, has an interest in getting the movie into theaters that fit its sense of audience interest in the film. If the film will have a limited or exclusive release, the distributor will want to place it in locations where members of the film's target audience live. Executives may try to place a movie aimed at African American moviegoers, for example, in areas where many African Americans live. If distribution executives anticipate that a film will be a blockbuster, they will insist that an exhibitor that wants to carry the film place it in the largest theaters within its multiplexes. In areas where a couple of exhibition chains have competing theaters, the distributor may try to satisfy them all in order to keep its long-term business

bookers
people who license movies from distributors for theaters

relationships solid. The distributor may offer the film exclusively to one chain in one area and to another in another part of the neighborhood. Or it may offer one potential hit to one company and another potential hit to the other company.

Financial Agreements Between Distributors and Theater Chains Negotiations on the issues that are important to distributors and exhibitors may continue until just a few weeks before a movie's opening. Eventually, distribution and exhibition executives negotiate an **exhibition license** for each theater, specifying the date the distributor will make the picture available to the theater, the number of weeks the theater agrees to play the picture, and when and where competing theaters can show the same film. The exhibition license also sets the financial arrangements between the distributor and the theater chain. These arrangements take into consideration the distributor's huge expenditure on the film and the exhibitor's need to cover its costs and make a profit.

One common approach is for the distributor to take a certain percentage of the ticket revenues from the film, with the exhibitor keeping the rest. Another approach is the **percentage-above-the-nut approach**, which works in the following way: The executives of the theater chain and the distribution firm come together to agree on what it costs to operate each theater (electricity, salaries, rent, maintenance, and the like). That break-even point is called the nut. For each picture, the theater chain negotiates what percentage of the amount "above the nut" it will pay to the distributor. Typically, an exhibitor will return around 90 percent of ticket revenues above the nut to the distributor. That percentage may get lower several weeks into the run of a film. "Discount" theaters, which may show movies a few months after they were first released, typically pay a substantially lower percentage above the nut to the distributor.

In the end, distributors typically get back about half the box office receipts. As a general rule, the 50 percent that exhibitors get covers their costs, plus about 10 percent. Although a 10 percent return isn't bad, theaters typically make a lot more money than their cut of the admission take through their concessions—popcorn, soft drinks, candy, and other food. Big theater chains, such as AMC, fully control their concession operations and do not have to share the profits of these operations with other firms. Selling food can be quite a lucrative proposition, particularly in view of the high prices the chains charge. (Remember the last time you bought a soft drink at a movie?) An increasing number of theaters now sell pizza, nachos, and other non-candy foods. A small number offer even fancier meals.

exhibition license
an agreement between a distributor and an exhibition firm that specifies the date on which the distributor will make the film available to the exhibition firm's theaters, the number of weeks the theaters agree to run the film, and when and where competing theaters can show the same film; it also sets the financial arrangements between the distributor and the exhibition firm

percentage-above-the-nut approach
an agreement drawn between a distributor and an exhibition firm in which the executives of the exhibition firm and the distribution firm agree on the costs of operating each theater (electricity, salaries, rent, maintenance, and the like)—a break-even point called the nut; then, film by film, the distributor and the exhibition firm negotiate what percentage of revenues "above the nut" the exhibition firm will pay to the distribution firm

THINKING ABOUT MEDIA LITERACY

If you were a theater owner, which of the two financial arrangements do you think would be most lucrative—a percentage of ticket revenues or the "percentage-above-the-nut" approach? Would it make a difference if you knew the movie would be a blockbuster?

Digital Screens

In the not-too-distant past, every year distributors spent huge amounts of money sending films to theaters. This may sound like a very basic activity: placing reels of movie film in a box and shipping them to the theaters that will use them.

Distributors and theaters have collaborated on the tens of millions of dollars required to install state-of-the-art digital projectors on which to play 3D films.

digital cinema package (DCP)
a hard drive that's encrypted and shipped to a theater that has the password

satellite cinema package (SCP)
the theater downloads the movie from a satellite and then projects it onto a screen

Although the activity was basic, it was a monetary and logistical nightmare. Traditionally, for every film that went out in wide release, distributors had to make more than 2,000 separate film prints. Every film had to be shipped to a theater and then shipped back to the distributor. Many of the prints could be used again overseas, but the distributor still had to pay shipping costs. Moreover, international releases of many films increasingly took place at around the same time as North American releases, in part to take advantage of global marketing activities. That practice meant even greater expense for creating prints, given that the same prints cannot be used simultaneously.

To address this problem, distributors and theaters collaborated on the tens of millions of dollars required to install state-of-the-art digital projectors on which to play regular and 3D films. (In 2017 there were 16,978 digital 3D screens in the United States.)[15] As a result, in nearly all movie theaters in the United States and internationally negatives are no longer relevant. Instead, distributors deliver movies to theaters in one of two ways. The most common is via a **digital cinema package (DCP)**. That is a hard drive that's encrypted and shipped to a theater that has the password. Of growing importance is the **satellite cinema package (SCP).** The theater downloads the movie from a satellite and then projects it onto a screen. As a result, virtually all of the theatrical "screens" in the United States and Canada during 2018 used digital projection. To foil piracy attempts, the distributors send the digital copy in a code that can be deciphered only by particular theaters.

Convergence and Nontheatrical Distribution and Exhibition in the Motion Picture Industry

Theatrical distribution is the pad that launches a film into many other exhibition locations. The importance of theaters as a movie's first platform explains why distributors pay a lot of attention to marketing movies when they are first released to theaters and why distribution executives must maintain good relationships with their counterparts in the theater business. When it comes to deriving profits from motion pictures, though, nontheatrical platforms—also known as nontheatrical windows—are often crucial. Recall that distributors keep only about half the theatrical box office receipts. If a movie reaps $30 million, then, the distributor takes back about $15 million, and the production firm receives only a portion of that. When movie companies distribute their products through other windows, they often can keep far more than half of consumers' payments. That business fact is a powerful incentive for Hollywood to develop many "post-theatrical" windows for its products.

For more than half a century, the movie industry has made extra money by circulating its movies through television outlets—broadcast networks, local stations, and beginning in the mid-1970s, cable television. As the movie timeline notes, the introduction of videocassette recorders, or VCRs, in the 1970s started an entirely new way for the movie industry to profit from its products. For the first time, Hollywood could create a major market for films sold directly to the consumer. Children's films were particularly popular, as parents bought or rented films that had been hits in the theaters (and even some that hadn't been) to show to youngsters at home. The digital video disc (DVD) replaced the videocassette in the mid-1990s. The popularity of these home-video technologies led moviemakers to lean heavily on post-theatrical earnings through sell-through outlets and rental outlets. **Sell-through outlets** are stores in which consumers buy the videos rather than just renting them. Some stores, such as Target and Walmart, sell videos in physical locations, whereas others, such as Amazon, sell only online. **Rental outlets** are companies that purchase releases from movie distributors and then rent them to individual customers on a pay-per-day basis.

The traditional way to carry this out has been to go to a physical ("brick-and-mortar") store such as one in the Blockbuster chain. In recent years, physical rentals shifted to companies such as Netflix and Redbox. With Netflix, for example, a person signs up online and can receive and return DVDs by mail, with Netflix paying the postage. A newer model has been pioneered by Redbox. This company has made deals with stores such as 7-Eleven, McDonald's, and Barnes & Noble to place vending machines in or near the stores so that you can rent a DVD directly from the machine using a credit card. If you are looking for a particular film, you can go online to find out which Redbox machine in your area (if any) has it and then reserve it. After viewing, you can return the DVD to any Redbox.

With the increase in the percentage of Americans and others who have broadband connections at home, an increasing number of rentals are taking place through cable and satellite firms, as well as through companies such as Amazon and Apple. These rentals often allow the playing of the movie across several digital devices—for example, the TV, laptop, tablet, and phone. With respect to movies with limited theatrical release, rentals may be available within several weeks of their appearance in theaters. There have even been cases where movies that are still in limited theatrical release show up for rental by cable systems and/or Amazon. The distributor clearly wants to take advantage of the marketing and publicity for the film in the hope that people who can't get to the theater where those films are playing will decide to watch it at home.

sell-through outlets
stores in which consumers buy the videos rather than just renting them

rental outlets
companies that purchase releases from movie distributors and then rent them to individual customers on a pay-per-day basis

The Shift to Digital Marketing

If you've ever checked the time a movie starts on a movie exhibitor website (e.g., through Fandango or Moviefone), you are quite aware of movie companies' ability to use digital snippets from their products to vie for your attention. Ads often have movie promotional segments (trailers) embedded in them. Moreover, those exhibition sites, as well as many other places online (such as Rotten Tomatoes which is owned mostly by Comcast), use short movie segments to start conversations among visitors about the film and whether (or not) someone should go. Encouraging such discussions

can be a double-edged sword for a marketer because some people can trash the product. (In fact, Brett Ratner, director of the *Rush Hour* franchise, called Rotten Tomatoes "the destruction of our business.")[16] Nevertheless, as we have seen, word of mouth is critical for pushing people to see a film. Movie distributors consequently seed the web with small pieces of their movies in the goal of sparking great interest. They also hope that people will share and repost videos and that this will get target audiences engaged in and excited by the release.

Video games represent another growth area for digital segments of theatrical films. Many popular movies become the basis for video games and video-inspired toys, and those products often have elements of the movies digitally stitched into them. Take *The Lord of the Rings: The Battle for Middle Earth*. This is a game based on *The Lord of the Rings* film trilogy that uses short video clips from the movies as well as a number of voices of the film's actors. Not only can such clips help make the game feel more like the movie that spawned it, but they also may encourage people to rent or purchase the films.

The Shift to Online and Mobile Downloads

Shifting practices in renting and buying films also point to digital convergence. In recent years, sales and rentals of movie DVDs and cassettes have diminished substantially. A key challenge for the movie industry is to keep post-theatrical sales high, even as people have the ability to interact digitally with so many other offerings on their digital devices inside and outside the home. Moreover, when so many of these offerings are free or available at low cost (including music, some books, and many handheld games), the movie industry must often convince people to pay more for its product. Hollywood executives point with hope to what they think will replace those revenues—downloads and streaming.

A movie download takes place when a person pays a company (e.g., Apple, via Apple TV) to send a digital copy of a movie to his or her computer, digital TV set, or phone. The person then owns the movie, can replay it, and may (depending on the purchase terms) be able to move it to another device. A rented digital movie, by contrast, is streamed to your device but not permanently stored. If you view an "on-demand" movie through your cable company or Amazon, for example, you might be able to view the movie on your digital TV, laptop, tablet, or smartphone (depending on the technology you have), but after a certain amount of time, you will not be able to see it without paying another fee to stream it again.

By this point in the chapter, you undoubtedly have picked up on the idea that, in the words of the website Deadline Hollywood, "When it comes to evaluating the financial performance of top movies, it isn't about what a film grosses at the box office." Rather, "[t]he true tale is told when production budgets, P&A, talent participations and other costs collide with box office grosses, and ancillary revenues from VOD to DVD and TV." Take a look at Table 12.2. It's a hypothetical example of the revenues and costs of a successful blockbuster release for a major producer-distributor (that is, a major studio), modeled after an example from Deadline.com.[17] Note that although the movie made $766 million at the global box office (with China here as a separate category from "foreign" because of its increasing importance), the actual

Table 12.2 Total Film Revenue + Profit/Loss (in Millions)

Domestic Box Office	$219
Foreign Box Office	$445
China Box Office	$102
Global Box Office	$766
Domestic Theatrical/Nontheatrical Rental	$111
Foreign Theatrical Rental	$174
China Theatrical Rental	$26
Domestic Home Entertainment	$87
Foreign Home Entertainment	$111
Domestic PPV/VOD	$26
Domestic Pay TV	$19
Domestic Network TV	$22
Domestic Syndication	$3
Foreign Pre-Sales and Overages	—
Foreign TV	$84
Merchandise	$27
Total Revenues:	**$690**
Net Production Cost	$275
Domestic Releasing Costs	$97
Foreign Releasing Costs	$2
Domestic Home Entertainment Costs	$26
Foreign Home Entertainment Costs	$38
Interest	$41
Residuals and Off-the-Tops	$32
Participations	$12
Overhead	$28
Total Costs	**$551**
Studio Net Profit	**$139**
Cash on Cash Return (Revenue/Cost)	$1.25

money the studio gets back (shown as theatrical "rentals") is less because exhibitors take a substantial amount. The studio makes extra revenues from its home entertainment and other release windows. In the end, the profit, $139 million, isn't nearly as great as you might expect for a major movie that made $766 million at the global box office. What seems from afar to have been a huge global success turns out to be a nice 25 percent return on investment.

THINKING ABOUT MEDIA LITERACY

Look over Table 12.2. How do you think this detailing of where movie revenues come from might influence what movies are made or how casting decisions might be made?

But the chart doesn't necessarily tell all of the story. The reason is that the production costs and releasing costs might be hiding money that the studio paid to itself. For example, it is possible that the company considers the money for filming on soundstages and recording the music for the film to be production costs even though the production company paid some substantial part of those costs to the production division of the larger firm. It is very difficult to know exactly what happens with the financing of a film; people snipe about Hollywood bookkeeping. As in the movies themselves, things are not always what they appear to be.

The Problem of Piracy

film piracy
the unauthorized duplication of copyrighted films for profit

data locker
a website that rents secure password-protected areas to store files

Profits in the motion picture industry are continually threatened in the United States and around the world because of **film piracy**, or the unauthorized duplication of copyrighted films for profit. The activity is illegal under international copyright laws, but it is rampant around the world, even in countries that have signed those laws. You can see it pretty openly in many US cities, such as when street vendors are selling videos of films that are still in theaters. It is even easier to find pirated copies of movies on the internet, especially through **data locker** sites—that is, websites that rent secure password-protected areas to store files. Sometimes pirated copies are produced by someone taking a video camera into a theater to record the movie. In more sophisticated cases, pirates smuggle a movie out of the theater, copy it as a video master, and then return the original. In recent years, technologies sold under the names Dragon Box and Tickbox have given people the ability to stream Netflix, Hulu, and other premium channels without paying.

Consider the ethical responsibility of the users of these illegal downloads as well as the behavior of the pirates. The head of the MPAA, the organization that represents the major studios, argues that although "it is difficult to quantify the exact cost of piracy, we know the unauthorized distribution of stolen content undermines the entire creative economy. It threatens millions of jobs and makes it harder to recoup the investments required to produce new movies and TV shows."[18] Consequently, the MPAA has helped the industry mobilize resources against piracy. It has, for example, with worked an organization called the Alliance for Creativity and Entertainment (ACE), founded in 2017 by thirty major production firms to combat privacy. Among other activities, ACE launched legal actions against Dragon Box and Tickbox and got a federal court to stop them from helping people get unauthorized access to streaming audiovisual content. Federal and local law enforcement groups have been trying to combat piracy within the United States. On a global level, the US government, aware of the importance of the film industry to US exports, has been pressuring the governments of countries in which enforcement of copyright regulations is particularly problematic. In addition, the MPAA, the group that represents the major production and distribution companies, has hired detectives who roam the world trying to identify pirates.

THINKING ABOUT MEDIA LITERACY

Have you ever watched a "pirated" movie (We won't tell). What are your justifications for downloading a movie for free? What are the negatives for the movie company? What positives might there be for the company?

Media Ethics and the Motion Picture Industry

Despite its expensive and risky nature, moviemaking, in many ways, lies at the center of American popular culture. Not only are movies shown, but they are also discussed. Especially when movie companies first release films, huge waves of publicity blanket the mass media. It often becomes impossible to avoid hearing about certain movies. Moreover, movie stars and songs that come from movies are themselves major topics on television, in magazines, in newspapers, around the water cooler, in the lunchroom, and in media classes.

Some observers of popular culture look at movie companies' activities with dismay. They point out that many of these performances and discussions found across so many media in so many parts of the world are sparked by just a handful of corporations—the major movie distributors. Moreover, all the majors are tied to huge mass media conglomerates—AT&T (which owns Warner Bros), Disney (which owns Disney and Twentieth Century Fox), Viacom (which owns Paramount), Sony (which owns Columbia), and Comcast (which owns Universal). These conglomerates use their Hollywood assets as content for their holdings in different media industries around the world. Materials get packaged, sold, and hyped many times. In this way, even extremely expensive movies have a decent chance of making their money back over time, and blockbuster hits have a chance of making stratospheric sums.

Starting from this position, critics voice two types of concern. One relates to the narrowing of cultural diversity. A second involves what they call cultural colonialism. Let's look at each of these.

Cultural Diversity and Cultural Colonialism

The Narrowing of Cultural Diversity Critics of the mainstream movie industry argue that movie executives are sending a rather narrow range of stories into American theaters and homes. Many contemporary Hollywood movies, they argue, are made according to simplistic formulas that use sex and violence in ways designed to ignite the interest of the central moviegoing audience: 14- to 24-year-olds. Expensive films that can become blockbusters are the name of the game in Hollywood because they have the potential to travel across so many different media and make so much more money for the majors than small films ever will. But the major studios will not take artistic risks on such films because the stakes are so high. As a result, films that push the envelope and challenge the audience to see the world differently are few and far between.

art films
movies created on small budgets that often do not fit into Hollywood stereotypes and standard genres

Exhibitors also work against cultural diversity, say the critics. By cultural diversity, they mean a reflection of the broad differences that exist in and across societies. Overwhelmingly, they book movies that fit the typical Hollywood profile. Few theaters in the United States show so-called **art films**—movies created on small budgets that often do not fit into Hollywood stereotypes and standard genres. Even fewer theaters show foreign-language films, dubbed or with subtitles. The theater chains defend their choices by saying that Americans simply won't go to see these movies in numbers that justify booking them. The critics respond that the movie industry worked for decades to keep such films out of the mainstream in order to protect the standard Hollywood product, so it will take time, they say, for Americans to develop the habit of watching non–Hollywood-style films. The critics add that by not encouraging Americans to see movies made in other countries, the US movie industry is keeping Americans isolated from important aspects of world culture. We live in a time, they say, when business is global, and Americans—especially young people—need to be able to understand the viewpoints of other people. Watching other people's movies can help enormously in building that understanding. The US movie industry's activities are counterproductive in this regard, they say.

Movie industry defenders note that low-budget specialty pictures and foreign movies routinely win Academy Awards and other movie kudos and so enjoy the publicity that goes with those honors. They note that Americans who watch the awards show and read the publicity can easily find those films on Netflix, Amazon, and other digital movie repositories. The critics retort that that kind of attention is miniscule compared to the heavy-duty cross-platform promotions the blockbusters get. Even on Netflix and Amazon, international films rarely make it to the home page. The lack of attention, critics say, both reflects and reinforces the more general lack of attention to other types of movies.

Cultural Colonialism Another strong criticism traditionally lodged against the Hollywood movie industry is that it represents a leading edge of American cultural colonialism. As we noted in Chapter 4, cultural colonialism is the process by which the media content of a dominating society (in this case, the United States) surrounds people of another society with values and beliefs that are not those of their own society. Rather, the values and beliefs reflected in the content tend to support the interests of the dominating society.

As you can see, this cultural colonialism is in some ways a mirror image of the narrowing of cultural diversity. The concern over the lack of cultural diversity in movies argues that American society is being harmed. The concern about cultural colonialism, in contrast, argues that American-based companies are harming other cultures. They are doing this, the argument goes, by drowning out the presentation of local cultural experiences in the media with Hollywood-based formulas.

The critics point out that this cultural colonialism helps American business by creating markets for their consumer goods. Moviemaking in the United States is big business. (In fact, filmed entertainment of all sorts, for television and home video as well as the theaters, is one of America's top exports.) At the same time, critics say, it erodes local cultures because they can't compete with US marketing glitz.

One result of the US movie industry's focus on the international market in recent years has been the search by the majors for smaller, more literary movies that might connect with relatively cultivated audiences around the world that are older than the typical moviegoing public. The conglomerates have set up divisions such as Fox Searchlight and Sony Classics to handle these films. You might think that critics and producers in other countries would be happy about this development. The problem is that, so far, all but a few of the movies that these divisions and others have picked up have been English-language pictures from the United States, England, Australia, or New Zealand. Distribution executives point out in frustration that American audiences, still the largest moviegoing audiences, don't like to watch movies that have been dubbed or that have subtitles. As a result, even European film companies have been moving toward making films in English and then subtitling them for non–English-speaking lands. Americans are colonizing even the art film world, critics say.

The critics point to the majors' worldwide success as evidence that cultural colonialism is taking place. The international power of the majors, they say, has made US films dominant in the box offices of many countries around the world. True, several of the conglomerates that own the studios, such as Sony, are not American. Their filmmaking activity, however, is very much based in the United States and presents the US view of the world. Furthermore, critics add, the popularity of US movies is merely the tip of a huge iceberg. Under the guidance of powerful multimedia conglomerates, US theatrical products blanket all sorts of print and electronic media. US stars, for instance, are favorites the world over. And the US way of life shown in the movies—with its strong commercialism, lack of environmental sensitivity, and urge toward immediate gratification—becomes an attraction for young people throughout the world.

Not surprisingly, Hollywood's supporters reject this view of their role in global culture. They point out that Hollywood employs many workers as a result of the movie industry's global reach. They add that many countries support local filmmakers and encourage them to make movies that reflect their own societies. It is not the US movie industry's fault, they say, that people like Hollywood films more than those types of movies.

Hollywood's defenders also argue that people around the world like US movies because they are good stories filmed in a high-quality manner. They also say that it is patronizing to believe that people in other countries see the movies in the same way that American audiences see them. Rather, these audiences accept or reject what they see in movies from the vantage point of their own cultures. They may even understand the stories differently because they are coming at them with different cultural "eyes."

In recent years, defenders of Hollywood have added a new argument. They note that America's cultural power is not nearly as great as when critics introduced the "colonialism" argument. In fact, China, the world's largest movie market, has placed major barriers on US movie distribution. For example, Chinese regulations limit the number of films that can be brought into the country, place blackouts on exhibiting US films during key moviegoing periods (such as the summer), and block Netflix from operating. Moreover, the major movie production and distribution firms are increasingly sensitive to making films that will not alienate the Chinese government or Chinese audiences in the hope the industry can lower the barriers.

Despite China's new clout, arguments about Hollywood's world power and its reflection of American values are not likely to go away. They may, in fact, become louder as the huge costs of Hollywood moviemaking increasingly require the movie studios to push their content globally (mostly with time-tested action and violence genres) in ways that take advantage of digital convergence. Where do you stand on these developments, and why?

CHAPTER REVIEW

 Visit the Companion Website at www.routledge.com/cw/turow for additional study tools and resources.

 ## Key Terms

You can find the definitions to these key terms in the marginal glossary throughout this chapter. Test your knowledge of these terms with interactive flash cards on the *Media Today* Companion Website.

A films	film piracy	release date
art films	film production firms	rental outlets
B films	green light	rough cut
back-end deal (percentage of the gross)	guilds	satellite cinema package (SCP)
block booking	independent producers	saturation release
blockbusters	line producer	scriptwriters
bookers	the majors	sell-through outlets
box office receipts	megaplex	star system
completion bond companies	multiplex	talent agents
data locker	negative cost	theatrical films
day-and-date release	on spec	title testing
digital cinema package (DCP)	percentage-above-the-nut approach	tracking studies
distribution rights	pitch	treatment
exclusive release	platform release	wide release
exhibition license	previewing	word of mouth
film distribution firms	publicity	

Questions for Discussion and Critical Thinking

1. Movie reviews used to be just word of mouth among friends or from critics hired by newspapers and magazines. How has the access to "audience" reviews in sites like Rotten Tomatoes changed the craft of movie reviewing? As a movie consumer, how much influence do differently "credentialed" reviewers have on your viewing choices? How do you think the rise of access to audience reviews has changed how movies market themselves?

2. Disney's *The Lion King* was originally released in theaters in 1994. In 2002 it was re-released in IMAX and in 2011 in 3D. Moreover, in 2019, Disney released a live action version. Why does Disney involve itself in this "recycling" of a single movie—and the remaking of an animated film into a live action one? Why or why not would Disney do these things with its entire catalog? Think, too, about "anniversary" showings of old movies and remakes (think of the forty-year anniversary of the Halloween franchise). What are the reasons a movie studio might do this?

3. Reflect on the demographics about movie goers: "People 12 to 24 years old buy 23 percent of the tickets even though they make up only 17 percent of the nation's population. People aged 25 to 39 buy 26 percent of the tickets, which is five percentage point higher than their percentage in the population. In contrast, Americans aged 60 and older, who make up about 22 percent of the population, account for only 16 percent of tickets." If you were a consultant asked to explain this, what points would you make to help understand audience behaviors?

4. The technology to create movies in 3D was developed in the 1890s. The first 3D movie was shown in theaters in 1922. But it wasn't until the 1950s that a surge of 3D movies came to the local theater. The 3D "fad" faded, and it wasn't until the mid-1980s that 3D movies made a resurgence. Now, many blockbuster movies are exhibited with the option to view in 2D or 3D. What was happening in the 1950s that made 3D movies an attractive option for movie producers? Why do you think the fad faded? Why is there a resurgence now in 3D viewing?

Activity

The growing influence of the motion picture industry in the 1920s and 1930s raised concerns about movies' impact on the youth of America. In order to circumvent calls for the establishment of government-set standards, in the early 1930s movie industry leaders developed their own Motion Picture Production Code. It presented a detailed list of "Don'ts and Be Carefuls" that would uphold the code's three "General Principles":

No picture shall be produced that will lower the moral standards of those who see it. Hence the sympathy of the audience should never be thrown to the side of crime, wrongdoing, evil or sin.

Correct standards of life, subject only to the requirements of drama and entertainment, shall be presented.

Law, natural or human, shall not be ridiculed, nor shall sympathy be created for its violation.

Today's letter ratings for movies were established by the Motion Picture Association of America in 1968. The letters (G: General Audience, PG: Parental Guidance Suggested, PG-13: Parents Strongly Cautioned, R: Restricted, NC-17: No One 17 and Under Admitted) are further enhanced by detail about the nature of the content ("disturbing images," "drug use"). For this activity, consider the following questions:

1. What are the key differences between the approach taken by the 1930s code and the 1968 ratings?
2. List three recent movies you've seen. Look over the detailed list of "Don'ts and Be Carefuls" from the 1930s code (found on Wikipedia at en.wikipedia.org/wiki/Motion_Picture_Production_Code). Which specific items from the code might the movies you listed violate?
3. Now, look up in Rotten Tomatoes or IMDB the rating given the movies. Would you agree with the rating?
4. Reflect on how ratings affect the movie itself—is there an impact on the box office? How do ratings affect your choices as a consumer? If you are or were a parent, what role would industry ratings of movies play?
5. Finally, consider whether the youth of America needs to be protected. Why or why not? To what extent are codes or ratings good ways to do it? Why?

The Television Industry

13

CHAPTER OBJECTIVES

1   Compare and contrast broadcast, cable, satellite, and over-the-top (OTT) television.

2   Explain the role of advertisers in these four forms of television.

3   Name and describe the different types of cable, satellite, and OTT services.

4   Identify the ways in which broadcasters, cable, satellite, and OTT companies produce, distribute, and exhibit programming.

5   Describe the issues facing the TV industry and society in a rapidly changing TV world.

"Did you watch television last night?" That used to be a simple question. Either you turned on that electronic box in your home and viewed it, or you didn't. Today, though, the question can hold different meanings for different people. For some, watching TV will always be associated with viewing the box, so if they streamed *The Voice* or *Game of Thrones* on their laptop computer, their phone, or their tablet, they would say they "didn't watch TV." Others might well say that they viewed television even when they saw *The Voice* or another program on their laptop or phone—or as in-flight entertainment—rather than on their traditional television set.

This ability to get programs across platforms is, of course, the very definition of convergence. Many in the audience—and many TV program creators—are happy with the activity, when it's done legally. Yet convergence is creating major tensions within the television industry. As we will see, the whole idea of what television means and how programming should be produced, sponsored, distributed, and exhibited is up for grabs as the traditional ways clash with new approaches and technologies. This chapter explores the US television industry at a time of enormous change. It presents the basic building blocks for understanding how things are done now, how they are changing, why they may be changing even more in the decades ahead, and how they relate to the trends toward conglomeration and globalization—but also toward independently generated and circulated material—that that we have mentioned in previous chapters.

> "Even the greatest of films is a one-night stand, where a TV series is a relationship—between the creators and the characters, and then between the characters and the audience—that can last years, with changes both subtle and inescapable along the way."

ALAN SEPINWALL, TELEVISION CRITIC AND HISTORIAN[1]

> "With thousands of hours of new TV coming out every year and an increasingly fractured marketplace demanding customers keep track of several different streaming services, how do we keep the truly excellent programming from being lost in the flood of mediocrity?"

SONNY BUNCH, TELEVISION CRITIC[2]

The Rise of Television

To understand the television enterprise and the tensions involved in its current transformation, you have to understand how it started. It's also useful to tie TV's rise to the three historical themes we've discussed in other chapters.

Television in Its Earliest Forms

Look at the timeline (Figure 13.1), and you'll immediately see the relevance of the first theme:

1   Television as we know it did not arrive in a flash as a result of one inventor's grand change.

The chronology indicates that the word "television" was used as early as 1907 in the magazine *Scientific American*. Even earlier, in 1879, the British humor magazine *Punch* published a picture of a couple watching a remote tennis match via a screen above their fireplace. Three years later, a French artist drew a family of the future watching a war on a home screen. Pretty prophetic, huh?

Although the idea of television was in the air, the reality of **television broadcasting**— scanning a visual image and transmitting it, generally with accompanying sound,

television broadcasting
scanning a visual image and transmitting it, generally with accompanying sound, in the form of electromagnetic waves that, when received, can be reconverted into visual images

in the form of electromagnetic waves that, when received, could be reconverted into visual images—was harder to accomplish. Laboratory work started in Germany during the 1880s and continued in the United States, Scotland, Russia, and other countries throughout the next several decades. Between 1935 and 1938, the Nazi government in Germany operated the world's first regular television service, sending propaganda broadcasts to specially equipped theaters.

Engineers did not consider the technology used for these performances very acceptable, however. The whirring mechanical disc that was used to scan the broadcast images had too many drawbacks. During the 1930s, a Radio Corporation of America (RCA) team brought together inventions that allowed electronic rather than mechanical scanning. RCA introduced the system at the 1939 World's Fair in New York; in introducing the new medium during formal ceremonies, President Franklin D. Roosevelt became the first US president to appear on TV. Regular broadcasts began, and TV sets went on sale, but television did not take off. World War II intervened, and resources were diverted to defense production. The few TV broadcasts that existed in New York related mostly to civil defense.

It was after the end of World War II—in 1946—that commercial television came into being in the United States. Even then, what was considered television continued to change. Over the decades engineers for major companies changed the television set, which had started out with black-and-white pictures, to include color. The technology for receiving television programs in most homes changed as well. It went from capturing local stations' transmissions over the air with antennas to allowing reception of those stations' transmissions—and far more program channels—via cable and satellite television. And as we noted in this chapter's introduction, reception possibilities expanded (mainly beginning in the late 2000s) to include a growing array of devices connected to the internet.

All of these transformations in the nature of "television" took place not just because engineers figured out new ways to send moving and talking pictures to the home. Rather, changes in what TV "receivers" looked like, as well as in the kinds of programs that viewers could access through them, resulted from a broad variety of influences from many areas of society on television executives. You might remember from previous chapters that this idea is reflected in the second historical theme. Here it is, applied to television:

2. Television as a medium of communication developed as a result of social, legal, and organizational responses to the technology during different periods.

For an example, let's take the development of the television networks' approach to programming during their first and second decades. You might remember from Chapter 12 (and note in the timeline here) that Hollywood executives saw the small home screen as an obnoxious intruder onto their turf. They attributed its popularity to the huge increase in parenthood that resulted from soldiers returning from World War II and getting married. They declared that when the children got old enough for the parents to leave them at home, their parents would give up the TV and return to the movie theater for their audiovisual entertainment.

This perspective led movie studio executives to refuse to deal with the executives of the major television networks (ABC, NBC, CBS, and a small one called Dumont) as TV gained a permanent hold on the population's interest in the

| 1875s | 1900s | 1925s |

1879: The British humor magazine *Punch* publishes a picture of a couple watching a remote tennis match via a screen above their fireplace.

1882: A French artist draws a family of the future watching a war on a home screen.

1907: *Scientific American* magazine uses the word "television."

1925: John Logie Baird successfully transmits the first television picture with a grayscale image.

1928: Stations in New York and Washington, DC, begin a limited array of live broadcasts, while in London the BBC has five-day-a-week programming by 1930.

1935–38: First regular TV service operates in Nazi Germany. This system sends propaganda messages to specially equipped theaters, rather than to sets in people's homes.

1936: The BBC begins regular electronic TV broadcasts in London.

1939: RCA introduces a television that scans images electronically rather than mechanically.

1939: RCA begins regular broadcasting during the formal ceremonies at the World's Fair in New York.

1946: Commercial broadcasting begins in earnest in the US, controlled by the firms that own major radio networks, NBC, CBS, and later ABC.

1948–52: FCC declares a freeze on new TV licenses.

1949–1955: The major LA-area (Hollywood) movie studios refuse to sell movies or create programs for television.

Figure 13.1
Timeline of the television industry.

1950s

1950–1960: The US sees a rapid uptake of television sets: just 9% of homes had one in 1950, 87% by 1960.

1950s onward: The A.C. Nielsen Company's rating system audits program viewing through an "audiometer" attached to the TV sets in a sample of American households.
1950: First community cable TV system is implemented in Lansford, PA.
1951: *I Love Lucy* is the first scripted situation comedy to be shot on film in front of an audience.

1955–1962: Warner Bros. sells a package of Westerns to the ABC television network for prime-time broadcasting.
Late 1950s and early 1960s: Especially in prime time (the evening), the major networks change their advertising model from full sponsorship (one advertiser supporting a program) to participating (inviting multiple advertisers to support a program).
1960s: NBC, CBS, and ABC develop enormous power over network television.
1970: Listening to critics of network power, government agencies establish prime-time access and financial syndication (fin-syn) rules, aimed at curtailing the power of the major TV networks.
1972: The federal government allows the expansion of cable television into metropolitan areas and for it to carry original programming.

1970s

1976: The US government allows businesses to use satellite communication.
1979: Warner Cable Communications launches Nickelodeon children's cable network.
1979: New FCC rules result in an increase in the number of UHF broadcast stations.
1980: Ted Turner founds CNN, a 24-hour cable news network.

1981: A joint venture between Warner Communications and American Express launches Music Television (MTV).
1986: Rupert Murdoch launches the Fox Network.
1994: DirecTV begins direct-to-home satellite services, followed by the Dish Network in 1996.

1996: Disney buys ABC.
1999: The first digital video recorders (DVRs), which allow viewers to record shows for later viewing, pause live TV, and skip commercials, are introduced.
1999: Netflix begins offering its subscription-based DVD-by-mail service.

2000s

2007: *Quarterlife,* a series about 20-something artists from successful Hollywood producers Marshall Herskovitz and Edward Zwick, appears in eight-minute segments on MySpace and its own site.
2008: NBC, ABC, and Fox launch Hulu, a platform for distributing their shows online.
2010: HBO launches its GO service to allow subscribers to access its programs when connected to the internet.
2011: Comcast buys a controlling interest of NBC-Universal from General Electric.
2013: Cable video on demand (VOD) grows in popularity, helping cable companies keep subscribers and offering hundreds of thousands of new viewers for network shows.
2015: The success of online video streaming services like Netflix, Amazon Prime, and HBO GO leads to a 20% drop in traditional TV viewership by young adults since 2011.

2015: 76% of American households DVR, subscribe to Netflix, or use VOD service through a cable provider.
2017: FCC reverses a 1975 rule banning a single media company from owning a newspaper and a broadcast station (radio or television) In the same local market.
2018: Netflix (with 7), HBO (with 6) and Amazon (with 5) are the major winners of Emmy awards, with traditional broadcast (ABC, NBC, CBS) programming winning only 2 awards.

broadcast live
broadcast as it was actually being performed, rather than being taped, filmed, or otherwise recorded

I Love Lucy was first broadcast in 1951 on CBS and was soon a beloved hit. Thanks to syndication, it actually runs more frequently today than it did in the 1950s. *I Love Lucy* ran for six years of original episodes (180 total) and stopped production in 1957, despite the fact that it was still the number-one show on American television. Lucille Ball and Desi Arnaz insisted on filming the shows in front of a live studio audience using three separate cameras, allowing the show to be edited into its final form with the best comedic angles. This audiovisual approach became the path many sitcoms took. More important, the filming of *I Love Lucy*—at a time when video recording was not used and most television was "live" and not well preserved— ensured that high-quality prints of *I Love Lucy* would allow viewing long into the future.

early 1950s. Most network television in its first commercial decade was therefore broadcast not from Los Angeles (the site of most TV production today), but from New York, the site of the broadcast networks' headquarters. In fact, rather than being made on film a la Hollywood, programs were **broadcast live**—that is, broadcast as the action was actually being performed, rather than filmed or otherwise recorded. (Videotape didn't come into wide use until the late 1950s.) Live variety shows with vaudeville and radio stars, as well as dramas from aspiring theatrical ("Broadway") writers and actors, gave television an accessible, real-world feel that was missing from many Hollywood films. The 1950s, which historians have nicknamed the first **golden age of television**, included powerful, original dramas such as *Marty*, *Judgment at Nuremberg*, and *Requiem for a Heavyweight* and such talented comedy performers as Milton Berle, Sid Caesar, Imogene Coca, Carol Burnett, and Ernie Kovacs. As in radio, sponsors leased time from the television networks and owned the shows, and their advertising agencies coordinated production.

It was an age that ended quickly. The grittiness of TV's live dramas made some major advertisers nervous. Hollywood, a world that was more upscale and populated with beautiful people, seemed to fit better with the advertisers' commercials for automobiles and other symbols of the good life. And Hollywood was finally getting interested in television. Even in the early 1950s, West Coast film producers and actors outside Hollywood's studio system had begun to sell new filmed series to television. The most important of these was created by Lucille Ball and Desi Arnaz, titled *I Love Lucy*, which became an enormous hit with audiences on CBS television. Movie and network executives were quick to recognize the advantages of having a hit on film as opposed to broadcast live. Unlike the live performances of Berle or Caesar, an *I Love Lucy* episode could be aired over and over again, or put into **syndication**.

By the mid-1950s, the major studios realized television wouldn't disappear from the scene, and they agreed to supply the television networks with old movies and new filmed TV series that would replace the live programming. By then television executives had accepted the idea that they were reaching as many people as the movie industry had in its heyday. And much like the movie executives of the 1930s, the TV people were worried that activist organizations angry with programming might encourage the federal government (in this case through the Federal Communications Commission, or FCC) to force changes in their programming. They therefore created a "Code of Good Practices" regarding morality in content that in many ways mirrored the self-regulatory code of the movie industry.

Despite the code, television executives of the early 1960s soon found themselves in the midst of political and social problems. Public anger over rigged quiz shows, over the large amount of violence on other shows, and over what many influential individuals in society considered idiotic entertainment ("a vast wasteland," the FCC's head called it) led to congressional hearings. Partly as a result, the networks changed their approach to selling advertising time on TV. Instead of advertisers buying the time and producing the shows themselves, network executives began to plan the schedule and order the shows, sometimes even producing them or taking part ownership in them. This planning allowed the TV networks far more control than in earlier years. Advertisers found it useful, too, because instead of putting all their television budget on one show, they could use it to buy time on various programs, thereby reaching people at different times and on different networks.

Brief though this description of the influences on the television networks' early approaches to programming is, it and the timeline should help you see the ways executives reacted to social, organizational, and potential legal reactions to their activities. The thumbnail history and the timeline also reflect the third theme:

3.   The television industry developed and changed as a result of struggles to control its channels to audiences.

The story of the networks' struggle to figure out the best ways to access programming and deal with sponsors is part of a larger story of the growth of the television industry. As we will see in this chapter, the TV industry today is far more than CBS, NBC, and ABC. Even during the 1950s and 1960s, though, those three networks made up only part of the larger television industry. The timeline reflects some of the most important players: the production firms (some owned by the networks, others part of the Hollywood studios, others independent) that created the programs; the television stations that took the network program feeds and broadcast them to geographical areas; the A. C. Nielsen company, which supplied **television program ratings**, or audits of people's viewing behavior, that helped the networks decide what programs to choose; the advertisers and advertising organizations that helped pay the bills; and even the FCC, which decided which channels would be available in different parts of the country.

These organizations and others have been very much involved in struggles to control what television audiences see, when, and how. During the 1960s and 1970s, for example, the television networks competed fiercely with one another for the largest audience as well as for advertising money. At the same time, advertisers competed with one another for the best slots for their commercials. The advertisers also often made it clear to the networks that the programs they put on should not present views that insulted the idea of buying products and living the good life. The FCC, for its part, tried to pressure the networks to tone down violence on their programming and to inject more educational elements into children's programming. Activists started advocacy organizations such as Action for Children's Television to encourage the FCC and other government agencies to keep the pressure on the networks and their sponsors. And Nielsen created an entirely different set of pressures: the ratings released by the firm became the basic criteria against which advertisers and networks judged the success of programs. Advocacy groups tried to persuade industry executives that they should evaluate the programs by quality as decided by groups of citizens rather than as popularity contests. Other critics carped that the ratings were flawed and didn't reflect popularity accurately.

Struggles among these organizations to create and control the various TV channels to audiences certainly didn't stop in the 1970s. As the timeline indicates, the organizations with power in the industry changed over time. Cable television firms, cable networks, satellite firms, and internet service providers (with many of the biggest also selling cable service) were among the most important players over the next few decades. Bolstered by changing government regulation that they influenced through lobbyists and new television technologies that they helped to produce, they dramatically changed the amount and kinds of "television" programming Americans

golden age of television
the period of time from approximately 1949 to 1960, marked by the proliferation of original and classic dramas produced for live television

syndication
the licensing of mass media material to outlets on a market-by-market basis

television program ratings
audits of people's viewing behaviors that gauge which shows households are viewing and how many are viewing them; they help network executives decide which shows should stay, which should be dropped from the lineup, and how much advertisers should pay to hawk their products during breaks in the program

Friends first aired on analog TV from 1994 to 2004, but it's seen a new lease on life since appearing on streaming services. *Friends* is now said to be one of the most streamed shows on Netflix.

receive and the amount of money Americans pay to receive the programming.

The television industry continues to change as companies react to new challenges, especially those involving convergence. As we suggested in this chapter's introduction, even the definition of "television" is in flux as programs that appear on the big home screen—or that are similar to those that appear on the big home screen—show up on the web and mobile phones. For the purposes of this chapter, we will define television programming as audiovisual material created by businesses to be part of a flow or gathering of material aimed at particular audiences and financed by advertising and/or audience payments. The definition is a mouthful. It is, however, meant to distinguish television from two other forms of audiovisual materials. One is amateur productions, such as the personal creations you can find on YouTube (hence "material created by businesses"). The other form to exclude is stand-alone movies. That's why the definition says a product must be created to be "part of a flow or gathering of material." It's "television" if a channel has a flow or gathering of stand-alone movies; think of the Turner Classic Movies (TCM) and AMC networks. Of course, television programming doesn't have to be a collection of movies. A hallmark of television output is the series—a collection of episodes with a continuity of characters, settings, and/or plot lines. *The Wire* (on HBO), *Sesame Street* (HBO and PBS), *Jessica Jones* (Netflix), *The Big Bang* (CBS), and *The Marvelous Mrs. Maisel* (Amazon Prime) are quite different types of series television. And although TCM and AMC do program lots of old movies, they also present original series. *Moguls and Movie Stars*, on TCM, is one example. *Breaking Bad* on AMC is another.

THINKING ABOUT MEDIA LITERACY

The majority of the 2018 Emmy awards for best television programming went to shows produced and distributed outside the major television networks. What do you think this means for network television?

An Overview of the Contemporary Television Industry

It's useful to think of the television world as divided into three domains:

- Television broadcasting
- Subscription cable and satellite services
- Online and mobile platforms

Each area has its own technologies, its own key players, and its own special programming. Yet convergence is very much at play here: the domains are quite connected to one another. Programming from the "television broadcasting" mode shows up in the subscription cable and satellite space, and programs from there can be found on the web and other digital platforms. Let's take a brief overview of each domain and then explore how production, distribution, and exhibition work in each.

Television Broadcasting

Television broadcasting, or the broad, over-the-air transmission of audiovisual signals, has historically been the most popular of these three domains. Its signals are transmitted from towers owned by local stations on frequencies allocated to them by the FCC. People with the right kind of television equipment can receive the signals without charge by simply turning on a television set.

About 1,800 television stations existed in 2014. Each station is licensed by the FCC to send out signals in a particular area of the country. Until recently, the FCC gave out licenses to operate on frequencies in one of two bands of the electromagnetic spectrum: the VHF band and the UHF band. Because VHF could deliver clear pictures to more people than UHF could, VHF stations were considered more valuable. By FCC ruling, however, in 2009 all stations moved to a new part of the spectrum, to broadcast using digital rather than analog technology. The part of the spectrum previously used by television stations was auctioned by the government for use by other companies and public service organizations. Newer TV sets are able to receive the digital signals. But Americans with older analog sets in their homes had to purchase special equipment so that their old TVs would be able to receive the new over-the-air digital signals. Nielsen estimates that around 96 percent of the 116.4 million US households receive "traditional"—that is, over the air—TV signals. Many of those homes also receive these signals in ways other than over the air, though, as we will see when we discuss cable, satellite, and internet vehicles for viewing television.

About 1,400 stations are what people in the TV industry call commercial; 400 others are noncommercial. **Commercial stations** make their money by selling time on their airwaves to advertisers. **Noncommercial stations** receive support in other ways, such as viewer donations and donations from private foundations and commercial firms in return for billboards. **Billboards** are mentions of a sponsor's name or products at the start or end of programs airing on the station. When a company pays to sponsor a program on a noncommercial station, that is called **underwriting**.

The Nielsen ratings firm divides the United States into 210 broadcast television markets. In 2018 they estimated that the nation had 112,143,960 households across those markets. New York City is the largest market, followed by Los Angeles and then Chicago. The New York City market boasts about 7.1 million homes. Glendive, Montana, the smallest market, has 4,030 (see Table 13.1).

More than 80 percent of local TV stations have linked up or affiliated with a television network for at least part of their broadcast day. A **television network** is an organization that distributes television programs, typically by satellite and microwave relay, to all its affiliated stations, or stations that agree to carry a substantial amount of the network's material on an ongoing basis so that the programs can be broadcast by all the stations at the same time. ABC, CBS, Fox, and NBC are the broadcast networks that regularly reach the largest numbers of people. They are advertiser-supported, as are the three major Spanish-speaking networks—Univision, TeleFutura (owned by Univision), and Telemundo (owned by Comcast's NBC Universal). Many smaller broadcast networks populate US airwaves. Three mid-size ones—the CW

commercial stations
broadcast television stations that support themselves financially by selling time on their airwaves to advertisers

noncommercial stations
broadcast television stations that do not receive financial support from advertisers, but rather support themselves through donations from listeners and private foundations and from commercial firms in return for mentioning the firm or its products in announcements at the beginning and end of programs airing on the station

billboards
mentions of a sponsor's name or products at the start or end of programs airing on the station

underwriting
when a company pays to sponsor a program on a noncommercial station

television network
an organization that distributes television programs, typically by satellite and microwave relay, to all its affiliated stations, or stations that agree to carry a substantial amount of the network's material on an ongoing basis so that the programs can be broadcast by all the stations at the same time

Table 13.1 The Top Five and Bottom Five Broadcast Television Markets in the United States, 2018

Rank	Designated market area (DMA)	TV households	% of US
1	New York, NY	7,074,750	6.309
2	Los Angeles, CA	5,318,630	4.743
3	Chicago, IL	3,299,720	2.942
4	Philadelphia, PA	2,869,580	2.559
5	Dallas—Fort Worth, TX	2,648,490	2.362
206	Presque Isle, ME	25,480	0.023
207	Juneau, AK	24,390	0.022
208	Alpena, MI	15,360	0.014
209	North Platte, NE	13,640	0.012
210	Glendive, MT	4,030	0.004

Source: Nielsen, "Local Television Market Universe Estimates," www.nielsen.com/content/dam/corporate/us/en/public%20factsheets/tv/2017-18%20TV%20DMA%20Ranks.pdf, accessed August 8, 2018. Copyrighted information ©2017, of The Nielsen Company, licensed for use herein.

Big Four commercial networks
the four largest television networks: ABC, CBS, Fox, and NBC

O&O
stations owned by ABC, CBS, Fox, and NBC

network affiliates
local broadcast television stations that are not owned by broadcast networks and yet transmit network signals and programs on a daily basis; in return, the network promises to compensate the affiliate with a portion of the revenues received from advertisers that have bought time on the network

program feed
the succession of shows sent from a network to its network affiliates

station groups
collections of broadcast television stations owned by a single company

independent broadcast station
a station not affiliated with one of the Big Four networks

(owned by CBS and AT&T's Warner Media), Ion, and MyTV (owned by Fox)—reach over 91 percent of US households. There are also more than a couple dozen smaller advertising-supported networks in English or Spanish that local stations contract to carry on extra digital signals that they send out. They air in fewer areas of the country and so reach fewer households. Examples are Me-TV and Antenna TV (owned by Tribune Broadcasting, which show reruns of so-called classic TV shows), This TV (owned by MGM TV and Tribune, which airs "classic" movies), Bounce TV (aimed at African Americans), and UniMas (a Spanish-language channel). The Public Broadcasting Service (PBS) is the major network for noncommercial stations. The **Big Four commercial networks**—ABC, CBS, Fox, and NBC—are the giants of the broadcast television business, primarily because of their role in coordinating the distribution of popular shows to hundreds of local stations, which then transmit the shows to homes. They also own lots of stations; those are called owned and operated stations—**O&Os** for short.

Many affiliates are part of **station groups**, or collections of broadcast television stations owned by a single company. In the wealthiest station groups, such as Allbritton Communications, each station is an affiliate of one of the major networks. Stations in other groups hook up mainly with CW, ION, or MyTV on their main signal. According to the FCC, no group may own more than two television stations in any market. That dictum is based on the desire to limit the power of broadcast groups in any one area. The FCC has also ruled, however, that a company can own two networks as long as both are not among the Big Four networks. A station not affiliated with one of the Big Four networks is called an **independent broadcast station**. (Industry executives often consider CW, ION, and MyTV affiliates to be independents because they air relatively few hours of network programming per week.) Practically speaking, independents must find all (or almost all) of their programming themselves. Actually, even network affiliates and O&Os must look to sources other than ABC, CBS, Fox, and NBC for some of their programming. The reason is that the Big Four do not distribute 24 hours' worth of shows. As we will see later in this chapter, the broadcast industry has no shortage of companies trying to interest independents, affiliates, and O&Os in programming.

With the help of advertising agencies (which Chapter 3 discusses in some detail), advertisers pay for time between programs and segments of programs. In return, broadcasters allow advertisers to use this time to air **commercials**—short audiovisual pieces that call attention to their products or services. In 2017 advertisers spent about $41 billion on television broadcast advertising.[3] Viewers of broadcast TV do not have to pay to receive the programming. Consequently, historically almost all the money that broadcast stations and networks receive has come from a single revenue stream—commercials. In recent years, though, stations and their networks have begun to make money from the two other domains—subscription television and online and mobile platforms—mentioned earlier. Local stations (and the networks that sometimes own them) now make about $6 billion a year charging cable and satellite systems for the right to pick their broadcasts off the air and retransmit them to subscribers; these are called **retransmission fees**. Stations and networks are also beginning to take advantage of digital media to develop sources of revenue other than broadcast

Subscription Cable, Telco, and Satellite Services

People in the TV industry sometimes refer to cable, telco (short for "telecommunications company"), and satellite services collectively as **multichannel subscription video programming distributors (MVPDs)**. Unlike with broadcasting (which anyone with the right technology in the right location can pick off from the air), consumers must subscribe to get these services. Table 13.2 indicates the top ten MVPD system owners along with the technologies they use. As you can see, most provide their services via cable, and two do it via satellite. In some systems, AT&T delivers the programming

commercials
short audiovisual pieces that call attention to advertisers' products or services

retransmission fees
the money television networks and local stations charge cable and satellite firms for the right to carry their material

multichannel subscription video programming distributors (MVPDs)
an organization that delivers video programming services, usually for a subscription fee

Table 13.2 Top Ten MVPD Systems Owners, 2017

Rank	MSO name	Total subscribers	Technology
1	AT&T-DirecTV	25,300,000	Satellite, Fiber, IPTV
2	Comcast Xfinity	22,500,000	Cable
3	Charter	17,200,000	Cable
4	Dish/Sling	13,700,000	Satellite/IPTV
5	Verizon	4,700,000	Fiber
6	Cox Communications	4,540,280	Cable, Fiber, IPTV
7	Altice	3,600,000	Cable
8	Frontier	1,500,000	Cable/Fiber
9	Mediacom	828,000	Cable
10	WideOpenWest	486,000	Cable

Source: Mike Farrell, "Top 2 MPVDs," Multichannel News, February 27, 2017, www.multichannel.com/news/top-25-mvpds-411157; and "List of multiple system operators," Wikipedia, via Kagan, https://en.wikipedia.org/wiki/List_of_multiple-system_operators, accessed August 8, 2018.

via cable-like wires but uses a format called IPTV, or internet Protocol television. It delivers the programming over a packet-switched network on the internet (see Chapter 6), streaming bunches of data to set-top boxes (and television sets) as if they were computers. In all these modes of delivery, advertisers pay the cable, telco, and satellite services to have their commercials shown during some of the programming. Most of these revenue streams are substantial, although the money received from subscriptions is far greater than advertisers' contributions. In 2014 American consumers paid around $101 billion to receive cable or satellite programming. Advertisers paid about $26.2 billion to advertise on these services.[4]

The Cable Television Business "**Cable television**" refers to businesses that provide programming to subscribers via a wire (historically a coaxial cable, but increasingly a fiber-optic line). The cable television business is by far the most developed in the cable and satellite area. Stripped to its basics, a cable is a type of flexible tube or pipe through which programs are exhibited in the home. The retailer that physically installs the cable and markets the program service to consumers in a particular geographic area is called a **cable television system**. A cable television firm that owns two or more cable systems is a **multiple system owner (MSO)**. Each system offers consumers in its community an array of channels that includes special networks as well as independent local broadcast stations and network affiliates. Though they are called cable networks because they first appeared on cable, the nonbroadcast channels are more appropriately called **subscription networks** because people pay a monthly fee (a subscription) to receive them via cable or satellite. In 2011 Americans spent $56.9 billion on cable TV subscriptions.[5]

The Telco Business In recent years, traditional telephone service providers, notably AT&T and Verizon, have also begun to offer multichannel television service in many parts of the country and now compete with the cable TV firms. Although they wouldn't be called cable companies by people in the business, Verizon and AT&T do use wire technologies (as opposed to the unwired satellite approach) to reach people's homes. Some people in the business call these firms the **telcos** (short for "telecommunications companies"). Verizon and AT&T have different technical philosophies, but they share the idea of using advanced communication lines called fiber-optic to send cable programming to TV sets. But the cost of running fiber-optic wires to homes is very expensive, so both AT&T and Verizon have also adopted alternative delivery systems. Verizon has been experimenting with using the upcoming 5G cellular standard, which will be ten to forty times faster than current 4G LTE wireless service, as the basis for a new cable and internet service. Instead of hooking up every customer with fiber-optic, Verizon customers would place standard internet routers near a window to receive internet and TV service signals from a nearby cell tower—one that might even be on a light pole outside the home.[6] All this technology is still in early stages, though, and it's not clear how much money it will really save. AT&T, in the meantime, has invested in satellite delivery as a complement to its fiber-optic operations.

The Satellite Business "**Satellite television**" means programming that comes directly to the home from a satellite orbiting the Earth. In 2018 about 29 percent of US households with a TV subscribed to a satellite operation. You may have seen old-style satellite dishes, the large structures that typically sat behind people's homes. The backyard satellite dish business was built in the 1980s on the proposition that a homeowner could cut out the cable system by installing a dish-shaped instrument in the backyard and getting programs directly from the satellite that sends them to

cable television
television service provided to subscribers by signals sent through a wire (usually a coaxial cable, but increasingly via fiber-optic lines)

cable television system
the cable television retailer that physically installs the cable and markets the program service to consumers in a particular geographic area

multiple system owner (MSO)
a cable television firm that owns two or more cable television systems

subscription networks
nonbroadcast program channels for which people pay a monthly subscription fee to receive them via cable or satellite

telcos
telephone companies that offer television and internet services

satellite television
programming that comes directly to the home from a satellite orbiting the Earth

the cable system. Unfortunately for the homeowners, though, most networks now encode their programs so that a person with a dish cannot view them free of charge. Most of the backyard receivers have been replaced by **direct broadcast satellite (DBS) technology**. Introduced in 1994, it allows a household to receive hundreds of channels. The signals are delivered digitally to a small dish installed on the side of a dwelling; a set-top box decodes digital signals so that they appear on the TV set. The DBS satellites operate from orbits directly above the Earth's equator and just over 22,000 miles up. DirecTV (owned by AT&T) and Dish Network are currently the largest DBS companies in the United States.

direct broadcast satellite (DBS) technology
technology that allows a household to receive hundreds of channels from signals that are delivered digitally from satellites operating in orbit to a small dish installed on the side of a dwelling; a set-top box decodes digital signals so that they appear on the TV set

Online and Mobile Platforms

By 2018 about 66 percent of US adults had broadband connections at home through which they could get online via desktop and laptop computers. Another 20 percent were "smartphone only" users—people who use smartphones as their primarily way to get online even at home. Overall 77 percent of Americans in early 2018 had smartphones and 50 percent had tablets through which they could use broadband Wi-Fi to access the web and apps.[7] The presence of broadband means they have speeds high enough to stream videos or download them much faster than older forms of internet connections (see Chapter 6 for more background). With more and more people owning tablets and other mobile-technology products, watching TV via the internet is becoming more and more prevalent. The notion of "watching TV" has fundamentally changed in recent years and will continue to evolve in response to new technologies.

The increasing ability of Americans to view video materials online and on mobile devices paralleled the growth of material for them to watch. Although many of these items were short and produced by amateurs (see most of the videos on YouTube, for example), broadcast networks, local stations, cable companies, satellite firms, and telcos have begun to use online and mobile technologies to distribute their programs as well. Why would broadcast and cable networks arrange for their programs to be viewed via the internet? Here we return to a central theme of this text: convergence. Executives for these firms realize that it is rather easy to make digital copies of broadcast and cable programs and make them available illegally on a variety of platforms. There is, in fact, a robust illegal circulation of television programs on the web. Television executives believe that they must find business models that encourage people to view programs legitimately in digital spaces. Many of their activities online and in the mobile realm are aimed at trying to experiment with different business models to find the best ones.

Another related reason cable and broadcast firms are allowing their programs to be viewed online and on mobile devices is executives' belief that in a fragmented media world they have to be on technologies their potential audiences use—and audiences, especially young audiences, increasingly take digital convergence for granted. The CW, for example, is a network that aims at teens and young adults. Its leaders know that their audiences might be at least as comfortable viewing programs on laptops and phones as they are using traditional television sets. They consequently place a lot of episodes online and try to sell advertisers on the idea of sponsoring both the broadcast and online feeds. Consider, too, Hulu. The broadband ad-supported and subscription programming service is owned by very traditional program distributors:

With more and more people owning tablets and other mobile technology products, watching TV online is becoming more and more prevalent. The notion of "watching TV" has fundamentally changed in recent years and will continue to evolve in response to new technologies

NBCUniversal (Comcast), Disney, and AT&T (through Warner Media). On Hulu you can view shows on your laptop you might also have viewed over the air or via satellite on your "traditional" TV set.

THINKING ABOUT MEDIA LITERACY

Is the term "television" outmoded? Think about what "television" means today. Is it the equipment? The format of the programs? What makes something "television"?

The television industry's acceptance of convergence does not, however, mean that the activity is always profitable. MVPDs *are* making lots of money providing general entry to the internet—about $55 billion in 2016.[8] But when it comes to making money from the professionally produced programming we associate with "television," it is hard to know how companies such as Netflix, Hulu, Amazon Prime, and YouTube are doing when it comes to return on investments; they don't report their expenses for specific programs or audience numbers for programs. Yet these and other firms represent important TV-like developments in the internet and mobile spaces, as we will see in this chapter.

To get an idea of how these providers are jockeying for viewers' eyeballs—and what the online and mobile domain adds to this mix—we have to understand the basic elements of the evolving television industry. To do that, we turn to our familiar categories of production, distribution, and exhibition. Production takes up the lion's share of this discussion, simply because there are so many different ways to look at it.

Production in the Television Industry

"Production" is a tricky word when it comes to the television business. In the broadest sense, at least three forms of production are going on at different levels of the industry. To get a sense of what this means, think of your local cable television system. Chances are your local cable system produces very few of its own programs. (Maybe it aids in the production of an access channel, where local officials and citizens can state their problems and parade their interests.) But making shows is not the only way a cable TV system can be involved in production. Your local system is very much involved in producing the number and nature of network channels that it offers potential subscribers; this menu of channels is called a **lineup**.

Trying to understand production in the television world, then, means getting a grip on the considerations that affect the lineup of channels, the formats of individual channels, and the elements of individual programs. Let's look at each of these categories as they relate to the subscription (cable/satellite/telco), broadcast TV, and online/mobile businesses.

lineup
the menu of channels that a cable television system offers potential subscribers

Producing Cable and Satellite Channel Lineups

Creating a channel lineup is a high-priority job for cable and satellite exhibitors. Executives from these companies believe that the number and kinds of programming networks that they offer potential customers are major features that attract people to pay for their service. For instance, take MTV, Nickelodeon, E!, CNN, AMC, Syfy,

ESPN, ESPN2, the Cartoon Network, HBO, or another network. For which of these networks would you consider subscribing to another service if your cable or satellite system didn't carry it?

With so much riding on customer satisfaction, you would think that cable and satellite executives would simply poll their customers and put on everything they want to see. The firms do, in fact, conduct surveys of consumers, and executives do look at ratings reports that indicate how many people watch different networks. Nevertheless, the choice of networks is based as much on three other considerations as on consumer feedback:

- The technological limitations of the system
- The amount of money a network demands from exhibitors
- Whether or not the exhibitor owns a piece of the network

Technological Limitations Technological limitations restrict the number of channels that a cable or satellite service can deliver. High-definition TV (HDTV) signals use substantially more bandwidth than standard TV signals, a factor that has affected the number of HDTV channels that cable and satellite firms have offered. As a telecommunications analyst said in 2007, "HDTV takes an enormous amount of (transmission) capacity. They're going to be sticking 10 pounds of potatoes into a 5-pound bag. Something will have to give." The increasing popularity of HDTV sets and competition with Verizon's very high-capacity FiOS system have been encouraging satellite and cable firms to add more HD channels. That feat is technologically easier for satellite firms than for cable companies, which have to implement major system upgrades across neighborhoods to add capacity. All the services, though, have to weigh the often huge cost of adding channels and other services against the additional subscribers they may bring.

Covering Costs In addition to technological limitations and the costs of upgrades, the lineups set by cable and satellite exhibitors depend on the amounts of money that particular networks charge exhibitors for carrying their networks. These costs are called **license fees**. The notion that a subscription video network should charge exhibitors for carrying it goes back to the early 1980s, when advertising support for cable networks such as CNN and A&E was meager and cable systems agreed to chip in to help the networks survive.

Cable and satellite systems pay wildly varying amounts for the networks they carry. The media research firm SNL Kagan estimates that MVPDs paid $1.50 to $2 per subscriber, per month in 2017 to broadcast affiliates of the major networks for permission to retransmit what those stations broadcast; these payments are called retransmission fees. The MPVDs shelled out money for nonbroadcast channels as well; the amounts varied based on the audience size of the network and the clout of its owner. As you can see in Table 13.3, Comcast's USA Network charged $1.07 per subscriber per month, whereas the Disney Channel charged $1.81 and Disney's ESPN, the king of fees, received $7.86. By contrast, AMC (owned by AMC Networks) received 44 cents per subscriber, Disney Junior 17 cents, and Viacom's BET Gospel received 5 cents. MVPD executives get angry about all these charges, as they do about the retransmission fees the broadcasters demand. The reason is that the programming costs cut into their profit margins. With millions of subscribers out there, consequently, when cable and satellite systems make decisions about their lineups, the mix of channels that they choose is influenced by the amount they will have to

license fees
the costs that particular networks charge exhibitors for carrying the networks' lineups in the exhibitors' cable or satellite systems

Table 13.3 Estimated Amount MPVDs Pay Top Networks Each Month per Subscriber

Network	Amount, per subscriber
ESPN	$7.86
TNT	$2.09
Disney Channel	$1.61
FOX News	$1.55
USA	$1.07
ESPN2	$0.98
TBS	$0.78
National Geographic	$0.28
Fox Business Network	$0.23
HLN	$0.00

Source: "Net Worth," Variety, March 21, 2017, https://pmcvariety.files.wordpress.com/2017/03/0321_041-nu.pdf, accessed August 9, 2018.

tiering
the strategy by which different levels of television programming are priced differently

pay-per-view (PPV)
a transaction in which a cable provider, satellite company, or telco charges the customer for viewing an individual program, such as a boxing event, a live broadcast of a concert, or a newly released motion picture

video on demand (VOD)
a television viewing technology whereby a customer uses the remote control to navigate to a menu of programs and then click on the program he or she wants to watch; unlike pay-per-view, in which the customer has to wait for the show to appear at a certain time, the program immediately appears for viewing

pay to those channels. A channel that charges more than another with the same level of audience popularity will have less chance of getting on a system than the one that demands lower license fees. The low audience numbers for HLN may be one reason Turner gives it away to MPVDs without charge.

Part of the way cable systems pay for many of these channels and make technological improvements is to make money from advertising on them. Advertising-supported channels such as CNN, Lifetime, or HLN typically leave room for the companies that carry them to insert commercials from national or local companies interested in reaching people in particular areas served by the satellite, cable, or telco operation. Of course, another way that a cable or satellite system can bring in revenues is to charge subscribers more money. Increasingly, though, cable and satellite firms worry that adding charges will drive customers to less expensive alternatives, as we will see. In general, the possibility of competition and a desire for consumer goodwill have led firms to keep their most basic rates relatively low and to charge more for extra packages of programs. The relatively low rate often offers the customer all the broadcast channels available in the area, channels with local government and other "access" programming, and a relatively small number of subscription channels, such as TBS and TNT. To get more clusters of channels, the subscriber must pay more. This strategy of charging different amounts for different levels of programming is called **tiering** (it's not spelled "tearing," though some people might cry when they see their bills—or they might want to tear them up). The number and variety of tiers have gone up dramatically in recent years, especially among cable firms. They include packages of movie channels (e.g., HBO and Cinemax), sports, Spanish-language channels, international channels, and more.

Another way to make money is through **pay-per-view (PPV)** or **video on demand (VOD)** or by renting DVRs. In pay-per-view programming, the cable or satellite company charges the customer for viewing an individual program, such as a boxing event, a live broadcast of a concert, or a newly released motion picture. The customer must wait for the specific time that the program airs to view it, or the customer can use the DVR he or she rents per month to capture the program at that time. With VOD, a customer uses a remote control to navigate to a menu of programs and then clicks on the program he or she wants to watch. Unlike PPV, where the customer has to wait for the show to appear at a certain time, the program immediately appears for viewing. As this description suggests, VOD requires the customer to be able to communicate directly with the computer providing the programming. That is possible in most cable and telco television systems because the wire connected to the television carries a signal two ways—from the system's regional delivery location (called the **head end**) to the home set and back. Satellite companies, however, don't typically provide the ability of a home television remote to communicate instantly with the computers delivering the programming. Consequently, they cannot offer true VOD. They try to make up for it by providing their customers with DVRs that download selections viewers might want to try, but the selections may be more limited than the ones that cable firms provide.

Some sporting events, such as Ultimate Fighting Championship matches, are available to view only on PPV.

head end
a cable system's regional delivery location

The Exhibitors' Ownership Role in the Network A third important consideration that influences the lineup of a cable system is whether the MSO or its parent company owns the network. It stands to reason that if a company has a financial interest in the success of a channel, it will include it. For example, if you live in an area served by Comcast, you'll probably find that it carries SportsNet, E!, Style, the Golf Channel, and G4—all owned wholly or partly by Comcast. AT&T similarly carries networks that it owns. This doesn't mean that cable systems that do not own these channels will not carry them. It does mean, however, that if a major cable MSO decides to create a channel, it will put it on enough systems in favorable channel locations to give it a good chance of success. That kind of boost would not be so easily available to independent companies with interesting channel ideas.

Producing Broadcast Channel Lineups

The practice of creating channel lineups is just beginning to happen in the broadcast industry. Recall that since late 2009 broadcasters have been sending all their programs in digital form. With digital technology, broadcasters now have the ability to send high-definition signals, which they could not do under the old analog system because their bandwidth wouldn't allow it. The digital frequencies do allow for **high-definition television (HDTV)**. They also, however, allow for more digital channels broadcast in non-HD. (If more than one is broadcast in HD, the images will degrade substantially.) This activity is called **multichannel broadcasting**—that is, splitting their new digital signals into two, three, or even four separately programmed channels and sending them in the form of a complex signal that is separated at the receiving end. (This is also called channel multiplexing.) So, for example, rather than just broadcasting channel 6, a network could broadcast on channels 6a (the main, HD, channel), 6b, 6c, and 6d.

This is where those digital networks mentioned earlier enter the picture. Me-TV, Antenna TV, Bounce TV (aimed at African Americans), and UniMas (a Spanish-language channel) are just a few of the many networks that companies are offering local broadcasters for channel multiplexing. The incentive is that the broadcasters can split the advertising money or sell advertising time on the network they choose

high-definition television (HDTV)
a television display technology that provides picture quality similar to that of 35mm movies with sound quality similar to that of today's compact discs. Some television stations have begun transmitting HDTV broadcasts to users on a limited number of channels, generally using digital rather than analog signal transmission

multichannel broadcasting (channel multiplexing)
sending multiple signals or streams of information on a carrier at the same time in the form of a single complex signal and then recovering the separate signals at the receiving end

to carry. The challenge for those networks, of course, is to draw audiences that will in turn draw advertisers. Because federal law (the Communications Act) requires MPVDs with more than twelve channels to set aside one-third of their capacity for local commercial stations, this effectively means that cable must carry the subchannels of these stations.[9] So, for example, the FiOS system in the Philadelphia area carries the earlier-mentioned networks. This carriage requirement gives them a greater chance of drawing a substantial number of viewers (and therefore more advertising money) than if they were just sent over the air.

Producing Online/Mobile Lineups

Many of the considerations that drive executives in the cable and broadcast arenas also come up among leaders of websites and mobile applications. Although you may think of a website or app as a single channel, chances are if it provides video choices, it actually offers its video options in arrangements by themes or types. Hulu's home page, for example, includes channel-like tabs that connect to collections of episodes of popular broadcast network programs (e.g., *Empire, Scandal, How to Get Away with Murder*), to movies, to Hulu Originals, and other types of material. A couple of other aspects of Hulu are important to point out because they reflect a larger point about online and mobile television. One is that its offerings of broadcast network TV programs are limited by the firms that own it: Comcast's NBC Universal Television Group, the Disney-ABC Television Group, and AT&T's Warner Media. If you want to watch CBS programs online, you have to go elsewhere—for example, to CBS All Access.

Hulu and CBS All Access are examples of services that people in the industry call subscription video on demand (SVOD). For a monthly fee to them, or to other SVOD firms such as Netflix, Apple TV, and Amazon Prime Video, a subscriber can access a wide lineup of movies and TV series, sometimes for the price of the subscription and sometimes for an extra fee. Some of the programming has commercial messages, but many does not. Getting to SVOD services (sometimes also called over the top—OTT—TV) means going online or to an app on a computer or tablet, accessing it through a "smart TV" with a built-in app for the specific service, or buying a device—an Amazon Fire, Roku, or Apple TV, for example, that connects to a TV set or computer.

It turns out that a majority of Americans who pay for OTT services do not use them as substitutes for traditional MPVDs. In 2017 only 30 percent of OTT households did not have a cable, satellite, or telco TV subscription.[10] But there is another area of programming distribution that virtually all of its subscribers leave to the MPVDs. These are the **vMVPDs**—the virtual multiple program distributors. They offer a smaller number of linear television channels than the traditional MVPDs through the internet for a substantially lower price. Industry practitioners call these smaller collections of channels **slim bundles**. There are dozens of vMVPDs, but the biggest are Google's YouTube TV, Hulu Live, Sony PlayStation Vue, AT&T's DirecTV Now, and Dish's Sling TV. While some cable, satellite, and telco firms may lose by not participating in this development, the MoffettNathanson research group flatly stated in 2018 that competition and low prices meant that being an vMVPD was actually bad business. MoffettNathanson also noted that other losers were the programming networks that were all over cable and satellite but that the vMPVD don't include in the slim bundle lineups. Despite these economic concerns, the public has been gathering interest in the services. Subscription to these "Big Five" vMVPs more than

vMVPDs
virtual program distributors; they offer a smaller number of linear channels than the traditional MVPDs

slim bundles
relatively small collection of channels offered by vMPVDs

doubled between 2016 and 2017. Still, penetration of vMPVDs into US households is still small. In early 2018 the Nielsen company put the distribution at 2.7 percent.[11]

Cutting the cord is the TV industry term for dropping cable, telco, or satellite TV subscriptions. The number of people doing that increases every year. For example, in the fourth quarter of 2018 the total number of MVPD subscribers dropped 3.4 percent from a year earlier. According to analysts at MoffettNathanson Research, this was the highest rate of decline since 2010, when the trend of cord cutting became evident. There are, of course, people who never subscribe to a cable, satellite, or telco service; some in the industry call them "cord nevers." The Leichtman Research Group found in a 2017 survey that 79 percent of Americans pay cable or satellite firms for their TV signals, down from 87 percent in 2011. Note, too, that many people who have kept their cable, telco, and satellite TV subscriptions have reduced the tiers they receive from MVPDs to save costs. The industry dubs these people **cord shavers**. To lure these people as well as the cord cutters, the OTT networks try to lure subscribers with programs they can't find on broadcast, cable, or satellite networks. We've already mentioned the series *The Handmaid's Tale* and *Casual* on Hulu, *Transparent* and *Mrs. Maisel* on Amazon Prime, and *Jessica Jones* on Netflix. They are series nested within the "original series" category of programming each subscription service presents. There are many other categories—for example, action movies, TV sitcoms, and documentaries. The idea is to create "channel" lineups that even people who subscribe to traditional pay TV will pay to watch.[12]

Producing Individual Channels

As the previous paragraph suggests, once a television service has a channel, it has to find a way to fill the time. The task of producing any channel itself is huge, whether it is carried out for a subscription TV network such as CNN or for a broadcast station. Programmers—the people in charge of operations as different as the Weather Channel and MTV on subscription video and WWOR (channel 9) in New York and KNBC (channel 4) in Los Angeles on broadcast TV—have to fill 24 hours of airtime every day of the year. Clock-based programming isn't typically a requirement for "on-demand" programs on cable or satellite or online. Offerings are set out for visitors to access as they wish; some are removed after a certain period. Populating these sorts of channels still requires a good deal of thought, however, for the menu of possibilities can either invite or chase away intended audiences.

Determining the Channel's Intended Audience The most basic issue that confronts a programmer online, in cable, or in broadcast relates to the intended audience: Whom should the programmer try to attract as viewers? This critical question is typically thrashed out by a number of top executives in the organization. The answer generally depends on four interrelated considerations:

- The competition
- The available pool of viewers
- The interests of sponsors
- The costs of relevant programming

"**Competition**" refers to the programming alternatives that already exist. If a channel that emphasizes history is already succeeding, starting a similar channel may not

cutting the cord
when people cancel their cable, telco, or satellite TV subscriptions

cord shavers
people who have kept their cable, telco, and satellite TV subscriptions but have reduced the tiers they receive from MVPDs to save costs

competition
the programming alternatives that already exist

be useful unless you are sure that you have a clearly more attractive way of doing it or that there are enough people who are interested in history to accommodate two somewhat different approaches to the subject. But even if there are enough history buffs around, executives who are thinking of starting a second history channel must ask whether there are enough advertisers that want to sponsor programs on such a channel. If the channel is in the cable/satellite domain (as it probably would be), the executives have to ask whether they could successfully place a second history channel on enough systems to interest advertisers. They also have to ask whether the costs of history programs would be appropriate in view of the projected revenues that would be received from advertisers that want to reach the projected audience. If the programs would be so expensive that the channel wouldn't be able to recover the costs from advertisers and cable subscriptions, such a channel wouldn't succeed, regardless of how interesting it was.

Programmers for cable/satellite/telco channels often focus on rather specific topics to guide their choices of materials. That's also true of many websites with video. They aim to reach people with particular lifestyle habits or interests—an available pool of viewers. Think of HGTV (Home and Garden Television) or the Golf Channel. In contrast, broadcast stations, because they are well known and accessible to virtually everyone in their area, do not differentiate themselves so narrowly. When they go after new audiences, they choose broad segments of the population that advertisers want to reach. In some large cities, for example, where the FCC added several stations and increased competition for audiences, a few stations have decided to pursue Spanish-speaking viewers, or non–English-speaking viewers generally to maximize their profits.

Ratings In the television industry, the audits of people's television viewing behavior that help determine where much of the money for programming and advertising should go are called **ratings**. The stations, networks, and major advertisers foot most of the bill for the firm's reports. Nielsen dominates this business, though it is not the only player. Periodically, networks or station groups, angry at the ways Nielsen audits viewing and charges for its services, have threatened to abandon it for others. In 2019 CBS complained about Nielsen's charges, as well as its inadequate measurement approaches to local viewing and to tracking viewing across many digital platforms. It threatened to use Comscore instead. The Gray Media station group, for its part, announced it was fed up with Nielsen's approach to local ratings and would use Comscore.[13] Nevertheless, Nielsen has managed to maintain its position partly because so much of the TV business is based on its measurement rules and partly because the company seems to be trying hard to find ways to reliably measure what people view across so many different platforms. Yet controversies about its work persist.

When it comes to TV sets, Nielsen uses meters and diaries to determine what people are watching and when. For a snapshot of what America is watching, Nielsen uses an instrument called a **people meter**. The company installs this small box on all of the television sets in about 27,000 homes that it has chosen as a representative sample population.[14] The meter holds a preassigned code for every individual in the home, including visitors. The research firm asks each viewer to enter his or her code at the start and end of a TV viewing session. Information from each viewing session on what the person watched on the TV and any device connected to the TV (for example, video game consoles, computers, VOD set-top boxes) is transmitted to Nielsen's computers through television lines and is the basis for the firm's conclusions about national viewing habits.

ratings
audits of people's television viewing behavior that help determine where much of the money for programming and advertising should go

people meter
a small box installed by Nielsen on television sets in about 20,000 homes that it has chosen as a representative sample of the US population. The meter holds a preassigned code for every individual in the home, including visitors. Nielsen asks each viewer to enter his or her code at the start and end of a TV viewing session. Information from each viewing session is transmitted to Nielsen's computers through television lines and is the basis for the firm's conclusions about national viewing habits.

However, meters in 27,000 homes scattered around the country can't tell stations in the 210 individual television markets around the country how many people are watching the stations and who these people are. To get these data, Nielsen uses three approaches. For nonstop research on the top twenty-five markets, Nielsen uses people meters. It explores the viewing habits of people in the other television markets during four months of the year—February, May, July, and November. Broadcast industry workers call these months the **sweeps** because the ratings measurements during these periods are comparable to giant sweepstakes in which winners and losers are determined. In the thirty-one markets below the top twenty-five, Nielsen uses household meters on every set to determine what the families are watching on television and all devices connected to the TV. It then applies a somewhat controversial statistical method it calls "viewer assignment" to determine what to say about the viewing habits of the people of different ages and genders who viewed various programs in those homes. A large part of the viewer assignment technique involves matching those household-meter homes with data about individuals collected in people-meter homes that are in the national sample but are geographically close to the metered homes. To measure viewing in most of the 154 markets below the top 56, Nielsen distributes more than 2 million diaries to samples of households in those markets. Nielsen asks the family members to fill in the viewing experiences for each member of the household for a month. Because this approach has well-known problems of accuracy (people forget to fill out the diaries on some days and so fill in what they think they remember), Nielsen is working to get rid of the diaries. Instead, it is making agreements with cable and satellite firms to send anonymous set-top-box viewing data of those homes to Nielsen.[15]

Nielsen's results are arrayed as ratings and shares. Ratings and shares, in turn, can be discussed in household and people terms. **Household ratings** represent the number of households in which the channel was turned on, compared with the number of households in the channel's universe (the local area, or the number of people who receive the cable network). **People ratings** refer to particular demographic categories of individuals within each household—for example, those aged 18 to 49 or those who are female. For a particular channel during a particular time, a **household share** represents the number of households in which the channel was turned on compared with the number of TV-owning households in the area where the channel could be viewed.

Because of their wide **reach**, or the percentage of the entire target audience to which they circulate, broadcast networks often answer to advertisers in terms of their **national rating points**. In 2015 every national household rating point represented 1,164,000 households (about 1 percent of US homes with a TV). Nielsen defines a home with TV as one that has "at least one operable TV/monitor with the ability to deliver video via traditional means of antenna, cable set-top box, or satellite receiver and/or with a broadband connection."[16] National people ratings are expressed in terms of the number of individuals in the United States who fit into a particular category. Each rating point in the 18- to 49-year-old category, for example, represents 1 percent of the US total for people 18 to 49.

For example, if *The Tonight Show Starring Jimmy Fallon*—which is exhibited nationally on NBC—receives a 3.4 household rating and a 16 household share, what does that mean? The rating means that of the 116.4 million households in the United States that own a TV set, 3.4 percent (about 4 million households) had at least one set or broadband connection tuned to *The Tonight Show*. That may look like a very

sweeps
the survey of TV viewing habits in markets across the United States, as performed by Nielsen four times per year—during the months of February, May, August, and November; competition among TV programmers is especially keen during these periods

household ratings
ratings that represent the number of households in which the channel was turned on, compared with the number of households in the channel's universe (the local area, or the number of people who receive the cable network)

people ratings
particular demographic categories of individuals within each household—for example, those aged 18 to 49 years or those who are female

household share
the number of households in which a particular channel was turned on compared with the number of TV-owning households in the area where the channel could be viewed

reach
the percentage of the entire target audience to which a media outlet will circulate

national rating points
a measure of the percentage of TV sets in the United States that are tuned to a specific show; in 2001 each national rating point represented just over 1 million US homes with TVs

small percentage, but the program airs at 11:30 p.m. (EST and PST), when many people are asleep. The 16 household share means that of the households in which people were viewing TV at that time of night, about one in six (about 16 percent) were viewing Fallon.[17] Of course, households often have people viewing different TV sets. Increasingly, then, networks and their advertisers prefer ratings and shares to be expressed not in terms of households but in terms of categories of individuals who are viewing. So, for example, you might read in the trade press that *The Late Show* received a 19 share among the 18- to 49-year-olds in its audience.

Nielsen reports each program's rating and share for a particular night to its clients (typically advertising executives). In the 2000s advertisers began to pressure Nielsen to report ratings and shares not just for the average viewing of programs but also in terms of the viewing of commercials within and around the shows. After all, for advertisers, the shows are there mainly to get the right people to watch the commercials. Nielsen determines ratings and household viewings during commercials and reports them in terms of the **average commercial minute**. That way, advertisers have measurements not just for each program taken as a whole but also for the commercials that run during the programs. In addition, Nielsen determines the ratings for a program and its average commercial minutes not just by counting the people who viewed it at the actual time it ran on broadcast or cable. The company includes in the ratings people who recorded it on a DVR and viewed it within a three-day period. The reason is that by 2015 about 49 percent of US households had a DVR-connected TV set. Some people also watch the latest episodes of network programs through their MVPD system's VOD capabilities.[18] The TV networks argue that advertisers should take viewing through DVRs and VOD into account as well as so-called live viewing. This approach—measuring the rating of the average commercial minute of a program within a three-day window—is called the **C3 rating** and is used for today's ratings reports. Some agreements between networks and advertisers use a **C7** criterion—the size of the target audience for average commercial minutes within a seven-day window.

Preliminary evidence suggests that the commercial ratings of some shows rise substantially when time-shifting via DVRs is added to the picture. However, the ratings do not consider viewing on the web and mobile media. For this reason, Nielsen has developed what the company calls its "Total Audience" solutions. As we noted, the company audits all video viewing by set-top boxes, desktops, laptops, game consoles, and other devices attached to the TV set. To measure what people watch on mobile devices, Nielsen pays companies that track people's internet usage to give Nielsen data about (anonymous) individuals' viewing activities.[19] Another approach the company has begun to use involves wearable devices given to a large and representative number of individuals. Programs that play on any platform emit coded sounds unhearable by humans that identify them. Nielsen uses the devices to capture those codes and learn what people are watching where.

One of the important developments that Nielsen's cross-platform ratings activities aims to monitor is nonlinear viewing. That is when people don't watch the programs networks prepare in real time and distribute across a preset schedule. Real-time (or "linear") viewing is slowly eroding as people increasingly watch programs when they want to view them via VOD services that various cable, satellite, telco, or online providers offer. Younger viewers (18 to 24) watch less of traditional TV than older ones. As they have done that, the ratings of cable television networks have declined. Michael Nathanson, an analyst of TV industry stocks, wrote in 2015 that "[i]t's hard

average commercial minute
Nielsen's reporting standard for determining ratings and household viewing during commercials; this information gives advertisers measurements not just for each program taken as a whole but also for the commercials that run during the programs

C3 rating
Nielsen technique of measuring the average commercial minute of a program by including in the ratings people who recorded commercials on DVRs and viewed them within a three-day period

C7 rating
Nielsen technique of measuring the average commercial minute of a program by including in the ratings people who recorded commercials on DVRs and viewed them within a seven-day period

to ignore our belief that technology is disrupting viewer consumption of linear network programming." Several years from now, most programming may be offered through "on demand" menus rather than on networks that present linear schedules of programming.[20] For the time being, though, most television viewing (Nielsen says 88 percent) is linear, and an important part of executives' work at a TV network involves preparing a schedule.[21]

Preparing a Schedule A TV schedule is a lineup of television programs that a station or network will present during particular hours on a particular day. Ratings are always on the minds of the programmers who produce schedules for their stations or networks. That is because the size of a program's audience helps determine the amount of money they can charge an advertiser for time during that program. Many broadcast and cable/satellite telco channel programmers break down their work into creating discrete **schedules**, or patterns in which programs are arranged, for different **day parts**, or segments of the day. The most prominent of these day parts is the period from 8:00 to 11:00 p.m. (or from 7:00 to 10:00 p.m. in the Central and Mountain time zones), when the largest number of people are viewing. Called **prime time**, these are the hours in which many networks put on their most expensive programs (see Figure 13.2 for a sample of a prime-time schedule) and charge advertisers the most money for commercial time (thirty seconds is the most common). Prime time is the most prestigious day part, although not necessarily the most profitable. CBS, for example, makes more profits from its afternoon soap opera schedule (for which it pays relatively little) than from its pricier evening fare.

In prime time, as in all day parts, the different goals of different channels lead to different schedules. As noted earlier, household ratings are usually not as important to advertisers and programmers as individual ratings. Age, gender, and sometimes ethnicity are particular selling points. When adults are the targets, most programmers start with the assumption that they must attract mostly people between 18 and 49 years old because this is the market segment that most television advertisers want to reach. Although people older than 50 actually have more money than those who are younger, many advertisers believe that once people pass the age of 49, they are not as susceptible as younger adults to new product ideas. Advertisers are also aware that people who are 50 and older are less likely than younger adults to be taking care

schedule
a lineup of television programs

day parts
segments of the day as defined by programmers and marketers

prime time
the hours from 8 to 11 p.m. during which many networks put on their most expensive programs and charge advertisers the most money for commercial time

Time Slot	Network			
	ABC	**NBC**	**CBS**	**FOX**
8:00 p.m.	The Goldbergs	Chicago Med	Survivor	The Masked Singer
8:30 p.m.	Schooled			
9:00 p.m.	Modern Family	Chicago Fire	SEAL Team	Almost Family
9:30 p.m.	Single Parents			
10:00 p.m.	How to Get Away with Murder	Chicago P.D.	S.W.A.T.	Local Programming
10:30 p.m.				

Figure 13.2
Prime-time lineups on Wednesday evenings for the four major national networks

series
a set of programs that revolve around the same ideas or characters

of children at home. More people in a household means more repeat purchases of goods such as soap, cereal, and frozen foods.

The building block of a television schedule is the **series**—a set of programs that revolve around the same ideas or characters. Series can be as varied as *Scandal*, an American political thriller about the owner of a crisis management firm; *Last Week Tonight with John Oliver*, a half-hour satirical look at the week in news; or *House Hunters*, where home buyers evaluate houses with their real estate agent, including one they have already chosen to purchase (though that isn't made clear to viewers).[22] Series are useful to programmers because they lend predictability to a schedule. Programmers can schedule a series in a particular time slot with the hope that it will solve the problem of attracting viewers to that slot on a regular basis.

Programmers generally try to bring viewers to more than just one show on their station or network. Their goal is to attract certain types of people to an entire day part so that the ratings for that day part—and therefore its ad fees—will be high. Keeping people tuned to more than one series also means keeping them around for the commercials between the series. In TV industry lingo, the challenge is to maximize the **audience flow** across programs in the day part.

audience flow
the movement of audience members from one program to another

That's a tall order when so many viewers clutch that ultimate ratings spoiler, the remote control, securely in their hands for the duration of their viewing sessions. The idea of audience flow is particularly precarious when a substantial portion of households have digital video recorders that can capture one network's program while they watch a different channel. Still, Nielsen ratings do suggest that certain scheduling techniques can improve audience flow. One is the use of a strong lead-in to programs that follow. A **lead-in** is a program that comes before, and therefore leads into, another program. Ratings suggest that a strong lead-in tends to bring its audience to sample the program that comes after it. The chance for **sampling**, or trying a new series for the first time, is also increased if the **lead-out**—the program that follows the new series—is popular. Many people who are interested in seeing the first and third programs will stick through the second if they consider it at all good.

lead-in
a program that comes before, and therefore leads into, another program

sampling
trying out a new program by watching it for the first time

lead-out
the program that follows the program after the lead-in

hammock
the strategic placement of a program between two other programs; positioning a new series between two well-established shows that appeal to the same target audience often gives the right viewers an opportunity to sample the new series

Say you're a programmer and have a new series that you want to give the maximum chance to succeed. By the logic of lead-ins and lead-outs, you should place the new series between two well-established shows that appeal to the same audience. This position, known as a **hammock**, gives the right viewers an opportunity to sample the show.

Sometimes what seems like a good program for a particular position in the schedule, or **time slot**, may be judged unacceptable because it is aimed at the same kinds of people (in terms of age, gender, ethnicity, or interests) who are flocking to a popular program on another channel at the same time. When programmers don't want to compete directly with a popular series, they turn to **counterprogramming**—scheduling a program that aims to attract a target audience different from that of other shows in a particular time slot. For example, in 2007 some local stations began to place game shows in the late afternoon (4:00 to 6:00 p.m.) time slot as counterprogramming to talk shows that their competitors were running at that time.

time slot
a particular position in the schedule

counterprogramming
scheduling a program that aims to attract a target audience different from those of other shows in the same time slot; often done to avoid competing directly with a popular series

Producing Individual Programs

To program producers, being successful doesn't just mean coming up with an idea that programmers like (as difficult as that may be). It also means coming up with an idea that programmers for local stations, broadcast networks, cable/satellite networks, or websites need—at a cost they can afford. During the past few years, SVOD firms have been pouring money into series and movies. High-profile Hollywood talent has been involved in web-initiated programming for several years. It's a new world for video professionals, and it stretches the term "television" far beyond what people would have thought a decade ago.

Consider Netflix, an SVOD that in March 2018 reached 125 million subscribers, including 57 million Americans. While Warner Bros. and Disney announced they would, respectively, release twenty-three and ten films that year, a Netflix source told the Indiewire media-business website that the studio aimed to roll out at least eighty-two movies or series. Some of them were evidently expensive productions—for example, Noah Baumbach's *The Meyerowitz Stories* follow-up starring Scarlett Johansson and Adam Driver, and the Sandra Bullock post-apocalyptic thriller *Bird Box*. The source also said that Netflix would produce or acquire 700 new or exclusively licensed programs, at least 100 of which are scripted dramas and comedies. These programs would come from twenty-one countries, among them Brazil, India, and South Korea. The UK business magazine *The Economist* wrote in early 2018 that Netflix had not yet turned a profit and was at the time $8.5 million in debt. Netflix replied that it was doing fine in terms of its current revenues compared to expenses.[23]

Either way, Netflix's budget gives certain powers a huge amount of program creation. Word was that the two other major SVODs, Amazon Prime and Apple, were also shelling out lots of money—$4 billion and $1 billion, respectively—content, some of which was newly created. YouTube has also been offering substantial funds to promising production firms with the goal of attracting large audiences for such "professionally" produced material on its territory. The executives believe advertisers will feel more comfortable placing ads alongside this fare rather than alongside the amateur and often raunchy videos currently typical of YouTube.

The upshot of all of this programming money is that the past several years have seen the rise of a large number of firms creating programs of various lengths for the digital world. Many, if not most, of these firms have track records (see Chapter 4). Less well-known and possibly more experimental video producers often take their chances on less well-known websites, on Myspace, or on YouTube without Google funding. Their goal is to get up-front funding from entrepreneurs who will also help them secure distribution in ways that will attract advertisers and pay for the shows. Many of the programs show topics not seen on mainstream channels as well as talented artists who have yet to get a break. A celebrated example is *The Mis-Adventures of Awkward Black Girl*, created and starring Issa Rae and posted on YouTube beginning in late 2011. The show follows the life of a black young woman named J in work and off-work life and was funded partly through donations received on Kickstarter. *Black Girl* won a Shorty Award for Best web Series in 2012.

An example of one production that paid for itself eventually is *High Maintenance*, created and written in 2012 by Katja Blichfield and Ben Sinclair. After its videos appeared on the Vimeo website, HBO made a deal with the *High Maintenance* creators and their Janky Clown Productions for six new episodes to air on the pay channel in 2016, with a second season in 2018. Such successes aside, production of programs aimed at the web and other digital spaces is risky from a business standpoint. Broadcast and subscription television are the places where production makes by far the most money. Moreover, according to the Vimeo site, all previous episodes of *High Maintenance* would be made available not only on HBO but also on HBO's SVOD services, HBO NOW and HBO GO.[24]

pitch
brief summary of a program idea

treatment
a multipage elaboration of a television series producer's initial pitch to network programming executives; the document describes the proposed show's setup and the way in which it relates to previous popular series

concept testing
research commissioned by network executives in order to determine whether the format of a proposed series appeals to members of the series' target audience; this often involves reading a one-paragraph description of series formats to people who fit the profile of likely viewers

pilot
a single episode that is used to test the viability of a series

preview theaters
venues to which members of a target audience are invited to engage in concept testing or to evaluate newly completed series pilots

license
the contract between a production company and network executives that grants the network permission to air each episode a certain number of times; usually thirteen episodes of a series are ordered

For many production companies, the biggest prize is often an order for a prime-time series from one of the broadcast networks. Landing this prize can be tough because often network-owned production companies seem to have an inside track. Even apart from the competition with the networks' production divisions, however, the chances of getting such an order are not high. Network programming executives meet with many producers to hear brief summaries of program ideas. Creators may present several of these summaries, called **pitches**, in one sitting. Most of the time, the network people say that they are not interested. Sometimes they tell the creators that they will pay for a **treatment**, a multipage elaboration of the idea. The treatment describes the proposed show's setup and how it relates to previous popular series. It also discusses the collection of elements that will propel the series and give it a recognizable personality—the setting; the characters; typical plots; and the general layout, tone, and approach. This collection of elements, which often are created using a set of rules that guide the way elements are stitched together with a particular audience-attracting goal in mind, is called the format of a show. (We have already seen how networks such as MTV can have formats.)

If network officials like the format and believe that it fits their programming strategy, they may commission research known as **concept testing** to try out this idea and the ideas of other producers with audiences. Concept testing involves reading one-paragraph descriptions of series formats to people who fit the profile of likely viewers. Sometimes these people are contacted by phone, and sometimes they are questioned in preview theaters where they have been invited to evaluate new shows. Researchers ask these viewers if they would watch the series based on the descriptions. If a producer's concept rates well with the appropriate audience, the interested network may contract for a sample script and a test program, called a **pilot**.

When the pilot is completed, the network tests it too. Often the process involves showing the pilot to a group of target viewers, either on specially rented cable TV channels or in **preview theaters**. When cable TV is used, the individuals chosen are asked to view a movie or series pilot on the channel at a certain time. After the program, the viewers are asked questions over the telephone about what they saw. Viewers in preview theaters sometimes sit in chairs equipped with dials that they can use to indicate how much they like what they see on the screen. These responses, along with the viewers' written comments, help network executives decide whether or not to commission the series.

Let's assume that everything works out fine with a series' concept testing and pilot. The network executives then give the production company a contract for several episodes—typically thirteen. The contract is for permission—called a **license**—to air each episode a certain number of times. You might think that with such a deal in hand, production firm executives would be wildly ecstatic, sure that the show will enrich their firm. Not so fast. For one thing, the network may reduce the firm's potential profits by asking for co-ownership of the show as a way of paying for the risk the network is taking to fund and air it. Moreover, even with network backing, the show may not last long. Many prime-time series receive bad ratings and are yanked by the networks even before their first thirteen episodes have aired.

Another factor that makes production executives nervous is that network licensing agreements typically do not cover the full costs of each episode—even for shows from companies the networks own. If an hour-long drama is slated to cost the production firm $2.5 million per episode, the network may pay $1.5 million. The producers then have to come up with $1 million per episode themselves. Over thirteen episodes, that will put them $13 million in a financial hole.

Why would any company do that? The answer is that in a convergence world production firms see network broadcast as only the first of a number of TV domains in which they can make money from their series. They can make money from local stations, from cable networks, from stores, from the internet, from mobile apps, and from broadcasters outside the United States. And if a show succeeds on TV, these extra windows can become gold mines. But to learn more about how the money comes in, let's shift the discussion from production to distribution.

Distribution in the Television Industry

As we noted earlier, a broadcast television network is involved in both the production and the distribution of material. When a network licenses programs from its own production divisions or from outside producers, it sends them to its affiliates, which then broadcast them (usually simultaneously) to homes. Cable and satellite networks similarly license shows from production firms and then send their feeds to the cable and satellite firms that have agreed to make them available to their customers. Similar to those other networks, distributors of television programming via the internet—for example, Hulu, Netflix, and YouTube—put together rosters of programs. They pay license fees for new shows but don't typically pay license fees for reruns. Rather, they give the owners an amount based on the viewers of the shows. YouTube doles out a percentage of the money it gets for ads around a typical YouTube video. It takes a different tack for its YouTube Premium subscription service, which does not carry ads. Instead, the Google-owned company splits its subscription revenues with the owners of the programming based on how many people watch the shows. YouTube didn't discuss how much of the split goes to the rights holder except to say that YouTube is paying out "the vast, vast majority of revenue."[25]

Note that local broadcast stations do not always rely on the broadcast "nets" for programs. One reason is that stations not affiliated with networks need to get their programming from somewhere. Another reason is that even network-affiliated stations do not broadcast the network feed all the time. Certain hours in the morning, in the afternoon, in the early evening, and after 1:00 a.m. belong to the stations. Therefore, they can take for themselves all the ad revenue they bring in during these periods, but first they must find programs that attract an audience at a reasonable price.

Many non-network distributors are willing to help local stations find attractive shows through syndication—licensing programs to individual outlets on a market-by-market basis (see Table 13.4, which presents ratings of the top fifteen syndicated programs during a week in 2018). Distributors of syndicated programs make three types of deals with stations: direct payment, barter, and a combination of payment and barter. When a station pays for a show with cash, it can sell all the commercial time (about seven minutes) during the program. In the case of **barter**, the distributor has the right to sell almost all the ad time to national advertisers. The combination of cash and barter means that the local station gets most of the time and the distributor gets a couple of minutes. Most deals—in fact, all of them for the shows in Table 13.4—are either full barter or cash plus barter.

barter
when a distributor provides a program to an exhibitor in exchange for the right to sell ad time to advertisers

One way to attract audiences "off network" is with programs that are newly created for syndication. Examples are the celebrity news program *Entertainment Tonight*, the talk show *The Ellen DeGeneres Show*, and the game show *Wheel of Fortune*, which are made to be shown every weekday, which is typical of new syndicated programming. This five-day-a-week placement is called **stripping** a show. Local programmers believe that, in certain day parts, putting the same show in the same time slot each weekday lends predictability to the schedule that target audiences appreciate.

Stripping is also a popular tactic in **off-network syndication**—in which a distributor takes a program that has already been shown on network television and rents episodes of that program to TV stations for local airing. Consider *The Big Bang Theory*, a prime-time staple on CBS for several years through much of 2019. The network licensed the show from Warner Bros. Television. As Table 13.4 indicates, Warner Bros.' distribution arm has been successful at syndicating it to local stations on a five-day stripped basis; Warner Bros.' syndication unit sells national ads and gives back some a number of minutes to the local stations for ads. Table 13.4 also indicates that not all off-network syndicated programs are stripped. *Modern Family, American Ninja Warrior, Blue Bloods*, and *Bob's Burgers* air once a week, typically on Sunday.[26]

If producers fail to place their reruns on local stations, there are other avenues that they can use. Cable and satellite networks have become voracious consumers

stripping
five-day-a-week placement of a television show; programmers believe that, in certain day parts, placing the same show in the same time slot each weekday lends a predictability to the schedule that target audiences appreciate

off-network syndication
a situation in which a distributor takes a program that has already been shown on network television and rents episodes of that program to TV stations for local airing

Table 13.4 Top Fifteen Syndicated Shows (Including Ties) in Households for May 28–June 3, 2018

Rank	Show	Dist	Days	Household rating	Women 25–54 rating
1	JUDGE JUDY (AT)	CTD	MTuWThF..	6.8	2.6
2	FAMILY FEUD (AT)	2/T	MTuWThF..	6.2	2.6
3	WEEKEND ADVENTURE	DAL	. . . . . Su	5.9	2.1
4	JEOPARDY (AT)	CTD	MTuWThF..	5.6	1.5
5	WHEEL OF FORTUNE	CTD	MTuWThF..	5.6	1.6
6	THE BIG BANG THEORY-SYN (AT)	WB	MTuWThF..	4.4	2.7
7	FAMILY FEUD-WK (AT)	2/T	. . . . . Su	3.6	1.2
8	LAW & ORDER: SVU-WKL (AT)	NBU	. . . . . Su	3.6	2.0
9	DATELINE WKLY (AT)	NBU	. . . . . Su	3.3	1.7
10	ENTERTAINMENT TONIGHT(AT)	CTD	MTuWThF..	2.9	1.2
11	INSIDE EDITION (AT)	CTD	MTuWThF..	2.9	1.0
12	DR. PHIL SHOW (AT)	CTD	MTuWThF..	2.8	1.1
13	WHEEL OF FORTUNE WKND	CTD	. . . . . Su	2.7	0.7
14	THE BIG BANG THEORY WKND (AT)	WB	. . . . SaSu	2.6	1.5
15	HOT BENCH (AT)	CTD	MTuWThF..	2.2	0.8

Source: "Syndicated TV Ratings . . . in the Week of May 28," TV by the Numbers, based on Nielsen Company data, June 3, 2018, https://tvbythenumbers. zap2it.com/weekly-ratings/syndicated-tv-ratings-may-28-june-3-2018/, accessed August 12, 2018. These are the top nationally syndicated shows, which Nielsen defines as shows for which the distributors sell national advertising. ("Simpsons repeats in syndication are not counted in the weekly ratings because they don't include any national advertising.") For syndicated shows that air on multiple days, the viewership shown is the average of all telecasts. "HH rating" stands for household rating. 2/T: Twentieth Television; CTD: CBS Television Distribution; ESP: ESPN; NBU: NBC Universal; NFL: National Football League; SPT: Sony Pictures Television; WB: Warner Bros; MGY: MGM. AT means additional time or telecasts; a station may air more than the typical number of episodes or time periods per week.

of off-network programming, in part because these programs are less expensive than new shows and in part because they reliably attract certain categories of viewers. Nick at Night and TVLand are two MPVD networks that air television programs that people in their thirties and forties viewed when they were young. Lifetime goes after programs that in their broadcast network lives were popular with women, and USA carries reruns of action series that have been popular on the broadcast networks in addition to new series it orders.

Another venue for making extra money from television programs is what marketers call **out-of-home locations**, sometimes called **captive audience locations**. These include such places as airline waiting areas and store checkout lines where people congregate and likely pay attention to TV clips and commercials. CNN distributes its news programming as the CNN Airport Network. NBC and CBS provide some of the news and entertainment programs they own to airlines; NBC also owns a network that sends some of its programs (with commercials) to health care offices. ABC News provides material for a company that puts video screens on gas station pumps.

out-of-home locations (or captive audience locations) places such as airline waiting areas and store checkout lines where people congregate and likely pay attention to TV clips and commercials

THINKING ABOUT MEDIA LITERACY

Take a closer look at Table 13.4 which lists the most popular shows in syndication. Do any of the programs there surprise you? Was a program missing that you thought would be there? Why does daytime television programming rely on these types of syndicated shows?

Foreign countries have also been a useful market for certain types of reruns. Broadcasters around the world purchase US-made series as components of their schedules. The popularity of programs from the United States rises and falls, and in many cases homegrown programming gets better ratings than the US material. Generally speaking, action dramas do better than sitcoms in this market because American humor doesn't cross borders as easily as sex appeal (*Baywatch* was popular around the world) and violence (so was *Walker, Texas Ranger*). During the late 2000s, the increase in digital television channels in some countries led both new networks looking to raise their profiles and established networks wanting to stem audience losses to scramble for highly polished programs at reasonable prices. US firms have been ready to fill the gap. In Spain, for example, the Telecinco network signed a deal with NBC Universal to show the new drama series *Trauma: Life in the ER* and the older *Parenthood* movies. "U.S. dramas bring prestige and work well for Spanish channels," said a Madrid-based research company executive.

Captive-audience locations, such as checkout lines, airports, airplanes, and even the backseats of New York City cabs, provide an opportunity for networks and advertisers to reach viewers (or potential customers, for advertisers) at a time when they are likely to actually view the programming that is put in front of them.

Note that a reverse flow of programs is also taking place. The increase in channels in the United States, combined with the need for less expensive programming, has led programmers to scour the world for series ideas. They may decide to copy an international series idea for use in the United States—even using the same basic scripts, but adapting the program to suit their idea of what their American audience wants. Examples include the NBC drama *The Office*, CBS's reality show *Big Brother*, and Showtime's drama *Homeland*, which were based on British, Dutch, and Israeli versions, respectively.

The internet has become a competitor to the traditional TV set for viewers' time, and so have video games and the DVD player. TV ratings are slipping as a result. Producers and network executives are trying to find ways to profit from the programs that they make and circulate.

Encouraging Viewers to View Programs With Commercials on the Internet An increasing number of homes have been paying for fast broadband connections to the internet. Such fast connections allow users to view audiovisual presentations with acceptable clarity, and as a result, just about every television network is posting much of its programming on the web for people to view. The shows **stream**—that is, they start playing when you click on their links—and they are not designed to be saved on the user's computer. The program streams come with commercials that are much fewer in number and shorter in time than the ones people see on traditional TV. The catch, however, is that online a viewer cannot speed through ads.

Current thinking on the part of network executives is that they must offer ways for people to stream their content from the web. NBC Universal, Disney, and Warner Media are among the firms invested in Hulu, which allows visitors to "watch current episodes, full seasons, original series, and hit movies all in one place," if they subscribe. The $7.99 version includes "limited commercials," while the "no commercials" version costs $11.99. (College students may pay less.) If you don't want to pay and still want to stream legally, you might find the show you want at a network's website. In 2019 for example, ABC.com was allowing access to a live stream of its local affiliate's broadcast and some episodes of current programs (such as *Modern Family*) on its site. CBS.com was also allowing viewing of the most recent episodes of select programs (*Big Brother, 60 Minutes*), but it was not allowing live TV viewing of a local affiliate. Instead it was trying to sell people subscriptions to CBS All Access, a streaming service for desktops, laptops, smartphones, tablets, game machines, and streaming boxes (such as Roku and Apple TV) that offers thousands of episodes on demand, new episodes on a CBS app the day after they initially air, and the ability to watch linear affiliate television. Urging viewers to try All Access, CBS.com enthuses that the OTT service allows people to "watch new episodes the next day just by streaming on your device of choice. Our app makes it easy for cord cutters to still enjoy their favorite CBS programs whenever, wherever!"[27]

Some observers contend that the major networks are—or soon will be—cannibalizing their audiences by placing their first-run prime-time programs for viewing on the web. That is, they say people will watch the programs online (where there are fewer and less expensive commercials) and so make it difficult for the networks to profit from prime-time showings. Network executives disagree, arguing that web versions allow fans to view shows they miss occasionally and that they create new fans who end up watching the programs in their broadcast time slots. Either way, cable and satellite executives are annoyed that the programs can be found for free online. They note that they pay money to carry those shows and other programming. They worry that increasing numbers of households will drop their subscription TV contracts and simply view many entertainment and news programs online—and purchase some from digital retailers such as Apple TV and Amazon. Nevertheless, as we noted earlier, to keep subscribers, Comcast, AT&T, and other MVPD firms have created "TV Everywhere" programs. They allow people who pay them monthly fees to view many of the networks they carry on multiple devices in or out of the home without extra charge through the use of a password.

stream
the act of sending digital materials so they can be heard or viewed as they are sent, without having to be saved first

GLOBAL MEDIA TODAY & CULTURE

TELEVISION FORMATS: LOCAL ADAPTATIONS OF TV PROGRAMS

Have you ever watched *American Idol*? If so, you were not alone: it has been one of the most successful TV shows in the United States in the last decade, drawing millions of viewers to the screen eager to find out who the new emerging music phenomenon might be. The singing competition prides itself in having launched the music career of many recording artists, including Kelly Clarkson and Carry Underwood, winners of season one and four, respectively.

Unlike its title suggests, however, this is not entirely an American show. Rather, it is an American adaptation of an international TV format—*Pop Idol*—distributed worldwide by a European media conglomerate, FremantleMedia. In the United States we are under the impression that we are watching an American show, as the contestants, judges, and hosts are American. But foreign audiences are watching their localized versions of the show airing in different countries around the world.

The local adaptation of TV programs is an increasingly relevant phenomenon in the global entertainment landscape, and other shows such as *Dancing with the Stars*, *The Voice,* and *Big Brother* are distributed internationally in the same way: A global format is adapted in different countries by local broadcasters. They combine global features—the format of the TV program—with local ones (usually hosts, contestants, and content of the show). What do you think of these TV shows? Is this genre bound to increase or decrease its presence in the TV landscape?

Exhibition in the Television Industry

Local stations, cable systems, satellite delivery systems, and wired and wireless phone companies take on the role of exhibitor when they deliver material directly to viewers. Like theaters in the movie business and stores in the book publishing industry, the broadcast exhibitors are retailers. Their business is to attract the number and the kind of viewers who can help them make a profit for their shareholders.

The early 21st century finds the television exhibition system in the midst of a major upheaval. Network affiliates are particularly worried about the declining ability of ABC, CBS, Fox, and NBC to grab the lion's share of the US television audience. Local TV executives are also concerned about the networks' strong and increasing participation in the subscription video world. Disney-owned ABC controls the multiplatform networks ESPN, the Disney Channel, and ABC Family, among others. Comcast's NBC Universal controls MSNBC, CNBC, USA, Syfy, and Bravo. All the broadcast networks are placing hit programs on the web, with the consequence that viewers don't have to watch local channels (and their commercials) to see prime-time TV. Network executives reply that their affiliates are important to them. Not only do they bring in a lot of advertising money, they bring in large retransmission fees—fees that the affiliates partly kick back to the networks for their programming. Therefore, the networks say, they would not do anything to fundamentally harm local service. They are also helping the local stations to beef up their websites, where they make money from advertising. Nevertheless, the tension between local broadcast stations and broadcast networks continues.

Tensions are also running high in the cable exhibition business. For decades cable systems were the only major exhibitors competing with local TV stations. Now cable operators worry that their power will be eroded substantially by satellite firms such as Dish and AT&T's DirecTV, as well as by broadband services from Verizon and AT&T (the telcos) that duplicate cable services. As we have seen, cutting and shaving the cord of all these services are activities that concern all these businesses. At this point it does not seem like a huge percentage of American households is doing that. Industry observers suggest that the numbers will grow substantially as ways to access television shows outside traditional "pay TV" services grow. The cable and telco providers will still be able to make money by selling the cord cutters high-speed internet service. Yet cord cutting will undermine the entire system of charging subscribers for a broad swatch of niche channels relatively few of them visit. Critics of the industry contend that people should not have to pay for so much they don't watch. Cable industry leaders respond that this approach is what has allowed the diversity of program networks that exist on cable television systems. They clearly hope that Americans will continue to subscribe to both their programming and their internet services.

THINKING ABOUT MEDIA LITERACY

In this era of converging technologies, cable providers worry that consumers want to "cut the cord" and just watch their favorite shows online when they want to. What advantages does this option offer consumers? What disadvantages does this option bring to cable providers and the networks? What, if anything, do you think cable providers could do to remain competitive?

THINKING ABOUT MEDIA LITERACY

The financing of television programming has become more fragmented. Think about you or your family's television viewing. What costs are involved? When television was first broadcast it was free. What types of charges are consumers paying now to view a wide variety of programming?

Media Ethics: Converging Screens, Social Television, and the Issue of Personalization

You may have noticed a basic point that has flowed through our discussion of television in this chapter: watching TV no longer only means viewing the box in your living room or bedroom. In fact, taking advantage of digital convergence, television industry executives are eager to move their programs across many platforms with the aim of eking revenue from advertisers as well as from viewers at every stop. The TV industry's realization that people use several screens in their daily lives has led to yet another development: **social television**. It refers to a person's use of one

social television
a person's use of one screen for viewing a program while he or she uses another screen for discussing it with others

screen for viewing a program while he or she uses another screen (e.g., a phone or tablet) for discussing it with others. Many people use Twitter to carry out social viewing, but other forms of messaging, including through Facebook, are also popular. Marketers have noticed this development, and they are eager to send ads to people's tablets or phones based upon their interactions around television programs. In 2015, for example, Twitter had a deal with Walmart that identified people discussing shows with Walmart commercials. Twitter then sent to their Twitter feeds Walmart ads that promoted the same products that were in the commercials.

In fact, advertisers are fascinated by the possibility of not just reaching but even interacting with people when they are viewing television on one or another digital screen. The activity is called "addressable television." It involves the ability to learn information about the individuals who are viewing and send them particular commercial messages. You may recall from our chapter on advertising that this type of activity is taking place quite actively online as well as on tablets and smartphones. Digital advertising leaders are trying hard to make it work for cable- and satellite-delivered channels, which don't share the same technical specifications as the internet-related media. Already it is quite possible for companies such as Visible World (owned by Comcast) to send different commercials to different homes based on information about the homes that the cable company provides that firm. Visible World can send variations of the same commercial—with different types of people or different music—to different homes based on information stored on the homes' set-top box. Although these activities are still expensive and experimental, many in the television industry expect that in years to come commercials will be customized based on data that cable firms, advertisers, ad agencies, and others hold about particular households and even individual viewers.

For example, your TV may get a commercial from Kay Jewelers while your neighbor gets one from Tiffany. Moreover, on the tablet you're using to send messages to friends about the program you're co-viewing, you may begin to see discount ads for Kay, whereas your neighbor finds an invitation to a special viewing of an expensive new Tiffany line at the nearby mall. When you learn about this difference during a conversation with your neighbor, you ask yourself, "Why is this happening?" Well, maybe the cable company has determined that your household income is lower than that of your neighbor, and your pattern of program viewing and the record the company has gathered of your supermarket purchases led it to suspect that you would be a Kay Jewelers type more than a Tiffany's type.

Insulted? Perhaps you should be. The more preferred outcome, for the purpose of this book, though, is for you to think more broadly about the possible impact of bringing huge amounts of data about individuals and households to the television screen, broadly defined. What will it mean for society when people wonder whether the commercials, the discounts, and maybe even the television programs they are receiving on various screens are being personalized based on what the advertisers know about them? Will people be nervous because they believe advertisers, networks, and exhibitors are defining them in ways that conflict with their understanding of themselves? Will people try to change their mobile, online, and even cable TV viewing habits in order to get better profiles that yield them better status and marketing offers? What are the ethics of media and marketing firms personalizing the screens and social media environments you receive based on information—even anonymous information—they have attached to you without your knowing it or giving your permission?

You may remember from the advertising chapter that critical observers see this issue as a major one for a lot of online and mobile advertising today. So far, these data-collection and personalization activities have not become part of the environment of the big home TV set or the little screens around them. Yet because television reaches so many Americans with powerful news, entertainment, and sports stories, marketers are chomping at the bit to bring the data techniques they have been developing for the web to those home screens. Do you think their audiences should have a say in whether and/or how they do it?

CHAPTER REVIEW

Visit the Companion Website at www.routledge.com/cw/turow for additional study tools and resources.

Key Terms

You can find the definitions to these key terms in the marginal glossary throughout this chapter. Test your knowledge of these terms with interactive flash cards on the *Media Today* Companion Website.

audience flow	household share	prime time
average commercial minute	independent broadcast station	program feed
Big Four commercial networks	lead-in	ratings
barter	lead-out	reach
billboards	license	retransmission fees
broadcast live	license fees	sampling
broadcast outlets	lineup	satellite television
C3 rating	multichannel broadcasting	schedules
C7 rating	multichannel subscription video	series
cable television	programming distributors	slim bundles
cable television system	(MVPDs)	social television
commercial stations	multiple system owner (MSO)	station groups
commercials	national rating points	stream
competition	network affiliates	stripping
concept testing	noncommercial stations	subscription networks
counterprogramming	O&Os (owned and operated	sweeps
cord shavers	stations)	syndication
cutting the cord	off-network syndication	telcos
day parts	out-of-home locations (or captive	television broadcasting
direct broadcast satellite (DBS)	audience locations)	television network
technology	over-the-top TV (OTT)	television program ratings
format	pay-per-view (PPV)	tiering
golden age of television	people meter	time slot
hammock	people ratings	treatment
head end	pilot	underwriting
high-definition television (HDTV)	pitch	video on demand (VOD)
household ratings	preview theaters	vMPVDs

Questions for Discussion and Critical Thinking

1. Over the past decade the number of "reality TV" programs has grown. If you were a television producer, what would be attractive about creating a "reality TV" program? As an advertiser, why is "reality TV" programming a good media buy for placing your commercials?

2. Companies initially involved solely in distribution and exhibition of television and movies programming have now moved into production. Why would the expense and risk involved in program production be beneficial to companies like Netflix, Amazon, and Hulu? Do you think they are smart to get into this type of "vertical" business model? Why or why not?

3. Sweeps—when every area of the country's audience for television is surveyed—have traditionally taken place four times a year. The ratings determined during sweeps help set advertising rates for different programs. How have the new methods for watching television programming made the analysis of television viewership more difficult? How have they made it easier? Does it matter what method is used for how someone views television content?

4. The 1950s have been referred to by media historians as "the golden age of television" because this newly available medium made "powerful, original dramas such as *Marty, Judgment at Nuremberg,* and *Requiem for a Heavyweight*" (quote from Turow, p. 388). Some television critics are saying we are in a new "golden age of television." Would you agree? Why or why not?

 ## Activity

In radio, a station's format defines the content it will offer the audience. The content choices are usually consistent throughout the hours the radio station is on the air. With the exception of specific niche topic or audience channels (e.g., ESPN, Animal Planet, Nickelodeon), general broadcast stations cannot be defined by a particular format or genre. How, then, are programming choices made?

For this activity, look at the local listings for television stations in your area (you can put your ZIP code into the TV Listings service on TVGUIDE.com). Examine the programming on ABC, NBC, CBS, and Fox. Reflect on what is similar, or different, about their programming options during different parts of the day (early morning, morning, early afternoon, early evening, evening, late night). What does this programming indicate about the audience the network is pursuing in each of these parts of the day? How does the array of programming options, and the audience it pursues, serve the television station's or network's financing needs?

The Video Game Industry

14

CHAPTER OBJECTIVES

1   Sketch the development of video games.

2   Describe video game genres.

3   Review the production, distribution, and exhibition of video games.

4   Chart major social controversies surrounding video games.

In 2018 the Cowen investment firm named *Grand Theft Auto V* (GTA 5) the most financially successful media title of all time. From the time of its 2013 launch, the game sold 90 million copies for its publisher, Take-Two Interactive, and in doing that generated around $6 billion dollars. Although more people may have seen individual films and listened to particular songs, no work of media content has made as much money, even when you take physical purchases, streaming, and inflation into account.[1]

GTA 5 was unusual from the start. Out of the starting gate the game became the fastest revenue-generating entertainment product in history. It earned $800 million on its first day and $1 billion in its first three days—and that was when it was being sold for use only on the PlayStation 3 and Xbox 360 consoles.[2] At the time of its release, the *International Business Times* wrote that "[t]he enormous budget for 'GTA 5' dwarfs what were formerly the largest video game budgets and rivals Hollywood blockbusters."[3] Actually, Activision's *Call of Duty: Modern Warfare 2* wasn't that different in price; it reportedly cost $250 million to create and market in 2009—$276 million in 2015 terms.[4] Increasingly, though adventure video games do cost as much as expensive Hollywood films, and as with the fruits of the movie industry, some do gangbusters and others fizzle.

Outside the big action games there are huge moneymakers, too. A website that follows gaming estimated in 2017 that the mobile game *Candy Crush Saga* had been installed on Android devices between 500 million and a billion

> "I like video games, but they're really violent. I'd like to play a video game where you help the people who were shot in all the other games. It'd be called 'Really Busy Hospital.'"
>
> **DEMETRI MARTIN, COMEDIAN**

times and had "produced total revenue somewhere near $1.7 billion for its developer King."[5] "Videogames are a much better business than [movie] studios," an analyst for the KeyBanc investment consultancy told MarketWatch. She added that because games are interactive (and often connected to the internet), their creators can see what works for players and what doesn't and make changes to the games or to new ones based on what they learned.[6]

These huge numbers associated with video games raise a key point: video games are a big business in the United States and around the world. According to the NPD research firm, in the United States alone, industry revenue hovered around $36 billion in 2017—$29.1 billion for content, $4.7 billion for hardware such as gaming consoles, and $2.2 billion for accessories, including headsets and virtual reality glasses.[7] This chapter explores this important media industry. It looks at the kinds of games that are out there; the production, distribution, and exhibition processes that create and circulate them; and social issues that surround them.

The Video Game Industry and Convergence

Including a chapter about the video game industry is rather unusual for an introductory text on media and society. Yet the production, distribution, and exhibition of video games have in the past few decades become major industrial activities that ought to be included in mainstream discussions of media in society. As we explore this relatively new industry in the final chapter, it's important to point out that convergence is a major theme.

That shouldn't be surprising. Throughout this book we have noted that media industries in the 21st century must be understood in terms of convergence, with companies and audience members moving content across media boundaries and often reshaping the content to fit different needs. We have seen how the relatively recent desktop and mobile business worlds have become important parts of the converging system. People experience convergence when they watch television, read newspapers, listen to radio, and read books and more on their mobile devices, tablets, and desktop computers, as well as on their television sets. Digging deep into that media system, we have seen how leaders in traditional media fields—advertising and public relations as well as the book, newspaper, magazine, recording, radio, movie, and television industries—understand that they have to link their products to a variety of media, analog as well as digital, to survive and grow. Fashion magazine publishers, for example, tie their periodicals' names to fashion shows in various cities, on television, and on the web in order to reach their audiences. Here we will see how video games fit into this pattern.

The Rise of the Video Game Industry

So what are video games? Here we will define them as entertainment products powered by computer chips and displayed on monitors that require users to

1930s	1940s	1950s	1960s	1970s

1931: David Gottlieb introduces the first coin-operated pinball machines.

1947: Gottlieb introduces Humpty Dumpty pinball game.
1948: Thomas T. Goldsmith and Estle Ray Mann develop a "cathode ray tube amusement device" on which a player uses knobs and buttons to simulate firing a missile on a screen.

1958: Scientists at the Brookhaven National Laboratory set up a video tennis game, an early precursor to *Pong* and the first video game designed to be played on a display screen.

1961: MIT students create *Spacewar!*

1971: Coin-operated *Galaxy Game*, the first commercial video game, is installed in Stanford University's student union.
1972: Nolan Bushnell and Ted Dabney found Atari and create *Pong*.

1972: The Magnavox company releases Odyssey.

1976: Mattel introduces Auto Race, the first handheld electronic game device.
1977: Atari releases its 2600 console.

1979: Video arcade games overtake pinball machines in popularity.

Late 1970s–mid-1980s: Arcade games like *Pac-Man, Donkey Kong*, and *Space Invaders* peak in popularity in what is often called the "golden age of video arcade games."

Figure 14.1
Timeline of the video game industry.

experience and interact with challenges in a series of tasks. The products leading to today's video games go back several decades. Read through the timeline (Figure 14.1). You might notice that the development of video game technology—and the development of the video game industry—echoes the three historical themes we have explored in other chapters. Let's take a look.

1. The video game did not arrive in a flash as a result of one inventor's grand change.

The birth of video games can be traced back to two separate developments that initially were unrelated to the computer.[8] The first development was the advent of the **pinball machine**, a coin-operated game in which a player scores points by causing metal balls to move in certain directions (often using flippers) inside a glass-covered

pinball machine
coin-operated game in which a player scores points by causing metal balls to move in certain directions (often using flippers) inside a glass-covered case

1980s	1990s	2000s	2010s

1983: The GamBit company in Minnesota introduces *Scepter of Goth*, the first commercial online role-playing game in the United States.
1983: A major economic downturn befalls the console industry.
1985: Nintendo introduces the Nintendo Entertainment System video game console in the United States.

1989: Nintendo releases the Game Boy.

1995: Sony releases the PlayStation.
1996: The 3DO company releases *Meridian 59*, the first massively multiplayer role-playing game (MMORPG).
1998: Nokia installs the game *Snake* on its mobile phones.

2001: Microsoft releases the first Xbox.
2003: Linden Lab launches *Second Life*, an MMORPG featuring a virtual world that avatars can explore—complete with a currency with a real-world exchange rate.

2004: Release of the handheld gaming systems Nintendo DS and PlayStation Portable.
2006: Nintendo releases the Wii.

2006: Ailin Graef becomes the first person to become a real-world millionaire via virtual real estate development in *Second Life*.
2007: Social network game company Zynga is founded.
2009: Zynga launches its best-known game, *FarmVille*, on Facebook, reaching 10 million users within six weeks.

2010: Microsoft introduces the Kinect motion sensing input device for the Xbox 360, allowing users to interact with games without a controller.
2012: OMGPOP, a struggling mobile-app firm, launches *Draw Something*, a mobile interactive word game. Within 50 days of its release, *Draw Something* is downloaded 50 million times.
2012: Zynga purchases OMGPOP for $180 million.
2015: NVIDIA releases GeForce Now, a subscription-based cloud gaming service that allows users to stream games to their devices from the digital cloud.
2014: Amazon purchases live streaming video game playing site Twitch for $970 million.
2016: Global revenue on video games is $101 billion, which is more than video and music sales combined.

entertainment arcades
commercial locations featuring coin-operated machines such as pinball machines, fortune tellers, and shooting games

case. These games were made popular by David Gottlieb beginning in the early 1930s at **entertainment arcades**—commercial locations featuring coin-operated machines such as pinball machines, fortune tellers, and shooting games.

While the mechanical pinball game was a fixture of arcades, scientists working on video electronics and computers were amusing themselves with games that could be played on TV-like displays. In 1958, for example, scientists at the Brookhaven National Laboratory set up a video tennis game on an oscilloscope for play during its annual visitors' day. Similarly, computer students at MIT, Stanford, and other schools began to use their universities' computer systems to create games such as *Spacewar!* that were tied to their love of science fiction. Activities like these that were taking place at the University of Utah influenced Nolan Bushnell and Ted Dabney to start Atari in 1972—the first successful US company to create and sell video arcade games. It was Atari that really got the ball rolling toward a video game industry.

2. The video game as a medium of communication developed as a result of social and legal responses to the technology during different periods.

As this brief description of the beginning of the video game industry suggests, the development of the technology initially took place in the social context of what today would be called "geek" culture. It was developed by highly educated computer science students at top universities who applied their skills in order to have fun as well as meet new technical challenges. In the 1970s, enterprising businesspeople who knew about these developments took the gutsy step of adapting for broad interests what those young, highly educated niches of US society were doing. Their console games struck a chord with large segments of the nation, as well as with many people in other parts of the world.

Yet social responses to the growing console industry changed in the early 1980s. A severe downturn in console-based video games during this period severely hurt Atari and other console-game makers. Instead, many gamers were attracted to games that could be used with the newly available personal-computer technology. Companies sold disks that could be played on specific computers—for example, the Commodore 64, the Apple II, and the IBM PC. Strategy video games and simulation video games—genres that had already been used for some consoles—caught on as particularly appropriate for computer play, with hits including *Dune* (strategy) and *SimCity* (simulation).

bulletin boards
software that allows users to exchange messages with other users, read news and public articles, and perform other activities such as play games

multiuser dungeons (MUDs)
early text-based online fantasy role-playing games

massively multiplayer online role-playing games (MMORPGs)
video games in which a large number of players—as many as hundreds of thousands—interact with one another in virtual worlds

Through the 1980s, social change connected to a different new technology again affected video games. This time it was the internet, and again the new approach to gaming related to "geeky" circles. As the internet began to be used by more and more academics in the 1980s, it, too, became a location for playing games. People even figured out how to use internet **bulletin boards**, in which many users could send messages to one another, as a place where many people could share a game. Multiplayer computer games that combined elements of chat rooms and fantasy role-playing games, such as *Dungeons & Dragons*, emerged as extremely popular in these environments, and the games became known as **multiuser dungeons (MUDs)**. They were the predecessors of today's popular **massively multiplayer online role-playing games (MMORPGs)**, such as *World of Warcraft*, that boast millions of players worldwide.

By the time the early 1990s came around, then, the basic types of video game vehicles had been established. Although some platforms lost popularity, the next decade would reveal that many different types of video game platforms—consoles, computers, handheld, and internet—could coexist.

3. The video game industry developed and changed as a result of struggles to control its channels to audiences.

The movement of video game makers toward a number of different technologies reflects larger changes that were taking place within American society and within the industry. As Americans began using computers and mobile phones, game makers created software for those channels. They also developed different types of games for men and women. For example, the idea was (and still is) that men are more interested in action-adventure games that may take a long time to finish, whereas women are attracted to short puzzle-like games that avoid violence. (Clearly these are generalizations that don't have to fit you.) Different companies tended to gravitate toward creating or distributing different types of games as well (we'll discuss more of that later). Over time, some software companies, such as Electronic Arts and Activision, became powerhouses with the ability to spend the most money on game production, advertise the most, and grab the most press attention.

A similar concentration of power eventually developed among console manufacturers, with three firms—Sony, Nintendo, and Microsoft—controlling that video game channel. Before Microsoft entered the fray in 2001, the competition was between three companies—Sony, Nintendo, and Sega. Sony's PlayStation became so popular that Sega stopped making consoles in 2001, and Nintendo lagged far behind in sales. Moreover, it took a while for Microsoft to be a serious competitor. Over time, Microsoft's Xbox and its successor, the Xbox 360 (released in 2005), cut into Sony's lead. In 2007 Nintendo came roaring back into competition with Sony and Microsoft via its new console: the Wii. The Wii represented a kind of counterprogramming to the gaming approaches of Sony and Microsoft. Hard-core gamers—mostly male 15- to 34-year-olds—preferred the Xbox 360 platform or PlayStation 3 for its superior graphics, more "hard-core" adventure titles, and strong online capabilities. The Wii, by contrast, was a gaming platform that Nintendo purposely built for people who may be intimidated by PlayStation and Xbox controllers. As a result, the Wii captured a broader audience than its competitors, proving very popular with women and children.

Through these struggles among firms, and similar to the other industries we have seen in this book, the industry players have had to contend with controversies. Most of the public anger directed toward them has revolved around sex and violence in games, though there also have been strong complaints about stereotyping of various ethnic and racial groups as well as women in the video games; *Grand Theft Auto V* is among the games most skewered on this account. Evident in the timeline, however, is a reaction that we have seen in many of the industries covered in *Media Today*: self-regulation. In 1994, stung by criticism of violent content in video games such as *Night Trap*, *Mortal Kombat*, *Lethal Enforcers*, and *Doom*, the video game industry association, the Entertainment Software Association, established the Entertainment Software Rating Board (ESRB). The approach it adopted is similar to what goes on with movie and television self-regulation. As Chapter 5 notes, the board assigns ratings to games based on their content, and next to the ratings are descriptions of problematic content in the games. By July 2012 the ESRB had assigned more than 22,000 ratings to titles submitted by more than 350 publishers.[9] The ratings have not stopped controversies about game content. We will discuss this topic in more detail later in the chapter. First, let's get an overview of the industry.

Nintendo continues to revolutionize the world of consoles. The Switch is multifunctional, and a separate "Labo" kit can even be purchased that transforms the console into a piano, racing cars, and much more.

The Contemporary Shape of the Video Game Industry

Today, video games are extremely popular with a wide segment of the population. According to the Entertainment Software Association (ESA), in 2017, 64 percent of Americans played video games. The ESA further reported that the average female video game player is 36 years old and the average male is 32. Females make up 45 percent of the US gaming population, and males constitute 55 percent. To disabuse people of the stereotype that most players are teenage boys, the association points out that "adult women represent a greater portion of the video game-playing population (33 percent) than boys under 18 (17 percent)." To counter the notion that gaming is an isolating activity, the association reports that it is in fact highly social, with 42 percent reporting they play with friends most frequently and 19 percent reporting that they play with family. The association also states that "most gamers feel computer and video games provide more value for their money" by large percentages compared to DVDs, movies, and music, and by a small percentage compared to video/music streaming services.[10]

THINKING ABOUT MEDIA LITERACY

Consider this statistic: "adult women represent a greater portion of the video game-playing population (33 percent) than boys under 18 (17 percent)." Does this surprise you? Why or why not?

All that playing drives a lot of spending. According to data compiled by the NPD Group and released by ESA, consumers spent $29.1 billion on video gaming content during 2017.[11] Of revenue gained from content sales, 21 percent was from purchases of physical games—for example, console discs or computer software. The proportion of money people spent on various digital downloads of games—for example, on the web or mobile apps—has grown substantially. In 2010 digital downloads represented only 31 percent of sales, whereas in 2017 it had increased to 79 percent.

As the preceding data suggest, today the term "video game" stands for a complex industry with several different types of products and different production, distribution, and exhibition processes. They make up a big business. According to the NPD research firm, in the United States the video game industry brought in about $36 billion during 2017, including the sale of consoles, accessories, and games.[12] From the preceding discussion and from what you may know about video games, you can understand that any discussion of the business has to take into consideration two key features: the hardware and the software.

THINKING ABOUT MEDIA LITERACY

Think of all the ways games are distributed and exhibited. List the variety of options for engaging with games. What is your preferred method? What do you think about the costs associated with different methods for getting access to games?

Video Game Hardware

"**Hardware**" refers to the devices on which the video games are played, and a number of types of hardware coexist. Games are sold for gaming consoles, desktop or laptop computers, interactive television connections, handheld game devices, and mobile devices. During 2017, Americans spent about $6.9 billion on hardware and physical accessories (such as virtual reality head-mounted displays) for the hardware. Let's look briefly at each type of hardware.

Gaming Consoles Gaming consoles are optimized for the speed and graphics that many games require. You could get many of the same features on a desktop or laptop computer, but you'd likely have to know a lot about ordering special components, and you'd undoubtedly pay a lot more money than if you bought a standard computer. Three companies—Sony with its PlayStation, Microsoft with its Xbox, and Nintendo with its Switch—make the consoles that people associate with contemporary gaming. The sales of various consoles rise and fall depending upon how recently they have been introduced; new models sell strongly at first and then fade, as fans wait for newer versions. A 2018 PWC analysis pointed out that console sales in the United States have been holding up even with the introduction of powerful general-purpose computers that have the ability to play the complex console games. The analysis concluded that "rumors of consoles' death are exaggerated—for now." But it predicted that by 2022 the spread of cloud computing linked to increasingly smaller and powerful general-purpose devices in the home would allow for the same kinds of gaming on consoles and so "may render further console purchases redundant for all but the most dedicated gamers."[13]

One bid that console makers have tried to get users to see their value beyond game playing is by building media convergence into the design and functionality of video game consoles. Whereas early consoles were used solely for game play, today's models can serve many different functions. Certainly, consoles connect to the internet so users can download games and play with other users. But various apps can also be downloaded, allowing users to stream video (via apps such as Netflix, Hulu Plus, and Amazon Prime), check sports scores (via the ESPN, NFL Sunday Ticket, or MLB.tv apps), or play music (through apps such as Spotify and Pandora). Microsoft's hype on the Xbox website revels in these cross-platform connections: "With Xbox, you'll find the best apps, TV, movies and sports all in one place so you'll never miss a moment," it promises. "It's all the entertainment you love. All in one place." Through convergence, consoles are quickly becoming more than just vehicles for game play. They are acting as multipurpose entertainment portals.[14]

Desktop or Laptop Computers Computer game players seem to prefer strategy games over the adventure games that console players tend to buy. Although games purchased to play on the computer were extremely popular in the 1990s, sales declined as consoles became attractive to hard-core gamers and as broadband connections to internet gaming increased and allowed for more sophisticated graphics and animation. Whereas buying game software for stand-alone computers is becoming less common, playing games online is rapidly gaining popularity. Gambling on US-based websites can be explicitly legal or illegal depending on the state and the game.[15] In addition to in-US activities, Americans do access sites elsewhere in the world to participate in these activities.

Aside from gambling sites, you can go to many websites that offer games to play. Most fall under the casual gaming category; this is a popular category supposedly

hardware
the device or console on which video games are played

preferred by women aged 25 years and older. It includes puzzle, card, board, and word games, sometimes with fictional characters. Pogo is a website that specializes in these sorts of games, featuring titles such as *Mahjong Garden* and *Jet Set Solitaire*. Pogo (along with MSN Games and other sites) also has arcade-like games and sports games. If, as a **casual gamer**, you want to play games for free, you will see a lot of ads; some even interrupt game play. Pogo allows you to get rid of the ads by paying a fee to play, and you can join Club Pogo to play a wide range of games without ad interruptions.

People interested in the more intense, complex, and often violent adventure platforms aimed at hard-core gamers can also find them online, along with chat rooms to discuss them. For example, on the Steam platform (which is available in versions for Windows and Apple computers), you can find games such as *Rise of the Tomb Raider, Farming Simulator,* and *Ultraball*. Some of them are free, whereas others charge users to play. Popular with hard-core gamers are sites for MMORPGs. In an MMORPG, a player uses a client to connect to a server, usually run by the publisher of the game, which hosts the virtual world and stores information about the player. The user controls a character represented by an **avatar**—a character that represents the user and that can be directed to fight villains, interact with other characters, acquire items, and so on.

MMORPGs have become extremely popular since the wider debut of broadband internet connections, boasting millions of subscribers from hundreds of different countries. *League of Legends* is the number-one subscription-based MMORPG in the world, with approximately 27 million players daily.[16] Other popular MMORPGs with active forums are *World of Warcraft, The Elder Scrolls Online, Star Wars: The Old Republic,* and *Final Fantasy XIV.*

Handheld Devices, Interactive Television, and Mobile Devices **Handheld game devices** are portable machines that are primarily designed for game play. During the early 2000s and early 2010s, the Nintendo DS (and its successor, the Nintendo 3DS) dominated the market, outselling the PlayStation Portable (and its 2012 iteration as the PlayStation Vita). More recently fans give the Nintendo Switch kudos for its portability. With the increasing popularity of multipurpose mobile devices, however, handheld game device sales have fallen steadily in recent years.

Interactive television (iTV) is another area in which games have been growing strongly. Cable, satellite, and telco operators are charging customers beyond basic fees to access playing areas with their remote-control devices. Much of the iTV gaming is done via the set-top box, so that even satellite companies (whose technologies do not allow for two-way interactions with customers) can get in on the action. In 2018, for example, Dish Network was one company offering a game subscription service. Its customers could get various game collections with different themes at different prices. The company offered Dish Games, a grouping of games, including *Yahtzee* and *Scrabble Scramble*, at $5 per month.

An increasingly popular portable gaming platform is the **mobile device**. The devices' capability for carrying games with sophisticated graphics has grown as the mobile system and devices have gotten faster at sending, retrieving, and processing data, with better graphics and memory capability. Typically, phone and tablet owners purchase games through the app store of the device's manufacturer or the creator of its operating system. Steam, for example, is available in versions for Apple and Android mobile devices.

casual gamers
women and men who are older than the hard-core types and/or who like to play less intense (though not necessarily less difficult) games than the hard-core types; these games include puzzle, card, board, and word games

avatar
a character that represents the user within a virtual world

handheld game devices
portable machines used primarily for game playing

mobile device
multipurpose handheld computing device that can be used as a portable gaming platform

Visitors to a video game convention in Cologne, Germany, playing *World of Warcraft*.

Although some games cost money, many run on the "freemium" model that has been discussed in previous chapters. Basic versions of freemium games are free to download, but users must pay to eliminate advertisements, access additional levels of the game, or purchase in-game items (such as weapons or character accessories). Game companies have learned that gamers are sometimes more willing to spend money within the game once they have tested it and like it than they are to pay a high price for the game up-front. *Fortnite* is a freemium mobile battle game that has been a spectacular success. Its Apple (iOsS) version made $500 million dollars in in-game purchases in just 326 days during 2018.

Many mobile games are played through social networks such as Facebook and are set up to allow many players to make their moves at different times. These **social games** are among the world's most popular, attracting tens of millions of players. By linking to their Facebook accounts, players serve as promotional agents for the game, advertising their in-game activities to their friends. Among the companies that make such games are Zynga and Playfish (which was purchased by gaming giant Electronic Arts in 2009). *FarmVille*, *Words with Friends*, *CityVille*, *Mob Wars*, and *The Sims Social* are a few of the most popular social games.

A huge number of Americans play games on mobile phones and tablets. eMarketer research reports that mobile devices downloaded games 4.3 billion times in 2017.[17] Moreover, close to one of two men and 60 percent of women play mobile games daily. Although around 33 percent of both genders say they play for between one and fifteen minutes, around 30 percent report playing for over an hour.[18] According to 2018 findings reported by eMarketer, 72 percent of mobile gaming takes places at home, 4 percent takes place on the commute to and from work, 11 percent occurs during work breaks, and 13 percent happens at "other" times.[19] The Verto Analytics research firm found that in 2017 the most popular games played by US adults were matching puzzle ("match 3") games—including the *Candy Crush* franchise—and "word/quiz" games, such as *Words with Friends*. The former drew about 31 million and the latter about 24 million unique monthly users.[20] The other top game genres in order of popularity were alternative/augmented reality games (*Pokémon Go*), action/strategy games (*Clash of Clans*), and casino games (especially nongambling, "for fun" slot machine diversions). Mobile gaming is a world onto itself. It turns out that the order of the top game genres on smartphones isn't the same as it typically is on consoles and PCs. On those game-playing platforms, role playing and shooter games most often make up the most popular genres; things look very different when it comes to mobile games.

Virtual Reality and Augmented Reality Hardware The Gartner consulting firm provides good, concise definitions of both of these technologies, which are developing in gaming as well as in other media industries. **Virtual reality (VR)**, says a Gartner analyst,

> provides a computer-generated 3D environment that surrounds a user and responds to an individual's actions in a natural way, usually through immersive head-mounted displays (HMDs). Gesture recognition or handheld controllers provide hand and body tracking, and haptic (or touch-sensitive) feedback may be incorporated. Room-based systems provide a 3D experience while moving around large areas or can be used with multiple participants.[21]

By contrast, **augmented reality (AR)** "is the real-time use of information in the form of text, graphics, audio and other virtual enhancements integrated with real-world objects and presented using a head-mounted-type display or projected graphics

social games
games played through social networks

virtual reality
the creation of a computer-generated 3D environment that surrounds a user and responds to an individual's actions in a natural way, usually through immersive head-mounted displays

augmented reality
the real-time use of information in the form of text, graphics, audio, and other virtual enhancements integrated with real-world objects and presented using a head-mounted-type display or projected graphics overlays

overlays. It is this 'real world' element that differentiates AR from virtual reality. AR aims to enhance users' interaction with the environment, rather than separating them from it."[22]

Although companies use VR for a variety of purposes, including training people for complex aspects of their jobs, you probably know it most for its use in video gaming. The head-mounted displays companies offer gamers change fairly often. In 2018, the most well-known ones were Facebook's Oculus Rift and Oculus Go, Sony PlayStation's VR, HTC's VIVE, Samsung's Gear VR, and Google's Daydream. Typically software producers release gaming titles for use with specific head-mounted displays. So, for example, in 2019 *Borderlands2VR* was aimed at PlayStation users, whereas *Star Trek: Bridge Crew* accommodated the Oculus Rift.

Unlike the complex and often expensive hardware associated with VR, readily accessible smartphones are devices that can be used for AR. Partly because of that AR is ahead of VR in terms of being used by marketers. So, for example, with some apps you can point your phone at a product on a store shelf and see more information about that item; industry prognosticators expect these sorts of uses to grow in the next several years. When it comes to gaming, the most popular use of AR by far has been with *Pokémon Go*. It is a mobile game developed and published in 2016 by Niantic for Apple and Android handheld devices. The aim is to use the mobile device's geolocation capability to find, capture, and battle virtual creatures, called Pokémon, which appear as if they are in the player's real-world location. So, for example, you could walk into a museum and, hunting with your phone, find one or more Pokémon to engage. That has annoyed the staffs of museums and other locations where hordes of Pokémon searchers have prowled. In fact, the concept has been so popular that by May 2018 the game had been downloaded over 800 million times. Although free to play, the firm supports in-app purchases, so that by late 2018 it had grossed over $2 billion dollars worldwide—about $124 million of it in the United States.[23]

The Production of Video Game Software

The Pokémon gross, though large, is a small part of the amount people pay for software. We noted earlier PWC's estimate that in 2017 Americans spent about $29.1 billion on gaming content. To serve this market, there is a huge number of video games fitting a wide variety of tastes. The companies that coordinate the production of video games are called **video game publishers**. Publishers in the video game industry serve a function similar to that of publishers in other media industries we have seen—for example, the book industry. Video game publishers search for products they believe will succeed in the marketplace. Often the publishers finance the games' creation or have staffs of video game developers that develop the games themselves. Large video game companies arrange for the marketing and distribution of their games to their intended audiences. Smaller publishers will partner with special distribution firms (sometimes the larger video game firms) to help them get the material out to the marketplace.

The major hardware makers have publishing divisions that produce games specific to their systems; the intention is to persuade people to buy their systems because of the games exclusively associated with them. For example, Nintendo turns out the *Super Mario* and *Pokémon* titles, among others, exclusively for the Wii, Nintendo 3DS, the Switch, and so on. Sony turns out the *Gran Turismo* racing game

video game publishers
companies that coordinate the production of video games

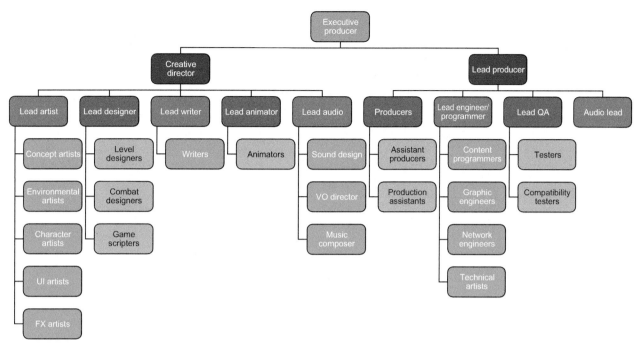

Figure 14.2

Organizational structure of a typical video game production firm. As you can see, people with many different talents are involved in the creation of the games.

for PlayStation devices. Microsoft has an exclusive deal with Bungie Studios (which it used to own fully and in which it still has an equity stake) to produce the *Halo* series for Xbox.

The launch of *Halo 3* in 2007 illustrates the utility of this sort of exclusivity from the console-maker's standpoint. The game's global sales reached $170 million on its first day, making it the biggest launch in video game history to that point. By the end of the first week, it had reached sales of $300 million globally.[24] Not incidentally, from Microsoft's standpoint, the game's release was associated with a spike in sales of the Xbox 360, the only console on which anyone could play the game. According to initial reports from retailers worldwide, Xbox 360 console sales nearly tripled compared with the weekly average before the launch of the new game.[25]

Although video games made by console and handheld manufacturers exclusively for their devices get a lot of marketing and press attention, by far the largest number of games are made by what the trade calls **third-party publishers**—companies that are unaffiliated with hardware companies. Because of their unaffiliated status, third-party publishers typically create games that work on a variety of systems. Electronic Arts is probably the most powerful third-party game publisher. Some of its top sellers include *The Sims* series, the *Need for Speed* series, the *Battlefield* series, and the *Madden NFL* series, which are all available on a myriad of platforms. Other key third-party publishers are Activision Blizzard (*World of Warcraft* and *Call of Duty*), Ubisoft (*Assassin's Creed* and *Far Cry*), and Take-Two Interactive (*Grand Theft Auto* and *NBA 2K*).

The titles just mentioned reflect that video games are often quite expensive to create and produce. That's particularly true for console games, especially those for the Xbox and PlayStation. The reason is that the console makers increasingly improve the graphics capabilities of the machines. If a game development company wants to compete on

third-party publishers
companies that are unaffiliated with hardware companies and that typically create games that work on a variety of systems

Candy Crush Saga and *Plants vs. Zombies* are two popular social games that can be played from your smartphone, tablet, or any electronic device. They are often part of social media sites such as Facebook.

those platforms, its leadership must hire more—and more sophisticated—programmers to create the games. Their work probably also takes a lot more time to finish than was the case with earlier games. As a result, the most high-profile console games today can cost as much to produce as theatrical films. Activision Blizzard's *Spider-Man 3* game, for example, cost $35 million, not including the marketing and sales expenses.[26] (The associated movie, Sony's *Spider-Man 3*, did have a production budget of $258 million, but this large of a budget is unusual even for blockbuster films.)

GLOBAL MEDIA TODAY & CULTURE

VR AND AR: THE NEXT FRONTIER OF VIDEO GAMES AND THE ENTIRE MEDIA ENTERTAINMENT LANDSCAPE?

The evolution of communication technologies has shaped the media landscape in the 21st century. Just think of the technologies we take for granted as part of our media experiences, which once were not available in media entertainment. Some revolutions have proved to be long lasting, such as sound: since the arrival of talking pictures in the 1920s movies have been incorporating synchronized sound and audiences have been expecting visual entertainment comprising sound. Other technologies have failed to leave a similar long-lasting mark on media entertainment—for example, Panavision, which was short-lived.

Will the same happen with the new technologies of VR and AR? Through digital technology VR completely immerses us in a world outside our reality, whereas AR enhances our experiences with the physical world, adding features to our devices such as smartphones or cameras. Video games are using both VR and AR. For example, the video game *Pokémon Go* utilizes any available mobile device's global positioning system (GPS) to engage the player with virtual creatures, called Pokémon, appearing as if they were in the player's real world. New video games consoles include VR headsets providing access to an immersive experience within the environment of the game. What do you think? Will their impact change the way the video game industry operates, creating a new standard, or will they fade? Will the impact of these technologies go above and beyond interactive media platforms and influence other legacy media, such as movies and TV shows?

These high costs lead to the third point: observers of the industry agree that it has become more and more "hit driven" through and since the 2000s. The high cost of making console games means that even the biggest firms such as Activision Blizzard and Electronic Arts concentrate their attention and marketing on just a few games, with the goal of making sure they are the top sellers. Sequels of hits become common because firms want to lower their risks when they spend huge amounts of money on games. The result, say critics, is that the biggest firms with the most expertise are pursuing formulaic blockbusters rather than exploring creative uses of technology and storytelling.

Despite the high risks associated with producing games today, companies are still producing a variety of types of games for the different devices on which people play games. Let's take a look.

Software Genres As we saw in Chapter 2, creators in every mass media industry think of content in terms of categories, or genres. This approach helps them understand how to create in that genre; it often helps distributors and exhibitors in selecting, marketing, and choosing titles for certain outlets; and it sometimes helps consumers who are thinking about what materials they want to watch, play, or hear. Most of the people who create video games for consoles, portables, and computers broadly categorize what they do as entertainment, meaning that the games are intended primarily for enjoyment. In fact, the variety of video games is so great that aficionados have developed several subgenres of entertainment to describe them and even subtypes to further differentiate content. Following, adapted from writings about video games posted on Wikipedia, are short explanations of the ten most important entertainment subgenres.

Action Games

Action games are those that present challenges that emphasize combat or involve attempts to escape being captured or killed. As a category, action games probably have the largest number of subtypes among video games. Three popular subtypes are shooter, competitive fighting, and platform games.

- Shooter games involve a character going through a dangerous environment hunting for bad guys. First-person shooter video games show the environment from the perspective of the character with the weapon; that character (whose full body you don't see) is controlled by the player. In third-person shooter games, by contrast, the player does see his or her character moving through the environment as the players uses the controls. Popular examples of shooter games include *Halo*, *Call of Duty*, *Fortnite*, and *Resident Evil*.
- Competitive fighting games emphasize one-on-one combat between two or more characters, one or more of whom may be controlled by the computer. Examples are *Mortal Kombat*, *Virtua Fighter*, and *SoulCalibur*.
- Platform games involve traveling by running and then jumping between levels and over obstacles in order to avoid being eliminated and to reach a goal. *Super Mario Bros.*, one of the best-selling video games of all time, released by Nintendo in 1985, is a well-known example. More recent entries include *Temple Run 2* and *Mighty No. 9*.

Gamers get a first look at the first-person shooter *Call of Duty: Black Ops 4* by Activision Blizzard, Inc., during the E3 Electronic Entertainment Expo in June 2018.

THINKING ABOUT MEDIA LITERACY

Over the years a number of different media options have elicited concern that they are damaging to young consumers. What do you think about the current concerns about video games, particularly ones with violent scenes? What are your arguments either supporting or negating the concern that video game violence promotes violence in young players?

Adventure Games

Adventure games are characterized by their focus on exploration and a story rather than on challenges that require the quick use of reflexes. One Wikipedia writer states, "Because they put little pressure on the player in the form of action-based challenges or time constraints, adventure games have had the unique ability to appeal to people who do not normally play video games. The genre peaked in popularity with the 1993 release of *Myst*."[27] Games that fuse adventure elements with action game-play elements are sometimes referred to as adventure games. A popular example is Nintendo's *Legend of Zelda* series.

Casual Games

As discussed previously, casual games are challenges with fairly straightforward rules that make them easy to learn and play. Social games tend to be of the casual type. The word "casual" probably comes from the idea that a person can get into the game quickly and doesn't have to devote a major commitment of time to learning rules and developing skills for the game. Such commitment is often required for people who want to play adventure games and games from other genres listed. Note that being deemed "casual" doesn't mean that a game is easy to master. As discussed in prior sections, these games often take the form of puzzle, card, board, and word games.

Simulation Games

Sometimes called sim games, simulation games involve players in the creation and cultivation of certain worlds that are designed to be realistic. The idea is to see whether you can excel at accomplishing a task. The task might be sprawling—for example, building urban environments (*SimCity*) or a farm (*FarmVille*). Or it might be narrower in focus, related to particular industries (*Stock Exchange*, *Roller Coaster Tycoon*). It might be even narrower still, focusing, for example, on raising pets (*Neopets*) or flying jets (*Microsoft Flight Simulator*).

Strategy Games

Think of chess. Strategy games require a careful assessment of a situation and wise actions in order to win a competition or war. The difference between strategy and action games is that action games center almost entirely on actual combat, whereas strategy games expect the player to focus on political diplomacy, the historical context, the procurement of resources, and the larger placement of troops. Two subcategories of this genre are real-time strategy (RTS) games and turn-based strategy (TBS) games. In TBS games, each player gets turns to move the units. After a user completes his or her turn, the opponent gets a chance; examples are *Poxnora* and *Silent Storm*. In RTS games, a story unfolds, participants play ongoing roles, and events of the game's story take place in real time and keep happening even if one of the players takes a break. *Company of Heroes* and *Halo Wars* are prominent examples.

Sports Games

One could argue that some sports games really belong to the category of action games and that others are a combination of action and strategy games. But producers, distributors, exhibitors, and consumers of video games consider sports-related games to constitute a separate category. Some games focus on playing the sport (the *Madden NFL* series is an example). Others focus on the strategy behind the sport, such as *Football Manager*.

Of course, not all video games fall under the entertainment genre. A much smaller, though socially important, segment falls under the education genre. To quote a Wikipedia article on the topic, educational video games "are specifically designed to teach people about a certain subject, expand concepts, reinforce development, understand an historical event or culture, or assist them in learning a skill as they play."[28] You may be familiar with *Reader Rabbit*, *Zoombinis*, *Mavis Beacon Teaches Typing*, or *The Big Brain Academy*. Instead of education, some in the video game industry use the term "**edutainment**" to describe such teaching-oriented games. The reason is that they are designed to be a lot of fun as well as provide educational outcomes for specific groups of learners.

edutainment
teaching-oriented video games that are designed to have educational outcomes for specific groups of learners

---

THINKING ABOUT MEDIA LITERACY

Imagine you are a video game designer. If you were going to pitch a new game idea to a game company, what factors would you consider when coming up with your idea? How would you convince the game company that your concept for a game was a good one to support?

Advertising Content and Video Games

It stands to reason that advertisers would be interested in a rapidly growing medium such as video games. Prior to 2009, their interest in video games centered on a desire to reach young men, who were assumed to be the dominant players. Beginning around 2009, though, the rise of casual social games (especially *FarmVille*) online as well as in the form of mobile apps marked the entry of a wider representation of the American public to the gaming world. Older players and females began participating at rates that, in some cases, matched or exceeded the proportion of young males.[29] This influx of a large, diverse audience of players led advertisers to believe they could target different types of people by gender, race, marital status, and more, based on the games they play. As a result, advertisers began to apply techniques to target game audiences and lead them to feel favorably toward products and hopefully buy them. The two most prominent ways in which they go about this are by creating custom games and by embedding ads in games.

Creating Custom Games To create a custom game (sometimes called an "advergame"), an advertiser partners with a game company or hires developers to create a game that is exclusive to that marketer. Once the game is created, it is usually linked to the advertiser's website or Facebook fan page. Doritos is a brand that for several years has given away branded video games to encourage players who like snacks to think of the chipmaker's products. For example, a game called *Doritos Crash Course 2*, released online right before summer 2013, followed the adventure genre. According to one review, it brought players' avatars "to new exotic locations while giving them crazy objectives and power-ups that can only come from spiced tortilla chips"—Doritos chips, naturally.[30] By 2016 Doritos was joining the VR bandwagon, with *Doritos VR Battle*, available on YouTube and Steam. It contains three difficulty levels of a type of casual game where the player wearing a headset has to collect Doritos chips. In phase 1, for example, "you must grab Doritos with your hands to score points while also dodging obstacles that slowly move into the play space. If you grab Doritos with extra Dorito Dust, you'll gain a bonus."[31] Does that make you hungry?

Speaking of hungry, the Chipotle restaurant chain released an advergame during fall 2013 that a *Venture-Beat* writer said "will, without a doubt, go down as one of the most successful marketing campaigns in history."[32] The chain partnered with Moonbot production studios to produce an animated film and mobile game to promote the view that, unlike giant companies, it makes food in sustainable ways that is also fresh and wholesome. The commercial, called "The Scarecrow," reached 6.5 million views on YouTube in under two weeks. The related *Scarecrow* game rose to the top fifteen free apps in the Apple's US App Store. An arcade-style mobile game guided users through four worlds and twenty levels. Users who unlocked all game worlds with at least one star at each level gained entry into Chipotle's "buy one get one free" offer at one of 1,500 international locations.[33] There was, however, pushback against the game by critics who thought Chipotle's claims in the game about its food were exaggerated. Search online and you'll find angry comments as well as parodies of the game and its messages.

Not all games promote specific commercial products and services. Some organizations create and distribute games to encourage players to adopt commercial or political beliefs through the playing of games. The US Army, for example, has released multiple versions of its action game *America's Army* free in CD/DVD form and for online play. The army released a 2018 version of *America's Army: Proving Grounds* for PlayStation and for Steam play on computers with the Windows operating system. It has an industry rating as acceptable for teens—the target audience for military recruitment. The "About This Game" section on Steam asks, "Do you have what it takes to train like a U.S. Army Soldier?" It implies the game will help answer the question as you

> take on the role of an 11B infantryman practicing combat maneuvers at JTC Griffin, a fabricated MOUT (military operations on urban terrain) environment. This training is crucial to your success as part of a Long Range Combined Arms—Recon (LRCA-R) unit, a full spectrum capable team that embarks on special operations missions behind enemy lines.[34]

Clearly, the army means for its ideology to be built into this advergame and internalized by potential recruits.

Embedded Ads Some companies or organizations don't want to go through the trouble of paying for and distributing games, but they do want to reach certain target audiences. To accommodate them, game publishers increasingly place ads or products in the action so that players will see the commercial messages or use the products in the course of their play. The game publishers realize that ad insertion increases their revenues without adding much to development costs. To draw advertisers, they have learned to make embedded ads look realistic and "natural." In racing games, for example, cars often pass billboards with the names of products whose companies have paid for their presence. In fact, even the model of the car that the player is driving may be offered because its manufacturer paid the gaming company. As this activity becomes routine, some companies are going one step further by giving people free add-ons that provide more characters or levels to the games.

A common use for in-game ads involves **rewarded ads**: asking a player to watch a short video commercial in return for extra life or a better weapon. The company that owns the game app makes money by selling to advertisers the ability to reach its players through those messages. Google's AdMob advertising service is one of the companies that helps game app owners do that. AdMob runs a marketplace by which firms can bid to advertise in games and then serve ads into the specific games. Many of the advertisers in games are themselves game creators, and AdMob has one type of rewarded ad that actually allows the game player to pause the current game and play a short version of the video game inside the ad in order to get the reward. Clearly the advertiser's hope is that the player will like the new game enough to download it.[35]

Marketers and game publishers see these activities as only the beginning of a highly sophisticated process of targeting players with ads and add-ons that are specific to what the companies know about them. They realize that with increasing numbers of gamers playing online, it will be possible to send them these features on the fly, while they are playing, and to change the ads and offer different sponsored downloads depending on different criteria. This activity is called **dynamic in-game advertising**. Rapidfire, one company that carries it out, defines it as "advertising inside of video games that can be implemented, updated, or changed in real time." Rapidfire notes that it can target players in real time based on their age and their geographic location. Expect in coming years to see the number of targeting categories expand dramatically.

Many sports video games, such as *NBA 2K* games, include in-game ads from various companies that both fund the production of the video game and create a real-life game experience, mimicking the ads seen in sports stadiums.

rewarded ads
asking a player to watch a short video commercial in return for extra life or a better weapon

dynamic in-game advertising
the process of sending ads into video games while individuals are playing and of changing the ads and offering different sponsored downloads depending on the players' game setting and level

Distribution and Exhibition of Video Games

There are many ways to get games to the player. As noted, some cable systems and telcos stream games to computers; the games do not remain on the computer. In the case of mobile games, the software is downloaded, and it must come directly to the mobile device; some of the payment is shared by the creator with the mobile service provider. Video games for consoles and handhelds and sometimes for PCs are downloaded from the internet or distributed on discs or cartridges to wholesalers and a variety of stores. In the brick-and-mortar world, you can find collections of the top games (and consoles) in huge retailers such as Walmart and in in consumer electronics stores such as Best Buy. There are also specialized video game retailers, such as GameStop, that sell a wider variety of titles. In addition, you can purchase video games online at Amazon.com or through many other online retailers. Used games show up in GameStop as well as on many websites, including eBay. Video games can also be rented through mail services such as GameFly and at physical locations such as at Redbox kiosks.

Part of the process of distribution and exhibition involves signaling to prospective players whether a particular game will fit their technology. As we have seen with Microsoft and *Halo*, sometimes a company with a financial interest in a particular operating system or console will want to have exclusive rights to certain game software, at least for a while. Sometimes, a publisher may get different companies to help with different platform versions of the same game. Consider *Tomb Raider: Legend*, the video game credited with revitalizing the Lara Croft adventure franchise. The publisher, Square Enix, formerly known as Eidos Interactive, enlisted Crystal Dynamics to develop PlayStation 2 and Xbox 360 versions. It had Nixxes Software work on the Windows PC and Xbox versions of the game, while Buzz Money Software developed the PlayStation version, with some platform-specific features. Humansoft worked out the Nintendo DS and Game Boy Advance versions. Fathammer and Sixela Productions created a version for mobile phones, Starting with Windows PC and Xbox in April 2006, the platform-specific incarnations rolled out across months. The game was so popular that an updated version for the PlayStation 3 (in HD) came out in 2011.[36] It also inspired sequels.

Video Games and Convergence

The cross-platform nature of the games we've just discussed is evidence of digital convergence at work. In fact, much of video game publishing involves deciding whether, when, and how to roll out digital versions of software across boundaries created by different systems for play. When it comes to multiplayer games, publishers will enable users to play the games online as well as on their individual consoles. For example, some Microsoft multiplayer games allow people who have an Xbox One to interact with people who are playing on their Windows PC or on their Windows-based Surface tablet.

As you might expect from the other media we have explored throughout this book, convergence doesn't stop with the movement of entire copies of games across different platforms. Game publishers have a strong interest in leading as many people as possible in their target audiences to learn about and buy their products. So

Tomb Raider, which has been a success in both the film and video game worlds, has also been the subject of controversy with respect to the way Lara Croft's character is typically portrayed as a very sexualized, scantily clad woman.

when Activision Publishing released *Call of Duty: Black Ops II* (developed by Treyarch) in 2012, for example, the company also released the soundtrack of the game. It hyped the soundtrack by publicizing that its main theme was written by Trent Reznor, leader of the band Nine Inch Nails and Academy Award–winning composer of the score for the English-language version of the movie *The Girl with the Dragon Tattoo*. The aim was clearly to give fans of the *Call of Duty* game series and fans of Reznor (perhaps an overlapping population) an additional reason to pay attention to the *Black Ops II* release.

Publishers of especially popular games encourage convergence—not all of it digital—because they make money from licensing characters, music, plots, or other aspects of their games to companies in other media industries. For a familiar example, just type Super Mario Brothers into Amazon's search engine. Results will include a variety of the kid-friendly Brooklyn plumbers' adventures on various Nintendo platforms. But you will also be able to buy Super Mario Brothers toys (several types of figurines and plush dolls), TV episodes, peel-and-stick wall decals, bedsheet sets, pillowcases, party napkins, hats, and cherry-cola lip balm, as well as the game's music track and more.

Lara Croft, of the *Tomb Raider* series, is an especially noteworthy example of a video game character who crossed media boundaries to become a major cultural figure. She first appeared in the 1996 *Tomb Raider* video game, where she competed with a rival archaeologist to find an ancient artifact. Even as she enjoyed other adventures in *Tomb Raider* games, she moved into other digital and nondigital media. These included dozens of comic book issues, two novels, three motion pictures (including a 2001 and 2018 *Tomb Raider*), movie soundtracks, and short animated films on the web. You can also buy Lara Croft paraphernalia such as character outfits, wigs, figurines, mouse pads, toy pistols, and shoulder holsters. Although Super Mario Brothers and Lara Croft represent characters originating within the video game landscape and migrating to other platforms, video games also provide a vehicle for extending storylines originating in other media forms. For instance, the book series *Lord of the Rings* has spawned a very successful movie franchise as well as a popular video game series.

Media Ethics: Confronting Key Issues

By this point in the book, you have probably noticed that all the media industries we discuss are embroiled in controversies that touch on ethical issues. The video game industry is no different. Three enduring concerns center on content, privacy, and self-regulation. Let's take a look at some examples. As we sketch them, consider how they make two broad points. First, think about how the controversies reflect the unique nature of the video game industry. But second, think about how quite similar issues can and do arise in virtually all of the other industries we've explored.

Concerns About Content

Advertising is a sometimes-controversial activity in many media businesses, and the video game industry is no exception. Critics have especially voiced concerns about commercial messages that are integrated into the plots of video games aimed at children who might not have the critical abilities to distinguish between a work of storytelling and a piece of propaganda for a company. The Berkeley Studies Media Group, affiliated with the School of Public Health at Portland State University has, for example, argued that advergames are frequently released by food companies to "instill brand loyalty in children through repetitive exposure to company products, logos and spokescharacters," often for firms that push candy, cereals, and fast food.[37] The popularity among children of the *Scarecrow* advergame by the Chipotle fast-food chain led an article in TheNextWeb, a popular tech-oriented website, to worry about the effect of that content on "unsuspecting audiences" who are too young to know that the video entertainment is also one long commercial.[38]

THINKING ABOUT MEDIA LITERACY

Have you ever engaged with an "advergame"? What do you think about the role of advertising in games? Do you think this is an effective way for a product to promote itself? Why or why not?

A very different concern about content, in video games as in other media, involves the depiction of women. For this chapter, Lara Croft is a good place to start. The *Guinness Book of World Records* calls her "the most recognized female video game character." She has many admirers who point out that she is athletic, strong, and proactive—which they claim is a great image for women in a video game. But the Croft character also has touched off strong negative reactions. Critics say that her sexy frame reinforces unrealistic ideals about the female body, that she is there to embody male fantasies, and that she is a negative role model for young girls. They also claim that the game's publisher and developer downplay the character's sex appeal when they are speaking to groups but emphasize it in their advertisements.

Images of women, as embodied by Lara Croft and other characters, are by no means the only controversial aspect of video games. Consider the *Grand Theft Auto* series. Published by Rockstar Games (which is owned by Take-Two Interactive), it had created fifteen editions of the popular game by 2018. It has sold tens of millions of copies worldwide, mainly for the PlayStation and Xbox consoles, though some versions are available in mobile versions. From its first incarnation in 1997, the game raised consternation because of its violence and sexual content. In 2005 *Grand Theft Auto: San Andreas* was skewered by angry parents and advocacy groups as morally bankrupt. They argued that it teaches people how to engage in a crime spree with gusto. Other games within the *Grand Theft Auto* series were castigated for their stereotypes of groups such as Haitians and Cubans as belonging to criminal gangs. In 2009 the *Guinness Book of World Records* called it the most controversial video game series in history. It calculated that over 4,000 articles had been published about it. Such articles have included laudatory comments about its innovativeness, but also many accusations of glamorizing violence, corrupting gamers, and even encouraging real-life crimes.[39] Video games such as *Grand Theft Auto* often enter the public debate about violence—especially teen violence. For instance, in the aftermath of the Columbine High School shooting in 1999, the games *Doom* and *Quake* moved to the center of a renewed nationwide debate about the possible harmful effects of violent video games. Although research on the subject suggests that video games have little causal effect on adolescent propensity for violence, the subject remains central in public discourse.

What factors encourage the creation of video game content that substantial numbers of people consider offensive? There is no easy answer. One view is that when creators of the games present sexist, violent, and/or ethnically derogatory portrayals, they are reflecting the attitudes of the people who play the games. The players may not shout those views in public, but they have no problem connecting with stories that build conflict or excitement by giving characters various negative sexually, ethnically, or racially stereotyped characteristics and pitting them against one another.

Many people in the video game industry believe that such images are socially harmful because they reinforce the idea that violence is the solution to problems and that particular groups in society have undesirable characteristics. These workers believe they have a responsibility to convince their colleagues and industry leaders to be sensitive to problematic depictions. One way some industry players have attempted to improve these presentations is by increasing the number and prominence of game creators with diverse backgrounds so that they can quash negative portrayals and be at the forefront of thinking up creative ways to use people of various backgrounds in less violent but compelling ways that will attract large audiences.

One of the major issues raised among people who observe the gaming industry is why there are so few women involved. According to a 2017 article on IGN.com, women account for only 22 percent of the entire video game industry. The article goes on to describe how male-targeted advertising, sexism, harassment, and lack of advancement opportunities have been alienating to women in the industry. A flashpoint of such activities occurred in 2014, when a vicious campaign of insulting antiwomen comments—and many threats of violence—targeted two female game developers, a feminist video game analyst, and those who supported them. Actor Alec Baldwin called the situation Gamergate; the title stuck, as did the impression that many in the video game industry don't respect women. One woman involved in video games noted to a journalist in 2017 that "the massive amount of news about harassment led me to believe that could happen to me too."[40]

Unfortunately, she may not be wrong. In 2017 a reporter interviewed fifty-five women who work in the video game industry and concluded that "sexism, harassment and inappropriate conduct in the workplace continue to be major issues for women throughout the video game industry, as they do for women in the tech world—and indeed the whole world—at large." The reporter added that some of the women she interviewed didn't want to talk about personal harassment, but the ones who did said they "had experienced [inappropriate conduct] on a micro level, while some had experienced it to a major, life-changing degree. Nearly all had accounts of seeing it happen to someone else."[41] Her words recall the 2012 comments by the female gaming practitioner and editor of a site for gaming practitioners who also works in the industry. "Every single one of us [women] can tell you at least one horror story," Leigh Alexander wrote. "Most of us have more than one. Booth babes, incidences of sexism, [and] using attempted rape as a *Tomb Raider* 'character builder.'" She then added, "None of these are things we should shut up about." It's important, she noted, to ask game developers "harder questions" with the aim of creating "a healthy industry with diverse products by and for anyone that wants to participate."[42] It's a worthy goal that many say is still far from being realized.

Concerns About Privacy

Many people probably think of the issues we've just discussed when they think about concerns with video games—sex, violence, and possibly social stereotypes. It is probably less likely that they think they are being followed and profiled when they play a game. Increasingly, though, that ought to be a consideration.

Consider *FarmVille*, *CityVille*, and the many other games published by Zynga. Perhaps you've played them on your web browser or while on a social networking site (SNS) such as Facebook. Well, if you read Zynga's privacy policy, you'll learn that Zynga is collecting loads of information about you as you play. Depending on what the SNS considers public information by default as well as your privacy settings, Zynga may access and store your first and last name; your profile picture or its URL; your user ID number, which is linked to publicly available information such as name and profile photo; the user ID numbers and other public data for your friends; the login email you provided to that SNS when you registered; your physical location and that of your access devices; your gender; and your birthday.[43]

Not sure what Facebook gives up about you by default? Not sure about your privacy settings? Research shows that many people don't know these things, and it's likely Zynga gathers a lot of information people might not have wanted the company to know. Zynga also uses cookies and other tracking devices to follow what you do if you visit its website or play one of its games in an app. Moreover, the privacy policy states,

> we use cookies and other similar technologies (e.g., beacons, pixel tags, clear gifs, and device identifiers) to recognize you and/or your device(s) on, off, and across different Services and devices. We also allow others to use cookies and similar technologies as described in our Cookie Notice. You can control or opt out of the use of cookies and similar technologies that track your behavior on the sites of others for third-party advertising, as described in our Cookie Notice.
>
> We, our service providers, and our business partners use these cookies and other similar technologies to collect and analyze certain kinds of technical information, including:
>
> - IP address;
> - the type of computer or mobile device you are using;
> - platform type (like Apple iOS or Android);
> - your operating system version;
> - your mobile device's identifiers, like your MAC Address, Apple Identifier For Advertising (IDFA), and/or Android Advertising ID (AAID);
> - application performance and de-bugging information;
> - your browser type and language;
> - referring and exit pages, and URLs;
> - the number of clicks on an app feature or web page;
> - the amount of time spent on an app feature or web page;
> - domain names;
> - landing pages;
> - pages viewed and the order of those pages; and/or
> - game state and the date and time of activity on our Services.
>
> In some cases, we will connect the above information with your social network ID or Zynga user ID. If you play Zynga games on a mobile device, in addition to your device identifiers (described above), we may also collect:
>
> - the name you have associated with your device;
> - your country;
> - your telephone number (if you provide it);
> - your specific geolocation (with your permission);
> - your mobile contacts (with your permission, as described further in Information About Your Contacts); and/or
> - information about the Zynga games and other third-party apps you have on your device.

Even when Zynga or other game companies are not linking your actions to personally identifiable information, they are often carefully tracking your in-game activity.

By embedding triggers in the game, publishers can observe user patterns that can provide useful marketing data and guide future game design.

Zynga's tracking of the visitors to its website and apps is by no means unusual. As we noted in Chapter 6, most publishers and marketers follow people's activities online and use—and trade—that information for marketing purposes. In addition to these funds of knowledge, marketers themselves have been taking advantage of the constantly decreasing costs of computer power to create their own databases from information they learn about their customers by asking them and by keeping records of their purchases. These storehouses of information are called **transactional databases**. A marketer that wants to learn more about the customers in its transactional database can turn to a data-gathering firm such as Acxiom. The company will match the names and addresses of the marketer's customers against its data on more than 124 million households. The resulting merged file could supply the marketer with a wealth of new information about each customer's purchasing behavior, estimated income, credit extended by mail-order firms, investments, credit cards, and more.

transactional databases
databases that store and sort large quantities of data that reflect transactions—such as logs of phone calls, emails, mailings, or purchases

Concerns About Self-Regulation

As you might imagine, this controversy about privacy has reached the halls of government. Critics of data collection by media firms have tried to persuade regulators and lawmakers to enact laws to stop those activities. Critics of the content of certain video games have also complained to lawmakers for action on the grounds that young people have been harmed. In both these cases, government response has tended to center on pressuring the companies that make up the industry to clean up their act. Industry critics and industry leaders disagree about how much this self-regulation has succeeded in erasing problems in the video game industry, on the web, or in the mobile space. Let's take a look at the arguments as they relate to privacy and content.

Privacy and Self-Regulation When it comes to privacy, the US government has mixed laws about collecting data. The existing laws relate to personal data about children, people's health records, and aspects of their bank and credit card records. Chapter 5 discusses the Children's Online Privacy Protection Act (COPPA), a law that requires websites (including game sites) to get parents' permission to ask children for information about themselves. By federal law, some aspects of medical privacy and credit data (e.g., your prescription drugs and specific purchases on your credit card) also require permission from the individual. These exceptions aside, the federal government in the early 21st century stayed away from imposing particular rules on the use of personal information by websites. The reason: to encourage web commerce.

Instead, lawmakers at the federal level have agreed with digital marketers and publishers that the best way forward is through self-regulation. Consistent with this approach, the Federal Trade Commission (FTC) has suggested four broad principles that it expects those engaged in the web and mobile industries to follow when it comes to handling information about people that identifies them personally through items such as their names, postal address, and email address. These "fair information practice principles" (FIPPs) include the following:

- Notice (or Awareness): Visitors to a site or app should be made aware of the company's information practices—and the information practices of other firms who take people's information at those locations—before any personal information is collected from the visitors.

- Choice (or Consent): The visitors should have the option of making decisions about how their data will be used during the current session on the site or app, as well as in the future. That is, the visitor should have the option of opting into the company's collection of data (the firm should not collect data unless the person gives the okay) or opting out (the firm will collect the data unless the visitor says no).

- Access: The visitor should be able to view the data collected and challenge it if the visitor considers it inaccurate.

- Security: The data collection and storage should take place in ways that stop people and firms from getting the data if they have no right to the data.

These principles are quite broad, they are not backed up by law, and they relate only to data that the FTC suggests will lead to the specific knowledge of the name and address of the person. Nowadays, most web marketers and game publishers contend that self-regulation will work to safeguard the public's privacy. They say that they understand people's desire to keep certain information confidential and secure. They also insist, however, that many individuals are willing to give up information about themselves if, in return, they get something that they consider valuable. Many privacy advocates agree that people should have the right to decide whether they want to give up private information as part of a transaction. But they insist that the FIPPs should cover all data, not only obviously personal data. They also disagree with the web marketers and publishers on the way in which consumers should be informed about the data that will be collected about them, often without their knowledge.

Industry representatives continue to insist that interactive sites and marketers could regulate themselves through an opt-out approach, although some sites still tell their visitors nothing about the information they collect about them. Compounding all these arguments is the international nature of the issue. The European Union requires an opt-in approach, for example, and US companies have to promise to accept the stricter EU rules when they deal with European consumers.

Note, too, that these privacy issues are related not only to the web but also to mobile apps and video games on several platforms that are connected to the internet. Moreover, as home-based television viewing becomes a two-way activity, getting data about what individuals do with the medium will also interest marketers and, possibly, certain branches of government. As these types of surveillance take place, various advocacy groups will argue against them and ask for legal safeguards against the misuse and abuse of people's data. Clearly, the fight over US consumer privacy and the merits of self-regulation in the digital age will continue.

Video Game Content and Self-Regulation The success of self-regulation is also in dispute when it comes to the content of video games. As discussed previously, the video game industry has set up a rating system much as the movie and television industries have done. Government regulators don't want to censor games out of concern that they would be overriding the firms' freedom of speech, but they also try to pressure the industry to act responsibly, to calm anger around the sex and violence of certain games on the part of consumers, especially parents. Like the movie and TV businesses, the video game industry argues that its ratings system

Table 14.1 ESRB Ratings of Top-Rated Video Games

Title	ESRB Rating
God of War	Mature
Celeste	Everyone 10+
Bayonetta 2	Mature
Shadow of the Colossus	Teen
Monster Hunter: World	Teen
Into the Breach	N/A
Owlboy	Everyone 10+
Ikaruga	Everyone 10+
Injustice 2	Teen
Pillars of Eternity II: Deadfire	Mature
Hellblade: Senua's Sacrifice	Mature
Subnautica	Everyone
Street Fighter V	Teen
Dragon Ball FighterZ	Teen
Just Shapes and Beats	Everyone 10+
Iconoclasts	Teen
Crypt of the NecroDancer	Teen
Donkey Kong Country: Tropical Freeze	Everyone
West of Loathing	Teen
Shantae and the Pirate's Curse	Everyone 10+

Source: The table combines data from www.metacritic.com/browse/games/score/metascore/year/all/filtered and www.esrb.org/ratings/search.aspx, accessed on June 19, 2018.

effectively categorizes games so that buyers can make informed purchase decisions. The six ratings (apart from "rating pending") are EC (early childhood), E (everyone), E 10+ (everyone 10+), T (teen), M (mature—17 and older), and AO (adults only). Content descriptors run a wide gamut from "alcohol reference" to "intense violence" to "use of tobacco." Table 14.1 presents a look at top video games and their ratings.

Despite this ratings system, some games have raised consternation among critics. Regardless of the public outcry surrounding *Grand Theft Auto: San Andreas* (discussed previously), the game was given an M by the ratings agency. Critics claimed that the rating and the accompanying descriptors were problematic because they didn't inform parents regarding the true level of violence and sex in the game. The controversy got hotter when players discovered that use of a certain code would unlock an explicit sex scene in the game. Even though Rockstar insisted that the sex scene and code were the work of a hacker, advocacy groups and politicians such as Hillary Clinton attacked the company for misleading the ESRB, retailers, and parents. Rockstar pulled the game from the shelves at great cost, deleted the scene, and put it back on the market. Nevertheless, the incident served as an opportunity for groups to rail against retailers for allegedly selling games to kids as young as nine years old.

One video game sparked so much negative reaction in 2018 that its publisher withdrew it. *Active Shooter*, a game developed by a small firm called Revived Games, is a first-person shooter that lets the player commit a mass killing in a school environment. According to *Variety*, "Depending on what role they picked, players were tasked with either neutralizing the target or hunting and killing civilians in a school setting. A counter in the corner of the screen tallied the number of cops and civilians killed." The developer, which also owns the game's publisher, Acid, was due to place the game on Steam through a Steam Direct program through which Steam's parent, Valve, allows any game on its system apart from hate speech and pornography, as long as the publisher pays $100 and the game works. Acid paid the fee, as it had with other titles. *Active Shooter* posted an adults-only ESRB rating.

When the game's story became known ahead of its release, though, anger swelled as people pointed out that twenty-three school shootings had taken place in the United States in 2018 alone. In fact, just several days before the game's release date ten students and teachers were killed at Santa Fe High School in Texas. Revived Games seemed to dismiss the pain its game might cause. It stated on its Steam page, "Please do not take any of this seriously. This is only meant to be the simulation and nothing else. If you feel like hurting someone or people around you, please seek help from local psychiatrists or dial 911 (or applicable). Thank you."[44] Responding to public anger and to what it called the publisher's general abusive behavior toward the industry and its audience, Steam pulled *Active Shooter* from its game roster.

The Entertainment Software Association praised Valve for "removing the tasteless game that so heinously exploits recent national horrors. It's the right call." The association then praised its self-regulation regime. "ESA and its members take its responsibilities seriously, as illustrated in its support of the ESRB rating system and broad compliance with strict industry marketing guidelines." Yet the game would have made it to homes had not members of the public noticed and pushed back. Clearly, controversies surrounding video game producers, distributors, and self-regulatory regimes are not over.

In fact, it's pretty safe to say that this is true about all the media industries we've covered in this book, as well as those we haven't looked at in detail. As we have noted more than once, media practices often affect the ways members of a society—you and I—see our world and carry out our daily lives. It should not be surprising that we all argue about them as well as enjoy them and try to influence them.

CHAPTER REVIEW

Visit the Companion Website at www.routledge.com/cw/turow for additional study tools and resources.

Key Terms

You can find the definitions to these key terms in the marginal glossary throughout this chapter. Test your knowledge of these terms with interactive flash cards on the *Media Today* Companion Website.

augmented reality (AR)
avatar
bulletin boards
casual gamers
dynamic in-game advertising
edutainment
entertainment arcades

handheld game devices
massively multiplayer online
   role-playing games
   (MMORPGs)
mobile device
multiuser dungeons (MUDs)
pinball machine

rewarded ads
social games
third-party publishers
transactional databases
video game publishers
virtual reality (VR)

Questions for Discussion and Critical Thinking

1. Think about the games you play that have characters in them. To what extent do they negatively stereotype certain genders, ethnic, racial, or other groups (including "aliens")? To what extent do they present diverse images of social groups? Do you think about these stereotypes when you play the games? If yes, how does it affect your game playing? If not, why not?

2. The use of games for all sorts of purposes—entertainment, advertisement, education—has been growing. There is also a category of "serious games," such as *Syrian Journey*, which was produced by the BBC to help educate about the plight of Syrian refugees. Take a few minutes to look through this "news game" at www.bbc.com/news/world-middle-east-32057601.

   What are your reactions? Would you consider this a game? Why or why not? Do you think this format is an effective way to promote understanding or awareness of serious issues? How does it compare to other methods for letting people know about the Syrian refugee crisis?

3. Massive amounts of user data are collected by websites providing access to games. Privacy advocates have concerns about how the data are protected and used. What are your concerns about privacy and personal data usage protection? Do you believe that industry self-regulation is sufficient, or do you believe there should be more government-enforced regulation of privacy guidelines?

4. Video game addiction is considered a diagnosable and serious psychological condition in several countries. Do you agree that this is a serious problem? Why or why not?

Activity

In September 2014 Amazon purchased Twitch, the live-streaming video platform that connects gaming communities across the globe. The $970 million cash purchase of Twitch created a great deal of speculation about why, or if, this is a good strategic purchase for Amazon. Spend a few minutes on Twitch.tv and answer the following:

1. Why do you think Amazon was willing to pay this much for this gaming video stream?
2. Think about audience research, finance, production, distribution, and exhibition in media organizations. How has the purchase of Twitch.tv benefitted Amazon in each of these aspects of Amazon's core business? In particular, how has having Twitch under the Amazon umbrella helped Amazon develop its audiences and the offerings it provides, improved or created new financial streams, or added new distribution and exhibition channels?
3. Do you think Twitch has been a good investment for Amazon? Why or why not?

Epilogue

The Need For Transparency

> "Let us not look back in anger, nor forward in fear, but around in awareness."

JAMES THURBER, AUTHOR

> "It is easy to sit up and take notice. What is difficult is getting up and taking action."

AL BATTISTA, BASKETBALL OFFICIATOR

As the examples we've explored throughout this text suggest, a central concern in the converging world of media today relates to people's lack of knowledge about what powers and what agendas lie behind the news, information, and entertainment that confront them across so many channels. People find it difficult to keep straight the maze of ownerships, alliances, and entanglements that affect so much of what we see and hear today. Corporate relationships within Sony affect the circulation of music and characters from video games to recordings to movies and back. Internal organizational rearrangements within Comcast affect everything from the lineup of your local cable system to the kinds of comedies or dramas you get from Universal Pictures and NBC, as well as the news you get from NBC, CNBC, MSNBC, and more.

The easy (and understandable) reaction is to simply throw up your hands and say, "It's impossible to follow these issues. All of the media world is manipulated in ways we can't understand, so I'll just distrust it all." This is the path of cynicism. It's an approach that will make you suspect everything you come across in almost every medium, even when that response isn't warranted. You'll shut yourself off from good stuff, and you won't learn to be an educated critic of what is going on in the media or the world at large.

The other, better reaction is to apply the media literacy skills that you've learned through this book in two ways. The first way is to try to keep track of the connections among the media that produce, distribute, and exhibit the materials that you use on a regular basis. What companies create these materials? Are they part of conglomerates, joint ventures, or alliances of other types? Do any of these relationships explain the kinds of content you are getting in the ways you are getting them? If so, can you figure out whether any corporate strategies might explain why these materials and not others are being released—and why one perspective and not another is being used?

The second way to apply your media literacy skills is to take action. Work with individuals or groups to convince mass media organizations to be more open about the corporate connections that go into creating their content. Demand that entertainment and news organizations routinely disclose when press releases or public relations organizations are involved in instigating or contributing to a story. Insist that media firms prominently divulge all product placements. Write to executives of public relations and "communication services" firms to demand that they work with media companies to inform the public when the products of their activities make it into print, on the air, on film, or on the web.

It's unlikely that media executives will take kindly to such requests. It's also unlikely that the government can force these sorts of corporate disclosures, because that is probably unconstitutional. Yet consistent, insistent pressure by various public groups for openness about the ways in which marketers and public relations practitioners influence 21st-century mass media might, over time, lead corporations to provide substantially more background about the commercial and political influences behind the mass media than the public now receives. Working toward more transparency in media today might well pay off big time in terms of what we will know about media tomorrow.

Notes

Chapter 1

1. Kenneth Olmstead, "A Third of Americans Live in a Household with Three or More Smart Phones," *Pew Research Center*, May 25, 2017, www.pewresearch.org/fact-tank/2017/05/25/a-third-of-americans-live-in-a-household-with-three-or-more-smartphones/, accessed January 29, 2018.
2. "Addressable TV: Harness the Power of Audience Data for One-to-One Targeting," *Experian Marketing Services*, July 2015, www.experian.com/marketing-services/addressable-tv-advertising-white paper.html, accessed January 29, 2018.
3. "Weekly Time Spent by US Users Watching Video Content on Smartphones . . . by Age Group (in minutes)," *Statista Citing Nielsen, University of Pennsylvania Library Database*, accessed January 29, 2018.

Chapter 2

1. p. 1.
2. Ellen Seiter, "Television and the internet," in Joseph Turow and Andrea L. Kavanagh (editors), (Cambridge, MA: MIT Press, 2003), p. 102.

Chapter 3

1. PWC, "USA Entertainment and Media Revenue," www.pwcmediaoutlook.com/country/US, accessed February 19, 2018.
2. Leo Sun, "Is Baidu Losing China's Search Market to Alibaba?" *The Motley Fool*, February 15, 2018, www.fool.com/investing/2018/02/15/is-baidu-losing-chinas-search-market-to-alibaba.aspx, accessed February 19, 2018.
3. Anne Wujcik, "MDR's School Spending Update 2015–2016," *MDR*, https://mdreducation.com/2017/10/13/mdrs-school-spending-update-2015-2016/, accessed February 26, 2018.
4. Calvin Reid, "Students' Textbook Spending Falls," *Publishers Weekly*, www.publishersweekly.com/pw/by-topic/digital/content-and-e-books/article/74614-students-textbook-spending-falls.html, accessed February 26, 2018.
5. PWC Global Entertainment & Media Outlook 2018–2022, "TV Advertising Market in USA," www.pwcmediaoutlook.com/segment/TVADV, accessed June 5, 2018.

Chapter 4

1. "Marketers and Ad Spending: US," *Advertising Age DataCenter*, http://adage.com/datacenter/, accessed June 6, 2018.
2. "MTV Closes 9 Consecutive Months of Primetime Growth and Ranks as Fastest Growing Top 40 Cable Entertainment Network," *Business Wire*, February 28, 2018, www.businesswire.com/news/home/20180228006300/en/MTV-Closes-9-Consecutive-Months-Primetime-Growth, accessed June 7, 2018.
3. John Moulding, "Viacom Puts Social Media TV at the Heart of Its Digital Strategy," *Videonet*, May 25, 2017, www.v-net.tv/2017/05/25/viacom-puts-social-media-tv-at-the-heart-of-its-digital-strategy/, accessed June 7, 2018.
4. Quoted in Joseph Turow, *Niche Envy: Marketing and Discrimination in the Digital Age* (Cambridge, MA: MIT Press, 2006), p. 43.
5. "Our Expertise," *Hill + Knowlton Strategies*, www.hkstrategies.com/global/en/our-expertise/, accessed June 7, 2018.
6. www.linkedin.com/company/pbn-hill-knowlton-strategies/media-relations-1186338/product?trk=biz_product, accessed January 21, 2013.
7. www.linkedin.com/company/hill-knowlton-strategies/
8. "Mission to the Edge of Space," *Redbull*, www.redbullstratos.com/, accessed April 10, 2015.
9. Andrew Hampp, "SXSW: Doritos Shells Out $2.5 Million for Lady Gaga Performance, Receives Tepid 'Applause'," *The Hollywood Reporter*, March 14, 2014, www.hollywoodreporter.com/news/sxsw-lady-gaga-performs-doritos-688577, accessed April 10, 2015.
10. Dodge Partners with Universal Pictures on The Fate of the Furious, Which Opens Nationwide on April 14, www.prnewswire.com/news-releases/dodge-partners-with-universal-pictures-on-the-fate-of-the-furious-which-opens-nationwide-on-april-14-300416999.html
11. Scott Cutlip, *The Unseen Power* (New York: Lawrence Erlbaum, 1994), p. 768.
12. www.columbia.edu/itc/journalism/j6075/edit/ethiccodes/PRSA.html, accessed January 21, 2013.
13. Sut Jhally, "Advertising at the Edge of the Apocalypse," www.sutjhally.com/articles/advertisingattheed/, accessed January 21, 2013.

Chapter 5

1. Editorial Board, "Trump Gambles and Loses on AT&T," *The New York Times*, June 12, 2018, www.nytimes.com/2018/06/12/opinion/att-cnn-time-warner-antitrust.html?action=click&pgtype=Homepage&clickSource=story-heading&module=opinion-c-col-left-region&region=opinion-c-col-left-region&WT.nav=opinion-c-col-left-region, accessed June 13, 2018.
2. The quote is from the US Supreme Court case *New York Times Co. v. Sullivan* (1964), pp. 271–272. The case quoting it is *Time Inc. v. Hill*, 385 U.S. 374 (1967).
3. *Roth v. United States*, 354 U.S. 476 (1957).
4. Bill Katovsky and Timothy Carlson, *Embedded: The Media at War in Iraq* (Guilford, CT: Lyons Press, 2004).
5. Paul Weidman, "Rules of Embeddedness," *Sante Fe New Mexican*, September 10, 2004, p. 32. See also Kevin Smith, "The Media at the Tip of the Spear," *Michigan Law Review* 102, no. 6 (May 2004): 1329.
6. Julie Bisceglia, "Parody and Fair Use," *Entertainment Law Reporter*, May 1994.
7. "Weird Al Yankovic Still Weird and White and Nerdy," *New Zealand Herald*, March 3, 2007, via Nexis.

8. Federal Communications Commission, "Best Practices for National Spectrum Management," http://transition.fcc.gov/ib/sand/irb/best practices.html, accessed January 21, 2013.

9. "Comcast-Time Warner Cable Merger," *Wikipedia*, accessed April 13, 2015.

10. Tricia Duryee, "Two Consumer Groups Try to Block Google's Acquisition of AdMob," *PaidContent.org*, December 28, 2009.

11. Jim Puzazzanhara, "FCC to Fine Univision $24 Million," *Los Angeles Times*, February 25, 2007, A20.

12. "Skechers Pays $40 Million to Settle Toning Claims," *Advertising Age*, May 16, 2012.

13. Stuart Elliot, "A Coalition of Marketers Is Accelerating Efforts to Sponsor 'Family Friendly' Prime-Time Television," *New York Times*, March 31, 2000, www.nytimes.com/2000/03/31/business/media-business-advertising-coalition-marketers-accelerating-efforts-sponsor.html, accessed January 21, 2013.

14. Stuart Elliot, "A Coalition of Marketers Is Accelerating Efforts to Sponsor 'Family Friendly' Prime-Time Television," *New York Times*, March 31, 2000, www.nytimes.com/2000/03/31/business/media-business-advertising-coalition-marketers-accelerating-efforts-sponsor.html, accessed January 21, 2013."

15. Association of National Advertisers, "Alliance for Family Entertainment," *PaidContent.org*.

16. Bob Steele, "Ask These 10 Questions to Make Good Ethical Decisions," www.poynter.org/latest-news/everyday-ethics/talk-about-ethics/1750/ask-these-10-questions-to-make-good-ethical-decisions/, accessed January 21, 2013.

17. Clifford Christians, Kim Rotzoll, and Mark Fackler, *Media Ethics*, 4th ed. (White Plains, NY: Longman, 1995).

Part II

1. "Internet/Broadband Fact Sheet," *Pew Research Center*, February 5, 2018, www.pewinternet.org/fact-sheet/internet-broadband/, accessed August 24, 2018.

Chapter 6

1. David Kirkpatrick, "Forrester: 94% of 18–29-Year Olds Stream Content Online," *Marketing Dive*, June 29, 2017, www.marketingdive.com/news/forrester-94-of-18-to-29-year-olds-stream-content-online/446129/, accessed June 15, 2018.

2. Steve Smith, "'What Did I Miss?' TV Attention Suffers a Big Hit from Second Screens," *Media Post*, May 24, 2012.

3. http://pewinternet.org/~/media//Files/Reports/2012/PIP_Digital_differences_041312.pdf

4. Monica Anderson and Jingling Jiang, "Teens, Social Media & Technology, 2018," *Pew Research Center*, May 31, 2018.

5. "Advertising Spending Online Expected to Surpass Print This Year," *Los Angeles Times*, January 20, 2012, http://latimesblogs.latimes.com/technology/2012/01/advertising-spending-online-expected-to-surpass-print-this-year.html, accessed February 11, 2013.

6. Sarah Perez, "Report: Smartphone Users Using 9 Apps Per Day, 30 Per Month," May 4, 2017, https://techcrunch.com/2017/05/04/report-smartphone-owners-are-using-9-apps-per-day-30-per-month/, accessed June 18, 2018.

7. Pew Research Center's Project for Excellence in Journalism, "Future of Mobile News," October 1, 2012, www.journalism.org/analysis_report/device_ownership, accessed October 27, 2012.

8. "Mobile Fact Sheet," *Pew Research Center*, www.pewinternet.org/fact-sheet/mobile/, accessed June 18, 2018.

9. "Cumulative Number of Apps Downloaded from the Apple App Store from July 2008 to June 2018 (in Billions)," www.statista.com/statistics/263794/number-of-downloads-from-the-apple-app-store/, accessed June 18, 2018.

Chapter 7

1. Paul R. La Monica, "Can Barnes & Noble Survive?" *CNN Money*, September 10, 2015, http://money.cnn.com/2015/09/10/investing/barnes-and-noble/, accessed December 23, 2015.

2. Adam Rowe, "Traditional Publishing E-Book Sales Dropped 10% In 2017," *Forbes*, April 29, 2018b, www.forbes.com/sites/adamrowe1/2018/04/29/traditional-publishing-ebook-sales-dropped-10-in-2017/, accessed June 18, 2018; "Kindle Direct Publishing," *Wikipedia*, https://en.wikipedia.org/wiki/Kindle_Direct_Publishing, accessed June 18, 2018.

3. Frank Catalano, "Seattle and King County Library Systems Rank at Top of Global Digital Lenders as Growth Continues," *GeekWire*, April 8, 2018, www.geekwire.com/2018/seattle-king-county-library-systems-rank-top-global-digital-lenders-growth-continues/, accessed June 20, 2018.

4. PWC, "Global Entertainment & Media Outlook, 2018–2022," www.pwcmediaoutlook.com/segment/CEBP, accessed June 20, 2018.

5. Susanna Hinds, "AAP StatShot: Trade Book Publisher Revenue Increased by 4.6% in 2018," *AAP*, February 11, 2019, https://newsroom.publishers.org/aap-statshot-trade-book-publisher-revenue-increased-by-46-in-2018/

6. Rachel Deahl, "Is Mass Market Dying, or Just Evolving—Again?" *Publishers Weekly*, May 19, 2017, www.publishersweekly.com/pw/by-topic/industry-news/bookselling/article/73668-is-mass-market-dying-or-just-evolving-again.html, accessed June 20, 2018.

7. "Zondervan Released Enhanced eBook of Rick Warren's Best-Selling 'The Purpose Driven Life'," *PR Newswire*, January 26, 2011, via LexisNexis.

8. For the larger number, see "Dan Poynter's ParaPublishing.com," www.parapublishing.com/sites/para/resources/statistics.cfm, accessed July 8, 2015.

9. "Number of Firms in the U.S. Book Publishing Industry from 2008 to 2010, by Firm Size," www.statista.com/statistics/185643/number-of-firms-in-the-us-book-publishing-industry-2008/, accessed July 8, 2015.

10. Alex Stedman, "'Fifty Shades' Spinoff 'Grey' Copy Reportedly Stolen from Publisher," *Variety*, June 10, 2015, http://variety.com/2015/biz/news/fifty-shades-spinoff-grey-stolen-from-publisher-1201516843/, accessed July 8, 2015.

11. Nielsen BookScan is now NPD Bookscan.

12. Clare Swanson, "The Best-Selling Books of 2014," *Publishers Weekly*, January 2, 2015, www.publishersweekly.com/pw/by-topic/industry-news/bookselling/article/65171-the-fault-in-our-stars-tops-print-and-digital.html, accessed July 9, 2015.

13. John Biggs, "Publisher Revenues Down as Ebook Buying Slows," *Techcrunch*, March 3, 2015, http://techcrunch.com/2015/03/03/publisher-revenues-down-as-ebook-buying-slows/#.usfnpf:Ji4u

14. Frank Catalano, "Traditional Publishers' ebook Sales Drop as Indie Authors and Amazon Take Off," *GeekWire*, May 19, 2018, www.geekwire.com/2018/traditional-publishers-ebook-sales-drop-indie-authors-amazon-take-off/, accessed June 21, 2018.

15. Michael Meyer, "My Advance," *New York Times*, April 10, 2010, www.nytimes.com/2009/04/12/books/review/Meyer-t.html?_r=1, accessed June 21, 2012.

16. Rachel Deahl, "The Rise of the Seven-Figure Advance," *Publishers Weekly*, November 21, 2014, www.publishersweekly.com/pw/by-topic/industry-news/book-deals/article/64848-the-rise-ofthe-seven-figure-advance.html, accessed July 9, 2015. Emily Temple, "A Brief History of Seven Figure Advances," *Literary Hub*, May 8, 2018.

17. Data Guy, "US Trade Publishing by the Numbers," *Digital Book World*, 2017, AuthorEarnings.com, http://authorearnings.com/report/dbw2017/, accessed June 21, 2018.

18. Communications Industry Forecast, 2011–15, section 14, p. 4.

19. Data Guy, "Children's Books Sell Online," *Indie Kids Books*, https://indiekidsbooks.com/childrens-books-sell-online/, accessed June 21, 2018.

20. Julie Bosman, "Jonah Lehrer Resigns from the New Yorker After Making Up Dylan Quotes for His Book," *New York Times*, July 30, 2012, http://mediadecoder.blogs.nytimes.com/2012/07/30/jonahlehrer-resigns-from-new-yorker-after-making-up-dylan-quotes-forhis-book/, accessed July 30, 2012.

Chapter 8

1. "Newspaper Circulation Volume," *Newspaper Association of America*, www.naa.org/Trends-and-Numbers/Circulation-Volume/Newspaper-Circulation-Volume.aspx, accessed July 12, 2015.

2. Douglas A. McIntyre, "America's 100 Largest Newspapers," *24/7 Wall Street*, https://247wallst.com/media/2017/01/24/americas-100-largest-newspapers/, accessed January 24, 2017.

3. Chris Roush, "More Than 50 Percent of WSJ Subscribers Are Now Digital," *Talking Biz News*, February 9, 2017, http://talkingbiznews.com/1/more-than-50-percent-of-wsj-subscribers-are-now-digital/, accessed July 3, 2018; Matt Snider, "Gannett Reports 4Q Loss Despite Growth in Digital Initiatives," *USA Today*, February 20, 2018, www.usatoday.com/story/money/media/2018/02/20/gannett-reports-4-q-loss-despite-growth-digital-initiatives-beats-wall-st-expectations/350877002/; and Sidney Ember, "New York Times Co. Reports Rising Digital Profit as Print Advertising Falls," *New York Times*, May 3, 2017, https://www.nytimes.com/2017/05/03/business/new-york-times-co-q1-earnings.html, accessed July 3, 2018.

4. Tony Biosotti, "Turnaround at San Francisco Chronicle Shows Way for Legacy Newspapers," *Columbia Journalism Review*, September 11, 2017, www.cjr.org/business_of_news/san-francisco-chronicle.php, accessed July 3, 2018.

5. Thanks to Leo Kivijarv, research director of PQ Media, for these data, July 17, 2015.

6. [no author], "Circulation of U.S. Community Weekly Newspapers by Circulation Groups," Editor & Publisher 96th Annual Newspaper DataBook (Irvine, CA: Duncan McIntosh Company, 2018), p. ix.

7. https://lasentinel.net/about, accessed January 7, 2019.

8. Annalies Winny, "America's 'News Deserts': The Death of the Great Alt-Weeklies," *The Guardian US Edition*, August 23, 2017, www.theguardian.com/cities/2017/aug/23/america-alt-weeklies-baltimore-city-paper-village-voice, accessed July 2, 2018.

9. "Print," *Oncampusadvertising*, www.oncampusadvertising.com/services/, accessed July 4, 2018.

10. "Community Newspaper Facts and Figures," *National Newspaper Association*, www.nnaweb.org/about-nna?articleCategory=community-facts-figures, accessed July 4, 2018.

11. "Newspapers: Daily Readership by Age (2016)," *Pew Research Center*, www.journalism.org/chart/5802/, accessed July 6, 2018.

12. "Unique Visitors of Newspaper Websites," *Pew Research Center*, www.journalism.org/fact-sheet/newspapers/, accessed July 6, 2018.

13. James Madore, "Edward Bushey Leaving Newsday: Debby Krenek to Continue as Publisher," March 27, 2018, www.newsday.com/business/bushey-leaving-newsday-krenek-to-continue-as-publisher-1.17700672, accessed July 7, 2018.

14. New England Newspapers, "Total Market Coverage," www.neni.news/print/tmc/, accessed July 7, 2018.

15. Corey Hutchins, "Warren Buffett's Newspapers Deploy Familiar Playbook as Fortunes Dim," April 13, 2017, www.cjr.org/united_states_project/berkshire-hathaway-newspapers-layoffs.php, accessed July 8, 2017.

16. Yemile Bucay, "America's Growing News Deserts," *Columbia Journalism Review* (Spring 2017), www.cjr.org/local_news/american-news-deserts-donuts-local.php, accessed July 8, 2018.

17. Communications Industry Forecast, 2011–15 (Veronis Suhler Stevenson, 2011), part 16, p. 9.

18. Corey Hutchins, "Warren Buffett's Newspapers Deploy Familiar Playbook as Fortunes Dim," *Columbia Journalism Review*, April 13, 2017, www.cjr.org/united_states_project/berkshire-hathaway-newspapers-layoffs.php, accessed July 8, 2017.

19. Pete Vernon, "The Denver Post's Rebellion and 'A Crisis in American Journalism'," *Columbia Journalism Review*, April 9, 2018, www.cjr.org/the_media_today/denver-post-editorial.php, accessed July 8, 2018.

20. Trevor Tan, "Facebook, Google Need to Start Paying for News," *Singapore Times*, December 20, 2017, www.straitstimes.com/tech/facebook-google-need-to-start-paying-for-news, accessed July 9, 2018.

21. Cris Velazco, "Google Just Made Paying for the News Dead-Simple," www.engadget.com/2018/03/20/google-subscribe-news/; Gerry Smoth, "Google Will Prioritize Stories for Paying News Subscribers," *BBloomberg*, March 13, 2018, www.bloomberg.com/news/articles/2018-03-13/google-is-said-to-prioritize-stories-for-paying-news-subscribers, accessed July 9, 2018.

22. Max Willens, "It's Dangerous to Chase the Shiny Thing," *Digiday*, March 20, 2018, https://digiday.com/media/thesis-qa-neil-vogel-ceo-dotdash-digiday-publisher-year/, accessed July 9, 2018.

Chapter 9

1. John Morthanos, "No, There's Not a Glut of Magazine Titles at Newsstand," *Publishing Executive*, June 23, 2016, www.pubexec.com/post/not-glut-magazine-titles-at-newsstand/, accessed July 12, 2018.

2. "About IDWE," www.idwentertainment.com/about/, accessed July 13, 2016.

3. "Entertainment and Media Market in USA," *PwC Global Entertainment and Media Outlook*, 2018–2022, www.pwcmediaoutlook.com/segment/CMAGPUB, accessed July 13, 2018.

4. http://hawthorncreative.com/hospitality-marketing-services/, accessed July 13, 2018.

5. http://files.pharmtech.com/alfresco_images/pharma/2014/08/21/8e795aaf-c1df-4162-83b5-20b9e5967316/article-465301.pdf

6. *Time Media Kit*, www.timemediakit.com/digital-audience/, accessed July 13, 2018.

7. "Magazines," www.pwcmediaoutlook.com/segment/CMAGPUB, accessed July 13, 2018.

8. "Publishing with Apple News Format," https://developer.apple.com/news-publisher/, accessed July 14, 2018.

9. www.forbes.com/sites/tonysilber/2018/05/29/big-ideas-for-a-magazine-newsstand-industry-in-distress/#29bc93195930

10. Tony Silber, "Big Ideas for a Magazine Newsstand Industry in Distress," May 29, 2018, www.forbes.com/sites/tonysilber/2018/05/29/big-ideas-for-a-magazine-newsstand-industry-in-distress/#15a175ce5930, accessed July 14, 2018.

11. J.W. Click and R.N. Baird, *Magazine Editing and Production* (William C. Brown, 1990), p. 2661.

12. Stephanie Hepburn, "From Storm to STEM," *Forbes.com*, July 23, 2015, www.forbes.com/sites/jpmorganchase/2015/07/23/from-storm-to-stem-rebuilding-xavier-university/?sr_source=lift_polar, accessed July 23, 2015.

13. "Our 360° Approach," *Meredith*, www.meredith.com/marketing-capabilities, accessed July 14, 2018.

Chapter 10

1. See "ASCAP 2017 Annual Report," p. 3, www.ascap.com/~/media/files/pdf/about/annual-reports/2017-annual-report.pdf?la=en&hash=E33B24B38F4AD2D1FADAE1593BD5CDE255D8B57E, accessed July 21, 2018.

2. Quoted in Becky Blanchard, "The Social Significance of Rap & Hip-Hop Culture," *EDGE*, n.d., https://web.stanford.edu/class/e297c/poverty_prejudice/mediarace/socialsignificance.htm, accessed July 21, 2018.

3. "USA Music, Radio, and Podcasts Market," *PWC Global Entertainment & Media Outlook 2018–2022*, www.pwcmediaoutlook.com/segment/MUSIC, accessed July 16, 2018.

4. "Global Music Report 2018," *IFPI*, https://www.ifpi.org/downloads/GMR2018.pdf, p 26.

5. IFPI, "Fixing the Value Gap," www.ifpi.org/downloads/GMR2018_ValueGap.pdf, accessed July 16, 2018.

6. "Smash (The Offspring Album)," *Wikipedia*, https://en.wikipedia.org/wiki/Smash_(The_Offspring_album), accessed July 17, 2018.

7. "About Us," *Bandcamp*, https://bandcamp.com/about

8. See "ASCAP 2017 Annual Report," www.ascap.com/~/media/files/pdf/about/annual-reports/2017-annual-report.pdf?la=en&hash=E33B24B38F4AD2D1FADAE1593BD5CDE255D8B57E

9. "It Doesn't Have to Make Sense," *Wikipedia*, https://en.wikipedia.org/wiki/It_Doesn%27t_Have_to_Make_Sense, accessed July 19, 2018.

10. "2017 Year-End Music Report, US," *Nielsen*, p. 4, www.fairnessrocks.com/wp-content/uploads/2018/01/Nielsen-2017-year-end-music-report-us.pdf, accessed July 19, 2018.

11. "2017 Year-End Music Report, US," *Nielsen*, p. 16 www.fairnessrocks.com/wp-content/uploads/2018/01/Nielsen-2017-year-end-music-report-us.pdf, accessed July 19, 2018.

12. "Vevo," *Roku Channels*, www.rokuchannels.tv/vevochannel/, accessed July 19, 2018.

13. Chris Morris, "Taylor Swift Made $54 Million for 6 Days Work," *Fortune*, June 1, 2018, www.nielsen.com/us/en/insights/reports/2018/2017-music-us-year-end-report.html, accessed July 18, 2018.

14. http://en.wikipedia.org/wiki/Live_Nation_(events_promoter), accessed December 11, 2012.

15. DJ TT Gut, "Your Favorite Rapper Is Poor," *DJBCoth*, https://djbooth.net/features/rapper-poor-artist-devlepoment, accessed July 19, 2018.

16. Chris Welch, "Spotify Hits 75 Million Paid Subscribers as It Releases First Earnings," *The Verge*, May 2, 2018, www.theverge.com/2018/5/2/17312686/spotify-75-million-premium-subscribers-q1-2018-earnings

17. "Best Sites to Buy MP3s," April 1, 2018, *CNET*, www.cnet.com/pictures/best-sites-to-buy-mp3/, accessed July 20, 2018.

18. Paul Resnikoff, "Apple 'On Schedule' to Terminate Music Downloads by 2019," *Digital Music News*, December 6, 2017, www.digitalmusicnews.com/2017/12/06/apple-terminate-music-downloads/, accessed July 20, 2018.

19. www.ibtimes.com/record-store-day-2015-how-merchants-rock-era-streaming-digital-downloads-1887422

20. Amanda Svachula, "Drake's 'Scorpion' Is the Year's Biggest Album. But Can You Find It in Stores?" *The New York Times*, July 20, 2018, www.nytimes.com/2018/07/20/arts/music/drake-scorpion-physical-cds.html, accessed July 20, 2018.

21. Becky Blanchard, "The Social Significance of Rap & Hip-Hop Culture," *EDGE*, n.d., https://web.stanford.edu/class/e297c/poverty_prejudice/mediarace/socialsignificance.htm, accessed July 21, 2018.

Chapter 11

1. "Radio," *Wikipedia*, http://en.wikipedia.org/wiki/Radio, accessed August 21, 2012; "Edouard Branly," *Wikipedia*, http://en.wikipedia.org/wiki/%C3%89douard_Branly, accessed August 21, 2012.

2. FCC, "Broadcast Station Totals as of June 30, 2018," https://docs.fcc.gov/public/attachments/DOC-352168A1.pdf, accessed July 25, 2018.

3. FCC, "FCC Broadcast Ownership Rules," www.fcc.gov/consumers/guides/fccs-review-broadcast-ownership-rules, accessed July 25, 2018.

4. Radio-Locator, https://radio-locator.com/cgi-bin/locate?select=city&city=Philadelphia&state=PA&band=Both&is_lic=Y&is_fb=Y&format=&dx=1&radius=&freq=&sort=freq, accessed July 26, 2018; also the Entercom Radio, iHeart Media, and Beasley Radio Group websites, accessed July 26, 2018.

5. See also "As the Audio Landscape Evolves, Broadcast Radio Remains the King," Nielsen, February 14, 2018, https://www.nielsen.com/us/en/insights/news/2018/as-the-audio-landscape-evolves-broadcast-radio-remains-the-comparable-king.print.html, accessed May 27, 2019.

6. "Fan Faviorite," *Nielsen*, December 5, 2017, www.nielsen.com/us/en/insights/news/2017/fan favorite-radio-listeners-spend-58-percent-of-their-tune-in-time-with-fave-station.print.html, accessed July 26, 2018.

7. "Radio Facts," *Why Radio?* www.rab.com/whyradio.cfm, accessed July 26, 2018.

8. "Why Radio Fact Sheet," *Radio Advertising Bureau*, www.rab.com/whyradio/images/full_fact_sheet_v2.pdf, accessed November 4, 2012; and "Why Radio Fact Sheet," *Radio Advertising Bureau*, www.rab.com/whyradio/Full_Fact_Sheet062415.pdf, accessed November 4, 2012.

9. "How Many Radio Stations Are There in the United States?" *Radio World*, April 11, 2014, www.radioworld.com/article/how-many-radio-stations-are-there-in-the-united-states/269915, accessed November 6, 2015.

10. *Communications Industry Forecast, 2011–15* (New York: Veronis Suhler Stevenson), section 18, p. 10. This volume presents only the 2011 data. The 1981 data comes from an earlier VSS forecast.

* Metropolitan area, 12 year olds and older.

* Metropolitan area, 12 year olds and older.

11. "Tops of 2017: Audio," *Nielsen*, December 13, 2017, www.nielsen.com/us/en/insights/news/2017/tops-of-2017-audio.html, accessed July 27, 2018.

12. See "Guide to Radio Station Formats," *News Generation*, May 2015, www.newsgeneration.com/broadcast-resources/guide-to-radio-station-formats/, accessed November 6, 2015.

13. www.insideradio.com/mid-year-report-what-formats-rule-the-radio-dial/article_36bff806-801e-11e8-92c6-57cfad5cd867.html

14. "Radio: Time-Tested Methods," *Harker Research*, www.harkerresearch.com/radio.php, accessed July 27, 2018.

15. www.srnonline.com/show/the-dennis-prager-show, accessed July 28, 2018.

16. "Kagan: Radio Revenues Climb 1.1% to $17.8 Billion In 2018," *SNL Kagan*, June 28, 2018, www.insideradio.com/kagan-radio-revenues-climb-to-billion-in/article_fa5faeee-7a94-11e8-b009-07a867dfdbc9.html, accessed July 28, 2018.

17. "How We Do It," www.nielsen.com/us/en/solutions/capabilities/audio.html, accessed July 28, 2018.

18. "SiriusXM Beats 2017 Suscriber Guidance," *SiriusXM*, January 10, 2018, http://investor.siriusxm.com/investor-overview/press-releases/press-release-details/2018/SiriusXM-Beats-2017-Subscriber-Guidance-Issues-2018-Subscriber-and-Financial-Guidance/default.aspx, accessed July 29, 2018.

19. Nathan Bormey, "SiriusXM to Buy Pandora Streaming Radio Service for $3.5 Billion," *USA Today*, September 24, 2018, www.usatoday.com/story/money/2018/09/24/sirius-xm-radio-pandora-media-acquisition/1408114002/, accessed January 10, 2019.

20. Tom Hals, "Largest U.S. Radio Company iHeartMedia Files for Bankruptcy," *Reuters*, March 15, 2018, https://uk.reuters.com/article/uk-iheartmedia-bankruptcy/largest-u-s-radio-company-iheartmedia-files-for-bankruptcy-idUKKCN1GR0IA, accessed January 8, 2019.

21. Marc Schneider, "iHeartMedia Reports, $853M in Quarterly Revenue, Says Chapter 11 'Moving Along as Anticipated," *Billboard*, August 1, 2018, www.billboard.com/articles/business/8468098/iheartmedia-quarterly-revenue-chapter-11-update, accessed January 8, 2019.

22. Source: www.nielsen.com/us/en/insights/news/2018/howamerica-listens-the-americanaudio-landscape.html, accessed February 7, 2019. Copyrighted information ©2018, of The Nielsen Company, licensed for use herein.

Chapter 12

1. "2017 Theatrical Home Entertainment Market Environment," *MPAA*, April 2018, p. 4, www.mpaa.org/research-docs/2017-theatrical-home-entertainment-market-environment-theme-report/, accessed August 2, 2018.

2. "2017 Theatrical Home Entertainment Market Environment," *MPAA*, April 2018, p. 4, www.mpaa.org/research-docs/2017-theatrical-home-entertainment-market-environment-theme-report/, accessed August 2, 2018.

3. "2017 Theatrical Home Entertainment Market Environment," *MPAA*, April 2018, p. 4, www.mpaa.org/research-docs/2017-theatrical-home entertainment-market-environment-theme-report/, accessed August 2, 2018.

4. www.boxofficemojo.com/movies/?id=scream.htm, accessed January 29, 2013.

5. Overlord (2018 Film)," *Wikipedia*, https://en.wikipedia.org/wiki/Overlord_(2018_film), accessed August 2, 2018.

6. Patrick Brzeski and Scott Roxborough, "After 'The Great Wall,' Can China-Hollywood Co-Productions Be Saved," May 18, 2017, www.hollywoodreporter.com/news/great-wall-can-china-hollywood-productions-be-saved-1005240, accessed August 2, 2018.

7. Dade Hayes, "Powering Up the Last Indie," *Variety*, January 21, 2009, p. 1.

8. www.the-numbers.com/movie/budgets

9. www.the-numbers.com/search?searchterm=cloverfield

10. www.imdb.com/title/tt1125849/companycredits

11. Pamela McClintock, "Summer's Bottom Line," *Variety*, August 20–26, 2007, p. 42.

12. Edward Douglas, "Dwayne Johnson and Kevin Hart from the Set of Central Intelligence," *ComingSoon.net*, May 23, 2016, www.comingsoon.net/movies/features/689053-dwayne-johnson-and-kevin-hart-from-the-set-of-central-intelligence, accessed August 3, 2018.

13. Lauren A.E. Schuker, "Indie Firms Suffer Drop-off in Rights Sales," *Wall Street Journal*, April 20, 2009, B-1.

14. Kelly Konda, "The 12 Most Profitable Blockbusters of 2014: Those Prints and Advertising Costs Are Killing Them," *We Minored in Film*, March 16, 2015, https://weminoredinfilm.com/2015/03/16/the-12-most-profitable-blockbusters-of-2014-those-prints-advertising-costs-are-killing-them/, accessed August 2, 2018.

15. MPAA, "2017 Global Cinema Screens by Format and Region," *2017 THEME Report*, p. 9, www.mpaa.org/wp-content/uploads/2018/04/MPAA-THEME-Report-2017_Final.pdf, accessed August 6, 2018.

16. Ashley Rodriguez, "How Hollywood Created Its Own Worst Enemy in Rotten Tomatoes," *Quartz*, September 26, 2017, https://qz.com/1073208/how-hollywood-created-its-own-worst-enemy-in-rotten-tomatoes/, accessed August 6, 2018.

17. See http://deadline.com/2015/03/amazing-spider-man-2-profit-box-office-2014-101389608/

18. Jeremy Kay, "MPA Chief Charles Rivkin on Piracy, #MeToo and Netflix Challenges," *Screen Daily*, April 10, 2018, www.screendaily.com/features/mpaa-chief-charles-rivkin-on-piracy-metoo-and-netflix-challenges/5127855.article, accessed August 6, 2018.

Chapter 13

1. Alan Seppinwall, *Breaking Bad 101* (New York: Abrams, 2018), Afterword.

2. Sonny Bunch, "Overload: Will Any Shows from the Golden Age of TV Endure?" *Weekly Standard*, March 16, 2018, www.weeklystandard.com/sonny-bunch/overload-will-any-shows-from-the-golden-age-of-tv-endure, accessed January 12, 2019.

3. "US TV and Radio Ad Spending, by Segment, 2017–2019," based on Jack Meyers Company Data, http://totalaccess.emarketer.com/chart.aspx?r=213757, accessed August 8, 2018.

4. PwC Media Outlook, "TV Advertising," www.pwcmediaoutlook.com/segment/TVADV, accessed August 8, 2018.

5. www.ncta.com/Stats/CustomerRevenue.aspx

6. Aaron Pressman, "Verizon Testing Super Fast 5G internet with Customers in 11 Cities," *Fortune*, February 22, 2017, http://fortune.com/2017/02/22/verizon-testing-5g-11-cities/, accessed August 9, 2018.

7. "Mobile Fact Sheet," *Pew Research Center*, www.pewinternet.org/fact-sheet/mobile/, accessed August 9, 2018.

8. "internet Market in the USA," *PWC*, www.pwcmediaoutlook.com/segment/INTACC, accessed August 9, 2018

9. "Cable Carriage of Broadcast Stations," *FCC*, www.fcc.gov/media/cable-carriage-broadcast-stations, accessed August 10, 2018.

10. Sarah Perez, "Over-the-Top Only US Households Nearly Tripled Since 2013, Impacting TV Ad Dollars."

11. "The Nielsen Total Audience Report, Q1 2018," *Nielsen*, p. 11, www.nielsen.com/content/dam/corporate/us/en/reports-downloads/2018-reports/q1-2018-total-audience-report.pdf, accessed August 11, 2018.

12. "83% of U.S. Households Subscribe to a Pay-TV Service," *Leichtman Research Group, Inc., Press Release*, September 3, 2015, www.leichtmanresearch.com/press/090315release.html, accessed December 7, 2015.

13. Al Tompkins, "CBS Threatens to Drop Nielsen: Gray Already Moving Away."

14. Joe Mandese, "Nielsen Unveils Plan to Model About Half Its National TV Ratings Beginning This Fall," *Media Daily News*, September 4, 2014, www.mediapost.com/publications/article/233528/nielsen-unveils-plan-to-model-about-half-its-natio.html, accessed December 7, 2015.

15. www.mediaaudit.com/media-watchdog/spot-tv-advertisers-understanding-nielsens-measurement-updates/, accessed August 8, 2018.

16. "Nielsen Estimates 116.4 Million TV Homes in the U.S. for the 2015–16 TV Season," *Nielsen*, www.nielsen.com/us/en/insights/news/2015/nielsen-estimates-116-4-million-tv-homes-in-the-us-forthe-2015–16-tv-season.html, accessed December 8, 2015.

17. "Nielsen Estimates 116.4 Million TV Homes in the U.S. for the 2015–16 TV Season," *Nielsen*, www.nielsen.com/us/en/insights/news/2015/nielsen-estimates-116-4-million-tv-homes-in-the-usfor-the-2015–16-tv-season.html, accessed December 8, 2015.

18. Jason Lynch, "Don't Panic, Says CBS," *Adweek*, August 10, 2015, www.adweek.com/news/television/dont-panic-says-cbs-more-people-are-watching-tv-now-decade-ago-166313, accessed December 8, 2015.

19. "Nielsen Cross-Platform Homes—Extended Screen Ratings," www.nielsen.com/us/en/measurement/television-measurement.html, accessed September 29, 2012.

20. "Nielsen Total Audience Report," *Nielsen*, p. 3, accessed August 11, 2011.

21. Cecilia Kang, "Americans Are Moving Faster Than Ever Away from Traditional TV," *The Washington Post*, March 11, 2015, www.washingtonpost.com/news/business/wp/2015/03/11/americans-are-moving-faster-than-ever-away-from-traditional-tv/, accessed December 9, 2015.

22. "The Truth About House Hunters on HGTV," *Hooked on Houses*, June 2, 2010, http://hookedonhouses.net/2010/06/02/the-truth-about-house-hunters-on-hgtv/, accessed December 9, 2015.

23. Jenna Morotta, "Netflix's Content Budget for 2018 Balloons to $13—Report," *IndieWire*, July 6, 2018, www.indiewire.com/2018/07/netflix-original-content-spending-13-billion-1201981599/, accessed August 12, 2018.

24. See Steven Kurutz, "Brooklyn's Favorite Pot Dealer Returns," *New York Times*, January 18, 2018, www.nytimes.com/2018/01/18/style/high-maintenance-hbo-ben-sinclair-weed.html; and High Maintenance on Vimeo, https://vimeo.com/channels/highmaintenance, accessed August 12, 2008.

25. Josh Constine, "YouTube Red, a $9.99 Site-Wide Ad-Free Subscription with Play Music, Launches October 28," *TechCrunch*, October 21, 2015, http://techcrunch.com/2015/10/21/youtubered/#.usfnpf:CBLG, accessed December 10, 2015.

26. "Syndicated TV Ratings . . . For Oct. 5–11," *TV by the Numbers*, based on Nielsen Company Data, October 21, 2015, http://tvbythenumbers.zap2it.com/2015/10/21/syndicated-tv-ratings-oct-5-11-2015/, accessed December 10, 2015.

27. "CBS All Access," www.cbs.com/all-access/live-tv/?intcid=CIA85fa358, accessed August 13, 2018.

Chapter 14

1. Max Cherney, "This Violent Videogame Has Made More Money Than Any Movie Ever," *Marketwatch*, April 9, 2018, www.marketwatch.com/story/this-violent-videogame-has-made-more-money-than-any-movie-ever-2018-04-06, accessed August 17, 2018.

2. Jeffrey Matulef, "Grand Theft Auto Series Has Shipped Over 220m Copies," *Eurogamer*, August 21, 2015, www.eurogamer.net/articles/2015-08-21-grand-theft-auto-series-has-shipped-over-220m-copies, accessed January 3, 2016.

3. Luke Villapaz, "GTA 5 Costs $265 Million to Develop and Market, Making It the Most Expensive Video Game Ever," *International Business Times*, September 8, 2013, www.ibtimes.com/gta-5-costs-265-million-develop-market-making-it-most-expensive-video-game-ever-produced-report, accessed January 3, 2016.

4. John Funk, "How Much Did *Modern Warfare* 2 Cost to Make?" *The Escapist*, November 19, 2009, www.escapistmagazine.com/news/view/96227-How-Much-Did-Modern-Warfare-2-Cost-to-Make, accessed January 3, 2016.

5. "These 25 Wildly Popular Android Games Are Raking in the Most Cash from In-app Purchases," *ZDNet*, April 17, 2018, www.zdnet.com/pictures/25-wildly-popular-android-games-raking-in-the-most-cash-from-in-app-purchases/25/, accessed August 17, 2018.

6. Even Wingren, quoted in Max Cherney, "This Violent Videogame Has Made More Money Than Any Movie Ever," *Marketwatch*, April 9, 2018, www.marketwatch.com/story/this-violent-videogame-has-made-more-money-than-any-movie-ever-2018-04-06, accessed August 17, 2018.

7. "Essential Facts About the Computer and Video Game Industry," *Entertainment Software Association*, 2018, www.theesa.com/wp-content/uploads/2018/05/EF2018_FINAL.pdf, accessed June 8, 2018.

8. Much of this brief historical sketch is based on a wide variety of articles on Wikipedia as well as on Steven Kent, *The Ultimate History of Video Games* (New York: Three Rivers Press, 2001).

9. http://en.wikipedia.org/wiki/Entertainment_Software_Rating_Board, accessed December 7, 2012.

10. "Essential Facts About the Computer and Video Game Industry," *Entertainment Software Association*, 2018, www.theesa.com/wp-content/uploads/2018/05/EF2018_FINAL.pdf, accessed June 8, 2018.

11. "Essential Facts About the Computer and Video Game Industry."

12. "Essential Facts About the Computer and Video Game Industry."

13. www.pwcmediaoutlook.com/segment/VIDESPT, accessed August 19, 2018.

14. www.xbox.com/en-US/entertainment, accessed on June 12, 2018.

15. Michael Bluejay, "Is Online Gambling Legal in the US," *VegasClick*, June 2018, https://vegasclick.com/online/legal, accessed August 19, 2018.

16. www.forbes.com/sites/insertcoin/2014/01/27/riots-league-of-legends-reveals-astonishing-27-million-daily-players-67-million-monthly/#56d1403b6d39, accessed June 12, 2018.

17. Chart, "Top 5 Countries, Ranked by Mobile Game vs. Nongame App Downloads, 2016–2022," *eMarketer*, http://totalaccess.emarketer.com/chart.aspx?r=218687, accessed August 20, 2018.

18. Chart, "Daily Time Spent Playing Mobile Games Among US Mobile Gamers by Gender, July 2017," *eMarketer*, http://totalaccess.emarketer.com/chart.aspx?r=211587, accessed August 20, 2018.

19. Chart, "Occasion When US Mobile Games Most Often Play Mobile Games, by Gender, Jan 2018," *eMarketer*, http://totalaccess.emarketer.com/chart.aspx?r=217920&ipauth=y, accessed August 20, 2018.

20. "Consumer Behavior in 2018: Three Trends to Watch," *Verto Analytics*, 2018, https://research.vertoanalytics.com/hubfs/Files/Verto-Analytics-Trend-Forecast-2018.pdf?hsCtaTracking=4321115a-86b3-4d21-ac4e-8390c04498ce%7C07ce56ba-42a4-47a3-93dd-c46c68e316a9, accessed August 20, 2018.

21. Brian Blau, "Virtual Reality," in Svetlana Sicular and Kenneth Brant (editors), *Hype Cycle for Artificial Intelligence* (Gartner, July 24, 2018), p. 62.

22. Tuong Huy Nguyen and Brian Blau, "Augmented Reality," in Svetlana Sicular and Kenneth Brant (editors), *Hype Cycle for Artificial Intelligence* (Gartner, July 24, 2018), p. 59.

23. [No author], "Pokemon Go," *Wikipedia*, https://en.wikipedia.org/wiki/Pok%C3%A9mon_Go, accessed January 14, 2009; [no author], "Annual Revenues Generated by Pokemon Go in the United States from 2016 to 2020, by OS (in millions of dollars)," *Statista*, www.statista.com/statistics/664985/revenue-from-pokemon-go-usa-android-apple/, accessed January 14, 2019.

24. Michael Sansbury, "X-Box Outplays Rivals and Movies," *The Australian*, October 11, 2007, 36.

25. Langston Werz Jr., "Video Games," *Charltte Observer*, October 11, 2007, 36.

26. "Video Game Publisher," *Wikipedia*, http://en.wikipedia.org/wiki/Video_game_publisher, accessed November 5, 2012.

27. "Video Game Genres," *Wikipedia*, http://en.wikipedia.org/wiki/Video_game_genres, accessed January 30, 2013.

28. "Outline of Video Games," *Wikipedia*, http://en.wikipedia.org/wiki/Outline_of_video_games, accessed January 31, 2013.

29. See Paul Verna, "Gaming for Marketers," *eMarketer*, October 2011, p. 3.

30. "Doritos Crash Course," *Giant Bomb*, www.giantbomb.com/advergames/3015-910/games/, accessed August 21.

31. "Doritos VR Battle," *Giant Bomb*, www.giantbomb.com/doritos-vr-battle/3030-57182/, accessed August 21, 2018.

32. George Deglin, "Chipotle Scarecrow Is the Future of Advergaming on Mobile," *VentureBeat*, September 30, 2013, http://venturebeat.com/2013/09/30/chipotle-scarecrow-is-the-future-of-advergamingon-mobile/, accessed August 13, 2015.

33. Lauren Maffed, "The Legal Loophole of Advergames," *TheNextweb*, June 29, 2014, http://thenextweb.com/dd/2014/06/29/legal-loophole-advergames/, accessed August 13, 2015.

34. "America's Army: Proving Grounds," *Steam*, https://store.steampowered.com/app/203290/Americas_Army_Proving_Grounds/, accessed August 21, 2018.

35. Frederic Lardinois, "Google Is Launching Playable In-game Ads," *TechCrunch*, March 15, 2018, https://techcrunch.com/2018/03/15/google-is-launching-playable-in-game-ads/, accessed August 20, 2018.

36. http://en.wikipedia.org/wiki/Tomb_Raider:_Legend, accessed November 11, 2012.

37. "State-Law Approaches to Address Digital Food Marketing to Youth," *Berkeley Media Studies Group*, December 19, 2013, www.bmsg.org/resources/publications/state-law-approaches-address-digital-food-marketing-youth-gaming#ref9, accessed August 13, 2015.

38. Lauren Maffed, "The Legal Loophole of Advergames," *TheNextweb*, June 29, 2014, http://thenextweb.com/dd/2014/06/29/legal-loophole-advergames/, accessed August 13, 2015.

39. http://en.wikipedia.org/wiki/Grand_Theft_Auto_(series), accessed November 15, 2012.

40. www.ign.com/articles/2017/12/20/women-in-video-game-development-in-2017-a-snapshot

41. Lucy O'Brien, "Women in Video Game Development in 2017," *IGN*, www.ign.com/articles/2017/12/20/women-in-video-game-development-in-2017-a-snapshot, accessed August 23, 2018.

42. Leigh Alexander, "Opinion: In the Sexism Discussion, Let's Look at Game Culture," *Gamasutra*, July 16, 2012, www.gamasutra.com/view/news/174145/Opinion_In_the_sexism_discussion_lets_look_at_game_culture.php#.ULkmW-Oe85R, accessed December 7, 2012.

43. http://company.zynga.com/privacy/policy, accessed November 15, 2012.

44. Stephanie Fogel, "What Is 'Active Shooter'," *Variety*, May 30, 1978, https://variety.com/2018/gaming/features/active-shooter-game-explained-1202824568/, accessed August 22, 2018.

Photo Credits

Prelims

Page vi: Photo credit: Kyle Cassidy

Part I

Chapter 1
Opener: © George Rudy/Shutterstock
Page 7: © Rawpixel.com/Shutterstock; Page 12: © Rasulov/Shutterstock; Page 14: © iofoto/Shutterstock; Page 17: © yvasa/Shutterstock; Page 23 © F-Stop boy / Shutterstock.com

Chapter 2
Opener: © Thomas Concordia via Getty images
Page 31: © Library of Congress; Page 34: Sony Pictures Classics/Photofest © Sony Pictures Classics; Page 35: © ensiferum/Shutterstock; Page 41: PBS/Photofest © PBS; Page 43: Walt Disney Pictures/Photofest © Walt Disney Pictures; Page 46: © Alinari via Getty Images; Page 50: HBO/Photofest © HBO; Page 52: CBS/Photofest © CBS

Chapter 3
Opener: © Kiev.Victor / Shutterstock.com
Page 69: © Drop of Light / Shutterstock.com; Page 70: CBS/Photofest © CBS; Page 77: © Kathy Hutchins / Shutterstock.com; Page 83: © OlegDoroshin/Shutterstock; Page 88: © lev radin / Shutterstock.com

Chapter 4
Opener: © pixinoo / Shutterstock.com
Page 98: ABC/Photofest © AMC; Page 102: © littlenySTOCK / Shutterstock.com; Page 118: © KPegg/Shutterstock; Page 123: © Twin Design / Shutterstock.com; Page 125: © Showtime

Chapter 5
Opener: © The Asahi Shimbun via Getty Images
Page 133: © Sharaf Maksumov / Shutterstock.com; Page 134: © New York Public Library/Oscar Lion Collection; Page 140: Fox Network/Photofest © Fox Network ; Page 152: ABC Family/Photofest © ABC Family ; Page 156: The Weinstein Company/Photofest © The Weinstein Company; Page 160: ABC/Photofest © ABC

Part II

Preface
Opener: © Alena.Kravchenko / Shutterstock.com
Page 167: © Monkey Business Images/Shutterstock; Page 169: Walt Disney Studios Motion Pictures/Photofest © Walt Disney Studios Motion Pictures; Page 171: © LoudDoor; Page 172: © Hmong Windows / Shutterstock.com

Chapter 6
Opener: © Dmitri Ma/Shutterstock
Page 185: © Denys Prykhodov / Shutterstock.com; Page 187: © Google and the Google logo are registered trademarks of Google LLC, used with permission.; Page 189: © Pe3k / Shutterstock.com; Page 192: © Zeynep Demir / Shutterstock.com; Page 194: © Karolis Kavolelis / Shutterstock.com

Chapter 7
Opener: © DW labs Incorporated / Shutterstock.com
Page 208: © Hand Robot/Shutterstock; Page 212: © Anna Mente/Shutterstock; Page 218: © ARTYOORAN / Shutterstock.com ; Page 221: © Karel Noppe/Shutterstock

Chapter 8
Opener: © Dedi Grigoroiu / Shutterstock.com
Page 235: © Library of Congress; Page 239: © iStockphoto.com/GoodLifeStudio; Page 245: © Lisa Fischer/Shutterstock; Page 247: © Paul Marotta via Getty

Chapter 9
Opener: © Andrew Cline / Shutterstock.com
Page 262: © Niloo / Shutterstock.com; Page 265: Marvel Comics Group/Photofest © Marvel Comics Group; Page 270: © FOOTAGE VECTOR PHOTO / Shutterstock.com; Page 274: © Opachevsky Irina / Shutterstock.com; Page 277: © iStockphoto.com/Lya_Cattel

Chapter 10
Opener: © dennizn / Shutterstock.com
Page 287: © ruigsantos / Shutterstock.com; Page 296: © Kevin Winter via Getty; Page 300: © Kathy Hutchins / Shutterstock.com; Page 302: © Kathy Hutchins / Shutterstock.com; Page 310: © Washington Post/Getty Images

Index

Note: **Boldface** page references indicate tables and photographs. *Italic* references indicate boxed text and figures.